Information space

Information space

A Framework for Learning in Organizations, Institutions and Culture

Max H. Boisot

London and New York

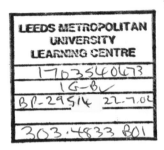
First published 1995
by Routledge
11 New Fetter Lane, London EC4P 4EE

Simultaneously published in the USA and Canada
by Routledge
29 West 35th Street, New York, NY 10001

© 1995 Max H. Boisot

Typeset in Garamond by
Solidus (Bristol) Limited
Printed and bound in Great Britain by
T. J. Press (Padstow) Ltd, Padstow, Cornwall

British Library Cataloguing in Publication Data

A catalogue record for this book is available from the British Library

Library of Congress Cataloging in Publication Data

Information space : a framework for learning in organizations,
    institutions, and culture / edited by Max H. Boisot.
        p.   cm.
    ISBN 0–415–11490–X
    1. Information technology—Social aspects. 2. Information
    services industry—Social aspects. 3. Information services–
    –Economic aspects. 4. Knowledge, Sociology of. 5. Learning.
    6. Information society. I. Boisot, Max.
    HC79.15515364   1995   94–48389
    303.48'33—dc20   CIP

ISBN 0–415–11490–X

Contents

Figures

Tables

Foreword

The assumptions underpinning mainstream neoclassical economics derive primarily from the conditions pertaining in the nineteenth century. As these have steadily lost relevance, the need for a new paradigm has become increasingly urgent. In this book, Max Boisot makes a major contribution towards its formulation.

Mainstream economics still depends upon static equilibrium-based theories which are unable to account for the most evident characteristics of the modern economic order, namely the transacting of information and the role of institutions in shaping the conditions for such transactions. Information transacting is central to the operation of key features of the modern economy such as inter-firm collaborative networking and is integral to the competitive advantage gained through organizational learning.

Boisot offers the outlines of a political economy of information, concerning both its production and exchange. The exposition is built upon two simple ideas. The first is that the emergence of organizational, institutional and, more broadly, cultural processes is shaped by flows of data within social systems. The second idea is that data flows themselves are subject to physical laws. The data processing and communicative strategies of individuals and groups reflect a coming to terms with these laws. Such strategies are driven by a need to economize which has so far escaped conventional forms of economic analysis. Economics has tended to focus on the diffusion of information and particularly on how it is used to support transactions, rather than on its production and its role as the *object* of transacting. In addition to taking information as an input into the process of exchange, Boisot provides an analysis of information as the product of an economizing effort, a product that is shaped by prevailing social institutions.

The analysis of data flows and of their institutionalization builds a bridge between the study of tangible objects and the study of meanings. As such, it provides a foundation for what Giddens refers to as the process of structuration.

The need for an analytical framework to handle the production and exchange of information has become pressing through the advent and rapid development of the data-based society. Practice in this respect is now running far ahead of our conceptual tools for understanding it. The result is that we are still running our economies on the precepts devised for the transformation of material goods through the application of physical energy. This book recognizes the growing importance of both information transformation and the trade-off in contemporary production functions between the application of informational and physical resources as distinct factors of production.

This is one of those rare path-breaking books which thoughtful people, be they academics or practitioners, should not ignore.

John Child
Guinness Professor of Management Studies
University of Cambridge

Acknowledgements

Information Space is the outcome of conversation and reflections that accumulated over fifteen years. In an age that has rediscovered that tiny causes can have big effects – one of the insights of Chaos theory – it is hard to tell which conversations or fragments of conversation have been critical in shaping the thinking contained in these pages. To list those that I readily recall is not to suggest that others have been unimportant, but extended discussions with J.M. de Anzizu, Horst Bender, Keith Blois, Philip Boxer, Chen Derong, Angela Dumas, Allan Gibb, Ken Ideus, John Irvine, Philippe Lasserre, Terry Lemmon, Judy Lowe, Tom Lupton, Henry Mintzberg, Rita McGrath, Ian McMillan, Bernard Ramananstoa, Gordon Redding, Jean-Michel Saussois, Haruo Shimada, Thanos Skouras, Nicholas Stern, David Wall, and Xing Guo Liang have all been helpful.

I should particularly like to thank Ed Schein, Douglas Hague, John Hendry, John Child, Ken Ideus, Jason Spender, Laurence Lynn, Ervin Laszlo, Dorothy Griffiths, Charles Hampden-Turner, Manfred Mack, and Bob Garratt for reading the manuscript in whole or in part and for giving me valuable comments and suggestions. Responsibility for the taking or leaving of these, of course, rests with me.

The work that led to the book was initiated many years ago when I was a research associate in the Euro-Asia Centre at INSEAD in Fontainebleau, and the support that I received from Henri-Claude de Bettignies, its founder, is gratefully acknowledged. The writing of the book was made possible by virtue of a two-year Senior Research Fellowship at Ashridge Management College that was generously made available to me by its chief executive, Philip Sadler. The book was finished with the financial and administrative support of ESADE in Barcelona and with the tireless secretarial support of Margareta Bellander Puyoles, Anna Balaguer, and Tere Octubre. Let them all be thanked. Finally, Rosemary Nixon, my 'friend at court' in Routledge, shared with me most of the anxieties and hassle involved in bringing this work to fruition. Given what I put her through, she gets the biggest thanks of all.

Introduction

0.1: THE MARKET FOR AIR

I have always been casually fascinated by the potential of inflatable structures. Are not balloons, in which a maximum of structured volume is achieved with a minimum of material (because the latter is under tension), marvels of material economy? In an earlier incarnation as an architect I had often wondered at the remarkable possibilities offered by inflatable structures. At one time it had looked as if inflatable technologies would penetrate all the nooks and crannies of our daily existence: in the 1960s, for instance, no progressive architectural magazine was without its quota of inflatable stadia, tennis courts, shunting yards, etc.; and even single-storey open plan offices occasionally fell under the spell of the new pneumatic technology.

Inflatables at that time also made their appearance in furniture stores. Who does not remember the inflatable sofa into which one reclined at one's peril? Of course, this Freudian contraption was not particularly comfortable – but then, what pioneering product ever is? What it lacked in convenience, it made up for in originality.

The next obvious candidate for inflation to my mind would be the car; large chunks of mostly empty, heavy, energy-consuming metal, blocking up the highway or the kerbside, would be replaced by featherweight, inflatable, rubber structures that would be deflated on arrival at home or at the office and then hung up on the nearest coat-hook. Fanciful? Perhaps. But in those days my fantasizing on inflatable technology was fairly unrestrained. Consider, for example, the next idea that I also toyed with. It was inspired by the Michelin man, a multilayered creature, all tyre and no brains – but inflatable! The thought struck me: why not use the concept of inflatability to create a hyper-responsive and adaptive environment around the human body and in close proximity to it? Clothes became a natural candidate for such treatment; with the right kind of instructions they could selectively inflate to become, say, an instant sofa allowing their wearer to sit down wherever he finds himself. At a pinch they could convert into a bed. In a car, clothes could offer the instant inflatable protection that Detroit is seeking to place in the car itself in the form of airbags – unless, of course, the clothes became the car itself in which case there would be no need to hang them on a coat-hook on arrival at the office as suggested above!

Pneumatic clothing offers further possibilities. Should wearers want to wash themselves they plug the inflatable outfit into the nearest taps and fill it up with warm water. A number of programmes are available to regulate the speed and temperature at which water circulates around the body, its soap content, the length of the cycle, and so on. In the last phase of the cycle, water is expelled from the outfit and replaced by a rush of warm air.

In such musings, a technology fit for astronauts is brought into the home and does away with the need for bathrooms and much of the furniture. Of course, the clothing industry, now having gone 'high tech', is put on a collision course with the furniture and the sanitationware industries, both of whose services would be increasingly dispensed with should the concept of an inflatable 'home away from home' really take off. And the threat posed to the steel and the car industries by a technology that can put clothes on wheels, thus turning them into vehicles, needs no elaboration.

Yet these are but musings. To bring them to any kind of fruition would require years if not decades of development work, with little guarantee that the final products or their derivatives would find a market, or that if they did, the market could be profitably defended against competing offerings – more air for your money? – once the technology had been mastered.

My problem – and doubtless also that of others who in their leisure hours like to give free play to their imagination in this way – is that I enjoy having such ideas rather more than the prospect of devoting several years of my life to improving their viability in the real world by actually having to make them work. They may turn out to be worth millions of dollars when successfully embodied in marketable products, but I would far rather sell them for a more modest sum to potential buyers in their raw unprocessed form and leave it to them to endure the pain of refining them into the pure gold of market winners.

In a world ruled by the principles of *caveat emptor*, however, any prospective purchaser of my mental ore would quite reasonably want to scrutinize my ideas more closely before reaching for a chequebook, and would then want to question me in detail on the technology of inflatables, on its reliability, on its applicability to the garment industry, and so on. It makes sense, after all, for anyone buying a new product in the open market to want to satisfy themselves as far as they can of its quality and potential utility.

But satisfying the prospective purchaser's legitimate curiosity concerning the attributes of a product that is as fuzzy and vague as what has been described could involve me in time-consuming explanations, descriptions, efforts at persuasion, and so on. If I was willing to go that far towards refining my ideas, then I might as well go right through to the patenting stage and set them down on paper. Yet it is precisely that part of the process of converting the ore into gold that I find tedious and would wish to leave to others. I may be prepared to outline the main features of the idea in a clear and forceful way, but no more than that.

Here I run into a familiar problem. For once the prospective buyer has had my ideas revealed to him in this way, what is to compel him to pay me for them should he now wish to exploit them? In the act of describing the goods for sale have I not actually transferred them and lost control of them? Not completely; for they are now transformed from a private into a joint possession, since two of us now have the same potentially exploitable ideas on inflatable structures. The only way that I could then extract a payment for my initial disclosure of the ideas is to threaten further disclosures to others, who might also wish to pursue the ideas further in competition with my first prospective purchaser. This would reduce the monopolistic value of our joint possession since with each new disclosure of the ideas their potential profitability would be further eroded. It follows from this that the cash I could extract from each new disclosure also goes down. This way of looking at things makes it clear that it is not so much for my ideas that I would be receiving payment as for my silence once these ideas become a joint possession. Indeed, it would not matter much if the idea had originated with the other party: once two of us possess an exploitable idea I can extract a payment for preserving its monopoly attributes by non-disclosure.

But then what should that payment be? Suppose for the sake of argument that my first prospective purchaser were in fact willing to invest in inflatable futures and to speculate some cash up front. He or she would still have a problem knowing how much to pay me for an idea coming straight off the top of my head. Recall that I do not particularly wish to spend endless hours refining the idea, defining the kinds of products it could give rise to, calculating their likely manufacturing costs, the size of the potential market for them, and so on. I wish the purchaser to do all that. I just want to be able to collect my cash, walk off, and launch myself into another round of profitable fantasizing. In other words, in the case under consideration, I am not selling neatly packaged and tested information that can be subjected to economic calculations; I am selling something that is not just unique – and hence already hard to price – but also fuzzy and vague, and characterized by rough edges and a great deal of uncertainty. My raw mental ore could be refinable into a brilliant end-product that secures for its purchaser the kind of wealth that industrial dynasties are made of, or it may end up in the graveyard of also-rans which make up 90 per cent of innovations today.

It will by now have dawned upon the reader that, given the uncertainties involved, the market for the raw product of idle musings is likely to be a thin one if it exists at all. I am unlikely to place as low a value on my ideas as a wary purchaser might and for that reason we shall find it hard to converge on a mutually acceptable price. There is no established market price for nascent ideas to guide us in this area so that if we were to strike an acceptable deal it would have to be reached through another approach.[1]

We might, for instance, agree that should the purchaser exploit the idea successfully I would receive a royalty payment on the resulting sales. This, of course, is how the patent system works, although, as we saw, to be patentable an idea has to be made explicit rather than left in a fuzzy state. Presumably, then, what I could expect to receive for my half-formulated ideas would be something less than what I could negotiate if I were to go to the added trouble of working it up to the level of detail required to file for a patent. This, however, does not affect the fact that a royalty formula could be applied in both cases.

It does not solve my problem, however. For one then has to ask how patent royalties themselves are set. What determines that an inventor or a firm granting a licence to exploit its patent will be paid 5 per cent, 7 per cent, or 15 per cent of sales achieved? The answer, it seems, is not much other than custom or straight bargaining clout.

So is it likely that a royalty formula will ensure an equitable outcome to someone trying to sell ideas in the raw? After all, by offering to pay me a percentage of his or her future sales, the purchaser is shifting a good part of the risk back on to me. To be sure, if my idea is not worth much the purchaser will not sell much and might therefore, justifiably, feel that I should share this risk. But my idea may in fact be worth a great deal and still the purchaser may not sell much. He or she may, for example, be lacking in motivation or in commercial competence, and in both cases I will end up receiving less than I could have done from a more viable prospect. How would I find such a prospect? I could go out and look for one and spend the required amount of time assessing the purchaser's willingness to develop my ideas further and his or her ability to push them into the marketplace. But this, of course, would impose upon me search costs, and possibly quite heavy ones, and for reasons already discussed I may be ill-disposed to make the effort involved. Alternatively, I could solicit bids from several prospective purchasers and select the best offer. But here again, in order to organize a fair bidding process, I would have to disclose to several prospective purchasers potentially valuable information on the contents of the ideas up for sale and hence once more reduce what I could expect to get paid for them.

Royalty payments involve some sharing of risk between buyer and seller so that prudence requires each party to 'size up' the other before it commits itself. I may prefer cash in hand to the sharing of risk but, as we saw, this only worsens my problem since a prospective purchaser and I are unlikely to agree on a price.

Yet, if it is cash that I am after, could I not simply sign a royalty deal and then just sell it on to someone willing to shoulder the risks of dealing with the purchaser? Possibly, but how am I to describe the contents of the royalty deal in sufficient detail to a prospective purchaser without lowering its intrinsic value?

It is in fact unlikely that I would be legally allowed to disclose the contents of the royalty deal to a third party – the original purchaser has after all bought the rights to the idea from me. It would seem therefore as if anyone buying future royalty payments from me is getting a product whose key attributes are unknown, i.e., a 'black box',[2] together with the original purchaser's reputed ability to turn it into a viable product. Since such a black box is unlikely to fetch the kind of price I am looking for, I am, in effect, no nearer a solution to my problems: I possess potentially valuable information that I cannot sell for cash at a price that a prospective purchaser and myself would both consider reasonable. No market for nascent ideas can emerge, on account of their inherent uncertainty, and so trading is unlikely to take place.

0.2: KEY ISSUES ADDRESSED

This is a pity. In the knowledge-intensive society that we are in the process of creating, the kind of exchange that I have just described is likely to become the key to wealth creation.

What is the issue raised by the above example? Simply this. We have an economic theory that can help us to understand and hence to manage the production and exchange of tangible objects like cornflakes and houses, but, as yet, no satisfactory economic theory to help us manage the production and exchange of intangible objects like knowledge. This book does not offer an economic theory of information as such. Rather, it maps out the contours of the territory that such a theory would have to cover. The territory's basic features can be outlined in a few words.

Perhaps its most important feature, the one that will serve as our main point of reference, is that knowledge and information do not behave economically like physical objects and for this reason cannot be subjected to the same laws of production and exchange. What is so special about the production and exchange of knowledge and information? Our basic proposition is that the way that useful knowledge is produced – essentially, as we shall see, through a process of codification and abstraction – facilitates its subsequent diffusion, and hence the terms on which it can be exchanged, to a far greater extent than is the case with a physical object. Stated bluntly, cornflakes and houses cannot be photocopied; the formula for Coca-Cola can.

In the book we present a conceptual tool, the Information Space or *I-space*, that can be used to study the codification, abstraction, and diffusion of knowledge – i.e., its production and exchange – in a social system. The I-space allows us to study how knowledge and information flow through the system and how they evolve as they do so. Such flows describe a social learning process by means of which new knowledge and information can enter the system.

Recurrent information flows give rise to transactional patterns which under certain circumstances crystallize into organizations and institutions whose characteristics reflect their specific location in the I-space. Where this happens, the resulting structures exert a reciprocal influence on the flows, and subsequently help to shape them. We thus obtain an information-based version of what Anthony Giddens has labelled a structuration process.[3]

In the I-space, culture emerges as a particular configuration of flows and structures, as the expression of information production and sharing strategies that take place within and between social groups. It follows that a political economy of information – i.e., the theory of its production and exchange – is coextensive with a theory of culture.

0.3: PLAN OF THE BOOK

Although our discussion will be conceptual it will not be – to repeat a point made earlier – narrowly economic. Our focus will be on the indirect effects imposed on economic processes by information ones, effects mediated by cognitive, social, institutional, and cultural structures, themselves also modified by the encounter. Our agenda is thus a broad one; more explicitly economic thinking creeps into it from time to time and in particular at the end of each chapter when we informally link its contents to certain economic issues, but our discussion does not have the pretension to pass itself off as economic theorizing as such.

The book is structured as follows. In Chapter 1 we discuss the problems that economics has experienced in coming to terms with the information phenomenon. We argue that these problems result from a prior conceptual commitment to energy as the primary form of wealth with information playing a support role. When, therefore, information becomes a form of wealth in its own right, economics finds itself wrong-footed and tackles the phenomenon with the wrong conceptual tools. The next two chapters describe the basic processes of information production and exchange. Chapter 2 is about the production of information – that is, the way that data is processed to produce information – and also about how this information is subsequently internalized to become knowledge. The emphasis at this stage is very much on the individual knower and on the knower's access to the world of phenomena through the data that he or she physically intercepts, processes, and then stores. Individuals differ in the way that they acquire and build up their knowledge, and a simple conceptual framework is presented to allow us to apprehend these differences. We then assess how an individual's propensity to communicate might be affected by these differences and conclude by briefly comparing the individual's data-processing attributes with those of his or her economic counterpart, economic man.

Chapter 3 embeds the individual knowing subject described in Chapter 2 in social situations which confront him or her with information exchange possibilities. When is he or she willing or able to share information and under what circumstances? Are certain kinds of knowledge subject to hoarding and what does this depend on? In what way do the conditions for the exchange of information interact with those of its production? The answers put forward to such questions complete the static formulation of our conceptual scheme.

Chapter 4 looks at the production and exchange of information as a dynamic process. It examines how production and exchange possibilities evolve over time and give rise to the creation of new knowledge in the social system. The perspective adopted is thus an evolutionary one: we are interested in how new knowledge emerges from complex information flows occurring within a target population, and also on how, at a later date, it gradually takes leave of that population. In sum, we are interested in the social system's information metabolism.

It is then the task of Chapter 5 to put some institutional flesh on to the conceptual structure presented and to bring it a bit closer to the kind of world that the reader will be familiar with. Here, the argument is advanced that institutions are themselves an outcome of information production and exchange processes and not merely devices for their governance; they are thus effects as well as causes. Four different institutional arrangements are identified and related to variations in the information environment from which they emerge. Institutional and governance structures are then distinguished from each other. The first type of structure is taken to define the means through which economizing on information will be sought; the second type, the purposes to which such economizing efforts are to be applied. In the real world, of course, the two interfuse.

In Chapter 6 we move beyond the analysis of individual institutions and develop the proposition that a political economy of information is in fact coextensive with a theory of culture so that cultural processes, far from being located on the other side of some imaginary boundary beyond which economic generalizations cease to apply and other social sciences (anthropology, sociology, etc.) take over, in effect inform the very core of such generalizations. An informational interpretation of cultural evolution is developed and then compared with more conventional economic representations of the phenomenon.

Although the conceptual framework presented in this book is not articulated to the point of yielding directly testable hypotheses, its potential usefulness as an interpretative tool can still be indicated. This is attempted in Chapter 7. It presents a case study of economic reforms in the People's Republic of China and then uses the framework to interpret them. It is shown that the difficulties experienced by the country in implementing economic reforms are primarily cultural and institutional rather than economic in the conventional sense. China's development experiences are then compared with those of Japan – still drawing on the framework as an interpretative guide – and then used as a point of reference in order to analyse the reform efforts currently under way in Eastern Europe and in the former Soviet Union. The potential usefulness of our conceptual framework is thus further illustrated.

Chapter 8 is our concluding chapter. It briefly recapitulates the main features of our conceptual framework and maps out possible directions for its future development. The main differences between the economist's perspective on information and the one developed in this book are highlighted, in effect also recapitulating the last section of each chapter.

Chapter 1

Orienting thoughts on information*

ABSTRACT

The value of information, if taken in the Walrasian sense of utility and scarcity, is indeterminate and can never be fully ascertained. The very act of ascertaining its utility reduces its scarcity. As a consequence, only those information goods whose utility is manifest can be traded unproblematically.

Until quite recently, economics treated information almost exclusively as a support to transactions rather than as an object of transactions in its own right. Yet today, with information becoming increasingly the focus of transactions, its indeterminacy, with respect to value, poses an important theoretical challenge. Nevertheless, in spite of the fact that information issues have now become central to much of modern physics, chemistry, and biology, mainstream economics continues to address them within an outdated nineteenth-century equilibrium framework.

What is now needed is a far-from-equilibrium information economics which allows for innovation, evolution, and learning. In the closing years of the twentieth century, the way that information is created and shared between economic agents has become a crucial determinant of corporate and national competitive advantage. Information is an extract from data, itself a form of low-level energy subject to the ravages of entropy. Nature minimizes the production of entropy by economizing on its consumption of both low-level and high-level energy. Such economizing can best be visualized by creating a production function that treats data (low-level energy) and physical resources (space, time, and high-level energy) as distinct factors of production.

We currently have an economics for the physical axis of our proposed production function but not for the data axis. While the information content of economic goods was low, this theoretical deficiency was hidden from view. No longer. The need for a plausible economics of information becomes ever more pressing.

1.1: THE INDETERMINATE NATURE OF INFORMATION

The second half of the twentieth century will be remembered as the period in which information came to replace energy as the central fact of life in post-industrial societies. Information forms the core of what Freeman and Perez[1] call a 'techno-economic paradigm ... a combination of interrelated products and processes, technical, organizational and managerial innovations,

---

*This chapter is an adaptation of an article that was published in *World Futures*, 41, 1994, pp. 227–56.

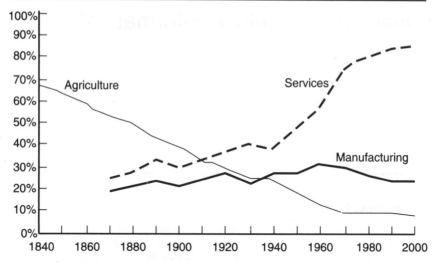

Figure 1.1 Employment as percentage of total labour force
Source: J.B. Quinn, *Intelligent Enterprise*, New York, Free Press, 1992, p. 4

embodying a quantum jump in potential productivity for all or most of the economy and opening up an unusually wide range of investment and profit opportunities. Such a paradigm change implies a unique new combination of decisive technical *and* economic advantages.'[2]

The centrality of information in social and economic life is evidenced, as Figure 1.1 indicates, less by the much-debated decline of manufacturing than by the market growth of service employment (Figure 1.1). In Japan, for example, according to figures published by the Management and Coordinating Agency of Japan, among the top 50 industrial companies, R and D spending exceeded capital spending for the first time in 1986.[3]

Powerful as the new paradigm may be in reshaping our lives, we continue to confront the numerous challenges it poses for us with the conceptual tools of the paradigm that it is replacing – those of the energy-based economy. Stated bluntly, we go on treating economic goods that come out of our heads as if they could be dropped on our feet. They are fundamentally different.

Walras, in his *Elements of Pure Economics*, established that only things which exhibit the joint properties of utility and scarcity can have value and contribute to social wealth: 'By *social wealth* I mean all things, material or immaterial (it does not matter which in this context), that are *scarce*, that is to say, on the one hand *useful* to us, and, on the other hand, only available to us *in limited quantity*.'[4]

Appropriability is a key requirement for Walras's theory of value to hold. It allows an economic good to be examined and its potential utility to be assessed without fundamentally altering the terms of the transaction. In cases of adverse selection or moral hazard[5] assessment is problematic and transactional efficiency is lost. Yet utility and scarcity still drive the transaction. The exact utility of a second-hand car may be hard to assess but either the vehicle stays with the dealer or its ownership is transferred to a purchaser.

Information, as we know, is not like that. Its utility can only be properly ascertained by disclosure, and disclosure inevitably compromises its scarcity. Patents, trademarks and the institutions of intellectual property are devices designed to cope with this phenomenon by giving scarcity a legal rather than a physical basis. But they do not do away with the phenomenon; they merely mitigate its effects under highly restrictive circumstances and at considerable cost. The irreducible economic fact is that an information good incurs a loss of scarcity in the very process of having its utility ascertained. No less than a subatomic particle, it is afflicted by the economic equivalent of Heisenberg's Uncertainty Principle which states that it is impossible to determine with accuracy both the position and the momentum of a particle simultaneously. The more accurately the position is known, the less accurately can the momentum be determined. Below a level of resolution set by Planck's constant, the energy expended in measuring a particle's position alters its momentum. Conversely, measuring its momentum alters its position.

Heisenberg's Uncertainty Principle, by introducing indeterminism into physical processes at the microscale – at the macroscale the effects of the Uncertainty Principle could be swamped by statistical effects – transformed our conception of the physical world. Our guiding proposition in this book is that information as an economic good is also indeterminate so that its value cannot be fully ascertained: its utility cannot be accurately measured without compromising its scarcity and hence its value, likewise its scarcity cannot be fully secured – i.e., it cannot be made fully appropriable – without to some extent limiting its utility. Information on information goods is not there for the taking; it first has to be extracted from the data, an uncertain and costly process that favours cases in which the utility of the good is in some sense manifest rather than elusive. In practice, therefore, only well-formed information goods – as we shall later see, those characterized by a high degree of codification and abstraction – will be subject to trading. Less well-formed information goods, by far the larger part of them in an information society, thus confront market failure.

1.2: NEWTONIAN ECONOMICS

That, contrary to the perfect information assumption of neoclassical economics, the acquisition of information carries a cost, is now accepted by most economists, and if this makes market clearing more difficult to attain, then so be it. Information costs thus highlight the limitations of the traditional competitive paradigm to which mainstream economists still subscribe, in situations where the information required for trading is either incomplete, ambiguous, or asymmetrically distributed. Some economists like Coase[6] have argued that complete competitive markets are not in fact necessary to achieve economically efficient outcomes since people can get together and negotiate their way to efficiency providing that nothing obstructs the bargaining process.[7] But the 'Coase Theorem', as it has come to be known, appears to be somewhat implausible unless restricted to situations in which people know one another exceptionally well, which by itself moves one away from the kinds of efficiencies promised by impersonal trading.[8]

The point we are making here, however, is that information costs are not the only issue – nor even, perhaps, the most important one. They introduce some friction into the equilibrating process that leads to market clearing – sometimes fatally – but we do not challenge the coherence of the process itself. Things change, though, when we treat information not just as a *support* to economic exchange but as its *focus*. For then the central problem ceases to be the cost of information but its indeterminism with respect to value. As far back as 1962, Arrow had fingered inappropriability and uncertainty as the chief culprits in accounting for the tendency to underinvestment in information goods.[9] Uncertainty concerning the utility of an information good poses a problem of disclosure and thus of appropriability. Yet even if uncertainty were wholly absent, that is to say, if the utility attributes of the information good were fully known, appropriability would still remain a problem. The reason is that information, unlike physical goods, is virtually costless to reproduce and can very quickly become everyone's *possession* even if, in strictly legal terms, they can claim no property right over it. Indeed, as we shall see in later chapters, reducing the uncertainty associated with an information good actually facilitates its diffusion and thus effectively exacerbates the appropriability problem.

In spite of its apparent robustness, then, informational issues have been nibbling away at the competitive paradigm for some time, and this both from the inside and from the outside. From the inside they challenge the putative efficiency of markets as a theoretically viable proposition. Such efficiency, as we have seen, is predicated on the ubiquity of well-structured information purged of any ambiguity and subject neither to hoarding nor to leakages. Only then can the price system function as a reliable signalling device[10] – if information turns out to be costly to acquire then prices cannot perfectly reflect its availability as if it was costless since, if it did, those who spent resources to obtain it would receive no compensation.[11] The result is a fundamental conflict between the supposed efficiency with which markets spread information and the incentives that exist to acquire that information.

For those who situate themselves outside the competitive paradigm, informational issues not only challenge the vaunted efficiencies of market clearing, but also call into question the scope of market institutions in the regulation of economic activity. In the words of Joseph Stiglitz:

Traditional economic analysis was predicated on three maxims. The first, due to Marshall, was that nature abhorred discontinuities. The second, due to Samuelson, was that nature abhorred non-convexities: not only could individual and firm behaviour be described as the solution to simple maximization problems ... but the behaviour of the economy as a whole could be described as if it were the solution to some maximization problem.

The third is the law of supply and demand; it has played a central role in the traditional economist's tool kit ...

Recent work in the economics of information has cast doubts on all three maxims. The world is not convex; the behaviour of the economy cannot be described as if it were solving any (simple) maximization problem; the law of supply and demand has been repealed.[12]

Stiglitz goes on to observe that 'Informational considerations [are] a central part of the "Foundations of Economic Analysis"' but also that 'There seem to be a myriad of special cases and few general principles',[13] and this in spite of the fact that work on the economics of information has been going on in economics for over three decades, attracting researchers such as Marschak (1959), Stigler (1961), Alchian (1969), Radner (1961), Hirschleifer (1971), Rothschild (1973), Spence (1973), and Arrow (1971, 1974).[14] Information economics has also provided some of the microfoundations for macroeconomics and created the basis for a New Theory of the Firm, a New Welfare Economics, and a New Theory of Economic Organization.

The discipline's paradigmatic core, however, remains essentially untouched by this work. We should not be too surprised at this. Referring to the sciences in general, the French physicist Pierre Duhem long ago pointed out that the theoretical core of any established discipline is protected by a belt of auxiliary hypotheses which adjust and adapt to challenges as they emerge and allow the core to survive in comparative tranquillity.[15] A Popperian type of refutation may well function within the protective belt itself but it rarely burrows through to the core, which is only likely to lose adherents when a new, more marketable, alternative paradigm is set up to compete with the dominant one.[16] Thus only when a competing paradigm has been developed and becomes available is the discipline's theoretical core genuinely threatened.[17]

The reason, therefore, that the traditional paradigm of perfectly competitive markets based on the theory of general economic equilibrium remains so ensconced in spite of the continued nibbling away at its central assumptions by information economics is that this new body of work has not yet produced a viable alternative paradigm. There is fermentation, there is interest, but a paradigm, in the sense of a conceptually articulate framework[18] that can compete with the neoclassical one in explanatory scope, there is not.

And yet the competitive paradigm is increasingly vulnerable to challenge.

It is, as Stiglitz has put it, 'an artfully constructed structure: when one of the central pieces (the assumption of perfect information) is removed, the structure collapses'.[19] Its continued inability to deal convincingly with knowledge and information, in the shape that they are usually encountered when they roam the open spaces of the real world, is limiting its territorial claims to those small islands of institutional practice where the perfect information assumption can still be plausibly sustained: some commodity and some financial markets – not beyond the real world, to be sure, but no big part of it either.[20]

The failure of orthodox economics to accommodate a credible theory of information within its paradigmatic core owes something to its early choice of intellectual role model within the natural sciences. Like many of the social sciences that were seeking to gain recognition at the end of the last century, economics aspired to the rigour and elegance achieved by classical physics,[21] an intellectual edifice which, by the early decades of the twentieth century, had itself fallen victim to paradigmatic change. Interestingly enough, that *change was partly brought about by incorporating information and communication concepts into the very core of physics as a discipline.*

The transformation of classical physics was hastened firstly by the quantum theory inaugurated by Max Planck's paper of 1900, and secondly by Einstein's theory of relativity in both its special (1905) and its general formulation (1915). Twentieth-century physics has, in effect, achieved much of its spectacular progress through an identification and exploration of the limiting cases in which data concerning a physical event can be said to be available to an external observer – given by Heisenberg's Uncertainty Principle – and also by identifying physical limits to the transfer of such data in space–time – given by Einstein's relativity equations. In each instance, data, the raw material from which information can be extracted, is viewed as an energetic phenomenon in space–time, a discernible difference between energy states that have both duration and location. Information, then, although itself not physical, has a physical basis.

Within the physics community itself the new paradigm has remained controversial. It no longer competes with the old classical model, which it has now superseded, but which has also been incorporated as a special case; in this sense the triumph of the new physics is complete. Yet physicists have split into two camps, with some taking the physical limits on information and communication imposed by the quantum and relativity theories as being essentially *epistemological* in nature, thus telling us how little *we* can know of the world in our capacity as observers, and others taking them to be *ontological* and hence revelatory of some basic existential properties of the world itself.[22]

Economics did not merely look to classical physics for general inspiration; it heavily adopted many of its conceptual models. As Mirowski puts it, 'The further one digs, the greater the realization that those neoclassicals did not imitate physics in a desultory or superficial manner; no, they copied their models mostly term for term and symbol for symbol and said so.'[23] What were these models? Essentially a product of Descartes' mechanical philosophy and Newton's law of universal gravitation. Descartes had reduced all phenomena to matter in motion, a reduction which, when coupled with the Newtonian conception of action at a distance, allowed the universe to be thought of as a giant clockwork mechanism running according to immutable laws which in the absence of friction could run on forever. In the 1840s the 'simultaneous discovery' of the conservation of energy recast nineteenth-century physics. By linking previously disjunct and disparate studies of motion, heat, light, electricity, and magnetism, energy provided an organizing principle for the conduct of physical research. It allowed a reduction of all phenomena to their energetic foundations.[24]

In the second half of the nineteenth century, the energy concept gave birth to the theory of the field, 'a spatial distribution of energy that varies with time' and which liberates energy from all dependence upon matter.[25] The formalism of the field, however, is only of use in cases where one can safely abstract away all considerations of process and the passage of time. Path dependence violates the conservation principles assumed by the formalism and undermines its coherence. It introduces dissipative processes such as friction into the system, so that any initial concerted motion gradually gets dampened until the system reaches thermodynamic equilibrium – i.e., all its initial high-grade energy has been dissipated into random thermal motion. In the absence of friction a classical system is reversible and can be run backward with no loss of energy or information; with friction, though, it moves irreversibly towards a deterministic thermal equilibrium.[26] The thermal equilibrium of dissipative processes thus threatens the timeless mechanical equilibrium of classical systems.

One of the main challenges confronting mid-nineteenth-century physics was to reconcile existing theories of heat with the new notion of energy. The reconciliation was brought about by Rudolph Clausius who in 1865 founded the science of thermodynamics. It rested on two laws: the first, that the energy of the universe is a constant; the second, that in the universe an opaque quantity called *entropy*, which measures the disorder in a system, increases to a maximum. The concept of entropy threatened the determinism of the classical system, what Mirowski labels 'the physics of the Laplacean dream'. In our own century such determinism has been further eroded by quantum mechanics which stipulates that every act of measurement or intervention in the world is at some level fundamentally irreversible.[27] Under such circumstances the energy concept dissolves; it fails to provide a metric independent of our endeavours to know it.

Thermodynamics, like general relativity, quantum mechanics, chaos theory, and the grand theories of unified forces, characterizes *modern* as opposed to classical physics; it has contributed to a revision of the very structure of explanation in physical theory. Economics, particularly the neoclassical variety, has been unable to follow. Guided as it has been by a pre-thermodynamic energy metaphor in its conception of economic value – in his posthumous *Principles of Economics*, Jevons wrote explicitly that 'the notion of value is to our science what that of energy is to mechanics'[28] – it has been unable to absorb the concepts of modern physics. They threaten the discipline's paradigmatic core. It thus remains wedded to a straw man of *c.* 1860 vintage.

Economics achieved its status as a science by appropriating a mid-nineteenth-century physics of energy which it then got stuck with. In such a scheme the second law of thermodynamics has no purchase: microscopic diversity, expressed as the fluctuation of variables and parameters around average levels, is then treated as so much 'noise' that gets attenuated – even if not actually eliminated – as the system as a whole moves towards mechanical equilibrium. In competitive markets regulated by Walras's auctioneer, for example, errors in pricing are gradually corrected through feedback mechanisms that refer continuously back to the disequilibria generated.[29] Only the most probable, 'average' states will subsist in such a system, which can then be likened to a 'machine' represented by a set of differential equations that govern its variables.

For the majority of applications, physical or social, dealing with macro-scopic phenomena, average values in effect create few problems and the classical paradigm thus retains its utility. Average values, however, can be quite misleading if what matters turns out to be dynamic behaviour at the boundary of the system. Here local values may count for more than average values so that dissipative quantum effects may then come into play. As Allen puts it, 'In non-linear systems, it is no longer sufficient to simply suppose that if there are many individuals involved the law of large numbers will ensure that the average value will be a good representation of reality...'.[30]

Of course, this is precisely what is assumed in a classical system. After all, its beauty resides largely in the computational economies yielded by such assumptions: with a minimum amount of data on the system's initial position and velocity, both expressed as averages, its future states can be completely determined.

As early as the eighteenth century, social philosophers were trying to capture these economies in ways that would allow a similar aggregation of social and behaviourial phenomena.[31] The law of large numbers, it was argued, would allow a reduction of complex social processes to simple mechanical ones that would be amenable to analysis and prediction. In the nineteenth century, Comte, in his *Cours de Philosophie Positive*, would label the new social science he was laying claim to, 'social physics'. As conceived by him, this science consisted of the statics and dynamics of society.[32]

Yet since individuals are not pieces of inert matter moving exclusively under the influence of external forces – they are more plausibly viewed as autonomous intentional agents[33] – how is one to get them to behave with such mechanical predictability? How can countless individuals each pursuing personal and sometimes quite idiosyncratic objectives be convincingly tamed by the law of large numbers?

Since the Enlightenment, the answer that has gradually emerged is the fruit of an abstraction from the myriad features that make up an individual, an abstraction that singled out those information-processing powers that he or she shares with others and that are held to constitute the hallmark of the species: it is rationality that makes behaviour predictable. Under the rationality postulate, individuals with similar objectives, in possession of identical information and endowed with average computational skills, will be led to make pretty much identical choices, individual variations between them being cancelled out as their number increases. Average values could thus replace individual values, and economic man, a mechanical information-processor that could be made to maximize a simple set of objectives based on self-interest, narrowly construed, could then be allowed to do duty for the messy complexities of human behaviour that lay beyond the reach of analysis.

Some requirement, such as the one for identical information endowments, could be a source of difficulty for economic man since it rarely seemed to be met in practice. In the neoclassical scheme, the problem was therefore simplified in two ways. The first was to assume that in addition to knowledge of their own production possibilities and tastes, individuals need only possess one other item of information for rationality to do its work, and that was price information. The elusive complexities of exchange in tradable goods would then be all encoded in a summary piece of data, the price,[34] thus relieving an individual involved in exchange of an information-processing burden that might overload him and impair his rationality.[35]

The second simplification was to assume that, providing that there was no overt information hoarding by traders, price information would be sufficiently ubiquitous in the economy to drive a self-regulating process of market exchange towards equilibrium. The equilibrium-seeking properties of the economic system so construed could be viewed as the equivalent of inertia in the Newtonian scheme, a tendency to continue in a given state in space and time in the absence of external disturbances. An information plenum of well-articulated and ubiquitous price data was to play the same role as the luminiferous ether in a mechanical universe – that is, to provide a fixed and objective system of reference around which equilibrium might occur. Less noticed, perhaps, it also called for a fairly mechanical concept of human rationality in which price data was to be processed by individuals in ways amenable to statistical aggregation and prediction.

Neoclassical economists were concerned to demonstrate that this self-regulating process, the market, exhibited a much-prized mechanical property: *efficiency* – an expression of economy in mechanical systems measured by the ratio of output to inputs. If, at equilibrium, a market could be shown to be efficient then it was held to be less wasteful than alternative ways of allocating society's resources. Just as a more efficient engine was to be preferred to a less efficient one, so a market that met the stipulated efficiency requirements – these included, but went beyond, the perfect information assumption – was superior to ones that did not. Institutional arrangements and policy measures therefore should be oriented towards the meeting of such requirements and should generally favour market-driven solutions over competing alternatives.[36]

The continued appeal of the neoclassical economic paradigm in spite of its increasingly Ptolemaic appearance rests in large part on the simplicity of its information assumptions, a simplicity that, to be sure, has allowed considerable progress to be made in our understanding of the market mechanism. Much of the theoretical debate that has taken place in economics over the last ten years, however, can be traced to a growing recognition of just how fragile those assumptions turn out to be. Critics of the neoclassical paradigm attack the sheer implausibility of perfect information requirement and its otherworldly quality. In the real world, transactionally relevant information is mostly local,[37] asymmetrically distributed,[38] and sometimes only tenuously connected with the events it purports to describe;[39] people interpret it in different ways.

More importantly perhaps, even if information was as bountiful as required by the paradigm, economic agents could not handle it with the degree of efficiency that delivers the requisite level of rationality: their information-processing capacities are limited and their rationality consequently bounded.[40] It is the failure of markets on information grounds that gives rise in the real world to alternative institutional arrangements such as firms for the governance of economic transactions.[41]

Such criticisms do not aim to jettison the concept of the perfectly competitive market which has served economists so well, but rather to limit its territorial claims over the field of economics. It has exercised a hegemonistic influence over economic theorizing out of all proportion to its effective explanatory scope. Some forms of real economic exchange are found to approximate the competitive paradigm, but they form only a small part of economizing activity in general, and it is increasingly felt by economists and non-economists alike that the paradigm itself should not continue to dominate economic thinking as it has done until now.

1.3: THE NEED FOR A POST-NEWTONIAN ECONOMICS

Just as classical physics, unrefuted, became a special case in conceptual schemes of greater generality – i.e., the general theory of relativity and the quantum theory – so neoclassical economics and its cherished lodestar, market equilibrium, may turn out to be less than the whole story when information and communication processes are given their proper place in the economic scheme of things.

At this point, however, the defenders of mainstream economics might lodge an objection. Newtonian physics, they may observe, for all its limitations, continues to serve perfectly well as a rough and ready guide for our daily activities: does it not help us intuitively to avoid falling tiles, to enjoy a game of billiards or table tennis, to jump on or off buses and so on? Why should economics, which operates neither at the quantum nor at the cosmic scale, not remain operationally valid as a theory of the middle range,[42] at that level of statistical aggregation for which the classical scheme still largely holds good and at which human behaviour becomes intelligible as such? After all, does economics, as a *social* science, really *need* the level of generality achieved by the new physics?

The argument has a certain practical force and the great majority of economists and their paymasters are nothing if not practical people. They do not feel driven to burrow down into the world of the quantum or to roam at the speed of light through intergalactic space in their search for practical solutions to pressing human problems.

The reply to such a practical objection comes in two parts, the first theoretical, and the second itself also practical.

The theoretical part draws on some important conceptual advances recently achieved in physics – in far from equilibrium thermodynamics – and mathematics – in the theory of chaos. Both advances show that the evolutionary potential of any system is ultimately linked to the existence of microscopic freedom, represented as stochasticity or 'noise'.[43] Even a Newtonian mechanical system has stochasticity at its core and hence offers scope for evolution. A Newtonian system, however, also known as a Hamiltonian system, is one in which no dissipation of energy is allowed to occur and in which the second law of thermodynamics, the entropy law, is consequently held in abeyance. It turns out that chaos is nevertheless present in such a system, as a persistent instability at the microscopic level. The fact that such chaos is deterministic challenges the nineteenth-century probability theories upon which much of the competitive paradigm in economics has been modelled.[44]

Chaos is pervasive in the natural world; it is a consequence of non-linearity. On close examination most phenomena turn out to be non-linear, a discovery that should provoke a greater amount of rethinking about the nature of the world we live in than has taken place so far. As Ian Percival, writing on the subject in the *New Scientist*, has aptly quipped, 'the very word non-linearity is deception: it is as if most of biology were called the study of non-elephant life'.[45]

Yet we must persist with our question: why should such theories having their effects at the microscopic level matter to economists concerned with the human realm? Essentially because stochastic effects, far from being a minor and corrigible irritation to a modeller concerned with long-run equilibrium results, have the power to drive an economic system from one state of organization to another, in effect provoking *evolutionary* rather than *mechanical* change. Allen and McGlade argue that 'Just as fluctuations in variables and parameters can radically affect the evolution of the spatial and structural organization of complex systems, so the real microscopic diversity underlying simple kinetic models is the real source of innovation and change in the nature of elements which make up the system.'[46]

In another paper Allen has pointed out that the discovery of so-called dissipative structures has ushered in an entirely new paradigm in the natural sciences, one which places *choice* at the heart of physical processes. 'In systems far from thermodynamic equilibrium, non-linear interactions between the microelements can give rise to macroscopic states of organization and behaviour that undergo *bifurcation*, that is, for identical external conditions, various possible structures can exist, each of which is perfectly compatible with the microcopic interactions ... This new description allows us to understand *innovation*.'[47]

And innovation is precisely what the neoclassical paradigm, given its orientation towards static equilibrium, has been unable to explain. In the new physical paradigm, innovation emerges from the very 'noise' that competitive market theory has chosen to ignore. The reason for its neglect is understandable since such innovation is in a fundamental sense unpredictable: past states of the system do not yield sufficient information to establish its future states. Yet if *microscopic* causes can have such unanticipated *macroscopic* effects can economists really afford to ignore them in the name of analytical tractability? Do the simplicities of the classical physics paradigm in economics offer anything more than false economies?[48] The second part of our reply builds on the first: in the age of molecular engineering and of the 'Galileo' space probe telescope the effective interpenetration of the microscopic and the macroscopic in human affairs allows no artificial distinction to be maintained between them for the sake of analytical convenience. With the dematerialization of production – i.e., the progressive reduction of energy content per unit of value created and the progressive increase in its information content[49] – we are moving towards an economic system in which information can no longer continue to be treated by economists simply as an external *support* for economic exchange; it has to be considered increasingly as its main focus. Indeed, is innovation – the phenomenon that the neoclassical paradigm has found it so difficult to account for – anything other than the creation and diffusion of new information within a social system, information embedded physically in goods, symbolically in documents, or biologically in cognitive and behavioural patterns?

Creating and sharing new information constitute the core of a modern nation's competitive advantage. To illustrate the point, we can refer to Dennison's exercise in 'growth accounting' for the United States for the period 1929–1982.[50] Smoothing away the business cycle he finds that education per worker accounts for 30 per cent of the increase in output per worker over the period and that advances in knowledge account for 64 per cent. Thus technical change remains the dominant engine of growth, with investments in human capital taking second place. Both are information phenomena and yet neither can be adequately accounted for within the competitive paradigm.[51]

Arrow has identified three areas in which information phenomena today pose a challenge to the neoclassical paradigm: (1) the economic relevance of non-price signals – i.e., information that is not captured in prices; (2) the costliness and economic value of information; (3) the differential possession of information by individuals.[52] These phenomena all point in the same direction: towards a treatment of information as a focus for economic exchange and not simply as a support for it. The information revolution, by transforming information into the dominant form of wealth generated by industrialized societies, dramatically increases the stakes for the neoclassical paradigm in meeting this challenge. If economists want to be listened to they will have to accommodate information-based concepts of wealth alongside the energy-based ones they have been working with up until now.

Recent developments in the world economy add to the urgency. Trade in information and services is now on the agenda at the WTO in belated recognition of the fact that it accounts for a growing proportion of world trade.[53] More importantly, perhaps, recent upheavals in the post-communist countries have made more credible theorizing on information issues a pressing matter. Following the widespread collapse of Marxism-Leninism as a viable ideology, economists in Eastern Europe, in the former Soviet Union, and, in spite of political setbacks, in China[54] are all seeking help from western economic models in bringing about a peaceful transition from a totalitarian to a more democratic order. Their economies initially got themselves into a rut by building on Marx's outdated conception of economic processes.[55] They could yet again repeat their mistakes if the only economic models that western economists can make available to would-be reformers are those about to be rendered obsolete by the information revolution.

1.4: IN QUEST OF A 'GESTALT SWITCH'

While this book aims to contribute to the creation of a new information-based economic paradigm, hopefully of use to economists among others, it is primarily about information rather than economics. Where the latter puts in an appearance, it is at the margin of the discussion. The book sets out a broad conceptual scheme that indicates the kind of thinking about information that economists and those in related social science disciplines will have to undertake if information is to be credibly incorporated into their theorizing. The scheme explores the conditions in which information is produced and exchanged in human affairs and, using broad qualitative strokes, it brushes in the outlines of what could be called a political economy of information.

In what follows, a certain number of working assumptions concerning the nature of information are presented. We are concerned to understand how it affects and is affected by physical processes over time. We start by reaffirming the distinction that is often drawn between knowledge, information, and data.[56]

As Popper has stressed, knowledge is dispositional, a readiness to act on the basis of beliefs, more or less firmly held, concerning the world or some part thereof.[57] In effect, knowledge might be represented as a set of probability distributions that we deploy with respect to the phenomena that we encounter: distributions on sets of expectations shaped by repeated encounters with information.[58] The latter by contrast constitutes an *extraction* from data that acts upon our probability distributions and either modifies or reinforces them – i.e., information makes a difference to the way we think about things or to our disposition to act. Data that does not bring about this modification to the knowledge that we possess carries no information; it is uninformative.

But what about data itself, the raw material out of which information is metabolized; how shall we characterize it? Knowledge describes our internal dispositional states as knowing and acting subjects; these are modified by acts of information extraction that we ourselves perform on data that reaches us through our senses. Data itself can then be thought of as an energetic phenomenon that links us in our capacity as knowing subjects to an external physical world.[59] Data in its most basic formulation is a discernible difference in the energy states of phenomena as they occur and propagate in space–time, whether as matter or electromagnetically.

Let us elaborate a little. Any state, to qualify as such, must have spatiotemporal extension, however brief, and be potentially discernible to an 'observer'; that is, it must register as *data* with some entity that can process it as such as well as being a purely energetic phenomenon.[60] It must thus be capable of extending itself and reaching out in space and time beyond the phenomenon that constitutes it. Consider a state, for example, that falls below the threshold of discernibility and does not propagate data; like an ideal isolated system that exchanges neither matter, energy, nor information with its surroundings, it remains unknowable. As a rule of thumb, it is not possible to see something smaller than the wavelength used to probe it and since smaller wavelengths are equivalent to higher energies – microwaves are more energetic than radio waves, and gamma waves more energetic still – it is only at very high energies that the smallest physical entities can be identified and explored, thus existing as data for observers.

Energy is not only required for probing; it is also needed to overcome the forces that bind matter together if its microscopic constituents are to be successfully isolated. Today's most powerful man-made provider of energy is the Tevatron at Fermilab outside Chicago, capable of accelerating protons to an energy of 1 TeV (1 trillion electronvolts). In the microworld, however, duration as well as size poses problems for observers. Some 'mass structures' or particles may survive for only a trillion trillionth of a second before decaying into other particles. These may decay in turn until stable particles are formed.[61]

Since such microscopic and short-lived energy states cannot be detected by a human observer unaided they need to be transformed into other states with more accessible spatiotemporal characteristics. The extraterrestrial macroworld presents observers with similar problems, however, since the velocity of light sets an upper limit to the speed at which electromagnetic energy acting as a signal, and hence as data, can reach us. Thus if in the microworld the constraints on our access to data are mostly energetic, in the macroworld they are mostly spatial. Physical phenomena can therefore only manifest themselves as data to observers within certain regions of space–time and within certain energy ranges, and this whether they do so directly or indirectly. In space–time the outer limits of the spatiotemporal region are set by the speed at which light can travel and the lower limit by Planck's constant. The upper limits of the energy range have not yet been identified or reached and its lower limits are set by the so-called 'zero point energy' – that is, the point below which according to quantum theory it is impossible to further remove energy from a system. Zero point energy is also known as vacuum energy.

The physical constraints on an observer's access to data can be described by means of a diagram (Figure 1.2) in which the size of the spatiotemporal region is represented by the vertical scale, and the energy level by the horizontal scale. An observer can only exist *qua* observer where physical phenomena can exist as data, an area notionally bounded by the dashed lines AA' and BB' in the figure. Modern science and technology have dramatically extended the spatiotemporal and energy ranges within which man as an observer currently has access to data. Radio telescopes allow us to pick up signals emitted billions of light years away and electron microscopes can achieve a resolution of a few angstroms. At the same time events occurring within the energy range from 1 TeV down to 1 photon can now be detected. Data that would be well beyond the unaided reach of our five senses can now be captured and processed. Five hundred years ago what was accessible to men as data would have been much more severely circumscribed by the science and technology then available. Figure 1.3 depicts this second situation as a set of more narrowly spaced dashed lines AA' and BB'.

If our horizons have expanded, it is because more of the universe that we inhabit is today available to us as data. Science and technology both continue to expand the region in Figure 1.2 within which we enjoy the status of observers.

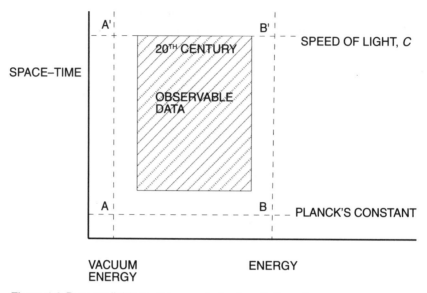

Figure 1.2 Data available to observers in the twentieth century

But does not the term 'observer' in the sense that we have used it carry a somewhat passive connotation when applied to man? Should we really be casting ourselves in the role of mere spectators, bearing witness to the wonders of God's creation with a certain detached interest?[62]

Could the knowledge thus gained not be made to serve a more instrumental purpose if by furthering man's understanding of his place in nature it provides him with a set of values that enhance his survival prospects? Beyond the values that can be distilled from such knowledge, moreover, lies the opportunity it affords for man to secure some direct and active mastery over nature, and with it not only a greater chance of survival but also, and more importantly perhaps, a higher quality of survival. Human beings, like all biological entities, seek to maintain – and in some cases extend – their spatiotemporal identity with minimum expenditures of energy or increases in entropy. Such parsimony reveals an economic principle at work in evolution. Brooks and Wiley describe it thus: 'Evolution is a process that slows down the entropic decay of lineages, minimizing their entropy increases. This suggests that, as the interplay of information and cohesion, biological evolution should exhibit an intrinsic tendency towards efficiency or parsimony which in turn should relate to the principle of minimum entropy production.'[63]

Minimizing entropy production, however, is not a characteristic unique to biological systems. It characterizes all non-equilibrium systems.[64] Brooks and Wiley argue that in purely thermodynamic systems the ordering process through which entropy production is minimized is a direct by-product of

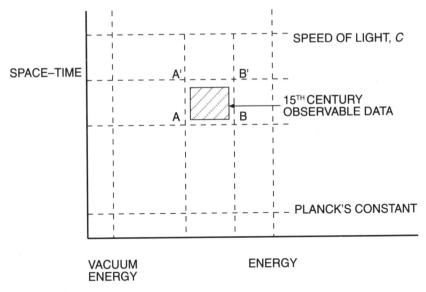

Figure 1.3 Data available to observers in the fifteenth century

energy flows, whereas in evolutionary systems it is a by-product of information and cohesion changes.[65] Yet to the extent that an ordering process can itself be considered as a generator of information it acts as a bridge between thermodynamic and evolutionary phenomena.

The idea that nature behaves parsimoniously has a respectable ancestry. Cartesians such as Malebranche, for example, made explicit use of metaphors that referred to 'the economy of nature'.[66] But it was in 1744, with the publication of Maupertuis's Principle of Least Action, that general extremal principles were introduced into mechanics.

Maupertuis defined a mathematical quantity which he termed the *Action* and which involved the product of mass, velocity, and distance travelled by bodies.[67] Maupertuis's Principle, which subsequently became known as the Principle of Least Action, was that 'If there occurs some change in Nature, the amount of action necessary for this change must be as small as possible.' The Principle turned out to be equivalent to Newton's laws of motion, only this time formulated teleologically.[68] The Principle was later generalized by Maupertuis's friend, the mathematician Leonhard Euler, into an integral theorem, valid for the continuous motion of a single particle acted on by an arbitrary conservative force. Euler's own action principle was in turn extended by Lagrange in 1760 to the case of motion of a system of interacting particles and given a particularly useful formulation by Hamilton in 1835.[69] Such formulations were not popular in an age which preferred mechanical causes to divine providence as explanations of the physical world, but they certainly were in the air; indeed, a century before Maupertuis's discovery,

Fermat had already put forward something analogous in the principle of least time: out of all possible paths that it might take to get from one point to another, light takes the path which requires the shortest time.

In both Maupertuis's and Fermat's teleological schemes, *nature economizes*. In words that foreshadowed the entropy concept, Maupertuis, referring to the action, observed that 'it is this quantity of action which is here the true expense (*dépense*) of nature, and which she economizes as much as possible'.[70] In the twentieth century, Einstein completed Maupertuis's Principle of Least Action with his general relativity theory. The geodesic hypothesis introduced by the theory states that the path of any free particle is a geodesic in space–time.[71]

We can grasp the essentially *economic* nature of the Principle of Least Action by delving a little into the economist's toolkit and making use – albeit with some adaptations – of what he terms a production function.

Any productive action can be characterized as a mix of inputs required to perform it; in the economic literature these have traditionally been defined in terms of land, labour, capital, etc., because these were the categories that economists were used to dealing with; they reflected the taken-for-granted institutional order. Yet there is in fact no specific restriction on how inputs are defined. A production function then specifies different quantities and mixes of inputs or *factors of production* required to produce a given level of output efficiently at current levels of knowledge. In Figure 1.4, for example, a given quantity of widgets might be produced by different mixes of capital and labour each representing a distinct choice of technology and each located at different points on the curve AA'.

Moving along the curve from A to A' one engages in factor substitution – that is, holding output constant, one shifts from technologies that are labour intensive to technologies that are capital intensive. Factor substitution occurs in response to changes in the relative price of capital and labour as measured by the slope of the tangent to the curve AA'. What economic efficiency dictates is that one should seek out the point on the curve that will minimize the cost of the inputs given different factor prices.

The shift to a curve closer to the origin, say from curve AA' to curve BB' in the diagram, represents an absolute saving in one or both inputs and hence, in contrast to factor substitution which merely represents technological *change*, it constitutes technological *progress*. Moving along a production isoquant by substituting one factor for another, and shifting from one isoquant to another closer to the origin, thus represent two quite distinct forms of economizing.

The first, because it deals with technological options that can be known beforehand, presents few problems for neoclassical economics. The second, however, involving as it does a *discontinuity*, receives no satisfactory treatment in economic theory. Technological progress follows from irreversible acquisitions of new knowledge over time – i.e., from *learning* – a process

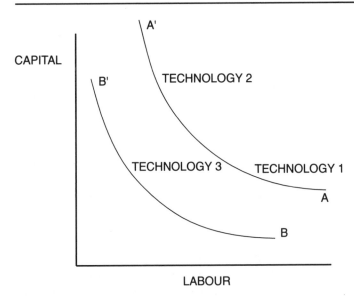

Figure 1.4 A neoclassical production function

which cannot be accommodated in essentially static and time-reversible representations such as production functions. The shift from curve AA′ to curve BB′ thus remains unexplained. The usefulness of production functions other than as expository devices is further limited by the fact that in practice it is almost impossible to distinguish factor substitution from technical progress with any clarity; technical change in the real world always turns out to involve a blend of both.[72]

As already mentioned, the productive factors that make up a production function often express the institutional and economic arrangements of the day. When Great Britain was still predominantly an agrarian economy, for example, production functions were Ricardian and the key productive factors were land and labour.[73] With industrialization and the need for large-scale investment, capital came to replace land as a key factor of production.[74] Yet in both the agrarian and the industrial economy, the choice of productive factors reflected the economist's identification of value with energy.[75] This is well illustrated in the writings of one of the pioneers of the engineering production functions, Hollis Chenery, who observes that:

> To an economist 'production' means anything that happens to an object or set of objects which increases its value. This action is most often a change in form, but it may merely be a change in space or time. The basic physical condition necessary to effect any of these changes (except the last) is that energy must be applied to the material in some form ... The application of energy is one element common to both the economist's and

the engineer's conception of production ... From an analytical point of view, production might be broken down into single energy changes ...

In one sense, a production function measures the effectiveness of various combinations of factors in producing a specified energy change ... The output of any productive process may be measured in terms of any of these forms of energy, using units of either work (force × distance) or heat (calories) ...[76]

The sociologist Daniel Bell, noting how economic theory has been unable to account for technology, innovation, or entrepreneurship in its analysis of production, has put forward the suggestion that information now be acknowledged as a factor of production in its own right given its importance to the post-industrial economy.[77] We shall discuss this suggestion in more detail shortly but to do so we first need to strip the production function of its existing institutional associations. This will free it up for a novel application: to the Principle of Least Action.[78] At the most general level we might argue that any physical system that performs work – i.e., acts teleonomically[79] – consumes inputs of space, time, and energy, in various degrees. This is as true of the solar system or the nervous system as it is of the economic system. Going further we could then devise a production function with, say, space–time as one productive factor and energy as another, and thus avail ourselves of a purely economic interpretation of Maupertuis's Principle of Least Action. As depicted in Figure 1.5, it translates into a tendency for all physical systems to move towards the

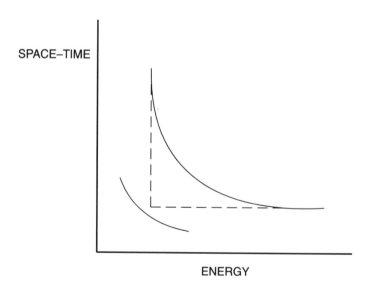

SPACE–TIME

ENERGY

Figure 1.5 Maupertuis's Principle of Least Action as a production function

origin as they seek to minimize their use of space–time and energy inputs.

The limitations of our new production function should be recognized. It may help us to visualize the 'economy of nature' at work but it still does so in a somewhat static, Newtonian fashion. However, although neither factor substitution nor curve shifts can as yet be given any rigorous operational interpretation in the diagram – the neoclassical production function can at least explain factor substitution – they do represent distinct physical processes. In effect, they invite us to consider two variants on the Principle of Least Action: the first, the one put forward by Maupertuis himself, shows up as a move along an isoquant in search of some minimum point – we consider this to be a short-term adaptation response of physical processes to the immediate possibilities of minimization with reference to some objective function which, like prices in the economic system, will vary from case to case; the second variant shows up as a curve shift towards the origin and amounts to a long-term adaptation of the physical system to its environment as mediated by its inherent *evolutionary* possibilities.

What conditions such possibilities? The production function of Figure 1.5 by itself does not tell us. A clue, however, is offered in a comparison of Figure 1.2 and Figure 1.5. The first figure shows *data* to be an emergent property of all physical phenomena consuming energy in space–time. Data accumulates over time in physical systems in the form of *memory* – the persistence over limited stretches of time of certain energy states – and gradually substitutes itself for both energy and space–time in a form of economizing that constitutes *learning*.[80]

We recall that data is a discrimination between states or microstates that is built out of low-level energy acting informationally – it acts only on observers, and this only when they behave as such – rather than mechanically within a physical system. To the extent that it participates in a process of factor substitution with space–time and high-level energy – i.e., energy that is available for mechanical work – data can be considered to be an input or factor of production in its own right. We accordingly now modify our new production function as in Figure 1.6 to accommodate data as a productive factor.

Note that our new factor of production is data and not information as advocated by Daniel Bell, and thus its availability to observers is limited by the range of physical conditions that can handle energy informationally. Some of these were discussed above, but others exist as well. The very capacity of an 'observer' to detect, store, and process data, for example, sets its own limit to the quantity of low-level energy that can count as data *for him or her*. Van Wyk, for example, discussing the amount of data that can be contained in a given quantum of matter, informs us that a self-contained data processing system can process up to 2×10^{47} bits per second per gram of mass that it contains. This is a theoretical limit which is never reached in practice since most physical systems have but a limited capacity to store and process data.[81]

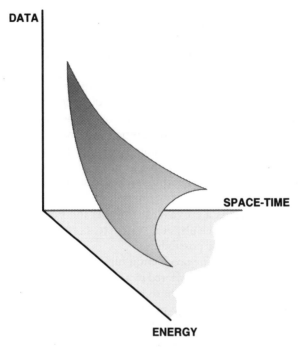

DATA

SPACE-TIME

ENERGY

Figure 1.6 Bringing data into the production function

On account of the data storage and processing capacities of observers – to which we must add transmission – data, like energy and space–time, must also be the focus of efforts at economizing, *and this is achieved by converting data into information*. It thus becomes apparent why information cannot be a factor of production in its own right: information is the fruit of *economizing* on data where data itself is the input into productive activity.

In effect, it is the conversion of data into information that brings about a shift from one isoplane to another in the three-dimensional production function of Figure 1.6 and which registers as a shift from one isoquant to another in the two-dimensional production function of Figure 1.5. As the curve shifts themselves indicate, the conversion of data into information is discontinuous. If we are to improve on the neoclassical account of production – and this is one of our aims – we must account for this shift (see Figure 1.7). This is the task of the next chapter. Yet it is already clear that the gradual accumulation of data in a physical system, depicted in Figure 1.7 as a process of factor substitution in which energy and space–time inputs are replaced by data inputs, allows time to be represented in our production function in contrast to those of the neoclassical scheme. It is, however, but one symptom of learning processes at work. A second symptom has already been mentioned. It is given by the sudden and discontinuous conversion of

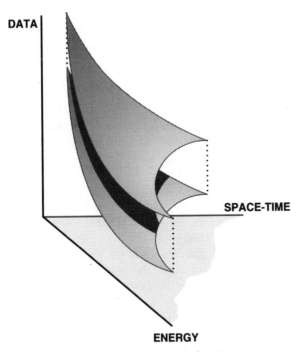

DATA

SPACE-TIME

ENERGY

Figure 1.7 A shift in the production function

accumulated data into information, a singularity which is analytically inaccessible within the conventions of neoclassical production functions. Data thus drives learning processes, and its incorporation into our new production function transforms it from a timeless representation of reversible Newtonian physical processes into one that accommodates historical and hence evolutionary time. It is the specific trajectory taken by factor substitution towards a greater use of data and a corresponding decrease in the use of the other two factors which, when coupled with the curve shifts associated with discontinuous learning phenomena, express the workings of evolutionary time.

We can summarize the foregoing in a simple postulate upon which the theoretical scheme to be presented in this book will implicitly rest. It can be simply stated:

> *In any physical system, learning processes bring about the substitution of data for energy, space, and time, as one expression, over the short term, of the Principle of Least Action. Data is then itself economized upon by its conversion into information in a second, evolutionary expression of the same Principle.*

The gradual build-up of complexity in evolutionary physical systems is then somehow linked to their ability to metabolize data into information and subsequently to internalize it, using it to enhance their responsive and adaptive capacities and thus to preserve their relative autonomy. Maturana and Varela label such self-organizing systems *autopoietic*.[82] The knowledge possessed by such systems offers a measure of these capacities, physically expressed as an ability to act in a given way in specified circumstances.

The postulate, I believe, is broadly consistent with the story of biological and, indeed, physical evolution as we know it. Brooks and Wiley, for example, view the evolution of biological systems as a product of increasing information complexity.[83] They point out that some aspects of evolution which appear to be manifestations of increasing thermal efficiency – the example they cite is that of photosynthesis in multicellular plants versus photosynthetic protists – are really products of an increase in information complexity.[84] How do they characterize information complexity? As a 'phase space' of a system's possible configurations over the number of microstates available to the system, the dimensions of the phase space itself being defined as $H_{max} = \log_2 A$, where A is the number of available microstates and $\log_2$ is chosen to represent the system in bits; that is, as *data*.[85]

Even more in line with our production-function-based representation is the suggestion put forward by Salthe[86] and Eldredge[87] that biological evolution be interpreted as the interaction of two hierarchies: the first, the 'genealogical hierarchy', manifests itself as trajectories of information flows; the second, the 'ecological hierarchy', shows up as a set of environmental constraints on the flow of energy needed to 'drive' the genealogical trajectories. When either hierarchy alters the structure of the other we get a non-reversible evolutionary change.

Brooks and Wiley take the view that only biological systems display evolutionary potential. Pure thermodynamic systems are inherently random and thus can have no 'memory' of initial conditions. Whatever ordering they achieve through fluctuations is but a by-product of energy flows.[88] Biological systems, by contrast, can have 'conversations with the past'[89] on account of stored information. This makes them self-referential. Yet as we have already suggested, even thermodynamic systems can acquire rudimentary memory over time.[90] As Nicolis and Prigogine put it, 'the idea of complexity is no longer limited to biology. It is invading the physical sciences and appears to be deeply rooted in the laws of nature'.[91]

The growth of complexity in purely physical systems takes us back to the beginning of time. As the early universe expanded and cooled after experiencing the intense and spatially highly concentrated energies of the primordial explosion, enough stability was achieved for simple data-bearing structures to appear – initially in the shape of elementary particles and later as atoms, heavy molecules, and finally simple forms of carbon-based life. Even in the pre-biotic universe a form of rudimentary natural selection was at work: data-bearing structures subsisted, replicated themselves, and spread out in space and time, clumping together into ever more robust combinations whose survival further contributed to the evolution of complexity and to the accumulation of data.

We can represent the process intelligibly in our new production function by collapsing the space–time and energy factors into a single dimension of physical factors and retaining data as an independent factor. The resulting two-dimension production function is shown in Figure 1.8.[92] In the diagram, the Big Bang is a singularity consuming a microscopic amount of space–time but unimaginable quantities of energy at A. Cooling and expansion increases the spatiotemporal content of the process at the expense of its energy content. With cooling, the first data structures appear, clumping together in spatial concentrations that move us from A towards A' in the diagram. The emergence of life can be located as a discontinuity – a downward shift towards the isoquant BB' – somewhere along this path. Intelligent life might then be associated with a third isoquant CC' with much of the learning ocurring along the path between C and C' taking a cultural rather than a biological form.

What the diagram indicates is a saw-toothed progression along the horizontal axis towards the origin representing successive accumulations of data in physical systems and their subsequent reduction through a conversion to information. The moves along the isoquants, from A to A', from B to B', and from C to C', accumulate data in physical systems; they represent factor substitution. Vertical downward movements, on the other hand, from A' to B, from B' to C, extract information from the data in what we shall refer to in the following chapters as *codifications and abstractions*;[93] they represent factor savings. Downward movements describe discontinuities that might correspond to the emergence of dissipative structures in the purely thermodynamic systems located towards the right in the diagram and to the emergence of self-replicating organization in biological and cultural systems located towards the left. In each case the depth of the vertical lines between isoquants measures a system's data processing capacity, and the horizontal distance between isoquants measures the energy saved in the transition per unit of output. Towards the left in the diagram the increasing depth of the vertical lines tells us that we are dealing with intelligent forms of life endowed with very large data processing capacities. It should be apparent that the moves towards the origins decribed in Figure 1.8 have the effect of minimizing entropy production in a physical system. In line with Brooks and Wiley we use the entropy concept as an abstraction that is common to energy flows in ecological processes and information flows in genealogical processes – respectively the horizontal and vertical axes of the production function shown in Figure 1.8.[94] The minimization of entropy production thus amounts to a reformulation of the economizing process first expressed in the Principle of Least Action.[95] The irony is that such an irreversible path-

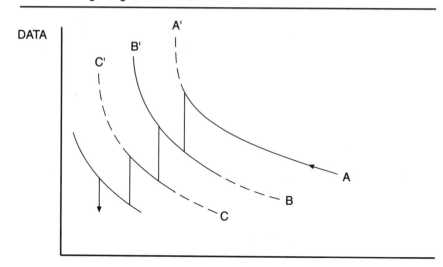

DATA

PHYSICAL FACTORS

Figure 1.8 Collapsing energy and space–time into a single dimension

dependent phenomenon could so readily be represented by the metaphor of the production function.

1.5: THE POWER OF THE INFORMATION PERSPECTIVE

Figure 1.8, to be sure, greatly oversimplifies the economizing process since the number of upward movements along the curves and of downward movements across the curves is countless. The diagram is thus a highly schematic presentation of a process far too complex to be accurately depicted in all its rich detail.

The figure oversimplifies in another way that must also be mentioned: it ignores horizontal discontinuities, those that describe a sudden and unexpected horizontal shift towards the left across the isoquants, savings in physical resources unprovoked by an accumulation of experience (i.e., data), or its articulation into knowledge (a vertical downward movement). Such shifts, in effect, represent pure serendipity, fortuitous empirical discoveries that hold the level of data constant and that offer, initially at least, little purchase for a learning activity.[96]

For all its limitations, however, Figure 1.8 brings out in an immediately apprehensible form the difference between the focus that we are developing in this book and that which orthodox economics has traditionally adopted. Simply stated, whereas the factors that have until now formed the object of economizing were almost exclusively identified with the horizontal axis in economic thought, in the following chapters we shall concentrate on the relevant properties of the vertical axis. Of course, the purely physical factors of production located along our horizontal axis were never labelled such since the institutional articulation of the economic world effectively concealed them. Thus space–time, for example, variously appears as land, necessary labour-time, or, less frequently, as market area,[97] whereas energy appears as labour power or as the productive capacity of capital equipment. As Mirowski has so persuasively demonstrated in his study *More Heat than Light*, the thinking of nineteenth- and twentieth-century economists largely crystallized around the energy concept.[98] In all these cases, data is latently present, embedded in the physical factors themselves. Yet it has no explicit role to play *qua* factor and it is therefore not the focus of economizing efforts as the physical factors are. Its ubiquity is taken as axiomatic and for this reason it is not subject to scarcities; its acquisition therefore carries no opportunity cost.

At this point it may be useful to recall from sections 1.1 and 1.2 the reasons why data has presented problems for economic analysis. Data does not appear to behave as an economic good in the sense ordinarily understood by economists. One minute it is locked up as tacit knowledge in someone's head and thus impossible to externalize efficiently into a viable object of exchange; the next minute it is proliferating quite costlessly, escaping all attempts at appropriation. Concentrating on the horizontal component of economizing in Figure 1.8, therefore, the one that involves saving on things that can be physically grasped and measured, made practical sense even at the cost of a loss of realism. Yet as the information revolution gets under way, and productive activity finds itself located ever further up along the vertical axis of Figure 1.8 where data has become cheap and plentiful, it becomes increasingly apparent that the very abundance of data will begin to butt up against our capacity to handle it in its raw form. Economizing on data here is called for not so much on account of its own intrinsic scarcity but because of scarcities in the means available to us to make good use of it – that is, because of the limitations of either our own brains as information processors or those of the equipment to which we delegate the task. When this happens major factor savings will only be achieved by concentrating on the vertical component of economizing, that is to say on the conversion of ever-larger quantities of data into information through downward movements in the production function of Figure 1.8 – in short, on codifications and abstractions.

The intellectual and practical challenges posed by the information revolution are only now being recognized. Paul Hawken, in his book *The Next Economy*, writes that 'The single most important trend to understand is the changing ratio between mass and information in goods and services',[99] and James Heskett in *Managing in the Service Economy* observes that 'Manufacturing is substituting information for assets. Nearly every program to reduce inventories has this character.'[100] George Gilder, writing in a more popular vein, describes the information revolution as essentially one of 'mind over matter'.[101]

Yet in an age where the material costs of our most important product, the electronic chip, account for less than 2 per cent of the total cost of making it, the dominant economic paradigm continues to focus our attention disproportionately on that 2 per cent.[102] Such a focus is reflected, for example, in the way we classify economic activity: only 6 per cent of IBM's employees worldwide are directly engaged in industrial manufacturing; the firm, however, continues to be classified as industrial in the Standard Industrial Classification (SIC) scheme.[103] We remain hypnotized by things rather than the information they carry.

Lags between scientific and technological developments and the social and intellectual frameworks designed to accommodate them are nothing new. Perez has interpreted the replacement of energy-intensive by information-intensive technologies in terms of Kondratieff long waves. Building on Freeman's concept of 'new technological systems' she sees information technology driving a new wave and with it a new mode of growth. She notes that long wave recessions and depressions result from a mismatch between the socio-institutional framework available to absorb the changes associated with a new wave, and the new dynamics operating in the techno-economic sphere. The resulting crises then constitute signals calling for the redefinition of the general mode of growth and its associated institutions.[104]

Our new production function is a metaphor for these new insights rather than an analytical tool for their systematic exploration. It signals the fact that as we move to dematerialize production we continue unwittingly to retain the economic and institutional paradigms of an energy-driven economy. We therefore have an economics for the horizontal scale of Figure 1.8 but none as yet for the vertical one. Surprisingly, this is an old problem and not a new one: we have been here before. The physiocrats, in their day, resisted the idea that manufacturing, by adding information to raw materials, was engaged in productive activity, hence Quesnay's characterization of artificers, manufacturers, and merchants as the 'sterile class'. Indeed, in his *Tableau Économique*, even farm labour is not classified as productive. Only land is. It was physiocracy's founding belief that nature's renewable energy bounty, exploited through agriculture, was the primary source of a country's wealth.[105] Marx, in turn, consistently downplayed the economic value of knowledge embedded in labour skills or machinery. Capital for him was nothing more than 'frozen labour' and technical progress a common possession of mankind; it reflected what he termed 'socially necessary labour time' and was thus only subject to scarcities that had been artificially contrived.[106]

The metaphor nevertheless points us in the direction of our task in this book: a study of the production and exchange of information as a phenomenon subject to economizing – production now taken as data *reduction*, and exchange as the prerequisite to data diffusion and accumulation in the social system. What we offer here is not an articulate and refutable theory but a rough conceptual guide to further thought and action in this area, a framework based on a heuristic principle in Simon's sense of the term.[107] For our purposes the metaphor offers certain advantages over more conventional ways of thinking about economic processes. Here I shall list three:

1 It offers *greater generality*, covering any physical system existing in space–time and exchanging energy and data with its environment. In our scheme, economizing is thus more than a human phenomenon; it is inherent in the order of things and thus helps to place man back in nature.[108]

2 It is a paradigm in the general systems tradition but one that is oriented towards evolutionary change rather than towards equilibrium.[109] It is thus more *realistic*, and promises *greater explanatory power*.

3 By making energy, space–time, and data – the three key resources that make possible our existence as sentient beings – the constituent elements of our new production function, the metaphor throws into stark relief what has been intuitively obvious in the closing years of the twentieth century, namely, that space–time and energy resources are finite and that we shall only effectively be able to economize on them by shifting towards a data-based economy. Douglass North has hypothesized that *Homo sapiens* has only twice experienced revolution at the species level.[110] The first, termed the Neolithic Revolution by V. Gordon Childe, described the passage from hunter-gatherer societies to settled agriculture[111] approximately ten thousand years ago. The second, known as the Industrial Revolution, was initiated just over two hundred years ago. Both of these revolutions were energy based even though the second derived much of its power from the growth of scientific knowledge in the seventeenth and eighteenth centuries.[112] This book is written in the belief that a third species-level revolution, this time based not on energy but on information, is upon us. Given the unforgiving Malthusian pressures exerted on our available physical resources, it comes none too soon. The three species-level revolutions are depicted in the production functions of Figure 1.9. They indicate that our metaphor also offers the advantage of *relevance*.

   Motivated by the metaphor presented in this chapter, those that follow take accumulating and then economizing on data as the key to a system's evolutionary potential. Although this introductory chapter reflects our basic concern with the production and exchange of information as a universal physical phenomenon, in what follows we shall confine our attention to its manifestation as a *human* activity. The metaphor of the production function that we have developed in this introductory chapter thus serves as no more than a backcloth to our analysis. We shall, however, only be interested in that region of the production space in which data has accumulated to a sufficient

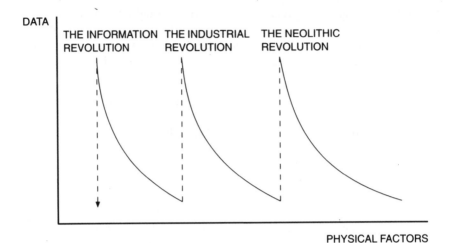

Figure 1.9 An evolutionary production function

extent to allow for the exercise of human intelligence – better illustrated by Figure 1.9 than by Figure 1.8. Human action is what we seek to understand[113] even if we believe such action to be ultimately driven by fairly general physical principles.[114]

Chapter 2

The structuring of information

ABSTRACT

How is data extracted from data by human information processing agents? Man intercepts low-level energy – i.e., data – from his external environment in such a way that if it is subsequently processed, it acts upon him informationally rather than mechanically. Data processing is subject to two distinct yet interrelated economizing strategies.

The first, coding, is an act of selection from a repertoire of possibilities that is performed with varying degrees of efficiency. Such coding organizes sense-data into perceptual categories. The second, abstracting, generates concepts that in turn economize on perceptual categories. Abstraction leads to generalization, a process that links together ostensibly different categories, whether these are perceptual or conceptual, allowing them to be handled for certain purposes as a single entity.

Coding and abstracting constitute the two dimensions of a space that we label the *E-space* (the E stands for 'epistemological'), a conceptual tool that allows us to examine in what form an individual processes and stores data over time. Movements in the E-space can be viewed as the outcome of interactions between percepts and concepts. Such movements trace out trajectories that are expressive of the learning strategies of individuals. These trajectories are not reversible. They dig the channels through which the individual personality flows and comes to structure itself. A personality is thus a spatiotemporally conditioned disposition to handle the data of the world – i.e., to construe it – in a particular way.

Economic man, as defined in orthodox economic theory, is only allowed to operate in that part of the E-space where data is both highly coded and abstract. Strictly speaking, therefore, economic man has no past.

2.1: PERCEIVING AS CODING

The neurological basis of perception

Adaptive behaviour can be viewed as the product of two distinct yet interrelated selection processes. The first, natural selection, constructs and defines us as a species, giving contours and direction to our capacity to act. The second, which Edelman terms somatic selection,[1] reflects our ability to make good use of that capacity through the creation of both a repertoire of representations and a repertoire of adapted responses. The kinds of representations and responses available to us are thus species-specific. Bees, for example, can detect ultraviolet light, and snakes have pits for electromagnetic waves in the infra-red range; pigeons have ferromagnets for orienting themselves with respect to the earth's magnetic field, and flies have gyroscoping strain gauges.[2]

The intuition that we can only know the world as it is presented to us goes back to Kant. It has been central to philosophical and, more recently, to neurobiological theorizing about how the mind and the brain work. As Churchland has put it, 'Our brains are massive mounds of excitable cells, which somehow contrive collectively to contain a rich representation of the outside world, as well as to enable the muscles to accomplish such feats as catching a ball, playing the violin, and talking, in addition of course to the fundamental feeding, fleeing, fighting, and reproducing.'[3] Such excitable cells are known as neurons. Those on the sensory periphery are called sensory neurons; they transduce physical signals such as light or mechanical deformation into electrical signals that they pass on. Neurons on the motor periphery are called motor neurons; they terminate on muscles to produce contractions. Between sensory and motor neurons lie the interneurons, a mixed bag of everything that cannot be classified as pure sensory or pure motor neurons. Synapses are the points of communication between neurons and, give or take an order of magnitude, there are estimated to be about 10 to the power of 15 such connection points in the human nervous system. These can be taken as a measure of evolutionary complexity.

Nervous systems have evolved in response to the need of animals, and later humans, to successfully predict events in their environment.[4] The evolutionary step that interposed interneurons between sensory and motor neurons, however, can be considered revolutionary in that it allowed complex and sophisticated representations of both events and environments as well as an updating of these through learning.[5] Several theorists have suggested that we store such representational knowledge in terms of structures variously termed scripts, frames, or schemata.[6] Yet useful as these may prove to be for encoding knowledge, they fail to fully capture the generative capacity of human understanding in novel situations. A new approach, labelled *connectionism* by Feldman and Ballard,[7] likens neural activity to a *parallel distributed processing* (PDP) system and, indeed, much contemporary PDP work can be traced back to neurologists such as Jackson and Luria.[8]

Neurons can be thought of as instruments of communication, receiving, integrating and sending signals. Where these have to be sent over distances greater than one millimetre, they are coded into action potentials, all-or-none spike discharges lasting for about one millisecond and carrying information by their presence or absence.[9]

In sum, when data from the outside world reach sense organs, they are converted into neural signals. Eyes, ears, touch receptors, etc., can be seen as so many transducers – photocells, microphones, strain gauges – that convert patterns of incoming energy into signals that can be read according to some code. Perception can then be thought of as a coding activity in which subtle and elaborate inferences are drawn from neural signals that bear some homomorphic relationship to incoming energy patterns.[10] Such inferential activity is the very process through which information is extracted from data. It yields results that for everyday purposes are usually adequate but by no means infallible, as the existence of perceptual illusions – i.e., the creation of incompatible inference structures – indicates.

Clearly, only that part of incoming energy that registers as a signal can be treated as data. The rest acts energetically, not informationally, and thus does not give rise to a coding or information extraction effort.

Perceptual inferences – or hypotheses, as Gregory prefers to call them – that individuals are able to draw are limited in their scope by the constraints of physiology which channel them in certain directions. Once the channels have been selected, repetition and habit then dig some of these channels deeper so that early coding behaviour largely shapes later coding practices.[11]

Communication and data processing models

An understanding of coding is basic to many of the themes that we develop in this book and requires a brief reference to information and communication theory. The distinction between the two terms is somewhat blurred and they are in fact often used interchangeably in casual discourse. Yet it is as well to bear in mind that whereas communication theory presupposes the existence of a sender and, by implication, a conscious intention to communicate, this is not true of information theory. Little of the data which reaches us at any moment through our senses and from which we extract information, for example, has been intentionally communicated to us by a sender. It is an impersonal energetic manifestation of our physical environment that we register as data.[12]

Some of the confusion arising from the ambiguous use of these two terms can be explained by the fact that early information theorists such as Nyquist, Hartley, and later Claude Shannon were engineers and primarily concerned with the communicative efficiency of artificial channels.

They were thus led to develop concepts and measures of information within the context of fairly limited and well-defined communication situations, those in which an information source selects a desired message out of a set of possible messages. It is then coded by the transmitter into a signal capable of being sent down a communication channel. The message, now in signal form, then travels down the channel from the transmitter to the receiver – a sort of inverse transmitter – which then converts the signal back into the original message before passing it on to a destination. In the course of transmission, the signal may become distorted with extraneous elements being added or taken away in ways that make effective communication problematic. We then say that there is noise in the channel and make corrective adjustments either to the channel itself, to the way we code our messages into signals, or in the rate at which we send information down the channel.[13]

In a communication model, the function of coding is to communicate effectively and efficiently, and we are thus led to describe the recipient as *de*coding the message. He or she is nevertheless still involved in coding (i.e., extracting information from data), however, for what is physically transmitted is always data, albeit data with an information content – the message – that has now been intentionally placed there by a sender. For our purposes, therefore, coding and decoding will be treated as interchangeable activities.

Although our understanding of neural processes has been enhanced by the communication perspective, Churchland has argued that it would be parochial to assume that communicative structures could serve as an adequate model for cognitive ones.[14] Such structures have led researchers in the past to think of neural activity as similar to the kind of data processing that goes on in a digital computer – a machine with the so-called Von Neumann architecture.[15] Ironically, Von Neumann machines were themselves heavily influenced by prevailing views of how the mind operates, views which have come to be thought of as somewhat naive by contemporary researchers in the neural sciences. According to data processing models, peripheral neural signals are encoded and retransmitted through increasingly sophisticated relay systems until they are cortically processed to generate output.[16] Such models, as Bullock points out,[17] rely on a very specific interpretation, both of the way that neural coding occurs and of the way that information is transferred from one particular neuron to another. Each interpretation owes much to Claude Shannon's communication model.

If we take the task of neuroscience as being to account for how the structure and function of the nervous system allow perceptual categorization to occur in particular species as a basis for learning and meaningful adaptive behaviour, then the computer-inspired data processing models just referred to put forward a very specific account of brain behaviour. They hold that like a digital computer, the brain processes information by means of programmes dictated in part by the environment and in part by neural wiring.[18] A consequence of this is that categories of natural objects are implicitly assumed to fall into defined classes or typologies accessible to programming.[19] Information processing models, then, are required to posit the existence of prior categories residing either in the brain, or in the environment or both. And just as Claude Shannon, in developing his communication model, had to specify *a priori* an agreed-upon code as well as a means of specifying the probability of receiving a signal under the code, so do information processing models of the nervous system. Data processing is thus transformed into sequential symbol manipulation.[20]

Connectionist or PDP models of cognition adopt a different approach. Whereas under the computer metaphor a representation is a symbol, in the connectionist world it is a pattern of activity distributed across a network. As Feldman and Ballard state it, 'The fundamental premise of connectionism is that individual neurons *do not transmit large amounts of symbolic informa-tion* ...'[21] Our connectionist model, developed by Edelman, goes by the name of *Neuronal Group Selection* (NGS) theory. It accounts for categorization without making information processing or computing assumptions. It takes the brain to be a selective system dynamically organized into cellular populations containing individually variant networks, the structure and function of which are selected by different means during development and behaviour.[22] This population theory of brain functions relies minimally upon neural codes and acts dynamically by selection upon potential orderings *already* represented by variant neural structures. It does not require these structures to be determined by 'information' in some sense already present in the environment.[23]

One of the objections that can be made against the computer metaphor resides in the fact that although brains are ponderously slow compared with computers – neuronal events are measured in milliseconds (10^{-3}) whereas silicon events are measured in nanoseconds (10^{-9}) – when the two are pitted against each other in perceptual recognition tasks, the brain leaves the computer back in the dust. This implies that whatever the means used by the brain to achieve perceptual recognition, it cannot be in the millions of steps arranged in a sequence that the computer adopts as a strategy. There is simply not enough time.[24] The great advantage of the PDP approach is that with hundreds of thousands of highly interconnected processors, i.e., neurons, a sequence that would require millions of cycles in a conventional serial computer can be carried out in a few cycles.[25]

Coding in a connectionist regime

Connectionist models want to replace the 'computer' metaphor as a model of the mind with a 'brain' metaphor. Each has a quite different way of depicting the way that representations, or knowledge, are stored. The first takes knowledge as stored in the state of certain units in the nervous system; the second takes knowledge as stored in neural connections. In the second case, learning becomes a matter of establishing the right connection strengths so that patterns of activation are appropriate to the circumstances.[26] Rules for adjusting connection strengths do so on the basis of information that is locally available to the unit[27] and in this sense rules can be said to emerge from the local interactions of simple processing elements. Such interactions can be *excitatory* and increase the probability of a neuron firing, or *inhibitory* and thus decrease it; they stand for hypotheses about data inputs at different levels of abstraction.[28] In every organism studied, for example, sensory neurons have been found to interact with interneurons in such a way as to inhibit neighbouring sensory neurons. Known as *lateral inhibition*, this arrangement is common in nervous tissues, being found in the retina, the skin, the olfactory epithelium, and the gustatory epithelium. The effect of a lateral inhibition circuit is to enhance the contrast between stimulated and inhibited neurons, the former firing at a higher rate and the latter at a lower rate than their base rate.[29] Through the interplay of neural excitation and inhibition, input signals are abstracted and filtered by sensory transducers, feature detectors, and feature correlators, which taken together make up a global mapping system. Active neuronal groups within particular repertoires receiving such signals are selected over others in a *competitive* fashion.[30] Such selection is the basis of perceptual categorization.

Researchers in the PDP tradition argue that the brain's primary mode of computation is best understood as a kind of *relaxation system* in which the computation proceeds by iteratively seeking to satisfy a large number of weak constraints. Thus neural connections, instead of playing the role of wires as in an electrical circuit, represent constraints on the co-occurrence of pairs of units. As Rumelhart and McClelland put it, the system should be thought of as *settling into a solution* rather than *calculating* a solution,[31] moving in a Bayesian fashion from less probable and towards more probable hypotheses as the result of 'voting' interactions.[32] One alternative to the relaxation system worth mentioning is the 'single shot' algorithm which can converge in a single pass through a neural network. Yet as Sejnowski has argued, 'relaxation' and 'single shot' options should be thought of as extreme points in a continuum of cognitive strategies any of which may be adopted by the cortex. For the recognition of common objects, for example, a network that could process the relevant image in a single shot might be developed through experience. For novel or more complex objects, on the other hand, a relaxation strategy may offer more flexibility on a higher processing capacity.[33]

Whether the search strategy is of the 'relaxation' or of the 'single shot' type, the issue is to ensure that it is computing something sensible and that it will eventually settle down. Each possible state of activity of the network has an associated cost and whatever rule or device is used for updating activity levels should be chosen so that this cost keeps falling. A good approach to a solution will thus be one that progressively reduces the value of a cost function. Hopfield (1982) has labelled his cost function 'energy' so that repeated iterations can be thought of as seeking out an energy minimum. Smolensky's *harmony* is computationally equivalent to Hopfield's energy,[34] and both approaches are convergent with the economizing perspective on data processing that we presented in Chapter 1.

One question that we need to address concerns coding. Does the connectionist premise that individual neurons do not encode or transmit large amounts of symbolic information sequentially mean that coding is not a useful term for describing neural processes? Claude Shannon makes coding procedures a fundamental feature of his theory of communication. In the theory, coding is almost entirely a response to the technical needs of transmission and, as Edelman points out, the nature of the coding process relies heavily on the fact that a symbolic repertoire exists *a priori* for the construction of codes.[35] How the symbolic repertoire itself initially came into existence is not addressed by the theory, concerned as it is primarily with transmission. It should be obvious, however, that from a broader data processing perspective – in which information transmission figures, but only as a component – a symbolic repertoire must at some point be the product of a pre-symbolic coding process in which certain data configurations or complexions are selected from among those possible and stabilized. In effect, such *complexions* become points in phase spaces in which the function of coding is to effect transitions between phase spaces. A particular pattern of activation of a neural network, for example, would constitute one point in a phase space, and the network, acting as a connectivity matrix, would then transform one pattern of activation into another.[36]

Yet is this not precisely what is achieved by relaxation strategies and single shot algorithms? And is not the difference between them that the single shot algorithm, as evidenced by the speed with which it can attain a stable economic configuration, is working with complexions that could form the basis of a symbolic repertoire, whereas the slower search patterns of relaxation strategies suggest that we are dealing with something pre-symbolic? Both processes involve selection from a repertoire and hence coding but only single shot algorithms, dealing with patterns made familiar through prior experience, can make use of *a priori* coding strategies the way that Claude Shannon does. If one had to summarize the difference between relaxation and single shot strategies, one could say that both are involved in a coding process but that while in the first case one is dealing exclusively with a repertoire of states or complexions, in the second one is dealing with a repertoire of complexions, some of which have achieved symbolic status.

Clearly, the second type of coding strategy, symbolic coding, facilitates communication to a greater extent than the first. It is faster and requires less search. The implication of this point is that effective coding strategies must seek two quite distinct kinds of energy economies. The first, identified by Hopfield, has already been mentioned; it is associated with the *state* of the network. Has the least cost complexion been selected in response to an external stimulus? The second energy economy concerns *process*: has the least cost configuration been attained economically in terms of the time and energy expended in seeking it out? What emerges from the distinction between the two forms of economizing is that economies of state establish the scope for economies of process but that a concern with the costs of cognition will impart a bias in both forms of economizing away from the relaxation strategies and towards single shot algorithms. Symbolic coding is then simply an expression of this economizing bias.

We have presented coding as an activity in which information is extracted from data. But what exactly *is* information in the scheme that we have just described?

It cannot be identified directly with a given sequence of data complexions but rather with the choice of complexion sequences available at a given level of neural processing; not with what *is* but with what *could be*. Information, in other words, measures one's freedom of choice to select a complexion sequence.[37]

Most complexion sequences fit this multiple choice process, even though, as Shannon has shown, all of them could, in principle, be reconfigured to produce a sequence of dichotomous or binary choices such as can be found in the game of 'Twenty Questions'.[38] Whether or not it is cast in a binary form, the quantity of information carried by a given data complexion sequence can be described mathematically as the binary logarithm of the number of choices necessary to define the sequence without ambiguity. According to Shannon:

$$H = \sum_{i=1}^{i=n} Pi \log Pi$$

where H stands for the amount of information and the Pi's are the probabilities of occurrence of the complexions – Shannon uses the term 'symbols' – drawn from a repertoire of n complexions and assembled into a sequence of length Nt.[39] If all the Pi's are equal, that is, if $Pi = p = 1/n$, then the quantity of information will increase in direct proportion to the length Nt of the complexion sequence and H will not vary from one part of the messages to another.[40] The resulting quantity will therefore describe the maximum amount of information yielded by a given complexion sequence – its originality. Information, under such conditions, can only be increased by expanding the repertoire of complexions n covered by the summation from which a choice is made, thus reducing the probability value of each. Information and choice are clearly closely related. Following Boltzmann, Shannon called the maximum information contained by a complexion sequence its maximum *entropy*.[41]

Where information does vary from one part of the complexion sequence to another then some complexions, in effect, have a higher probability of occurrence than others so that Pi does not equal $1/n$. They are less unexpected by the receiver and in that sense more redundant. By suitable recoding, these high probability complexions can be 'chunked' together to produce combinations that have a lower probability of occurrence and that once more increase the information content of the complexion sequence as a whole.[42]

But how do probabilities become attached to complexions in the first place? How come that in Shannon's scheme, they enjoy so much stability that they are amenable to the kind of 'information engineering' that he proposes? Recall that a stable complexion, accessible through a single shot algorithm, can be used as a symbol, and when so used, a complexion can be partly rule-governed. In language, for example, probabilities are assigned to individual letters according to the position that they are allowed to occupy in words. Words themselves have probabilities assigned to them according to the position that they can occupy in sentences, a position dictated in part by rules of syntax. In both these cases, the probabilities are given *a priori*. When complexions are selected through relaxation strategies, by contrast, they initially lack the stability required for the efficient *a priori* application of a rule. It follows that many more complexions have to be processed during the selection process and that for any single complexion, one is likely to be operating at much lower levels of probability than in the case of single shot algorithms. In contrast to single shot algorithms, therefore, relaxation strategies are dealing with high entropy processes, those in which the information content latent in a sequence of complexions is too high – i.e., too original – to be efficiently communicable. Reaching a stable state is one way of reducing this entropy; progressing from a relaxation to a single shot strategy is another. We have here another example of the equivalence, established in Chapter 1, between economizing and minimizing the production of entropy.

Information is about originality. It is the unexpected, that which causes surprise. Some experiences, however, are so original as to become well-nigh unintelligible; nothing can be made of them at all. Pushed to the limit intelligibility and originality find it hard to coexist. The closer you move to the one, the further you move away from the other. Coding, by imposing a measure of structure on the data of the phenomenal world, tries to tame it, to restrict its myriad manifestations to categories that gradually become familiar that we can then recognize and can cope with. Structure limits the range of choices that have to be made and the quantity of data that has to be processed. The understanding expressed in structure then acts on expectations in such a way as to increase the perceived level of redundancy of stimuli received. Understanding aims to reduce our data processing requirements by making the world *a priori* intelligible. However, taken too far, the quest for intelligibility carries its own dangers. Pushed below a certain information threshold, stimuli become banal and may then be missed altogether, the proverbial dog that did not bark.[43]

In sum, good coding aims to structure the repertoire of complexions in a sequence in such a way that the high probability elements – i.e., those with a lower information content – are 'chunked' together, thus freeing up data processing capacity to deal with the lower probability elements. What effectively constitutes a high or low probability element, of course, depends on the statistical characteristics of the data processing agent – that is, on the structure of its prior expectations and on its coding skills. Let us call these its *memory*. This can be viewed both as a store of past experiences captured by particular complexions and as an *a priori* statistical disposition to structure future complexion sequences in particular ways based on such experiences.[44]

Coding brings about the perceptual differentiation and integration of data with a view to achieving information efficiencies. Efficient coding, however, calls for an investment in time and effort that tends to give an existing repertoire of complexions a life of its own. With repeated use, it acquires inertia and becomes in consequence hard to modify or replace.[45] New stimuli are then filtered through an already established perceptual structure according to assignment rules set by existing codes. Where stimuli herald the emergence of new and complex phenomena, calling perhaps for a fresh coding effort, they may not even be detected by a fully committed data processing apparatus that lacks 'perceptual readiness',[46] let alone responded to. They will then very likely flow through or past the perceptual apparatus unattended on account of their ostensible lack of interest. A lack of perceptual readiness, then, is often symptomatic of a fundamental mismatch between prior investments in coding capacity and the kind of coding required by new phenomena. These, if they are detected at all, will need to be processed through relaxation strategies rather than single shot algorithms, a reflection of their perceived complexity and the need to respond to it with a more extensive search process.

Miller has shown how easily our sensory apparatus can be overwhelmed by complexity and how information overload – i.e., data that cannot be processed by existing coding schemes – can lead to a failure of perception.[47] He hypothesizes that our immediate span of apprehension for a single stimulus is about 7 bits of information; in other words, the average person can estimate at a glance the number of dots scattered at random on a white surface when these number no more than seven. Even the most skilled human operator in fact enjoys a surprisingly limited capacity to absorb information. A silent reader, for example, can absorb a maximum of 44 bits per second; an expert pianist, 22 bits per second. To put such figures into perspective, they should be compared with the tens of thousands of bits per second that can be handled by computer circuitry. In a series of experiments conducted at Cambridge, Hicks[48] demonstrated that in performing a skill with clearly defined choices such as pressing a response key on seeing a light flash, the decision time t for a human subject increases with the number N of possibilities by $t = k \log (N + 1)$. Choice or decision time turns out to be very nearly proportional to the number of bits per stimulus.

Attempts at coding thus become an intelligent response to excessive amounts of data or unmanageable complexity. In the language of connectionists, if we have x binary units (on–off or 0–1) in a neural network, then there are $2x$ possible states in which the system could reside; that is, in which each of the x units could have the value 0 or 1. Where we are dealing with continuous units – i.e., units which can adopt any value between 0 and 1 – the system can in principle take on any one of an infinite number of states. Only by building constraints into the network unit can we limit the number of states into which the system will settle.[49] This is the function of coding. The effective amount of data that can be taken in by one's perceptual span can thus be greatly increased by 'chunking' it into larger bits. These can be learnt more easily and thus more effectively stored in memory, whence they can be drawn upon and in turn reinjected into future events so as to reduce their own information requirements. Chunking, it should by now be clear, is what happens to data when it has been processed in a neural network through a single shot algorithm.

Chunking is not always possible, however. Many situations that we confront are simply too complex. According to Edelman, 'even to animals eventually capable of speech such as ourselves, the world is initially an unlabelled place. The number of partitions of potential "objects" or "events" in an econiche is enormous if not infinite, and their positive or negative values to an individual animal, even one with a richly structured nervous system, are relative, not absolute.'[50] Where the experienced complexity of phenomena outruns the capacity of our perceptual apparatus to code for them, then, a second-best coding strategy, that of *scanning*, must be adopted.[51] With scanning, all data or complexions are in effect treated as equiprobable: no prior coding scheme, therefore, is available to guide the processing effort and coding efficiency is hard to achieve. Consequently, information content is initially at a maximum, which aligns scanning with relaxation strategies in neural networks.

With most phenomena, there are often several levels at which 'chunking' can occur, each with its own type of code, and each with its own repertoire of n complexions. These might correspond to different levels of abstraction, but not necessarily. Abraham Moles illustrates this point with the printed page. A child or an illiterate would receive the raw visual message it contains in the form of black and white dots spread horizontally across the page in what appears to be random fashion. Here the elements in the repertoire would number about one billion. A proofreader or a foreigner not knowing the language, on the other hand, might face a repertoire n of approximately 200 letters. Between the two extremes an ordinary reader will have to deal with a repertoire of some 50,000 English words which can then be reduced to manageable proportions through the chunking operations performed by syntax.[52] For each of these individuals there is an accessible repertoire, a corresponding type of redundancy, and a measure of originality. These will reflect his prior knowledge, his mental habits, and his education.[53]

Most of us, of course, do not confront the complexities of daily life armed with just a single repertoire of codes. We deploy whole batteries of them and readily switch from one to another as we try to make sense of different

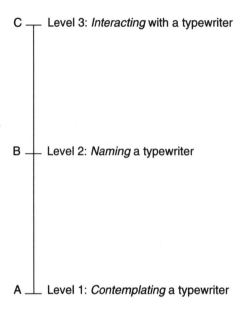

C — Level 3: *Interacting* with a typewriter

B — Level 2: *Naming* a typewriter

A — Level 1: *Contemplating* a typewriter

Figure 2.1 Coding for a typewriter

types of stimuli. This often means *discovering* the coding repertoire that will yield the minimum level of processing effort called for by a given situation.

An assortment of repertoires, then, gives us access to an overlay of distinct complexion sequences, each with its appropriate matching signs, codes, sub-repertoire, etc. An event that enters our awareness could thus yield a number of information measures, $H1$, $H2$, $H3$ ... as well as a parallel set of redundancy measures, $R1$, $R2$, $R3$ which, following Moles, we might call its *information blueprint*.[54] Each set of measures (H, R) would require its own coding strategy. The codes actually used could then be placed along an ordinal scale which indicates the amount of data that an appropriate response under each strategy would have to consume and brings out the inverse relationship that consequently obtains between information and redundancy. Such a scale is depicted in Figure 2.1. As the figure indicates, a complex object such as, say, a typewriter might be experienced at different levels:

1   At the level of an object that one merely *contemplates* with a certain detachment. Neither clarity nor resolution are ardently sought, and some ambiguity might even be actively enjoyed. Little coding effort, therefore, is required at this level, indicated by point A on the scale; it is low in structure and high in complexity and information content.

2   At the level of an object that one has to *name* in order to identify it and distinguish it from other objects in the visual field. One is not concerned

to structure the object beyond the minimum necessary for a crude classification. Some coding is required but not much. This level is indicated by point B on the scale. Some articulation has been achieved so that both complexity and information content have been reduced relative to point A.

3   At the level of an object that one has to *interact* with in order to use it. Here there is a need to identify both the object itself and its constituent elements, and to understand how these fit together: a measure of differentiation and integration is now required, and, by implication, a higher degree of coding. Point C on the scale indicates the necessary coding level. It is characterized by a more finely articulated structure, a lower degree of complexity, and a lower information content than the other two levels.

Each mode of apprehending the typewriter, corresponding to a different point on the coding scale of Figure 2.1, requires a prior investment in the mastery of an appropriate coding scheme at that point. Mastery of codes at one level of apprehension, however, does not in any way suggest mastery at another. A copy typist, for instance, who achieves a typing speed of 100 words per minute by developing coding skills corresponding to point C on the scale is not necessarily capable of conceiving a typewriter as a 'soft sculpture' as did the American artist Claes Oldenburg in the 1960s. This would require that the typewriter be apprehended contemplatively at a level corresponding to point A. Nor do we necessarily infer, when contemplating Oldenburg's 'soft typewriter', that it must be the work of a man who can reach typing speeds of 200 words per minute and thus possesses coding skills appropriate to point C. Operative and contemplative coding skills produce separate universes of discourse with respect to the same object. At some points they may come together – but only because we *make* them do so, not because they are destined to. They represent complementary ways of knowing a typewriter.[55] It follows that relaxation and single shot processing strategies might be used at any point on the scale even though the need for single shot strategies will increase as one moves up the scale and becomes increasingly involved with the object. The skilled use of single shot algorithms by, say, a typist, however, does not imply that a higher level of understanding of typewriters has occurred – a point emphasized by John Searle.[56]

The ordinal coding scale of Figure 2.1 can be converted into an interval scale by relating each of the different ways of knowing an object – in the case given above, a typewriter – to the minimum number of bits of data required to describe it at the corresponding coding level. These are the H of Shannon's formula.[57] The higher the degree of coding, the less the amount of data required to describe the object. Thus, for example, the contemplative experience of the typewriter turns out to call for much larger volumes of data

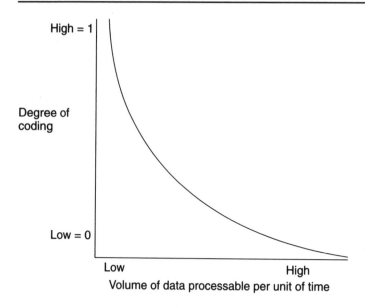

High = 1

Degree of
coding

Low = 0

Low   High

Volume of data processable per unit of time

Figure 2.2 The influence of coding on data processing

processing than are required for actually typing with it. Contemplation might lend itself more easily to a scanning than to a chunking strategy in the sense that myriad possibilities are non-committally explored and combined. The typewriter thus becomes a kaleidoscope of transient images which cannot be reduced to one another through further coding.[58] The volume of data then required for naming and discussing the typewriter as an object turns out to be less than is needed for its pure contemplation but more than the minimum required to operate it. In the latter case single numbers or letters referring to the different parts of the machine will usually suffice if supplemented by a simple line diagram relating them to each other. The typical beginner's manual is a fairly laconic affair.

A typewriter is one possible object of experience, a headache is a second, and a general election is a third. Each will vary in the amount of data required to achieve a minimal satisfactory description at a given level of coding. We can factor out such variations by focusing our attention on the maximum volume of data that can be processed *per unit of time* by a given coding scheme and then use the total time required to process a complexion sequence as an independent measure of the cognitive effort imposed by an object of experience.[59]

In Figure 2.2, therefore, we express the degree of coding as the reciprocal of the amount of data required per unit of time to describe an object of experience. The extreme points of our scale represent, respectively, those points at which either description is impossible on account of the infinite amount of data that make up the experience or the object – i.e., $C = 1/\infty = 0$ – or description is unnecessary since it can be reduced to a single bit of information – i.e., $C = 1/1 = 1$. In this way we create a coding scale whose values vary between 0 and 1. The scale forms our point of departure for the analysis that follows.

To summarize, in attempting to identify and respond to recurrent regularities in our environment, we must develop coding strategies that make a good and timely use of the data available. Jerome Bruner has used the term 'perceptual readiness' to describe such strategies. They serve, where appropriate, to minimize the surprise value of the environment by matching accessible categories with probable events and less accessible categories with less probable events, thus increasing the overall chance of apprehending sought-after objects. In effect, perceptual readiness is nothing more than the ability to take up in good time one or more appropriate positions on the coding scale we have presented in Figure 2.2 as circumstances require.

It may be, however, that in certain circumstances it is impossible to take an appropriate position on the coding scale because a coding repertoire is not yet available there. It will therefore have to be created. Code creation is one of the ways in which the new knowledge emerges, one that helps to fill in gaps in the coding scale. Different ways of knowing a phenomenon can thus be expressed as a continuum on our coding scale along which we are free to move providing that we have first created and mastered the codes that define it.[60]

Creating new codes involves moving either up or down the scale from a given position – or creating them at that spot. A move up the scale is a move towards greater data processing economies and hence greater structure. Gaining the necessary insights into the structure of phenomena to be able to code them is itself an activity that requires prior knowledge and some mastery of the context within which insights can emerge. A move down the scale, by contrast, is one in which a code that one has already mastered is tested out in a variety of new situations – that is to say, it gets contextualized. This second move is more costly in terms of data processing and, to the extent that context is open ended, it leads one to operate at a lower level of structure.

Code creation may be termed *efficient* to the extent that moves up or down the coding scale, whether they involve shedding or gaining data – upward moves shed it and downward moves acquire it – remain information preserving so that ultimately the same quantity of information can be extracted from a code, whatever its position on the coding scale. A moment's reflection should persuade us that coding moves up the scale can never be 100 per cent efficient. The reason is that codes, like formal mathematical systems, are subject to Gödel's Incompleteness Theorem so that their use and interpretation will always partly depend on their context; that is to say, on a set of codes further down the coding scale.[61] In like fashion, contextualizing a code by moving down the coding scale can never be fully information preserving since, starting from the code itself, context cannot be exhaustively specified. The information losses incurred as one moves up or down the coding scale are evidence of entropy at work in all data processing systems. Schopenhauer expressed the point somewhat more poetically when he observed that 'thoughts die the moment they are embodied in words'.

In Chapter 1 we hypothesized that data processing organisms would seek to minimize the production of entropy through a judicious use of information. What we have concluded here is that using information is also subject to entropy. A well-chosen coding strategy is one way of reducing entropy production. Yet such a strategy cannot fully function unless it is accompanied by insights into the structure of phenomena that give codes their initial purchase. Insight calls for a skill which is quite distinct from coding. It is called *abstraction*. We turn to it next.

2.2: CONCEIVING AS ABSTRACTION

Categorization

Coding is simultaneously an act of selection and of categorization. What is selected? How is it then categorized? Only that which is in some way stable and reproducible can be selected. The totally ephemeral cannot be coded, it has no structure; it cannot even be identified. Yet coding builds upon identification, upon those elements in the flux of sensation whose existence is sufficiently durable to make them good candidates for the selection process. Edelman contends that the basis of memory resides in the neural structures that are responsible for categorization.[62]

What is selected, however, has to be placed into categories that to some degree, at least, must already be available even if only embryonically. Knowledge and categorization are intimately intertwined since knowledge can be thought of as a prior disposition to assign stimuli to classes of objects and events that we ourselves have somehow constructed. A simple example of categorization is furnished by the process of looking into a shop window where the glass pane has been tilted at a slight angle so that buildings on the other side of the street as well as the skyscape are reflected in it. Two classes of objects then have to be distinguished: the set of objects placed behind the shop window and hence located inside the shop, and the set of objects that are reflected in the shop window but that are located outside the shop.

Categorization is initially a matter of trial and error subject to improvement; the assignment of stimuli to classes is carried out probabilistically on the basis of prior learning and experience. If the assignment of sensations to pre-extant categories is competently carried out it economizes on data processing since it relieves the organism of the burden of storing large numbers of single instances.[63] The more efficient the coding the less data it requires for processing. Where the assignment is problematic, however, where the fit between the sensation and the category is an uncomfortable one, then either some restructuring of the category will be attempted or other available categories offering a better fit might be sought. More rarely, a sensation that cannot be accommodated by an existing repertoire of categories will give rise to the creation of new ones.[64]

Selection and categorization of sense data is performed in a routine, almost unconscious fashion in our daily commerce with the world. It is often in fact quite tentative and risky. Where coding is primarily a perceptual activity, it involves making inferences that Gregory[65] has labelled 'perceptual hypotheses'. Sensations are then components of perceptual hypotheses and the various dimensions of sensation underpin the structure of perceptual hypotheses. Making an inference invokes a decisions process, and learning a new perceptual category amounts to making a series of interrelated decisions in which each step in a performance results from a choice between alternative possibilities. Coding *within* an existing category, and coding *for* a new category, therefore activate search procedures which, from a decision-making perspective, are not so very different from each other. To choose between options in accommodating a given stimulus, the cognitive apparatus, as we have seen, will be concerned to economize on data processing effort and will consequently show some preference for what already exists over what has to be created anew. Well-tested and available perceptual categories, wherever these might be located on our coding scale, will therefore be drawn upon first, only being abandoned reluctantly.[66] To be of adaptive value to the organism, however, categorization must entail generalization – that is, on the basis of a few stimuli, to recognize and respond to a much larger and possibly more varied class of stimuli. People are good at this. If they learn a new fact about one object, it will modify their expectations about a whole class of similar objects.[67] The knowing subject then emerges from the activities of a nervous system organized according to two mathematical principles: classification and conditional probability.[68] The first provides structures derivable from a generalization of prior knowledge and experience; the second a mechanism for accommodating both new experiences and new structures at the margin along lines that might loosely be described as Bayesian.[69]

Percept versus concept

Edelman distinguishes between perceptual and conceptual categorizations – that is, between coding activities that are rooted primarily in *local*, immediately given stimuli, and those that are more dependent on *non-local* stimuli originating in memory and experience.[70] It is the way that these combine that gives rise to the detection of law-like regularities, what Churchland terms *nomological generalizations*.[71] Although in information-theoretic terms both perceptual and conceptual categorization can be treated in a similar way, they lead to very different strategies for economizing on data, and these, as we shall see in the next section, whilst constantly in interaction with each other, are not necessarily mutually compatible. Perceptual categories are rooted in the five senses of sight, hearing, taste, smell, and touch. They are a first line of interception of data from the external world which, left to their own devices, would allow only a limited and fragmentary classification of immediately apprehended phenomena. But as we now know, perception is never left to its own devices; it may be *constrained* by physiology but in its activities it is largely guided by concepts. Conceptual schemata may be thought of as data complexions that represent generic concepts – objects, situations, events, sequences of events, actions, and sequences of actions – that are stored in memory.[72] Configurations of schemata are constantly being brought to bear on the process of perceptual categorization in seeking out an economic account of a given set of input stimuli; it is thus only in strictly developmental terms that perceptual categorization can be taken as prior to conceptual categorization.[73] Only to unreconstructed empiricists are perceptions always immediately given;[74] to those who accept the research findings of modern physiology, sensation can never be totally naive but is always to some extent 'theory-laden'.[75]

The above point can be illustrated by referring to our earlier discussion of Figure 1.3 in Chapter 1. Technology in the form of radio telescopes or electron microscopes can extend the range of data that we can capture from the external world well beyond what is immediately given to our senses and thus offers us the opportunity of developing more discriminating codes. The differentiation and integration of sensory stimuli can then be taken much further when augmented by appropriate data capturing and processing technologies than what is possible by the five senses unaided.[76] Yet the development of such technologies itself inevitably draws upon knowledge of physical phenomena that is theoretical in nature and hence conceptual. All observation, whether assisted by technology or otherwise, is in this way guided by theory.

Conceptual and perceptual categories, then, interfuse in such a way that perception is never wholly free of a conceptual element, and the perceptual coding of sense data invokes prior theoretical knowledge, itself the fruit of earlier successful generalizations.

Perceiving and conceiving share a common aim: complexity reduction – making sense of the world with a minimum consumption of the organism's scarce data processing resources. Data overload is a permanent threat and the larger the number of attributes or instances to be dealt with, the larger the number of hypothetical perceptual or conceptual categories in which the elements may be grouped.[77]

Bruner and his co-workers have suggested that the number of hypotheses compatible with the first positive instance of an event can be expressed by the formula $H = f(A)$ where H is the number of hypothetical concepts possible after a first positive instance of an event, and A is the number of attributes in an array. To illustrate: if 3 attributes can be grouped under 7 possible categories, 4 may be grouped under 15, 5 under 31, and 6 under 63. Choices rapidly proliferate out of control. Clearly the larger the number of attributes in an array, the larger the number of hypotheses that will have to be processed before an input can be interpreted.[78]

Bruner's formula allows us to distinguish two ways in which we economize on our data processing resources when confronted with complexity:

1   By reducing the number of attributes that have to be attended to in sense data. This is the function of coding: it economizes on the quantity of *data* to be processed.
2   By reducing the number of categories that will be used to filter sense data. This is the function of *abstraction*: by the creation of suitable concepts it economizes on the number of categories through which data will have to be processed.

Simplifying somewhat, we might say that coding economizes on the raw materials and abstraction economizes on what they have to go through to be rendered useful.

The different possibilities for economizing that we are describing here are shown schematically in Figure 2.3. What the diagram cannot show is how far these different possibilities interact. Since concepts shape the process of perceptual categorization, they have a further selective effect on the data that will be drawn up for coding. This issue will be discussed further in the next section.

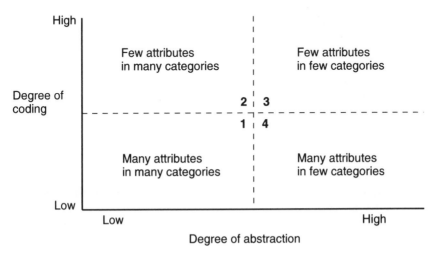

Figure 2.3 Coding and abstraction

Of course how far one is actually seeking data processing economies will depend on the circumstances of the case. In the previous section we saw that complexity elicits two kinds of cognitive response. The first strives to reduce information overload by better chunking – i.e., choosing a code that makes better use of available redundancy or structure in the data. The second, invoked when no chunking is possible, is a form of scanning. It is not inevitably to be treated as a second-best solution as earlier implied, however. If there is little or no cognitive pressure to *resolve* the complexity – whether by using existing codes or creating new ones – or if it is simply intended to be experienced rather than interpreted, then scanning strategies may offer more scope for casual non-committal exploration than coding strategies.

Scanning can be viewed as a form of openness to experience, of acceptance. It is close to what we have called contemplation. It may indeed be less efficient or economic of our time, but we do not systematically approach all experience with a view to economizing on it. Complexity may on occasions be enjoyed for its aesthetic richness rather than pared down or eliminated. Chunking or coding, the first response to complexity, involves reducing the number of attributes that have to be attended to by moving up the coding scale of Figure 2.3 towards greater structure and redundancy. The second response, scanning, involves staying put on the scale at a lower level of coding, and working there with a given stock of attributes.

Coding will be attempted when difficult cognitive conditions create noise and ambiguity in a message at a time when an efficient and well-directed response is called for. As a minimal step, one will want to clarify the context in which the message is received. Contextualising a message, by placing brackets around the specific circumstances of its occurrence, is a first step in coding it since it sets a provisional limit to the size of the database or the repertoire of complexions that one will subsequently draw from. If the context turns out to be benign, one may then relax and switch from an efficiency-oriented problem-solving mode to a style that is more detached and exploratory – i.e., one in which the data is scanned in a gentle, non-committal way. If, on the other hand, the context suggests continued vigilance, then one may continue to seek out ever more articulated and economical perceptual or conceptual structures.

Abstraction

The use of concepts greatly reduces the amount of information the cognitive system needs to encode. Recalling a point that we made in the preceding section, if a perceptual object exhibits f binary features, then the probability distribution associated with that object will require 2^f numbers to specify. If, however, we can group the features into s groups corresponding to schemata, each involving f/s features, then only $s2^{f/s}$ numbers will be needed. This can amount to an enormous reduction since even with such small numbers as f

= 100 and s = 10, the reduction factor is $10 \times 2^{-90} \approx 10^{-28}$. Yet if abstraction involves economizing on conceptual categories, it means reducing s, which, unless f is correspondingly reduced, at the limit leaves us back where we started and with little to show for it by way of economies. Luckily, as we saw above, f and s interact; that is to say, percepts and concepts are in some kind of feedback relationship which allows an iterative reduction of both f and s as one moves further towards abstraction.[79]

Like coding, abstraction economizes on categories by an act of selection from competing alternatives. Edelman aligns such selection with evolutionary processes:

> Darwin (1859) stated that the origin of taxa was natural selection acting upon variants within a population to yield differential reproduction of the most adapted (Mayr 1982) ... The theoretical principle I shall elaborate here is that the origin of categories in higher brain functions is somatic selection among huge numbers of variants of neural circuits contained in networks created epigenetically in each individual during its development; this selection results in differential amplification of populations of synapses in the selected variants. In other words, I shall take the view that the brain is a selective system more akin in its workings to evolution than to computation or information processing.[80]

Abstraction, then, can be thought of as a choice among competing hypotheses concerning which categories better capture a perceptual attribute. In contrast to the computation paradigm, the categories are not given *a priori*; they have to be discovered through a process of hypothesis creation and testing that make them *emergent* properties of the microstructure of cognitive process. Such properties are *non-linear*, which is to say that they cannot be inferred from the statistically salient features of the input stimuli alone. Abstraction can thus never be reduced to a process of summarizing inputs; the operation has holistic qualities that we associate with the distributed nature of neural networks.[81] Beyond a certain level of abstraction, however, clusters of relationships sometimes acquire cohesiveness and hence a life of their own independently of the perceptual attributes they play host to. They can then form a *symbolic* repertoire amenable to manipulation, and to further coding and economizing. Symbolic coding, however, is quite a different business from perceptual coding. It allows one to build new structures out of elements that refer to other, more complex structures without requiring that these be represented in all their cumbersome detail.[82] Yet to the extent that symbols are required, they must emerge from the subsymbolic level at which neural processes function. As Rumelhart has pointed out, the currency of these is excitation and inhibition, not symbols,[83] even if at some point sequential symbol processing takes over from parallel processing.[84]

Coding and abstraction can work either in tandem or independently of

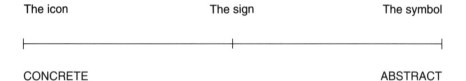

Figure 2.4 The abstraction scale

each other, abstraction being considered an independent dimension which can be scaled to rank the minimum number of categories required to handle a given hypothesis, whether this turns out to be predominantly perceptual or conceptual. Coding can thus occur at different levels of abstraction from the lowest level at which concrete experiences are given structure, form, and stability, to the highest level at which conventions regulate the use of symbols and give them theoretical content. It is generally accepted, however, that the greater the level of abstraction at which coding takes place, the deeper must be the insight and understanding into the causal texture of phenomena.

In sum, abstraction might be described as a move away from a process of manipulating images or other objects of experience that have been given form – call this iconic coding – and towards operating with symbols that are more easily manipulated, stored, and retained in memory because they have been largely drained of perceptual content. The move from one to the other can be scaled. Semiotics, for example, gives us three useful points on such an abstraction scale (Figure 2.4). In addition to icons at the concrete end of the scale and symbols at the abstract end, the theory identifies a midpoint which it labels 'the *sign*'. It stands halfway between the image with its homomorphic mapping of percepts on to concrete regions of the world, and the symbol, floating above the world and tethered to it only at one or two points. The sign has concrete referents but remains more detached from them than the icon.[85]

Symbolic coding, then, offers simultaneously the two types of data processing economies discussed above, reducing both the quantity of data that must be handled as attributes and the number of categories to which these must then be assigned. Such coding vastly reduces the load on memory and frees up information processing capacity for other uses.

For this reason, perhaps, even if symbols are not the currency used by neural processes, they have become the currency by means of which much data processing and exchange activity is conducted between individual minds. A currency acts as a measure of value, a store of value, and as a means of exchange.[86] If information is then taken as having value – this, after all, is one of the basic themes of this book – then symbols act as a measure of information, as a store of information, and as a means of information exchange. It is because of the contribution made by symbolic processing that in Figure 2.3 information reaches its highest value in quadrant 3.

As with monetary assets, symbols have varying degrees of liquidity that reflect how much data they have been able to shed through coding and abstraction and which determine the ease with which they enter into a variety of cognitive exchanges. Here, just as money begets more money, so, through crafty manipulation, symbols beget more symbols. Beyond the symbols of everyday language, and at a higher level of coding, are to be found those of symbolic logic, symbols which formalize and articulate thought processes that lie outside the descriptive reach of such language.[87] They require less data for their operation than everyday language and activate fewer categories.

Yet the very considerable data processing economies offered by symbolic knowledge are only available to those who invest the necessary time and effort in mastering the relevant coding skills and the associated concepts. An algebraic formula, for example, stores information more efficiently and economically than the corresponding mathematical table and at the same time promises greater generality. But mastering the use of algebraic formulae requires a different kind of learning skill than simply remembering in serial order and by rote the value of entries in a mathematical table. In effect, it calls for a cognitive investment that moves one by degrees along the two dimensions of Figure 2.3 towards both greater codification and greater abstraction. The move is depicted in Figure 2.5.

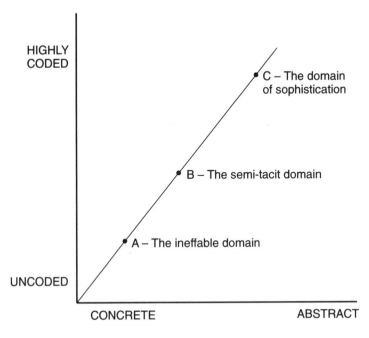

Figure 2.5 Different modes of knowing

Modes of knowing

As with the coding scale of Figure 2.1, the different points labelled A, B, and C in Figure 2.5 correspond to different modes of knowing. Research into cognitive styles suggests that different modes of knowing are more congenial to some than to others; each has his favourite spots – not necessarily located at any of the three points shown on the diagram. Such spots reduce the cognitive load imposed on an individual, requiring less personal effort or strain.[88] Partly following Michael Polanyi,[89] we can label the three points in the figure:

1 *Point A: The ineffable domain* – that mode of knowing which cannot be put into coded form at all. Since it is located on the left of the diagram it deals with concrete experiences rather than abstract phenomena; these can be shared, but only with those who are co-present. Whatever limited communication is possible in the ineffable domain is achieved by simple gestures such as pointing or by force of example. The great paradox of the ineffable domain is that by itself it requires virtually no investment in the acquisition of codes or the mastery of concepts, and for this reason, as a way of knowing, it is potentially available to all. Yet the need for the co-presence and physical proximity of would-be communicators – sometimes over extended periods of time if they are to share successfully the same 'wavelength' – itself occasioned by the same lack of codes, in practice severely restricts the number of participants in a given experience of the ineffable. This domain, then, has the least structure and, whatever effort at coding might be undertaken, the results are rarely stable enough to be developed, stored, and shared outside the here-and-now. It is the purest case of what Polanyi himself terms 'personal' knowledge.

2 *Point B: The semi-tacit domain* (this is our term) – in this part of the space one encounters natural discourse, drawing upon a repertoire of non-specialized symbols and concepts acquired through a process of collective socialization and thus widely shared. Here, people are willing to invest in the acquisition and mastery of codes and categories in so far as they offer participation in the activities of a wider community. Effective communication here depends upon a mix of words and gesture, text and example. Any loss of data entailed by coding complex messages into words, or by abstracting from a concrete situation, is now compensated by gains in communicative potential offered by an increase in structure.[90] Transacting parties may still need to be co-present, but now no longer necessarily so. The people and things addressed might be elsewhere. Codes and concepts of the semi-tacit domain prise open large tracts of experience to comparatively effortless shared understanding. Yet it is always a limited understanding resting on substrata of more personal concrete knowledge that cannot itself be shared. Heroic

attempts have been made by some writers to bring such tacit knowledge into the public domain, James Joyce's *Ulysses* being one of the best-known examples.

3 *Point C: The domain of sophistication.* This is pure text or speech, drawing mainly on highly coded and abstract categories. Tacit and explicit ways of knowing now part ways; they become disjointed as the data embedded in earlier arrays of attributes and categories – the source of their richness – is gradually shed and lost to view. In the domain of sophistication, a speaker or writer can never know *quite* what he is talking about since the process of articulating itself encumbers the tacit element as well as representing it.[91] Novel modes of thought become possible here and often result, paradoxically, from the capacity of our abstract symbolizing skills to outrun our understanding. The quantum theory, for example, emerged from an interplay of symbols and concepts so abstract that at first they eluded all attempts at intuitive understanding.[92] In the domain of sophistication, language or other symbol systems shape thought explicitly through procedural and inferential rules. In the semi-tacit domain, by contrast, the reciprocal influence that language and thought exert on each other remains more elusive.[93]

These three modes of knowing, and particularly the latter two, can only be mastered with some effort. The developing child, for example, does not display competence in all three domains simultaneously. As it grows older its cognitive abilities gradually spread out from the origin in Figure 2.5, extending from the ineffable domain first into the semi-tacit domain and then later, with the acquisition of specialized skills in symbolic coding, into the domain of sophistication. Piaget[94] and Bruner[95] have put forward similar descriptions of this evolution. Piaget, for example, has shown that with a gradual mastery of concrete operations, the child by degrees comes to develop an internalized structure underpinned by the logic of classes and the logic of relations. The 'concrete' that Piaget refers to deals with the here-and-now, with an immediate reality that the child can directly apprehend through the senses; it ignores things that are absent or more general categories. When the child builds up an internalized structure, therefore, it is mostly coding perceptually and only just beginning to abstract. That is to say, it is moving up the coding dimension of Figure 2.5, but on the left, still largely in the realm of the concrete.

Bruner perceives the process of abstraction in a child's cognitive development much as Piaget does. He distinguishes three complementary systems of representation that the child moves through as it grows: the enactive, which is based on action and involves pointing at things; the iconic, based on imagery; and the symbolic, based on language and involving both labelling and sentence construction.[96]

While neither Piaget nor Bruner explicitly formulate their views in the terms used here, they each describe a sequential process of coding and abstracting, of first giving form and structure to experience and then of generalizing on the basis of these. The attainment of concepts according to Bruner is achieved by quantum jumps that are impossible to analyse experientially: we reach a concept but we do not quite know how we got there – as already indicated, the process is non-linear. Also, we fail to notice that on arrival at our conceptual destination we still have a fair amount of enactive and iconic knowledge in tow. Polanyi[97] has argued that this mysterious process has consistently led us to ignore the tacit component of articulate knowledge and the important part played by sense perception in building up our symbolic capacities. Abstract symbols may come to *acquire* autonomy, but they are not born with it.

Trajectories

If we choose to view intellectual development not so much as 'stages' that one first moves into and then out of, as hypothesized by Piaget, but as a cumulative process in which increasingly large areas of the space of Figure 2.5 are occupied and then dwelt in, then the interfusion of ineffable, semi-tacit, and sophisticated modes of knowing – among others – becomes possible, creating a highly individualized and complex cognitive trajectory for each one of us, a trajectory rich in meanderings that reflect both personal predilections we may have for certain regions of the space, and the amount of time we invest in it.[98] It should be intuitively clear that the effort gradient runs from the ineffable domain to the domain of sophistication. Progress up the gradient depends on the effort invested. Obviously a greater investment will be required to create new cognitive resources than to exploit those already available. Yet symbolic processing remains intrinsically difficult and hence not universally accessible. Zuboff has documented the difficulties that confront people who are called upon to operate at a higher level of coding and abstraction than their training and education has prepared them for.[99] The information generated by symbolic processing may have the highest value, but its obtention also calls for the greatest prior cognitive investment. Not everyone will think that the payoff justifies the investment, and their cognitive trajectory will reflect this fact.

Novelty

In spite of the different purposes they serve, coding and abstraction are easily confused. One reason may be because they each deploy similar strategies for saving on data.[100] Both involve selecting and placing stimuli into equivalence classes; both call for the establishment of probabilistic relationships between events belonging to the various classes; and finally, both require some manipulation of the classes themselves through the application of trans-formation rules.

For the most part, coding and abstraction are routine activities guided by the ready availability of well-tested repertoires of percepts and concepts. Where an adequate repertoire is not available, however, cognitive innovation becomes necessary. Langley and his co-workers term such innovation 'data driven' when it originates with percepts, and 'theory driven' when it emerges from purely conceptual deliberations.[101] Researchers in the PDP tradition assimilate cognitive innovation to learning and describe it as 'bottom-up' when it is data driven, 'top-down' when it is theory driven, and interactive when it integrates the two.[102]

Although in practice innovative coding is hard to disentangle from innovative theorizing, the latter, over time, has a far greater impact than the former on how we perceive and interpret the world. The French mathematician, Henri Poincaré, for example, describes theory creation thus:

> There is a hierarchy of facts. Some are without any positive bearing, and teach us nothing but themselves. The scientist who ascertains them learns nothing but facts and becomes no better able to foresee new facts. Such facts, it seems, occur but once and are not destined to be repeated. There are, on the other hand, facts that give us a large return, each one of which teaches us a new law. And since he is obliged to make a selection, it is to these latter facts that the scientist must devote himself.[103]

In practice, away from the frontiers of science, cognitive processes remain quite conservative. And with good reason. The human organism's cognitive apparatus, buffeted by the turbulent flows and eddies of experience, seeks to anchor itself to solid meanings and structures, themselves resting on comparatively secure foundations of prior learning, an accumulated stock of percepts and concepts that constitute its inertial frame of reference. Too much choice, too many new possibilities, become destructive of the needed stability and meaning. Bartlett[104] held that an organism's 'effort after meaning' was for this reason constantly being diverted towards the familiar and the known by the action of memory. Such cognitive conservatism, however, makes the unfamiliar hard to perceive and to remember correctly; it therefore increases the organism's data processing load when it is confronted with novelty. In simple terms unfamiliar stimuli are hard to code for or to abstract from.

The unfamiliar is in consequence also hard to talk about. Communication is only possible where some measure of overlap exists between the categories drawn upon by the parties to an exchange. We described this requirement in the previous section as being a precondition for the sharing of experience. Yet while cognitive conservatism might bias communicating parties towards shared categories – whether perceptual or conceptual – their irreducibly provisional or hypothetical character robs them of any epistemological permanence. They may thus help to render an individual's world communicable to others, but what is then shared may turn out to be nothing more than a mirage, permanently subject to revision if not to outright refutation. Coding and abstraction, then, may help to make experiences more communicable – the subject of the next chapter – but do not thereby convert them into valid knowledge. We explore the epistemological issue next.

2.3: THE E-SPACE

The value of abstraction

In the preceding section, the process of deriving abstract categories from a collection of concrete individual instances was viewed as discontinuous. Abstraction is an emergent property of neural activity and not merely a summary description of data points. The transition from one level of description to a higher, more abstract level therefore entails crossing an inductive gap, a point first made by Hume and much explored in our own day by Popper.[105]

The epistemological status of induction, the question of whether it yields reliable public knowledge, remains a matter of some controversy. Are the stars, for instance, inferred from spectral lines objects of the same cognitive order as, say, the steak on my plate? Both the formal abstract models of science that help to structure and interpret problematic observations *and* more casual and naive acts of direct perception aim to achieve predictive value, albeit often at different levels of certainty, and to go, as Bruner puts it, 'beyond the information given'.[106] If they fail to do so, they have no surplus value; they are trivial. But the difference in surplus value aimed for in scientific observation is not usually of the same order as that created by a casual act of immediate perception as one goes about one's daily business. The challenge, in science, is to grow fruitful generalizations from the compost of experience, generalizations that extend their range of useful applications while maintaining a high degree of validity.[107] In other words, science aims at a much higher level of abstraction than most other human activities.

Perceptions are rooted in immediate events, in the here-and-now, in what you can see, hear, feel, and touch. Concepts, by contrast, have no particular habitat. Floating above events at an indeterminate distance, they can glide frictionlessly across space–time boundaries into new realms of experience. The experiences processed by an act of conceptualization may be quite concrete but concepts themselves remain abstract. By implication, perceptions are far more limited in range and application than concepts, whose power is generally related to their degree of abstraction – that is, the extent to which the generalizations they occasion are removed from the specific instances to which they are applied or to the concrete data from which they may be derived.[108] In sum, if perceptions offer vividness, concepts offer coverage.[109]

In the act of perceiving, as we have already noted, the concrete and the abstract thoroughly intermingle. Consider the following passage from Churchland's book *Neurophilosophy: Towards a Unified Science of the Mind/Brain*:

> A beginning neuroscientist's first observation through a microscope may produce puzzlement – it may be difficult to know what is artefact and what is part of the cell ('*That's* endoplasmic reticulum ... ??'). Theory informs observation, and after a short while it becomes hard not to see, say, the end bulb. Notice that if I see something as an end bulb, then I imply that the whole range of additional properties will obtain: that it is at an end of an axon, that if tested it would be found to contain synaptic vesicles, that if we looked at it under an electron microscope we would see synapses, and so on. To apply the term 'end bulb' to what is seen in the microscope is not a sheer naked observation: it implies an indefinite number of generalizations applicable to the object. This cascade of indefinitely many applications is a general feature of the observational application of any descriptive term, whether it is 'coyote', 'red', or 'synaptic vesicle'.[110]

Empirical philosophers in the tradition of Bacon and J.S. Mill have always demanded a solid well-built platform of reliable perceptions from which to launch conceptual probes. But what if the platform itself is discovered to rest on a conceptual substructure subject to shifts and adjustments? Have we not argued earlier that the act of observation itself is from the outset 'theory laden'?[111]

Epistemological issues

We can push any enquiry into the epistemological status of abstract concepts along two paths. The first leads to an examination both of the empirical base from which abstraction is claimed to derive and of the nature of the derivation itself. On most accounts, following this path, abstract objects appear to be epistemologically fragile creations. The second path leads to a questioning of whether concept attainment – taken here as the creation of an abstract object – inevitably requires an articulate empirical base. Bruner takes concept formation as an instance of 'generic coding' which he defines as a 'contentless description of the ideal case, empty in the sense that geometry is empty of particulars'. He argues that it is this emptying operation that constitutes the creative step in invention or in producing a coding system, and tentatively concludes that 'Generic learning and the abstracting or emptying operation are the same thing I think.'[112]

What Bruner refers to as 'generic coding' is of course none other than

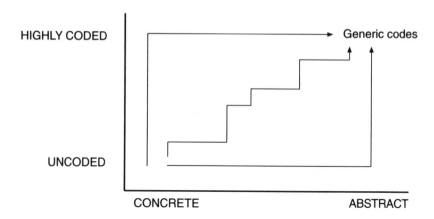

Figure 2.6 The evolution of generic codes

symbolic coding, discussed in the previous section. Recall that both perceptual and symbolic coding describe upward movements located respectively on the left and on the right of Figure 2.5. Symbolic coding thus offers an alternative path for the creation of well-defined abstract objects to the one which proceeds to the right in the diagram from already well-coded concrete experiences towards well-coded abstractions. Such rightward movement can effectively occur either in the upper part of the diagram based on well-formed percepts – the resulting abstraction becoming an articulate structure of generic elements or relations – or it can occur in the lower region where data is more vague and ambiguous and where the outcome remains conceptually fuzzy – a structure still undergoing development rather than fully formed. A subsequent coding movement up the space might then follow, which removes the concept's fuzzy edges and gives it definition. Empirical support exists for a move to the right operating at a low level of coding. Studies on pigeons, for example, by Herrnstein and by Cerella, indicate that some language-free organisms have a capacity for forming generalizations. Furthermore, even language-based organisms inherently possess a number of categorization processes which, while quite complex, arose prior to language acquisition.[113]

In sum, we are hypothesizing that the evolution of generic codes might follow any one of the alternative paths shown in Figure 2.6, or possibly some combination of them all. Once developed, of course, a new generic code can subsequently be applied to concrete situations in which it can help to generate innovative perceptions. Thus while we can agree with Poincaré that an innovative conception turns upon what concrete facts – coded or uncoded – one selects in performing an abstraction, it can also be argued that an innovative perception in turn depends on what concepts are selected in carrying out an observation.

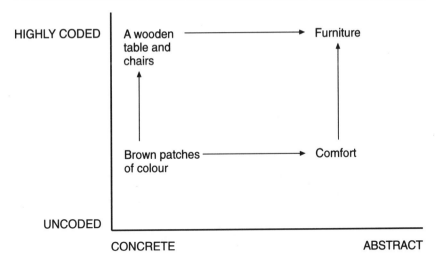

Figure 2.7 The E-space

The two dimensions of coding and abstraction allow us to visualize graphically in what form an individual processes and stores the data available to him. We shall label this simple scheme an epistemology space or an *E-space* for short. It can be used to give us a snapshot of how the knowledge held by an individual is distributed at a given instant – for an illustration see Figure 2.7 – or it can allow us to trace the evolution of a particular item of knowledge by following its trajectory in the space – also shown in the figure.

The E-space is a personal space, being confined to what is going on inside one individual's head. The way that the knowledge held by an individual is configured in the E-space is affected by the way he learns and by more general personality factors. These are discussed in the next two sections of this chapter. The E-space, unlike a closed system, exchanges energy and information with its external environment; it is thus open to outside influences. In the next chapter we expose the individual's cognitive processes more explicitly to social influences in order to assess how far these modify the contents and evolution of his E-space.

Popper's three worlds

I have found it helpful to think of the E-space within the framework of Karl Popper's evolutionary epistemology.[114] Popper describes himself as a realist who believes that a world of abstract objects – which he labels World 3 (W3) – is no less real than one of concrete objects which he labels World 1 (W1). According to Popper, it is human consciousness, World 2 (W2), that mediates between W1 and W3. Just as there is a competition and an evolutionary struggle for an existence in W1, so there is in W3, and abstract

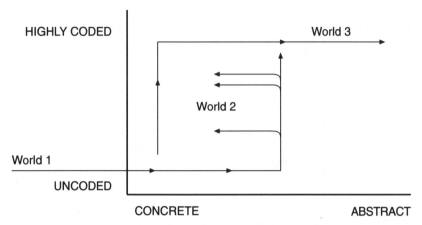

Figure 2.8 Popper's Worlds 1, 2, and 3 in the E-space

objects that have been inadequately constructed fare less well over time in the selection process than more robust competitors. What determines their prospect for survival in W3? According to Popper, the nature of their incubation in W2.

Popper's evolutionary epistemology has been both influential and highly controversial.[115] Since in what follows we are not required to take up a strong position on the epistemological status of W3 objects, we can sidestep the controversy and simply make use of Popper's scheme as an expository device. I believe that the E-space articulates Popper's W2 in a way that highlights what is required for the creation of useful epistemological products. Figure 2.8 shows the E-space – now taken as our equivalent to Popper's W2 – receiving data inputs from a concrete W1 within which it is immersed. As the data is processed in W2 it traces out a slow and approximately diagonal path towards the north-east corner of the E-space to emerge eventually as an abstract and well-coded object with a life of its own – i.e., as a W3 object. Much of the controversy concerning W3 objects is whether they can have a life of their own outside W2. In other words, do they survive if they move out of the E-space on the right? Whether they do or not – we take no position on this – their life expectancy, however, ultimately depends on the uses to which they can be put: a W3 object sooner or later finds its way back to W1 in some guise and embeds itself there if it is to be of any service. The return journey is shown as a feedback loop in the diagram – again we need not decide whether it originates from within W2 or from a position outside the E-space to the right of it. Returning W3 objects now act as data filters that help to code new W1 inputs and to give them form. As a result of their intervention such inputs now enter W2 at a higher level of coding than inputs unmediated by W3.

An individual E-space blends epistemological products that are the fruits of ontogenetic development with those that are imported in as a cultural inheritance. The latter enter the E-space preformed by coding and abstraction and materially influence an individual's subsequent data processing efforts through the feedback loops just described. Popper's W1, W2, and W3 thoroughly interpenetrate – Popper is an interactionist. W2, for example, the world of consciousness, is an emergent property of biochemical behaviour occurring in W1; its existence rests on nothing other than minute and not so minute variations in energy states that can be physically detected and stored. W3 in turn is entirely dependent on the workings of W2 for the creation – Popper would say the discovery – and often the storing of abstract objects. Popper believes that W2 cannot be reduced to W1; that is, that mental states cannot be reduced to brain states. He also believes that W3 does not reduce to W2 and that any regularities that we discover in nature have an independent existence.

Storing knowledge

Where a W3 product is deemed sufficiently valuable and where it has survived the selective effects of competition with other W3 objects, it may be given a more durable substrate in W1 than the human brain with its limited life and its tendency to forget.[116] It might then be stored in books, on stone, in works of art, or on computer tape. W3 objects that have been 'externalized' in this way and that find an independent existence outside the perishable human brain subsequently become the artefacts of a culture, infusing inert matter with the information they contain and transforming it into objects of immediate use. Technology, here, plays a mediating role between W3 and W1 since it is often through technical applications that W3 objects are required to demonstrate their worth in W1. W3 objects embedded in W1 artefacts can also be more easily transmitted to other brains, thus becoming inputs to other E-spaces.[117]

Not all products emerging from W3 can be stored in W1, however. Only those that have received enough structure to be intelligible and hence communicable are likely to be candidates. Some degree of coding and abstraction in W2 thus becomes a critical precondition for any externalization to take place, and this may call for a considerable investment in time and effort. Yet an externalization of W3 objects, by making in turn more of W1 intelligible and communicable, economizes on data in W2 – the E-space – and thus reduces both the memory and the data processing load upon it. With a more manageable W1, W2 can now *afford to forget much of what it had been required to know* and to open itself up to new and more diverse experiences.

Our physiological capacity for storing external data is limited and vastly inferior to our daily information needs. Our cranium is not an infinitely expandable neural repository; it imposes limits to what we can carry in memory and to what we can process.[118] The need to make room for fresh data requires that we clear our heads of information that can better be stored elsewhere.

Effective learning thus requires selective forgetting and a related ability to draw upon external memory stores. Luria, in *The Mind of a Mnemonist*, describes the problems faced by a patient of his condemned to drag along with him throughout his life the excess luggage of useless memories. He could never hold down a job long because he found it difficult to understand what was being said to him; even a simple phrase elicited an almost endless recall chain.[119] Too much data languishing on a storage shelf somewhere in the inner recesses of our mind is a sign of faulty stock control, cognitively speaking, of knowledge that has not been moved out or externalized in a timely fashion.

Externalization

W1 aids to remembering are thus, paradoxically, also aids to forgetting. Writing down a lunch appointment in a diary, for example, allows one to forget it until the relevant day. It is much easier to remember the general rule that the diary must be regularly consulted than it is to remember a sequence of individual entries giving names, dates, times, and addresses. External aids – diaries, books, libraries, etc. – greatly amplify our access to useful knowledge and simultaneously relieve the strain on internal memory.

External aids, however, need not necessarily take a written form. The world of artefacts as a whole can be treated as an external memory store, an objectivization of thought. By externalizing ideas and embedding them in objects one can play around with them, change them, and perfect them. They become bodily extensions that can be amplified and can evolve without requiring corresponding bodily changes.

Externalization, however, is not costless. It amounts to an empirical test of E-space products in which, through their interaction with W1, reality is given a chance to 'kick back'.[120] Well-corroborated W3 objects, those that have survived successive acts of coding and abstraction as well as the 'kicks' that accompany them, can subsequently be externalized at a lower cost than those which have not. Such objects, furthermore, on account of the data economies they have already achieved, are also more easily communicable to others.

Only in the case of scientific products, however, will attempts at corroboration be self-consciously and epistemologically rigorous.[121] To externalize is to express oneself, and in most instances self-expression is quite free of any epistemological claim. Many expressive gestures, cries, facial tics, etc., occur below the threshold of consciousness, and hence of intentionality. Where expression is intentional, we talk of communication, an externalization which requires a minimum of coding and abstraction to be effective. Even as obscure an object as a De Koonig painting has its abstract code: at

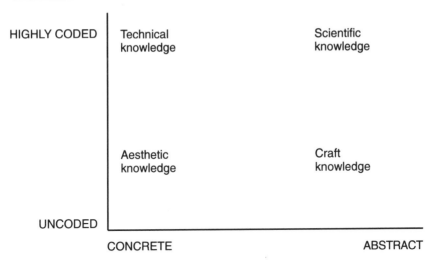

Figure 2.9 W3 artefacts in the E-space

some level of consciousness it was intended. Figure 2.9 locates a variety of epistemological products, each of which will incorporate W3 content to some degree, in various positions in the E-space from which each might be externalized. All may become embedded in W1 objects but in different ways. Scientific knowledge, for example, will find its way directly into stores of symbolic information such as books, scientific journals, and so on. Technical knowledge may also be stored in this way, but for the most part it is directly embedded in physical products designed for specific uses. The latter may therefore often get externalized at a lower level of abstraction and corroboration than the former, securing its aims over a more limited domain.[122] Reality may still kick back here, but perhaps with less force.

The way that a culture's externalized epistemological products are distributed in the E-space largely determines the learning opportunities that will be made available to its members. How effectively those opportunities are seized is a question of individual learning style and personality. We discuss learning next.

2.4: MOVING IN THE E-SPACE: LEARNING

Learning and evolutionary processes

Learning is an acquired capacity either to adapt to an environment or to modify it in ways that enhance an organism's well-being or its survival prospects. In a pure natural selection regime, learning is a strictly ontogenetic phenomenon. Phylogenetic adaptation is the product of environmental selection acting on purely random mutations. Contrary to what Lamarck believed, what is learnt in one generation cannot be biologically transmitted to the next. With the evolution of culture, what is learnt on one generation, although still not biologically transmissible to the next, can be passed on through socialization processes and artefacts. In this sense cultural evolution is 'Lamarckian' not 'Darwinian'.[123]

Learning has been and continues to be many things. At the most basic level it includes habituation, sensitization, imprinting, one trial learning, classical conditioning, instrumental conditioning, and place learning. To these rudimentary kinds of 'plasticity' must be added the higher kinds of learning through which complex representations of the environment, both present and absent, become possible.[124] From a connectionist perspective, both kinds of learning can be subsumed under a simple idea: the gradual acquisition and modification of connection strengths within a neural network. To reformulate this point in E-space terms, learning then becomes something that takes place in W2 as, assisted by W3, it comes to terms with W1. As a developmental activity, it describes how cognitive structures are initially developed, tested, and used over time by a growing organism in different circumstances. In fully developed organisms, the study of learning takes these structures as broadly given in order to study how they process new data and convert it into usable knowledge. Since effective learning is a precondition for survival both at the individual and the species level, it is a basic premise of evolutionary epistemology that knowledge which does not contribute, however indirectly, to survival enjoys a lower life expectancy than knowledge that does. It is less likely to be retained in consciousness, to evolve into a W3 product, or to be externalized and shared; in sum, over time it is more likely to be selected against. We leave open the question of whether knowledge that is selected against is in some epistemological sense less 'true' than knowledge that survives.

Learning requires a capacity to acquire and process data in adaptive ways. If we refer back to the diagram of the evolutionary production function of Chapter 1 (Figure 1.9), it becomes clear that learning can only take place in systems or organisms that have travelled sufficiently far up and towards the left in the diagram to have crossed a certain threshold in their data processing capacity. Only beyond such a threshold will the complexity of the data processing mechanism allow for internal representations of the external environment. The E-space can then be used to indicate how far, and at what level of abstraction, such representations are structured – i.e., coded.

In higher level learning, however, we are not just interested in knowing how knowledge can be distributed in an individual E-space but also in how it is mobilized and integrated in particular situations: building up cognitive resources is one way of expressing learning capacity, deploying them in appropriate circumstances is another. The first is a matter of investment, the second a matter of style. The first has been discussed in some detail in preceding sections; we must now say something about the second as it affects the individual human learner.

Learning styles

The theory of human learning that is most consistent with the structure of human cognition represented by the E-space, as well as with accepted theories of human growth and development, is that of David Kolb.[125] Kolb's *experiential learning theory* incorporates a theory of learning styles and both will now be presented and discussed. What follows draws heavily on Wolfe and Kolb.[126]

Experiential learning conceptualizes the learning process in a way that allows an identification of differences in individual learning styles. The core of the experiential learning model is depicted in Figure 2.10 as a cycle in which experiences are translated into concepts which are in turn used to channel new experiences. The learning cycle has four stages. In the first, immediate concrete experience forms a basis for observation and reflection in a second stage. These observations are assimilated into a 'theory' in a third stage which is translated into action in new situations in a fourth and final stage. A new cycle is then initiated. In Kolb's model, a learner needs to develop four distinct kinds of generic abilities; those that promote: (1) concrete experience (CE); (2) reflective observation (RO); (3) abstract conceptualization (AC), and (4) active experimentation (AE). These abilities, according to Kolb, are polar opposites so that the learner must continually

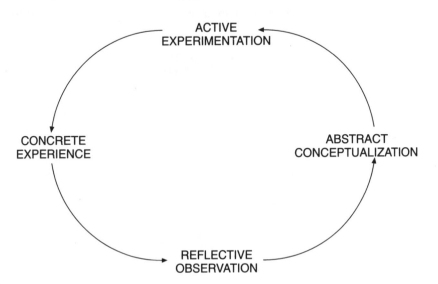

Figure 2.10 The Kolb learning cycle

choose which set of learning abilities he will invest in and which he will apply in particular learning situations. The learning process can be structured along two dimensions on which all four generic abilities can be located. The first dimension represents the concrete experiencing of events at one end and their abstract conceptualization at the other. The other dimension has active experimentation at one end and reflective observation at the other.

These two dimensions represent the major directions of cognitive development identified by Piaget as well, according to the latter, as those of science. The concrete–abstract dimension has been identified by many cognitive psychologists as a primary one for cognitive growth and learning[127] and we ourselves have it as a constituent dimension of our E-space. The active–reflective dimension also finds empirical support in the work of Singer (1968) and Kagan (1964, 1970).[128] Our own interpretation of active experimentation and reflective observation differs somewhat from Kolb's. Although we agree with Kolb that they stand in opposition to one another, he takes the first to be an externalized physical activity and the second to be an analytical one based on internal representations and symbolic manipulation. The first would then be located in W1 and the second in W2. Under this interpretation, however, this second dimension stands in danger of losing its orthogonality to the first. The issue can be resolved if we think of active experimentation as the deliberate and conscious manipulation of well-coded data complexions – whether this is carried out in one's head, on things, or in documents – and we think of reflective observation as a detached, noncommittal search for patterns, operating either internally or externally, at a lower level of coding. The first takes place in the world of the given, of things with hard edges that can be moved about without dissolving; the second in

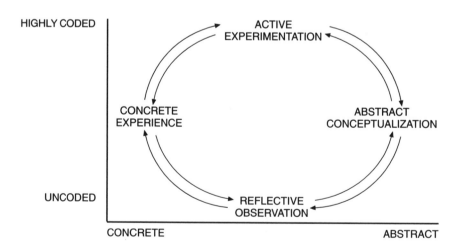

Figure 2.11 The Kolb learning cycle in the E-space

the world of the possible, one in which things shade into one another to yield new configurations. Under this second interpretation active experimentation and reflective observation become the two end points of our coding dimension, and Kolb's conceptualization of the learning process can be mapped onto our own. This is shown in Figure 2.11. Our reinterpretation of Kolb's second dimension calls for some modification in the functioning of the learning cycle. For it becomes apparent that if active experimentation is the locus of analytical activities then the cycle, still starting from concrete experience, could plausibly be run in both directions. The original idea that in learning one first abstracts from experience and then reinjects abstractions into new experiences is in no way compromised. Yet such a modification aligns the learning cycle with the schema of Figure 2.8.

Kolb argues that over time individuals are led to resolve the dialectical tensions that exist between the different generic abilities discussed in a characteristic fashion. Hereditary equipment, past life experiences, and the demands placed upon them by their present environments all impel them to emphasize some of these abilities over others. As Kolb himself puts it:

> Some people develop minds that excel at assimilating disparate facts into coherent theories, yet these same people are incapable of, or uninterested in, deducing hypotheses from the theory. Others are logical geniuses but find it impossible to involve and surrender themselves to an experience. And so on. A mathematician may come to place great emphasis on abstract concepts, while a poet may value concrete experience more highly. A manager may be primarily concerned with the active application of ideas, while a naturalist may develop his/her observational skills highly. Each of us in a unique way develops a learning style that has some weak and some strong points.[129]

Kolb, in his researches, has been able to identify four statistically prevalent types of learning styles based on the two dimensions. He calls them, respectively, the converger, the diverger, the assimilator, and the accommodator. These are located along his dimension and in the E-space as shown in Figure 2.12. Kolb hypothesizes that in the early stages of development, progress along one of these four dimensions can occur with some independence from the others. With maturity, however, a continued commitment to adaptive learning produces a strong need to integrate the four adaptive modes. In effect, complexity and the integration of dialectic conflicts among the adaptive modes become the hallmarks of creativity and growth.

The appealing similarity between Kolb's scheme and our own gains from the fact that we each arrive at them by very different routes. Kolb's two dimensions are empirically grounded in a statistical analysis of individual learners and their cognitive preferences – in E-space terms they amount to an abstraction from concrete data. We derive our own two dimensions analytically from a theory of information. Kolb's empirically based typology

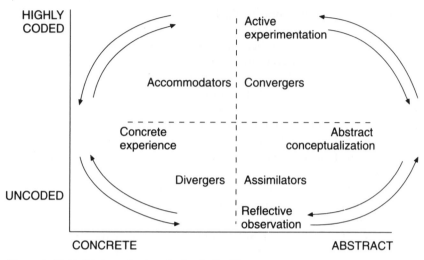

Figure 2.12 Kolb's learning typologies in the E-space

of learning styles thus provides independent corroborative evidence in support of our own theoretical scheme. What does Kolb's learning model add to our understanding of the E-space?

Learning and epistemology

Epistemology has been largely concerned with those transformation rules that legitimate moves from the left to the right in the E-space and very little with the path actually chosen by the individual learner in the space seeking as best he/she can to put his/her cognitive assets to good use. This task is left to psychology. Certain areas of epistemology, most notably those that touch on the field of science, have been more narrowly concerned to define the conditions on which knowledge gains admittance to the north-east region of the E-space, a region where a limited number of abstract and symbolic W3 objects claiming the highest level of generality dwell, sometimes far removed from the uncoded and concrete realities they purport to explain. Scientific epistemology, then, has acted as this region's custodian, controlling and validating entry into it and showing little interest in what goes on elsewhere. It has thus been more concerned with what Reichenbach has called the 'context of justification' of scientific knowledge – that is, how a W3 object makes good its claim to residence in the north-east region of the E-space – than with the 'context of discovery'[130] – i.e., the path it followed in getting there.

Not surprisingly, therefore, scientific epistemology has focused on knowledge in its most evolved, communicable, and hence public form[131] to the detriment of that less tangible and more personal form of knowledge which might later evolve into scientific knowledge but which for now still inhabits other parts of the E-space. The assumption is made that well-built W3 objects sooner or later will come back and exert a corrective influence on these other W2 processes and thus facilitate the learning process.

W3 objects, however, as Durkheim has argued, yield a paradoxical sort of understanding: 'Our concepts never succeed in mastering our sensations and in translating them completely into intelligible terms. They take a conceptual form only by losing that which is most concrete in them, that which causes them to speak to our sensory being and to involve it in an action; and in so doing they become something fixed and dead. Therefore we cannot understand things without renouncing the understanding of it.'[132]

As we move towards that region of the E-space patrolled by scientific epistemology, therefore, personal understanding in the ineffable domain is traded in for public understanding of a communicable kind – in the domain of sophistication. Furthermore, as we move towards the north-east region of the E-space, the one in which scientific discourse becomes both possible and legitimate, we move into cognitive territory occupied primarily by convergers (see Figure 2.12). Kolb himself views scientists and engineers as typical convergers, people whose cognitive style shows a marked preference for *reducing* the size of a problem space through coding and moving up the E-space rather than *expanding* it – a strategy that one might associate with divergers[133] – and moving down the E-space.

Yet the history of science is replete with descriptions of scientists who are anything but convergers. Einstein, to take but the most prominent example on offer from the first half of our own century, does not fit the description at all. He has been termed by those who knew him well as 'not so much a scientist as an artist of science'[134] – *prima facie* evidence for a strong capacity to diverge.

Convergers in science correspond to what Kuhn[135] calls 'puzzle-solvers', people who tackle well-formed – i.e., coded – problems in an incremental, comparatively secure fashion. Kuhn distinguishes between puzzle-solvers and paradigm creators, scientists who offer radical departures from the accepted ways of doing things and who tend to found new research traditions often in competition with existing ones.[136]

Yet new paradigms in science by their very nature tend to originate *away* from the north-east corner of the E-space and only slowly move towards it as they gain in structure and abstraction. They are thus the fruits of cognitive processes and skills that are not only substantially different from those deployed by 'normal' scientists – Kuhn's 'puzzle-solvers' – but also, and in consequence of this, from those that furnish science with its legitimating epistemology. Could the cognitive bias of current scientific epistemology in favour of certain learning styles be working against a more varied and dynamic progression from W2 towards W3? Does not our analysis point towards a premature selection operating against potentially

valuable epistemological products, not so much at the level of overly
rigorous methodological requirements – these may well turn out to be
necessary – but rather at that of the type of individual attracted into science
and of the type of problem he will feel it worth while to invest in?

Moving through the E-space in a learning mode is a delicate art that is full
of pitfalls and that has to be painstakingly acquired. Polanyi had just such an
art in mind when he suggested that 'to classify things in terms of the features
for which we have names, as we do in talking about things, requires the same
kind of connoisseurship as the naturalist must have for identifying specimens
of plants and animals. Thus the art of speaking precisely, by applying a rich
vocabulary exactly, resembles the delicate discrimination practised by the
expert taxonomist ... The process of applying language to things is also
necessarily unformalized: that is, it is inarticulate. Denotation then is an art,
and whatever we say about things assumes our endorsement of our own skill
in practising this art.'[137]

Otherwise stated, the skilled application of a code or the creation of a new
one requires a sound appreciation of context, and context is precisely what
is excluded from the north-east region of the E-space. Classification and
denotation only gain acceptance as part of the scientific enterprise when the
element of artistry – i.e., the personal appreciation of context – they call for
has been expunged from its products. For this to be possible, both the
attributes and the classes to which they are assigned must be free of any
ambiguities or vagueness that might give scope to personal discretion.

Failure to meet this particular requirement, for example, has long
undermined psychoanalysis's claim to scientific status. Freud's theory of
repression, to take one example, is one which lacks the power of a strongly
corroborated and well-articulated (coded) abstraction, and for that reason
when applied clinically to concrete cases it is in need of strong doses of the
connoisseurship that Polanyi refers to. The skill of the psychoanalyst
consists in first mapping out and interpreting the latent structure of a
discourse or a dream, and then in working back from a set of iconic symbols
that have been unconsciously and idiosyncratically coded, to the concrete
biographical events in which they originated. We hypothesize that an
individual's dream symbols occupy the top-left corner of the E-space, and
the personal experiences to which they give form the bottom-left-hand
corner. Repression can thus be thought of as a form of unconscious coding
in which the process of selection is overwhelmingly driven – and distorted
– by the subjective experiences of pleasure and pain rather than by external
and objective references. What is selected in this way is stored in such a way
as to be inaccessible to consciousness, even though it forms part of the data
on which an individual is driven to act.[138]

The case for psychoanalysis rests on a belief that the concrete experiential
data lost to view in such a coding process remains in fact ultimately
retrievable and therefore available for a more balanced recoding of the initial

and subsequent experiences. The case against psychoanalysis put forward by many practising scientists is that it is connoisseurship writ large and nothing but connoisseurship. To be acknowledged as a science outside its own disciplinary community, psychoanalysis needs a body of systematic, empirically testable generalizations to its credit that move it away from the concrete clinical situation and towards something more abstract – i.e., it needs to gain admission into the north-east region of the E-space.

Learning as a social activity

Kolb's message is that no man is an island, cognitively speaking, and that progress through the E-space, in whatever direction, is likely to be a collective enterprise linking very different learning styles and cognitive resources. We might like to think of the outcome as an extension of the connectionist model now operating across brains as well as within them. With such an extension, communication processes suddenly loom very large as determinants of social learning. These will be the subject of Chapter 3. Before we embark on this new topic, however, we have to consider why learning styles differ as they do. This brings us to the role of individual personality in cognitive processes.

2.5: MAPPING THE INDIVIDUAL IN THE E-SPACE: PERSONALITY FACTORS

Psychological types

Although we are placing coding and abstracting at the heart of our analysis, man is a warm-blooded creature that does not live by data alone. He lives by and through experiences through which the data flows. What he makes of the data therefore depends at least as much on what he makes of the experience as an object of *value* as on his data processing faculties themselves. His likes and dislikes, hopes and fears, thus have a direct bearing on how he structures his world.

The influence of personality on cognitive processes is now well established. Jung's theory of psychological types, for example, is built upon the way that individuals capture and process the data of experience and on the orientation that they adopt towards it.[139] Jung identifies two basic personality orientations: the first, which he labels *extrovert*, places a high value on an external objective reality, whether the objects that populate it be concrete or abstract; the second, which he labels *introvert*, values internal subjective reality. These orientations largely determine the data that will be processed and how it will be processed. Some individuals, for example, might only respond to concrete sensuously perceived objects or processes of the kind that everyone, everywhere would sense as concrete. Others, by contrast, might be more intuitive and allow themselves to be guided by unconscious processes towards what is possible rather than simply what is given. If sensing and intuiting filter the data that will be processed then some combination of thinking and feeling will do the processing. In the first, data processing outcomes will be the fruit of intellectual deliberation, in the second they will reflect the workings of preferences – these may or may not be subjectively determined.

The three dimensions that Jung develops to analyse his psychological types – extroversion–introversion, sensation–intuition, thinking–feeling – impose a template on the experiences processed in the E-space. The first, extroversion–introversion, orients individual data processing either towards Worlds 1 and 3 or towards World 2; the second, sensation–intuition, biases it towards coded or uncoded data; the third, thinking–feeling, establishes the part that will be played respectively by cognitive and by affective factors in the manipulation and evaluation of data. E-space data, extruded through such a template, incorporates elements of the individual personality that find their way into any epistemological product such data eventually gets embedded in. Kelly called such extruded data *personal constructs*. We shall now discuss these in greater detail.

Construct theory

The theory of personal constructs first developed by Kelly in the 1950s aims for a broader view of man's cognitive activities than that which the somewhat bloodless focus on data processing alone can offer.[140] A construct for Kelly is not a thought or a feeling – it is a discrimination. It is part of the way that one stands towards the world as a *whole* person.[141] Kelly tells us that a person's construction system is composed of a finite number of dichotomous constructs and that the two poles of the construct have a relationship – a contrast. He argues that two poles – an affirmative and a negative pole such as black and non-black – are more useful to us than unipolar concepts or categories such as black or white on their own. In effect, Kelly is highlighting the cognitive contribution made by the act of negation. He is asserting that a given stimulus does not elicit a class A in isolation for categorial assignment, but a relationship between A and not-A.

The use of dichotomous constructs, however, does not preclude the use of a more graduated scale between A and not-A in the early phases of developing a discrimination. The bipolar relationship he describes constitutes more of a point of arrival than a point of departure in efforts at construing. Thus, black and not-black admit of nearly black as a viable position on the scale, but one that will be increasingly forsaken for the end points of the scale as the construct develops; it will eventually disappear.

Kelly's description of the evolution of constructs bears a striking resemblance to the dynamics of the coding process as we have described it. The gradual move towards a dichotomous construct turns out to be a data processing and shedding operation that creates a code with optimal information content: a binary choice between 0 and 1 in which both values are equiprobable. Construing, however, cannot be reduced to coding; as a careful reading of Kelly makes clear it also involves abstraction.[142]

Construing does not inevitably move the individual towards greater coding and abstraction in search of structure and security. Although there are circumstances which, by virtue of the opportunities or threats that they foreshadow, effectively impose a need for clarification – and hence a need for tight construing – on most of those who experience them, unstructured situations are not, *per se*, viewed as threatening. Most people, most of the time, are quite happy to settle for a pretty loose construal of their circumstances – indeed some individuals positively thrive on the absence of structure.

Constructs, in sum, describe a highly generalized state of readiness of the whole person to respond selectively to classes of events in the environment. These become integrated with more general hypotheses – i.e., abstract superordinate constructs – concerning environmental events to produce a map of cognitive and behavioural possibilities available to the individual.

But what is it, one might ask, that leads an individual to avail himself or not of these possibilities? Our answer comes in five parts.[143]

1   The frequency of past confirmation of the construct – what Popper in a scientific context would call its degree of corroboration – whether it is perceptual or conceptual.
2   The construct's monopoly power: the smaller the number of constructs used the greater their strength will be – how small the number turns out to be is a function of their degree of abstraction.
3   The cognitive consequences of adopting the construct: the better integrated the construct is with existing ones, the stronger it will be.
4   The motivational consequences of adopting the construct: the more basic the information of the construct becomes to the realization of cherished goals, the more strongly it will be held. To hold a construct strongly on motivational grounds is to hold it in a bipolar form – often a source of prejudice and stereotyping.
5   The social consequences of adopting the construct: when confirming or infirming data is lacking, the more people that have already adopted the construct, the more strongly it will be held.[144]

The more highly corroborated, monopolistic, integrated, motivating, and widely shared a construct turns out be the more it is likely to push data processing up the E-space in the direction of the north-east region. It does not, however, necessarily vouchsafe us a shared and objective W3. Those coded and abstract constructs that make up W3, and that are held in common, have more the character of shared hypotheses that are implicitly held. In spite of the fact that they might actually be experienced by individuals as a shared objective facticity they often enjoy only a limited amount of overlap in their content.[145] A plurality of symbolic abstract worlds may therefore coexist and sometimes compete with each other in claiming to represent the world as it really is. The ongoing debate between realists and relativists turns on the possibility of arbitrating in an epistemologically reliable way between such competing claims.

As with perceptual hypotheses, the development of a construct rests on a blend of deductions from explicit theory in which the role of *a priori* knowledge predominates, of inferences from observations, and of scanning. The theoretical component of a construct binds the elements that are subordinate to it and, while it must conform to events if it is to maintain its relevance, it is often not so much determined by them as by the superordinate view of the theorist himself.[146] Like perceptions, subordinate constructs are 'theory laden'. It is in effect through the feedback loop that brings elements of W3 into W1 that superordinate constructs inject a theoretical element into subordinate ones.

Culture and personality

The acquisition and elaboration of constructs, and their subsequent trajectory and distribution in an individual E-space, express a subtle interplay of cognitive, personality, and cultural factors. The contribution of culture to our theme will be examined in more detail in Chapter 6. Here, we shall confine ourselves to a few preliminary remarks on the subject.

The interplay between cognition and personality does not take place in a vacuum; it is largely mediated by socialization processes that vary considerably in their content, intensity, and duration, yet are deeply embedded in a culture. By means of experiments showing how children develop the concept of time, of number, or of movement, for instance, Piaget has shown that a child construes events essentially the same way that other members of his or her culture construe them.[147] Their geometry over time becomes the child's geometry, and where they laugh he or she will uncomprehendingly giggle. Pushing the mediating role of culture to extremes, the sociology of knowledge asserts that we live in a world that is socially constructed[148] and that individual knowing and choosing is always hemmed in by the forces of acculturation. If we believe in and act upon our experiences it is not because they have been epistemologically validated according to narrowly scientific Popperian criteria, but because they have been socially validated by groups that count for us. Such reference groups become important sources of cognitive and affective legitimation.

By placing the control of personal trajectories in the E-space so completely in the hands of society, however, the sociology of knowledge robs individual cognitive and personality processes of much of their potential autonomy.

More specifically, it becomes hard to see how any new codes or abstractions could ever emerge as other than purely social phenomena.[149]

Kelly's fundamental postulate holds that 'a person's processes are psychologically channelled by the way he anticipates events'. Anticipations of this kind often amount to cognitive commitments that may prove hard to extricate oneself from. The flexible personality holds back from irrevocable commitments, even when these are socially demanded, and can as a result move between coded and uncoded, or abstract and concrete forms of thought.[150]

The challenge for the individual is to learn how to hedge his cognitive bets, to strike a balance between levels of cognitive investment in a given region of the E-space; if too high they lead to stereotyped responses, but on the other hand little investment anywhere in the E-space means that he can be shunted around at will by social and natural forces external to himself – in effect relinquishing control of his capacity for autonomous cognition.

Some cognitive openness to outside influences is a requirement for any individual in social interaction. Social communication is only feasible if there is some convergence or overlap between the constructs we respectively use. Totally idiosyncratic constructs and construct relations make it difficult if not impossible to get on to the same wavelength as others. In extreme cases, the result is paranoia. 'The paranoid person with ideas of persecution and grandiosity may have an organized way of viewing the world, but it is a peculiar view; there is a dictionary but it is a private dictionary.'[151] The paranoiac will experience a structural communication problem in dealing with others and consequently difficulties forming stable relationships. Paranoia isolates.

The isolation experienced by the paranoiac reflects the closed and self-contained nature of his E-space. Communication between individuals only becomes possible above some threshold of shared codes, constructs, and experiences. To some degree, therefore, individual E-spaces must overlap; the question is: how much? A minimum overlap is initially given to us on the left of the space to the extent that some precoded concrete experiences are accessible to us all by dint of our common biological make-up: the wetness of water, a rustle of leaves, the action of gravity, etc.[152] It is what we each individually choose to abstract from these shared experiences that subsequently sets us off on different cognitive paths towards a variety of possible symbolic worlds; the organizing power of these then reaches back into the process of perceptual coding itself to generate further divergencies. As we each progress along our chosen path, then, we gain in individuality.

How an individual distributes himself in his E-space tells the story of his development and subsequent struggles. He must reconcile cognitive, personality, and social requirements that frequently pull him in different directions. He seeks autonomy, yet he wants to belong; he needs clarification, yet he fears the inconsistencies this may produce. For most of us, the E-space is a mix of idiosyncratic constructs rooted in the unique circumstances of individual biography as well as of shared constructs brought into mutual alignment through social interaction. Shared constructs, however, are not identical constructs; the only social requirement that they have to meet is that they be intelligible and communicable. Much of the power and richness of W3 results from a continuous encounter between cognitive objects that challenge or complement each other in beneficial ways. Variety in W3 is a precondition for evolutionary progress, offering scope for selection and for further development. Variety in W3, however, depends entirely on the progress going on in W2, in individual E-spaces, as with some W3 help they metabolize W1 data into new W3 objects.[153]

In this section we have examined the role played by personality factors in shaping the topography of W2 – the way that an individual spreads himself out in the E-space. We have seen that whatever configuration he achieves will be both facilitated and constrained by his social situation. For this reason, in what follows we shall bring the E-space out of the splendid isolation in which we have placed it and treat it as a socially embedded phenomenon.

2.6: CONCLUSION

Recapitulation

We now briefly recapitulate and discuss the main points presented in this chapter and then explore what they contribute to this book's theme.

1   Both perceiving and conceiving are data processing activities best modelled as parallel distributed processes in highly connected networks. In order to avoid overloading the cognitive apparatus, data must be shed in the course of processing but selectively so. Perceiving and conceiving do so in different ways: perceiving, by focusing selectively on the discriminable attributes of concrete experiences – infused as these may become by abstract categories – gives these definable contours; conceiving invokes memory – stored experiences – to organize percepts into stable data complexions of a higher order that exhibit generalizable properties. More data is thus shed but the conceptual structure which is then revealed is thereby removed from perceptual immediacy. Perceiving is a coding activity and conceiving is an abstracting one. Coding economizes on data by assigning it into categories and then dealing only with the latter; much of the assigned data can then be discarded. Abstracting achieves its data economies by then reducing the number of categories that have to be employed in apprehending W1 events. In practice coding and abstracting are closely intertwined.

2   Coding and abstracting constitute the two dimensions of an epistemological space or E-space that help us to identify and track the data

processing strategies by means of which an individual maps out his world. Physiology initially predisposes him to certain kinds of cognitive organization – and hence to certain trajectories in the E-space – but it only partially determines them. Growth in an individual's knowledge and understanding is registered as an accumulation of cognitive assets in certain regions of the E-space over time, assets that are subject to shifts reflecting an interplay of learning and personality processes. The actions of coding and abstracting are subject to economizing efforts by individuals who will then invest either in those regions of the E-space where the marginal costs to them are the lowest – i.e., regions where they already have effected substantial prior cognitive investments – or those in which the prospective benefits of a fresh investment are likely to justify the effort required. A fresh cognitive investment, however, must be considered not only costly but risky as well since both coding and abstraction retain an irreducibly hypothetical character. This may become attenuated by corroborative experiences but it can never be wholly eradicated.

3   Empirical work on learning styles offers some support for the view that an individual's personality participates in the structuring of his E-space and subsequently acts to restrict his freedom of movement within it. In consequence, individuals will vary in their orientation towards the risks, costs, and prospective benefits associated with cognitive investments. Construct theory teaches us that an individual's cognitive activities cannot be treated in isolation from other aspects of his personality which are likely both to predispose him towards distributing his investments initially in certain regions of the E-space and then, on account of the cognitive inertia thus created, subsequently to limit his ability or willingness to wander out from there and explore other regions.

4   Only cognitive assets that have acquired some minimum degree of structure – i.e., that have already shed data – can be externalized and communicated. The further we move away from the south-west corner of the E-space the more data we shed and the easier it therefore becomes to express what we know. It follows that not all knowledge in the E-space is equally communicable and that the nature of the communication problem incurred by externalizing one's knowledge will vary with its location in the space. Restrictions placed on the sharing of knowledge with others by communicative and institutional constraints in their turn exert an influence on the data processing strategies chosen by individuals and hence on their personal trajectories in the E-space. Such an influence is amplified by an individual's cultural inheritance. The largest proportion of cognitive assets that are at his disposal is socially transmitted to him, the fruit of a cumulative investment by the culture in which he participates. The inheritance, however, is double-edged. If it spares a socialized individual the pains

of learning everything he needs to know about the world on his own by trial and error alone, the data processing economies on offer also predispose him to channel his cognitive efforts at the margin into those areas of the E-space where his individual learning costs are likely to be low – i.e., those in which socially inherited assets are most readily available. In a sense, cognitive convenience is purchased at the cost of cognitive freedom with the result that both his perceptual and his conceptual processes become by degrees domesticated by his culture. To paraphrase Rousseau, we might say that while man is born cognitively free, how far he will be subsequently cognitively chained by his culture is likely to vary both across individuals and across cultures.

Some forms of social organization are less restrictive in this respect than others, allowing their members greater freedom and scope for cognitive exploration and experimentation. Western societies, for example, over the last two centuries, have come to believe that progressive social evolution depends on the generation of cognitive variety from which competitive selections are made, and to that end they are prepared to grant their members considerably more cognitive freedom than they used to.[154]

The E-space versus the prevailing economic perspective

Whatever the degree of cognitive restriction placed on an individual by his social inheritance, his data processing strategies in the E-space stand in stark contrast to those attributed to him by conventional economic theory.

What, in effect, is asked of economic man, cognitively speaking? Simply this: that he should know the market prices of the goods he wishes to trade in, that he should understand how variations in the quality of goods relate to variations in price, and that he should be able to use this knowledge in allocating his scarce resources in an optimal way to the trades available to him.[155]

But what kind of cognitive product is a price? A price is a measure of value, a coding device that economizes on data processing by substituting itself in the computations of buyers and sellers for the complex of attributes – themselves more or less coded – that make up an object of exchange. A price shares a code's hypothetical character in that it is subject to testing and revision in the market: people take it or leave it. Only in so far as there exists some overlap in the ways that buyers and sellers respectively code for price will a trade occur. In the absence of overlap one gets a great deal of haggle with no guarantee of convergence towards a price acceptable to both parties.

How is overlap achieved? The answer given to us by the E-space can be framed as two propositions:

Proposition 1: An object of exchange can be priced in so far as its *valued* attributes can be coded for. Price then effects an *attribute reduction* by capturing the information these contain and then discarding them as transactional data.

Proposition 2: The price of an object becomes its *market price* when, through a process of testing and adjustment in multiple bilateral trades, it becomes abstracted from these to become itself an information input into future transactions. The abstraction is made possible by a *category reduction* in which only those categories that regroup *commonly* valued attributes of the object over multiple trades are retained and the rest are discarded as transactional data.

The two propositions taken together describe price formation as a cognitive event that moves a given price through an individual E-space in the way depicted in Figure 2.13. It then becomes immediately apparent that a *market* price is a W3 object in Popper's terminology that can be reinjected into W1 to influence subsequent E-space activity.

Economic man only ever apprehends price as a fully formed W3 object. He occupies the north-east region of the E-space and trades from there. He is therefore deemed to possess from the outset the data resources necessary to his trades in that region, and is not expected to enter into exchange relationships from any other location in the space. Price thus enters the E-spaces of economic agents as a fully fledged W3 product and acts to channel their internal data processing activities in the direction of an equilibrating abstraction: the market clearing price.

Is there not a striking parallel between the predilection of epistemologists of science for the north-east region of the E-space and that of neoclassical economists for prices sufficiently well coded and abstracted to be assigned

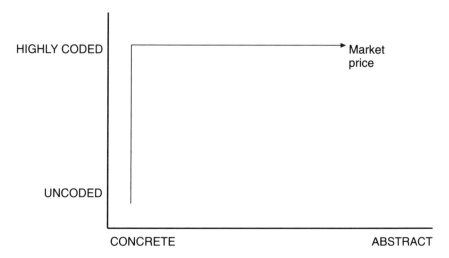

Figure 2.13 Price formation in the E-space

there? Does economic man, in effect, express anything other than the positivist's disdain for the 'context of discovery'?

Economic man has been criticized by some economists for his toy-town lack of plausibility. One line of criticism developed by Keynes and particularly by Keynesian 'revisionists' such as Robert Clower and Axel Leijönhufvud, for example,[156] pointed out that the failure of markets to clear could be taken as a sign that ignorance was present in trades and that such ignorance was due to frictions in the transmission of market prices. Abstract coded knowledge in the north-east region of the E-space did not always communicate instantaneously and market adjustment processes were thereby impaired. Keynes and his followers did not challenge the status of prices as well-formed W3 objects but merely asked whether such a status entailed instantaneous price formation and communicability as required by the prevailing theory.

Hayek[157] shared Keynes's scepticism concerning the instantaneous transmission of knowledge in market processes and consequently held ignorance to be pervasive. But Hayek's scepticism had different roots from Keynes's.

Hayek emphasized the irreducibly *local* nature of economic transactions and therefore viewed price formation as a tentative coding exercise occurring on the left of the E-space. For him, it was the business of economics to explain how concrete local transactions originating in the south-west region of the space could gradually move market prices towards the north-east region and hence towards better-tested coding and abstraction. The neoclassical orthodoxy had assumed the problem away by locating economic man in the north-east region from the outset.

Both Keynes and Hayek focused on the asymmetric *availability* of market data to economic agents.[158] Neither called into question their ability to make good use of the data once it came into their possession. The Carnegie school, and most notably Herbert Simon,[159] did so, pointing out that if the costs of processing available data are taken into account then an added friction must be reckoned with in moving a cognitive resource through the E-space, a friction not imposed on the individual from *outside* by the availability of data or by communicative constraints, but one that arises from *within*, resulting from limits to her computational capacities. For Simon, coding and abstraction are intrinsically costly and uncertain enterprises that cannot be guaranteed to yield a steady progression through the E-space towards the north-east corner, towards the creation of viable W3 objects. It is the differential performance of economic agents in their respective E-spaces that gives rise to market disequilibrating phenomena such as strategic behaviour, moral hazard, and adverse selection, and transaction costs.[160]

At stake here was the rationality postulate that had underwritten the reign of economic man. It was the rationality imputed to economic agents that firstly had justified the assumption of an agent's steady progress in the E-space towards a transparent world of well-coded objects of exchange and that secondly had legitimated the economist's almost exclusive focus on the north-east region – i.e., on the 'context of justification' rather than 'the context of discovery'.

In an economic regime in which rationality is 'bounded' – that is, subject to limitations in data processing capacity – the quest for data economies through coding and abstraction may itself be vulnerable to inefficiencies and distortions.[161] The 'economic problem' then ceases to be how to aggregate whatever local rationality is present in individual trades – as expressed by coding and price formation processes originating in the lower left-hand region of the E-space – into the universal and abstract rationality of a market price, but rather whether coding and abstraction are productive of rationality in sufficient quantities for aggregation to be a worthwhile intellectual enterprise.

The shift from a concern with the availability of well-coded and abstract data and its communication between economic agents to an examination of how well these use the data – however fuzzy – once obtained, calls for a theory of *learning* that can adequately account for progress, if any, towards the north-east region of the E-space. Two very different theoretical accounts of the learning process have been put forward by economists.

The first has been developed by the so-called New Classical School and goes by the name of *Rational Expectations*. Its basic premise is that data processing errors committed by individuals as they move through their personal E-spaces, whether originating in their cognitive apparatus or in the data itself, are in fact corrigible and that they will learn from their mistakes at least sufficiently to eliminate systematic error.[162] In other words, if and when coding and abstraction do occur, they will in fact display a built-in tendency to move the knowledge held by economic agents in the direction of well-formed and epistemologically viable W3 products located in the north-east region of the E-space. The economic focus on that region is thereby vindicated.

The second account, although not cast explicitly as a theory of learning, nevertheless implies one; it is associated with the *New Institutional Economics*. It holds that learning is personal, often tacit, and hence hard to articulate and generalize. Even when it builds on a common stock of well-structured and shared data – i.e., a market price – it becomes 'impacted' in individual minds in idiosyncratic circumstances that become a source of opportunism and that are as likely to move agents away from the equilibrating processes associated with a frictionless W3 as towards them. In other words, even if economic agents were all to start off with identical information endowments in the north-east region of the E-space, their personal data processing strategies, i.e., their individual cognitive styles, would redistribute them over time into different regions of the E-space.[163]

Institutional economics argues that markets fail on information grounds and that the economic agenda must be consequently broadened to accommodate alternative institutional arrangements better suited to data processing as it is found in the real world and, by implication, in the different regions of the E-space.

If we choose to view these two theories of learning as complementing rather than competing with each other we can treat them as covering related yet distinct phases in a learning cycle of the kind depicted by Figure 2.10. In our discussion of learning, we saw how individual learning processes in part condition what can and cannot be shared with others. Recast in economic terms, the problem of what kind of data is available and of how it is subsequently distributed among economic agents and processed by them suddenly reappears, not as an exogenous issue that can be casually relegated to some 'context of discovery' and then ignored, but as one which, being inherent in the dynamics of the E-space itself, has to be taken as central to our conception of economic processes. Such a conclusion becomes all the more compelling if we take information not merely as a support to economic exchange – still the prevailing tendency among economists – but as its object. The question of what can and cannot be shared between E-spaces then translates into one of deciding at what level of coding and abstraction information is capable of becoming an economic good in its own right, surely a crucial issue for an emerging information society.

In this chapter, the focus has been primarily on the individual data processor, on what goes on inside a single brain. Expository convenience rather than a belief in 'methodological individualism'[164] dictated the approach. After all, if we are prepared to argue for the existence of emergent properties within a single brain, can we afford to exclude them as a possible explanation of what goes on between brains? What goes on between brains is the subject of the next chapter.

Chapter 3

The sharing of information

ABSTRACT

If the last chapter focused on the production of knowledge, this one is primarily concerned with its distribution. Taken together, the two chapters lay the groundwork for a political economy of information.

All communication is costly and hence selective. Communication, to be effective, must overcome technical, semantic, and pragmatic barriers to the transmission of information. Meaningful communication always requires some minimum sharing of context between sender and receiver. Where this is difficult one must resort to shared abstractions in order to be understood. Abstraction facilitates the diffusion of a message since it increases the number of particular situations in which a message can have utility and relevance.

The U-space (U stands for 'utility') explicitly links the diffusibility of a message to its degree of abstraction. Trajectories in the U-space towards well-diffused and abstract knowledge are affected by the prior distribution of knowledge in the space as well as by the social power of those in possession of such knowledge. Both are stabilized by institutions, structures designed to economize on social information processing as well as to minimize the social production of entropy.

Coding, or codification as we shall henceforth call it, also facilitates diffusion. This is indicated in the C-space (C stands for 'culture'), where different kinds of knowledge can be represented.

Effective communication requires the sharing of either abstract codes or contexts between sender and receiver. The choice is affected by the communication technologies available. The *data field* emerges from a sequence of such choices, a product of the way that the forces of codification, abstraction, and diffusion interact. The data field exhibits self-organizing properties that challenge the conventional economic view of information as a ubiquitous and static phenomenon.

3.1: INTRODUCTION

Cognition as a social process

In the preceding chapter, we examined data processing as a phenomenon occurring within a single brain, a highly dense and connected network of neurons capable of emergent responses to patterns of incoming stimuli. In this chapter we are less concerned with connections within brains than with connections between them; the focus is thus on the communicative component of data processing now taken as a social activity. Does the connectionist perspective, however reformulated, have something to offer at this level and what kind of emergent phenomena might it give rise to?

We can only partly address such questions in what follows and we do so very indirectly, relying on later chapters to flesh out our reply. Our emphasis will be less on the production of knowledge – the subject of the previous chapter – than with its distribution, with how and with whom it is shared once it has been produced. We cannot, of course, entirely ignore the production of knowledge since the prospect of having to share it with others will usually influence how it gets articulated and how it subsequently evolves.

The production and distribution of wealth in society have traditionally been the concern of political economy. If we take information to be the dominant form of wealth in most post-industrial societies – that is to say, if we treat it as an object of, as much as a support for, economic exchange – we can view our mission in the preceding chapter and in this one as preparing the ground for a political economy of information. The production of information results from a complex interplay of data coding and abstraction;[1] its distribution, as it turns out, activates the same variables. Does this open up the prospects of developing a unified scheme?[2]

3.2: COMMUNICATING

Transmitting tacit knowledge

How can the experience of a concert be properly shared with someone who was not present? How can riding a bicycle be taught except by force of example? What exactly is it about someone's facial expression that signals to intimate friends that he/she is in a bad mood? All these questions butt up against what Polanyi has called 'tacit knowing':[3] large tracts of conscious experience and behaviour located in the south-east region of the E-space, as we have already seen, habitually escape verbal formulation or coding. Few genuinely creative people, for instance, are able to articulate in a convincing way the processes that lead from initial inspiration to the execution of their work. For this reason, Picasso, as a painter, is often better understood by reading his critics and interpreters than by perusing his own pronouncements. Even then, there will remain a large uncodifiable residue in his art that can never be completely grasped. This residual Picasso will remain the object of continued speculation and successive reinterpretations which are more likely to reveal something of their authors as they grapple with the unfathomable, than anything objectively ascertainable concerning the artist himself.[4]

Tacit knowing describes the form in which we hold our least communicable knowledge assets in the E-space. It was to these that the early Wittgenstein referred to in the *Tractatus* when he asserted that 'whereof one cannot speak, thereof one must be silent'.[5] Yet speaking up or shutting up are unnecessarily stark choices[6] given the potential richness of our communication resources. After all, a painting by a Picasso or a Jackson Pollock remains an intentional act of communication even if what is actually externalized in paint is weakly coded and can only partially convey what is experienced by the artist at the moment of executing the work. Communication between the artist and his audience, however, is only possible in so far as some overlap exists between their respective E-spaces. And whether in fact communication occurs will depend on how well the artist successfully reconciles his divergent needs for autonomy in the processing of personal experiences on the one hand, and for sharing these with a sympathetic audience on the other; a balance must be struck between the claims of self-expression and those of effective communication.

Individual cognitive and affective processes and communication needs thus exert a reciprocal influence upon each other so that the way that we know something affects the way that we express it and, conversely, a concern to express something affects the way that we know it.

The cost of communicating

In his book *Personal Knowledge*, Polanyi's interest is centred almost exclusively on the individual knowing subject. Although he pleads in favour of a social system that can restore to individual (personal) knowledge its sense of wholeness through an acknowledgement of its tacit component, having stated its requirements, he then tends to leave it at that. He does not go on to ask what kind of social system is likely to do this or what influence it might exert on this tacit component.

In this chapter we explore social knowing, moving from personal knowledge individually held to personal knowledge collectively held, and from thence in Chapters 5 and 6 to differences in forms of social organization and cultures that express variations in the distribution of knowledge. Our guiding thoughts will be the following: communication, like data processing, is an entropy-generating phenomenon that will be subject to economizing efforts.[7] The marginal cost of communicating from certain regions of the E-space, for example, will be lower than from others and, other things being equal, these will be the regions preferred for communicative exchanges. Yet such a cost – largely a matter of communicants having built up shared codes that are then available to them in that region – is only part of the story: to properly exploit the value of the message communicated (i.e., its perceived relevance to recipients) will also call for a prior investment in the build-up of shared knowledge assets in the region, assets that can then create a suitable context for the subsequent interpretation of the message. The expected value of the message establishes its terms of trade, so to speak, and hence the productivity of any exchange relationship associated with it. Where perceived message value is high, one will be willing to incur greater communication costs than where it is low, and in recurrent situations one may additionally invest in data processing activities in order to shift knowledge assets into the regions of one's E-space from which effective communication is achievable at lower cost.

From this perspective, auto-communication, the processing and transmitting of data internally within the individual organism, is always a moment in a wider communicative act as well as at times a preparation for it. The requirement of social exchange, therefore, and the benefits that can be derived therefrom, must be counted among the key forces that drive the evolution of knowledge in the E-space. However these are measured, it is often the expected returns to one's communicative efforts rather than to one's data processing activities alone that compel us to shift at least some of our cognitive assets into the north-east corner of the E-space from where they can most easily be transmitted.

Freedom to choose: communication as selection

An ability to communicate is intimately related to an ability to abstract and to code. An experience that is refractory to coding and that cannot be fitted into any category or system of categories is, in the final analysis, incommunicable. To quote Bruner: 'If perceptual experience is ever had raw, that is, free of categorical identity, it is doomed to be a gem, serene, locked in the silence of private experience.'[8] Yet such gems turn out to be constituent elements of *all* experiencing, in effect a residue of data and information sacrificed through the selective action of the coding process itself. It is in the paradoxical nature of *all* acts of communication that they must forever remain partial in order to be effective. *Pace* Wittgenstein, the ability to talk can thus never be wholly disentangled from the willingness to stay silent.

Silence, as a component of the communication process, holds more appeal for some than for others. It may appeal more, for example, to individuals whose personal cognitive or learning style locates them in a part of the E-space where their experience is hard to articulate and hence costly to communicate. We must therefore expect considerable variation in the effort individuals are willing to invest in pushing what they know tacitly towards greater articulation and generality. For much will depend on where in the E-space they set out from; on what cognitive risks and costs they incur in trying to shift, even if temporarily, from one way of knowing to another; and on what returns they can expect for their pains.

The somewhat utilitarian mental calculus just described robs the communicative process of its simplicity and its directness. In particular it poses something of a challenge for those who believe that an individual's mental processes can be inferred from nothing more than a knowledge of his/her material situation. To a cultural materialist like Marvin Harris, for example,[9] the high degree of dependence of W3 products and W2 processes on the physical constraints imposed by W1 robs the 'private language' of situated individuals, and indeed the private – i.e., emic – language of a situated group of any ability to achieve any 'real' or objective understanding of their respective situations.[10] Only the language of external observers can do this using 'etic' description.

We shall have an opportunity to explore the cultural materialist position further in Chapter 5. Here we must merely note that while such materialism does not go as far as behaviourism in denying 'mind' any reality at all, by making its workings overly dependent on W1 it saps it of any emergent properties and hence of its scope as an autonomous level of explanation for an account both of the evolution of W3 and of the way that W3 objects embed themselves in W1. Yet any effort at representation – whether for internal use or for external transmission and whether emic or etic – confronts us with different coding possibilities and choices, some being more parsimonious than others with respect to the amount of data to be processed; how we choose to represent events to ourselves, for example, may not correspond to how we might describe them to intimate friends or to how we would communicate them to strangers. The materialist is committed to the view that these choices, being grounded in a single objective physical reality, are highly constrained in the way that they can legitimately represent it. He holds, in effect, a 'correspondence theory of truth'[11] in which representations that diverge from the templates provided by objective material conditions in W1 are treated as so much 'superstructure'.

Communicative strategies

Coding choices have to satisfy both internal representational and transmission needs which can only themselves be formulated through further representations. To an outside observer, according to Dennett, someone involved in making such coding choices has to be treated as an *intentional system*, one whose behaviour can usually be explained by ascribing to it beliefs, desires, hopes, hunches, fears, intentions, etc.[12] Does she wish vaguely to connote something in a poetically elliptical fashion only intelligible to a restricted circle of illuminati, or does she aim to denote it with the precision of an American contract lawyer? It may not always serve one's best interests to be clear with everyone. Argyle[13] has spoken of the valuable property of vagueness whereby interactors are not committed to a particular relationship and shifts in attitude can be made quite easily. Much body language has this property. Skill in communication, then, can be described as the ability to select positions on the coding and abstraction scales that are appropriate to the circumstances and knowing when to switch from one position to the other. It is a skill that helps each individual to establish, within the limits of what he can articulate, the degree of permeability to outsiders of his personal E-space.

Not all positions that might be chosen along the two scales, however, are equally well endowed in readily usable codes. In the lower section of the coding scale, for example, the codes are harder to articulate; they are less numerous and more ambiguous, and thus can at best meet the needs of internal representation rather than external communication. And at the zero point of the scale, arguably, no codes exist at all; as one moves up the coding scale, however, the codes available increase as do the number of communication channels within which they can be deployed. Furthermore, channel combinations greatly extend the complexity and subtlety of messages that can be sent. When several channels are used in combination for the transmission of a given message, however, by increasing the coding choices available relative to the length of the message they bring us once more *down* the coding scale and thus effectively reduce the message's degree of coding.

In the upper segment of the coding scale, message data has to be highly compressed to exploit the specialized codes and artificial communication channels that may be available. Unlike the sensory channels that we use, almost unconsciously at times, to communicate with our immediate environment, artificial channels are created by technology. Their spatial reach may be greater than that of sensory channels but they are more costly to develop and use. To transpose a message from a sensory channel to an artificial one may require a non-intuitive effort to adapt and translate it and may call for the mastery of a new coding repertoire.

Here one's communicative strategy indeed reflects material conditions – i.e., the technical choices available – but only in the trivial sense that without a conscious effort at coding no communication at all takes place. Material conditions in such circumstances might therefore *constrain* communication possibilities but they do not necessarily *dictate* them; indeed, with technological evolution, communicative constraints are being decreased in ways that progressively extend our freedom of choice. Thus the cognitive autonomy of W2, far from being eroded by W1 as materialists would have it, may actually be enhanced by it when the latter incorporates W3 objects that embody the fruits of technical change. It would follow, however, that the greater the constraints actually imposed by material and technological circumstances, the more compelling becomes the materialist position. The primitive societies discussed by Marvin Harris in his book on cultural materialism[14] thus provide better exemplars for his thesis than post-industrial societies like our own. They are indeed more constrained by material circumstances than our own in what they can articulate and communicate, but no more than ours are their styles of representation actually determined by such circumstances. In this respect, a connectionist model of social interaction offers the degree of plasticity required by the emergent properties of collective representation that we are arguing for.

Design as a communication process

All artefacts that embed W3 products in W1 extend our communicative choices and freedom even if few of them are expressly designed to serve a communicative function. Some have communication purely as a by-product, while others – perhaps the majority – merge the communicative function with other attributes. Created physical extension systems, or artefacts that embody a communicative element, exhibit some degree of intentionality. Good design, for example, is nothing other than the ability, firstly, consciously to come to terms with and master this intentional element while respecting whatever constraints circumstances impose, and secondly to let the object or system of objects communicate that which we wish it to, that which it can, and that which it should – and no more. Yet it is a characteristic of all artefacts that over time they become established physical facts independent of their creators and hence take on a life of their own. To slightly misuse a Marxist term, they become 'alienated' and eventually migrate from the site of their creation.[15] Artefacts encapsulate knowledge and store it either within their own physical forms or within the design traditions associated with their evolution – Abernathy and Utterback call the products of such traditions 'dominant designs',[16] and when collections of related artefacts are involved, Freeman and Perez refer to them as technical systems.[17] Some of these traditions can be highly coded and therefore easily transmissible; others, less coded or structured, can only be acquired slowly and in much more restrictive circumstances.[18]

Culture is a prime vehicle for the transmission of artefacts. Some of the knowledge they encapsulate, being explicit, can be transmitted in writing or through other artificial channels in a fairly impersonal way. Some of it, however, will remain implicit and can only be properly imparted over a long period of time and in face-to-face situations that we associate with the process of socialization. If impersonal transmission can occur through artificial channels and reach a large number of people in a short period of time, it nevertheless allows little scope for direct feedback and, like any form of broadcasting, therefore becomes a somewhat 'hit and miss' affair. Personal transmission, by contrast, uses sensory channels in parallel and for this reason can only reach a few people at a time. However, feedback here becomes possible and communicative intentions can be made clear by successive adjustments of codes and messages. The first approach thus offers greater coverage; the second greater control.

Three levels of communication problem

Cultural evolution, like biological evolution, is a matter of generating variety, selecting from it, and transmitting what has been selected to contemporaries and descendants. But its chosen vehicle for the generation and transmission of variety is artefacts instead of genes, information-bearing W3 products that have to survive the selective rigours of W1. How effectively these W3 products communicate, therefore – i.e., pass on their information content – is crucial to their chances of being selected and adopted, and hence to their future prospects for survival. What are the requirements of effective communication? Shannon and Weaver, in their classic text on the subject,[19] identify three types of problem operating in any communication system:

- Level A problems: How accurately can a given message be transmitted? (The technical problem.)
- Level B problems: How precisely does the message convey the desired meaning? (The semantic problem.)
- Level C problems: How effectively does the received meaning affect the conduct in the desired way? (The effectiveness problem.)

Note that a problem at level A automatically implies a problem at levels B and C but that the converse is not true. And at all three levels, communication problems are greatly reduced by the spatiotemporal proximity of communicating parties. Whatever the level, the further one moves away from the here-and-now, where feedback and multichannel adjustments and corrections are possible, the more problematic communication becomes. Beyond a certain spatiotemporal distance one is led to switch from sensory to artificial channels. To those living in industrialized societies the need to switch may seem fairly obvious; yet it has not always appeared so compelling. Oral traditions still prevailing in certain parts of the world, for example, can handle intergenerational transmission processes tolerably well even though the anthropological evidence points to much information being lost en route.[20] Oral traditions nevertheless suffer from spatial as well as temporal limitations that confine them to the transmission of the most central messages of a culture's repertoire. While they transmit messages exclusively through sensory channels, the high degree of selectivity applied to the message itself, together with the highly ritualized context in which transmission often takes place, makes oral traditions in practice a highly coded business quite removed from the more natural and sensory forms of interpersonal communication normally associated with spatiotemporal proximity.

Communicative efficiency versus communicative effectiveness

The switch from sensory to artificial channels will often be costly. New codes have to be learnt by all parties to a communication process and these may not be readily mastered. Furthermore, a communication infrastructure – transmitters, channels, receivers, etc. – may also have to be set up, thus further consuming scarce resources. The greater the resources that have to be devoted to the creation of a communication infrastructure, the more sensible it becomes to develop specialized codes that economize on its use. Thus, coding skills consist essentially in choosing that level of redundancy which minimizes transmission costs without sacrificing the clarity of a message. Conceivably, similar coding skills will be required for the processing of data within an individual E-space and for exchanges of data between E-spaces. If so, the connectionist perspective could be extended beyond the strictly neural level to cover the case of individual E-spaces acting as communication nodes within a social network. Relaxation and single shot algorithms would then become social information processing strategies that reflected the degree of cognitive cohesion present within a social system.[21] At each level a balance would have to be struck between communicative *efficiency* – minimizing transmission costs without incurring a problem at level A – and communicative *effectiveness*, which might call for considerable volumes of technically redundant information for the message to be not only understood (the level B problem), but also acted upon, thus avoiding a problem at level C.

How can the balance between efficiency and effectiveness be operationalized? Shannon defines a message's relative information as H/H_m where H measures a message's actual information content and H_m the maximum amount of information it could carry.[22] The ratio varies between 0 and 1 and represents the message's relative originality. By implication, the complementary magnitude $1 - H/H_m$ gives us the message's redundancy. Thus for a given channel we can assess the efficiency of a chosen repertoire of symbols – i.e., type case, vocabulary, and sentences in the case of a written natural language – for the transmission of a certain type of information.

Our coding scale (Figure 2.2) offers increasingly fast transmission rates and achieves ever-higher levels of compression of data into codes as one moves up along it; but at each point on the scale an efficiency–effectiveness trade-off will have to be faced. Taken in the purely technical sense (Shannon and Weaver's level A), redundancy will be a function of the statistical laws governing the collection of symbols and their relationship. Thus, for example, Shannon has estimated the redundancy of the English language to be about 50 per cent,[23] and Moles, using a similar approach, puts the redundancy of the French language at about 45 per cent.[24] In both languages, therefore, only half of what is said can be freely chosen, the other half being governed by the structural properties of the language itself – its syntax.

At the semantic level (Shannon and Weaver's level B), choosing an appropriate code is initially a question of establishing some measure of 'fit', or a mapping, between the statistical character of a chosen set of symbols and their interrelationships, on the one hand, and the statistical profile of the phenomena to be apprehended through the code on the other. Yet even if this is well done, it is still only half the story; for the chosen code, if it is to serve the needs of effective communication as well as of data processing, must also be known to the receiver. What repertoire of symbols is the *receiver* likely to have at his/her disposal? Would T.S. Eliot's recondite and coded references to classical mythology in his verse, for example, be accessible to the average contemporary reader? Did Eliot *intend* them to be?

Art and poetry pose the problem of effective communication in an interesting way. The artist's skill consists either in devising original high-level codes for describing and communicating phenomena, or in modifying existing ones in original ways. Yet inevitably, the closer artists get to achieving genuinely novel descriptions, the further they are likely to remove themselves from the coding conventions that allow them to reach their audience. Conversely, the greater the concessions they are willing to make to the coding needs and expectations of their audience, the greater the danger of vulgarization – that is, of resorting to a facile or commonplace coding of the phenomena they are trying to express. All works of art thus harbour an irreducible opposition between the artist's need for self-expression and the need to communicate.

The aesthetic experience, as we saw in Chapter 2, is one in which clarity is not always sought, the effectiveness of the message residing at least in part in its ambiguity. Powerful artistic statements are often those that have a certain tautness about them, keeping redundancy – i.e., rhetoric – to a minimum, and converting the resulting semantic difficulties into an enjoyable and instructive predicament for a given audience. Communicative effectiveness at level C, in such cases, is effectively achieved by *not* resolving all the semantic problems that might arise at level B.

Semantic versus aesthetic information transmission

Sensory channels offer an important advantage over artificial channels in that one can use them in combination with relative ease and for the most part almost unconsciously. This is perhaps just as well, since in our day-to-day encounters with our immediate environment, relatively few of the incoming messages that we register lend themselves to processing by a single sensory channel just for our convenience. Sensory stimuli are highly correlated in their sequencing and continually reinforce each other's internal probability structures: we first *hear* the train approaching the platform and *then* turn around and catch sight of it. If the train is close enough as it passes we may then *feel* the rush of air as it speeds past. Should the sound of the locomotive only reach us a few seconds *after* it had gone past we would be puzzled indeed.

Artificial channels are usually much more difficult to coordinate and combine than sensory channels. They are more cumbersome to use, and hence more costly in time and effort. For this reason any collapse of the multichannel experiences of the sensory mode into the single channel experience of the artificial one usually involves some sacrifice of data and therefore some compensating selectivity that preserves communicative efficiency in the way it is processed. In other words, the use of artificial channels usually calls for a greater degree of coding.

Switching messages between one sensory channel and another presents us with similar difficulties and also entails a loss of data. When can such data losses be countenanced? When they do not incur a concomitant loss of information; that is to say, when the underlying structure of what is being transmitted is sufficiently well understood or *conceptualized* that through careful coding or recoding it can survive the switch from one sensory channel to another – or for that matter from sensory to artificial channels. The abstract objects of W3, in so far as they express such a conceptual understanding, are thus better candidates than the concrete objects of W1 either for a transposition across sensory channels or for one from the sensory multichannel communication mode to the single channel artificial ones.

Messages that can be translated from one channel to another without undue information – as opposed to data – losses can be labelled, following Moles, *semantic* messages.[25] They have a universal abstract quality that is accessible to anyone who can grasp their underlying principles. They tend to be more highly coded and articulate than what Moles calls *aesthetic* messages; these are untranslatable from one channel to another without information losses since what they describe are the concrete if sometimes ambiguous internal states specific to individuals. Aesthetic messages are thus confined to the channel or channels that transmit them and they are profoundly altered by any transfer from one channel to another. They have, as Moles puts it, 'only equivalents, not equals'.[26] Moles's views on aesthetic information are clearly convergent with those of Polanyi on personal or tacit knowledge.

In sum, we might say that semantic messages survive moves up the coding scale – particularly those moves that associate a change of code with a change of channel – by shifting away from the sensory channels that give us access to the concrete world on the left of the E-space, and, through successive acts of abstraction, by moving towards the more artificial channels that allow such a transposition of codes. Much data is shed on the way with consequent efficiency gains. Communicative effectiveness, however, is only maintained to the extent that information-preserving structures are successfully abstracted from such data before it is shed.

Aesthetic messages, by contrast, are required to preserve data to the extent that such data is required to convey the full richness and complexity of a

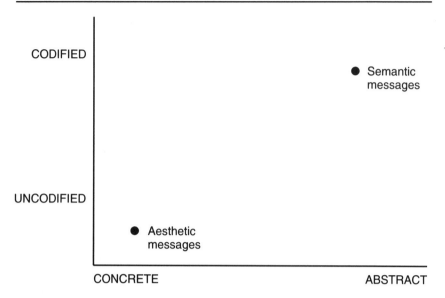

Figure 3.1 Semantic and aesthetic messages in the E-space

concrete personal experience. Moves up the coding scale are possible and often necessary in order to give a minimum amount of outline and definition to a personal experience. Yet these moves are limited by the constraints identified by Moles: no transposition of codes is possible across sensory channels, and, to the extent that a personal experience is conveyed exclusively by means of such channels, aesthetic messages will tend to cluster in the south-west corner of the E-space. The location of each type of message in the E-space is shown in Figure 3.1.

Interesting consequences follow from the foregoing analysis which will be further explored in subsequent chapters. What we need to note here is that the more coded and abstract the epistemological objects that populate W3 can be made, the more adapted they will be to transmission by means of artificial channels. Thus not only, by dint of their abstraction, can they become independent of time and space in what they *refer* to, but in addition, by moving through artificial channels, they achieve a mobility and a diffusibility that further frees them from spatiotemporal constraints in their choice of audience. The concrete qualitative data that inhabits the south-west corner of the E-space does not enjoy such mobility and is thus more parochial in nature. Where it is communicable at all it is thus more confined, both in its choice of references and in its choice of audience.

In conclusion we might say that knowledge assets located in the north-east region of the E-space have the properties of ubiquity and universality while those located in the south-west corner enjoy those of uniqueness and identity. The closer one comes to securing one of these two sets of properties, the more of the other set must be given up. How does this affect the way that these different kinds of knowledge get shared? We turn to this next.

3.3: COMMUNICATING MEANINGFULLY: THE SHARING OF CONTEXTS

Technical and physical constraints on information diffusion

Figure 3.2 describes the diffusion of a given item of information in a target population of data processors as a function of time. The population chosen for the exercise could be of any size ranging from a handful of people to a nation-state or larger. It need not even refer to people necessarily: any entities capable of receiving, processing, storing, and transmitting information – dolphins, nerve cells, viruses, microprocessors, harmonic oscillators – could make up a diffusion population for our purposes. The target population is placed on the horizontal scale of the diagram and is expressed as a percentage; thus, for instance, on the left-hand side of the scale, only a small percentage is reached by a given message, whereas on the right the majority or even all of it is. Time is shown on the vertical scale. Clearly, the flatter the gradient of any curve, the faster the diffusion process at any given level of coding, and the steeper the gradient, the longer the time required for an item of information to diffuse through the population. If one assumes a population to be evenly distributed in physical space and homogeneous in its character-istics, then we might even expect the diffusion curves to be relatively smooth

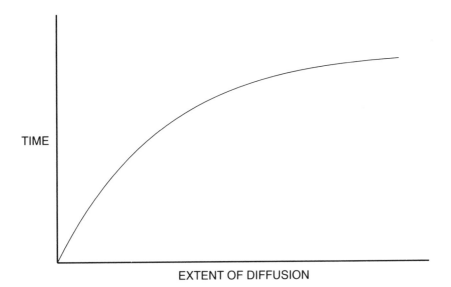

Figure 3.2 Diffusion over time

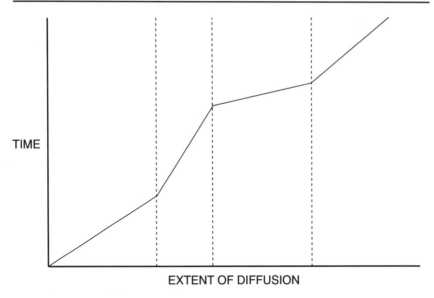

EXTENT OF DIFFUSION

Figure 3.3 A non-homogeneous diffusion population

and continuous whatever their gradient. If, on the other hand, the population is structured into subgroups that differ in their spatial distribution and in their internal characteristics, then the diffusion curve may show a number of breakpoints as in Figure 3.3. In this second case, the first phase of a diffusion process, for example, might take place face to face in a primary group and the second phase through more impersonal specialized media. Such a two-step process might describe how news of a research breakthrough comes out of a research laboratory, being firstly communicated to work colleagues and then, after their comments and suggestions have been received, to a larger professional audience through professional journals.[27]

Available communication technologies also affect the slope of the diffusion curve. As might be expected, the larger and more spatially scattered the population to be reached by a given message, the more costly effective communication becomes in the natural mode and the more it will depend on the ready availability of artificial channels and an appropriate communications infrastructure.

Yet such an infrastructure imposes its own constraints on would-be communicators: limitations on the size and number of channels and on the availability of time slots for message transmission; coding restrictions designed to make efficient use of a given channel; queuing rules for various categories of message, etc. The social and physical configurations of a target audience – its internal structure and spatial distribution – thus interact with technical possibilities to establish the scope that exists for different types of communication. Where message transmission is deemed to be costly, a priority ranking system will be established so that certain audiences will gain privileged access to messages before others.

The transmission of meaning

The differential distribution of a society's stock of knowledge, whether or not it results from communication constraints, inevitably skews the initial endowment and subsequent evolution of individual E-spaces. The cognitive asymmetries that result further stimulate the process of differentiation, as well as a pattern of interaction between individuals and larger groupings that comes under the heading of the sociology of knowledge.[28]

Referring back to Shannon and Weaver's three levels of communication problems – the technical, the semantic, and the pragmatic – the sociology of knowledge to date has shown relatively little interest in the technical level, somewhat more interest in the semantic level, and the greatest interest of all in the pragmatic level, the one at which the problem of socially validated meaning appears. Recall that the technical problem as discussed by the authors is rooted almost exclusively in the physical characteristics of the communicative situation, and for that reason it is addressed largely independently of what is going on in the minds of senders and receivers. To be sure, these often adjust to physical communicative constraints by selecting suitable codes common to both. But in doing so they are then addressing semantic problems at Shannon and Weaver's second level, not their first. Meaning, by contrast, lies at the heart of Shannon and Weaver's pragmatic problem at level C. It is a wholly relational concept that unites sender and receiver; it is defined by Donald MacKay as

> the selective function on the range of the recipient's state of conditional readiness for goal directed activity; so the meaning of the message to you is its selective function on the range of your states of conditional readiness.[29]

Otherwise stated, a meaningful message in some way changes an individual's disposition to act. Like coding, it affects an individual's probability structures but at a higher cognitive level. A communication becomes meaningful when it modifies the expectations that shape behaviour.[30] It activates a receiver's cognitive and affective structures in such a way as to bring them into temporary alignment with those of a sender. Our sense of what is real is partly built up through multiple resonances of this kind, through the gradual acquisition, from infancy to adulthood, of meanings shared with individuals and groups that mediate our access to the life-world.[31] To quote Sahlins:

> the creation of meaning is the distinguishing and constituting quality of men – the human 'essence' of an older discourse – such that by processes

of differential valuation and signification, relations among men, as well as between themselves and nature, are organised.[32]

In sections 3.7 and 3.10 we shall further develop the proposition that the level of abstraction and coding at which meanings are shared is consequential for a sociology of knowledge. As we have already suggested, translating experience into symbolic form does more than extend what can be talked about by allowing for remote reference: it also broadens a message's potential audience. Experience mediated through language and other coded forms is released from immediacy since signs become detachable from their context; they can be used outside the here-and-now to describe things that are absent to people who are not there.

Technology and the sociology of knowledge

Suitable coding gives access not only to new thoughts but to new technologies for communicating them. Technological and cultural evolution go hand in hand. If before Gutenberg's experiment with movable type in the mid-fifteenth century the transmission of knowledge required a strong spatial proximity between social groupings – indeed, Braudel has shown that even after the development of printing, the diffusion of books was confined to the channels through which the trade in luxuries flowed: the fairs of Lyon and Frankfurt in the sixteenth century, that of Leipzig in the seventeenth[33] – today, with modern communications technology and for large tracts of human experience, the transmission process has become virtually instantaneous whatever the physical distance.

In principle, it should be new knowledge that flows most forcefully through the social system; such knowledge is likely to make the biggest difference to the prior expectations of receivers and hence carries the most information. New knowledge, however, often experiences difficulty in passing itself off as meaningful. Modern communications technology may overcome level A technical problems, and universal education may give us all a sufficient number of codes in common to skirt around level B semantic problems, but pragmatic level C problems can only be overcome by a mutual sharing of contexts, something that effectively gets more difficult with increases in spatial distance. A lack of shared context between sender and receiver thus becomes one of the main obstacles to the effective diffusion of meaningful innovation.[34]

3.4: SCANNING AND DIFFUSION AS SOCIAL PROCESSES

Invention and imitation

An early and sophisticated version of the thesis that cultural evolution was above all a communication phenomenon was developed by the nineteenth-century French sociologist Gabriel Tarde. In his book *Les Lois de l'Imitation*,[35] Tarde argued that imitation was the most elemental communication activity and that it was to social processes what 'undulations' (i.e., vibrations or resonance) were to physical processes. With social evolution, Tarde claimed, imitation has become independent of hereditary transmission and hence of space–time constraints. Cultural diffusion did not necessarily require spatial or temporal contiguity, although clearly the denser the communication network the greater the scope for imitation and hence for cultural integration. A society, in this view, is nothing other than a group linked by a high degree of imitation or what he termed counter-imitation, i.e., a conscious collective striving to avoid imitating an exemplar which thereby confirms its identity in the repertoire of cultural symbols.[36]

But what, it might be asked, initially gets the imitative process under way? How does an exemplar worthy of imitation get to emerge in the first place? And how does it then get 'selected' for subsequent diffusion? Tarde's reply, reflecting his century, is essentially Darwinian. All repetitive imitation originates in an individual invention that survives a process of competitive selection, criticism, modification, and further invention.[37]

Invention, then, forms a bridge between individual and social processes. Although in our daily activities we imitate far more than we invent, invention can be thought of as the coding of a novel thought or experience which, under certain circumstances, will be subject to diffusion. One basic requirement that was discussed in section 3.2 is that the new creation be sufficiently coded to be communicable even if not always in verbal or written form. Forces are at work, however, which tend to blur the line that divides the initial act of invention from acts of imitation that subsequently diffuse it. When communication is ambiguous or otherwise problematic, where there is noise in the channel, when senders and receivers do not fully share the same codes or the same context, then information is lost and imitation is perforce incomplete. Consciously, or otherwise, the imitator then has to make up the shortfall with inventions and adaptations of his own.[38]

All imitation thus carries the seeds of new inventions. For this reason, following Schumpeter, we shall use the term 'innovation' rather than 'imitation' as it does not preclude that incremental inventive activity which follows diffusion and helps to adapt an original invention to the specific circumstances of an adopter.[39] The steady accumulation of adaptive incremental inventions can often outweigh the novelty of the original invention to which they were responding.[40]

An invention is an act of encoding new knowledge that is performed in a *single* mind. Such knowledge remains undiffused on the left-hand side of Figure 3.2 until it is communicated; that is to say, it remains embedded in an individual E-space until externalized whether by accident or design. It becomes an innovation to the extent that it travels towards the right along the diffusion scale of Figure 3.2. The region of an individual E-space in which externalization occurs will establish an invention's initial communicability and hence its scope for diffusion, its clarity and force as an exemplar, and to some extent the need for further invention and adaptation. Once an invention has been externalized, it will spread through a population in a manner and at a pace that reflect the nature and extent of the coding process as well as the spatial and social characteristics of the target population. The social trajectory of a new piece of information or knowledge, whether embodied in objects, in documents, or in minds, is thus given by an interplay of internal and external forces that can profoundly modify a message's form and content in the course of its travels through a given population. Yet not only will the first and the last recipients of a given message in a population then gain access to different information, they will also bring to its interpretation quite different contexts and orientation.

Private and public coding

On the far left of Figure 3.2, coding activity, inventive or otherwise, is likely to be a mostly private affair. Indeed, it may not even be conscious. An individual inventor is rarely fully aware of the tortuous path that she followed in arriving at a new concept or idea. Much of it will be the product of a mental activity under no conscious direction.[41] More importantly, the stored knowledge that the individual draws upon in articulating her experience on the left of the diffusion scale, and the way she combines various elements into patterns, appears to be largely idiosyncratic. She may be drawing upon the same external stimuli as her neighbours but each will make something quite different of them. The differences, for the most part, will be trivial and inconsequential. On occasions, however, they may become a source of radical new insight.[42]

As one moves towards the right along the diffusion scale, however, the knowledge and experience contained in individual E-spaces gets shared with an ever-larger percentage of the population and gives rise to collective forms of representation.[43] It now becomes easier to communicate what one sees, hears, and feels since more of the knowledge that makes up the context of a communication has become common property. Coding performed towards the right of the scale will consequently appear less idiosyncratic and more consensual. While it may feel quite free of any sense of social coercion or pressure, it will nevertheless be channelled by perceptual and conceptual categories collectively held; what might then appear to an individual to be purely personal coding preferences will in fact be guided by values that he/she holds in common with different groups to which he/she belongs.[44]

In sum, towards the right of Figure 3.2 social constraints impose themselves on the act of giving form to personal knowledge. On the far left of the diffusion scale one sometimes comes upon the social deviant construing a strictly private world according to his own lights; on the far right by contrast one meets the conformist, largely dependent on others for the creation of his *Umwelt* as well as for some direction on how he should move through it.[45] In the short term, society has fewer problems dealing with conformists than dealing with deviants since the former reinforce rather than threaten the established order. In the long term, however, a society without deviants deprives itself of the cognitive variety essential to social evolution.[46]

To call the horizontal scale of Figure 3.2 a diffusion scale is, in one sense, misleading and needs elaboration. In the next chapter, for example, we shall see that information flows from right to left as well as from left to right. At first sight this may appear puzzling since it seems to imply that knowledge which has already been diffused and is thus held by a large proportion of a given population can become suddenly undiffused again and unknown by the same population. Are we trying to run a film backwards?

Things become clearer if we bear in mind that what is flowing *physically* between data processors is not information as such but *data* and that each individual extracts information idiosyncratically from this data to construct her own schemes within her E-space. On the right such schemes are widely shared and on the left they are not, even though in both cases the *same data* may be used for their construction. The leftward movement in the diagram in effect describes a process of cognitive individuation through which an individual's perceptions or concepts gradually come to lose features that they had in common with those of her neighbours. Sometimes physical isolation may be the cause of such individuation; at other times it will be personality factors that lead an individual to build up and use her E-space in idiosyncratic ways. Either way, part of her cognitive resources shift leftward along the diffusion scale of Figure 3.2.

From coding to codification

Only the unique individual occupies the extreme left-hand point on our diffusion scale, and even then only episodically. The point is important enough to warrant a change in terminology. In this chapter and those that follow, therefore, the term *codification* will henceforth be used in preference to *coding* to reflect the fact that giving form to experience is rarely a completely autonomous process carried out by unique individuals located on the extreme left of the diffusion scale. It is at least in part a socially structured process. In effect, coding can be thought of as an idiosyncratic and limiting case of codification located at the origin of our diffusion scale. Suitable candidates for codification are those areas of experience – customs, laws, knowledge – that are stable enough to be shared with others and that express either a common group preference or the workings of power relationships within a group.[47] As we have already seen, most of the information through which we initially build up our world is socially inherited and thus already codified.[48] Berger and Luckmann put it thus:

> I live in the commonsense world of everyday life equipped with special bodies of knowledge. What is more, I know that others share at least part of this knowledge and they know that I know this. My interaction with others in everyday life is, therefore, constantly affected by our common participation in the available social stock of knowledge.[49]

Yet this 'common participation in the available social stock of knowledge' remains problematic. For a start, only a small part of what passes for human experience is actually retained in consciousness, and whatever is held remains for the most part implicit and inaccessible. It can only contribute to the *social* stock of knowledge when it is in some way objectivated in a sign system, i.e., when it is codified to some degree. Then, there is the added complication that not all sign systems offer the same communicative scope. While anyone with a good command of a spoken language has a reasonable chance of being understood at least by his fellow countrymen, this is not necessarily the case with other forms of communication for which the required codes – whether these be abstract symbols, dress codes, or behavioural signs – may be the property of restricted groups.

Constraints on codification become simultaneously constraints on new ways of knowing *and* on sharing them. What is not objectivated in some kind of a sign system is exclusively available to the individual as personal knowledge within his own E-space. He can know his own experiences better than his neighbour can, having access to them in a way that the latter can never have. Incommunicable personal experiences of this kind are extreme examples of what Hayek has termed 'local' knowledge; that is, knowledge intimately tied to circumstances of time and place.[50] Our myriad encounters with the world – a favourite walk, a fishing trip, a casual conversation, etc. – are of this kind. Even in our dealings with those who are co-present at an event, the element of shared experience offers but limited overlaps. Much stays largely local.

Personal versus impersonal exchange

What Alfred Shutz has called the *life-world*, our common intersubjective yet unspoken stock of shared experiences, is built up and continuously reaffirmed using information filtered through the codification constraints just described.[51] On the most intimate level, usually the one we enjoy with a primary group, relationships have a spatiotemporal immediacy that is absent from our dealings with contemporaries. In face-to-face interactions, multiple channels are available which, together with the possibilities of giving and receiving feedback, and hence of correcting for distortions and information losses, preserve the richness of exchanges. They do so, however, only by keeping them local.

Contemporaries by contrast are not bodily present. In our dealings with them the here-and-now recedes into a bland anonymity as concrete experience is thinned out to render it communicable over larger regions of space and time. Such anonymity, of course, can also be injected into face-to-face relationships: the intimacy *available* in the here-and-now, after all, need not be much drawn upon. Market transactions, for example, have often been held to depersonalize face-to-face relationships, abstracting from the complexities of concrete individuals and situations, and codifying exchange into a featureless encounter between a buyer and a seller – in effect, transforming them into more manageable W3 objects.

It is in situations where the pressures of the social situation push for transactional efficiency that one can no longer react to individuals in their fullness; one is led to codify them into impersonal abstract roles that require a less discriminating response so that one can then react more narrowly to types: not to M. Jefferson who lives in the brick house in Chipstead Street, but to the baker, the ticket inspector, the newsagent, and so on.

Yet if anonymity can be injected in this way into a face-to-face relationship, an impersonal relationship can in turn sometimes be personalized. A rock star's fan club, for instance, is a shrewd commercial device for personalizing at least one of the parties in what can only be for the majority an anonymous relationship.

One can stratify communicative relationships, then, according to the degree of anonymity involved. The more anonymous the transactions between people the more 'objective' appears to be the meaning system that underpins it. At the highest level of anonymity, the world appears to be objectively given and self-evident, even to outside observers of the transaction. Anonymous relationships, the joint products of spatiotemporal distance and large transacting numbers, are more likely to be found on the right of our diffusion scale than on the left. Here too, it will be shared symbols – conventions that refer to abstract codifications – rather than shared experiences that contribute to the building of mutually intelligible worlds or components thereof. Shared experiences, particularly those that are the fruits of socialization within the primary group, have an important part to play in this construction but, being strictly local, they cannot involve contemporaries to any great extent. The reality that we can take for granted in our dealings with others – the life-world – will therefore of necessity reflect the numbers involved and by implication the degree of anonymity of interactions with them.

To summarize, each of us possesses knowledge whose characteristics would locate it at different points along the diffusion scale of Figure 3.2. Towards the left, as we have seen, the knowledge we possess tends to be more idiosyncratic, personal, and possibly proprietary. Some of it will remain in our sole possession, locked inside our skull and inaccessible even to our most intimate acquaintances. We take such knowledge with us to our grave and it perishes with us. Towards the right, however, such knowledge becomes an increasingly common possession: public, freely available, and, if codified, largely impersonal. Acts of communication can then move this knowledge either to the left or to the right along the scale, its mobility being a function of its codifiability. Knowledge that is hard to codify will move more slowly and in smaller volumes than knowledge that is easy to codify; the latter will always travel best along the scale.

Yet such mobility, as Shannon has taught us, is a purely technical property of well-codified knowledge. Barriers to movement along the scale exist at the semantic and at the pragmatic level.[52] For the effective transmission of codified knowledge also presupposes the prior existence of shared substrata of uncodified meaning that can unite sender and receiver by placing them on the same 'wavelength'. How far they can be united in this way is partly a matter of the spatiotemporal distance that separates them and partly of whether they are in fact intimates or merely contemporaries. Both Tönnies and Durkheim saw in the ability to communicate with contemporaries rather than intimates one of the driving forces of social evolution, shifting social and economic exchange away from the local and parochial and towards the universal.[53]

The authority of the transmitter

In the early phases of an individual's development, any idiosyncratic knowledge that he/she possesses on the left of the diffusion scale is likely to be overwhelmingly concrete rather than abstract.[54] Yet, even though such knowledge remains highly personal and by implication hard to share, it will still be largely bounded by the abstract categories which the individual inherits from his/her culture and which are themselves widely available within it.[55] In actually making use of inherited abstract categories, the individual typically begins life on the right of the scale; he/she *may* then move towards the left, but only as specialized concepts and experiences are acquired. Any position occupied by an individual other than at the extreme points of the scale, however, makes him/her a potential communication link in a scanning or a diffusion chain, picking up knowledge from others, possibly processing it a bit, and then passing it on. When the individual passes it on to those located to the left of him/her, he/she participates in a scanning process; when it is to those located on the right, in a diffusion process.

Playing a link role confronts an individual with new requirements. If he/she is the recipient of well-codified information, the decision to adopt and transmit it is made easier by the fact that the data is visible and can therefore be assessed for plausibility and internal coherence. As with the Ten Commandments, the very clarity and consistency of a message can make its adoption compelling. If, on the other hand, an individual has to grapple with uncodified data, his course of action is much less clear. Since the meaning of uncodified data has to be teased out of it and may only emerge slowly, much of it, at least in the early stages of a transaction, may have to be taken on trust. Polanyi illustrates the need for trust in the transfer of knowledge between a master and apprentice:

> To learn by example is to submit to authority. You follow your master because you trust his manner of doing things even when you cannot analyse and account in detail for its effectiveness. By watching the master and emulating his efforts in the presence of his example, the apprentice unconsciously picks up the roles of the art including those that are not explicitly known to the master himself. These hidden rules can be assimilated only by a person who surrenders himself to that extent uncritically to the imitation of another.[56]

In cases such as the one above – and it typifies a large number of social relationships ranging from a Zen master with his acolytes to a father proffering career advice to his children – the power of the receiver resides essentially in her ability to grant or withhold her trust, to 'surrender', as Polanyi puts it, to the higher power of the transmitter. While the feeling of trust exists, the power of the transmitter, often charismatic in nature where knowledge is personal and uncodified, will dominate the relationship and keep lines of communication open between the parties. Nevertheless, what the receiver will actually construct out of what the sender transmits will remain indeterminate where uncodified data is involved. In such cases the act of imitation can never be complete and some of the work of codification and abstraction will be left for the receiver alone to perform – the topic of the next section.

3.5: THE REACH OF ABSTRACTION

Coercive and non-coercive codifications

Scheler has argued that in any society, *all* human knowledge is given as prior to human experience.[57] Order and meaning are imparted to the individual from outside. The acquisition of language is a *conditio sine qua non* for gaining access to them; language, by coercively patterning individual experience, gives it a facticity that is rarely challenged. To adapt a term that we used in Chapter 2, once language has been internalized, it's single shot algorithms all the way. Powerless to resist the force of linguistic articulation, the developing individual locates himself at the outset on the right of the diffusion scale of Figure 3.2, with respect to both concrete and abstract knowledge. Personal efforts at codification, being socially determined, are unlikely to move him leftward towards more personal and idiosyncratic forms of knowledge until much later in his development, if at all. By then, of course, the die has been cast.

The flaw in Scheler's formulation, it seems to me, resides in its over-reliance on language as the coding paradigm. The less articulate the code, the greater the discretion one enjoys in deciding how it is to be applied and what it is to be applied to – and by implication, therefore, the more one enjoys some freedom of choice in *interpreting* its various applications. Moreover, if, in a simple, undifferentiated society, socially mediated stimuli can be presented to the individual as mutually reinforcing and unproblematic, as soon as a minimum level of social complexity is reached stimuli emerging from diverse social groupings will often appear contradictory and destabilizing. The codes through which these are then filtered will lack their former apodictic quality.

Tarde,[58] like Scheler, had also noted the coercive nature of social codes and the constraints that they place on individual freedom and fantasy. Yet in certain circumstances they lost their totalitarian character. Tarde claimed that in imitation, there were two despots, custom and fashion, and that of the two, custom was the more tyrannical. A hierarchical society, he argued, will be dominated by custom, a democratic one by fashion. With development, fashion replaces custom, for fashion according to Tarde is driven by rational selection processes and over time rationality will win out.

The key difference between custom and fashion is that the first is transmitted unilaterally from ancestors to contemporaries, whereas the second is transmitted interactively between contemporaries. Both originate in a codification that occurs at a given moment on the left-hand side of our diffusion scale. But in the case of fashion, the power of adoption or rejection resides mainly with the recipient. Fashion operates through a competitive process that results in a much higher rate of innovation than that which is possible in the case of custom. Where custom reigns, on the other hand, messages originating on the left tend to be accepted unquestioningly by those on the right. There is no way of communicating with ancestors and hence no way of negotiating with them. One can take or leave what they say, but if they are endowed with authority by the social order, then the tendency will be to take it.

With contemporaries, the situation is different. Novel messages emerging on the left are accepted or rejected on their intrinsic merit following large-scale sampling, testing, and deliberation by potential adopters, with the outcome feeding back to would-be innovators and trend-setters – a scanning process that now sets up a flow of information along the diffusion scale from right to left. Feedback in turn stimulates additional efforts at adaptation on the part of potential innovators, efforts which act competitively to limit the lifespan of any single fashion cycle and thus to weaken its dominion over the social order as new alternatives loom into view.

Multichannel versus single-channel communication

Whether one is dealing with custom or with fashion, the more abstract and codified messages become, the more likely they are to travel beyond the environment in which they originated and the greater the power they have of establishing remote reference. Conversely, less codified, concrete messages are more temporally and spatially confined. In pre-literate societies, for example, such as the !Kung's, the bushmen of the Kalahari, only the immediate context is available to children to learn from, and the lack of any broader institutional effort at codification leads to an almost total absence of formal teaching.[59] The power of remote reference is therefore denied to !Kung children owing to the absence of an adequate coding repertoire. Recall, however, that efficient coding itself presupposes a shared context within which meaningful messages may be exchanged, even if such a context operates at a more implicit level than the coded message itself. Spatio-temporal distance reduces the probability of sender and receiver sharing a common context and thus requires that the codes used do more of the work required in getting a message across. This carries a cost. The contribution of a shared context to the effectiveness of even well-codified exchanges is not always obvious to members of western literate societies. Edmund Leach suggests that

> In our own western, literate, mechanically organised society, so much 'true' Aristotelian knowledge is built into the cultural system that we mostly take it all for granted that logic of this kind is an essential component of common sense. Yet in practice, we only exploit formal logical principles in the relatively rare instances in which we are seeking to convey exact information at a distance using a single channel of communication, as in writing a letter or a book, or speaking to someone over the telephone. When two people are in face-to-face communication, so that they can use several channels of sensory information simulta-neously – touch, sight, hearing and so on – the logical ordering of individual messages is much less obvious. If you record unrehearsed conversation on tape, you will find that on playback, very little of it is immediately comprehensible; yet in context, all those present would have understood what was being said.[60]

I read Leach to say that multichannel communication reduces our need as well as our ability to resort to artificial codes. Multichannel communication is communication in the natural mode, it is the coordinated deployment of gesture, speech, tone, clothes, movement, in the service of messages whose complexity would normally overwhelm the single channel. Communicating at a distance denies us the rich coding resources of the natural mode. Beyond a few metres, facial gestures lose their crispness so that, for example, stage actors need to use make-up to articulate (i.e., to code) the physical features of the characters they portray; they also have to dramatize relevant behaviour patterns to get them across – film, which unlike the theatre allows close facial shots, calls for very different acting skills. A few metres' distance more between transmitters and receivers and microphones has to be used, voices raised, and many modulations of tone and pitch forgone to maintain the requisite level of verbal comprehension. More coding, more data lost. Now stretch the communication distance a fraction further and visual contact itself is broken. To the adoring throngs below, the Pope is reduced to little more than a white speck on the balcony of St Peter's. Here, the visual component of the message has all but disappeared, and the microphone, if used, is then left to say it all. With increasing distance, therefore, the natural multichannel mode of communication gives way to the artificial single-channel mode in which the need for efficient coding of necessity leads to a repression of expressive subtleties, unless these, in turn, can successfully be codified through stylistic conventions. Yet even then, much data is lost.

Abstraction as an alternative to shared context

Chapter 6 will explore the hypothesis that as western culture has extended itself spatially across the globe – and partly in consequence of this it has experienced the need to develop single-channel communication technologies – it has developed a marked preference for codified and abstract over uncodified and concrete forms of exchange with telling consequences for the functioning of its institutions. Here, we simply make the point that in overcoming the spatiotemporal distance that separates sender from receiver, efficient coding often only solves the technical communication problem by creating new problems at the semantic and at the pragmatic level where the issue of shared context looms largest. Messages are then efficiently transmitted but are not necessarily understood, or, if understood, they do not lead to the desired behaviour. We discover, sometimes rather late, that communicative efficiency and communicative effectiveness make uncomfortable bedfellows. Efficiency is concerned with the resources deployed to achieve a given communication effect – the coding effort involved, the channel capacity used up, the required transmission time, etc. Effectiveness, on the other hand, is measured by the degree of 'fit' that obtains between the outcome of a given communication act as intended by a message source and its actual outcome. The first is concerned with economizing on means, the second with achieving ends. Effective messages have to be both plausible and useful in the sense that their recipient will consider them to be substantially true and relevant to his/her circumstances.

A sharing of context by senders and receivers is one way of enhancing the effectiveness of a message while saving on data transmission as well as coding effort and time. An alternative approach available for economizing on communication costs while maintaining effectiveness, however, is to use coding categories that succeed in retaining their validity across multiple and variable contexts. This moves message content towards a higher level of codification and greater abstraction.

Abstraction is a crucial requirement. Highly codified messages, whether abstract or not, travel fast and far, spanning cultures remote from each other both in space and time. Their effectiveness, however, is not guaranteed since, particularly in situations where they are transmitted anonymously, they cannot easily be authenticated. They may be deemed potentially relevant; but who, or what, stands behind their claim to truth?

From a transmitter's point of view, this effectiveness problem is compounded by the fact that as an audience grows either in space or over time, it can be subdivided into groups with sometimes radically different approaches to the validation of truth claims. The Kuba of the Kasai, for example, take historical truth to be whatever is accepted by the majority as worthy of belief – a specification not unknown in those western cultures whose judicial system admits of trial by jury. The Tobriand Islanders, on the other hand, take historical truth to be whatever the ancestors claim to be true.[61] In each society, consequently, acceptable messages are likely to emerge from quite different sources, to go through different authentication procedures, and to require a different context.

It can also be safely anticipated that the Kuba will examine messages less critically and will therefore be more vulnerable to communicative manipulations, whether for public or private purposes, than will the more conservative Tobriand Islanders.

A more political view of how truth claims are handled takes message acceptability to be a function of power relationships between senders and receivers, the ability to make people believe being rooted in the ability to make them conform.[62] The 'might is right' position has two possible interpretations. The first, which we might call 'Orwellian', is that a coercive use of power has a direct impact on an individual's cognitive capacity and that the use of force or the threat to use it can lead people to actually believe as well as to affirm propositions contrary to the evidence of their senses.[63] The second interpretation, which we might term 'Machiavellian', is that power can be used non-coercively to control the flow of data along the diffusion scale and thus to regulate the access of various social groups to the different cognitive categories that can be derived therefrom. In the second instance, the exercise of power over cognitive processes remains indirect.[64]

Will such power always be used cynically and in self-serving ways? Marxists and non-Marxists will disagree on how far communication filters placed at different points on the diffusion scale can genuinely contribute to the detection of errors and to the systematic falsifications of unwarranted truth claims on the one hand – the justification usually given by power holders for attempts to control the diffusion of information through censorship practices – and how far they invariably end up in the service of dominant groups and of the cognitive order that they seek to promote on the other. Many non-Marxists will be quite happy to go along with the view that the control of information flows, at least on occasions, should also be justified on efficiency grounds.[65]

Universalistic versus particularistic exchange

The dialectical tension that exists between social and individual thought reflects the terms on which they transmit to each other. Marx, perhaps its most articulate observer in the nineteenth century, believed that the dialectic has a physical basis, that material and social conditions establish both the scope and limits for human thought.[66] He believed that mental activity is founded in physical activity – i.e., labour, broadly defined – as well as in the social relations brought about by this activity.[67] He termed physical activity the *substructure*, and the articulate mental world it gave rise to, the *superstructure*. In Popperian terms, Marx held that only W1 was causal and that W2 and W3 – the latter one being the superstructure – were both epiphenomenal. Yet if, instead of treating physical and mental activities as distinct categories, we broaden Marx's concept of physical activity to include data processing of the kind that takes place in an E-space, we arrive at a view of W1 and W3 quite at odds with Marx's own, and somewhat closer to that of Berger and Luckmann when they say that

> It is an ethnological commonplace that ways of becoming and being human are as numerous as man's cultures. Humanness is socioculturally variable. In other words, there is no human nature in the sense of biologically fixed substratum determining the variability of sociocultural formations.[68]

The above comment, however, confronts us with a dilemma: for how can the reality of W3 proclaimed by Popperians be reconciled with the cognitive relativism implicit in Luckmann and Berger's views of human nature? It is after all the putative reality of well-tested W3 objects that gives a measure of legitimacy to the products of abstract thought. It is the reason why, as spatiotemporal distance increases in social exchange, we feel entitled to blend in a measure of abstraction with our codification in order to ensure communicative effectiveness. If concrete situational contexts lack a sufficient overlap to purge meaning of its ambiguities as exchange develops, then an abstract context can be developed for the purpose instead. In sum, the larger and the more spatially scattered the population brought into a communication nexus, the more important it becomes that this should be universalistic in its orientation rather than particularistic.[69]

Such an orientation, however, need not imply a realist stance. An alternative to the view that W3 objects have to be true to partake in the discourse of society is one which takes them to be nothing more than useful and reliable tools that can be applied to W1 problems. This pragmatic approach to abstract knowledge goes by the name of *operationalism*.[70] The utility of knowledge is explored further in the next section.

3.6: THE UTILITY SPACE

Abstraction and diffusion

If, as Marx believed, W1 material and social conditions directly shape human thought in W2, unmediated by an autonomous W3 – he was, in effect, denying thought any emergent properties – how do they effectively impinge upon consciousness in W2? In the previous chapter we argued that the process was at best indirect and that W3, whatever cognitive autonomy it is actually granted, will help to dig the channels through which the data of the external world will flow as it irrigates our thinking.

Such data, however, does not reach all of us at the same time or in the same volume. Sociologists of knowledge claim that strategically placed power holders seek to regulate its flow by operating filters that control its distribution among various groups. They implicitly assume that in the absence of such filters, it would flow freely and voluminously in all directions. Hence the *internal* structure of the data – i.e., its degree of codification and abstraction – remains unproblematic for the sociology of knowledge, its effective distribution in a given population being almost exclusively determined by external factors such as social organization and power relationships.

Our own analysis of information and communication processes leads us to challenge the adequacy of a purely sociological approach to data flows and to offer an alternative augmented by epistemological considerations. Power relationships are not thereby occulted. Far from it. But the influence they exert over how knowledge is actually allocated to target groups is attenuated by distributional problems: the perishable nature of the commodity; the consequent need to package it securely for travelling; the extension of its shelf-life both at the wholesale (broadcasting) and at the retail (one to one) end of the communication channel, and so on. In sum, a blend of technical, semantic, and pragmatic problems ensures that a given item of knowledge at one time and place is not necessarily the same product it might be at another.

We start by bringing into an orthogonal relationship the abstract–concrete dimension of the E-space and the diffusion dimension discussed in this chapter. For expository purposes, we dichotomize each dimension as shown

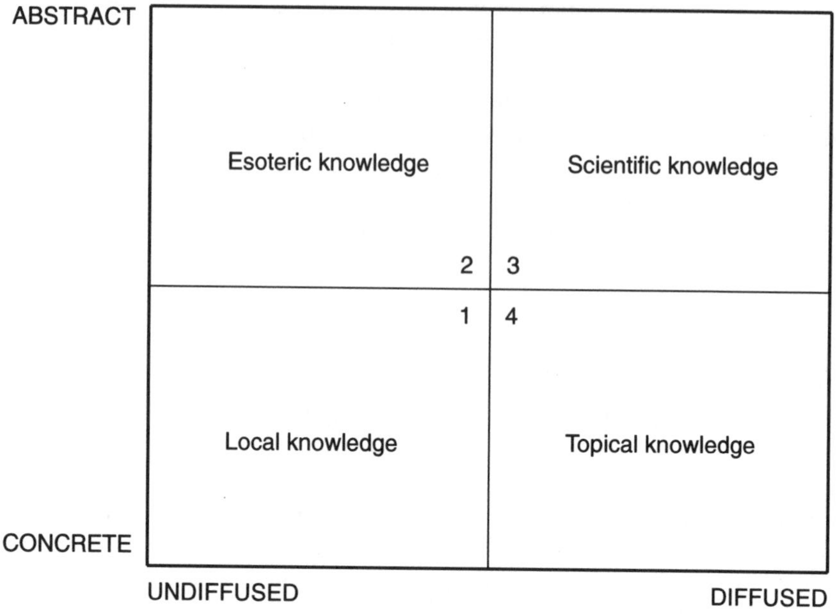

Figure 3.4 A typology of knowledge (1)

in Figure 3.4 to produce a fourfold classification of knowledge that reflects its degree of generality along one dimension and the extent of its diffusion along the other.[71] We then obtain:

Quadrant 1:   Knowledge that is concrete and undiffused: what Hayek has termed 'knowledge of particular time and place' – i.e., local knowledge.[72]

Quadrant 2:   Knowledge that is abstract and undiffused: such knowledge may be lawlike in character but is the property of an individual or a small group – i.e., esoteric knowledge.

Quadrant 3:   Knowledge that is abstract and diffused: Boyle's law, the melting temperature of ice, etc. – i.e., scientific knowledge.

Quadrant 4:   Knowledge that is concrete and diffused: gossip, rumours, news of current events – i.e., topical knowledge. With repetition topical knowledge gives rise to legends, myths, histories, etc.

This classification does not distinguish between codified and uncodified knowledge, and therefore leaves out of consideration one of the major variables that affects the distribution of knowledge along the diffusion scale. The relationship between codification and diffusion will be examined in section 3.11. What we want to examine here in somewhat more detail than in the previous section is how the diffusibility of knowledge might be affected by its degree of abstraction.

Exploring the quadrants

Quadrant 1 holds local knowledge. An extreme of this is the isolated, immediately given, concrete private experience, the reverberations of a mental event forever locked inside a single mind. It cannot move in any direction out of quadrant 1 without shedding its information content along with its data, and this whether it moves towards abstraction in order to achieve greater generality, or towards communicability (through coding) and hence greater diffusibility.

Quadrant 1 experiences may be meaningful but they cannot easily be shared. The knowledge they yield may have some utility, but while it is confined to the south-west region of the diagram, it can only be a local and personal utility accruing to the individual in possession of the experience, not a social utility from which others may collectively benefit.

Any increase in the social utility of quadrant 1 experiences would have to come from an extension of their scope, from an increase in the range of their potential applications. Utility can be increased in this way by a move towards greater abstraction and generality; that is, a move up the vertical axis of Figure 3.4 and towards quadrant 2.

Although we have so far placed only one individual in quadrant 1 for illustrative purposes, it is quite possible to locate intimate small groups in it, groups whose collective encounter with reality is likely to be idiosyncratic and parochial in so far as they draw their epistemological resources solely from this region. At times, non-rigorous validation procedures may help to bestow a high degree of social legitimacy to knowledge and experience emanating from quadrant 1, but again only at the price of a limited diffusibility that does not pose too rigorous a challenge to the procedures actually used. The hallucinatory experiences of the Yaqui Indian Don Juan and his circle as described by Carlos Castañeda, for example, gave them prestige and charismatic power in their community but perhaps only because it was a small one.[73] A more familiar example is provided by the work of the sociolinguist Basil Bernstein who showed how the limited and highly situational coding practices of working-class British children has the double effect of implicitly shoring up the limited world they construct with their peers, whilst at the same time cutting them off from a wider, more impersonal and abstract universe of discourse that might ultimately challenge it.[74]

Quadrant 2 yields knowledge that, by dint of its higher degree of abstraction and generality, would enjoy a wide social application were it not the monopolistic possession of some individual or group – it has potential utility. There exists a strong social demand for such knowledge whether it is actually diffusible or not; but because it meets the two key requirements of economic value – i.e., it is scarce as well as useful – it is subject to appropriation.[75] The mechanism of appropriation will vary with the codifiability of such knowledge as well as with the relative power of senders and receivers in the communication nexus. But except perhaps for the case of small, isolated pre-literate groups, there is usually a greater demand for the social diffusion of knowledge residing in quadrant 2 than for that located in quadrant 1. The audience for which it promises to be relevant is larger and its own potential utility is also more manifest. For this reason a horizontal diffusion of knowledge out of quadrant 2 and into quadrant 3, by dint of its higher degree of abstraction, is likely to be much faster and more certain than one from quadrant 1 to quadrant 4, and this in spite of whatever attempts might be made by its initial possessors to prevent or retard the process.

Concrete knowledge originating in quadrant 1 is for the most part highly parochial. In his field observations of oral traditions, Vansina has observed that many pre-literate groups only narrate their own history and refuse to recite traditions belonging to neighbouring groups, particularly where these are protected by rights of ownership. Illustrating his point with another Kuba example, he describes an event that occurred once in the Ngongo tribal council in Natumba, when a speaker was reprimanded by his listeners for reciting traditions belonging to the neighbouring Ngeende and had to break off.[76]

We need not reach out as far as pre-literate societies for evidence of a preference for concrete local knowledge. Even in industrial societies, a predilection exists for news that is topical and focused on the immediate community rather than news which describes more general trends and developments that occur elsewhere. Abstract issues, to be sure, are of some interest, but only when they can be brought down to earth and their relevance for local concerns made manifest. A preoccupation with the environment in western industrial societies, for example, only became pressing when people could start relating what was being said in remote international forums on the subject to concrete realities such as polluted rivers and oil-smudged beaches that they could experience directly for themselves.[77]

It is not just the limited interest that concrete knowledge has to offer outside its immediate locality that limits its diffusion from quadrant 1 to quadrant 4. The information losses incurred in its transmission must also rank as an important factor. Recall from Chapter 2 that abstraction is one way of economizing on data to be transmitted, codification (alias coding) being the other. Although we defer a fuller treatment of how codification affects the sharing of information to section 3.11, here we note that to the extent that concrete local knowledge is less likely to be codified than abstract universal knowledge – this was one of the conclusions of our earlier discussion of the E-space – it will tend to diffuse more slowly, and will do so through a process of personal contact rather than through speedier and more efficient means.[78] The transmission of many intangible skills, for example, requires intense personal multichannel contact between teacher and pupil. Polanyi maintains that given the right degree of contact, one can in fact become a proficient performer simply by following a set of rules that one may never become fully conscious of.[79]

The fragility of moves towards abstraction

Imitating a teacher is a slow business and often an uncertain investment requiring a great deal of practice and repetition. Yet without these, according to Tarde,[80] science becomes impossible. For continuous practice and repetition furnish a statistical base capable of corroborating acts of abstraction or generalization. In the case of intangible skills such as piano playing or painting, the outcome may be nothing more than a well-tested rule of thumb or heuristic that cannot be further explained – in effect more a case of codification than one of abstraction as such; but with other activities, repetition and practice may yield intelligible principles which extend understanding to new areas.

A move towards greater abstraction thus offers the prospects of genuine gains in utility.[81] We anoint this insight by labelling the diagram of Figure 3.4 a *Utility space* or *U-space*. The insight must be applied with care, however. For moves up the U-space may also offer no gain in utility at all: the statistical base accumulated through repetition and practice may be too flimsy to sustain an inference, or the inference itself may turn out to be faulty. The history of science abounds with examples of spurious generalizations that initially appeal but that do not stand up to the test of time. The failure of the pioneers of hypnosis from Mesmer to Braid comes to mind as one example of inferential inadequacy. Hypnosis only gained popularity when an adequate hypothesis – i.e., inference – was put forward to account for and bring order to the facts that had already accumulated.[82]

Yet if a move up the U-space towards abstraction and the creation of W3 objects is provisional, as Popper claims it is, and always subject to revision,[83] does this not undermine its presumed utility? Is it then appropriate to allow the diffusion of potentially fallible abstract knowledge into quadrant 3 where by dint of its scope it might cause extensive damage?

In science, where the problem is most acutely felt, the institutionalization of validation procedures is designed to minimize any diffusion either within or beyond the scientific community of faulty abstract knowledge. Scientific validation procedures themselves, however, whether sponsored by the transmitter of knowledge or by its recipient, often express a particular philosophical commitment, whether this be to realism, to operationalism, to epistemological anarchism, or to whatever 'ism' happens to be topical. Despite the confusion, the most robust validation procedure will remain the performance of abstract knowledge in W1.

Rounding off our discussion on the U-space we observe that the propensity to abstract and the propensity to diffuse, interact. If abstract knowledge, by dint of its greater utility, finds a wider potential audience than concrete knowledge, the increasing size of such an audience and its active involvement with the material being diffused itself offer greater opportunities for practice, repetition, inferential learning, and validation. The two movements out of quadrant 1, towards abstraction and diffusion, thus feed upon each other. It should not be assumed, however, as we have already seen, that there is a generalized tendency for all types of knowledge to move towards quadrant 3. The move along the abstract dimension is often blocked by the coding propensities or capacities of a given group or culture. Diffusion, in turn, may be retarded or brought to a halt by discontinuities in the social fabric.

Knowledge thus gets partitioned into what Schutz called 'finite provinces of meaning'.[84] What accumulates in quadrant 1 constitutes a source of social differentiation; what ends up in quadrant 3, by contrast, acts as a source of social integration. Within a given group, however, integration is often only brought at the price of its own differentiation from a larger one. Only by sustaining a continuous movement of knowledge towards the north-east region of the U-space, together with a steady accumulation of universal abstract knowledge therein, could one possibly talk of the emergence of a single, widely shared world view. Societies, no less than groups or individuals, adopt various configurations in the U-space, partly in response to forces set in motion by their own internal development. These forces create vast tidal movements of knowledge both within and across their boundaries whose ebbs and flows are continuously remoulding the cognitive maps of their members – those at least not landlocked by tradition.

Does the foregoing commit us to the view that all epistemological progress is ultimately illusory and that human knowledge is irreducibly contingent?[85] Or do the tidal movements of knowledge described above throw up geological formations over time that are more durable? If so, how durable? We discuss this next.

3.7: RELATIVISM

The language of participants versus the language of observers

Husserl maintained that the techniques of the natural sciences could not apply to social acts. Social acts involve meaning and meaning can only be grasped intersubjectively as 'lived experiences'.[86] Intentional acts, according to Husserl, cannot yield purely abstract and objective knowledge; and, given the need for context in the decipherment of meaning, nor can they be communicated to those who do not share a common base of experience. In other words, an inability to share meanings, whether due to a lack of common codes, common backgrounds, or common values, prevents or retards the flow of knowledge from quadrant 1 into quadrant 3.

Anthropology acknowledges the problem of meaning in the distinction it draws between *emic* and *etic* description (see section 3.2). With the first, a native informant is made the judge of descriptive adequacy: a given set of observations and conclusions will be considered valid if they are acceptable within his community. Etic description, on the other hand, places the power to arbitrate on descriptive adequacy with an external observer. A native narrative then becomes just another object of description. At issue is whether the descriptive terms employed by the external observer are those that other outsiders, placed in similar circumstances, would have used.

The problem of meaning, of grasping context, is believed to create an epistemological bias in the social sciences in favour of quadrant 1, of the concrete and the local, or in Windelband's terms, away from the nomothetic and towards the idiographic.[87] At stake is the possibility of moving out of quadrant 1 without incurring unacceptable information losses. A shift into quadrants 2 or 4 decontextualizes knowledge and robs it of meaning. The belief that the natural sciences are free from this bias is due to a widespread assumption that unlike the social sciences, the natural sciences deal exclusively in universal codes and etic descriptions.

The cultural anthropologist Edward Hall has questioned the value of the emic/etic distinction by claiming that it is not possible to describe a culture solely from the inside or solely from the outside. As an alternative, he grades communication possibilities according to how far a common context can be shared between participants themselves on the one hand, and between observers and participants on the other. He cites the language used between airline pilots and control tower personnel as an example of what he calls highly contexted situational dialect. A shared knowledge of the operational situation by the actors allows them to use a language of great parsimony and low ambiguity in circumstances that are clearly defined and highly restricted.[88]

Like the East End children studied by the sociolinguist Basil Bernstein, airline pilots and control tower personnel communicate through a highly restricted code[89] which economizes on data transmission when communication resources – channel capacity, attention span, etc. – are scarce. Their language might be considered emic in so far as an external observer might have to master both their code and the context in which it is used in order to make sense of what he hears. Much of their discourse, however, derives its operational effectiveness by drawing upon technical knowledge and concepts located in quadrant 3, so that a familiarity with local circumstances will need to be complemented by a more abstract and universal non-local type of knowledge, as well as by some mastery of the etic codes which give access to such knowledge.

In the Husserlian perspective, the purely external observer of social acts is a figment of the positivistic imagination. A minimum dialogue is necessary if an observer is to gain access to his subject and 'a dialogue can be sustained only if both participants belonging to a community accept on the whole the same teaching and tradition for judging their own affirmations. A responsible encounter presupposes a common firmament of superior knowledge.'[90] In our daily commerce with others, we unconsciously assume an ongoing fit between our respective meanings, between our world and theirs. In the natural attitude, we take our world to be unproblematic. Where a problem does arise between us, the natural attitude may have to give way to the more conscious theoretical attitude, but this will then require a special effort on both our parts. We may have to cease assuming a 'common firmament of superior knowledge' and begin to depersonalize certain aspects of our relationship. Each of us may then become aware of the other as an object of study as well as a co-participant in an exchange and may consequently hold back from an unrestricted 'we-relation'. Pushed to extremes, however, such circumspection removes us from the communication nexus altogether and converts the newly objectified 'other' into a scientific specimen that yields only data rather than meaningful messages. The other, in effect, then becomes little more than a statistical input into a nomothetic generalization.

Competing codifications

A moment's reflection, however, will show that the need for a meaningful dialogue with the subject of an anthropological observation hardly suffices as an adequate basis for the distinction that Husserl wishes to draw between the social and the natural sciences. For does not the familiarization of, say, a young biologist with the abstract and etic codes that are the tools of his/her trade inevitably pass through a dialogue with peers, custodians of a particular scientific tradition that constitutes *their* 'common firmament of superior knowledge'? Is the universality claimed by scientific discourse so uncontaminated by traces of its origins, of the concrete and the local circumstances that shaped its codes and its subsequent trajectory in myriad individual E-spaces, that we can declare it wholly free of emic description?[91]

If the relativization of knowledge calls into question the concept of scientific progress as objectification – and we do not prejudge the issue here – then such questioning surely applies to the whole of science and not just to the social sciences alone. As an 'observer' the nuclear physicist is as 'social' as the field anthropologist so that the 'hard' sciences no less than the 'soft' ones deal in categories that are socially mediated. In both, encounters between individuals who do not share the same context become potential sources of cognitive discrepancy and faulty communication. Discrepancies that occur in everyday matters can usually be accommodated within an existing, epistemologically undemanding, symbolic universe. We do not consider them cognitively problematic and what we call our commonsense knowledge is sufficiently pliable, with a little stretching and pulling, to absorb them without hiccups. Yet every symbolic universe is incipiently problematic. Sooner or later one crosses domains of experience where its writ ceases to run. It is in these lawless territories that rival and possibly quite deviant symbolic schemes may emerge, and if these are adopted, objectivated, and then diffused within the social fabric, they may come to develop a life of their own and one day rise to challenge the established institutional order itself. Since socially well-tested and objectivated knowledge is designed to yield compelling propositions about reality, any radical alternative to the existing symbolic order appears in its early formative phases as a departure from reality, a deviation, in extreme cases possibly a depravity or an illness.[92] The social system will move to neutralize it either by downgrading its ontological status, by making a special effort to incorporate it in existing schemes, or by attacking it outright.

Where this happens, new knowledge may move up the U-space from quadrant 1 to quadrant 2 towards greater abstraction, but will then find itself blocked from diffusing into quadrant 3. It may have great potential utility and this for a large audience; yet if it is perceived as deviant this utility may never get exploited. Scientific methodologies do not do away with such blocking mechanisms. At best they make them less arbitrary by subjecting new abstract knowledge to more rigorous and rational testing procedures prior to diffusion than might otherwise be used. This has certainly helped to speed up the flow of new knowledge, although even in the most developed societies the filters that are erected between quadrants 2 and 3 are never wholly free of what Munz has termed 'social bonding'.[93]

Why does the emergence of a new abstract order constitute such a threat? And correlatively, why do existing practices, customs, habits, and perceptions display such inertia and resistance to change? Among the many possible ways of approaching these questions, a promising one seems to lie in examining more closely the nature of codification.

Every new act of codification involves both an affirmation and a negation. To allow alternative codifications of reality to coexist or to compete with each other is in effect to live under greater existential uncertainty or ambiguity and to accept a lower degree of ontological structure than many social systems can tolerate.[94] In the neurological language of Chapter 1 they seek to avoid the conflict-laden explorations of relaxation strategies in their social transformation processing activities, preferring to apply single shot algorithms wherever they can. The distribution of power, authority, wealth, and status to their members requires stable, well-structured, and unambiguous cosmologies for their legitimation. It is to protect a brittle cosmological order that some societies impose such strict controls on new codifications. And even in systems where new ideas flow more freely, their diffusion will still remain a slow process of overcoming entrenched *a priori* presumptions in favour of an existing order and of bringing about a reconfiguration of prevailing beliefs and motivations.[95]

Trajectories in the U-space

According to Kelly, 'social psychology must be a psychology of interpersonal understandings and not merely of common understandings'.[96] Can common knowledge emerge from interpersonal understanding or does it require common understanding as a precondition?

A person's or a group's cognitive assets can be distributed across the U-space and assessed for how far they are shareable with others semantically and pragmatically.[97] The south-west corner of the U-space speaks of a private, possibly idiosyncratic world that is in certain respects incommunicable; the north-east corner of an objective world that appears to be shareable with others unproblematically. The question of how objective and how far shareable turns upon the epistemological and social conditions which are imposed on any attempt to move out of the somewhat solipsistic universe of the south-west region. Common knowledge resides in the northeast corner of the U-space. Yet only if the individual trajectories that link it to the south-west corner are identical can we properly speak of common understanding.

A relativistic stance holds that any trajectory up the U-space towards greater abstraction is as good as any other since the criteria by which these moves are judged are socially determined and hence contingent.[98] Furthermore, the abstract constructions available to us once we reach the northeast region of the space are also socially conditioned; they are possibly constrained by W3 but it does not follow that they are descriptive of it. Unlike materialists, relativists do not argue that only W1 is real and that W3 is all epiphenomena; their claim is that real as it may be, W3 can never be objectively known and that given the socially contingent nature of moves up the U-space, no progress towards knowing it better is possible.

Realists such as Popper, by contrast, take the position that while W3 can indeed never be known completely, progress towards knowing it *better* remains possible. A movement towards greater abstraction therefore, providing that it has been rigorously corroborated through testing, is not just a cognitive convenience that saves on data processing – essentially the operationalist view – but is also epistemologically meaningful.[99] A trajectory through the U-space that leads upwards and to the right is then for realists a move towards a shared objective world.

The move does not, however, take place in a vacuum. Certain forms of social organizations and their underlying belief systems will speed up the movement towards the north-east region, while others will slow it down or block it altogether. In so far as the distribution of power in a society affects its choice of organizational forms and belief systems, it will play an important but not exclusive role in shaping the evolution of knowledge in individual U-spaces.[100] We explore the issue of power in the next section.

3.8: THE SOCIAL DISTRIBUTION OF POWER

Codification as intellectual leadership

According to Tarde, to be social is to imitate.[101] Pure invention, in contrast to imitation, requires a certain freedom from social pressures, a minimum ability to escape society. Recall, however, that an inventive codification is simultaneously an affirmation and a negation, an act of selection in which the state that is chosen or coded for gains an identity at the expense of the larger number of states that are consequently rejected. Where innovative coding involves a kind of social competition between alternative states, each being sponsored by a powerful individual or group, the successful diffusion of one will both stimulate and inhibit the production of rival states.[102] The publication of a patent, for example, may place control of the diffusion of new technical knowledge in the hands of its creator and thus inhibit its unrestrained use; yet by demonstrating that a given approach is feasible, a patent effectively invites competitors to abandon alternative approaches and to devote more resources to the challenge of 'inventing around' the new patent. Thus by reducing technical uncertainty in one area, a patent may create a growing network of affiliations and cognitive commitments – 'connection strengths' in neurological parlance – based on demonstrated feasibility.[103] Patenting, then, as an act of codification, pits the ability of originators to control the flow of new knowledge against the mimetic abilities of followers.

What is true of technology is also true of science. Yet in science the selective emphasis is perhaps placed more on abstraction than on codification as such, an emphasis that often leads us down a quite different diffusion path. A technology gains adherents through a concrete demonstration project covering a limited portion of reality within which it is shown to 'work'; a scientific theory, by contrast, gains popularity if it can be shown to explain more than competing alternatives. Both technology and science achieve their effects in W1, but in the case of an abstract scientific theory, a W3 product, the test is usually at best indirect, inconclusive, and always subject to revision.

Not only is the testing of a scientific theory more problematic than the testing of a new technology, but the stakes are often much higher. For in science what are sometimes pitted against each other are not alternative physical contrivances, each with its own specific performance parameters, but competing and at times incompatible world views with ramifications that extend into the social order as a whole. The usurpation of a Ptolemaic cosmology by a Copernican one, for example, or of the creationist view of nature by Darwinian natural selection, in each case ushered in social and religious transformations that extended far beyond the specific and limited hypotheses in which they originated. Yet the lack of any scientific test that would be accepted as conclusive by opponents of the new ideas meant that decades had to pass – indeed in the case of the Copernican hypothesis, nearly two centuries – before the social and intellectual conflicts they engendered finally abated.[104]

Invention versus innovation

The ability to reduce cognitive uncertainty through codification in a way that is acceptable to others is a creative act of leadership and a source of power that sets those located on the left of our diffusion scale apart from those located on the right.[105] The key term here is 'acceptable to others' since many individuals located on the left may be highly productive sources of new and original codifications which subsequently turn out to be too eccentric or deviant to diffuse beyond a small group of acolytes. These are often social marginals in the system, a creative humus from which may emerge the tender shoots of valuable new ideas.

One of the major achievements of the late nineteenth century and of the twentieth century as a whole has been to capture the creative potential of such people through organizational innovations such as the research and development laboratory which, in effect, decouple the process of generating new ideas from that of diffusing them or of exploiting them.[106] Recast in evolutionary terms, the process of generating variety was institutionally separated from the process of selecting from it. For this to occur, invention had to be clearly distinguished from innovation.[107] An invention describes the first instance of creative coding or abstraction whether it is to produce new scientific knowledge, a technical device, a new aesthetic trend, and so on. It invites but does not actually compel imitation. Innovation, on the other hand, covers the process of adopting an invention that has already taken place, the taking up and passing on of a new idea. The two terms interfuse, however, when the act of adoption requires an effort of adaptation that is itself inventive.[108] This is more likely to happen when the respective loci and contexts of invention and innovation are far removed from each other.[109]

Science and technology are not the only sources of innovation and new knowledge. If, as the saying goes, imitation is the sincerest form of flattery, it is often just as likely to target an innovative personality as new ideas or contrivances. Imitation is a form of submission to an exemplar. If the object of imitation is a person rather than a thing, then the act of submission amounts to a recognition of personal authority and prestige rather than a pursuit of material utility, narrowly construed. One tries to emulate people one respects and admires.[110]

Who is recognized as an opinion leader in a social grouping will have an important bearing on what new codification or inventions are likely to be selected for imitation and on who is then likely to be doing the imitating. As de Tocqueville noted, in an aristocratic society, the object of emulation is one's hierarchical superior; in a democracy, it is likely to be one's neighbour.[111] In both cases, the tendency will be to imitate those who are felt to be within reach. Where the authority and prestige of a group is threatened by uncontrolled imitation, however, it may be coercively restricted to members of the group alone. The Indian caste system provides examples of behaviours, clothes, and rituals which get appropriated by particular socio-economic groups and the diffusion of which subsequently becomes strictly regulated.[112] Social structure thus simultaneously influences the propensity to invent and to adopt and often prescribes the channels that link the one to the other.

The power of diffusers versus the power of adopters

The decision to adopt is sometimes a risky business, riskier perhaps at times than the act of creating itself which in most cases can be kept discreet if not actually covert.[113] Acts of adoption performed by an opinion leader constitute selection judgements on which he takes his reputation and his prestige. He gambles what Bourdieu refers to as his symbolic capital in return for followers, measuring his success by their number and quality.[114] Where the social order is conservative, that is to say where the prevailing cosmology promotes stability and tradition over evolution and change, the judgements of opinion leaders in matters of adoption will most likely be negative, as will be the perceived returns to innovation. In such cases, the established hierarchy of social prestige can block innovation and sometimes invention as well and may on occasions resort to coercion in order to do so.[115]

In sum, the diffusion or non-diffusion of knowledge is linked in important ways to the distribution of power in society. At times, established power relations actively favour innovative diffusion where this serves to reinforce the prestige and authority of a dominant group: the French language, for example, first gained its ascendancy through the influence of the French court in Paris; it then spread throughout the Ile de France during the Middle Ages, all competitors being relegated to the status of a *patois*.[116] In other circumstances, entrenched interests will be threatened by the spread of new ideas and will block them: the failure of Jesuit missionaries in sixteenth- and seventeenth-century China to successfully diffuse Christian doctrine was due in great measure to their inability to consolidate their power base at the Ming court in the teeth of opposition from the literati following the papal interdiction on the preaching of the new Copernican doctrine. Thus is the diffusion of certain types of knowledge promoted and the flow of competing alternatives restricted. All social systems have their information hoarders and their proselytizers; their respective effectiveness will depend on where they are placed in the system and on the institutional resources they command within it. It seems reasonable to assume, however, that power holders will seek to position themselves towards the left in the U-space, where not only will they be among the first to receive new knowledge when it emerges but also they will be well placed to control its subsequent diffusion to those placed to the right of them.

Gabriel Tarde was one of the first to link a social system's capacity for development to the power distribution within it.[117] An early exponent of what later came to be known as the Convergence Hypothesis, Tarde argued that the moral and aesthetic community towards which the individual orients his behaviour was continually growing and that the dynamics of imitation were increasingly pushing for the adoption of common habits, customs, etc. He put this down to the spread of rationality and the growing power of fashion to overcome the conservative forces of tradition. Tarde's vision of societal development – for a vision it was – can be interpreted in our U-space as a gradual shift of society's cognitive assets from quadrant 1, where knowledge is parochial and its diffusion is either limited by local circumstances or subjected to strict controls, and into quadrant 3; there knowledge has become universal and widely available throughout the social system. Invention and imitation help to accelerate this shift of cognitive assets in the U-space, a process which has reached its most advanced stage, many social observers argue, in western industrialized societies.

We shall discuss the Convergence Hypothesis further in Chapter 6. We end this section by noting that any shift of knowledge in the U-space of the kind hypothesized by Tarde has been much assisted by the development of institutions explicitly designed to bring it about. What might be the contribution of such institutions to the diffusion of knowledge? The phenomenon of institutionalization is given a full treatment in Chapter 5. In the next section we confine our attention to the information processing role of institutions.

3.9: INSTITUTIONS

Economizing on social exchange through institutions

The relationship between knowledge and its social base is a dialectical one;[118] that is, knowledge is at the same time a product of social change and a stimulus for it. But their interaction does not proceed smoothly. The move from one quadrant of the U-space to another is therefore a hesitant, fitful business with frequent pauses that may indicate the presence of zones of stability and inertia in the workings of the dialectic, zones in which novel abstractions either challenge the prevailing social order or are further consolidated and integrated into it.[119] If a lack of movement in the U-space points to conflicts and blockages rather than consolidation and integration, it may be due to a confrontation between incompatible cosmologies that hinders the effective metabolizing of both existing and new knowledge. Movement or the lack of it may be given a number of interpretations that we explore in the next chapter. Here we note that where integration and consolidation rather than conflict occur in a given region of the U-space, we may expect to find institutionalization processes at work, building on the recurrent cognitive and communicative practices of individuals or groups.[120] The codification and generalization of recurrent social processes both facilitate and are greatly facilitated by the existence of a stable institutional order. By economizing on information processing transmission and storage, institutions release social and cognitive energies that can be more profitably redirected towards non-programmed activities.

Institutionalization offers large-scale economies of mental and physical effort, but only by paying the price exacted by any act of codification or abstraction, namely, a suppression of competing formulations. Institutions are in effect W3 objects and share with other W3 objects a certain facticity that masks the epistemological fragility of their foundations. To survive at all, institutions need to build up a certain level of structural inertia which makes them resistant to change. They achieve their inertia by a subtle application of coercion to social behaviour. Effective socialization to the institutional order, however, often conceals the latter's essentially contingent nature, allowing coercive measures to be applied selectively and economically; even behaviour that appears to occur quite spontaneously will for the most part have been gently channelled through the appropriate institutional forms. Stability will prevail in those areas where the institutionally prescribed order can be taken for granted and no competing alternative is in sight that might rise up to challenge it. Social action is then at its most predictable and controllable. Social marginals, to be sure, those who by definition have the lowest stake in the established institutional order, may attempt to corrupt or disrupt it, but unless they either form a sizeable minority or can offer an appealing alternative to more centrally placed groups, their strivings will remain peripheral and fruitless.

Institutions can only be constructed from a set of shared assumptions or world views that are accessible to all the relevant actors. They do not emerge spontaneously within the body politic but from a gradual articulation of shared typification that is itself slowly built up by accretion. Institutions, then, represent a long-term collective investment designed to lower the information costs of social exchange – what institutional economists, more narrowly focused on economic processes, label *transaction costs*.[121]

From what has just been said, it will be apparent that in U-space terms effective institutions cannot really be quadrant 1 phenomena. They express universal aspirations and aim at a wide-ranging consensus. In effect, they may best be thought of as relay stations on any one of a number of imaginary paths that link quadrant 1 to quadrant 3. One might even hypothesize that the closer they are located to quadrant 1, the more institutions will express the exclusive perceptions, values, and interests of particular groups. Conversely, the greater their proximity to quadrant 3, the more they will reflect the broader concerns of society as a whole.

The distinction we are drawing here between particularistic and universalistic institutions can be traced back to Parsons.[122] Societies with a universalistic orientation are less likely to suffer the pressures of social bonding that slow down or arrest the flow of knowledge from quadrant 1 to quadrant 3. The degree of abstraction associated with universalism imposes a degree of impersonal discipline on institutional processes that mitigates somewhat the arbitrary exercise of power associated with social bonding.

Controlling knowledge flows: the institutional legitimation of the social order

Power in society is, among other things, power to define and impose upon others the critical socialization processes upon which institutional integration can subsequently be built and by means of which a description of reality compatible with the power holder's own interests can evolve. Power holders aspire to institutional positions in the U-space that allow them to filter and regulate the information flows that reach different groups. Through control of the mechanisms of abstraction and diffusion they are in a position to determine what shall flow out of quadrant 1 and into quadrants 2 and 4, and thence ultimately into quadrant 3. The potential social utility of new knowledge will often only effectively be exploited therefore where it turns out to be aligned with the personal utility of key power holders where this is expressed in specific institutional practices.[123]

Control of knowledge flows in the U-space by power holders can be maintained as long as groups offering competing alternative and possibly quite deviant cognitive schemes cannot dislodge them. The threat of such destabilizing intrusions explains why, in most societies, access to the control of knowledge flows is institutionally regulated. In a pluralist society, regulation may be less restrictive than in a totalitarian one and access to the control mechanisms may be made subject to competitive processes. Nevertheless, the flow of large volumes of socially useful knowledge will remain subject to the monopolistic influence of groups strategically located in the U-space. What then remains available for processing by individual E-spaces is inevitably affected.

Is the control of knowledge flows necessary to the stability of the social system itself? Or merely to the survival of power holders within it? Unbridled rivalry between competing definitions of social reality produces a fragmented social order and transient constellations of subjective realities and identities. All worlds are then seen as relative, including one's own. The feeling that 'anything goes' sooner or later leads to a crisis in the perceived legitimacy of the established institutional order. As Berger and Luckmann put it, 'all social order is precarious . . . all societies are constructions in the face of chaos'.[124]

Legitimation of the social order aims to keep such chaos at bay. Competing claims, however, by weakening the collectivity's commitment to any single legitimate construction, bring chaos one step closer – unless, that is, the competitive process itself can be regulated with reference to some stable meta-order. A stable meta-order is what science aspires to provide in the case of secular western societies, in spite of the fact that what is actually on offer – realism, operationalism, epistemological anarchism, etc. – is itself the product of a competitive process.

Can institutional control of knowledge flows ever be really effective? Power holders must reckon with the fact that any given distribution of knowledge within the social system depends on how far it has been codified and abstracted. Knowledge travels more easily when it has shed data and been compressed into codes and categories. A social system's core schemata, however, the key assumptions about the world that hold it together, are usually implicitly held and only partially articulated.[125] This sometimes produces a dilemma. In large, diverse groupings subject to a variety of socialization processes, social cohesiveness requires that core schemata be suitably structured for transmission to a wider audience. Recall, however, that both codification and abstraction are hazardous as they may bring to the surface latent conflicts between competing groups or inconsistencies that would remain undisturbed if left unformulated. Articulating core schemata, therefore, when tempered by the need to avoid social conflict or confusion, is likely to produce distorting oversimplifications in the form of easily remembered and uncontroversial institutional formulae. Cultural and intellectual impoverishment will then be the price paid for the pursuit of cohesiveness in societies that cannot metabolize the conflict between competing core schemata. Paradoxically, where these simplified formulae turn out to be amenable to empirical testing and refutation, the cohesiveness sought through them may be placed even further out of reach.[126] The recent disintegration of formerly communist societies offers eloquent testimony on this point.

The limits to institutionalization

The dilemma of institutionalization can be summarized thus: the more people that have successfully absorbed or been socialized to a system's core schemata and values, the less will its governance be experienced by them as an external imposition. Less coercion and fewer external controls will then be required, with a consequent reduction in the costs of social exchange. In face-to-face or primary groups, socialization can take place quite unconsciously so that both the system's core values and its related institutional order can remain implicit. But as groups get larger and more diverse, and as they become more spatially scattered, interpersonal bonds loosen and face-to-face relationships give way to more anonymous transactions. Then, the tacit component present in all social communication no longer diffuses smoothly or uniformly through the social fabric.[127] An uncodified residue gets left behind in any cultural transmission, imposing a margin of personal discretion on any effort at interpretation by a would-be recipient that he/she may not even be aware of. The most conformist individual is thus turned into something of an inventor regardless of how reluctant he/she may be to exercise this talent. Data loss is inherent in all transmission of information. It is indicative of entropic processes at work in the system.[128] Institutions, no less than physical processes, must reckon with the second law of thermodynamics.

3.10: THE ENTROPY OF SOCIAL PROCESSES

Entropy as a social loss of memory

Institutions are a battle against entropy, against forgetting and the consequent loss of organization. Through judicious acts of codification and abstraction they structure and store knowledge that has or is deemed to have order-preserving properties. In an effort to minimize entropy production, institutions are continuously constructing or reconstructing the social order by selectively moving knowledge up and across the U-space from quadrant 1 to quadrant 3.[129]

Codification acts to select what can be stored and preserved, abstraction to establish how widely and usefully it can then be applied as an ordering principle. Here we are mainly concerned with the storage properties of codes and hence with codification. In discussing codification, however, we must guard against oversimplifications such as, for example, equating writing with codified communication and speaking with uncodified communication just because the first seems to have a more durable substrate: paper. Ordinarily, writing does seem to involve a greater effort at codification than does speech, but not always. An after-dinner speech, for example, may be a far more formal affair, even when given from brief jottings on a piece of paper, than, say, the automatic writing of a surrealist like André Breton which might be totally impulsive. Or, to take a more telling example, an oral tradition is effectively an exercise in codification that does not involve the use of writing at all. Here, of course, the degree of codification can vary considerably from one tradition to the next, being a random transmission from group to group or from generation to generation in one instance, and a carefully regulated affair using special mnemonic devices and techniques in the other.

The channels available for transmission and the physical mechanisms available for the storage of information will favour particular types of code.

To take one example, the *quipu* is used in Peru as a mnemonic device.[130] It is a series of knotted cords of different colours and lengths, tied together and attached to the head-dress as a fringe. The Quipu can be read since colours, knots, lengths of string all have mnemonic significance. The line that divides a mnemonic device as an aid to human memory from an external store of knowledge as an alternative to human memory is not always a clear one. For this reason the transition from an oral to a written tradition may sometimes be imperceptible. The design of an everyday object as an act of codification, therefore, could serve to reinforce an oral or a written tradition equally well.[131]

If mnemonic devices are individual aids to reliability, some societies . maintain the reliability of their oral traditions by social means. When the Kuba, for example, want to recite a group testimony, they set up a *Kuum* or secret conclave where a spokesman is appointed and the testimony rehearsed so that all are in agreement with it before it is recited in public. More coercively, in Polynesia, ritual sanctions are brought to bear on the speaker if his performance is less than word perfect. In New Zealand, not so long ago, the slightest deviation from the tradition brought instant death to its reciter – a pretty drastic response, one might think, to the threat of entropy.[132]

The risks incurred by the individual narrator when public control of the tradition is so punitive are such that he/she will always cautiously be confined to a minimal version of it. Yet even in the absence of punishment, according to Vansina, 'A group testimony is always a minimum testimony.'[133] Thus once more and as always, codification, this time verbal, entails a loss of data and possibly of information as well. And where the degree of social control is weakened by the availability of several traditions that the individual narrators can draw upon, personality factors will enter into both their selection and their presentation. An element of personal discretion thus pervades any description of the event, eroding the rigour of the codification process itself as well as the durability of what is subsequently stored. Entropy then wins out.

Vansina has suggested that another way of maintaining the accuracy of oral traditions is to limit their diffusion by making them the property of special groups. They then become esoteric knowledge that others may possess but are not allowed to transmit. In Rwanda, for example, certain families are entrusted with the guardianship of selected traditions in exchange for social privileges. If they want to hold on to the privileges, the chosen families must prevent the traditions from becoming public property. The link between uncontrolled diffusion and entropy has clearly been grasped here: the custodians of the *Ubwiiru*, the dynastic code of Rwanda, are not allowed to publish it, particularly in the Rwanda language, for fear that it might be transmitted clandestinely with who knows what additions and omissions.[134]

We are now in possession of an insight important to our later discussions: one way to control the diffusion of knowledge in a social system is to make it appropriable, to endow it with property rights. By establishing either exclusive or ordered access to valued resources, property rights effectively reduce the social production of entropy.[135] Among Tobriand Islanders of the Pacific, a tradition can actually be bought. Thus a certain Chief Omarakana once gave food and objects of value to the descendants of a certain Tomakam in exchange for the dance, the song, and the commentary on it that they owned.[136] A more familiar example drawn from our own industrial societies is the technical licensing agreement in which proprietary knowledge and know-how, subject to certain restrictions, is made available to others on a selective basis in exchange for royalty payments. Note that in both instances *it is the act of codification itself which, by giving knowledge a visible structure, makes it appropriable and hence the object of a controlled diffusion.* In some societies, the state itself will exercise control over the codification and diffusion of knowledge – in its day the Inca state was no less rigorous in this respect than was the former Soviet Union before *perestroika*.[137] In others, control will be delegated to trusted groups, custodians of a social order in which they have a stake. Yet whatever the control mechanism, and however loosely or restrictively it is applied, the transmission of socially meaningful knowledge – of clans, of family histories, of science, and of schools of thought – is institutionalized in such a way as to maintain its socially perceived accuracy and authenticity. In short, it is institutionalized so as to minimize information losses or entropy.

Entropy as a loss of socially derived meaning

Oral traditions, as might be expected, do not rank very highly in terms of accuracy and authenticity, being placed somewhere between the eyewitness account and the rumour. They are cases of weak codifications, of information diffused in face-to-face situations within comparatively small groups – more often than not pre-literate. Given the small numbers involved and their spatial contiguity, however, the socially meaningful knowledge made available to an individual can quite easily be institutionally and hierarchically regulated. By contrast, where numbers are much bigger, and constant spatial proximity less likely, the individual becomes a recipient of knowledge that flows much more anonymously, that is readily available from a variety of sources, and that is therefore much less amenable to rigorous hierarchical control. Such knowledge may well have originated on the left-hand side of Figure 3.4, but as it spreads informally through a population it becomes prey to entropic processes that sap both its accuracy and its authenticity. Any individual located to the right on the diffusion scale of Figure 3.4 – i.e., a recipient rather than a transmitter – is thus bombarded with messages of uncertain provenance that compete for his attention while often contradicting each other.

In industrialized cultures, television advertising is the paradigm example of such messages. Consciously or otherwise, the individual copes with the resulting cognitive overload firstly by downgrading the status of each message received from this source and then by becoming more selective and deliberative in his responses. In short, the individual, faced with an incipient information chaos building up on the right of the diffusion scale, is led to impose her own organization on the data through successive acts of rational choice. If on the left of the scale, the validity and utility of transmitted messages can still be underwritten through the legitimate exercise of institutional power, on the right, the individual recipient has to assess these for himself. She will be gauging message utility against a personal utility function rather than one that has been institutionally imputed to her, and the validity of the message, given its uncertain provenance, will be established with reference to its internal consistency rather than to its origins.[138] Do we not have here an explanation for the greater rationality of fashion as observed by Tarde when he compared it to tradition?[139]

The exercise of individual rationality, as we have already seen, carries a price tag. The pluralistic competition that takes place between a variety of implicit cosmological orders or meaning systems is subversive of a single stable, taken-for-granted definition of reality. At a moderate level of intensity, such competition may in fact be highly adaptive and may facilitate the process of change and adjustment that characterizes peaceful social evolution. Beyond a certain point, however, and particularly when the framework of rules that govern the competitive process itself becomes a target for change, unbridled competition can result in a total loss of meaning, a state of normlessness that Durkheim termed *anomie*, and eventually in a collapse of the institutional order which such meaning underpinned.[140] The social system's capacity for assimilating and accommodating new knowledge[141] then becomes overwhelmed and the world ceases to make sense under any conceivable definition of the term. A frequently cited example of such a process at work is the sudden contact between either a primitive or a traditional society on the one hand, and a modern industrial society on the other. The large number of new and unfamiliar categories imposed by the latter often leads to a destabilization or an atrophying of the former,[142] especially where its world view is narrow and brittle.[143] The simple apodictic notions that are capable of regulating the daily flow of events in a primitive culture are rapidly submerged in the complex currents and whirlpools that shape an industrial one.

Atrophy is one possible outcome of such exposure to overwhelming change: a ready example is provided by the lethargic and aimless existence on offer today in the residual cultural spaces of an American Indian reservation. In societies that have undergone some evolution, but which have done so within a social order moulded by tradition, however, destabilization imported from outside will be fought and might provoke a backlash. Islamic fundamentalism – a search for simple original virtues through which to combat the evils of industrialism and pluralism – here readily comes to mind as a contemporary example.

What accounts for the institutional fragility of societies whose traditions have proved so resilient in the face of nature alone? Berger and Luckmann have argued that the hyperstable order of traditional society can lead to a form of reification in which 'the objectivated world loses its comprehensibility as a human enterprise and becomes fixated as a non-human, non-humanizable, inert facticity'.[144] Imperceptibly, the abstract world of institutions merges with the concrete world of nature to occult the mediating role of human consciousness; Popper's W2 and our E-space as a whole either are then lost from view or their existence is denied altogether. In effect, no distinction is allowed between Popper's W1 and his W3; reality is seamlessly one. Pluralistic competition, when it hits these societies, then tears away the institutional veil that has been so tightly drawn over things, to reveal the frail contingent nature of their core premises – a traumatic experience for any culture that lacks the psychic resources to adjust.

Fighting entropy through institutionalization

If entropy erodes a society's sense of ontological security,[145] institutionalization aims to restore it. The scope for stable institutionalization in a given society, however, ultimately depends both on how widely shared its relevance structures turn out to be and on whether these are sufficiently broadly defined – i.e., abstract – to accommodate variety and change in concrete instances. It is variety and change that stimulate the conscious search processes through which W2 is explicitly brought into play as a mediating agency between W1 and W3. Note, however, that sharing relevance structures goes beyond the simple sharing of knowledge; it entails in addition a common valuation of the knowledge base in areas where it matters. The particular social conditions under which the diffusion of knowledge effectively occurs must therefore be well understood.

In this section and the ones that have preceded it, we have emphasized that the potential utility of knowledge acts as a stimulus to its diffusion and its subsequent institutionalization. The diffusion knowledge itself thus acts as a powerful antidote to entropy increases within a system. Effective transmission for this purpose can be thought of as overcoming both level B and level C communication problems in Shannon's terminology – that is, ensuring that messages firstly convey their intended meaning and secondly lead to desirable patterns of behaviour. Stated otherwise, for effective communication to occur there must be some minimal alignment of individual E-spaces. The technical problems associated with information transmission itself, however – Shannon's level A – must not be neglected. Their resolution makes a crucial contribution to the successful diffusion of knowledge and hence to the process of social evolution. Shannon presented level A communication problems as being wholly independent of the other two levels, its own influence on them being unidirectional. Shannon was concerned with communicative efficiency: how best to transmit a message once it has been formulated. Yet one does not typically proceed by first formulating a message and *then* working out how to transmit it. Message formulation and transmission in most situations constitute a single project. Technical communication problems therefore can rarely be addressed in isolation as they are by the communications engineer, so that Shannon's three problem levels must be approached holistically. With that proviso we focus in the next section on some of the technical level issues raised by information sharing.

3.11: THE C-SPACE

Codification and diffusion: some propositions

One tenet basic to the theoretical perspective developed in this book is that the codification and diffusibility of information are systematically related. It is our contention that the relationship is a fundamental one – no less so than that which obtains between abstraction and diffusibility – with wide implications for both psychological and sociological processes. Although for expository purposes the diffusion properties of abstraction and codification have been treated separately, in practice, as was shown in Chapter 2, the ability to abstract and to codify are intimately related. Simplifying somewhat we might say that if abstraction as a cognitive strategy economizes on content, codification economizes on form. Economies of the one, sooner or later, lead to economies of the other.

Stated algebraically, our proposition is that:

$$D = f(C)$$

Our formula thus brings together the codification and the diffusion scales already discussed in earlier sections into an orthogonal relationship where D is the percentage of a given population of data processors that can be reached in a given unit of time with a particular message, and C is the degree of codification of a unit of length of that message, defined as the reciprocal of the number of bits of information required to transmit it. At the lower end point of the codification scale, for example, the number of bits required to transmit a unit message becomes infinite and we thus obtain:

$$C = \frac{1}{\infty} = 0$$

Here no conceivable structuring of the data is possible and not even scanning strategies can help; the data processing apparatus simply becomes overwhelmed by the sheer volume of data to be processed and data just runs off it. We are in the domain of the ineffable, of zero codification. At the other end point of the codification scale, by contrast, the information content of a given unit message can be captured by a single bit so that:

$$C = \frac{1}{1} = 1$$

No further coding of this particular message is possible: its data has been reduced to its theoretical minimum.

The function f is derived from the specific characteristics of the various communication elements that link the various members of the diffusion population into a complex communication system: the number of channels available between any two links, channel capacity, channel noise, the nature of transmitters and receivers available, etc. – in short, all the elements that make up a communication system as described by Shannon and Weaver[146] and that affect the choice of code and the time incurred by coding. The choice of system itself will reflect broader constraints such as the spatial distribution of the target population, the communication technologies available, their cost, and so on.[147]

A schematic description of the relationship between codification and diffusion is given in Figure 3.5.[148] Clearly, many different curves could be drawn to reflect a more realistic variety of communication situations and most probably few of them would be as smoothly drawn as the one shown. What they will all demonstrate, we nevertheless hypothesize, is that if abstraction and codification, working together, are the means available to us for overcoming constraints on *cognition*, then codification is also the activity

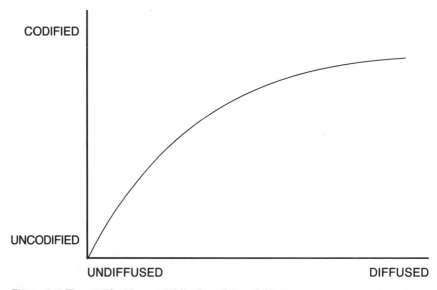

Figure 3.5 The codification and diffusion of knowledge

through which we overcome physical and energetic constraints imposed on acts of communication by dint of their occurrence in time and space. The extensive diffusion today of ever-greater volumes of codified data to ever-larger and more distant populations constitutes *prima facie* evidence in support of our claim.

Put thus, the proposition presented above has an almost embarrassing simplicity: knowledge that cannot be formalized in some way diffuses more slowly and less extensively than knowledge which can be. Such simplicity, as we shall presently see, is deceptive. To gain a more intuitive feel for the proposition's deeper meaning, let us start by dichotomizing our two dimensions as follows:

The codification dimension

1   Uncodified knowledge: knowledge that cannot be captured in writing or stored without losing the essentials of the experience it relates to – i.e., of the smile on your child's face; of a sunrise on Mount Taishan; of riding a bicycle; of playing a guitar; of a headache.
2   Codified knowledge: knowledge that can be stored or put down in writing without incurring undue losses of information – i.e., stock market prices; the Tudor Constitution; the chemical formula for benzene; a postal address.

The diffusion dimension

1   Undiffused knowledge: knowledge that stays locked inside one's head whether because it is hard to articulate or because one decides to keep it there – i.e., childhood memories; military secrets; sexual fantasies; skilled performance; a toothache.
2   Diffused knowledge: knowledge that is shared with others – i.e., the dates of historical events; a concert; a radio or television broadcast; Mae West's published biography; the law of contract; Boyle's law; a good laugh.

A typology of knowledge

We can intuitively assign the items of knowledge listed under each dimension to one of the four quadrants of Figure 3.6. Most entries will prove to be quite straightforward: the personal experience of a sunrise on Mount Taishan, for example, is both hard to codify *and* hard to share with those not present; knowledge of stock market prices on the other hand is at the same time easy to set down on paper and easy to diffuse. Some entries, however, will be more troublesome. What, for example, are we to make of a concert? It does not easily fit into a dichotomized structure. The *experience* of a concert might be

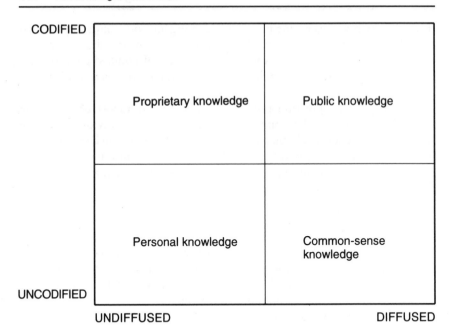

Figure 3.6 A typology of knowledge (2)

hard to codify and to share with those not present, but its *production* – i.e., following and responding to a written score – presents fewer problems in this respect and admits of a limited diffusion, albeit one that until the advent of broadcasting was spatially restricted to an audience sitting in an auditorium. If we make due allowance for the dangers of oversimplification, the result of this exercise is the fourfold classification of knowledge shown in Figure 3.6. Each category is now discussed in turn.

Public knowledge

Public knowledge is what most commonly passes as knowledge in society. It is structured, tested, recorded in textbooks, learned journals, and other publications.[149] Less loftily it may also appear as product information on beer cans or cornflakes packets, as television advertisements, as scandalous publications, and as railway timetables. In the case of scientific knowledge, gaining access to this quadrant for the purpose of diffusing new knowledge is subject to a certain number of restrictions, but once it is in there its diffusion is hard to control. As with other forms of public knowledge, people are free to take it or leave it, distort it, repackage it, add to it, and so on; it becomes a case of *caveat emptor*.

A key point about communication patterns in this quadrant is that where the communicating population is large, people often transact anonymously.

Transmitters and receivers may never meet, and even if the data they deal in is hard and codified, unless it has been *branded* in such a way that its source can be identified it will not be easy to authenticate. The branding of an item of public knowledge invests it with authority and improved its chances of adoption and hence of survival in the competitive marketplace.

Even where the diffusion of public knowledge involves face-to-face interaction it tends to be mostly impersonal. Few of the customers who buy their evening paper from a news-stand on the way home from work, for example, ever get beyond a brief verbal exchange with the vendor. Some prior familiarity with the paper itself and a knowledge of its price will usually suffice to keep the transaction brief and virtually silent.

Public knowledge by its very diffusibility is detachable from its origins and over time gains a certain facticity. It is, if anything, more attached to the coding procedures that gave it structure and form than to the situational context from which it emerged. Well-chosen codes bestow upon their data valuable powers of combination, allowing them to form novel patterns either on their own or by linking up with existing items of codified knowledge. In this way public knowledge slowly gets woven into a dense impermeable tissue of facts, categories, and concepts that may subsequently prove hard to modify – i.e., over time it acquires inertia.

Common-sense knowledge

Much less codified than public knowledge but no less widespread is common-sense knowledge. Common sense is acquired more slowly than specific items of codified knowledge and in a different way: public knowledge such as textbooks may provide the raw materials for its development but what gets internalized as common sense largely reflects a person's social situation and the power that others have in orienting what he learns about the world and how he makes sense of it. Common-sense knowledge thus has a more contingent feel to it than public knowledge. A person's stock of common sense is acquired gradually over a lifetime through an idiosyncratic distillation of personal learning experiences and face-to-face encounters that are initially confined to the family circle but that subsequently broaden out to cover peers and other members of the person's culture.[150] Common sense is context dependent and its exercise cannot be divorced from the social value and belief system that moulds the pattern of preferences with reference to which consistency of behaviour will be judged. What will appear self-evident to a family of Gansu subsistence farmers may leave a group of Wall Street stockbrokers scratching their heads. It is not, however, necessarily to indulge in cultural relativism to argue that although each may achieve a measure of internal consistency, some forms of common sense will prove more viable than others since there may exist superordinate grounds for preferring one value system to another. It may for example be able to handle a greater variety of contexts without loss of effectiveness or consistency.[151]

In dealing with common sense a dichotomized diffusion scale is somewhat misleading, since not only does this kind of knowledge diffuse inter-personally much more slowly than codified knowledge – this is in line with our main proposition – but because of this it also tends to spread only partially through a given population. Even within a single culture, therefore, subgroups will crystallize around implicit beliefs and value systems that may never diffuse much beyond their boundaries. The resulting discontinuities in the social structure will further limit the diffusion of what passes for common sense in different groups so that only those elements of it which are derivable from a culture's core values, and that are subscribed to by the population as a whole, will be widely shared.

Personal knowledge

Personal knowledge shares with common sense a diffuse and ambiguous quality but it is by nature much more idiosyncratic.[152] Both are hard to articulate and are usually communicated implicitly, often by force of example. Personal knowledge, however, even in face-to-face situations, is less accessible than common sense. It has almost by definition insufficient overlap with the experience of others – this also applies to the primary group – to create a shared context suitable for discourse. And with no shared context, personal knowledge cannot compensate for the absence of a shared code that would otherwise be needed for its transmission. Polanyi makes the point that personal knowledge is not necessarily subjective knowledge, arguing that 'the *personal* is neither subjective nor objective. In so far as the personal submits to requirements acknowledged by itself as independent of itself, it is not subjective; but in so far as it is an action guided by individual passions, it is not objective either. It transcends the disjunction between subjective and objective.'[153] Personal knowledge that gradually does diffuse towards the right-hand quadrants of Figure 3.6, and hence becomes shared, acquires a certain intersubjective validity and freedom from the purely subjective organization of the individual experience. It becomes 'objecti-vated' in the form of traditions, skills, recipes for conduct, etc.,[154] and might subsequently become the common possession of a group or society. Of course, none of this transmission need occur at an explicit level, at least in its early stages. As diffusion extends over larger reaches of space and time, however, some of the more recurrent features of a personal experience, now increasingly widely shared, may become candidates for some form of codification. Those that are not will remain ephemeral and are ultimately destined for extinction.

Proprietary knowledge

Where personal experience encounters discernible regularities in the flux of events that impinge upon it, stable patterns may emerge from it and generalizations may suggest themselves. We described this in Chapter 2 as a process of codification and abstraction that moves an individual through her E-space and makes her experience increasingly intelligible and articulate.

Typically, in structuring the E-space thus, an individual will draw upon a repertoire of existing codes and concepts made available by her culture: the individual inherits ways of knowing that over time help to align her personal experiences with those of ancestors, contemporaries, and descendants and thus renders discourse possible. Situations may arise, however, in which the cultural repertoire of codes available to an individual fail her, denying or distorting personal experiences that are irreducibly real and in urgent need of interpretation. Through a process of trial and error, the individual may then be led to devise a personal coding scheme that helps to make sense of her situation, even if a chosen scheme socially isolates her and causes the individual to be branded as a deviant.[155]

Where the experience thus codified is totally idiosyncratic and unique, it will lack the degree of overlap necessary to make it relevant or interesting to contemporaries and will not justify any effort on their part at mastering the new code. The individual in possession of such a code has, in effect, created a private language for himself, one which may facilitate autocommunication but little else. Where some convergence exists between an individual's idiosyncratic experience and that of others, however, pressures may grow either to diffuse the newly articulated knowledge and codes, or to block their diffusion. Blocking will occur where receivers perceive them as a threat; it will also occur where transmitters deem them too valuable to just give away.

We shall call the structured knowledge that emerges from idiosyncratic coding processes 'proprietary knowledge': once codified it becomes in effect technically diffusible but while it continues to reside in a single mind it cannot easily be appropriated by others. Proprietary knowledge, of course, is not necessarily useful knowledge: the codes and solution devised by an individual to make sense of a unique situation may have little general application outside it or may turn out to be faulty or distorting – i.e., poorly formulated perceptual or conceptual hypotheses.

But where such knowledge does prove to be useful, however, it may now be traded and bargained over. Being as yet undiffused it has a degree of scarcity which when combined with its utility gives it *value*.[156] Diffusing it into the right-hand quadrants of Figure 3.6 erodes its scarcity and hence its value. Diffusion barriers will therefore often be erected by possessors of proprietary knowledge between the top left-hand and the top right-hand quadrants in order to slow down or prevent uncontrolled leakages of potentially valuable information.[157]

Applying the C-space concept

The codification and diffusion dimensions of Figure 3.5 create a space which allows us to explore the way that different types of information and knowledge are structured and shared within a given population. The structuring of knowledge expresses cognitive activities that take place in individual E-spaces, an interplay of abstraction and formalization that gets registered in the figure as one moves up the codification scale. Chapter 6 will develop the proposition that information structuring and sharing are the defining attributes of a cultural process. For this reason we propose to label the space of Figure 3.5 a *culture space* or a *C-space* for short.

A C-space can be used at many levels. In so far as an individual, for example, is a recipient of existing and available knowledge as well as a generator of new knowledge, he/she can be profiled in the C-space drawing on the typology presented in Figure 3.6. His cognitive assets might first be located in his personal E-space and then subsequently in a C-space where their scarcity value can be gauged by asking 'what does he know that others don't know?' 'Others', of course, need specifying. This is done by defining the population to be placed on the diffusion scale – a village, the employees of a firm, customers, a nation-state, etc. Scarcity value is then measured with reference to this specific population.

Used thus, the E-, U-, and C-spaces combine into a single three-dimensional representation to give us the cognitive 'signature' of an individual, a small group, or a larger population, and point to the probable strategies they will respectively adopt in receiving, processing, and transmitting information. Strategies for the reception and processing of information were discussed in Chapter 2 under the heading of learning styles. We must now examine more closely the strategies available for the transmission of information.[158]

3.12: INFORMATION STRATEGIES

Sharing of codes versus sharing of context

Providing suitable communication channels were available, in theory any message, no matter how complex and consuming of data, could be technically transmitted between any two points aligned horizontally with each other in the C-space – i.e., operating at similar levels of codification. The time this would require, however, the degree of attentiveness it would impose on both senders and receivers, and above all the presence of noise all conspire to set practical limits on what can effectively be communicated. Intelligible communication is no free lunch.[159]

Since no absolute structural distinction can be drawn between noise and signal, the presence of noise in the C-space is problematic. According to

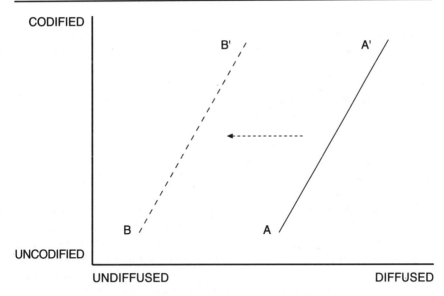

Figure 3.7 The effect of noise on the diffusion curve

Moles, noise can be thought of as a signal that a sender does not want to transmit or that a receiver does not want to receive.[160] The respective *intentions* of senders and receivers can then act as guides to help us distinguish noise from information. Yet, in the lower part of the C-space, intentions may be quite ambiguous or vague; consequently, the presence of noise there will be proportionately more damaging to effective communication than in the upper part of the space. Moles argues that 'The only way to reduce noise, is to reduce the channel's capacity, the extent of the repertoire of elements that it can convey ... The choice of elements is reduced [and] we particularize, *a priori*, the nature of the signals which we want to amplify or receive ... What is gained in sensitivity is lost in the variety of elements ... We have derived a principle limiting the amount of information which can be received from the external world ... As a consequence, in order to increase sensitivity indefinitely, it is necessary to know more and more about the nature (frequency) of the message to be received.'[161]

Moles's prescription for dealing with noise – a reduction of channel capacity – leads us in two directions. The first is towards a greater degree of codification of messages passing through the channel in order to make more efficient use of the channel capacity that is left; this, of course, requires a prior *sharing of codes* between senders and receivers. The second holds the level of codification constant and leads instead towards a greater *prior sharing of context* between the communicating parties. In both instances the *a priori* knowledge shared by the parties must be increased. But whereas in the first case anonymity and distance can be maintained, the second entails a much greater degree of face-to-face involvement: the mutual adjustment and alignment of expectations that the sharing of context makes possible requires a high degree of co-presence. This, of course, limits the numbers that can be involved in a communicative exchange so that sometimes the best results are obtained by mixing the two approaches. The example given by Edward Hall of an airline pilot communicating with air traffic control (section 3.7) combines the sharing of codes with some sharing of context. For the latter to occur it is not necessary that every airline pilot develop a face-to-face relationship with every air traffic controller he will have to deal with; it is merely required that each group be socialized to the other's values and ways of thinking concerning those tasks on which they have to collaborate and get on to the same wavelength.

Noise shifts the diffusion curve of Figure 3.5 leftward from AA′ to BB′ as in Figure 3.7. Responding to noise by sharing codes or by sharing context has the effect of placing the receiver on different points of the now shifted curve. One can either increase the level of codification of a message and hold the size of a target audience constant, or one can reduce the size of a target audience so as to handle noise-related ambiguities interpersonally.

Increasing the level of a codification of a message entails a sacrifice at least of data and possibly also of information, both of which may lead to communicative distortions.[162] Nuances that were present in the sender's mind have to be expunged from the message in the interest of clarity and efficiency; subtleties evocative of latent or alternative possibilities are bracketed out; personalized qualitative elements that express authorship, style, and preference must now give way to more bland and neutral forms.

Yet holding the degree of codification constant also has its problems. The threat of message distortions and information losses imposes co-presence and thus limits the size of the audience which can participate in more ambiguous transactions. One of the great advantages of face-to-face communication is that it is multichannel and, where required, it can therefore selectively increase the level of redundancy in order to compensate for the presence of noise. The meaning carried by a tone of voice, for example, can be reinforced by the raising of an eyebrow or a hand. Whether harsh words are pronounced in earnest or merely in jest can usually be intuited from, say, the nature of the accompanying smile. Skilfully correlated signals, therefore, emanating from different sensory channels, can be used to amplify or attenuate the central message. This requires physical proximity, however, and even then it can never by itself eliminate the ambiguity that some irreducible lack of shared codes – behavioural as well as verbal – imposes upon all social exchange. There will always be a sense in which the sender 'knows' more than the receiver, retaining a 'tacit coefficient'[163] which he is unable to articulate no matter how much he may wish to. Indeed, Freudian theory holds that the sender himself never really 'knows' how much he knows, much of his knowledge being submerged within the depths of his unconscious, and hence beyond the reach of any degree of articulation. Thus the communicative act, in an absolute sense, is always incomplete, even when it is reflexive, and thus addressed to oneself.[164]

Branding as the creation of trust

Asymmetries in the knowledge held respectively by sender and receiver, whether they are intended or not, pose the problem of trust and expectations as a determinant of effective communications. Where the message is uncodified, trust has to reside in the quality of the personal relationship that binds the parties through shared values and expectations rather than in the intrinsic plausibility of the message or other features of the communicative situation – i.e., it resides in their ability to get attuned to each other, to get on to the same 'wavelength'. Trust, in short, reflects a prior investment in the communication nexus, undertaken to counter the anticipated presence of noise in the channel and to speed up the pace at which ambiguous or uncertain (i.e., uncodified) messages can be transmitted. Trust requires 'high context' in Hall's sense of the term;[165] it allows the use of a shorthand – a form of coding based on shared contextual knowledge – that reflects the parties' attunement to each other, what Giddens describes a mutual knowledge.[166]

Yet trust is also called for in dealing with more codified messages where these are anonymous. For what, after all, might be their provenance? And what degree of reliability can be placed upon them? Being well structured they may be quite unambiguous but still designed to mislead. Where a sender cannot be known to a receiver, it is the credibility of the channel itself that has to be built up. It then becomes the focus of trust-building efforts – let us call them *branding* efforts. Brands confer authorship, and hence identity, on messages that one might otherwise be led to disregard for want of trust. In the world of commerce, brands aim to shape consumer expectations in positive ways and to build up goodwill towards a message source.

In the world of commerce, however, brands authenticate messages that refer to a limited set of concrete goods or services, W1 objects that can be eventually sampled and experienced directly. Risks, although certainly present, are confined to specific members of the set. Any attempt to extend unduly the class of objects covered by a brand – known in the jargon of advertisers as 'brand stretching' – sooner or later weakens its credibility.[167]

W3 objects, on the other hand, abstractions that can find their way into myriad W1 situations, have much more potency. And being consumed indirectly – through the W1 objects they embed themselves in – they can be 'brand stretched' to a far greater extent than specific consumer products or services can be.[168] The potential audience for such W3 products is consequently much larger and is often in need of some protection against either fraudulent or questionable message sources and the damage that these can inflict. In the case of the most abstract W3 objects, the products of science, the responsibility for protecting the integrity of the 'brand' is entrusted to the scientific community as a whole; it regulates the diffusion of new knowledge produced by its members through institutionalized publication procedures that are designed to weed out unsustainable claims.[169]

IT and the extension of strategic options

To summarize thus far: prior investments, both in communicative relations between social actors and in a given communication infrastructure and its associated technologies, will give the diffusion curve schematically depicted in Figure 3.5 a specific shape that will reflect, in addition to such investments themselves, the characteristics of a target population such as its size, its spatiotemporal distribution, its coding and abstracting skills, and so on. Effective communication strategies will be those that take such characteristics into account when tailoring a given message's degree of codification and abstraction to the possibilities and expectations of the chosen audience.

Our strategic options in matters of communication are today constantly being extended and amplified by the evolution of new information and communication technologies. Certain uncodifiable qualities of face-to-face interactions, for instance, can now be diffused more widely through the spread of videoconferencing which thus confers on selected events an immediacy that in earlier times was totally unavailable outside the here-and-now. The effects of such developments should not be exaggerated, however:

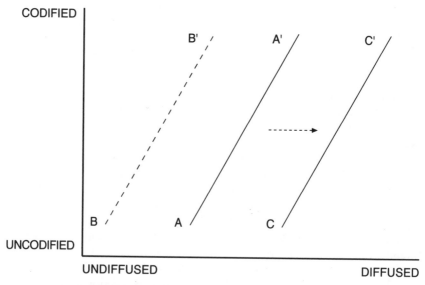

Figure 3.8 The effect of information technology on the diffusion curve

a televised concert and a live one are clearly not the same thing, and the prices that concert-goers are willing to pay to experience the latter directly bear witness to the difference.[170] Yet with ever-accelerating technical change, one could hypothesize a long-term shift of the diffusion curve towards the right in the C-space towards CC′ as depicted in Figure 3.8. The shift registers the ability of emergent telecommunication and computer technologies to handle ever-larger volumes of data, and hence, in many instances, also a diminishing need either for the communicative efficiencies offered by increases in codification[171] or for restrictions in audience size, each being in part a response to the presence of noise in the system. Figures 3.7 and 3.8 are in effect mirror images of each other. The leftward shift of the diffusion curve shown in Figure 3.7 amounts to a restriction on communicative options; the shift to the right in Figure 3.8, by contrast, amounts to an extension of communicative options.

The diffusion curve in the C-space, however, reflects little more than the *technical* characteristics of a communication system, an ability to overcome Shannon's level A problems at different levels of codification as measured by the number of people that can be reached. It describes the diffusibility of information rather than the level of diffusion actually achieved. It does not ask, for example, *how* a receiver came to share codes or contexts in common with a given sender. This is Shannon's level B problem – the semantic problem. It is a far from trivial problem, of course, since for meaning to be shared by communicating parties, not only must the same codes be learnt by each but they must also be given substantially the same referents; that is, they must be contextualized in a similar way. A lack of prior shared contexts, however, being symptomatic of the impersonal and codified communication nexus, makes it less likely that codes and referents will overlap to any great extent in any given exchange.

Restricted versus elaborated codes

In cases where the skilled use of a code promises access to knowledge with a high degree of utility, it will often justify an individual's prior investment in mastering the code – as for instance in technical or scientific training. Any differences in interpretation of a common pool of knowledge held by communicating parties are then brought into mutual alignment by coding conventions that facilitate the communication process. Yet in so far as a code's potential utility is tied to the degree of generality that it can achieve, the conventions that regulate its applications and its use in communication will crystallize in the north-east region of the E-space where knowledge is abstract as well as codified and can only be acquired by those willing to invest extensively in the appropriate type of theorizing.

But what is 'appropriate theorizing'? In highly codified and abstract fields of knowledge such as modern mathematics, for example, Shannon's technical-level problems present few challenges to effective transmission; yet those at the semantic level abound. If today no single mathematician is able to master more than a tiny fraction of the discipline's theoretical body of knowledge, how do mathematicians working in different subdisciplines with different symbolic codes and concepts ever manage to communicate?

In asking how different specializations communicate across conceptual and coding barriers, we are effectively invoking the distinction drawn by Bernstein between 'restricted' and 'elaborated' codes. For Bernstein a restricted code operates on the basis of a shared context and limited codification. The implicit nature of the code, and above all the requirements for a shared context, act to restrict the size of the linguistic community with which one is able to interact. This was the problem that confronted the working-class children that Bernstein studied. We would locate them in the south-east corner of the C-space. The more explicitly elaborated code that middle-class children were taught to use, on the other hand – these were also studied by Bernstein – placed them in effect higher up the C-space and thus served to extend the size of the linguistic community with which they could interact. An increase in codification here reduced the requirement for shared context.[172]

But does not the specialized mathematician also work with a restricted code, one that by its very abstraction and codification limits the number of people that have access to it? The mathematician incurs isolation by moving even further up the codification scale than Bernstein's middle-class children do. Viewed purely technically, the symbols he/she manipulates could in principle be transmitted faster and hence further in a given unit of time than anything verbally articulated by middle-class children anywhere – electronic networking, for example, can today link up scientific databases instantaneously on a global basis. Yet the investment in time and effort required to master the coding conventions used in different subfields of mathematics, given their high degree of abstraction, limits the number of people willing to master the code to a tiny fraction of those who could effectively be reached communicatively through it. It is in this sense that the code is 'restricted' and the restriction operates in a quite different way from what is described by Bernstein.[173]

The semantic curve

The mathematician has a communication problem at Shannon's level B, the semantic level. Figure 3.9 schematizes it as a semantic curve. The curve gives us the percentage of a given population potentially capable of understanding a given unit of message in a given unit of time. Here codification and diffusion are *inversely* related: the physical diffusibility of information as one moves up the space may still go on increasing but *effective* diffusion, taken in the sense of a message communicated, received, *and* understood, will actually reduce.

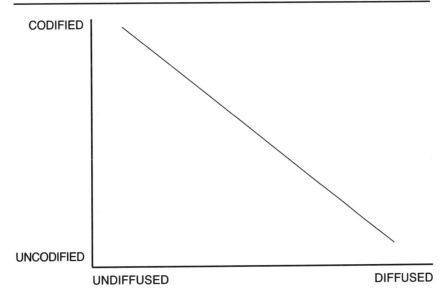

CODIFIED

UNCODIFIED

UNDIFFUSED   DIFFUSED

Figure 3.9 The semantic curve in the C-space

What accounts for this inverse relationship? Recall from Chapter 2 that abstraction is facilitated by codification and that they mutually reinforce each other. The relationship between them was depicted in Figure 2.5. Abstraction, however, as we have seen, can be performed in any number of ways and there is no assurance that what these will mean for different individuals can be brought into alignment unless it be by learnt coding conventions requiring time and effort to master. Our new semantic curve, now projected onto the U-space in Figure 3.10, also depicts an inverse relationship between the degree of abstraction of an item of knowledge and the size of the population that can master it. The curve strongly suggests that a negative utility or cost is incurred by individuals investing in abstract codes.

For anyone contemplating investment in the acquisition of abstract knowledge or coding skills, therefore, something must compensate him for the costs and effort involved. That something turns out to be whatever appropriable value is realized by the joint utility and scarcity of what is acquired. Utility gains are achieved firstly by moves towards abstraction on account of an increase in the generality of the knowledge thus obtained, and secondly by moves towards codification which give form and stability to such knowledge and render it manipulable. Scarcity, by contrast, is secured by the limited number of people willing to cognitively invest.

Many considerations dictate an individual's cognitive investment choices. Few abstract coding schemes, for example, can be acquired and used incrementally; they have to be mastered as a whole. One does not decide to learn only the first twelve letters of the alphabet just to see how things go;

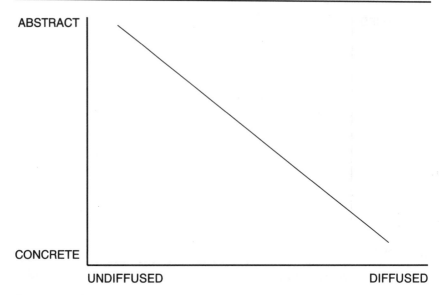

Figure 3.10 The semantic curve in the U-space

for the attainment of literacy, it is twenty-six letters or nothing. Many technical subjects likewise require the mastery of a whole corpus of codified knowledge for even a minimal proficiency in their use. Then there is the question of variations in individual aptitude. Our discussion of learning styles in Chapter 2 pointed to considerable individual differences in cognitive preferences and skills in handling abstraction. Any move towards it will clearly be experienced as more costly by some than by others. Finally, profitable opportunities for the exploitation of abstract codes, once mastered, are not evenly distributed across individuals. For every 'technical expert third class' working at the Berne Patent Office, for example, who makes it to the Princeton Institute of Advanced Studies – the case of Einstein – there will be countless dustmen and ticket collectors who will not think it particularly worth while to invest themselves in a mastery of the Kaluza–Klein theory or Fermi–Dirac statistics. The cost–benefit equation they face is stacked firmly against it.

Value in the U-space is the outcome of a tension created between the two curves A and B shown in Figure 3.11. The first, A, measures the utility of knowledge as a function of the number of people for which it has potential relevance – whether or not they are themselves capable of understanding such knowledge. The greater its degree of abstraction, the larger the number of situations in which a given item of knowledge will have potential utility. The second curve, B, is the semantic curve of Figure 3.10: it traces the increasing scarcity of knowledge as a function both of its degree of abstraction and of the risky prior investments in the mastery of codes it

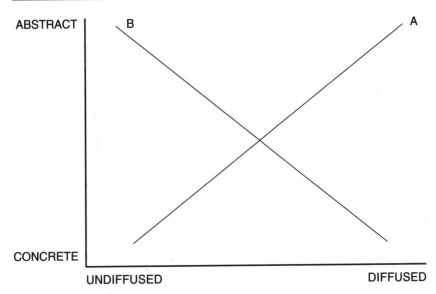

Figure 3.11 Value in the C-space

consequently requires. Curve A is a demand curve for knowledge, curve B a supply curve. The greater the horizontal gap between them, the higher the monopoly rents that can be extracted from the knowledge one possesses.

Information strategies in the data field

The three-dimensional integration of the E-, U-, and C-spaces shown in Figure 3.12 brings into focus forces that act upon human information processing and transmission activities. We can think of these forces as creating a *data field*,[174] a region in which an information-charged item of data exerts its influence and shapes the information environment that an individual confronts. The data field itself, however, forms part of the individual's *physical* environment. It consists of low-level energy which, being registered by the individual as data rather than mechanical energy, has the capacity of acting informationally. The data field is not static but evolves over time as a function of:

- the development of new codes assignable to different points along the codification dimension;
- the development of new communication infrastructures that increase the size of the audience reachable at different levels of codification across space and time;
- the size of the semantically competent audience created through investments in education;

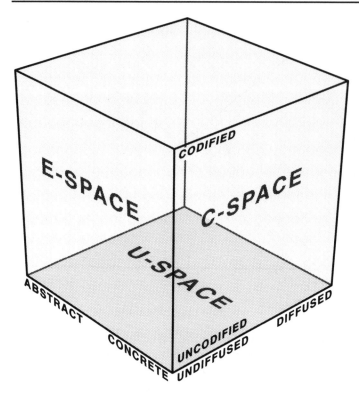

Figure 3.12 Integrating the E-, U-, and C-spaces

- the development of new abstract categories assignable to different points along the abstraction dimension;
- changes in the size of the audience for which an item of knowledge has potential relevance;
- the creation of barriers to communication, deliberately or otherwise.

An individual's life prospects turn on his ability to respond strategically to the opportunity and threats that operate in his information environment. He will need to develop an effective *information strategy*, one that creates value for him by making effective use of his location as a data recipient, processor, and transmitter in an evolving data field. This requires some knowledge of the dynamics that regulate the behaviour of the field and some sense of how to invest scarce data processing and communicative resources so as to harness the field's potential.

Since we are asserting that a grasp of the field's dynamic behaviour is a prerequisite for the elaboration of an effective information strategy, we make it the subject of the next chapter.

3.13: SUMMARY AND CONCLUSION

Four propositions

The main propositions derivable from this chapter will now be briefly presented and some of their implications touched upon.

1   The structuring and sharing of information are related: structuring, taken as any move through the E-space towards greater codification and abstraction, facilitates movement in both the U-space and the C-space and is in turn affected by these. The C-space relates both the diffusibility and the actual diffusion of information in a target population to how far it has been codified as well as to the prior mastery of codes; the diffusion and semantic curves respectively offer a graphic representation of Shannon's technical-and semantic-level communication problems. The U-space links the diffusion potential of information to its degree of abstraction, since together with codification, this affects the number of situations for which it has potential relevance or utility. It thus allows us to explore Shannon's pragmatic level communication problem.

2   Where abstraction calls for investments in specialized codes and coding conventions it becomes a source of information scarcity since fewer people will be, or perceive themselves to be, in a position to benefit from the cognitive investments required. Moves up the U-space towards greater abstraction simultaneously increase the utility of information and its scarcity. It achieves the first by increasing the size of the population for which it has potential relevance (whether this is consciously appreciated by this population or not); it brings about the second by increasing the size of the cognitive investment that has to be made and hence reducing the number of those willing to make it. Only when utility and scarcity are joined in this way does information actually acquire economic value.

3   The value of information is precarious and under a constant threat of erosion. Codification and abstraction simultaneously facilitate appropriability and diffusibility. It is this dual effect of information structuring that distinguishes its economic properties from those of physical goods. Unlike the latter, information goods cannot be spatiotemporally confined. Property rights in information, therefore, cannot enjoy the degree of institutional stability required for the effective operation of market equilibrating processes. The economic value of information must in some fundamental sense remain *indeterminate*.

4   The E-, U-, and C-spaces described in this and the previous chapter reveal the forces – resolvable into three dimensions – at work in the data field. The field evolves over time, creating and distributing new information and gradually eroding or eliminating old information.

Individuals create value for themselves by judiciously exploiting the forces at work in the field; for example, by generating abstract and hence potentially useful information and then by successfully keeping it local and scarce. But in doing so they incur costs measured in time and energy expended. An effective information strategy, then, is one that creates value while economizing on scarce cognitive and communicative resources. Such a strategy, however, to be effective, requires an understanding of how the field evolves over time and of how its dynamic behaviour can be exploited – the subject of the next chapter.

Implications

In one respect, the data field stands in a similar relationship to neoclassical economics as Maxwell's electromagnetic field a century ago stood in relation to Newtonian mechanics.[175] For Newton, space was empty, infinite, and timeless, a neutral medium in which the only reality was the encounter between pieces of inert matter regulated by the laws of celestial mechanics. In this space, continuity and equilibrium were taken as norms and change was perceived as a disturbance that had to be explained. James Clerk Maxwell, by injecting energy into empty space, imparted a structure and a dynamic to the latter that prepared the ground for the subsequent development both of the special and general theory of relativity and of the quantum theory. Suddenly it was stability and equilibrium that had to be explained, and change – increasingly of the evolutionary kind – that now constituted the norm.

Newtonian mechanics was not thereby done away with, far from it; but it was seen to explain less than it had hitherto claimed. Building upon Galileo's earthbound experiments with falling bodies it had retained an anthropocentric flavour that confined its cosmological possibilities to what could be intuited directly through the five senses. Maxwell's electromagnetic field, by contrast, was beyond the reach of naive sensory intuition; it thus represented a quantum leap in the degree of abstraction that would henceforth be expected in the thinking of physicists.

In coming to terms with data and information, economics is having to move along a path similar to the one taken by the physicists over a century ago. Neoclassical economists, however, set out on their journey with a particular handicap, since neither physical space nor historical time form any part of their discipline's paradigmatic core: economic activity is taken as occurring at a single point in space–time and for that reason neither evolution nor the differential distribution of information to spatiotemporally situated actors is registered as a problem: by assumption, information is ubiquitous. It follows, therefore, that while such information can have utility, not being scarce, it can have *no economic value*; it must therefore be considered to be what economists call a public good,[176] one whose consumption by one party does not increase its scarcity for other parties. Where information scarcity does occur – and economists are the first to recognize that in the real world, information scarcities abound and information does indeed have real value – it is either artificially engineered as in the patent system, or it is considered to be no more than a temporary hitch on the way to information ubiquity. The first case leads to a conceptualization of information as an object of exchange, the second to a conceptualization of information as a support for exchange. Clearly, information cannot be both at the same time. Only by restoring a spatiotemporal dimension to information processes can these conflicting conceptualizations be reconciled.

Historical space–time entered physics through the second law of thermodynamics and made its appearance in economics firstly in the writings of Marx and then later through the German Historical School, the Austrian School, and the Institutionalists.[177] Marx himself regarded information scarcity as nothing more than an artificial contrivance incapable of generating real value. Value creation was the task of labour conceived as a pure energy system. Information utilities might be embodied in labour – Marx was not about to deny that brains as well as brawn were necessary in the new industrial society – but they reflected the 'socially necessary labour time' required to produce a good and were decreed to be a common inheritance of mankind.[178] Pay differentials between skilled and unskilled labour were to be accounted for by the efforts expended by labour in acquiring specialized knowledge and information, not by the relative scarcity of those once acquired. Both the information embodied in past labour and that incorporated in new technology were by implication public goods made artificially appropriable by capitalistic property relations; they did not participate, therefore, in Marx's theorizing on historical time.

If Marx in the last century stressed the irreversible temporal aspects of economic processes,[179] the Austrians in the first half of this one also attended to the spatial ones. Friedrich Hayek in particular repeatedly emphasized that all economic knowledge is at bottom local knowledge and that any plausible explanation of economic coordination must reckon with this fact.[180] In the past three decades something close to a Pauline conversion has taken place in economics with respect to the role attributed to information in economic activity, professional interest focusing mainly on the way it gets distributed across economic agents,[181] on its evolutionary possibilities,[182] and on the institutional implications derivable from an information perspective.[183]

Nevertheless, a unitary view of information as both a sociological *and* a physical phenomenon is still lacking. Economists, for example, are often quite happy to conflate data, information, and knowledge in their theoretical discussions. Take Hayek in his discussion of the problems of knowledge in society:[184] he argues that all knowledge is local. We have to agree with him since knowledge is located in individual E-spaces. But are data and information local in the same way that knowledge is? And to the same extent? Does not Hayek's stress on methodological individualism, by keeping knowledge strictly local, in fact reveal a pre-Newtonian aversion to information-based action-at-a-distance and to the emergent properties of a data field as it moves towards greater abstraction and codification? And is not the consequence of this localism – in effect an epistemological predilection for the concrete over the abstract – that organization and self-organization must be treated as epiphenomenal, thus robbing the information perspective of its paradigmatic possibilities?[185]

This book develops the hypothesis that codification, abstraction, and diffusion have to be the constituent dimensions of an information economy: the E-space indicates how increases in mutually reinforcing codifications and abstractions save on data processing, and the C-space highlights the economies in transmission that can be achieved by increases in codification – whether this is supported by abstraction or not. Codification, the information-preserving act of shedding physical data, is common to both spaces. The U-space then allows one to relate the utilities gained through the greater abstraction and diffusibility of created knowledge to the cognitive and communicative investments these require in both the E- and the C-spaces – i.e., it establishes both the demand and supply conditions for knowledge. The information economy, foreshadowed in the information production function of Chapter 1, now emerges almost naturally from intelligent attempts to deal with the scarcities that condition our own human existence as finite energy and information processing systems bounded in space and time.

One of the most important propositions to emerge from the preceding chapters is that information has a physical basis: it originates in attempts to economize on the energy and time consumed by data processing and on its spatial transmission. In a fundamental sense, then, information must be considered a product of economic behaviour itself, whether consciously intended or not. The urge to economize on energy and space–time appears to be present in all living organisms and may even inhere in nature as a whole.[186] Learning systems, whether living or inert, are those which have the capacity to channel this urge to economize into the creation of new knowledge.

To claim a physical basis for information processes is not to push a reductionist thesis. Knowledge is not merely information, just as information is not merely data. The data field, as we have just hinted, displays a potential for self-organization that imparts to it an evolutionary dynamic. The next chapter examines this dynamic in greater detail.

Chapter 4

Dynamic behaviour
The social learning cycle

ABSTRACT

If we bring the E-space, the U-space, and the C-space together into a single, unified, three-dimensional representation, we obtain the I-space ('I' stands for 'information'). By examining how codification, abstraction, and diffusion interact to move information through the data field, we can see how new knowledge gradually builds up in a social system.

New knowledge can be described as a clockwise, cyclical movement in the I-space that can be decomposed into six distinct components:

1   Scanning – a leftward movement in the I-space through which data which is generally available and diffused crystallizes into singular and idiosyncratic patterns that then become the possession of individuals and small groups.
2   Problem-solving – an upward movement in the I-space through which these new patterns gain a definite form and contour.
3   Abstraction – a movement towards the back of the I-space through which the newly codified patterns extend their range of useful applications and gain in generality.
4   Diffusion – a rightward movement in the I-space that makes the newly created knowledge available to a larger population.
5   Absorption – a downward movement in the I-space by means of which the newly created knowledge is internalized through repeated use and becomes largely implicit.
6   Impacting – a movement towards the front of the I-space through which the new knowledge becomes embedded in concrete practices and physical artefacts.

Taken together, these six components create a *social learning cycle* (SLC). The first three steps of the SLC are value generating, the last three are value exploiting. Many SLCs are possible; they reflect the opportunities and constraints imposed by the distribution of prior cognitive investments in the I-space. An effective strategy in the I-space is one that extracts value from an SLC by successfully negotiating the constraints and opportunities that it encounters on its journey.

Economics has tended to focus on information diffusion at the expense of codification and abstraction. It has therefore been dealing more with effects than with causes and cannot convincingly relate information exchange to information production.

4.1: INTRODUCTION

The I-space

Our examination of codification, abstraction, and diffusion in the first three chapters points to further possible developments of the analysis.

Our newly created data field is structured by forces traceable in E-, U-, and C-spaces, – let us henceforth for the sake of convenience bring them together and treat them as a single three-dimensional entity that we can label the Information Space or *I-space* (see Figure 4.1) – forces that channel the flow of knowledge and its distribution in the field; forces, then, which by implication give the field its evolutionary orientation over time. The data field through which information processing agents have to navigate in order to survive is far from being an empty chamber reverberating with the random echoes of solitary utterances; it is rather a richly structured information plenum, built up dynamically from past accumulations of knowledge.

New acts of codification, abstraction, and diffusion trigger off data flows which have the same effects as the flow of mountain water on a river bed,

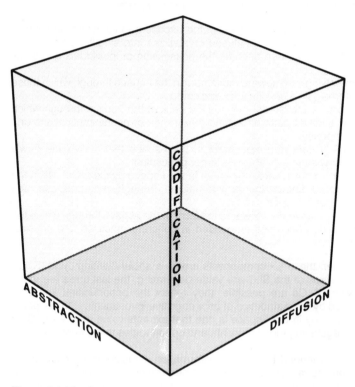

Figure 4.1 The I-space

dislodging particles here, silting up the channel there. Eddies may appear where the flows are turbulent and stagnant pools may form in pockets of calm elsewhere. By examining the interplay of forces that shape the data flow patterns in different parts of the field over time, one should gain a sense of how knowledge gradually builds up – or metamorphoses, if you will – in the brains of individual agents, in written records, and in the artefacts of a culture and in organizations, as well as of how long-term migrations of knowledge from one part of the field to another might occur. The analogy with the dynamics of plate tectonics and continental drift in geology is too inviting not to be mentioned in passing, but, alas, it will not take us much further than would any vivid metaphor. The self-organizing nature of data fields expressed through the metaphor of flows may be somewhat closer to what Rupert Sheldrake has termed *morphic fields*,[1] although here again, perhaps, too much should not be made of the similarity since our own use of the field concept differs in important ways from Sheldrake's.

In this chapter, we shall be solely concerned with those movements in the data field that lead to the emergence of new knowledge, and we shall use the I-space as a tool for the identification and analysis of such movements. We shall argue that knowledge-creating movements combine to produce a discernible pattern that distinguishes them from the myriad other kinds of data flow that also occur in the I-space. The hypothesis, as developed here, receives only a general formulation and is therefore not cast in a form that would make it easily refutable. As Duhem has argued, this is a characteristic of all general theories.[2] It is not, however, inherently untestable and it would take, I believe, only a little more work to derive from it a number of auxiliary theories and predictions which would themselves be refutable. Our purpose, however, is not to practise turnkey theorizing, in which a theory is delivered complete with conclusive empirical tests – an approach that works better with auxiliary than with general theories – but to sketch out a broad theoretical approach. If the sketch is judged sufficiently promising it will invite further articulation and, subsequently, empirical testing.

The structure of the chapter

The chapter is organized as follows. In the next three sections we re-examine in summary form the nature of the movements that can take place in the I-space along the three dimensions of codification (section 4.2), abstraction (section 4.3), and diffusion (section 4.4); in section 4.5 we briefly discuss the general character of knowledge flows in the data field as captured by the I-space and the grounds we have for believing in the specific flow patterns adopted by new knowledge as it emerges; sections 4.6 to 4.11 describe in more detail the trajectory followed by new knowledge in the I-space as it moves around the field, and section 4.12 examines the forces that power new knowledge through this trajectory. In section 4.13 we discuss the strategic behaviour of data processing agents who seek to exploit the dynamics of knowledge flows in the data field, and in the concluding section, 4.14, we once more assess the relevance of the chapter's findings for current economic thinking on information.

4.2: CODIFICATION

Cognitive filtering

A data processing agent is free to select any position along the codification dimension of the I-space for cognitive and communicative purposes and then to move from there in either direction along the dimension as circumstances and her personal preferences dictate, *always providing* that at each point so selected there exists both a coding repertoire on which she can draw, as well as a body of accumulated experience guiding the use of that repertoire – i.e., a coding convention. In other words, a prior stock of knowledge must exist at such points. Lower down the codification scale, the required knowledge will be less structured and the available codes more ambiguous and more prolific in their consumption of data. Further up the scale, the codes will offer more structure, less ambiguity, and more economy in their use of data. All this was established in Chapter 2 and needs no further elaboration here. At points on the scale where no suitable coding repertoires are available, cognition is problematic and no communication is possible. Two options then present themselves to a data processing agent: either to move to a point on the codification scale where a coding repertoire has already been created and to cogitate and communicate from there; or to invest in the creation of the necessary codes at that point. Pursuing the first option may lead to suboptimal cognitive or communication strategies if it entails a loss of valuable data – as will happen with premature codification – or a loss of data processing time and communicability if the codes available turn out to be unsuitable. Yet pursuing the second option may incur data processing costs that far outweigh the benefits on offer from a given cognitive or communication strategy. The movement of the agent up and down the codification scale, therefore, is by no means unfettered; it reflects the constraints imposed upon her by gaps in the pattern of prior cognitive investments – her own and those with whom she interacts.

Aristotle believed that the act of codifying was largely fettered, that the relationship between words and things was fixed and that the definition of a thing captured its essence. This was one variant of the doctrine of essentialism.[3] It effectively did away with our codification dimension altogether by collapsing it arbitrarily into a fixed point: that at which ordinary speech operates. Much contemporary philosophy has granted ordinary language a privileged role in mediating our access to the external world and has thus also implicitly downgraded the epistemological status of other locations along the codification dimension.[4] Language becomes the filter through which all created knowledge is required to pass and it occupies a specific region along the codification dimension. Knowledge may then subsequently spread itself along the codification dimension towards both greater and lesser degrees of structure; but valid knowledge, the kind of knowledge, for example, that is associated with the scientific enterprise and is granted institutional legitimacy, typically moves from a linguistic to a more highly codified formulation further up the codification dimension.[5]

I remain agnostic on the role of language acting as a primordial filter in the creation of knowledge. Fortunately what follows does not require me to take up a position on this matter. Our discussion of the E-space in Chapter 2, however, indicates that one filter at least is created by a data processing agent's cognitive style. This second filter, however, unlike the one that might be created by language alone, may be located at different points along the codification dimension, skewing the distribution of the agent's data process- ing efforts, favouring certain regions of the codification dimension rather than others and thus making his knowledge more or less useful or communicable to others. No point along the codification dimension, however, enjoys a privileged *epistemological* status by virtue of its degree of codification alone. Only when evolving knowledge has met other conditions, set by its parallel trajectories in the E- and C-spaces, will movement along the codification dimension towards greater codification be acknowledged as contributing to its epistemological status. Such movement entails a trans- formation of the vague into the structured, of hazy intuitions into verbal statements and, more demandingly, into numerical measures and perhaps even mathematical formulations. Each step in this transformation moves the stock of knowledge further up the vertical dimension of the I-space towards increasing codification. Each step up this dimension, however, also leaves behind a residue of more tacit knowledge that cannot be captured at the new level of coding. It cannot easily be shared and discussed and is somewhat refractory to the kind of testing that allows for generalization and abstrac- tion. This residue nevertheless forms part of our experienced reality – indeed the largest part – retaining its cognitive influence on us and silently exerting its own powers of selection on our data processing efforts as we move up the scale. As Polanyi puts it, 'Within any articulate system, there is present a personal component, inarticulate and passionate, which declares our stand- ard of values, drives us to fulfil them and judges our performance by these self-set standards.'[6]

The personal element in codification

Whatever degree of codification we attain, then, and perhaps particularly where we ourselves are participants in the act of code creation, a personal element, to some extent incommunicable, remains with us to become a source of individuation and differentiation in the skill with which the code is applied. Personal, no less than social, validation shapes our convictions and with these our sense of what is real.[7] It would therefore be premature, to say the least, to conclude that uncodified knowledge has no part to play in the epistemological validation of what moves up the codification dimension. After all, what else is a scientist drawing on when he or she claims to prefer one theory to another on grounds of elegance or aesthetics?

The move up a codification scale, of course, is by no means ineluctable and may be blocked for any number of reasons. For a start, the tacit hunches or intuitions that are required in the lower part of the scale to initiate an upward movement may be wholly absent or, if present, the belief that they can be further articulated may not itself be intensive enough to elicit the requisite data processing effort. Typically, in our waking moments, we are often prey to transient feelings of puzzlement, wonder, curiosity, anxiety, fear, hope, or desire. They pass through us without necessarily having engaged our attention and may thus have no perceptible effect on our motivations or behaviour.

Secondly, even where an upward movement towards greater codification is contemplated, it might be seen to carry risks and to be exceedingly costly in time and effort. Codifying means making consequential choices under conditions of uncertainty and possibly conflict, choices that can occasionally lead up a blind alley and sometimes to disaster.

To illustrate: should I, as an individual, take as given, i.e., as codified, current scientific pronouncements on greenhouse gases and global warming? Or more cautiously, should I wait a while longer and suspend judgement? After all, there is little consensus within the scientific establishment on whether the global temperature patterns observed amount to a trend or represent a statistical freak. There is even less consensus on the consequences of the trend if trend it be. What, for example, would be the consequences for our planet of a one-degree rise in the Earth's surface temperature? What would the consequences of a two-degree rise look like?

If I were temperamentally disposed to avoid feelings of uncertainty, I would feel compelled to decide for or against global warming whatever the quality of the evidence available to support my judgement, and to act accordingly. If I believed in the phenomenon, for example, I might then feel morally obliged to invest in the development of patterns of behaviour that would transform me into a good environmental citizen. I could, for instance, sell my car and commit my family and myself to the use of public transport. This in turn might require me to live close to the centre of town if the regional transport infrastructure proved to be inadequate. But since property prices in the large cities are now so high, I might be forced to settle for life in a smaller provincial city, and then to accept the limitations this places on my possible career choices.

Should I reject the scientific evidence in favour of the global warming hypothesis, on the other hand, say in circumstances where others accept it, I might be able to invest my savings in a nice beach house at a knock-down price that reflects the market's expectation of an eventual rise in the sea-level and coastal flooding. Either way, by codifying my beliefs and fixing them in action I am taking a gamble, and betting either my career or my savings. A refusal to decide, of course, also carries a cost, but in some indefinite future which may never come and which, therefore, could be heavily discounted. Who could blame me for feeling hesitant?

There is often a tendency to play down the element of risk and uncertainty involved in making choices in retrospective accounts of efforts at codification. The history of science, for instance, is often portrayed as little more than a long cumulative sequence of successful acts of selection each building on a base provided by its predecessors. It would be more accurately portrayed as a slow and painful search process up countless blind alleys in which frustration is the rule and successful codification (and for that matter abstraction) very much the exception[8] – at least in the early phases of scientific discovery: data processing risks and uncertainties are far greater in the lower regions of the codification scale where search processes originate than in the upper part where problems are better articulated and the area of search is necessarily more constricted. And it is such differences in the level of data processing risk involved at different points along the codification scale that help to distinguish what Kuhn has termed normal science from what he has called revolutionary science.[9] The first tends to be a much more structured and codified activity than the second.

Codification as a generator of conflict

Finally, codifying is conflict laden. To assert A is also to reject not-A and thus, by implication, to challenge or reject those – possibly including oneself – who have a stake in not-A as an outcome.[10] New knowledge is always to a degree a threat to the established order, to the stability of at least part of the old knowledge on which this order has been built up, and hence also to the ascendancy of those who have invested themselves in good faith in the continued validity of such knowledge. The Copernican Revolution is often taken as a paradigm example of the displacement of old codified knowledge by new codified knowledge, a displacement that had profound consequences for the social order. The Church of Rome, by committing itself to the defence of a geocentric world view, greatly weakened its hold on the minds of men when that view turned out to be scientifically untenable. Over three centuries later, Church teaching was again to be challenged by Darwin's theory of natural selection but this time its defence of its position was somewhat more circumspect. No evolutionist was burnt at the stake for heresy as Giordano Bruno was in 1600, or even threatened with it as was Galileo.[11]

Old knowledge is not necessarily invalidated by new knowledge; it may simply be rendered less useful or made peripheral in some way that diminishes its scope. The shift occurring today from mechanical to electronic technologies, for example, does not kill off the science of mechanics as such; but it does place it at a competitive disadvantage in attracting funds and talent for its future development. As an active force in the data field it begins to wane.[12]

The downward movement in the I-space

In the above we have associated the creation of new knowledge with an upward movement along the codification scale. But then what exactly are we to make of a downward movement? In what sense might already codified knowledge become uncodified? Wordless thought can be, and often is, founded on language.[13] Sapir, writing over sixty years ago, suggested that:

> The relation between language and experience is often misunderstood ... [it] actually defines experience for us by reason of its formal completeness and because of our unconscious projection of its implicit expectations into the field of experience ... language is much like a mathematical system which ... becomes elaborated into a self-contained conceptual system which previsages all possible experience in accordance with certain accepted formal limitations ... Categories such as number, gender, case, tense, mode, voice, 'aspect', and a host of others ... are not so much discovered in experience as imposed upon it.[14]

If this is true of language, is it not also likely to apply to other codes once these have also been mastered? A structure, in short, whether linguistic, mathematical, binary, or whatever, tends to exert a structuring influence on what is unstructured.

It appears, then, that causal influences on cognition do not all run one way and that codified and uncodified knowledge exert a reciprocal influence upon each other; that if some tacit component unconsciously acts as our guide in the differentiation and subsequent articulation of experience, the codes thereby created become the apparatus through which fresh and as yet uncodified experiences can be piped, filtered, and blended. Thus if a move up the codification scale serves to convert selected components of such experiences into unambiguous elements and relations, a downward move draws upon these in turn for the seeding of new patterns. Elements and relations thus get embedded in a wider context which, whilst itself remaining resistant to full codification, may nevertheless gradually gain in structure and intelligibility as a result. A downward movement reflects a mastery of codes and an ability to apply them, possibly unconsciously, within a variety of different situations. Compare for example the speed with which a skilled mechanic can diagnose an engine fault with the time it takes a novice, or the experienced accountant's ability to assess a firm's position from a quick glance at its balance sheet with the plodding analysis of a freshly minted MBA graduate. A downward movement initiates a process of internalization or absorption which, by restoring a certain primacy to the tacit dimension of knowing, releases conscious attention for further information processing. In effect, knowledge absorption economizes on data processing by providing ready-made templates for the handling of uncodified experiences. It thus often reduces the need for inefficient 'scanning' strategies.[15]

The value of habit

Code mastery, however, has two necessary if interrelated components. The first, which we have just discussed, consists in recognizing the range of circumstances or contexts in which the use of a given code is appropriate – i.e., the use of a given algebraic formula to calculate the tensile strength of a steel cable, of a particular type of drill to bore through masonry, of a specific choice of words in composing an after-dinner speech. Such a skill moves one down the scale when it gets exercised instinctively or intuitively. It is properly thought of as an interpretive or diagnostic skill. The second has to do with performance rather than diagnosis, with the proficiency with which a codified skill is applied, whatever the context. Here, knowledge absorption reflects a process of repetition and habituation – possibly preparing a move in the E-space towards greater abstraction – in which the rate of information yielded per unit of time in working with a code decreases as the binary logarithm of the number of repetitions.[16] Habituation and repetition diminish the overall originality of a message and hence the attention and the amount of conscious data processing it requires.

Within our own nervous system, for example, continuous stimulation results in a gradual reduction and then disappearance of neural activity. When I enter a room for the first time, I look around. In a few swift glances, my eye has taken in the main features – tables, chairs, walls, windows, etc. – that I need to categorize in order to move with confidence and purpose in the space. If I then proceed to sit down, these elements, now assigned to categories of varying degrees of abstraction, are consigned to the back of my mind, allowing me to attend to whatever might present itself as a priority item, perhaps a painting, a particular view, or a conversation. Very quickly the room and its objects will move out of focus to become mere background knowledge for me. And when out of focus they may all come to lose some of their sharpness, providing but a rough outline for the anchoring of perception and the stabilizing of context.

The 'chunking' of perceptions described in Chapter 2 in effect involves both an upward and downward movement along the codification scale, a kind of to-ing and fro-ing. In the upward movement an experience is differentiated and given some degree of structure following a conscious

174 The social learning cycle

effort at problem-solving. In the downward movement, a newly codified experience is consolidated and integrated into the perceiver's existing stock knowledge through a process of trial, error, correction, and repetition, much of which may be unconscious. It then acquires a penumbra of uncodified associations that reflect the variety of situations in which it might find applications and which cannot be derived from a knowledge of the code alone. These uncodified associations, however, may themselves get further structured if they can be coaxed once more up the codification scale.

To illustrate: both the chess master and the novice may be in possession of the codified knowledge that constitutes the basic rules of chess. But the chess master, unlike the novice, also carries in his head countless possible movement patterns allowed by these rules. Any particular distribution of the pieces on the chessboard can immediately be 'chunked' in ways that match one of these patterns and interpreted accordingly. Whereas the novice has to build up his understanding of a given distribution laboriously, piece by piece, the chess master draws upon a repertoire of what has now become uncodified knowledge built up by years of practice. Both are having to deal with uncodified data the complexity of which cannot remotely be captured by the rules of chess; that, after all, is what makes the game interesting. But whereas for want of a usable repertoire of patterns the novice has to scan the data,[17] the chess master can chunk it. The first stays put in the lower regions of the codification scale when confronted with complexity; the second moves nimbly up and down along it.

Blockages to absorption

Knowledge absorption, then, can be thought of as a form of 'learning by doing'. Like codification itself it is subject to blockages: it may, for example, be difficult or impossible to achieve a satisfactory fit between newly codified knowledge and the uncodified background knowledge that provides a context for its interpretation. In such a case the codes cannot be given any convincing meaning or interpretation. At times the problem is a cultural one as when, for example, agents from an industrializing country seek to acquire an advanced technology. Many technologies impose forms of social organization and thinking that may be quite at odds with those sanctioned by local values and belief. The result is frustration, underperformance, and sometimes outright rejection of such knowledge by the recipients. At other times the problem resides in the cognitive orientation of particular individuals. The scientific community's response to quantum theory in its early stages provides an interesting illustration of this second case, when even physicists of Einstein's stature, who had actively contributed to the theory's creation, found it almost impossible to incorporate its core propositions on indeterminism into their implicit but deterministic schemes.[18]

4.3: ABSTRACTION

How it differs from codification

Moves towards greater abstraction share one thing in common with moves towards greater codification: they both economize on data and its processing, and in so far as data processing has spatiotemporal and energetic attributes, they also economize on space–time and energy. Beyond that, codification and abstraction achieve their savings in very different ways. The first saves on data by giving a better definition to form, removing its fuzzy edges and allowing a sharper discrimination and focus. Abstraction saves on data by correlating features of the forms so defined on the basis of shared attributes, thus avoiding the need for independent description or treatment. Simplifying somewhat, we might say that codification reduces the complexity of forms whereas abstraction reduces the complexity of content. The first proceeds by *differentiation*, and allows us to enumerate finite sets of discrete elements; the second aims for *integration*, and brings elements so created into some limited and specifiable relationship with each other. In practice, of course, the two processes merge and are not easy to factor out. Abstract categories are drawn upon in guiding the way that we define things and so intimately participate in acts of codification, and the latter in turn provide the initial discriminations around which correlations and hence integration will subsequently be sought.

At this stage in our discussion, the alert reader might be asking himself whether there is any discernible difference between the kind of integration achieved by abstraction and that brought about by 'chunking' – i.e., by moving up and down the codification scale.

I would cite two. Firstly, abstraction builds up discrete correlations between individual phenomena whereas chunking builds up whole patterns or Gestalten. Patterns may indeed emerge from a clustering of correlated phenomena but need not do so. Alternatively, patterns may help to identify promising candidates for correlation but again not necessarily so. Secondly, the correlations established by abstraction move knowledge towards greater generality, and hence beyond the data in which they originate, whereas the patterns generated by chunking remain confined to the specific data being processed. To be sure, the pattern may be symbolic and hence quite abstract, but it can also be quite concrete and immediate.

Abstraction as reality versus abstraction as descriptive convenience

Abstraction constitutes a delocalization of knowledge in the data field, a construction of free-floating W3 objects that have no particular spatio-temporal habitat. Embedded in our minds, W3 has subjective reality and exists for us in a personal way that is mediated by our consciousness in W2.

Embedded in the world of physical objects, on the other hand, a world of forms, documents, and other observable phenomena, W3 acquires an objective reality, albeit one which is not always unambiguous or immediately accessible. As Popper points out, reality sometimes only manifests itself by 'kicking back',[19] and this it does in W1. This process of embedding, whether it occurs in W2 or in W1, endows W3 knowledge with a material substrate as well as spatiotemporal coordinates: it may be delocalized but it can only effectively propagate in space and time by respecting physical and social constraints on its transmission. We shall use the term *impacting* to describe the embedding of W3 objects in W2 or in W1.[20] It is a return movement along the abstraction dimension away from the abstract and back towards the concrete.

The move towards abstraction has a tentative, hypothetical character[21] and the data saved by the move may prove to be a false economy. Abstraction, like codification, offers choices between competing hypotheses not all of which are guaranteed to prove viable under rigorous testing. Reality, if properly solicited, may do us the favour of 'kicking back', thus handing down to us, sometimes quite violently, its oracular judgements on the viability of the competing candidates. Abstraction, also like codification, is therefore a conflict-laden activity. The passion and anguish it can sometimes provoke, however, suggests that something much deeper than data processing economies are at stake. Abstraction aims at achieving generality and therefore has to move beyond the realm of what can be readily apprehended through the senses or through simple perceptual categories. As it does so it becomes increasingly guided by the most basic and implicit assumptions that we make concerning the nature of reality, by the non-testable and founding propositions that help us to make sense of our experiences when concrete or perceptual knowledge no longer suffices for the task. In this new realm, reality may actually be quite sparing of its kicks and may maliciously decide to keep its own counsels, leaving us to grope our way forward as best we can.

We might label the founding propositions that act as our guide in the dark regions of W3 a cosmology or a metaphysic. Such a guide, however, sometimes turns dictator. Those who believe in the existence of an abstract reality, for example, will not be disposed to react in the same way to competing hypotheses as those who view abstractions as nothing more than a convenient symbolic shorthand for describing a concrete reality. The former believe in the independent existence of W3 objects, the latter do not. Imprisoned in incompatible founding propositions, realists and nominalists are led to develop incompatible world views.[22]

The power of uncodified abstraction

The move towards abstraction may or may not itself occur in a codified form. It is not a strict epistemological requirement that the move be formalized, although this may help. When objects of thought have definite contours they can be more readily grasped and manipulated, and rigid rules of transformation can then be developed and applied to them. Uncodified abstractions, by contrast, may be difficult to handle with any degree of precision and may not yield anything solid. Think of the intrinsic vagueness of terms such as truth, beauty, love, etc., and of the endless debate they provoke unless they can be clearly defined – i.e., codified – before being fed into a discussion. Yet have philosophers ever really succeeded in reaching a consensus on the definitions of such terms?

There is often a tendency to assume that all abstraction requires codification, that only language or formal symbol systems can possibly yield viable abstract objects. But is this not to confuse cognitive and epistemological viability? We may indeed be more *conscious* of abstractions performed at the linguistic level but that may only be because they are easier to stabilize and to hold in awareness. The point, however, does not argue against the epistemological or even the cognitive viability of uncodified abstraction as such. If anything, the empirical evidence points the other way, to the proposition that uncodified abstraction may well be for many a dominant form of thought.

We have discussed in the preceding chapter the possible role played in individual thinking by uncodified abstract entities such as Jung's archetypes.[23] A historian of science such as Holton and students of scientific creativity such as Arthur Miller, Pat Langley, and Herbert Simon similarly argue in favour of uncodified abstract objects when discussing the wellspring of scientific creativity.[24] Holton's investigations, for instance, show creative scientists to be guided in their thinking by themata that are universally shared even though scarcely articulated.[25] These play an important role in the early phases of a scientist's investigation when she disposes of few structured elements on which to build. Themata are then used as heuristic devices that consciously or unconsciously serve to limit the scientist's search of her problem space and hence contribute to keeping her data processing efforts manageable.[26]

Abstraction versus anthropomorphism

In our discussion of the E-space, it was argued that codified abstraction would prove more cognitively tractable than uncodified abstraction. What is codified might indeed be easier to manipulate than what is not, but blockages to abstraction will occur whatever the level of codification. Beyond simple linguistic categorization which allows us to deal with everyday objects, effective abstraction does not come easily. Perhaps the biggest obstacle we face in developing viable autonomous abstractions is our incorrigible anthropomorphism, a deeply rooted belief that W3 is in some fundamental sense isomorphic to W1, that the deities we create for ourselves are pleased to share our concrete circumstances, and that our microworld is but a shrunken version of the macroworld. We have a built-in disposition to believe that what you see is epistemologically what you get. What is mythology, after all, if not cosmological thinking at its most magnificently and poetically anthropocentric?

Twentieth-century physics could only progress when it managed to free itself from the limitations of concrete thought habits and started deriving its schemes directly from the properties of abstract codes or abstract themata themselves. Such cognitive freedom, however, has placed many physical concepts well beyond the reach of direct experience and intuition, a development which has alarmed physicists like David Bohm who fear a gradual loss of shared understanding and communicability within the scientific community itself.[27] Other sciences, such as biology, are today moving in the same direction as physics, albeit with somewhat less loss of visualizability.

Blockages to abstraction and impacting

Our abstractions, no matter how remote they be from our everyday experience, only ever become credible when, whether directly or indirectly, they offer some scope for testing in W1; when, that is, they offer reality an opportunity to 'kick back' , thus fulfilling Popper's falsifiability requirement. This return movement from W3 back to W1, however, which we have labelled impacting, is also subject to blockages. For one thing, there may not be any readily available path from W3 to W1 which would allow such impacting to take place. A totally abstract theory cannot be tested directly; it can only be tested through a set of auxiliary hypotheses that are derivable from it and that are closer to the world of direct and concrete experience.[28] If no auxiliary hypotheses can effectively be derived from a given abstract theory, or if these in turn prove to be refractory to any conceivable form of empirical testing, then the theory is doomed to remain a metaphysical and uncorroborated possibility. It may attract but it cannot command assent.

Another important source of blockage to the impacting and testing of abstract knowledge is its sacramental use for social bonding. Islam does not allow any concrete or pictorial representation of the Prophet, for example, and sixteenth-century European churchmen, it is said, did not deign to peer through Galileo's telescope lest it trouble their clear theological conception of the sublunary sphere. Yet even where concrete representation is allowed and social bonding is not an issue, an abstraction may remain too uncodified to allow anything other than an allegorical representation. Many nineteenth-century railway stations in France, for example, are barnacled with finely sculpted figures doing duty for prudence, industry, thrift, etc. In such cases, W3 will once more remain disconnected from W1 and its contents will be all the more vulnerable for it.

4.4: DIFFUSION

Communicative effectiveness

The position that an item of knowledge occupies on the vertical codification scale influences the ease with which it diffuses within a given population and hence the scope for information sharing. The distribution of knowledge along the codification scale indicates the nature of a society's communication problems; it also tells us something about the different communication technologies which various audiences horizontally distributed along the diffusion scale must deploy if they are to gain effective access to relevant information. To each position on the vertical scale will correspond one or more appropriate communication technologies capable of reaching a chosen target audience in a given time and at a given cost.

Whether the communication that does take place is effective in the sense of Shannon's level B or level C problems – respectively the semantic and the pragmatic levels – is another matter. If the knowledge to be diffused has generality, that is, scope for a wide variety of applications, the potential audience for it may be much larger than the one that is actually reached. The reason for the gap may be that generality has been achieved by moving towards greater abstraction, and towards codes that are not widely shared. In such cases, unless the codes are mastered by receivers willing to invest the required time and effort, the potential audience is likely to become a frustrated audience.

Of course, in interpreting this point, one must be cautious. Communicative effectiveness does not always consist in maximizing the size of the audience in receipt of a message. Esoteric codes, for example, are specifically designed to frustrate all but the most persevering of audiences. Such information hoarding behaviour is at its most visible in the context of technological innovation where esoteric technical codes are often developed as 'black boxes' and embedded in a matrix of more common codes that are widely available to users.

Individual versus collective knowing

The largest part of an individual's stock of concrete and abstract knowledge is not built up through vertical upward movements performed by himself alone on the codification scale – i.e., through personal problem-solving or structuring activities. It is acquired, more often than not, off the shelf through a process of social interaction, internalized by force of repetition, and gradually embedded into an individual's world view. English school-children will eat porridge for breakfast, go to church on Sundays, learn about equilateral triangles in class, and come to expect Christmas trees to appear in their and their chum's living rooms from mid-December onwards. These

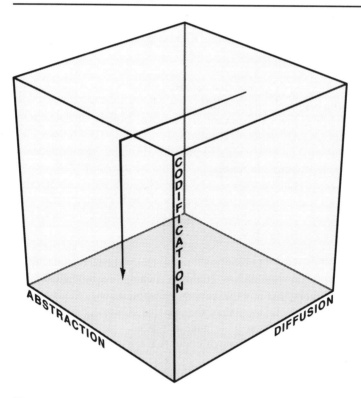

Figure 4.2 Individual learning by doing

events form part of a 6-year-old Anglo-Saxon's cognitive inheritance; it is acquired from others. In the Picardie region of France, farmers can tell from a glance at their fields whether the harvest will be a good one and when it will be the right political moment to start agitating for state or EC subsidies. It is a lifetime's concrete and intimate involvement with the land and local weather patterns that gives a farmer intuitive knowledge and 'feel' for the issues that must be dealt with. Yet if experience was nothing more than an isolated accumulation of individual trials and errors, the difference in productivity between a Sichuanese peasant and an American cornbelt farmer would have to be viewed as essentially a random phenomenon once differences in the quality of land and climate had been allowed for, explainable by purely personal factors such as intelligence, age, constitution, etc. The fact is that most of the farmer's knowledge, augmented as it may be by appropriate doses of personal experience, is socially inherited, whether directly through parents, teachers, friends, colleagues, or indirectly through textbooks, newspapers, or trade magazines. Such social learning is first and foremost a leftward horizontal scanning movement along the diffusion scale in which socially held knowledge is made available to individuals; it is then

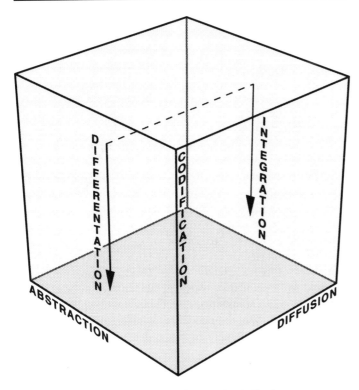

Figure 4.3 Differentiation versus integration in the I-space

followed by a downward movement in the I-space along the codification scale towards absorption, a process that reflects individual learning by doing (see Figure 4.2).

In its individual biographical articulation, social learning blends together a unique combination of skills, of practical and of personal knowledge not all of which can be shared with others; a society's accumulated stock of knowledge, therefore, always retains a substantial undiffusible private component that accumulates towards the left on the diffusion scale and in the lower uncodified regions. An individual scans for socially derived – and hence generally available – problems and solutions located towards the right on the diffusion scale but then gradually internalizes and often absorbs them in ways that make them idiosyncratically his/her own on the left.

In sum, if society's stock of knowledge becomes cognitively articulated by a move up the codification scale it also becomes socially differentiated first through a move leftward along the diffusion scale towards greater individu- ation and then downward towards individual absorption and internalization. By contrast, a move downward in the I-space that occurs towards the right along the diffusion scale is a move in the direction of both increasing cognitive and increasing social integration. Figure 4.3 depicts these two trajectories in the I-space; the abstraction dimension is not activated here.

Blockages to scanning and diffusion

Both scanning and diffusion movement along the diffusion scale are subject to blockages. Scanning in the lower part of the I-space, as we have already seen, is fraught with problems. Uncodified signals are ambiguous and vague and usually require considerable redundancy to overcome background noise effects.

Although the ability to detect improbable signals may be important for dealing with unusual situations, it is less likely to be developed in the lower regions of the I-space than in the upper ones. Where scanning is conducted through social exchange, for example, through casual conversation or the observation of others, the propensity to accept an improbable signal rests either on interpersonal familiarity or on an act of faith which presupposed that an acceptable level of trust already exists between communicating parties. Hence the need for a prior investment in face-to-face interaction or trust-building alternatives when transactions, or the information that underpins them, cannot be codified. Where uncodified scanning does not involve social exchange, the up-front investment in signal detection is, if anything, even greater.

Scanning one's physical and social environment for meaningful signals is an exercise in anticipation. Events that portend an experience of pleasure or of pain must be at least detected, and, if possible, predicted. Suitable responses must then be devised in the time allowed by circumstances between signal detection and what follows from it. Yet in most crucial respects the world remains opaque; where signals are weak or have to be teased out of the noise that enshrouds them, time is required for both detection and interpretation, and often in unpredictable quantities. Before we know it, therefore, the event is upon us. The uncodified realm is one in which events cannot be reliably construed, expectation cannot be realistically formulated, utilities cannot be accurately calculated. In this realm we quixotically charge at houseflies masquerading as monsters while blithely ignoring monsters that we take to be flies. Unless it is understood and properly handled, the cognitive disorientation that threatens can at times strike at our very capacity to survive as a race as two brief examples drawn from contemporary history will illustrate.

In the past sixty years two singular events have done much to shape American foreign policy and consequently recent world history as a whole. The first was the surprise attack on the US Pacific fleet by Japanese carrier-borne aircraft at Pearl Harbor on the morning of 7 December 1941, which triggered America's entry on the side of the democracies into the Second World War. The second was the Soviet attempt to place medium-range offensive missiles on the island of Cuba during the summer of 1962, a move which in October of that year produced the first nuclear confrontation between the superpowers and took the world to the very brink of a nuclear war. As scholarship has later shown,[29] both the attack on Pearl Harbor and the Cuba Missile Crisis could have been forestalled had they been detected early enough.

And they could have been. In each case, sufficient data on what was being planned was already available to the American intelligence community prior to the specific actions which triggered off the crisis; data, which if it had been properly *interpreted*, could have led to timely preventive action. The data, however, was circumstantial and ambiguous. Reasonable men could differ as to its meaning, so that time was needed to process it (i.e., to codify it) and to cast it into a pattern whose plausibility could command enough consensus among senior intelligence officers to justify recommending a swift and risky response.

In the case of Pearl Harbor, the time needed to extract a reliable signal from the mass of ambiguous data proved to be tragically insufficient.[30] In the case of the Cuba Missile Crisis, confirming data became available just before the missiles were to become fully operational and a nuclear catastrophe was only just averted by a mixture of military pressure, luck, and skilful diplomacy.

As one moves towards the upper part of the I-space, scanning gains in confidence and efficiency. Signals are better formed and the relationship between the sign and what it stands for becomes less tenuous. We might say that where uncodified information connotes, codified information denotes, whatever the object's degree of abstraction. In routine applications, therefore, scanning well-codified data, being less likely to lead to error, can often be performed semi-automatically or unconsciously. This facilitates chunking. Were that not so, our attention would be permanently in bondage to our immediate data processing needs and it would never acquire the freedom to explore the world beyond them. In effect, we would always be looking down at our feet to see where to place them next and never up at the horizon.

Positioning receivers on the diffusion scale

Blockages to diffusion are not all attributable to a lack of codification. They are sometimes associated with a message's degree of codification and abstraction – the very attributes designed to speed up diffusion. Our earlier discussion of the tacit component that inheres in all personalized knowledge has alerted us to the problems of diffusing uncodified knowledge. Yet, the further to the right we place a recipient with respect to knowledge emanating from the left of the diffusion scale, the more diluted and impoverished becomes the message she is likely to receive, however codified. It has either been purged of its idiosyncratic richness through the acts of codification that render it transmissible, or, if left uncodified, it has been transmitted slowly through interpersonal processes that have drowned large chunks of the message in noise. In the second instance, data losses are incurred for what Shannon labels technical reasons – his level A problems. In the first, however, blockages to diffusion may be due to semantic or pragmatic causes – Shannon's level B and C problems.

Recipients, for example, allocate a limited time budget to various message sources. What factors will direct their attention towards one source rather than another? What conscious or unconscious cost–benefit calculation drives their allocation decision? Few signals out of the total on offer will be deemed to justify great efforts of attention and reflection. It is an awareness of this fact that leads advertisers, to take one example, to package their offering in such speedily digestible form. Indeed, it is the very blandness of what passes for common sense and public knowledge that helps to make it so easily digestible – the fast food of epistemology, we might call it – and many consumers of such knowledge would not have it any other way. After all, for the most part, they have other things to attend to. Like blockages every-where, therefore, semantic and pragmatic blockages to the diffusion of information have to be dealt with by a process of thinning out and of dilution. Codification can only take us part of the way since even in a message that has been structured for effective transmission, further data filtering must often take place to align the message with the expectations and dispositions of the receiver. An important idea follows from this: the density of data contained in a message of unit length is likely to be at its highest in the south-west corner of the I-space at the concrete end of the abstraction dimension and at its lowest in the north-east corner at the abstract end of the abstraction dimension.

4.5: KNOWLEDGE CYCLES

Analysing data flows by means of the I-space

At any point in the data field, there are forces at work that act on the structure and distribution of knowledge moving it through the three constituent dimensions of the I-space that contains it. Each orthogonal component of these forces was described in sections 4.2, 4.3, and 4.4 above. Movement in the data field, then, must be thought of as the norm so that stable regions in the field become the exception rather than the rule. In consequence, what has to be accounted for is a lack of movement in the field rather than movement itself; equilibrium rather than disequilibrium.

Each point in the I-space can be considered to have orthogonal forces acting upon it as in Figure 4.4. Whether some part of the stock of knowledge becomes dislodged from a given location in the I-space and which direction it moves in turns on the balance of forces acting on it at that location as well

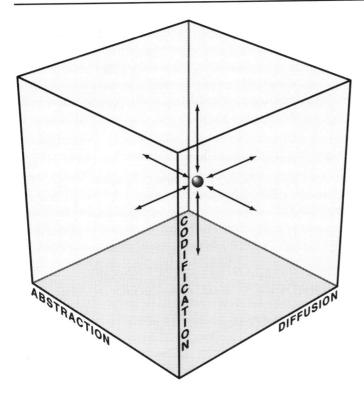

Figure 4.4 The forces acting at a point in the I-space

as on the presence or absence of barriers to movement, some of which will be presently discussed.

Any analogy that might be made between our field of forces and a physical field should not be pushed too far. We are trying to depict in an intelligible form something that is extremely elusive. If we were concerned with *data* alone, then the analogy with fields as they are thought of in physics – i.e., as the region in which a force is effective – would indeed be a close one; for data is a discrimination between physical or energetic states: black versus white, hot versus cold, large versus small, etc. And data is transmitted in physical space and time only in so far as physical entities that serve as its substrate can be projected from one spatiotemporal region to another, whether this be brought about by the movement of matter or by electromagnetic propagation.

To be sure, our whole theoretical edifice rests, in the final analysis, on the physical flow of data within the field, but that is not what we aim to represent in the I-space.[31] As the term implies, we are concerned with *information*, that extraction from the data the processing of which is characteristic of intelligent behaviour – i.e., it modifies those prior probability distributions that pass for expectations and accumulated knowledge among data processors. If we were accountants we would think of knowledge as a stock of usable assets distributed in the data field, and information as a flow of data that modifies the size and distribution of the stock. Knowledge, however, unlike tangible assets, is not an entity that can be easily observed empirically; we only come to sense its presence by tracking the flow of physical data in the field as it shows up in the I-space and by drawing the appropriate inferences.

New knowledge as a clockwise cyclical flow

For the most part, the patterns traced by data flows through the I-space will appear to be random, or at least not resolvable into a coherent scheme that we can readily apprehend. The forces that we have described will be pulling the data in all directions at once. Not much sense can then be made of what happens to it. But that may be in part because we are standing too close to the data and that our focus needs adjusting. After all, if you were to hover with your nose only two feet away from a pointillist painting by Seurat, you might also have problems seeing the wood for the carefully regimented blobs

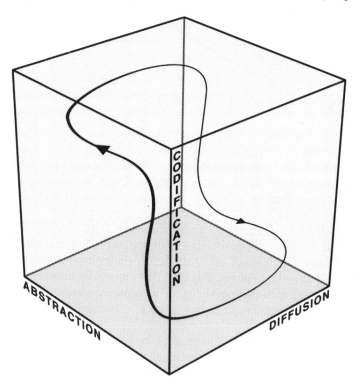

Figure 4.5 The social learning cycle (SLC) in the I-space

and splashes of variegated colours that populate his canvas. Should you then step back, however, a more ordered pattern of objects and settings would become discernible, one that suddenly emerges from the background noise of seemingly random elements. Recall the chunking process. Could it apply to the I-space?

To assess what is going on in the I-space and chunk it appropriately, some stepping back will also be necessary. The hypothesis that we shall now develop is that one of the patterns that may then become discernible is a three-dimensional cyclical flow of data progressing clockwise in the I-space as in Figure 4.5. It describes the creation, distribution, and absorption of *new* knowledge that can be extracted from what is currently available in the data field. The cycle, one of many that could be teased out of the innumerable patterns created by the complex flows of data in the field, could of course turn out to be a pure figment of our imagination and to have absolutely no basis in reality. But this is a character it shares with all abstract hypotheses until they can be properly tested. Since our whole enterprise in this book consists in articulating a series of linked hypotheses for testing, we cannot allow ourselves to be deterred by the hypothetical character of our chosen hypotheses. If it ceases to be hypothetical, it also ceases to be interesting.

Those who have followed the arguments of the preceding two chapters will of course already be aware of the hypothetical character of the cycle we are about to describe. We shall henceforth refer to it as the *social learning cycle*, or the SLC for short, reflecting the fact that the way that knowledge is created, distributed, and absorbed by a given population effectively expresses its learning processes. But what grounds do we have for imputing to social learning processes the cyclical configuration we have given in it Figure 4.5?

One answer to this question would be that the SLC is simply a statistical pattern, what one would gradually see emerging from the I-space if one were to study the trajectories of a sufficient number of cases of technological or social innovation or of scientific discovery. Its shape and direction would then be the product of a statistical inference based upon a suitable sample of observed cases. The cycle, then, becomes just a handy way of summarizing complex observation data.

But why should we accept one cycle configuration rather than another? To label the SLC a convenient descriptive shorthand hardly adds much to its explanatory power. Yet in hypothesizing that the SLC will follow the trajectory traced out in Figure 4.5 we need to give good reasons for thinking so. Only by providing such reasons can we justify directing the gaze of researchers towards what may in practice be extremely elusive and problematic observation data. Applying some of the insights gained in our discussion of the E-space, we are in effect claiming that the cycle is more than just an inductive generalization, a move from a set of concrete observations towards an abstraction that merely summarizes the data. It also embodies a theoretical element that has to be independently formulated and that in turn incorporates, albeit implicitly, the metaphysical assumptions that were discussed in Chapter 1.

The SLC expresses the battle against entropy

Recall that individuals strive to maximize the value created by their cognitive and communication effort and, in some undefined sense, to appropriate for themselves the returns on such value. We have taken value here to mean economic value in the narrow sense defined by Walras[32] when he described it as a combination of utility and scarcity.

Is there a location in the I-space where value, taken in this specific sense, is at a maximum? The answer is yes. Is there somewhere in the space where value is at a minimum? The answer is also yes. These two locations are shown in Figure 4.6, respectively as points of minimum and maximum entropy, or, if you will, of maximum and minimum structure. In the first location uncertainty is at its lowest and scarcity of information at its greatest; in the second uncertainty is at its highest and information scarcity is at its lowest.

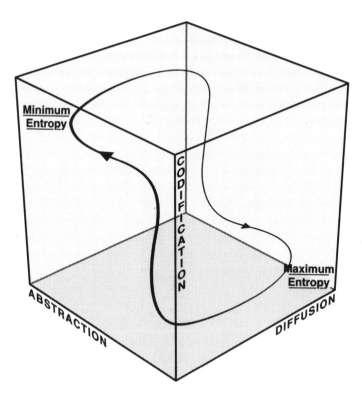

Figure 4.6 Entropy in the I-space

Associating the value and entropy concepts in this way highlights an important property of the SLC: the point of maximum value – or minimum entropy – of the cycle in the I-space is an inherently unstable one. It is subject to forces of diffusion and destructuring (absorption) that are constantly eroding whatever value has been created. These forces are nothing other than the expression of entropy at work. Over time, both the scarcity and the utility of structured knowledge are drained out of it as it drifts towards the pole of minimum value in the SLC. To reactivate the SLC and generate further value, new knowledge must be created and made scarce by moving it towards the north-west corner of the I-space. A physical analogy would be with the adiabatic compression phase of the Carnot cycle for a reversible heat engine except that here one is dealing with an information engine that extracts from data a capacity to do work measurable along the three dimensions of codification, abstraction, and diffusion.

The components of the SLC

The SLC of the information engine has two distinct phases, a value creation and a value extraction phase, each of which can be broken down into three sequential components, as shown in Table 4.1.

The cycle, subdivided into its different components, is shown in Figure 4.7. To prevent our discussion from becoming unwieldy on account of the terms used, we shall develop a simple notation to describe both the I-space itself and any movement through the SLC within it.

The field's three constituent dimensions of abstraction, codification, and diffusion will be referred to respectively by their initials given as capitals, i.e., A, C, D. If we wish to refer to the absence of abstraction, codification, or diffusion we shall put a bar over the letters thus, $\bar{A}$, $\bar{C}$, $\bar{D}$, so that the three letter pairs $\bar{A}A$, $\bar{C}C$, $\bar{D}D$ completely describe our I-space, albeit in a dichotomized form.

Table 4.1 SLC phases

Phase one – the creation of value: (1) Scanning; (2) Problem-solving; (3) Abstraction
Phase two – the exploitation of value: (1) Diffusion; (2) Absorption; (3) Impacting

---

Table 4.2 Components of the SLC phases

---

(1) Scanning: *s*; (2) problem-solving: *p*; (3) abstraction: *at*; (4) diffusion: *d*; (5) absorption: *ar*; (6) impacting: *i*

Note: A complete SLC then reads as *spatdari* with phase 1 being *s, p, at*, and phase 2 being *d, ar, i*

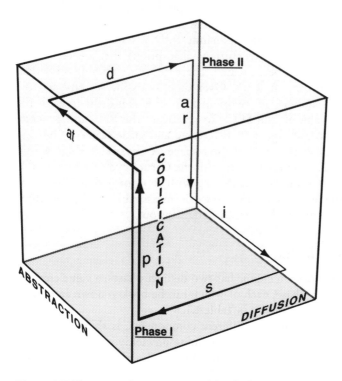

Figure 4.7 Phases and components of the SLC in the I-space

The six components that make up the two phases of the SLC will in turn be labelled as in Table 4.2.

We now discuss each component in more detail. In doing so we shall be covering territory already explored but from a somewhat different perspective.

4.6: SCANNING (*s*)

Meaningful stimuli as the violation of expectations

Any living creature will generally strive to organize its perceptual field, however rudimentary it might be, in such a way as to give priority to stimuli relevant to current needs and expections, pushing those that are not into the background.[33] Perceptual distortions may then result from the organism's general orientation as determined by its level of arousal, its drives, its fears, its hopes, and so on; dispositions labelled 'wishful thinking' when they become too disconnected from what reality has to offer – i.e., when they are observed in romantic adolescents or in Californian gold diggers. Nevertheless, perceptual distortions may continue to operate beyond the reach of consciousness as long as the actual outcome of events does them no violence. What possible harm could befall the ample Belize, for example, in Molière's *Ecole des Femmes*, for believing that every young man that she met was secretly in love with her? After all, the more ardently he might disavow such amorous sentiments the more he was admired by their object for his perfect discretion and his self-mastery. Perceptual distortions, however, are not always that benign, and in most cases a feeling of anomaly, that something is not quite right, sooner or later burrows through to consciousness. When that happens, as Bruner remarks, 'It is either a very sick organism, an overly motivated one, or one deprived of the opportunity to "try and check" which will not give up an expectancy in the face of a contradicting environment.'[34]

But how often are such anomalous feelings in fact experienced? Max Scheler was not the first to argue that a determining feature of the world we construct for ourselves as human beings or that is received from others in our culture is that it is *unquestionable*: a sedimentation of group experience that has passed the test and that needs no further scrutiny.[35] William James[36] also held that uncontradicted objects posit an absolute reality, an assertion that can be applied not only to the objects themselves but also to object relations. Yet such unquestionable experiences, while they may help to consolidate the existing stock of knowledge, in effect add little to it.

Only stimuli that violate expectations, that have a capacity to modify them, carry information and with it new knowledge. Can we say anything about the circumstances in which this is more likely to happen?

External stimuli, which assail us at every waking moment, generate a continuous stream of hypotheses to be tested, challenging the expectations we form as we go about our daily business, either helping to consolidate them or disconfirming them. Through a selective attention to such stimuli our environment is being continuously sampled. Extend the environment and you enlarge the population of stimuli from which the sample can be drawn. Where stimuli can be sampled from environments which are non-local to the data processing agent, they acquire an abstract quality; and the objects whose existence they posit can come to be thought of as abstract objects. Those that survive the hypothesis-testing stage and that violate no unquestionable expectation may then go on to become the building blocks of an abstract reality.

Perceptual recklessness

A failure to perceive anomalous or conflicting stimuli can arise from defects in the perceptual apparatus itself or from the circumstances in which such stimuli are registered. It can also arise when the organism is predisposed to categorize and structure them in a particular way in order to fit them to premature perceptual hypotheses. In such cases the data processing agent generates his/her own noise, indulging in a 'perceptual recklessness'[37] that masks important signals. Sometimes this occurs because the stakes involved are high and the agent is overly motivated, driven more by internal disposition than by the stimulus event itself. The event may then flow past, unregistered. Or, if a perceptual hypothesis crystallizes too early, after receiving only a minimal amount of confirmation, it subsequently acts as a barrier to the recognition or proper categorization of incongruous stimuli.[38] An extra hurdle then has to be negotiated: more information may then be required to *correct* a faulty perception than would have been needed to create a valid one in the first place. Cure, as always, is more costly than prevention.

Perceptual recklessness creates false data processing economies; the sample size of stimuli attended to is unjustifiably reduced. Whether those that remain in the sample have a predominantly local or non-local character will subsequently tell us something about the cognitive style of the agent and indicate his preferences for concrete or for abstract thinking, a preference that may further distort valid perceiving.

The difficulty of detecting novelty

An inability to perceive or construe events leads to anxiety. Things that mysteriously go bump in the night frighten us more than things that talk in the night. We need to make sense of our world and to do so we are usually ready to knock it about a bit in order to make it fit familiar categories, those that we feel comfortable with. For this reason, stimuli that threaten a fundamental restructuring of our categories – those that foreshadow the creation of fundamentally new knowledge – are often much harder to detect and interpret than those that call for only minor categorical adjustments.

Do we not find here, in the mechanism of perception itself, the distinction Kuhn has drawn between the requirements of normal science and those of revolutionary science, between the perceptual clarity associated with well-delineated puzzle-solving activities and the opacity and ambiguity that shroud the creation of new paradigms? Kuhn's[39] somewhat artificial subdivision of the history of science into normal and revolutionary periods has not gone unchallenged[40] and in many fields of endeavour normal and revolutionary phases will often overlap or run into each other. Yet whatever the validity of the Kuhnian distinction as a *historical* hypothesis, the perspective it opens up on the cognitive and perceptual conditions that accompany the emergence of fundamentally new knowledge has considerable value. If retained, it leads us to conjecture that the stimuli that provoke radically new knowledge creation will travel from right to left predominantly in the lower regions of the I-space, in the uncodified realm, where they are hard to categorize with any confidence. In the language of our new formalism such stimuli could in theory be located at any point along $\bar{C}C$, as it moves from

D to D̄, but where the knowledge created is basically new they are more likely to drift downward towards C̄.

The sources of scanning

But why, we might ask, does scanning shift information processing from right to left in the I-space? What exactly is the meaning of a move from D to D̄ in which knowledge which appeared to be diffused and hence available to all gradually becomes undiffused and the property of a single person or a small group? The answer to this puzzle requires us to keep in mind the distinction drawn earlier between data and information.[41] The data that triggers off the scanning process is generally available to a large number of people who mostly tend to construe it in broadly similar ways. Whether it is actually experienced as being anomalous when so diffused is less important than the fact that if it is in C̄ the experience cannot easily be given an unambiguous form or articulated. In fact only a few, located in D̄, might be capable of doing so and when they do they are likely to extract information from the data in novel or idiosyncratic ways.

How far towards the right of the diffusion dimension a stimulus triggering a scanning process will emerge will depend on the population under study. Yet in studying innovation processes, a correct specification of the diffusion population is problematic. There are those who argue that anomalous stimuli registered in D̄ effectively express the concerns and needs of the population at large and that the SLC as a whole is effectively market driven. Evidence in support of such a view has been presented by Jacob Schmookler in the case of technologically based knowledge.[42] Others, on the other hand, claim that novel stimuli emerge from the work and experiences of a much smaller community of specialists – scientists, technologists, or other experts – located much closer to D̄.

Two types of argument can be cited to support this second view and they are mutually reinforcing. The first rests on the specialized nature of the codes and on the uncodified knowledge that are is required to gain access to the relevant stimuli in the first instance: how many lay people, for example, ever get to use liquid phase epitaxy techniques or to operate a Plasma Millimetre-Wave reader? And of those who do how many are in a position intuitively to make any sense of the data that emanates from such instruments?

The second argument advanced is more sociological in nature. The triggering stimuli are as likely to be scanned through the informal face-to-face interactions that occur among members of a specialized community possessing the relevant codes as they are to emanate from inanimate physical objects. In the case of new scientific knowledge, it is held, the triggering stimuli are not mediated by data that is generally available to a larger community located in D, but by data emerging from specialized discourse already confined to networks of individuals or small groups in D̄.[43] The problems and opportunities these stimuli foreshadow are therefore those being experienced primarily in $\bar{D}$ and not those that may confront the wider community.

We are not required to choose between these competing perspectives on the scanning process. Providing that we hold on to the view that in both cases we are dealing with a leftward movement from D to $\bar{D}$ and that it is only the *extent* of the movement that is at issue we do not have to specify any specific source region from which anomalous knowledge-creating data originates. Scanning can be thought of as a stochastic process akin to a fluctuation in thermodynamics,[44] a way of bringing about a spatiotemporal concentration of the information required to transform a disordered into an ordered state. In D, it might be said, the information latent in the data is held in a less concentrated form than in $\bar{D}$ so that any leftward shift of this information into one or two minds capable of extracting it through the creation of novel patterns – let us call the resulting Gestalt a cognitive singularity – has a lower chance of occurrence the further along D the shift originates. This is hardly surprising since at D's extremity, particularly in $\bar{C}$ (the lower region of the C-space) we find ourselves in the region of maximum entropy, a region from which the emergence of ordered states is increasingly improbable. On the other hand, this diluted information is now lodged in a greater number of heads each capable of harbouring unique insight and hence of provoking a leftward movement along $\bar{D}D$. The chances of generating new patterns and with them valid knowledge from scanning efforts in D thus depend in part on the density of relevant data available in that region. A thermodynamicist might describe such data density as the region's free energy level.

Scanning and idiosyncratic perception

The crucial point to retain, however, is that the leftward movement of available stimuli in the I-space embeds them in increasingly idiosyncratic and unique perceptions. As raw data they may effectively be available to all; yet individuals will inevitably interpret them and act upon them in ways that reflect their different circumstances. 'The distinctive ability of a scientific discoverer', according to Polanyi, 'lies in the capacity to embark successfully on lines of enquiry which other minds, faced with the same opportunities would not have recognized or not have thought profitable. This is his originality. Originality entails a distinctively personal initiative and is invariably impassioned, sometimes to the point of obsessiveness.'[45] The history of science is not short of examples that illustrate Polanyi's point, one of the most popular ones being that of Sir Alexander Fleming's discovery of penicillin – he first labelled it 'mould juice' – following a chance observation of its antibacterial effects on staphylococcal colonies that had grown on a discarded culture plate.[46]

Inventiveness versus selectiveness

Note in parenthesis that the originality Polanyi refers to may express an inventive disposition, but not necessarily. The idiosyncratic view of the world that differentiates many creative minds from the rest is often a highly stable – not to say conservative – product of personal circumstances rather than any expression of a native ability to flutter like a butterfly from one promising Gestalt to another. Inventiveness is an adventurous but essentially detached exploration; it does not commit one's whole being to a particular way of seeing things to the extent that idiosyncratic perceptions slowly internalized and worked over a lifetime might. Figures like Copernicus, Kepler, or even Darwin were not inventive in the sense that they would lightly or non-committally explore a wide range of alternative formulations of their problem and its possible solutions – the favoured approach in brainstorming seminars. Their search was confined to the neighbourhood of what they knew, and it was what they knew, or, perhaps more importantly, how they came to know it, that made them distinctive and separated them from more common mortals.[47] Inventiveness, taken on its own, typifies the creative advertiser more than it does the creative scientist. Where it occurs in science, in fact, it may well play a secondary role, expanding in a controlled way the range of alternatives from which judicious selection subsequently has to be made. Indeed, if selection is codification, a move towards C, then inventiveness is a move *away* from codification and towards $\bar{C}$. If, as we shall see in the next section, problem-solving is both about generating possible alternatives and about making promising selections, it must entail, in effect, a sequence of movements up and down $\bar{C}C$. Making promising selections, however, is a large part of what creativity is about, and such selections, when effective, *eliminate* alternatives, thereby increasing the overall level of codification of a problem situation. If effective scanning is about generating novel patterns to be explored, effective problem-solving brings about a gradual move up the $\bar{C}C$ scale of selected patterns so generated. Novel patterns may be produced either by inventive individuals or by individuals eccentrically located with respect to patterns currently in use within a given community. In either case they will find themselves located towards the left in the I-space.

4.7: PROBLEM-SOLVING (*p*)

Problem-solving as assimilation and accommodation

Jean Piaget has characterized the learning process as one in which the organism comes to terms with his environment through a process of assimilation and accommodation.[48]

Assimilation involves filtering a given experience through one or more provisional interpretative schemes available along $\bar{C}C$ and, consciously or unconsciously, moving it up or down the scale until a good 'fit' is established between the experience to be processed and the cognitive structure available for doing so. The term 'fit' of course could mean many things, none of which can be explored here. We shall simply take it as referring to the maximum speed at which incoming data can be processed whilst remaining free from blockages of the kind identified by Claude Shannon in his discussion of different levels of communication problems,[49] namely, those of a technical, semantic, or pragmatic nature. Unproblematic assimilation favours routine problem-solving: the smooth and speedy assignment of experiences to pre-extant categories.

Accommodation, by contrast, calls for a modification of the interpretative schemes themselves when they either get blocked in ways described by Shannon, or for some other reason can no longer perform their cognitive filtering function. Accommodation can then be considered a form of non-routine or creative activity which involves a reinterpretation of experience. It can be achieved either through the extension of an existing coding repertoire or through the creation of new codes. Both approaches trigger an upward movement along $\bar{C}C$, which, if it occurs in $\bar{D}$, is likely to be idiosyncratic in nature. It is from this upward movement on the left-hand side of the C-space that new knowledge emerges, gaining in articulation in the initial stages of the upward thrust in one or two minds only, but with increasing codification spreading outward to reach an ever-expanding population of contemporaries and descendants.

Scientific discovery as problem-solving

Both Simon[50] and Laudan[51] have presented the process of scientific discovery as a special case of problem-solving. In Simon's case the reduction of the first to the second aims to demystify, to show that scientific discovery, far from operating in the inaccessible realms of divine inspiration, shares with problem-solving a rational foundation which makes it analytically tractable. According to Simon, any being of average intelligence in possession of the right information and training is capable of codifying solutions to the kinds of problems posed in science. Rationality, then, broadly conceived, rather than divine inspiration or ineffable genius, drives p, the upward movement along $\bar{C}C$.[52]

I interpret these authors as arguing that it is more likely to be differences with respect to s in the SLC than differences with respect to p that account for what passes for scientific creativity. How do such differences arise? Langley and his colleagues[53] explain differences in s as arising, among other things, from constraints on search: very few scientists are so free from distractions or the pressures of professional obligations that they can devote to a given problem the time required for an adequate exploration of the problem space. Were they able to devote more time to search, many more of them would stumble on to the same discovery at the same time. The established rarity of simultaneous discoveries on this view – i.e., of the calculus by Newton and Leibnitz independently of each other; of the principles of natural selection by Darwin and Wallace – is evidence not so much for the singularity of creative genius as for the constraints on problem-solving activity imposed on intelligent data processing agents operating in D.

Note that little in the argument put forward by Langley and his co-workers in favour of s as a determinant of creativity contradicts what we have said about it. The insights and understanding developed in $\bar{D}$ with respect to issues and problems experienced either at D or at different points along $\bar{D}D$ may indeed be unique, but not so much on account of the extraordinary intellectual powers of those to whom such insights are given as because individual circumstances have allowed them to invest time and effort in s and as a result they have been able to slowly build up the information differential that justifies their assignment to $\bar{D}$. The only modification to our own presentation of s that might be called for by their arguments would be in the probability processes that describe the leftward thrust $\bar{D}D$. The latter would now no longer be purely random as we have implied but would become partly a function of a prior investment of individual time and effort – such a modification would clearly favour what has been labelled an internalist's account of scientific discovery, one in which s is confined to $\bar{D}$ rather than acting as a bridge between D and $\bar{D}$, and by implication one in which the signals attended to originate within a small community of specialists.[54]

Showing that problem-solving capacity of the kind used in scientific discovery is widely distributed – i.e., that under suitable circumstances p could take place in D thus cutting short the leftward movement of s before the SLC turns upward – does not in itself demystify it. For it remains a possibility that we could all be divinely inspired. It has to be shown in addition that problem-solving activity is sufficiently rational as to leave little explanatory scope for inspiration and other intangible personal qualities that might serve to distinguish between individuals similarly endowed with information and the computational skills required to process it. At this point the Langley *et al.* programme to 'rationalize' the process of scientific discovery becomes vulnerable to a number of objections, only one of which need be dealt with here.

Heuristic problem-solving

Early efforts at codification – i.e., those located predominantly in $\bar{C}$ – are, as Langley would be the first to agree, *heuristic* in nature; that is to say, they take the form of rules of thumb that are incapable of rational justification. When does one resort to the use of heuristics? Either when the size of the problem is unknown or when it is known to be so large that systematic search becomes computationally inefficient or impossible.[55] In $\bar{C}$, the abundance of data makes the use of heuristics inevitable. There, systematic search is a poor cognitive investment. Rationality in the use of heuristics, according to Langley and his co-workers, consists in selecting those that are believed likely to yield the best result.[56]

But how, in effect, is such a selection to be justified if not itself on rational grounds? This is not the strategy adopted by Langley *et al.* They appear to adopt the 'reasonable man in English law' type of justification: the choice of heuristic becomes justified if other scientists in possession of the same information would have been led to adopt it. They demonstrate the power of their approach by feeding that information to a computer program already in possession of a repertoire of heuristics and watching it derive a number of scientific laws therefrom. Yet all they have effectively succeeded in showing is that much scientific discovery is further up $\bar{C}C$ than might be supposed, closer to puzzle-solving than to paradigm creation. It leaves the problem of dealing with $\bar{C}$ essentially untouched. Moreover, to argue that a choice of heuristic becomes reasonable if other scientists in possession of similar data would have selected it moves us towards relativism, not towards rationality in any sense intended by Langley or by Simon. In $\bar{C}$, an inventor or discoverer initiates a search process that is highly personal in style and quite uncertain in its outcome. The more personal the search process, the more likely it is to be autonomous and located in $\bar{D}$, free of the pressures or the collective rationality of groups or communities located in D.

Algorithmic problem-solving

Cognitive strategies in $\bar{C}$ differ in important ways from those available in C. A heuristic, for example, as Simon himself points out, must be distinguished from an *algorithm* which is a mechanical search process in C and possibly in D that offers a guaranteed outcome. An architect, for example, playing around with spaces and volumes and seeking a suitable configuration of these for a restricted site, adopts a heuristic approach. No established search procedure can systematically integrate all the factors that she must consider – the client's budget, available construction technologies, the range of activities that the spaces must accommodate, local building regulations, the local climate, the topography of the site, and so on – in ways that yield a guaranteed outcome for her stated problem. When she finally alights upon a solution that is satisfactory, she cannot be sure that better ones are not available.[57] Her problem-solving strategy remains open ended with no specifiable point of departure or point of arrival. The architect must decide when she has arrived. Contrast the architect's problem with that of a schoolgirl learning to carry out long division in her maths class. Not only is a procedure available to her that offers a clear point of departure and of arrival, but she is guaranteed a solution if she manipulates the right numbers and correctly carries out the specified operations on them. Here it is the *algorithm* itself that decides when to terminate a computation, but it does so in a process which, as it undergoes successive refinements in its moves from $\bar{C}$ to C, has been completely drained of any personal element of choice.

Relating heuristics to algorithms

Moves further up $\bar{C}$C embed knowledge emerging from p in an existing stock of codified knowledge. Much of the search process will continue to remain heuristic but now, in certain regions of the problem space, algorithms become available. Problem-solving becomes less uncertain, outcomes more predictable. To the extent that newly codified knowledge establishes positive links with the existing stock of codified knowledge, creative problem-solving in $\bar{C}$ gradually gets transformed into routine puzzle-solving in C. Cognitive activity respectively at $\bar{C}$ and at C draws upon different skills and temperaments: the creative problem-solver requires a greater measure of 'intuitive familiarity'[58] with his material to guide him towards those codified combinations that will prove to be effective rather than absurd; the routine puzzle-solver, on the other hand, may need a greater technical mastery of his codes.

But even in the latter case the tacit element is never wholly absent. Nor is creativity. For things will not always go smoothly in p. The move from $\bar{C}$ towards C is fraught with pitfalls. Newly codified knowledge may resist integration with the existing stock in C and may even be perceived as a threat to it. Codes may compete with each other rather than collaborate, thus in effect disintegrating rather than integrating the knowledge base. Yet, over the long term, in both cases the result is likely to be a further move towards C, albeit a fitful one. Where codes compete, empirical testing, crucial or less-than-crucial experiments, and the cognitive habits of the scientific community[59] all impose a process of natural selection that eliminates the weaker candidates; choices are made which for better or for worse increase the level of codification.[60] Where codes collaborate, on the other hand, the relationship between them gets stabilized and consolidated; it is thus rendered predictable. Here again degrees of freedom are reduced and this has the effect of increasing the level of codification.[61]

The foregoing considerations lead me to think that the Langley *et al.* view of scientific discovery better characterizes p as it approaches C than in its early phases in $\bar{C}$. They also highlight a possible difference between Kuhn's approach to puzzle-solving and our own. For in the scheme presented here, puzzle-solving only really takes over either when newly created codes can be properly integrated into a self-contained and coherent scheme, or when an *existing* stock of codified knowledge opens the door to an algorithmic approach through its own further codification. Yet where such algorithms fail to crystallize for one reason or another, then whatever further codification takes place could easily remain heuristic in nature and, although it will be less uncertain than in the early stages, it will nevertheless retain all the indeterminacy of open-ended problem-solving processes – until, that is, p itself is able to supply its own algorithms, possibly following an act of abstraction. In sum, data processing in C may facilitate puzzle-solving; it does not, however, entail it.

4.8: ABSTRACTION (*at*)

Categorizing possible worlds

Codification saves on data and on data processing by giving edges to things and form to experience. Yet the world will not necessarily appear any less chaotic to us because it is now populated by objects rather than raw sensations if we lack any way of apprehending them or formulating viable expectations as to what they might be. The codified objects within our immediate perceptual reach in Ā still constitute an environment of potentially staggering complexity for our senses. Unless we have some cognitive basis for directing our attention towards things that are relevant to us we quickly become disoriented.

Abstraction, as we saw in Chapter 2, saves on data processing by focusing on those regularities in the data field which, although of potential relevance to us as data processing agents, are not immediately given to perception as a set of self-contained forms. A chair, for example, is perceptually resolvable into a set of hard contours whose configuration varies quite rapidly as one moves around the object. Such codified perceptions, however, only become categorized as a chair when a subset of these is seen to covary in such a way that whatever one's angle of vision, topological and geometrical relationships between them are taken to be constant.[62] A chair, then, becomes an abstract object when it constitutes a generalization of these relationships, one that can be referred to and discussed in the absence of any specific concrete exemplar. That is to say, the abstract object serves to categorize not only the kaleidoscope of sense data that I experience when contemplating a given chair, but also any other possible cluster of perceptions in which the same constant topological relationships might be encountered. By categorization I save on data processing not just in apprehending *this* chair that I have before me, but also in *any* future encounter I may have with a chair-like object whether it be a Windsor chair, a Louis XV chair, a Marcel Breuer chair, or whatever. I save on data processing through increasingly competent acts of categorization repeated at each encounter with a chair-like object whenever and wherever it might subsequently occur. Repeated encounters with such objects help me to tease out what these events have in common and to embody my findings in a general proposition or statement that moves me from Ā towards A.

By expanding the set of spatiotemporal events that may share in its truth content, a general or abstract statement enlarges the problem space over which it extends dominion beyond what can be immediately apprehended and hence achieves a greater measure of utility than a more concrete statement could. Yet by removing itself from immediacy and from the here-and-now, it only becomes accessible to thought through a process of detached reflection. To simplify somewhat, we might say that concrete thought is 'hot' and immersed in the facticities of a world that once codified is unproblematically given; abstract thought by contrast is 'cool' and detached and tends to take experience as inherently problematic.

The requirements of valid abstraction

Because an abstraction is removed from the concrete immediacy of Ā, it is also beyond the reach of unambiguous empirical testing. Its link with concrete reality is indirect and open to competing interpretation. Duhem, Quine,[63] and later Lakatos[64] have all pointed out how difficult it is to refute unambiguously an abstract proposition. Not only is it likely to be woven into a dense fabric of implicit abstract relations that may themselves turn out to be a source of problems, but in addition the proposition itself, when abstract, is capable of potentially infinite adjustment and adaptations that can mitigate the severity of any empirical test it might be called upon to endure.

Yet because abstraction is potentially so powerful, because it is capable of finding its way into so many domains of experience and of structuring, not to say of dominating them, the urge to it has to be kept in some sort of check. A scientific abstraction, for example, before being accepted by a scientific community has usually to clear three hurdles, two of them quite visible and explicit, and the third often completely hidden from view.

The first hurdle is that of *consistency*: an abstraction is embedded in a network of interrelated propositions that obey a set of logical rules. These must not be violated; if they are, they destroy the epistemological status of the abstraction as a W3 object and with it any claim it may have on our attention.[65]

The second hurdle is that of *empirical testability*: as a W3 object an abstraction must have some discernible and predictable effect upon W1, the world of concrete events. The path that links these two worlds is often tortuous and barely visible, but some kind of path between them must exist. Where it does not, an abstraction is unrefutable and has only a metaphysical status.[66]

The final hurdle is that of *thematic compatibility*: this is a psychological rather than a scientific requirement, a W2 constraint designed to ensure that a sufficient number of potential adopters inside a given scientific community are willing to champion it. An abstraction will inevitably have a tacit component located in C̄ that is either the fruit of a learning by doing process or a precondition for it.[67] Such a component must fit in with the existing stock of implicit schemes that already inhabit C̄, the cognitive incumbents, if you will, that make up an important part of an individual's W2; failing a proper integration of implicit schemes in C̄, the abstraction will be treated as a foreign body and unaccountably rejected.[68] And without a stable anchorage point in W2, it becomes much harder for an abstraction to travel between W3 and W1 so that opportunities for empirical validation become correspondingly scarcer.

The nature of the moves from concrete to abstract thought, from Ā to A, and back again, was first discussed in Chapter 2 and then later in section 4.3. We add little to that discussion here save to note that the first type of move must be considered an important component of the SLC, activating as it does the third dimension of the I-space. It is more easily performed in C than in C̄ on account of the greater manipulability of codified knowledge. Our discussion of learning styles in Chapter 2, however, cautions us against assuming that codification always precedes abstraction.

In the next section we examine how abstract knowledge spreads in a population. If by increasing the level of generality of new knowledge we expand the audience for which it has potential utility, do we thereby facilitate its diffusion?

4.9: DIFFUSION (*d*)

Matching the bandwidth of senders and receivers

A move up C following *p*, as we have already seen, makes knowledge more readily diffusible.

Codification, by eliminating uninformative data and thus reducing average message length, makes it easier to process. But codification does more than that. By simultaneously shortening and structuring a message, it saves time and effort at every step involved in communicating it from its initial formulation in someone's mind to its final interpretation in the mind of a recipient. Codification thus saves on the transmission as well as on the processing of data. As new knowledge moves up the codification scale, it begins to diffuse, perhaps slowly at first to co-workers in face-to-face encounters at the workplace or in small professional meetings, but then more rapidly and to larger and more distant groupings. In the case of new scientific knowledge, for example, at the end of an initial period in which interpersonal exchange with co-workers predominates, the first preprints describing new concepts or data might be circulated to a limited number of professional colleagues working in external institutions both at home and abroad. The language used in preprints will be highly specialized and will still draw heavily on a tacit coefficient of shared experiences that helps to keep communicating parties on the same wavelength.

Such publications in effect require that their recipients draw on a repertoire of codes spread right across the $\bar{C}C$ and the $\bar{A}A$ scales that make up their E-spaces. There has occurred an increase in codification for some parts of the preprints' message content, to be sure, and this has enhanced their technical transmissibility. But since by virtue of their specialized nature only a limited audience possesses the necessary skills to decode them, their diffusion takes the form of narrowcasting: in such case the spatial distance between communicants might be increased more easily than their number.

Moving selected elements of new knowledge further up towards C whilst leaving a significant part of it still in $\bar{C}$ has the effect of increasing what we might call the communication 'bandwidth' available. If receivers want to receive the whole of the transmitted message, they must be able to detect signals right across the bandwidth. Failing this they are likely to incur communication problems of the kind described by Shannon, with possibly semantic and pragmatic issues predominating. It is only when the tacit coefficient has been further reduced by additional efforts at codification that the new knowledge can become intelligible to a wider professional audience and hence diffusible within the scientific community at large. The bandwidth then narrows once more but now centres around C instead of $\bar{C}$ to reflect a gain in articulate understanding and an increased mastery of the knowledge created.

Diffusion, d, of new knowledge, a rightwards movement from $\bar{D}$ to D, takes place most rapidly as might be expected in the upper regions of the I-space. The major constraint on effective diffusion, however, will still lie in a shared possession by communicating parties of the necessary codes, whether these be abstract or concrete. Outside the scientific community, for example, the potential audiences for a given message may be much larger but they may have at best an indirect interest in the new knowledge it contains. They may not, therefore, find it worth their while to invest in the acquisition and mastery of the necessary codes and may not even figure on the $\bar{D}D$ scale as a target population for this kind of communication if they perceived their interests to be too remote from the topic at hand. For this reason much popular diffusion of scientific knowledge takes place in a somewhat informal fashion at a lower level of codification than what might be typically found in professional scientific journals. De-jargonized verbal explanations and simple diagrams here replace algebraic symbols and abstract graphs, and average message length increases once more to something that may approximate casual conversation. Yet since popularization usually only really gets started once new knowledge has been tested and digested by the relevant scientific communities, it properly forms part of the absorption component of the SLC to be discussed in the next section. From a narrow scientific perspective this type of diffusion has lost its urgency. From a broader societal perspective, however, it may be the most important phase of the diffusion process since it contributes to the fostering of scientific literacy and helps to bridge the gap between the conceptual world of the specialist and that of the layman.

The valency of new knowledge

In the diffusion phase, newly created knowledge gets increasingly embedded into the existing stock of knowledge, an uneven process that reflects both the prior social distribution of this existing stock across $\bar{D}D$ and what for want of a better term we may call its valency; that is, its predisposition to combine with new and sometimes quite alien elements. Valency may reside in the properties of available codes – the logic of the combinatorial relations they allow or forbid – or in the scope granted by the tacit coefficient of existing knowledge for novel and unanticipated combinations.

As in the p phase of the SLC, in the d phase newly created knowledge must either compete or collaborate with an existing stock; its diffusion prospects depend ultimately on how it fares in its various encounters with established occupants of the I-space.

On one view, genuinely new knowledge, particularly if it builds on a new paradigm, may not interact with the existing stock at all. It may in effect be incommensurate with it. In such cases all talk of collaboration between new and existing knowledge becomes meaningless. Yet, if in consequence of this there has to be competition between them, no rules of the game can be devised which might allow a dispassionate comparison and evaluation of their respective epistemological claims. This is the relativist position. It denies the existence of any superordinate criteria that would allow us to choose between old and new knowledge on strictly rational grounds. As argued by epistemological anarchists such as Feyerabend[69] it transforms the diffusion of new knowledge into a propaganda or public relations exercise in which 'anything goes'. The only epistemological strategy worth investing in is the one that achieves what we might call 'share of mind' rather than 'share of truth'.[70]

On another view, rule-based competition and collaboration between old and new knowledge are both possible providing that the type of rationality on which effective choice is predicated is procedural rather than sub-stantive;[71] that is to say, it is concerned with the rigorous application of established methodological rules rather than with the specific outcomes which the rules produce. If well conceived, such rules will specify testing procedures and selection criteria that favour alternatives offering a higher degree of corroboration over a lower one and broader explanatory power over something narrower. Procedural rationality of this kind moves knowl-edge towards greater abstraction at A and consolidates its status as a W3 product. Old and new knowledge may well be incommensurate at some level of analysis but this does not necessarily place them beyond the reach of rational comparison. If new knowledge survives, it does so for a good reason to be found through testing in W1 and not on the cognitive whim of potential adopters indulging their W2 fantasies. Realism, not relativism, informs this position. It is that chosen by evolutionary epistemologists such as Popper and, in a more attenuated form, by Lakatos.[72]

Adopting new knowledge

Although neither science nor the philosophy of science is the primary focus of our discussion, the epistemological concerns presented above must lead us to ask whether the SLC leads to the build-up of valid knowledge in the I-space or to something more provisional and less durable. The question has, in fact, two parts. Firstly, does the SLC operate in such a way as to take us nearer to something called the truth in a specifiable time-frame? Secondly, is truth-bearing knowledge, by dint of its verisimilitude,[73] a durable phenomenon in the I-space once created, or is it also subject to the action of entropic forces as discussed in section 4.5?

Why do these two sub-questions matter? Essentially because the way that we answer them affects how we view the process of adopting new knowledge and hence the d component of the SLC as a whole. A durable truth may be an epistemological gain that some people are willing to die for, a transient one is not. Thus what can be reasonably believed concerning the nature of the cognitive assets being created through the action of an SLC in the I-space bears upon the cost–benefit calculations that will precede any investment in the cycle as well as on the level of personal commitment to its growth and development that will be elicited.

The risks involved in adopting anything new have been well studied,[74] in the case of technological innovations as well as in science. Adoption is not a random process but is related firstly to the perceived benefits that might flow from adoption (in the case of science those associated with the increment in utility that new knowledge offers over old knowledge); secondly to the capacity of an individual or a group to bear risk, as measured by income level in the case of technological innovation; and, finally, to the costs, psychological or material, incurred in adopting new knowledge, as measured by prior cognitive investment in alternative formulations that might now have to be forgone.

The fact that the questions posed matter does not mean that we are in a position to answer them. They will continue to fuel controversy among philosophers, sociologists, and historians of science for some time to come. In the light of our analysis, however, we can put forward a few tentative thoughts:

1   The rate of adoption of new knowledge in a population over time is often held to be plottable as a logistic curve, with a slow initial rate of take-up giving way to accelerated adoption in the case of successful innovations. We would hypothesize that the slope of the curve is itself explainable in terms of the SLC.

2   Moves towards C and A increase the potential utility of new knowledge whilst lowering its transmission costs; with such moves it also becomes better tested and more standardized. Beyond a certain point a switch occurs in the cost–benefit ratio associated with the use of this knowledge as perceived by potential adopters. Acceleration up the logistics curve would follow this switch. The diffusion rate is not explainable solely by the sociological characteristics of adopters alone as claimed in some of the adoption literature, but also by changes in the characteristics of new knowledge itself as it progresses through the SLC.

3   The diffusion of new knowledge from a position in C is less hindered by the existence of intangible obstacles still residing in $\bar{C}$ so that adoption might occur even where subsequent operational experience with this knowledge eventually proves problematic. At the moment of adoption such potential problems remain latent and are not yet visible on the horizon. Had diffusion taken place in $\bar{C}$, however, at an earlier phase of the SLC, intangible difficulties would have loomed much larger and been felt more quickly and adoption would have been less likely to occur. If we take adoption as a given, these difficulties will still be encountered, but now in the absorption process that follows adoption, in *ar*.

4.10: ABSORPTION (*ar*)

Restoring richness to experience

Codified knowledge, if adopted, is put to use. Recipients will endeavour to master it in a variety of situations that call for practice and adaptation, a learning process from which general, not to say abstract, principles can sometimes gradually be distilled. Return for a moment to an example that we used in Chapter 2. Imagine learning to use a typewriter. At first great concentration is required to correctly locate the keys on the keyboard. The fingers are slow and hesitant, and many mistakes are made. With practice, however, one's typing speed gradually improves until after a while one is bashing away at the keyboard without thinking. At this point the mastery and experience gained allow extrapolation and experiment: for instance one may try tabulations; or one may transfer one's newly acquired skills to the mastery of a telex machine or a microcomputer. In this way, a sedimentation of new experiences based on use acts to consolidate newly acquired knowledge, increasing its familiarity for a learner and its apparent givenness. Both the deepening and the broadening of new skills – whether cognitive or behavioural – are enhanced as they become second nature, not to say unconscious. Absorption (*ar*) makes of such learning-by-doing a constituent and vital component of the SLC.

Absorption is a vertical thrust back down the I-space towards $\bar{C}$. It reflects an awareness of nuance in the use of codes, a sensitivity to context and to the claims of complexity. If the world can never be fully reduced to codes, if subtleties and shades of meaning get stranded in $\bar{C}$ during the *p* phase of the SLC, then *ar* can be thought of as a rescue operation that restores a certain wholeness or richness to experience and a certain art to the use of codes selected for processing it.

The *ar* component of the SLC can originate at many points along $\bar{D}D$, although it is very likely that those who are responsible for performing the upward thrusts of the codification process in $\bar{D}$ will, in the nature of things, also be the first to initiate the downward movement; their co-workers will then be the next to do so, followed by other professional colleagues. In effect, although when discussing the SLC, for the sake of convenience we only describe a single *ar* component, the absorption process in fact occurs wherever there is adoption and active use of new knowledge, as, for example, in Figure 4.6.

Integrating old and new knowledge

Through *ar*, newly adopted knowledge, spread throughout the C region of the I-space, now encounters an intangible stock of well-embedded pre-extant knowledge located in $\bar{C}$. We thus face the familiar question of whether old and new knowledge will compete or collaborate. Will there be integration or collision? Here it is no longer the logic of codes and their combinational powers that give them their valency but the more elusive logic of values and of personal preferences. In science, for example, as we have noted in our discussion of thematic compatibility in section 4.8, a theory that is internally consistent and empirically well supported may still find itself rejected by individuals on aesthetic grounds, and sometimes on such grounds alone. Was not Copernicus's prime motivation in developing the heliocentric theory to render the Ptolemaic theory more aesthetically satisfactory by ridding it of its irritating epicycles? Did Einstein ever put forward a good scientific reason for his notoriously ambivalent attitude towards the new quantum physics?[75]

In $\bar{C}$, the same intangible considerations that guide an individual's initial choice of heuristic in the *p* phase shape his propensity to apply or to let atrophy newly adopted codified knowledge during the *ar* phase. In either case, his decision owes a great deal more to aesthetic preferences and to deeply and unconsciously held personal values than it does to rational deliberation. The cognitive forces at work in this part of the I-space are guided by patterns that Holton has labelled *themata* – hence our own use of the term 'thematic compatibility'. Interesting comparisons suggest themselves between these organizing Gestalten and, say, the Jungian archetypes discussed in Chapter 2.[76]

The *ar* phase, occurring as it does right across D̄D, encounters very different kinds of knowledge as it moves down towards C̄, reflecting cognitive and other variations in the diffusion population. Consider, for example, the two diffusion situations depicted in Figure 4.8. They might represent the diffusion paths taken by a certain type of technological innovation, say a revolutionary new pharmaceutical product or an electronic one. We see in SLC1 the *ar* phase initially taking place within a small community, possibly of specialists familiar with the new codes, and hence with few obstacles to a full and fruitful integration of old and new knowledge in C̄. A second cycle, SLC2, however, taking the newly created knowledge to a wider and less specialized audience, has run into problems. Here we find the *ar* phase blocked by incompatibilities with what currently occupies C̄. In the case of a new pharmaceutical product, it may be that its galenic formulation clashes with established cultural practices, or that it places unrealistic demands on prevailing patterns of behaviour. The problems

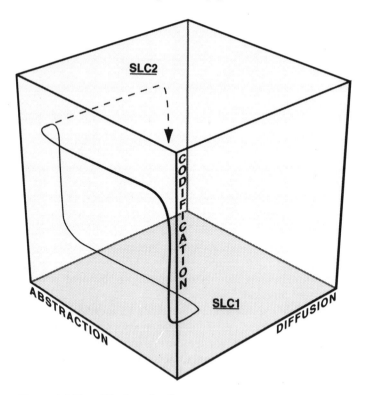

Figure 4.8 Two diffusion situations

encountered in getting people to use appropriate contraception measures in order to fight the spread of HIV infection readily come to mind as an example.

A new electronic product might pose similar problems of cultural adaptation. Imagine, for example, that we are dealing with the electronic tagging of individuals such as prisoners out on parole or patients in a hospital. There may be no problem in understanding the product's character-istics at a purely intellectual level; but its more general adoption and use might still clash with prevailing notions of individual freedom and dignity, thus leading to its rejection.

For this reason, the *ar* phase in the case of SLC2, if it occurs at all – the alternative being that the SLC just dies off and its constituent knowledge gets discarded – will require a much longer period of time to run its course and a possible adaptation of elements in the new knowledge that it carries with it to the constraints imposed in $\bar{C}$. Any conflict between old and new knowledge detected in that region might then serve to initiate a new SLC which, if successful, would gradually eliminate it. Failing this, then SLC1, being both relatively uncongested and confined to the left-hand region of the I-space, will run faster and serve to partition the diffusion population as a whole into two groups: those in $\bar{D}$ that have successfully mastered the new knowledge, but which by dint of their intangible investment in the *ar* phase of the cycle find it hard to transmit to those who have not; and those in D who must remain outsiders with respect to such knowledge until it can be fully integrated with an existing stock of knowledge in $\bar{C}$. It is blockages to the progress of the SLC such as the one just described which serve to cognitively differentiate a given population into subgroups.

Using new knowledge

Yet what tells us whether knowledge has effectively been absorbed by a given population and that it has actually been internalized by individual cognitive structures in the way we have described? The short answer is: by the use to which it is put. That short answer, of course, is not the easy answer since to infer the nature of knowledge in $\bar{C}$ from physical and verbal behaviour may turn out in practice to be quite a challenge.[77] Yet the point becomes obvious once we remind ourselves that behaviour in all its forms is a physical manifestation in W1, the world of concrete events in which all forms of knowledge, from whichever part of the field they may hail from, are sooner or later put to the test. Even quite abstract knowledge, therefore, must sooner or later gravitate back towards $\bar{A}$, perhaps in the form of auxiliary hypotheses,[78] to get itself embedded in the physical world. We call this impacting; it is the final phase of the SLC.[79]

4.11: IMPACTING (i)

Impacting in W2

The term 'impacting' has been borrowed from Williamson. In his book *Markets and Hierarchies*,[80] Williamson refers to 'information impacting' to describe the way that knowledge embeds itself in individual heads or organizations and, by inhabiting their implicit structures, thereby becomes hard to disclose or to share. The term is used here in a slightly more general sense since it traces the movement i from Ā to A in the SLC, a movement through which abstract knowledge becomes incorporated and expressed in specific concrete practices. Nevertheless, the intended connotation is the same: something that was once fluid and diffusible – in this case abstract knowledge – permeates a substrate – here the world of concrete events – from which it subsequently becomes hard to extract.

Williamson takes information impactedness to be a characteristic of idiosyncratic experience, what Hayek in another context has labelled 'knowledge of particular time and place'.[81] Such a view in effect makes impacting indistinguishable from what might be produced by scanning since idiosyncratic experience occupies D̄ rather than D. Yet impacting as we are using the term would, if anything, precede scanning and is probably a precondition for it where it creates a tension between an individual's concrete practices and his changing cognitive organization, a tension that will be experienced either as an opportunity or a threat. Information impactedness, therefore, may be idiosyncratic but not necessarily. Not all knowledge and experience that embeds itself in individual brains becomes unique as a consequence. We saw in Chapter 3 that much intangible knowledge can be collectively held as common sense or as implicit recipes. Our own use of the concept of impacting, therefore, makes it a necessary but not sufficient condition for the particularization of experience.

Impacting in W1

Impacting, i, is closely associated with absorption, ar, since it is through a process of learning by doing that knowledge gradually comes to achieve its embeddedness. Embedding information in brains, however, is only one way of bringing impactedness about: for information can also be embedded in artefacts – a process which, when performed consciously, is called design.

The first form of impacting moves one along the i component of the SLC from W3 to W2, from a world of freely floating abstractions to their biochemical or neuronal representation in the consciousness of individual minds. Note in passing that it is the representation of knowledge in consciousness that is located in W2; the neuronal or biochemical substrates which make representation possible are themselves located in W1[82] – we shall not deal with this point here. While such abstractions remain well formed in C, they can still be communicated to others, albeit at the discretion of the individual knower. But as they become absorbed, that part of them that moves down through *ar* from C to C̄ becomes increasingly hard to articulate and disclose – hence the impacting.

The second form of impacting moves one through *i* from W2 to W1, from internal representations of abstract possibilities to their concrete embodiment in physical things or processes. With this second type of move we find ourselves in the world of design and of technology. Recall, however, our discussion of the E-space in Chapter 2: any application of abstract knowledge in the real world always constitutes something of an empirical test for such knowledge. For this reason the *i* component of the SLC must continue to be regarded as part of a broad epistemological process and not as something apart from it, something tagged on to the process once it has come to an end. Design and development, contrary to the way they are usually depicted, can never be reduced to the mere application of an existing stock of knowledge which itself remains unmodified by the exercise.

The move from W2 to W1, like the one from W3 to W2 described above,

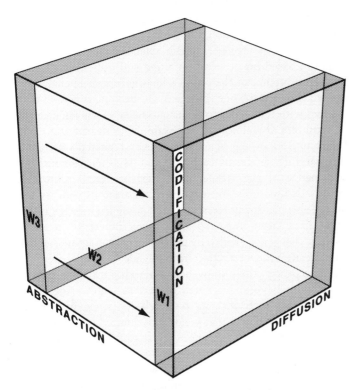

Figure 4.9 Impacting at different levels of codification

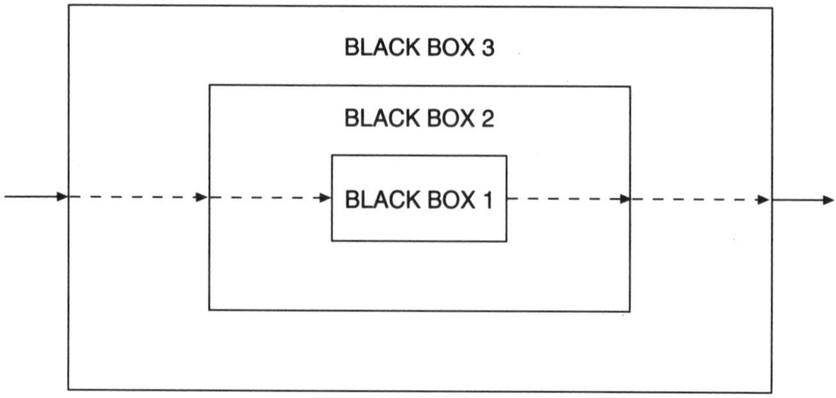

Figure 4.10 Nested black boxes

will also occur partly in C̄ and partly in C (see Figure 4.9). If in C, the knowledge so moved remains diffusible and can be acquired through imitation. Yet even when in C, imitation becomes harder if such knowledge is highly abstract. Simple objects such as, say, a cube made of wood may be reproduced by straightforward imitation. But what of a more complex object such as a computer which incorporates much science-based knowledge? Here, passive imitation based on observation alone will not easily of itself secure an effective reproduction of the object's key performance characteristics. More is needed. For a start, one must actively become *involved* with the object and interact with it in order to understand it. Reverse engineering is how would-be acquirers of technology, for example, both licit and illicit, obtain much of their understanding of an object. They repeatedly assemble and disassemble it, carefully analysing each part and its potential contribution to the performance of the whole, until they achieve an intuitive understanding of how it functions. Yet even such an arduous process will prove to no avail unless one also possesses at least some knowledge of the abstract codes that have been impacted in a given object or piece of equipment, knowledge that is not yielded by the object in interaction but that has to be brought to bear on the interaction from outside.[83]

Designers wishing to protect their know-how and to foil imitators have to keep these abstract codes beyond the reach of reverse engineering. They create 'nested' black boxes each with its own self-contained package of knowledge. A black box is an object that yields only limited information in response to questions. A black box is technology as oracle: manipulate the inputs one at a time and observe what happens to the outputs and eventually understand how they are correlated. But do not waste your time trying to probe further; i.e., to draw inferences concerning the nature of the causal links between inputs and outputs. Nesting black boxes make this extremely difficult if not impossible. For at each promising point within a black box one encounters another black box (see Figure 4.10), and inside each of these second-level black boxes lurks a set of third-level black boxes also carefully deployed, and so on. Even within a single organization a conscious nesting of black boxes inside the organization's products or processes can be used to create a differential access to technical knowledge for different groups of employees. Thus, for example, sales employees may have access to level-one black boxes because they need to know enough of what happens when they pull different switches to convince customers that their object of interest will not baffle them. Maintenance engineers, on the other hand, may have access to level-two black boxes in order to carry out repairs on the object. However, only a few people in a firm operating sophisticated technologies will usually enjoy effective access to black boxes at all levels in the nesting.

Impacting and entropy

Impacting restores to knowledge and information a spatiotemporal location in things or people. But with such physical embedding, knowledge also acquires a certain finitude as things wear out and people die off. Only knowledge that can be transmitted and that can find a new substrate before its own disappears will survive; and such knowledge is mostly in C, not in C̄. Embedding abstract knowledge in the concrete inanimate and living objects that populate our world exposes it to the physical ravages of entropy, to the erosion of structure over time and with it of memory. Knowledge in C̄ will be the hardest to preserve and hence the first to go, so that impacting in C̄, the end point of the SLC as we have depicted it, also turns out to be the most entropy prone.

Our discussion of impacting must not obscure the fundamental fact that even at their most abstract, information and knowledge are always embedded in a physical substrate of *data*. The move from A to Ā merely extends the scope for embeddedness, from, say, the laconic markings of a mathematical formula on a piece of paper to the massive and complex machinery of a nuclear power station. The SLC has portrayed abstractions as emergent properties of data, structures in the data field that, to be sure, save on data but do not in any way alter its physical nature. Physically, the data field, no matter from which part of the I-space we gain access to it, or in which phase of the SLC, remains just data.

Does impacting need W2?

One final thought on the question of impacting. We have depicted knowledge from W3 as necessarily passing through W2 on its way to W1; that is, as passing through human consciousness. Will this always be the case? Can we imagine a situation in which abstract symbolic outputs of a computer get channelled into physical processes with no effective intervention from the human mind at any point? This is in fact the dream of some researchers in artificial intelligence: to demonstrate that W2 is epiphenomenal. The debate currently centres on whether machine intelligence at some future level of development would actually be able to dispense with W2 altogether or would have to transfer it on to a new physical substrate that would, in effect, replace the human brain. In other words, do highly intelligent machines do away with the need for consciousness? Or on the contrary, by having to acquire it in some primitive form, do they show it to be indispensable?[84]

4.12: DRIVING THE CYCLE

The data field accommodates many SLCs

The impacting component, i, of the SLC completes the trajectory in the I-space through which new knowledge comes into being. By degrees it integrates it with old knowledge, weaving them together into what appears to be a seamless physical fabric with which to cloak reality. What we then perceive seems to be cut out of whole cloth. Seams, of course, may still exist but they are usually lost to view in the folds of the drapery and only become visible when an ill-fitting garment is produced that causes the cloth to get unduly stretched. Only then does one become aware of how some of our most elegant epistemological creations have been stitched together. If the cloth tears, it may be discreetly patched up; but if it continues to tear, then a new garment must be cut from a fresh SLC. Thus, it is only when the impacting process fails, when the presence of anomalies stubbornly blocks the process of unconscious mastery and internalization of knowledge through concrete applications, that a need arises for the further creation of new knowledge and the initiation of a fresh cycle. An anomaly will generate its own confused signals and these will once more be picked up in D; but not necessarily by the agents who had participated in the first cycle. The population located along $\bar{D}D$, like the molecules of a gas, does not stand still with respect to the knowledge it processes. Under the process of knowledge flows it is constantly moving about and relocating itself along $\bar{D}D$. Since the I-space does not identify the individual members of a diffusion population, it cannot bring out this point graphically.

This has important consequences. There is nothing in the present analysis to suggest that the evolution of knowledge through successive SLCs necessarily remains confined to a given epistemological domain. Much will depend on the distribution patterns of the existing stock of knowledge in the data field and on the ready availability of 'receptor sites' suitably located to capture the anomalous signals as they emerge – i.e., of individuals predisposed by training and attitude to detect such anomalies, to interpret them for what they are, and to respond to them. Each new SLC, therefore, may well

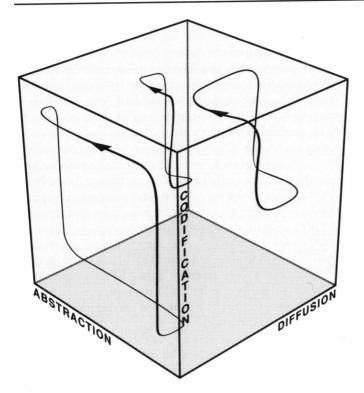

Figure 4.11 Different SLCs in the I-space

act upon its own, specific, diffusion population, and a move from one SLC to another will entail changes in the composition and the ordering of D̄D.

The SLC that we have described in this chapter is purely schematic. It is not the only possible cycle nor even, probably, a typical one. In fact, many different types of SLCs can activate in the data field, all of different shapes in the I-space. What they will all have in common however, we hypothesize, will be their clockwise flow pattern in the space. What then, if anything, gives the various knowledge cycles illustrated in Figure 4.11 their particular shapes in the I-space? The most plausible answer is the configuration of forces that make up the data field itself interacting with the current distribution of prior investments in knowledge that have already take place in the field. Such an answer, however, only takes us so far since the distribution of prior cognitive investments in the field, and by implication of the forces that they occasion, is itself the fruit of earlier SLCs whose shapes we are also trying to account for. Can we do better? Only a bit, I am afraid.

Potential and kinetic intelligence

Gregory[85] has drawn an interesting distinction between 'potential intelligence', the possession of knowledge, and 'kinetic intelligence', the creation of knowledge, observing that we cannot assess kinetic intelligence without knowing what contributions are made by stored intelligent solutions – potential intelligence. Gregory's distinction runs parallel to the one we are implicitly drawing between knowledge as a stock of assets that reflect prior cognitive investments, and knowledge as a cognitive performance partly made possible by the possession of such assets. The knowledge possessed by potential intelligence, however, can only be durably stored outside the brain if it is in a form that can be recorded – i.e., as books, documents, computer tapes, designs, paintings, etc. In other words, it must have undergone a minimum amount of codification. Uncodified knowledge, or the tacit component of already codified knowledge, is condemned to remain embedded for the most part within individual and perishable brains – and there, it would appear, often in only a very transient form. Effective individual learning, then, requires primarily an internalization of pre-extant and inherited potential intelligence secured by a steady yet comparatively modest accumulation of confirmatory experiences.

Gregory argues that most behaviour draws upon the stored knowledge of potential intelligence rather than the created knowledge of kinetic intelligence. Resting his case on a counterexample, he comments: 'It is worth noting that prodigies are found mainly in music or mathematics and other spheres where wide knowledge is not essential (as it is for history or biology)'.[86]

Otherwise stated, genius is usually attributed to high kinetic intelligence but in circumstances where potential intelligence is not in fact much required.

Translating Gregory's terms into our own, we can now see that when the existing stock of knowledge gets itself embedded, whether externally in W1 artefacts or internally in W2 brains, it will affect the scope given to kinetic intelligence in the I-space and by implication will affect the shape of knowledge cycles and on what flows through it.[87]

The descriptive scope of the SLC

The SLC is not only schematic; in the absence of a well-specified population along $\bar{D}D$, it can also be considered disembodied. With suitable adaptation it could be made to describe the knowledge held by an individual,[88] a group, or a larger aggregation of individuals such as a firm – in fact any well-specified data processing agents, physical or corporate. The diffusion of knowledge within and between related populations of different sizes is also possible. Figure 4.12, for example, relates the distribution of a given item of

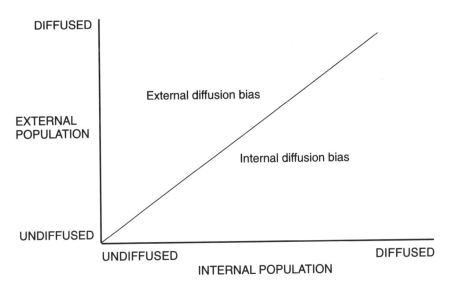

Figure 4.12 External and internal diffusion biases

knowledge as held by a focal population – say, individuals within a firm – to the distribution of the same item of knowledge as held by a larger, external population – i.e., firms within an industry. Knowledge located above the diagonal in the diagram is more readily available outside the focal population than it is within it. Conversely, knowledge located below the diagonal is more widely distributed within the focal population than outside it. The first situation might describe how specialist knowledge is distributed within firms and industries, the second how organizational knowledge is confined within firm boundaries.

An SLC activates the I-space as a whole and allows an integrated representation of epistemological (E-space), economic (U-space), and sociological (C-space) issues when discussing the production and distribution of knowledge within a population. Yet small groups only rarely have the complete cycle under their control. Unless an analysis is carried out at a high level of population aggregation, one will be dealing for the most part with fragments of cycles that somehow need to be combined together for knowledge to flow at all, rather than with whole ones. There are many possible reasons for this and some have already been touched on – the pattern of prior cognitive investments in the data field, blockages to communications that arise from the physical and structural characteristics of the focal population, the strategies pursued by individual data processing agents, etc. Yet however diverse its manifestation, one important explanation for the fragmentary nature of some SLCs will be found in the limitations of individual cognitive styles and learning capacities,[89] limitations that can only be compensated for by the statistical aggregation of data processing agents.

Is the SLC progressive?

Nothing about an SLC *per se* enhances the epistemological status of the knowledge it generates. It can put into general circulation wild absurdities no less effectively than eternal truths. The latter run a permanent risk of drowning in a sea of competing falsehoods and never more so than when they are in their infancy, in the early phase of their trajectory through the cycle. The survival prospects of genuine knowledge are nevertheless deemed to improve with age by evolutionary epistemologists such as Popper, providing that it has first been properly exposed to the elements and become weather-hardened by rigorous testing. The ability to survive such testing then becomes a criterion of demarcation that allows us to distinguish knowledge that approaches the truth – it usually does so incrementally through a continuous process of adjustment and refinement – from knowledge that is plainly false.[90]

The challenges to Popper's evolutionary perspective are of two kinds. There are those who broadly support his view that science is capable of evolutionary progress but who believe that new knowledge can rarely be tested with the severity that Popper himself requires. Lakatos, for example, has argued that it is whole research programmes rather than specific hypotheses that are tested, and that in such cases the tests are by their nature less conclusive and more tolerant of falsehoods than Popper would care to admit.[91] Then there are relativists like Feyerabend and Kuhn who question whether science is in fact capable of any progress at all in the sense of getting us closer to the truth over time.[92] According to them, tests have but limited powers for discriminating effectively between truths and falsehoods when the choice turns out to involve competing paradigms because such tests are themselves under the dominion of one of the paradigms on which they are supposed to adjudicate. The seventeenth-century witch trials, for example, in which a hapless creature's guilt or innocence was tested by drowning, are nothing more than an extreme application of Popper's principle.[93] Critical choices between theories, argue the relativists, owe more to the interplay of social forces such as power and domination than they do to the exercise of some disembodied rationality, so that the diffusion of new scientific ideas and their subsequent incorporation into the stock of socially validated knowledge turn out to be no presumption whatsoever in favour of their verisimilitude.

A more *nuancée* position is adopted by David Bloor who, in spite of being branded a relativist by his critics,[94] feels under no compulsion to choose sides in this debate. For Bloor, knowledge can be both progressive *and* socially conditioned. In our terminology, it can move from Ā to A in the E-space whilst acknowledging the influence exerted on its progress by considerations of social utility in the U-space and of social cognition in the C-space.

In what he describes as the *Strong Programme* in the Sociology of Knowledge Bloor requires an account in terms of *all three dimensions* of the I-space for what progresses towards abstraction in the E-space. Internal accounts of science would explain progress in the E-space in E-space terms alone; external accounts in terms of U- and C-spaces alone. Bloor requires that all three be combined.

All the protagonists in this debate, implicitly or otherwise, take progress along the E-space towards greater abstraction to be equivalent to progress towards greater verisimilitude. Popper's goal is to move autonomously towards ever higher, ever more general truths; Kuhn's is to show that such moves are confined within socially selected paradigms which cannot be reconciled to achieve ever-greater generality; and Bloor's is to argue that moves towards more general truths might indeed be possible but that we delude ourselves if we believe them to be autonomous and untainted by social influences.

Our own discussion of the SLC leads us to a quite different view, one which takes moves in the E-space towards greater abstraction and generality as driven by a need for *cognitive economy* rather than a disinterested quest for truth, and that takes a requirement for verisimilitude as a *constraint* upon these moves rather than as their goal. Verisimilitude is achieved by progressively weeding out the errors that sprout around these theories. When enough weeding out has been done, a theory becomes a fit candidate for moving along ĀA; 'enough' is a social category.

It is what the theory explains that gives it its appeal, not the fact that it has survived any weeding out. When Popper states that for equivalent degrees of corroboration achieved, it is the theory that offers the greatest explanatory power that will be chosen, no one will quarrel with him. Yet although explanatory power can be taken as a move towards abstraction, it must not be taken *in itself* as a move towards greater verisimilitude. It is a move towards greater cognitive economies that will only be valued if the requirements of verisimilitude – i.e., the weeding out of errors – have been met beforehand. If they have, then, since every territorial expansion by a theory into new explanatory areas will require a fresh weeding out of errors, moves towards abstraction will indeed be accompanied by gains in verisimilitude. If they have not, however, if weeds are allowed to sprout, then absurdities no less than truths will find their way along ĀA, there to offer their data processing economies to the unwary. In both cases, society has its say in how the gardening is carried out.

The deviance of new knowledge

One final point concerning the SLC. When viewed as a social process, the creativity that generates fundamentally new knowledge is at times indistinguishable from social deviance. Recall for a moment our discussion in section 4.6. The source of variation that expands the range of choices for the exercise of evolutionary selection may not be individual inventiveness at all, as is commonly supposed, but possibly the idiosyncratic conservativism of certain individuals who cannot help seeing the world the way that they do. They become cognitively committed to a vision that sets them apart from their fellow humans.[95]

Inventiveness, by contrast, is uncommitted; a playful, detached exploration of alternative worlds and possibilities that may indeed stumble upon something unexpected and fundamental. It can be a valuable skill for those operating at the frontier of knowledge who often need to shed old forms of thought. Yet in certain instances, genuine insight is the work of individuals who do not go in for carefree exploration of this kind at all but rather deepen their commitment to a singular view of the world that is the product of idiosyncratic circumstances. As Polanyi has remarked, tacit knowing cannot be critical and, for that reason, is hard to confirm and often hard to change. It sets its own standards of appraisal, drawing on personality factors that make such standards rigid or flexible.[96] Through a succession of circumstances that are largely biographical, an individual ends up seeing the world in a particular way. It is rarely wholly of her own choosing. It is mostly thrust upon him by her own life history within a given culture. By and by, however, some individuals build up world views that are idiosyncratic with respect to the norms prevailing in their group. Where others see trees they see elephants, and where others hear the wind rustling through the leaves they hear voices beckoning. To quote Shelley on the visions of the solitary poet: poetry 'purges from our inward sight, the film of familiarity which obscures from us the wonder of our being, "breaking into" a world to which the familiar world is chaos'.

Deviance has no reason to think of itself as anything but rational and therefore no reason to lack confidence in its judgements. The world inhabited by the deviant 'makes sense' to the deviant even if it differs from the world experienced by contemporaries in every respect. Technical or scientific specialization may be a source of cognitive deviance with respect to a lay audience or even other professional colleagues working in other fields. When for example a scientist formulates a hypothesis for testing, he will select one which he personally feels to have a high chance of being true. Yet, paradoxically, it is only *improbable* hypotheses that have a high information content and are therefore considered to be of potential interest to the scientific community. It is precisely because certain options sometimes strike an individual as highly plausible that he is willing to gamble on what peers would consider a hazardous enterprise. What we have here is a gap in the subjective probability estimates of the deviant or specialized individual and that of the wider community to which he belongs.

Karl Popper, in focusing on the logic of scientific discovery, was led to neglect both its psychology and its sociology and thus to argue for cognitive search strategies that would allow an individual researcher to unearth improbable hypotheses. In Popper's major works, the stress is all on individual boldness and inventiveness and the willingness to take risks in order to bridge the inductive gap that had been opened up by David Hume. Yet improbable hypotheses are just as likely to emerge from a deviant perception which, taking itself as a norm, is inclined to attribute higher probabilities to a particular outcome than others would do. After all, what is a gambler if not someone who believes himself/herself to be exempted from the tyranny of probabilities as they apply to others? Risk seeking is by no means excluded as an explanation for a gambler's behaviour, but what is at issue here is how risk is construed in the first instance, not how it is responded to once construed. An ostensibly risk-averse individual may actually pursue a course of action that would be judged highly risky if not outright dangerous by others, if she construes the situation using probability estimates that differ substantially from theirs.

Cognitive deviance may have been given an epistemological escape hatch in Kurt Gödel's demonstration that no system of knowledge can exhaustively demonstrate its internal consistency from within its own boundaries.[97] A deviant standing outside the system may well turn out to be in error more often than not, but who inside the system can ever be absolutely sure of when this is the case?[98]

Realism versus subjectivism in the SLC

The problem posed by the deviant in the SLC leads us back to issues of relativism and incompatible paradigms: how does one effectively choose between competing yet incommensurate alternatives? Popper seems to believe that over time subjective and divergent probability estimates gradually align themselves with objective ones through a process that, to borrow a Freudian idiom, we might call 'reality testing': no matter how crazy or deviant an individual's scheme might be, providing it is testable, directly or otherwise, it gives reality a chance to 'kick back'[99] and the individual an opportunity to improve his scheme. In other words there is no problem of incommensurability. There exists a single, objective world. Popper's realism can be contrasted with the subjectivist position of neo-Bayesians such as Howson and Urbach[100] who argue for a gradual convergence of different subjective probability estimates that will meet on their own, following extensive testing, with little need to invoke objective probability estimates at all.

The respective positions of realists, such as Popper, and subjectivists, i.e., Bayesians, can be clarified by use of the SLC. As we have already seen, Popper is moving almost exclusively in the E-space quite undeflected by the forces bearing down on him out of the U- and C-spaces. He wants to know under what conditions we can be said to be making genuine progress towards W3, the world of abstract objects, in A, the world of general truths. It is his belief in the reality of A that drives him on. For him, extending the E-space into a third, socially generated dimension to create an I-space is a dangerous distraction subversive of the scientific enterprise.

Subjectivists by contrast are quite comfortable in the C-space where, through the testing of new knowledge by ever-wider populations, initially divergent probability estimates can be made to converge and peak. Since such estimates are subjective, the E-space is considered to be a purely W2 phenomenon with no power to create autonomous epistemological products in W3. For subjectivists the E-space is then but a projection of the C-space into the third dimension which, towards A, encourages a reification of the products of social cognition.

In both the E- and the C-spaces codification reduces uncertainty: in the E-space it does so by facilitating the move towards A, towards more encompassing generalizations; in the C-space it does so through a diffusion process that fosters a mutual alignment of divergent probability estimates and a gradual collectivization of the codification process itself.

Since in the SLC, both types of uncertainty-reducing processes will be at work at different points in the cycle's trajectory, we are not in fact required to choose between them. Indeed, we do not even have to frame them as alternative interpretations of the knowledge creation process. For the SLC can accommodate various contingencies: in some, knowledge might have been well codified but inadequately tested so that false knowledge diffuses through the system and brings about a convergence of subjective probability estimates; in others, the diffusion of highly corroborated new knowledge might remain blocked by the political strength of an incumbent and inhospitable paradigm.

Deviant or misfit?

The capacity to produce an unexpected and original insight is a mark of creativity that requires singular vision. The deviance normally associated with such singularity, however, need not necessarily be framed as an inability to adapt to society and its expectations. The deviant must not be confused with the misfit as he sometimes tends to be in popular lore. The deviant may move among us wearing a pin-striped suit and may regularly lunch at his club; he poses no obvious threat. He remains nevertheless a most potent force for social change. The misfit, by contrast, is a victim of social change as well as sometimes its perpetrator; he cannot establish a legitimate position for himself or his views and so withdraws into a cognitive shell of his own creation to shelter from the social hostility that he provokes. To be sure, the misfit may then come to harbour deviant perception just as some deviants may well end up as misfits. Yet deviants and misfits remain distinct categories. Consider, for example, the case of Giordano Bruno: he was burnt at the stake in February 1600 on the Campo del Fiore in Rome for proclaiming his belief in an infinite universe and a plurality of worlds. As early as 1576 Bruno had had to abandon the Dominican order and leave Italy for his heretical views.[101] Could anyone seriously imagine that happening to him in Western Europe today? In 1600 he was branded a deviant and therefore a misfit; today he would merely be considered a deviant.

The deviant, one might say, is one positioned at the tail-end of a probability distribution with respect to a given set of social norms, cognitive or otherwise. The misfit, by contrast, is created by society's inability to tolerate any overt manifestations of variation around its norms. Individual cognition and values locate an individual at a given point on the distribution; society then decides whether he falls within that part of the distribution bracketed off as normal. An intolerant society will turn many deviants into misfits whereas a tolerant one will try to make good use of them to progress through the SLC.

4.13: STRATEGIC ACTION IN THE KNOWLEDGE CYCLE

The distribution of value along the SLC

The second phase of the SLC, the d, ar, i phase, is the one in which value created in the first phase is exploited. When acting on a heterogeneous population this second phase leads to a partitioning of the data field with respect to how knowledge is distributed within it. Figure 4.13 uses the I-space to illustrate such a partitioning with respect to medical knowledge.

Three levels of expertise can be identified in the diagram:

1   Knowledge held by the patient. In its most impacted and implicit form this is nothing other than the direct inarticulate experience of aches and pains that tell the patient he/she should visit a doctor. This kind of experiential knowledge is available to all sentient beings.
2   Knowledge held by the general practitioner or family doctor. The general practitioner helps the patient to articulate what he/she feels and possesses sufficient medical knowledge to decide whether the ailment is something that can be dealt with on the spot or whether further investigations drawing on more specialized knowledge than she commands are called for. The general practitioner's codified knowledge allows her to direct the patient towards the most relevant area of specialization in which treatment might be available. She performs a

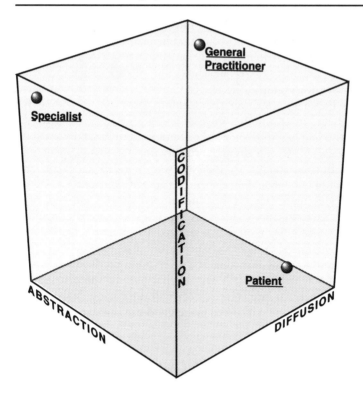

Figure 4.13 The distribution of medical knowledge in the I-space

linking role in the I-space, for if the general practitioner knows the patient well, she will be capable of interpreting the more personal and tacit context of the patient's problem – i.e., hypochondria, unemployment, marital problems, etc. – and modulate the prescription accordingly.

3   Knowledge held by the specialist – i.e., the neurologist, the cardiologist, etc. The specialist deploys a repertoire of undiffused yet codified and abstract models which she uses to formulate and test hypotheses concerning the patient's ailments – i.e., she makes a diagnosis. By the time a patient steps into the specialist's consulting room, 'common sense' approaches to the patient's problems will have been exhausted and only specialized problem-solving will be deemed to be an adequate response to what has in effect been a two-step scanning process (see Figure 4.14).

The kind of knowledge held by the patient is the least articulate and the least scarce even though it concerns only the patient: after all, the experience of pain is universally available. It is located in the I-space at the point of maximum entropy and for that reason has the least tradable value. The

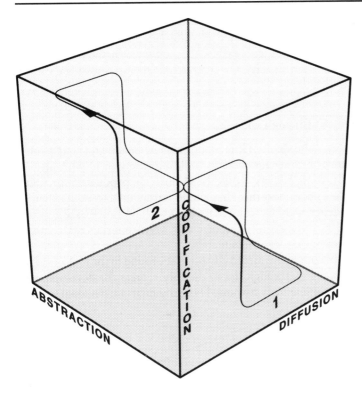

Figure 4.14 A two-step scanning process in the I-space

cardiologist, on the other hand, is in the opposite situation. He possesses abstract knowledge which is hard to diffuse – whether on account of lack of shared codes, where his knowledge is codified, or because of a tacit coefficient that has built up around the codes he possesses over years of accumulated personal experience. The cardiologist occupies the point of minimum entropy in the field and possesses a large stock of valuable medical knowledge assets on the basis of which he can trade.

Not only will the availability of such knowledge decrease as one moves along D̄D towards D in the I-space, but whatever part of it does eventually get diffused will encounter quite different tacit coefficients as it moves along D̄D, possibly impeding its effective absorption at the point of encounter. The reason is that there will only be a modest amount of horizontal movement of uncodified knowledge that might assist such absorption. The cardiologist's many years' accumulation of tacit knowledge, for example, is not easily passed on to the general practitioner, nor the latter's to patients.

Yet in C, where knowledge is more easily transmissible, the lack of common codes between senders and potential receivers will also act as a brake on a full flow of information from one region to the other. And, as we have just seen, what actually does get to flow is not picked up and interpreted in the same way by receivers located at different points along D̄D; it is absorbed into different 'mind sets', each with its own distinctive stock of tacit knowledge, its particular capacity for abstraction, its interest in the subject at hand, and so on.[102]

Blocks to movement through the SLC

The differentiation of the stock of knowledge in the I-space expresses a social division of labour. If knowledge were to build up solely in D̄ with little or no subsequent diffusion, society would be exclusively producing specialists who have so little in common that they could barely talk to each other. If, conversely, knowledge were to accumulate in D with no flows back towards D̄, people would become so like-minded and right-thinking that nothing new would ever emerge under their sun.

Such extremes, of course, are mercifully not to be found in the real world; no social system, however pathological, can durably repress the developmental forces that push simultaneously towards D̄ – individuation, personal growth,

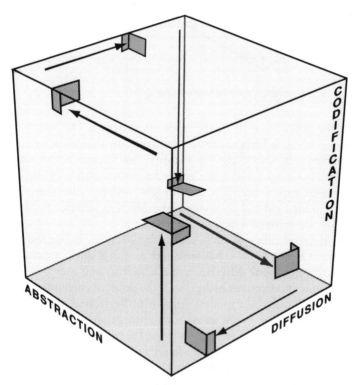

Figure 4.15 Blockages to the SLC

maturation, etc. – and towards D – socialization, fellowship, dependence, etc. If the cardiologist, for want of a common language, is prevented from sharing the most intimate insights afforded by his professional experience with a stock-broking neighbour, and if, for the same reason, the latter is condemned to keep technical knowledge of margin trading and put options locked up within his breast, then the British weather and test matches will still offer both a vast acreage of neutral conversational territory on which seeds of friendship may yet be sown and flourish.

The pattern created in the I-space by prior investments in the stock of knowledge provides a distinctive topography for the channelling of data flows through the SLC. The paths taken by such flows will depend on the nature of the terrain created – that is, on the presence or absence of barriers that might deflect or block them.

In one case, the barrier is a natural one created by the topography itself: existing knowledge creates an obstacle, a dam that blocks the flow of new knowledge. The entropic action of time, however, may gradually erode this obstacle through the process of forgetting, so that at a certain point new knowledge will begin to wash over old knowledge and possibly even hasten its disappearance.

Yet other kinds of barriers also inhibit the functions of the SLC and distort the flow of knowledge in the I-space. They can sometimes go as far as to block the learning process altogether. In Figure 4.15 vertical barriers describe blockages to individual learning; horizontal ones, mainly blockages to social learning. The causes of such blockages may be quite varied:

1   In *scanning*, individuals may filter out or block those incoming stimuli that do not square with their prior expectations or cognitive commitments where the emotional stakes for them are high. Instead of adjusting what they think to what they see in order to respond to the world in an adaptive way they try to adjust what they see to what they think. Festinger calls this gap between cognition and perception *cognitive dissonance*.[103] The blockage to scanning is likely to be most in evidence in $\bar{C}$, where an individual, if she is overinvested in C, may lack the cognitive flexibility to pick up uncodified signals. A rigid personality, for example, tends to place an undue, almost ritualistic, reliance on well-structured and unambiguous perceptions. Implicit signals are either misinterpreted or ignored.

2   *Problem-solving* or codifying calls for successive acts of choosing or selecting between alternatives. If these are all strongly valued, whether positively or negatively, the need to decide, to select, and by implication to reject, may provoke personal anguish and emotional upheaval. If others are affected by his decision, an individual's cognitive freedom to choose may be inhibited by the fear of any hostility he might encounter from those who might have to suffer its consequences. This is why

political choices are sometimes so difficult and why politicians often appear so ready to postpone difficult decisions. Alternatively, an individual's choice may be distorted by an undue concern with the personal rewards he might reap from those who stand to benefit from the way that he exercises it.

3   *Abstracting* skills, as we learnt in Chapter 2, are facilitated by a certain cognitive style. Yet their development can also be blocked by certain habits of thought that stress immediacy and discourage reflection. Because abstractions are less tangible than concrete facts, they are often dismissed by 'practical' people as empty theorizing and irrelevant to real issues. Perhaps the greatest external obstacle to the process of abstracting, besides cognitive ones that are innate, is the denial of its value and of the time – often considerable – necessary for its performance. Kurt Lewin's well-known quip that 'there is nothing so practical as a good theory' is for many a hard truth to accept.

4   The barriers that exist to the *diffusion* of new knowledge are well documented.[104] Differences in coding ability apart, a key obstacle appears to be an unwillingness either to communicate on the part of transmitters, or to listen on the part of receivers. Often, as in the case of proprietary knowledge, transmitters feel that more is to be gained by holding on to knowledge than in sharing it. Conversely, some receivers may perceive themselves to lose more than they gain in accepting new knowledge if its application is disruptive of established routines or of social relationships that have crystallized around existing knowledge – they become, in effect, cognitive Luddites.

5   The *absorption* of new knowledge will be slowed down or blocked when it threatens deeply and unconsciously held values or cherished attitudes and beliefs concerning the nature of the world we live in – we might think of this phenomenon as a more existential variant of cognitive dissonance. How else to explain the hostility of the Catholic Church to Copernicus's heliocentric theory or of the Anglican Church to Darwin's theory of natural selection? Unblocking the situation requires either that the new knowledge be modified or rejected, or that existing values and beliefs undergo a major transformation. Failing this, an unstable coexistence between the two will sooner or later result in a social schizophrenia, a condition not unfamiliar to the foreign-educated elite of many a Third World country today undergoing a rapid industrialization, who face the need to reconcile modern and traditional values.

6   *Impacting* takes place when information at varying degrees of abstraction gets embedded in a physical system – whether this be a technical artefact, a document, or brain cells – through which it finds some application in the real world. Finding a suitable physical application for itself constitutes an empirical test of the viability of new knowledge which, if successful, enhances its survival prospects. Physically embed-

ding such knowledge, however, is a prerequisite for testing it and success is not guaranteed. The lack of a suitable physical substrate available for its embedding can become a source of blockage which limits its use and hence the opportunities that it presents for learning.

Navigating through the SLC

One invests in the SLC consciously or otherwise in order to create value for oneself or for some specifiable group whose welfare one identifies with. Since value is only available in a certain region of the I-space, i.e., in $A\bar{C}\bar{D}$, one must learn how to navigate through the data field, and exploit the flows of data within it in order to route the SLC through the I-space's value-creating region. Effective navigation, however, requires some sense of how existing knowledge is distributed in the field and of whether it facilitates or inhibits progression through the cycle. An effective strategy in the data field is one that invests scarce information and communication resources in such a way as to exploit the dynamic properties of the SLC while keeping an eye open for sources of blockage or distortions that show up in the I-space and that could undermine one's efforts. In certain situations, value will only be created if new knowledge can be kept unconditionally scarce; at other times, its unrestricted diffusion will be a better bet.[105]

4.14: CONCLUSION

Recapitulation

In this chapter we discussed the dynamic properties of the data field as they appear in the I-space. To simplify our analysis we resolved flows of information into vectors moving along the three constituent dimensions of the I-space, $\bar{A}A$, $\bar{C}C$, and $\bar{D}D$. We also confined ourselves to an examination of those information flows in the data field that could be directly associated with the creation of new knowledge. In particular we hypothesized that:

1   New knowledge emerges in the I-space through a three-dimensional clockwise cycle of information flows that can be likened to a large feedback loop. The cycle itself has two phases, value creation and value exploitation, which taken together can be further decomposed into six distinct components: (1) scanning (s), (2) problem-solving (p), (3) abstraction (at), (4) diffusion (d), (5) absorption (ar), (6) impacting (i). We call the whole sequence a social learning cycle or SLC.

2   Many different shapes of the SLC are possible in the I-space and most have only a fragmentary and transient existence. Their specific trajectory expresses the distribution of forces at work in a given data field, many of them created by prior investments in knowledge. In some cases these

prior investments turn out to be synergistic with the new knowledge, in which case the flow of information through the cycle will be accelerated; in others they will act to block the progress of new knowledge through the cycle and either extinguish it altogether, or force it to re-route itself through other parts of the field.

3   The SLC describes a process of creation, destruction, and renewal of knowledge, of birth and rebirth. In its value-creating phase (s, p, at), the cycle is progressing towards a point of minimum entropy in the I-space, one at which the value-defining attributes of structure, utility, and scarcity are at their maximum. The move towards maximum value at CAD̄ requires a conscious effort to counter the ever-present forces of entropy. In its value-exploiting phase, on the other hand, the cycle moves towards that point in the field, C̄ĀD, at which structure, utility, and scarcity – and hence value – are at their minimum, and from which a new cycle may emerge through a fluctuation. In this second phase, value is extracted from knowledge by those who possess it in a process of controlled diffusion through which it gradually becomes available to all. Note, however, that knowledge only fully exhausts its potential utility when absorption and impacting are accompanied by a gradual erosion and atrophying of the stock of codified knowledge from which they originate.

4   An effective information strategy in the I-space is one that understands the latter's dynamic properties and in particular one that can properly distinguish between the value-creating phase of the SLC (s, p, at) and the value-exploiting phase (d, ar, i). If the effort and time invested in the creation of new knowledge are to be adequately compensated, then value must be extracted from the cycle before it gets dissipated by diffusion, absorption, and impacting. Investments in the SLC can be considered strategic when they express a value-maximizing behaviour that takes into account the possible blockages to information flows, whether these be created by cognitive or social factors or by prior investments in non-synergistic knowledge. Strategic value-maximizing behaviour in the I-space, however, is as likely to mean exploiting existing blockages to the functioning of an SLC as removing them.

The SLC and orthodox economic theory

This chapter takes us even further away than the previous ones from the orthodox economist's view of information. Until Keynes, information was treated as a parameter of the economic system, as something external to it. Keynes made the availability of information problematic for economic analysis since markets could fail for want of it.[106] Much of the debate within economics since the time of Keynes has been on the effects of information asymmetries between economic actors and on the way that they may or may not threaten economic efficiency. Is analysis better served by viewing information as a public good or as a private good? I think it would fairly summarize the current situation to say that macroeconomists prefer to think of information as a public good, albeit one subject to corrigible inefficiencies in its distribution, whereas microeconomists, those that study behaviour at the level of the firm, tend towards a private good perspective.

Both macroeconomists and microeconomists, however, focus almost exclusively on the distribution of information along $\bar{D}D$. Neither group has yet explored the properties of information along $\bar{A}A$ or $\bar{C}C$. And since neither macroeconomists nor microeconomists have any explicit theory of how an item of knowledge can *evolve* over time, they have no way of incorporating social learning as we have described it as a stimulus to the evolution of society's knowledge base. In effect, in their focus on $\bar{D}D$, economists have been dealing more with effects than with causes and have consequently made little progress in giving to information an economic role commensurate with its importance.

Neo-Austrian economists plead for a more process-oriented approach to their discipline, one that can take on board the irreversible spatiotemporal nature of the world we live in.[107] By implication, a process-oriented approach to the economics of information and knowledge would also be helpful. This is what has been sketched out in this chapter. The creation of knowledge is a process that simultaneously economizes on data (i.e., low-level energy) and on space–time (i.e., shrunk through speedy diffusion) through acts of codification and abstraction. These economies are the fruits of a conscious effort by data processing agents, of a strategic investment of their scarce resources. The SLC generates tradable values that are subject to the action of entropy: at one moment an item of knowledge has one value, at another it has none. It starts off in the head of a single individual as a private good and then by degrees becomes public. To treat it as inherently private or public is in effect to freeze it at a particular point in its trajectory through the SLC; it is also to deny the process of learning any economic status.

Successful strategies for handling the production and exchange of knowledge at different locations in the I-space can be stabilized and can subsequently emerge in the space in the form of institutions, acting as relay points that maintain and enhance the performance of selected SLCs. The character of these institutions will vary with their location in the I-space, as we shall see in the next chapter.

Chapter 5

Institutions

ABSTRACT

Social and economic transactions provide the impetus for the production and exchange of information. Transactions, however, entail effort and incur costs and are thus subject to attempts at economizing through institutional arrangements. In the I-space, we distinguish between four basic types of transactional structures:

1   Markets, in which transactionally relevant information is well codified, abstract, and widely diffused.
2   Bureaucracies, in which transactionally relevant information is well codified and abstract, but whose diffusion is under strict central control.
3   Clans, in which transactionally relevant information is uncodified, concrete, and only diffused to small groups.
4   Fiefs, in which transactionally relevant information is uncodified, concrete, and undiffused.

These transactional structures are both the products and shapers of information flows. Where such flows are stable and recurrent, such structures will metamorphose into institutions.

Institutions impart a certain facticity to their knowledge base and are treated as stores of potential intelligence. Since such stores help to economize on data processing, transactions tend to gravitate towards those regions of the I-space well endowed with prior institutional investments. Institutions, however, not only enjoy a limited reach in the I-space, but also are prone to obsolescence on account of the effects of new information flows.

As pointed out in the preceding chapter, economics, although acknowledging the importance of information in economic exchange, has tended to concern itself primarily with information asymmetries and hence with the diffusion dimension of the I-space. By largely ignoring the influence of codification and abstraction on the distribution of information, it has been led to an essentially static form of institutional analysis that greatly underestimates the creative scope for learning in an economic system.

5.1: INTRODUCTION

Investing in the I-space

Whether movement in the I-space occurs cyclically, as we have hypothesized that it does when new knowledge is created, or whether it is random, it entails efforts and incurs costs in time, effort, resources and so on. What specific activities are associated with these costs? Essentially, those of problem-solving and of learning by doing in the case of vertical movement along $\bar{C}C$ and back, those of repetition and testing along $\bar{A}A$, and those of transmitting and receiving information in the case of horizontal movement along $\bar{D}D$. For the larger part of our waking moments, many of these costs might be considered trivial and may not even be reckoned such. A mother reading a bedtime story to her child (transmitting information) or a schoolboy mastering a computer game on his father's PC (absorption) may not think of themselves as particularly burdened; indeed, they may actively enjoy what they are doing. From a more analytical perspective, however, this is just another way of saying that what they get out of their respective activities justifies the effort that they put into them so that each is willing to invest time while their satisfaction lasts.

The willingness of the mother to invest time in bedtime reading may not be simply a question of immediate enjoyment, much as this may also be present. She may have more complex investment criteria involving the need to give her offspring a good start in life, the desire to develop a strong parental bond, and so on. Even if she is tired and not particularly inclined to read, she may still pull herself together and make the necessary effort if she takes a longer-term view of the benefits that accrue from this activity. The schoolboy's interest in his computer game, however, is likely to be more volatile. His father may rejoice at the idea that he is acquiring sophisticated technical skills, but at the point that the game bores him, he will drop it without a further thought and move on to his Spiderman comic or his Lego set.

The cost–benefit calculations performed by the mother and the schoolboy are likely to be unconscious or at best intuitive and informal. The mother does not sit down with pencil and paper to *compute* how many increments of career progression for her child an extra five minutes of bedtime reading will yield. Yet certain types of movements in the I-space require such levels of effort that they will only be undertaken following a fairly searching analysis. The problem-solving activities that make up a major research and development project, for example, may call for several hundred man-years of highly skilled and painstaking effort; or again the advertising campaign required to educate a market to the use of a radically new technical product – a diffusion cost – may run into tens of millions of dollars, and so on.

An important distinction should be drawn between the example of the mother and that of the schoolboy. Since the mother is communicating with her child, there is a sense in which the movement of information in the data field is visible; the child smiles, laughs, gasps, and generally provides feedback. By watching for this feedback we know whether or not data has effectively been transmitted. In the case of the schoolboy, by contrast, everything is hidden or impacted; whatever skill he has absorbed sitting alone in front of his father's PC remains his unique possession until, through some form of social interaction, he is led to show what he knows. Indeed, it may be in anticipation of such a future interaction that he is striving for mastery. He may, for example, be practising for a casual game with friends, or even for a tournament. In the latter case, the expected benefits of his efforts will run beyond the enjoyment of the moment and he may become willing to invest a correspondingly higher level of effort in practising his game. Indeed, he might now try to calculate informally what such a level should be in terms of other activities forgone that he would have preferred to pursue – i.e., hanging out with the gang, going to a movie, etc. But now, as in the case of the mother and her child, movement in the I-space is prompted by the prospects of a future return, a form of exchange with the schoolboy's physical or social environment whose consummation is spread out in space and in time.

Transactions

The use of information may be central to a physical or a social exchange or may be quite peripheral to it; for our purposes it matters not. In either case information ends up as support for a *transaction* between an agent and its environment, steering it towards desired outcomes and triggering adjustments on the way. In this chapter, we shall take transactions as the driving force behind the creation and use of information, giving a purpose and a logic to its flow and evolution in the data field. Transactions, past, present, and prospective, energize the field and endow it with a characteristic structure, accessible through the I-space.

Clearly, we are here using the term transaction in a broader sense than is common in economics where it has been taken as the ultimate unit of microeconomic analysis.[1] Simplifying somewhat, we might say that if money drives economic transactions, information drives transactions in general. Yet what is money if not a physical store of information? Like money, codified information can be a store of value, a measure of value, as well as a means of exchange; at certain times, one of these functions will predominate, at others another one will. And just as making money and exchanging it productively for goods and services require an intelligent expenditure of effort over time, and, usually, well ahead of a transaction, so do the production and exchange of information. In short, effective transacting requires prior investment.

At times, the creation of information may appear to be only loosely related to the transactions in which it might be used. The schoolboy playing around with a game on his microcomputer, for example, may only decide that he is of 'tournament class' *after* he has already achieved a measure of proficiency and this may have been quite casually acquired. He may not initially have thought of consciously investing time and effort to achieve a particular skill level. Yet looking back, he discovers that intentionally or not he *has* effectively invested himself and that his 'learning by doing' has moved him down the I-space from C, where he possessed no more than basic knowledge of the rules of the game, towards C̆, where he had implicitly internalized strategies and a feel for promising patterns of play.[2] He can now transact from a position in the space which was possibly inaccessible to him six months before.

To summarize, the production of information and its use in transactions both incur costs and are thus subject to economizing. In the 1970s, there occurred a revival of interest among economists in the economics of transaction, and Oliver Williamson in particular, building on the earlier work of Ronald Coase and John Commons, has explored the different institutional arrangements which govern transactional choices.[3] In this chapter, we shall also concern ourselves with the institutional order built up from transactions, but our focus will be less narrowly economic than the one adopted by Williamson. Like him, we shall argue that institutional structures aim partly at achieving transactional efficiencies and that where such efficiencies are effectively achieved they act somewhat like a magnetic field – a mathematician would call them 'attractors' – drawing the uncommitted transaction into a given institutional orbit. Yet in contrast to Williamson's, our concept of transactions is underpinned by an explicit rather than an implicit theory of information production and exchange which yields a different way of classifying them as well as a distinctive approach to their governance. We find ourselves in consequence in the realm of political economy rather than of economics *tout court*.

In the next chapter, we shall show how the institutions that crystallize out of transactional structures mediate a cultural order; a powerful link between institutional economics and cultural analysis is thus established. Attempts to build such a link have been made before, notably by William Ouchi;[4] yet Ouchi, I feel, had underestimated the role that must be played by information in such an analysis. By treating, as we intend to do, transactional structures and institutions as *emergent* phenomena in a data field, we are placing the information environment in which a transaction occurs at the heart of our analysis.

5.2: TYPES OF TRANSACTIONS

Structures and processes

In what way might an individual's or a group's access to information influence the terms on which they enter into different forms of social exchange? Cast in the language of the I-space, the question becomes 'What roles do the codification, abstraction, and diffusion of information play in the way that an individual or a group construct and enact their social world?' We share Mary Douglas's ambition to go beyond the assertion put out by social phenomenology that the individual's life-world (*Umwelt*) is socially constructed.[5] Like her, we would like to know what kinds of worlds are likely to be constructed when social relations take on this or that form. Yet we could equally well run the lines of causal influence in reverse and ask what kinds of social relationships are brought forth by a given way of constructing the world. A materialist position sees the life-world as all superstructure, an emanation from the social and economic relationships which it expresses with modest, if any, causal powers of its own. An idealist position, conversely, subordinates the creation of social and economic structures to the imperatives of a particular cosmology or world view. It argues, so to speak, either from design or from an all-embracing universal concept.[6] The flow of information in the data field can effectively accommodate both approaches, since it is both channelled by structures – social, physical, cognitive, etc. – and in turn serves to build these up. Structures are zones of stability in a dynamic process that reach out into the field to modify its configuration. Structure and process here mutually determine each other. The resulting patterns can be exceedingly complex and no description of these will be attempted here. Our aim, more modestly, is to identify the type of structure that is likely to crystallize out of information flows in certain regions of the data field – what Max Weber, in another discourse, would have labelled *ideal types* – and briefly to investigate both its intrinsic social attributes and how these might be modified by the action of the SLC over time. Our approach remains consistent with the connectionist metaphor discussed in Chapter 2. Transactions activate complex patterns of information exchange within a network of agents in potential interaction with each other. The patterns themselves are the product of excitatory or inhibitory links between individual transactions that compete or collaborate with each other. The analogy with the behaviour of neural nets should need no further elaboration.

A transactional typology

It is the SLC itself which brings forth transactional structures in the I-space; articulations of distinct phases in its trajectory. In this chapter we identify four such structures. There may be more in practice but we believe these will be hybrids and thus not amenable to analysis as ideal types. The location of our four structures is shown in Figure 5.1. We have labelled them markets, bureaucracies, clans, and fiefs, the first three in deference to existing transactional typologies, and the last one on account of its provocative connotations.[7]

The fact that existing transactional typologies such as those of Williamson and Ouchi might be made to fit into the I-space amounts to a quick and dirty test for the plausibility of our claim that transactional structures can be

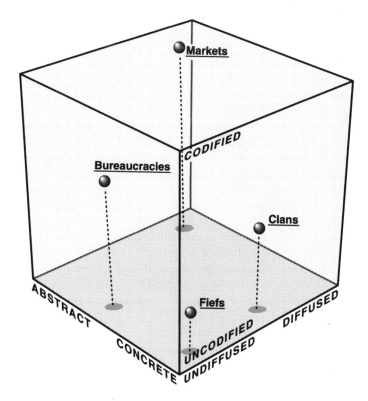

Figure 5.1 A transactional typology

viewed as an emergent property of information flows. What then needs to be established in the sections that follow is how far the social patterns of behaviour associated with each structure could reasonably be predicted from the characteristics of the information environment in which they occur. More challengingly, one would expect to discern some systematic relationship between the dynamic evolution of the data field brought about by information flows themselves and shifts of emphasis in the building up and maintenance of institutions away from one type of structure and towards one better adapted to new constraints imposed by the changing nature of the data. At a macroscopic scale, that at which the aggregation of transactional populations in the SLC yields discernible institutional patterns, one could then reasonably expect any shift that occurs between structures to tell us something about the nature of social evolution. This will be the subject of Chapter 6.

We next examine our transactional structures individually.

5.3: MARKETS

Information characteristics

In the case of pure markets we are dealing with transactions the effectiveness of which depends on the provision of two items of well-codified, abstract information being available to all members in a given population: quantities and prices. Yet if such information is so available it will be *because* it is abstract and well codified. Of course, much non-codified and concrete information is also often widely distributed in a population and is therefore collaterally available in market transactions, but since it tends to diffuse only slowly and mostly in face-to-face situations, it is subject to lags, leakages, and distortions. Given that with respect to this second type of information, one can hardly argue that everyone is in possession of *the same* transactional information as required by the theory of efficient markets,[8] it has tended until recently to be either underemphasized or ignored.

Codified, abstract information can be acquired and transmitted by impersonal means. Although impersonality is usually associated with large distances and in our day with modern communications technology, it is also quite viable in many face-to-face relationships. The key point is that in an impersonal social exchange, one is not essentially concerned with the identity of the other party even if this happens to be knowable. It would be unusual, for example, to enquire into the family background, personality, or value system of a street newspaper vendor before deciding to purchase an evening paper. If both the price and the type of contents of the paper are known beforehand, the transaction will be brief and to the point – indeed, in the typical case, it may even be wordless. Both parties will be concerned to minimize the time taken up by the transaction and get on with other business – if, say, it takes place during the evening rush hour when the vendor expects to make his/her best sales to large volumes of people hurrying home, personalizing the relationship with any one buyer will be bad business. Anyone, such as an out-of-town tourist, who starts asking for transactional information on the newspaper's price or its contents, may receive a pretty curt reply to his/her questions. The purchaser is in fact *expected* to know the paper's price and its contents.

On the other hand, transpose this hapless tourist to a Saudi Arabian *souk* where codified information on the goods displayed is neither much available nor much diffused, and the transaction acquires quite a different character. Here, personalizing the relationship will become the central requirement of a bargaining process which proceeds, like Walras's auctioneer, by *tâtonnement*.[9] Yet Walras's auctioneer strives for impersonal outcomes since these help to speed up the process. The auctioneer is helped in this by the fact that he/she finds himself in a multilateral bargaining situation in which buyers and sometimes sellers are anxious *not* to reveal their respective identities. In the *souk*, however, bargaining will be bilateral in nature. Since everyone does not possess the same information as to price, quality, or the level of demand, it pays both parties to find out more about each other. The seller, for instance, might wish to discriminate pricewise between buyers who are 'wised-up' and those who are not. The buyer may wish to know more about the product's quality and the seller's honesty in describing it. Both sides will therefore be attentive to nuance and context, looking for clues, and 'sizing up' the other.[10]

Although buying a newspaper from a street vendor and buying an article in a Saudi Arabian *souk* are both characterized as market exchanges, the key difference between the two kinds of transaction is that the ready availability of relevant codified information to both parties in the first case places the buyer and the seller on an equal footing. In contrast to the case in the Saudi *souk*, the cost of haggling is eliminated for both parties. The newspaper seller knows that she will not get a purchaser to pay more and the latter will not expect to pay less than the going rate for an evening paper.

Efficient versus real markets

This first kind of transaction is therefore somewhat closer to what economists refer to as efficient *markets*. Only somewhat, however, since the price of an evening paper does not respond to every fluctuation in supply and demand conditions but is set in anticipation of future market trends. Thus a knowledge of price by the parties avoids haggling and reduces transaction costs, but it only affects the price itself with a lag.

Depending as they do on the speedy and extensive diffusion of abstract codified information, efficient markets have become the paradigm case of economic exchange. In the real world, however, they are also extremely rare and, for the most part, represent something one aspires to rather than expects. Why? There are many possible reasons for this. Here we shall give only two. Firstly, as markets increase in efficiency, the larger the number of players that are made to compete on an equal footing. This requires the freedom to enter or exit markets in response to price movements. In reality, however, and for practical reasons, most markets are limited in size so that over time some players may acquire a disproportionate weight relative to others. They are then in a position to influence price–volume relationships and become price makers rather than price takers. In fact, it has only been with the advent of information technologies that allow continuous trading across space and time that certain types of markets have been able to approximate the economist's definition of efficiency. In earlier times markets were intermittent affairs that found it hard to bring together would-be buyers and sellers in one place. The Champagne fairs of the thirteenth century, for example, took place on certain fixed dates only – usually five or six times a year – and involved such high transaction costs for the parties that for the most part only luxury goods could justifiably be traded there.[11]

Secondly, and more problematically, a market only achieves efficiency where the prices at which trading occurs embody all the transactionally relevant information available to buyers and sellers. Thus not only does price behaviour reflect current trading conditions, but everything that is currently known about future trading conditions as well. This 'rational expectations' view of markets in effect amounts to a requirement that all such transactional information be fully codified, abstracted, and diffused.[12]

The workings of the SLC itself should alert us to the near impossibility of ever fully satisfying this requirement. A price that is the outcome of bilateral bargaining between economic agents (*a priori*, therefore, this excludes our newspaper vendor) is a *local* affair that has the character of a hypothesis to be tested *both* against knowledge of 'local circumstances of time and place'[13] and against non-local, abstract knowledge of prices practised elsewhere. Much of the local knowledge that goes to make up the price in fact stays local, but the price struck only effectively captures it as transactionally relevant information if the hypothesis is a good one, i.e., if exchange actually takes place at that price[14] and if that price effectively has implications for exchange practised non-locally.

Defenders of the rational expectation view will argue that it is not essential to start with good hypotheses concerning prices providing that subsequent hypotheses are corrigible and can be improved by learning. In other words, local prices are tested against the market price and all other available information and adjusted accordingly.[15] Learning so defined contributes to the movement of prices towards equilibrium, that unique price at which the market is cleared.

Markets and learning processes

Some light upon this issue can be shed by Ross Ashby's 'law of requisite variety'.[16] The law states that learning, to be effective, must operate at a rate that matches that of changes occurring in the organism's environment. The law does not guarantee that such learning, even if effective, will necessarily also be epistemologically correct: it may, after all, be built on a faulty hypothesis.[17] The rational expectations hypothesis ignores this feature of the law of requisite variety and takes market learning to be epistemologically unproblematic. Systematic errors are sooner or later weeded out and random errors do not impede the learning process.[18] It is thus, by assumption, that market learning contributes to an equilibrating process and movement towards a single equilibrium price. And if, as one approaches equilibrium, the rate of change in the market environment decreases, the rate of learning by economic agents is, so to speak, allowed to 'catch up'.

Yet our SLC points to the possibility that a move *away* from equilibrium is itself the fruit of a learning process – i.e., knowledge absorption – which impacts what might otherwise be available knowledge in the heads of a few well-situated individuals capable of using it opportunistically and in novel ways. It thus becomes once more concrete and local – i.e., undiffused. To present this disequilibrating process merely as an interlude between two equilibrium points, as rational expectation theorists are prone to do on the argument that disequilibrium will sooner or later be followed by equilibrium, is to miss the essence of the phenomenon.

Clearly, any breach of the two conditions mentioned above – namely, that market entry and exit should be unimpeded and that market price should capture all available information – will tend to push transactions out of the market region and towards other parts of the I-space. The smaller the number of players, for example, the more likely it is that their identity as well as their relative size will begin to matter and that their behaviour will in fact embody local information known to them but not to others. They can then behave 'strategically'[19] with respect to other agents in the market who are less well informed. Strategic behaviour, of course, shows up in price movements and is thus sooner or later communicated. But it usually does so too late to matter, particularly where early learning has been successfully impacted and has allowed strategic actors to move away from equilibrium in opportunistic ways. In the absence of equilibrium, therefore, a market sometimes becomes the location in the I-space where 'suckers' are to be found, and these are unlikely to gain much consolation from the knowledge that others will one day learn from their mistakes.

One way of avoiding the 'small numbers' condition, as we have seen, is to make entry and exit into the market unrestricted. Any profit resulting from monopolistic positions would then immediately attract new entrants. The small-numbers condition itself, of course, if persistent, moves one either towards bureaucracies or towards clans in the I-space as the transactionally relevant population shrinks. Where market-relevant information has not been fully abstracted, codified, and captured by the price, transactions are more likely to migrate towards clans than towards bureaucracies. Some of the more local uncodified information relevant to transactions will then only be transmitted face to face and will therefore no longer be available to all would-be participants. It will only be passed on to those close at hand: to colleagues, friends, and relatives who may consequently enjoy an information advantage with respect to 'outsiders'.

It is worth noting that the two impediments to market efficiency just described – i.e., barriers to entry and an inadequate codification and abstraction of transactionally relevant information – tend to mutually reinforce each other. Transacting among small numbers, for example, will tend to stabilize relationships and increase the opportunities for personalizing them and thus for transmitting uncodified information face to face. Yet transacting with uncodified and concrete information is an uncertain, time-consuming business that will automatically tend to limit the number of participants that can be involved.

Moving in the I-space towards clans and moving towards bureaucracies, however, involve quite different responses to the workings of SLC. In the first case, one follows the cycle out of the market region in a way that might almost be called 'natural' since the move away from equilibrium and towards small numbers in effect reflects a form of market learning (absorption) and impacting. In the second case one moves against the cycle by explicitly setting up barriers to the diffusion of codified abstract knowledge (see next section).

The markets which today are considered to come closest to achieving the efficiency ideal are financial markets in industrialized economies. Not only do they now benefit from a telecommunications technology that ensures a rapid diffusion of codified information – a price movement on Wall Street, for example, will be registered in a matter of seconds in both London and Hong Kong – but with the growing integration of national financial markets into a single global one, they have increased severalfold the number of players who can freely participate in their operations.

Yet, as the 'insider trading' scandals of recent years amply demonstrate, even in so-called efficient markets, information is never fully codified, abstracted, or diffused. Market prices continue to conceal as much as they reveal and small numbers lurk opportunistically within the large numbers required for transactional efficiency.

Markets and social values

Economists will continue to debate whether the asymmetric distribution of market-relevant information constitutes an insuperable barrier to the attainment of transactional efficiency as technically defined. Yet efficiency can also be impaired by how the presence of information asymmetries is perceived by participants themselves. Why else would insider trading scandals 'rock' Wall Street? Why should a few winks and nods between eminent and established figures of the financial community land them with four- or five-year jail sentences? There is little mystery here: by their behaviour such people may not have posed any great threat to market efficiency as technically defined by rational expectation theorists; but in being perceived to benefit unfairly from an information advantage they were challenging the *value system* of the market as an institution. It is this value system that keeps a market working as close to its ideal as is feasible under given circumstances and, in the absence of its lubricating effects, both confidence in the fairness of the institution and a willingness to use it for transactional purposes will be undermined. If too many people leave the market in search of more equitable alternatives, large numbers will once more give way to small numbers and the market's efficiency will be further compromised.[20]

Can components of this value system be identified? Perhaps the two core values that underpin market transactions are a belief in individual rationality and a belief in competition as a regulating mechanism.

A belief in individual rationality received its most powerful formulation in the philosophies of the Enlightenment as systemized by d'Holbach[21] and, in economics, its most popular articulation in the writings of Adam Smith. Simply stated, it holds that individuals are quite capable of deciding for themselves what constitute their real interests and of then going about satisfying these in sensible ways, always providing that they are adequately informed as to what their real options are. Individual rationality, to be effective, thus presupposes access to transactionally relevant information.

Individual rationality *per se*, however, does not necessarily yield socially desirable outcomes, and it would never by itself have commanded the attention it has done had not another important insight also been available. For if individuals can be shown to be rational in the pusuit of their own goals what is to guarantee that such goals, when aggregated across a large number of individuals, are in any way compatible with each other or that if they are not, social harmony can ever be preserved?

Adam Smith was certainly not the only one to see how the market might resolve this dilemma in the eighteenth century, but he gave the solution its most broadly intelligible formulation. He did not argue, as many have taken him to, that the selfish pursuit of individual interests was ethical,[22] but merely that it was reasonable. Smith held that if self-interested individuals could be put into regulated competition with each other in pursuit of their respective goals, then, from a social point of view, there was no need to pass judgement on the ethical worth of these goals; they were in effect a matter for the individual and his conscience. Socially efficient outcomes could be secured *in spite of* the selfish pursuit of individuals, providing the latter could be made to compete fully and fairly with each other. Under such circumstances individual rationality would be productive of social rationality and the information generated by countless local transactions would be used by the market to regulate itself.[23]

Social welfare will only be maximized in this self-regulating scheme, however, when competitors are numerous and small, when no transaction is of such a size as to produce distorting effects, when no barriers exist to prevent people from entering or leaving the market, and finally when competitors cannot collude to form powerful subgroups. It is, of course, this last condition that 'insider trading' violates, thereby demonstrating how difficult it is to satisfy these requirements in practice even in the most sophisticated and best-functioning markets.

Linked to these core values are other values that are not always made explicit but are none the less implied by markets as an equitable institutional order. For example, freedom to choose goes hand in hand with a belief in personal responsibility for one's own fate, which in turn translates into a social value stressing equality of opportunity rather than equality of outcome.[24] Put more harshly, rational men are equally free to make choices – some will be good, some will be poor; in all cases, though, they must bear the consequences. The doctrine of personal responsibility promotes both tolerance and impersonality. Tolerance, because if each individual is free to pursue personal objectives according to his own lights, then he must not be unduly constrained in doing so through the moral judgement of others – in this sense, markets are pluralistic as well as individualistic. Impersonality, because any concern with the identity and welfare of the other party to a transaction beyond that minimum required by civility and the preservation of the social order can act as a brake on one's own maximization objectives and hence to the detriment of a properly competitive relationship. Thus collusion between free economic agents, that is, those not bound by blood relationships or those of employment, translates into the pursuit of a group welfare function which threatens the atomism of the market, and by implication its efficiency as an allocator of social resources.[25]

Perhaps the most fundamental social value underpinning the institution of markets remains the belief that an individual must be left free to pursue his life chances as he sees them. Possibly originating in the medieval doctrine of the sanctity of the individual soul, the acknowledged primacy of individual over collective goals, coupled with a growing understanding of how the latter could be served by the former through the mechanism of self-regulation, gradually came to erode the perceived legitimacy of the mercantile state in the eighteenth and nineteenth centuries. Markets have existed in some form or other in most cultures and in most historical periods but nearly always in a subordinate role to other institutions. Only in western liberal doctrine were they later to be elevated into a dominant component of the social order, albeit one maintained by the regulatory power of the state – the latter exercised through a form of bilateral governance in which markets retain the leading role.

Markets as a social order

The automatic self-regulatory nature of efficient market processes, however, largely does away with the need for state direction in those regions where markets rule. Inspired by the politically as well as the economically liberating implications of ideas of self-regulation, 'He governs best who governs least' then became the slogan of *laissez-faire* capitalism in the nineteenth century, some of whose protagonists held that much of social life could be reduced to market processes supervised by a 'nightwatchman state'. What had initially evolved as a governance structure for certain classes of transactions then for true believers became elevated to the status of an ideology which could reign over the social order as a whole – indeed, by appropriating Darwin's theory of natural selection for its own purposes after the theory's publication in

1859, market ideology could expand hegemonistically to claim dominion over organic life itself.[26]

Although these hegemonistic impulses of market ideology have since been somewhat reined in, market processes still remain the dominant paradigm for economic transactions in those countries where free market institutions were allowed to flourish.[27] They increasingly came to be perceived as an integral part of the natural order with market equilibrium expressing an underlying tendency of the social system as a whole towards stability when this is unimpeded by external 'disturbances'.[28] The whole arrangement is magnificently Newtonian since once the metaphysics of equilibrium has been suitably established – this could only be done mathematically, not empirically – any move away from the equilibrium point became by definition an 'external' disturbance and hence of no threat to the metaphysical core of the doctrine. As Williamson puts it in *Markets and Hierarchies*, 'in the beginning there were markets',[29] and the economist's concept of 'market failure' is a normative presumption in favour of market transactions which implicitly casts alternative forms of governance as second best.

As we have seen above, where 'market failure' occurs on information grounds, it will move transactions towards those regions of the I-space occupied by bureaucracies or clans, in the first case pushing against the flow of the SLC, in the second, moving along with it and allowing it to run its course. We consider bureaucracies next.

5.4: BUREAUCRACIES

The informational characteristics of bureaucracies

Like market transactions, bureaucratic ones depend on the use of well-codified and mostly abstract information – financial budgets, monthly reports, economic assessments, statistical surveys, etc. But now this information is no longer available to all agents as it might be in a market. It is the authorized possession of a limited number of individuals who thereby stand to gain a legitimate transactional advantage from it.

The theory of the SLC is built upon the premise that information has a natural tendency to diffuse when it is codified and abstract so that in effect it has little inherent stability in that region of the I-space where bureaucracies are to be found. If information is to remain there, as it must if bureaucratic institutions are to emerge at all, barriers to its diffusion must be erected. And it is the very presence of such barriers that gives bureaucratic transactions their particular flavour.

Barriers are not necessarily designed to block the diffusion of information as such, but simply to make it controllable by designated individuals. In contrast to the market case, in bureaucracies diffusion ceases to be a random process with receivers colliding haphazardly into messages that are somehow 'out there' for the taking. Messages are now distributed discreetly on a point-to-point basis with further redistribution also taking place selectively. If the appropriate metaphor for the diffusion of information in a market is that of an Alka-Seltzer tablet dissolving in water, the one that best conveys bureaucratic information processing is that of the central nervous system, a hierarchically structured communication network. Of course, if we consider that knowledge is power, then the differential possession of transactional information confers considerable advantage to individuals who operate the barriers to its diffusion. The information resources under their control put them in a position of strength in many forms of social exchange, and the institutionalization of transactions in this region of the I-space is therefore designed to ensure that the circumstances in which such individuals come to possess valued information, and the use to which it is then put, are both perceived to be socially legitimate. A confidential report, for example, transmitted by a government's intelligence services to a head of state is not expected to be widely diffused; its restricted circulation will usually be granted a high degree of legitimacy by the country's citizens given the threat to their security posed by any leaks. A publicly quoted industrial corporation, on the other hand, which sought to prevent the publication of its financial accounts in order to avoid answering embarrassing questions at a shareholders' meeting might quickly provoke an outcry. The first type of transaction therefore is a plausible candidate for bureaucratic governance whereas the second should properly be assigned to market governance.

But how are individuals effectively selected for the privilege of operating barriers to information diffusion? What criteria are used? In the real world, these are numerous and they are applied with varying degrees of rigour. In the case of the pure bureaucratic transaction, however – the ideal type – we need only retain two: competence and accountability.

Competence and accountability

The competence criterion ensures that only those who know how to use the information they receive do in fact get it, and that those who do not are kept out of the distribution channel. The decision-maker has to be capable of *evaluating* and *interpreting* transactional information received prior to deciding how it should be used and to whom it should be further distributed. For this he/she needs a knowledge of *context* to guide his/her analysis. What the decision-maker then decides to retransmit up or down the communication hierarchy is always the product of an act of selection; i.e., an abstraction and a codification. Competence, therefore, has to extend beyond the identification of appropriate nodes in the communication network with which to interact, and cover as well an ability to formulate appropriate messages in an intelligible code in order to overcome Shannon's three communication problems.[30] The consummate bureaucrat is, above all, a consummate communicator.

The accountability criterion is required to ensure that the privileged possession of information does not lead to abuse. In a bureaucracy, individuals are no longer free to pursue their own personal objectives as they are in a market. Objectives are now hierarchically imposed from above. Individuals are granted power and authority in a bureaucracy to the extent that they accept as their own objectives that are handed down. They are not required to subscribe to these personally, merely to act as if they did. Yet it is sometimes easy for individuals holding such power privileges to exploit them for ends that have little or no institutional legitimacy. They must therefore be constrained in their behaviour either by the presence of external control systems designed to render their behaviour visible, or through the gradual development of a personal value system that can act as an internalized control system. Where transactions are well codified and based on abstract principles and can therefore be recorded and made visible, the first kind of control system might be preferred. Where the information used in transactions is concrete and cannot be so codified, however, only those who have been socialized to the required value system and can demonstrate a credible commitment to it will be entrusted with its possession. The latter case, however, ceases to describe a purely bureaucratic transaction; it properly belongs to the fief region of the I-space and will be further discussed in section 5.6. Yet in both instances the differential possession of information creates a hierarchical transactional structure; in bureaucracies this becomes a formal and specialized communication network based on impersonal authority. In contrast to fiefs, therefore, power in bureaucracies is constrained by structure.

Roles and routines

A formal communication hierarchy possesses distinctive properties. For a start, the authority relations it describes are built largely upon expertise. Eligibility for a particular position is determined by meritocratic criteria that stress both competence and accountability. Then, since such a hierarchy deals with codified information, its transactional style tends to remain largely impersonal. Roles – i.e., the codification and standardization of behaviour patterns – rather than the vagaries of personalities and of individual identities are what matter. Roles express behavioural clusters of specialized knowledge and expertise that serve to mutually orient both the senders and receivers of codified abstract information. Roles also allow transactions themselves to be standardized and subsequently routinized so that larger volumes of information can then be processed by the hierarchy. But since roles reflect the logic of standardized transactional requirements rather than individual idiosyncrasies, they also demand impersonality. Just as in a pure market transaction at a given price, one customer is as good as another, so in a pure bureaucratic transaction, providing that each party possesses the required competence and sense of accountability, one role incumbent is as good as another.[31]

Bureaucracies typically, but not always,[32] involve smaller numbers than markets do, although they tend to deal in more varied and more complex information than markets can properly handle. A market is designed to process large volumes of abstract data coded as prices and quantities. Bureaucracies also deal with abstract codified data, which can therefore be written down on paper, but it is often of a kind that cannot so easily be standardized. Disparate kinds of written data – on personnel records, legislation, budgets, etc., – have to be reconciled in ways that often call for a knowledge of context and the exercise of personal judgement. Of course, bureaucratic routines that integrate and structure transactional information into more manageable wholes are constantly being sought; yet since such routines cannot deal with every unforeseen contingency – remember that codification involves selection from a limited set of alternative possibilities – a certain number of transactions will inevitably fall outside their scope. These will be 'referred upwards' and thus travel up the hierarchy until they find a procedure – which may or may not be routinized – for dealing with them.

This upward drift of transactions for which no suitable code exists at a lower hierarchical level suggests that, whatever the nature of the organization, not all transactions in a hierarchy can be purely bureaucratic, and that as a consequence fuzzy, unanalysable, non-routine decisions must inevitably gravitate towards the top. As we shall see in section 5.6, such transactions belong in fiefs. The point that we wish to make here, however, is that since, in contrast to what prices are meant to do in markets, codes cannot completely capture all the information relevant to bureaucratic transactions, these occupy a position somewhat lower down the codification dimension than markets do in the I-space and remain somewhat less abstract (see Figure 5.1).

Bureaucratic values

How does the value system that underpins bureaucratic transactions compare with that of markets? Certain values the two institutional orders will share; in other respects they are totally different.

Take, for example, rationality. Both markets and bureaucracies aim at the rational integration of means and ends and both make use of codified and abstract information for achieving this. But here the resemblance ends. Defenders of markets believe that each individual exercises rationality in the pursuit of his own personal goals and that, providing that enough of the relevant information is available to all, this atomistic collection of goal-seeking individuals achieves optimum social outcomes through a process of self-regulation. Individual rationality under efficient market governance thus generates social rationality with little or no leakage. Defenders of bureau-cracy, by contrast, challenge this automatic transposition of rationality from the individual to the collective level. Not only might self-regulating processes not function properly, but even if they did they might still fail to bring about socially desirable outcomes. These must then be secured by hierarchical means. Certain carefully chosen individuals will therefore be legally empow-ered to represent the collective interest and to pursue it through a process of hierarchical coordination.[33] Relations between different levels of the hier-archy will then be based on the exercise of authority, legitimated by expertise rather than by market power. As Max Weber has defined them, bureaucratic relations are based on a belief in rational–legal order.[34]

Those in authority, then, are deemed to know more than their subordinates and this gives them the power to coordinate the allocation of resources; the use of that power will be considered legitimate by those who submit to it as long as it is applied to social rather than personal ends. By assuming at the outset an asymmetric distribution of information among social and economic agents, bureaucracy may be thought to require less heroic assumptions than markets. In practice this may be so, but a bureaucratic ideology, by positing the existence of the all-seeing professional administrator working selflessly in the service of society, strains our credulity in other ways.[35] The synoptic abstract rationality of markets has not been done away with, but merely monopolized by those who, now calling themselves 'central planners', sit atop the administrative hierarchy.

Bureaucracies also share with markets a concern for stability and a Newtonian world view that sees change as the externally generated disturb-ance of a system wanting to move towards equilibrium. Yet in bureaucracies, the system does not move towards equilibrium unaided: the invisible hand of the market is replaced by the visible hand of an all-knowing administra-tion drawing on information that is for the most part codified, abstract, but not diffused.

The stability of a hierarchical order is in fact incompatible with the widespread and uncontrolled diffusion of the transactional information on which it rests; the non-sharing of information consequently becomes a deeply entrenched bureaucratic value among those who cherish such stability. If market institutions struggle against insider trading and the exploitation of information asymmetries, bureaucratic ones by contrast strive to prevent 'leaks' of valuable transactional information: self-regulation requires information sharing; hierarchical coordination requires information hoarding. Interestingly enough, in both cases, institutional transgressions take the form of an uncodified and concrete transaction – a social exchange whose transient face-to-face nature remains hidden to all but the few involved in it and which subsequently leaves no trace.

A third important bureaucratic value briefly touched on above and irrelevant to the functioning of efficient markets is that of professionalism, which harnesses the privileged possession of specialized knowledge and competence to an ethic of service. Professionalism in fact operates in two modes:

1   It serves to legitimize the non-diffusion of diffusible information by arguing that such information 'getting into the wrong hands' would not serve the public interest. The implication here is that the 'right hands' do serve the public interest and are prepared to subordinate private goals to public ones. A professional bureaucrat or 'public servant', for example, is someone who not only has the technical competence to select the means once the ends have been decided, but, within certain politically definable limits, gives himself the moral right to select the ends themselves. The bureaucrat's commitment to an ethic of service qualifies him/her to specify social goals, whether this be done selectively (i.e., in situations where collective choice finds no coherent expression either in markets or through the ballot box[36] – in other words, where markets fail) or more comprehensively, as in command economies, where individual choice is granted from the outset a low level of legitimacy. The social counterpart to the technical and moral authority of the professional bureaucrat, of course, is obedience from subordinates and compliance or at least acquiescence from clients.

2   It serves to bolster the exercise of highly personal idiosyncratic skills in ill-defined situations where a high degree of interpersonal trust between the parties is required if a transaction is to take place at all. A doctor–patient relationship or a lawyer with his client typify this kind of social exchange. As in the first mode described above, there is information asymmetry between the transacting parties, but here such information is intrinsically hard to codify and thus does not transmit easily between a professional and her client. The latter, therefore, not only has to take on trust that the former has the requisite ability to perform the service that is being solicited for, but also that she is willing to use it exclusively in the client's own interest.[37]

As we shall see in section 5.5, the second mode in which professionalism operates properly belongs to the clan region of the I-space and is not in fact representative of the bureaucratic transaction as such. It is more personalized and involves smaller numbers than the latter, since in bureaucracies professional competence and accountability can be effectively achieved, and on a larger scale, by more impersonal means.[38]

Bureaucratic competition

Bureaucratic transactions, no less than market ones, involve competition between participants, and in both cases individual success involves moving from a position on the right in the I-space, where one is a net recipient of knowledge, towards a position on the left along the diffusion curve, where one becomes a net contributor.

But surely, it might be objected, on the right we do not find bureaucracies but markets. Was this not after all the burden of section 5.3? What would a bureaucrat be doing on the right anyway unless he had lost control of his stock of information? The answer is that transactional structures compete with each other throughout the I-space but are better positioned to survive in some parts of the space than in others on account of the fit that obtains between their information requirements and the characteristics of their local information environment. Thus, for example, a market represents a limiting case of hierarchical decentralization, the point at which information parity between all actors in an organization effectively allows self-regulating processes to take over from hierarchical coordination. Yet until one reaches the top right-hand corner of the I-space, some measure of hierarchical coordination remains possible. Where transactional possibilities overlap in this way, we may either view the situation as one in which bureaucracies extend themselves to the right along the diffusion scale reaching into markets to impose a measure of hierarchical structure – such would be the case, for example, where natural monopolies are regulated by the state – or, conversely, we may see market processes moving leftward along the diffusion scale and penetrating bureaucracies in the form of internal organizational competition – between divisions, functional units, individuals, etc. How does such competition work in practice?

Both Adam Smith and later Joseph Schumpeter realized that no player actually enjoys the rigours of pure competition and that players will do what they can to escape it by attempting to secure for themselves some monopolistic advantage – today the term used is 'competitive advantage': it sounds less offensive while retaining essentially the same meaning.[39] Smith saw the phenomenon somewhat statically as a source of economic inefficiency to be deplored, whereas Schumpeter thought of it in more dynamic terms as a stimulus to innovation.[40] He understood that the quest for competitive advantage and the flight from pure competition themselves constituted competitive processes that brought but temporary relief. Either way, a monopolistic control of markets resting on an information advantage amounts to a leftward move in the I-space and away from the purely competitive case.

The quest for competitive advantage characterizes a bureaucracy no less than a market. A move up an organizational hierarchy where there are fewer players confers an information advantage that is monopolistic in nature and that also translates into a leftward movement in the I-space: information has to be shared with a smaller percentage of the transactionally relevant population. Yet a leftward move in a bureaucracy remains in principle meritocratic and rests on competence and accountability rather than on raw market power. Nevertheless, both bureaucratic and market moves towards the left share a common aspiration to overcome the barriers to entry that will inevitably be found there in order to escape the turbulence of competition on the right. When these barriers have been crossed, transactions can then navigate in calmer waters; thoughtful people can now see where they are going and appropriate courses of action can be chartered. Competition has not of course been completely eliminated on the left of the diffusion scale, but it becomes a more leisurely, more gentlemanly affair involving but a few players.[41]

The bureaucratic order

If individual freedom in a self-regulating cosmos remains the dominant value underpinning market transactions, the necessity of subordinating individuals to collective interests and a belief in the power of orderly and rational planning characterize the bureaucratic outlooks. The 'blindness' of markets, with no competent hand to guide them, is abhorred and considered to be a social aberration. If, as Williamson claims, in the beginning there were only markets, then it must surely follow that in a progressive society the move away from a Hobbesian 'war of all against all' and towards the security and serenity of hierarchy must count as a desirable outcome. The regression towards markets, the drift towards the right in the I-space, must then amount to a form of 'bureaucratic failure'.

Many liberals would argue, however, that societal evolution actually requires bureaucratic failure. When citizens all enjoy high levels of education, then information asymmetries can no longer be justified on welfare grounds. The absolutist state of the seventeenth and eighteenth centuries, the paradigm case of a bureaucratic order,[42] was only possible while the coding skills conferred by education remained in the hands of an administrative elite. With industrialization and the spread of mass education this asymmetry ceased to be tenable. It was maintained in place on a large scale by the Marxist-Leninist state – a twentieth-century attempt at state absolutism – in those countries where mass education had not yet emerged: the USSR, China. Where mass education is available, however, it gradually erodes a pure bureaucratic order from within – witness Eastern Europe in 1989, and in 1991 the Soviet Union itself.[43]

In the People's Republic of China, on the other hand, where mass education is not yet widely available above – or even at – primary school level,[44] the bureaucracy, whilst failing to deliver, has not in fact 'failed' in favour of markets. An examination of the SLC reveals that markets are in fact not the only resting place for failed bureaucracies. Like markets themselves moving towards bureaucracies, the latter can also move against the cycle: towards fiefs. As we shall see in section 5.6 and illustrate in Chapter 7, this is a move towards feudalism. Before considering this alternative form of bureaucratic failure, however, let us first examine the second way that markets themselves can fail, when, allowing the SLC to follow its natural course, they move into clans.

5.5: CLANS

The information characteristics of clans

Markets fail when information asymmetries between transacting parties create a small-numbers condition and the self-regulating nature of the exchange process can no longer be assumed. A hierarchical governance structure might then emerge either to complement or to replace market processes. Is hierarchy the only option?

Information asymmetries, as we have seen, can arise in a number of ways. Those codifying new knowledge on the left of the I-space, for example, may choose to be selective in what they diffuse – such is often the case with patent disclosures: enough is revealed to secure the patent but not enough to allow imitation by would-be competitors. Alternatively, creators of new knowledge may actually be unable to fully codify or abstract from certain areas of their experience which must consequently remain concrete and personal to them. In both these cases the clockwise progress of the SLC itself is slowed down, thus maintaining existing information asymmetries.

Moving against the cycle in an anti-clockwise direction in the upper region of the I-space, on the other hand, is another way of either maintaining or creating information asymmetries. It can mean developing proprietary coding skills for oneself, and then using them to make one's own discoveries or using them to gain privileged access to newly codified, abstract, but as yet undiffused knowledge. Bureaucratic competition pursues information asymmetries through either option; it consists of a regulated manoeuvring for position as far to the left as possible along the diffusion scale.

Yet information asymmetries can also result from *following* the SLC rather than either slowing it down or moving against it, from an absorption of codified, abstract knowledge that is subsequently impacted in idiosyncratic and possibly creative – but now uncodified – ways. Put another way, markets also fail when the learning-by-doing opportunities that they offer are skewed in favour of a small number of individuals who thereby gain a 'first mover' advantage from knowledge that is hard to articulate or to disclose.[45]

The small-numbers condition

The communication constraints imposed by uncodified and concrete information tend by themselves to generate a small-numbers condition since the number of agents that one can maintain a worthwhile face-to-face relationship with remains of necessity limited. We shall label small face-to-face groups that operate on the basis of shared but largely uncodified and concrete, i.e., local, information, *clans*. They represent a case of limited information diffusion in which a group of 'insiders' collectively enjoys an information advantage with respect to 'outsiders'.

Some of the authors who have studied the dynamics of transactions in clans tend to see many of them essentially as the outcome of instabilities in political and economic markets. Both Michels in *Political Parties*[46] and Olson in *The Logic of Collective Action*[47] call into question the self-regulating character of market transactions. And Axelrod in *The Evolution of Cooperation*[48] further demonstrates that the payoff to small-group collaboration in recurrent conditions will always be higher than to competition involving large numbers. The implication seems to be that institutional attempts to keep small groups of regularly transacting parties in a purely competitive arm's-length exchange relationship will often be subverted by the interest they have in banding together and in personalizing their dealings with each other.

Oliver Williamson and Alfred Chandler, by contrast, both see small-numbers clan transactions as being themselves unstable and subject to erosion by the logic of markets. Chandler, for example, in his study of the repeated attempts by many US industries to cartelize their operations at the turn of the century, found them to be short-lived and plagued by defections. Relations between cartel members were characterized by a lack of trust and a lack of any durably effective policing devices that could compensate for the lack of trust.[49]

Clearly, interpersonal trust must be counted an important ingredient in bringing about stability in clan transactions. Yet this quality of personal relationships, so important to information sharing behaviour when transactional data is uncodified and local, is subsumed by Williamson under the catch-all label of 'atmosphere' and is thus not perceived by him as extending the range of transactional options beyond those that he originally identified; i.e., those of markets (the large-numbers condition) and hierarchies (what we have termed bureaucracies) which usually regroup larger numbers than clans (although not always) yet smaller numbers than efficient markets, these being in theory open to everyone.[50] William Ouchi, one of Williamson's collaborators, has analysed the concept of the clan as a governance structure in its own right[51] and others have at various times referred to communes[52] or federations[53] as equally viable transactional possibilities. Yet none of these authors have conceptualized clans as anything other than a transactional form located in an intermediate position along the diffusion scale between markets and hierarchies.

Clans, however, are assignable to the lower region of the I-space. They deal essentially in fuzzy information which is diffusible enough to be shared by clan members in a given time period but not by the population as a whole. Should we characterize the data used by clans as tending towards the abstract or the concrete? Given the location of clan transactions on the SLC, we are tempted to answer 'the concrete' and in most cases this is likely to be right. Clans will treat as critical the local, particularistic data that affects the day-to-day working of clan life. Yet one can conceive of groupings whose essential concerns and ultimate effectiveness might well require a shared base of abstract knowledge. This might be truer, though, of a purely scientific community than, say, of a professional association whose primary mission might be to defend the interests of its members in the wider society – even if it does this while proclaiming its adherence to abstract values.

Exceptions such as the scientific community apart, clans exemplify the distinction drawn by the cultural anthropologist Edward Hall[54] between 'high context' and 'low context' cultures. The distinction is almost directly derivable from differences in their respective information environments: high context cultures deal with rich, concrete, uncodified data in face-to-face situations that are complex, multidimensional and subtle, whereas low context cultures orient their transactions towards the selective use of codified abstract data in clear, simple, impersonal settings.

As with Williamson's typology, Hall's also turns out to be only half the story. If in the first case markets and hierarchies as institutionalized information processing structures can only be located along the diffusion dimension of the I-space on account of Williamson's almost exclusive theoretical focus on information asymmetries, Hall's high context and low context cultures can only be placed in the E-space. Hall is in fact aware that context affects information-sharing behaviour but his observations do not lead to any theoretical analysis of this phenomenon that might cause him to refine or extend his typology. The phenomenon of information diffusion is left out of the picture.

The issue of trust

Clan transactions are inherently uncertain. Markets can handle risk where the possible range of outcomes and their likelihood of occurrence can be specified sufficiently to shape expectations. They are less well equipped to handle uncertainty.[55] How does transactional uncertainty arise? When neither the range of external contingencies faced by transacting parties, nor their possible responses, can be identified and assigned probabilities in advance; when, for example, it is impossible to be sure that someone faced with overwhelming opportunities or threats will remain steadfast in honouring earlier commitments which turn out subsequently to be vague or leaky. Market contracting then becomes an unreliable device for securing such commitment since it acknowledges as legitimate any self-seeking behaviour not specifically constrained by enforceable contract clauses or external legislation. *Caveat emptor* is as much of a comment on the informational deficiencies of markets where complete contacts cannot be written as it is on human nature as we know it.

Clan transactions assume information parity among clan members and for this reason they partly escape the 'moral hazard' issue that arises when one party possesses transactionally relevant information that the other does not. I say 'partly' because one information asymmetry remains; namely, a transacting individual's knowledge of her own intentions. She may choose to disclose these or she may not. In markets characterized by spot contracting, such disclosure is hard to elicit; the parties meet, exchange, and go their own ways. They owe each other nothing beyond civility. In more continuous interactions, however, intentions may gradually be discerned. The extensive socialization efforts associated with effective clan governance are specifically designed to keep such intentions mutually aligned.[56]

The elimination of moral hazard through a shared pattern of socialization is best achieved with small numbers. In any dealings between clan and outsiders, the moral hazard issue is likely to retain its full force. Within the clan structure itself, participants develop implicit forms of communication which simultaneously affirm and reinforce their 'apartness' from non-members; i.e., their exclusive access to a collectively apprehended reality that is either opaque or possibly invisible to outsiders. Apartness bolsters a group's identity and creates 'barriers to entry' which can be as varied as the initiation rites to which novices must submit on entering a religious community and the screening that applicants are put through before being admitted as members of an exclusive golf club.

Moral hazard is extensively discussed by Williamson who comes very close to the concept of information absorption, the move towards $\bar{C}$, in his analysis of information impactedness – a condition in which information sharing is perceived to be too costly to undertake on account of a transaction's lack of codifiability. Yet impacted information in Williamson's analysis simply moves one along $D\bar{D}$ further to the left and towards hierarchies *tout court*; by leaving to one side issues of codification and abstraction, it can yield no further transactional options.

Uncertain and complex transactions pose the problem of trust in an acute way and the greater the uncertainty, the greater the amount of trust between the parties needed to overcome it. As we shall see in section 5.6, the need for interpersonal trust grows greater as one moves towards $\bar{A}\bar{C}D$ in the I-space. Yet trust effectively turns out to be a required ingredient of *all* transactions in the lower region of the space – i.e., in $\bar{A}\bar{C}$ – where transactional contingencies can never be fully specified and catered for.

Trust relationships cannot be decreed. They either evolve or they do not. An understanding of the circumstances in which trust flourishes can be helpful in building it up, but it will remain a hit or miss affair dependent on a wide range of factors such as personality, cognition, prior familiarity with issues and agents, and so on. Prior familiarity seems to be a particularly important requirement in fostering attitudes of trust towards expected outcomes. Is there in fact any difference between the paratrooper who trusts that his parachute will open when he tumbles out of the aircraft thus saving him from a certain death, and the wounded infantryman who trusts his 'buddies' not to abandon him to the enemy as they pull back under attack? The former 'knows' his equipment and the latter 'knows' his buddies.

Trust is primarily a matter of prior familiarity and grounded expectations: the attribution by those who possess it of a higher probability to ostensibly uncertain outcomes or events than those lacking such familiarity would be willing to grant. Yet since familiarity requires time to build up, trust cannot be given freely beyond the boundaries within which familiarity has had time to evolve. These boundaries may gradually be pushed outwards but since one cannot be familiar with everything, whatever stock of trust is available must of necessity either get spread more thinly across people and events or it must be more selectively invested. One is then moved by degrees to trust *classes* of events rather than events themselves, and *categories* of people rather than specific individuals. What is gained in extension by codifying and abstracting in this way, however, is lost in intensity so that trust becomes a form of taken for granted knowledge subject to revision.

Of course, the process cuts both ways: a loss of trust in an individual can rapidly contaminate the social categories he is placed in. One of the major purposes of professional codes of conduct, for example, is to maintain a high degree of public trust in a group of people who exercise uncodified skills on a fiduciary basis. Professions stand to lose a great deal should that trust disappear, which is why they are often allowed to police themselves. In attempting to do so, however, they face a paradox in that the built-in disposition to trust colleagues in clan organization creates a bias in favour of the insider at the expense of the outsider – in this case the client or the public at large[57] – so that self-policing tends to become self-serving.

Clans and shared values

How does one minimize the risks involved in the granting of interpersonal trust? One looks for clues: background, reputation, affiliations, etc. But what constitutes a promising clue in a given situation will itself be the fruit of prior familiarity, of 'learning by doing', of a downward and horizontal move towards AC̄ in which information is absorbed and impacted in intangible ways. In clans such learning is a collective process. For this reason, people who share a common background, a shared system of values, will be quicker to trust each other than those who do not. The process of transmitting transactionally relevant information will be more efficient since much of it can be done implicitly – the old school tie, a certain accent or choice of words, a particular way of dressing, etc. A would-be 'con-man' has to master a host of implicit codes before he is in a position to abuse people's trust. And it is precisely when the con-man fails to to 'absorb' the necessary codes – that is, when he has gained access to them as an outsider rather than as an insider, and thus leaves them in their unadapted, codified form – that he is unmasked. He treats them as stereotypes whose nuances escape him. He rings false for reasons that those who do possess the codes may not themselves be able to articulate. Is this not precisely the problem that 'new wealth' faces in passing itself off for 'old wealth'? Does not the hurried effort at mastering the appropriate codes show through? Not always as clumsiness, but sometimes as a kind of technical virtuosity that smacks of overachievement?

The scope for the effective exercise of interpersonal trust is limited either by the number of people that can be known personally – i.e., that can be the focus of prior uncodified transactional investments – or by the number of implicit or explicit categories available to an individual for deriving reliable behavioural predictions. The weakness of stereotyping in addressing such limitations is that it so easily achieves false data processing economies. It amounts to a hurried construction of explicit categories based on traits or features that more often than not offer poor predictive value. Stereotyping leads to false generalizations about individuals that one has had no time to know better; it becomes in effect a substitute for trust, one that is sometimes imposed by cognitive overload. It is primarily the need for trust that confines clans, in contrast to markets, to comparatively small numbers and in particular to that number with whom values can be shared and expectations made to converge.

Note that convergent expectations and values do not imply that transacting parties actually have to like each other or that they must necessarily share the same goals. They must, however, be able to anticipate each other and get on to 'the same wavelength' in a process of mutual adjustment. They must also be united by some superordinate values or goals, however remote, that are capable of maintaining the relationship in spite of divergencies in individual interest – some of these, indeed, might actually form the focus of the transaction. For unlike market transactions, which in their pure form are quite transient and disembodied, clan transactions are deeply embedded in, and shape, long-term social relationships.[58]

Consider, by way of illustration, the price fixing behaviour of a cartel. Much of the information used to reach a decision is not traded outside the group and much of it is exchanged informally in a face-to-face situation – the proverbial smoke-filled room. Since in most circumstances in a free market economy, a cartel is considered illegal, agreements must remain uncodified and must not be leaked to any party outside the group. A copious economic literature on the 'signalling' practices of cartels, the corporate winks and nods by which their members adjust their behaviours and align their expectations, bears witness to the uncodified and highly local nature of this communication process.[59]

And yet cartels, as Chandler and others have shown, tend to be unstable structures.[60] They tend to break down when eroded by the opportunistic behaviour of their members. After all, these remain competitors at least as much as they might be collaborators. As in the Prisoner's Dilemma, the payoff to defection tends to be higher in many cases than the rewards of conformity to group discipline.[61] In the face of such persistent divergencies of interests should we consider cartels to be viable clan structures?

When it comes to pure cartels, probably not. They only exist to serve a narrowly overlapping set of membership interests and no superordinate goal structure exists to make the payoff to adherence more attractive than that to defection where this can be practised either undetected or without penalty. Yet many structures economically organized as cartels successfully manage to survive by endowing themselves with a broader purpose, one which not only gives their members a collective identity that they can live with but one which also bestows upon the group a high degree of social legitimacy – in short, they find ways of increasing the degree of overlap in their members' individual interests.

Medieval guilds and corporations offer one example of such a structure.[62] To be sure, their demise from the end of the Middle Ages onward can be attributed to the gradual defections of their members lured away by the more attractive economic opportunities offered by nascent market relationships. Yet this only happened when the credibility of the superordinate goals guilds had been proclaiming had already eroded and they came to be perceived by both insiders and outsiders as pure cartels with no socially legitimate interests beyond narrowly sectional ones. Today many professions are confronted with a similar development: the ethic of disinterested professional service is increasingly viewed by the public and its representatives as a veil drawn over less altruistic economic motives.[63]

The scope of clan governance

The term 'clan' as used here will refer to a non-hierarchical group of limited size transacting on the basis of shared intangible knowledge and values. In theory, at least, tacit knowledge and values can be diffused to much larger groupings than clans since their inter-generational transmission from parents to children can often compensate for the spatial and other obstacles that exist to the intra-generational transmission of uncodified knowledge. In this way, much uncodified knowledge reaches populations in D beyond the reach of transactional structures such as clans, and certainly well beyond what appears to be indicated by the diffusion curve itself. Such knowledge, however, not only diffuses extremely slowly but is distorted by heavy information losses. The 'high context' in which various categories of receivers make use of such knowledge becomes ever more diverse and leads to a form of cultural 'speciation'[64] in which values and understanding get differentiated to create new and distinct groupings.

Yet, for all that, it still remains true that socialization mechanisms can be effective in larger groupings than clans. The shared sense of belonging to a single nation, or sometimes to a single species, diffuses beyond small numbers and works to mutually align the behaviour of even perfect strangers in ways that go beyond what is required for market exchange. Where does this shared sense of belonging come from?

Theories exist that purport to account for the coherency of such diffusion mechanisms. Carl Jung, as we have already seen, argued that we all share in the possession of primordial images, archetypes which as a species we have inherited from the earliest times.[65] These form what he called our collective unconscious. Yet if primordial uncodified knowledge can be universally shared in this way, on what grounds can we then argue that the use of uncodified knowledge will tend to confine transacting to small numbers? Are we not in fact capable of attuning ourselves with anyone with whom we are able to share some common elements of socialization?

Up to a point. Pushed to extremes, a Jungian definition of shared uncodified knowledge can easily become a *reductio ad absurdum* of our transactional categories. Whatever the personal and cultural variations in the way we choose to interpret events, there remains a sense in which we all 'know' that the sun will rise tomorrow and that nasty things tend to happen to people who jump off cliffs. This knowledge may be implicit but it is non-local. Thus to categorize someone as human is at the outset to set brackets around the range of experiences and behaviours that might be expected of him/her.

Yet categorization becomes trivial if it does not help to discriminate between prospective transactional partners. In a market the discrimination required may not run beyond a brief assessment of ability to pay – and even then enforceable contract law often keeps this requirement to a minimum. Personal considerations, therefore, need not be involved. The key requirement that sets a limit to the number of potential participants in any transaction, then, is the common possession of transactionally *relevant* knowledge. The fact that a banker and client both know that water does not run uphill in no way helps the first to decide whether the second will pay back the loan she is requesting. For that, a detailed knowledge of the applicant's background and what she is about is likely to be more helpful to the banker than a nodding acquaintance with hydraulics or geophysics. Some of the banker's knowledge concerning the applicant may be well codified – her university diploma, military or medical records, etc. But the banker's confidence will be greatly increased if the applicant has been recommended by a long-standing mutual friend, or, better still, if she has already been known to the banker for a number of years.

It is this interpersonal investment that creates transactionally relevant uncodified knowledge, a process limited by time and the availability of agents – what Hayek has termed *local* knowledge[66] and what in Chapter 2 we have defined as *concrete* knowledge. Small numbers merely reflect the spatio-temporal constraints that limit such interpersonal investments. We call them clans because they operate on the basis of *exclusion*, distinguishing between those who by dint of personal effort or good fortune possess the relevant knowledge and those who do not. Only the former are then admitted into the transactional arena.

Clans create in-groups and they create out-groups. In-groups are bound together by feelings of loyalty and mutual obligations and sometimes by feelings of hostility towards out-groups.[67] The polarization of such relationships is itself the product of information asymmetries and uncertainty since the former are known and hence understood and trusted, while the latter are often the target of ignorant speculation and prejudice.

The amount of knowledge deemed to be transactionally relevant varies considerably from one grouping to the next. We might hypothesize that the smaller the informational requirements of the typical transaction, the larger the feasible size of the clan that can handle it is likely to be. A team of research scientists working on an advanced basic research project, for example, has sophisticated and complex information requirements, much of the information being uncodified; it might therefore not run to more than a dozen colleagues.[68] A Chinese family clan in Fujian province, by contrast, may draw on little common knowledge beyond a rudimentary awareness of the clan's origins and subsequent history and for this reason could run to 6,000 or more members.

5.6: FIEFS

The information characteristics of fiefs

In transactional terms, fiefs are the antithesis of markets. If the latter are characterized by the rapid impersonal diffusion of abstract codified information (CAD) that works to achieve a self-regulating outcome, the former describe a transactional structure that deals in uncodified, concrete data ($\bar{C}\bar{A}\bar{D}$) that is hard to transmit – even face to face – and that leads to highly personalized hierarchical relationships, usually of limited reach, and expressive of cumulative information asymmetries between transacting parties.

Fiefs can either emerge spontaneously from interpersonal processes already occurring in $\bar{C}\bar{A}\bar{D}$, or more gradually from bureaucratic or clan failures. The first type of failure results from an inability of the bureaucratic rule to adequately encode transactional complexities. The second type of failure reflects information-sharing problems and the presence of durable information *asymmetries* between transacting parties. Both kinds of failures, each in its own way, end up placing hard to codify – and hence diffuse – transactionally relevant information in one or a few hands, thereby endowing them with considerable personal power.

One example of the fief type of transaction will be found in the patriarchal family units of pre-industrial societies, units which vest paternal authority with a primordial wisdom designed to inspire a feeling of awe and submission. Although such authority is deemed to be benevolent, it is also absolute and brooks no restraint within the immediate family unit. The father figure is sometimes charismatic; that is, endowed with special powers that guide its actions and confer on them an aura of infallibility.

Charismatic authority is, of course, not the only source of paternal power. Douglas[69] and Bernstein,[70] for example, distinguish between *personal* families in which parental authority rests on the manipulation of thoughts and feelings, and *positional* families in which a child grows into a set of unchallenged categories. Only in the first case, if authority is invoked, is it likely to be charismatic; in the second it will be traditional. Charismatic and traditional authority constitute two of Weber's three basic categories of authority – the third being bureaucratic.[71] Traditional authority, in effect, can be thought of as a halfway house between totally uncodified and personal charismatic authority on the one hand, and codified and impersonal bureaucratic authority on the other. To be sure, rules are involved in the exercise of traditional authority, but their interpretation and application remain more personalized and less rationally grounded in universal principles than in the case of bureaucratic authority.

In personal families authority need not be centralized; with the modern American middle-class family, a charismatic structure often gives way to something more akin to a clan. Relationships between family members remain highly personalized and a measure of decentralized social control can be achieved through an appeal to internalized family values. The process becomes consensual rather than authoritarian so that 'Dad' ceases to be a god and instead becomes a 'buddy'.

The highly personalized forms of knowledge that are a major source of power in fiefs are most effectively applied when there is little or no codified or abstract information to counterbalance it: the wisdom of the elders is always vulnerable to challenges originating in the growth of structured abstract knowledge visible to all and open to rational criticism. Yet, paradoxically, the reach of such personal power also remains limited unless it can be amplified by complementary transactional structures operating at a more codified and abstract level – a point we shall have occasion to discuss further in the next chapter. Within its own transactional orbit, however, the power available in fiefs can be absolute and offers its possessor considerable discretion as to how it is exercised.

The origins of the term

But why the label 'fief'?

Taken in its Eurocentric historical sense, a fief describes a territory and its inhabitants over which a vassal was empowered to rule by his liege lord. The granting of fiefs and, below them through a process of subinfeudation,[72] of subfiefs created a personalized hierarchy of authority in which protection and rights were granted by a superior in return for loyalty and the performance of certain obligations by a subordinate. The resulting social order went by the name of *feudalism*; it emerged in Europe in the ninth and tenth centuries in a decentralized form to fill the institutional vacuum created by the collapse of the Roman Empire in the fifth century.[73] The feudal economy was essentially manorial and was built around non-monetary exchanges that were highly local in nature.[74] Following the barbarian invasions, and in Southern Europe the Islamic invasions of the eighth century, the Roman transport infrastructure that had linked different parts of Europe to each other had fallen into disuse, fragmenting the economic space and offering little opportunity for large-scale specialization prior to the re-emergence of cities as centres of industry and commerce from the tenth to the twelfth centuries.[75]

Although feudalism as a form of economic organization has existed in many parts of the world – in China, unlike in Europe and Japan, it remained centralized[76] – it is no longer considered compatible with the needs of industrialization so that in many cultures it has become a term of abuse. Indeed, even Karl Marx, his devastating critique of nineteenth-century capitalism notwithstanding, credited capitalism with clearing away the cobwebs of feudalism and the forms of human bondage historically associated with it.[77] However, even today what might loosely be called feudal relations linger on or are deliberately maintained in a wide variety of social organizations. It follows that fiefs, although not necessarily institutionalized as a legitimate transactional form in their own right, may still constitute an effective driving force in many different types of social exchange.

Clearly, we are not using the word 'fief' here to describe the possession and control of a physical stretch of territory. Prior to industrialization, control over land was effectively control over resources. With industrialization, however, resources became more mobile and could therefore be owned independently of territory. And with the information revolution, resources have become more mobile still. Have fiefs therefore disappeared? In the institutional sense of a chunk of real property handed down by a territorial magnate to his vassal together with a bundle of personal rights and obligations attached to it, perhaps. But fiefs, taken as the exercise of personal power over highly localized people and things and based on the monopolistic possession of a scarce resource, live on.

In this section, therefore, we shall be discussing the fief as a transactional structure that crystallizes around the tacit and personal possession of potentially useful knowledge as a scarce resource. Under suitable circumstances such knowledge, in spite of its inherent lack of diffusibility, can be selectively imparted to others – albeit slowly and usually interpersonally – and hence can be traded for the loyalty and obedience of a privileged group of recipients. A successful entrepreneur or the head of a family business may both often operate in fiefs used in this wider sense no less than a *fudai daimyo* or a *tozama daimyo* did under the Tokugawa Shogunate.[78]

Fief values

What kinds of values and beliefs bestow on fiefs their legitimacy as a transactional order?

Perhaps the most crucial is a social acceptance of the exercise of personal power by those deemed to possess certain gifts and, by implication, of a duty of loyalty and obedience by those who do not. These gifts need not necessarily reduce to the simple possession of knowledge as such – they could for example alloy such possession with military prowess, the display of outstanding virtue, or a demonstration of magical powers[79] – but in all cases, and this is what concerns us here, the knowledge in question is likely to take the form of divine inspiration, of extraordinary insight, and will generally be deemed beyond the reach of the common run of mortals. Such knowledge may not be of the conceptual or intellectual kind and in certain cases it will only find expression in a display of physical or technical virtuosity. A world-class tennis player, for example, possesses this kind of knowledge, as do in their own way concert pianists, orchestra conductors, and painters. In all these cases, the gift is not transmissible other than by the force of example, and the knowledge and insights it embodies cannot be properly articulated in words. It can therefore only be conveyed very gradually, and with considerable risks of failure and misunderstanding, to disciples or followers willing to accept the authority of a 'master' on trust.[80]

Transmitting personal knowledge in this way requires the co-presence of communicating parties and, above all, time. Spatial proximity and a hefty time commitment are essential ingredients for the effective transmission of tacit knowledge. Given such constraints, a master may be able without too many difficulties to secure the devoted following of, say, twelve disciples;[81] but if he then wishes to extend his following to 1,200, the way that he transmits what he knows will necessarily undergo some subtle changes. With larger numbers, face-to-face communication will lose its nuance and some coding conventions will have to be introduced. It may even be that parts of the transmission process will have to be entrusted to others now acting as relays. The master's charisma will now run the risk of becoming routinized, to use Weber's term,[82] and his personal authority will be under a constant threat of challenge from the impersonal rule underpinning such routinization.

Like clan transactions, fief transactions of necessity involve small numbers and operate on the principle of *exclusion*. To personally serve a charismatic leader is a privilege available to only a few, a privilege that must be won by continued demonstrations of loyalty and devotion. Although charismatic authority can at times be exercised in a diffuse manner over very large numbers – witness the ability of a Napoleon or a Mao to win, at least temporarily, the affection of millions of followers – it only effectively commands absolute and unconditional obedience from small numbers and even there poses problems of transmission to successors. Fiefs, therefore, tackle the problem of agency by keeping numbers down to a minimum and imposing unusually rigorous selection requirements on potential followers.[83] In many cases, the criterion of eligibility to be considered a follower or a potential successor is often itself the possession of some charismatic power. In this way a charismatic community is created.

The power of fiefs

The exercise of purely personal power cannot easily be constrained by rules of accountability. Individuals may in time come to lose their charisma, but while they possess it, usually no direct causal links bind them in the use of their powers to the realization of specific outcomes or performances to which they are committed. Following floods or a famine, for example, the Chinese emperor might conceivably be deemed to have lost the mandate of heaven; yet natural catastrophes could usually only be loosely related to his conduct so that such a contingency was in fact extremely unlikely. Ambiguity is a solvent that allows personal power to remain capricious if it wishes to be, and hence always potentially dangerous. Its acceptance by followers therefore requires a high degree of *trust* on their part that it will be applied to ends that they consider legitimate and that it will not be exercised at their expense. Followers of a charismatic leader are always vulnerable. They therefore need to be reassured. The 'Son of Heaven', for example, kept his mandate in a good state of repair by a continuous display of benevolence just as the medieval lord and his vassal were bound to each other by a chivalrous code of honour that affirmed a broader set of principles.[84] In the patriarchal family, paternal wisdom is assumed to have only the welfare of children and the future security and prosperity of the household at heart.

The most egregious abuses of personal power will in fact often be tolerated as long as they can be veiled by a credible appeal to higher values.[85] Even as destructive a paranoia as Stalin's could be sustained while he was able to project himself to a sufficient number of immediate followers as an avuncular figure concerned only with the welfare of his people.[86]

The fragility of fiefs

Fiefs, dependent as they are on the judicious use of individual personal power, usually perish with it and perhaps for this reason constitute the least stable of our transactional categories. The way that such perishable powers are preserved for transmission to successors provides some clue as to how fiefs fail.

Followers seeking to maintain their prior transactional investment in a leader who has disappeared may attempt to routinize his charisma by embodying it in practices or rules over which they will exercise custody. Thus we have the Mosaic laws, the rule of St Benedict, the ancestral code, etc. In a first phase, we might move towards a form of traditionalism in which personal authority continues to be exercised by designated successors but where the scope for discretion is now restricted by precedent and customary practice. In a second phase, as the number of followers expands inter-generationally, rule-based authority, now rationally determined and impersonally applied, may gradually come to replace the exercise of personal power, and the uniquely gifted individual, acting on prior experience and intuition alone, gives way to the technically trained official applying an abstract rule according to purely rational and impersonal criteria. This move from fiefs into bureaucracy follows the SLC in the I-space and is consistent with a gradual articulation and structuring of the transactionally pertinent knowledge base. Here the fief fails where no mechanism is available either for the preservation of charisma or for its faithful transmission from one generation to the next. Religious leaders sworn to celibacy, for example, may be forced to designate their successors and thereby split their following. Where transmission mechanisms are available – as in the case of a royal blood line – charismatic authority may in fact be preserved for a considerable time across generations unless openly challenged or abused.[87]

Fiefs also fail when personal power is fragmented among followers. Hereditary charisma might be preserved intact through the institution of primogeniture, or it could gradually diffuse through all descendants of a particular blood line. In the second case, it might rapidly be dissipated through a competitive struggle for dominance among contenders. Yet it might also be successfully preserved as a communal possession through a collegial exercise of power – keeping it in the family, so to speak. Either way, the move towards the right in the I-space is one from fiefs to clans – albeit with possibly more stability in the latter instance – one that amounts to a successful move against the flow of the SLC.

In sum, as with the other institutional structures described in this chapter, fiefs can fail either by following the SLC or by moving against it. It is the specific configuration of information flows in the I-space that channels transactions towards or away from particular institutional structures and hence determines how these will evolve over time.

5.7: TRANSACTIONAL EVOLUTION

Transactions in the SLC

The main features of our transactional typology are given in Table 5.1. It is far from exhaustive since many forms of social exchange overlap or shade

Table 5.1 Profile of transactions in the I-space

Bureaucracies	Markets	Fiefs	Clans
Information is abstract, codified, but undiffused – i.e., its diffusion is under central control. Example: the monthly financial report	Information is abstract, codified, and diffused. Example: prices	Information is concrete, uncodified and undiffused. Example: personal childhood memories; expertise	Information is concrete, uncodified, but enjoys limited diffusion – i.e., to groups, rather than the target population as a whole. Example: myths, oral traditions, etc.
Relationships are impersonal, identity does not matter	Relationships are impersonal, identity does not matter	Relationships are personal, identity does matter	Relationships are personal, identity does matter
Control is external, shared values and trust are not necessary	Control is external, shared values and trust are not necessary	Control is internalized, shared values and trust are necessary	Control is internalized, shared values and trust are necessary
Coordination is hierarchical and formal	Coordination is horizontal and self-regulating (the invisible hand)	Coordination is hierarchical and informal	Coordination is horizontal and carried out through mutual adjustments
Goals are imposed from above	Each player is free to pursue his/her own goals	Goals are imposed from above	Goals are negotiated between players
Core institutional value: obedience to the rule	Core institutional value: transactional freedom	Core institutional value: loyalty and submission to a leader	Core institutional value: loyalty to the group

into each other to create new subcategories. Its significance derives from the fact that it is more than just a classification of empirically observed transactional behaviour – for all its magnificent erudition, this, in effect, is what Max Weber's *Economy and Society* amounts to;[88] it is the analytical fruit of a theory of information flows. Although we cannot specify here in any great detail the causal relationships that link particular transactional behaviour patterns and given information environments, we can offer the refutable hypothesis that they are related, and that any failure of a particular transactional order will be associated with changes in the underlying distribution of information available in the data field resulting from the dynamic action of the SLC.[89]

Transactions may either follow shifts in the distribution of knowledge in the data field or they may provoke them. To illustrate: a small firm manufacturing a complex technical product but relying essentially on the uncodified know-how of a skilled and experienced workforce may well be forced to codify and diffuse a part of its proprietary know-how in order to stimulate customer demand, particularly if the product is quite new and prospective buyers lack the information that would allow them to evaluate it. In so doing, the firm may open the door to potential customers mastering the procedures necessary to enter the business themselves. From what had originally been a strong monopolistic position in $\bar{C}\bar{A}\bar{D}$, the firm may be forced by degrees to shift to a more vulnerable one in CAD – a move along the SLC from fiefs to markets.[90] The move, although initiated by the firm itself, was prompted by the need for a stronger market orientation and the consequent need to relax its monopolistic grip upon its proprietary knowledge base. In this particular example, the transactional shift, although provoked by the firm's own actions, followed the SLC; but, as has been indicated in the previous sections, countercyclical shifts are also possible.[91]

Grid and group: Mary Douglas's typology

One way of bringing out the theoretical distinctiveness of our transactional typology is to compare it with one that shares its cognitive orientation but is less grounded in a specific theory. Recall from Chapter 2 that Mary Douglas in her book *Natural Symbols*[92] has analysed the relationship between the value systems and cosmologies held by different social group-ings on the one hand, and their cognitive and power orientation on the other. Using a conceptual tool that she labels *grid and group*, Douglas has produced a provocative analysis of belief systems and their associated forms of social organization in a variety of cultural settings. An illustration of her approach is given in Figure 5.2 which uses a modified version of grid and group to produce a typology of family values.

The vertical axis, *grid*, describes the communication style among group members as a function of the cognitive elaboration of categories and concepts used. Thus at the top of the scale, interpersonal discourse uses what Basil Bernstein has termed a 'restricted code', in which much content is left implicit, and shared and familiar experiences are left to fill in the gaps. At the lower end of the scale, by contrast, communications between family members draw upon an 'elaborated code'[93] which is much richer and conceptually explicit. Clearly, we have here a distinction similar to the one Edward Hall has made between 'high context' and 'low context' cultures[94]

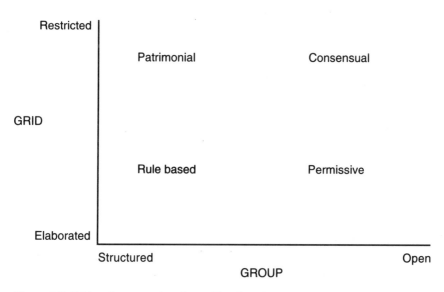

Figure 5.2 Grid and group: a typology of family values

and that we ourselves have established between uncodified and codified communications.

Turning now to the horizontal scale, *group*, Douglas analyses power distribution within a group, with individual freedom to pursue one's own goals being located on the right of the scale, and the necessity to submit to hierarchically imposed goals on the left. Commenting on her typology, Douglas observes:

> The area of maximum structuring of the family is on the left: the area of maximum openness and freedom from structuring is on the right. In the bottom right, the individual emerges as free as possible from a system of socially structured controls ... The people who have been freed most completely from structured personal relations are among those most involved in the complexity of modern industrial structure.[95]

In effect, we would argue, they are involved in market transactions as one can immediately see by inverting the vertical scale and superimposing our recently derived transactional categories on to Douglas's value typology (Figure 5.3). To those who have followed the transactional analysis presented in this chapter, the resemblance between Douglas's typology and our own should appear quite striking.

The key difference, of course, is that our own analysis is built upon a theory of information-based production and exchange whereas Douglas's classification is derived from observed attributes of thought and behaviour in different cultural settings. We might say, following Simon, that Douglas's

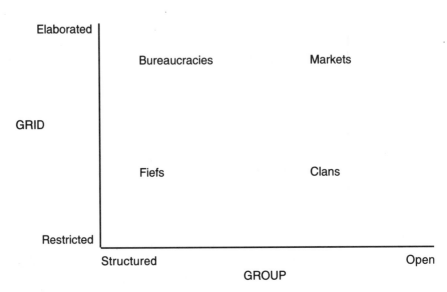

Figure 5.3 A transactional typology located in grid and group (vertical scale inverted)

typology is data driven whereas our own is theory driven.[96] That the two should be so close is encouraging but it should not obscure the fact that the scope of Douglas's approach remains somewhat circumscribed by its lack of grounding in a general theory. Our scheme offers her such a theory.

Douglas's work is certainly closer than our own to what Robert Merton has described as 'theories of the middle range'.[97] Yet by focusing on observed behaviour rather than on the information environment that supports it, Douglas has no way of explaining the evolution of structures and belief systems over time, or the possible shift from one structure to the other. Power and cognition in grid and group can yield a classification, and, to be sure, a useful and illuminating one at that, but they remain theoretically disjoint. We know that they interact and mutually influence each other, but the mechanisms are not articulated sufficiently to be theoretically relevant. In the absence of a dynamic theory of information processing and flows, Douglas has no way of moving from one part of the space she has created to another. Intriguing and suggestive as it is in many respects, her scheme is more of a taxonomy – a classification based on observed traits and only modestly guided by an underlying theory – than anything else, and for this reason it enjoys relatively modest predictive power.

It is, then, the derivation of our transactional typology from a dynamic theory of information behaviour that endows it with the power potentially to predict not only what belief and value systems might be associated with a given transactional structure – to some extent, Douglas's grid and group does this as well – but also how these are likely to evolve over time and under what circumstances. This claim will be further discussed in the next chapter and illustrated in Chapter 7. Here we shall confine ourselves to a couple of observations.

Transactional competition and collaboration

Transactions may originate in one region of the I-space alone but not necessarily.[98] A large project, for instance, may trigger off a complex pattern of exchanges which draw upon several different transactional structures simultaneously. When transactions occur in such clusters, there is no reason to suppose that they all exert their effects independently of each other, or that they are all drawn from neighbouring regions of the I-space. Indeed, transactions located in different regions of the space may well act so as to mutually reinforce each other, so that one is not necessarily led to make exclusive choices between markets and hierarchies, fiefs or clans; it may therefore be possible to operate with several transactional types concurrently and then subsequently to integrate them.

An example may help to make this clear. It is a commonplace that in the real world, the self-regulating character required of efficient markets is not sufficiently developed or pervasive to ensure socially equitable outcomes for all would-be participants.[99] The very act of codifying market knowledge such as prices, of course, opens the door to some possibility of control by reducing the degrees of freedom inherent in transactional knowledge. Yet the *locus* of such control along the diffusion dimension of the I-space remains as yet unspecified. Self-regulation, for instance, would embed it within each self-seeking participant in the market itself. Where transactional data is insufficient, however, much of the control process may still be left to self-regulation, but now judiciously augmented by some measure of hierarchical control. The market may be policed and would-be participants might therefore be required to register with some external authority prior to or subsequent to any exchange – a move away from the anonymity that results from absolute freedom of entry and exit in impersonal atomistic markets, and towards a hierarchically determined eligibility to participate. Bureaucratic and market transactions operate synergistically in such circumstances: the greater the potential volume of market transactions, the greater the pressure from potential entrants to achieve transactional eligibility, and the more rationally and fairly this can be achieved – even if through bureaucratic means – the greater the general willingness to transact and hence to increase the volume of market transactions.

North holds the rational–legal apparatus of the state bureaucracy to be an essential complement to market processes if transaction costs are to be brought down to the point where a sufficient number of players are willing to use markets in efficiency-promoting ways.[100] Yet as he himself points out, a political element is rarely absent in such transactions. To take our example one step further, the rationality or fairness of the regulatory bureaucratic transaction itself might on occasion be open to challenge and may need to be bolstered by the legitimating presence of a charismatic figure located in fiefs but sitting atop the bureaucratic structure itself. In Great Britain, the Monarch, with his or her reserve powers, performs the function of a charismatic backstop should a failure of the political or bureaucratic apparatus – here taken to include the military hierarchy – occur. In Spain, the effectiveness of this reserve charismatic power of a modern monarchy was demonstrated in February 1981 when an attempt was made to seize the state apparatus in a coup, a *pronunciamiento*, mounted by a group of military officers nostalgic for dictatorship. Yet with a single televised speech, King Juan Carlos was able to rally popular support against the coup which then fizzled out. In another context, the chairman of the Federal Reserve Board also requires a certain charisma if he is to keep the trust of financial markets at times when the regulatory mechanisms under his control are put under strain. In Britain, a few calming words by the Governor of the Bank of England can have a miraculous effect on the psychology of financial markets – another instance of collaboration between fiefs and bureaucracies.

Transactional pathologies

The trick in many situations, then, may be to find the right transactional mix rather than making exclusive choices between competing transactional structures. Put in too much bureaucracy and self-regulating market processes get crowded out. On the other hand, build up too charismatic a leadership at the top of a hierarchy and the rational–legal foundations of a well-functioning bureaucracy begin to erode. One might usefully frame the issue in terms of *countervailing transactional power*, an even-handed distribution of transactions in the I-space that works against the emergence of transactional pathologies – a situation in which *all* transactions are channelled through one type of structure to the exclusion of others, no matter how ill-adapted that structure turns out to be to the diversity of requirements placed upon it.

As an instance of such a pathology, consider the case of pure hierarchy in which *no* information is ever allowed to flow horizontally between agents (as it would in, say, a market or a clan) and all relationships are vertically ordered. The creation of such a pathological structure was in fact attempted by Stalin. It operated on the basis of absolute authority unmitigated by any trace of countervailing power. Polanyi explains how such a 'divide and conquer' strategy can be made to create absolute hierarchy:

> It is commonly assumed that power cannot be assumed without some voluntary support, as for example, by a faithful praetorian guard. I do not

think this is true, for it seems that some dictators were feared by everybody, for example, toward the end of his rule, everybody feared Stalin ... If in a group of men, each believes that all the others will obey the commands of their claimed superiors, each will obey.[101]

Other examples that at times got close to becoming transactional pathologies were furnished in the 1980s by attempts in the US and in Britain to force large tracts of social exchange best handled by other means exclusively through market processes. That the market should be ever present as a competitive transactional alternative is not disputed, but in their more extreme forms, Reaganomics in the US and Thatcherism in Britain amounted to an unbridled pursuit of individual self-interest, unmitigated by any feelings of fellowship or common sentiment. The alienating effects of markets on individuals had been the burden of the Marxist critique of capitalism in the nineteenth century, although it should not be forgotten that the Marxist-Leninist alternative to treating labour as a commodity that could be impersonally bought or sold was to treat it as a commodity that could be impersonally ordered about. As transactional pathologies, pure markets and pure hierarchies rival each other, and it should not be supposed that pure clans or pure fiefs offer any improvement.

The issue of transactional mix will be taken up again in the next chapter. We conclude this section by noting that transactions, as forms of social action, incur costs measured in terms of time, space, energy, and information. Where they occur in large volumes and on a recurring basis, some thought may be given to minimizing these costs for a given transactional effect. A structure might then be created to channel transactional energies more efficiently. Such a social investment in transactional infrastructure creates specific institutional forms that express the scope for economizing in different parts of the I-space. The economizing perspective on institutions is developed in the next section.

5.8: INSTITUTIONALIZATION

Characteristics of institutions

Institutions are stores of established social practices, structures through which we externalize collective memories, representations, values, norms, rules, etc., in order that they should outlast us. Giddens calls them 'chronically reproduced rules and resources'.[102] Only transactions that are unusually salient in their consequences for social life, or that are recurrent, will normally justify the costs of a specific effort at institutionalization; that is, of creating a structure tailor-made for their governance. The less salient or more transient interactions that form the stuff of everyday life are usually accommodated within existing institutional structures, and these may be only roughly adapted to their individual governance needs.

North argues that an organization stands somewhere between the evanescent transaction and the more permanent institutional order, a particular concretization of a given set of institutional practices.[103] The commercial firm, for example, expresses specific property and employment relations, forms of rationality embodied in particular accounting and managerial practices, and a set of economic values that originate in the tradition of possessive individualism.[104] The typical firm, then, constructs its internal organization from a pre-extant and available institutional repertoire; it does not start from scratch.

Transactions involve an exchange in which some knowledge and information is transmitted from one party to the other. Where transactions are regular in character and recurring, the knowledge they build on may come to acquire an absolute and objective quality that subsequently locates it in that part of our experience that Schultz calls the life-world (*Umwelt*) and that we take as 'given'.[105] The processes of abstraction described in Chapter 2 by degrees transform the concrete and local knowledge of individual transactions, provisional and uncertain as it might be, into a universal knowledge embedded in institutions and consequently perceived as forming an unalterable part of the natural order. Such knowledge may or may not satisfy strong requirements of epistemological validity. Yet whether or not it can be adequately corroborated according to specifiable universal criteria, for some identifiable social groups it becomes, through a process of absorption and impacting, part of the socially taken-for-granted stock of knowledge that is implicitly held, and hence comes to acquire a legitimacy and an inertia of its own.

Institutions as potential intelligence

Institutional knowledge of this kind can be thought of as a form of potential intelligence in the sense used by Gregory and discussed in Chapter 4. Gregory distinguished potential and kinetic intelligence as follows:

> We live off intelligence stored in artefacts designed by our ancestors. These solutions are of enormous potential use for our problem solving. We no longer have to invent roofs or scissors when we know about these things. So education increases our 'internal' potential intelligence, through giving knowledge of what problem solvers or aids are available.
>
> ... Kinetic intelligence is on this account mainly gap filling, necessary where solutions are not adequate as stored potential intelligence ... To the extent that problem solving follows established rules, it draws upon potential intelligence in discharging a kinetic function'.[106]

Of course, the potential intelligence of institutions is embedded in individual minds as well as in physical objects such as books, physical structures and so on. In Popper's terminology, then, institutions must be considered World 3 objects that are stored partly in World 2 and partly in World 1.

Potential and kinetic intelligence can be viewed as substitutes for each other: the more of the one is available to solve a given problem, the less the need to draw on the other. Yet in so far as potential intelligence is also a sunk cost borne by earlier generations, and hence not recoverable, the bias will inevitably be towards letting bygones be bygones and economizing primarily on kinetic intelligence, the cost of which is directly borne by an existing generation. In an economic sense, therefore, a predisposition to be bound by the past and inherited traditions is often a rational solution to a cognitive investment problem that requires a marginal cost approach. This remains so even though a marginal cost approach sometimes imparts a considerable inertia in the face of needed changes to the institutions that perpetrate such traditions.

Transacting at the margin in the institutional order

The foregoing observations lead us to a simple proposition: if we incorporate the intangible costs of aligning values and attitudes with choices made into our definition of transaction costs, alongside more tangible ones such as physical effort or search, then a concern with transactional efficiency will assign transactions to those parts of the I-space in which prior transactional investments – i.e., the ready availability of potential intelligence – will offer the greatest marginal returns; that is, to those parts in which institutionalization either has already occurred or is under way.[107]

Another way of saying the same thing is that prior institution building serves to lower the marginal cost of transacting and thus helps to channel the uncommitted transaction into those regions of the I-space where institutional structures are to some extent already available.

At this point, an objection might be raised. Surely, once the process of institution building has got under way, based on some initial cost advantage one institutional form will sooner or later come to predominate and all others must of necessity wither away for lack of competitiveness. After a while, therefore, genuine institutional choice will effectively disappear. Once a marginal cost advantage has been achieved, a vicious circle is set in motion in which the more transactions are drawn to a given part of the I-space, the greater the scope for institution building there and the further the marginal cost of transacting drops, hence attracting further uncommitted transactions, and so on. The institution becomes in effect what mathematicians call an *attractor* and what speaking somewhat more metaphorically we might call a *transactional black hole*: it draws into its orbit transactions that might initially be floating in quite remote parts of the data field and keeps them there, forbidding all escape.

Joseph Schumpeter conceived of the passage from a capitalist to a socialist order to be of this nature, with the giant industrial firm conferring an initial economic advantage on internal bureaucratic transactions which, as they grew in volume and scope, would gradually drain market institutions of their transactional content. Once the transition to a hierarchical order was complete, the state would only need to take over a few giant corporations to usher in a command economy.[108]

This 'winner takes all' objection elicits four counterarguments. The first is a purely economic one, namely, that the marginal costs of transacting beyond a certain point will cease to fall when scale and learning effects have been exhausted and will gradually start to rise again. Without major modifications to the institutional structure that will increase its transactional capacity beyond the limits that have now been reached, at some point it will begin to lose its attractions. Such a modification, however, represents a major investment the viability of which is by no means guaranteed when ranked against alternatives, themselves competing on the basis of incremental costs.

The second counterargument is linked to the first in that the psychological component of the cost of transacting – the values and beliefs that facilitate or constrain a transaction – frequently looms large and for the most part remains hidden. The comment 'he would sell his own grandmother', for example, points to implicit limits beyond which the market transaction would be in violation of deeply held social norms, and would be considered pathological in the sense discussed in the previous section. And just as not all forms of social exchange will be allowed to pass through markets, so too bureaucratic, clan, or fief transactions will discover limits to their dominion. For all its ideological ardour the communist leadership in China did not succeed in replacing the peasant family with the work brigade. The psychic costs to individuals proved too high, no matter how attractive such a form of social organization might be on other grounds.[109]

If the psychological costs of transacting through institutions in ways that are at odds with social values and norms is taken into account in any economic evaluation of competing alternatives, then one would expect to see these costs rise as an institution reaches out into the I-space to capture transactions far removed from its own natural information environment.

A third counterargument is that to rising marginal costs and psychic costs must be added the transaction costs of choosing between transactional options.[110] Options have to be discovered and evaluated and in the absence of full information the switch from one to the other is not frictionless. Suboptimal choices may thus allow competing transactional options to co-exist under a 'satisficing' regime.[111]

A final counterargument would point to the static nature of the information environment assumed by the objection. The knowledge underpinning the institutionalization of transactions, like all phenomena that rest on a physical substratum, is prey to the ravages of time.[112]

Firstly, it is subject to obsolescence which appears when prior institutional investments no longer meet current transactional needs. The inductive procedures that gave situation-specific and concrete transactional knowledge its objective and universal character break down, and taken-for-granted transactional arrangements are suddenly found wanting in corroboration. As the contingent nature of the assumed transactional order suddenly becomes discernible through the smooth and seamless surface of events, confidence in the solidity of the institutions that had underlain it gets eroded. At this point alternatives are sought.

Secondly, the action of the SLC itself is constantly redistributing knowledge throughout the data field so that, for example, information which might have been appropriable for the exercise of hierarchical control at a given point in the cycle ceases to be so as it diffuses to ever-wider populations: as they get hold of transactionally relevant knowledge these may begin to impose a market style on the marginal transaction that better reflects the emerging exchange possibilities offered by the new information environment. Attempts at a bureaucratic solution under such circumstances will prove to no avail.

The operation of black markets illustrates this last point: a central authority that lacks the appropriate administrative mechanisms for imposing a total hierarchical control upon a given class of economic transactions must resign itself to tolerating a parallel and competing transactional structure that is market oriented and that draws its strength from the wide availability of leaked information.

Or again, taking an example from further along the SLC, what may start out initially as an efficient market gradually gives way to clan transactions as locally recurring encounters reveal the identities of certain parties to each other and help to personalize their relationship. An in-group may then slowly crystallize in cases where participants prefer to do business with each other. Criteria of group membership can vary: ethnic background, a common education, religious affiliations, and so on. As with all clan transactions, however, personal identity matters, and in this example identity is built up by the SLC itself upon reaching a certain region of the I-space. There, the intangible experiences that transacting parties come to acquire of each other through ostensibly impersonal and arm's-length market transactions reflect the cumulative effects of learning by doing. Transactions, of course, may then move on further along the SLC – possibly towards fiefs.

Institutions as entropy-reducing devices

In sum, stored knowledge at any one location in the I-space *depreciates* over time and if institutions are the expression of a cumulative social learning process, they are also subject to *forgetting* – i.e., information losses that reflect either the disorganizing effects of entropy, or the onset of atrophy and a consequent loss of utility, with both working in harness most of the time. For this reason, the institutional order can never be static. Where it appears to be so, it is because a state of dynamic equilibrium has been reached in which for some unspecified period, the rate of transactional investment in the maintenance or development of a given institutional structure exceeds the rate at which it depreciates.

The consequences of this last point bear spelling out. Considered as a moment in the progress of the SLC, for example, market equilibrium would appear to be a much more precarious phenomenon than neoclassical economists – and indeed some neo-Austrians[113] – would have us believe. Their faith in the potential stability of market processes stems from an assumption that all transactionally relevant knowledge sooner or later finds its way into the market region of the I-space *and stays there*. It may start life as local knowledge, as Hayek maintains, but it gradually gets abstracted from its concrete particulars, becoming universal and available to all. In the neoclassical perspective, social learning is never a *disequilibrating* process; in the Austrian perspective, on the other hand, it is equilibrating in that phase of the SLC that precedes an entry into the market region and disequilibrating when it moves transactions out of that region and towards clans – a phase of the SLC that in a political context Roberto Michels has labelled 'the iron law of oligarchy'.[114]

Let us further elaborate the point. Those institutions with the greatest depth of prior investments will be the slowest to 'forget' through the disorganizing influence of entropy. In the language of Chapter 2, they will have the greatest capacity to minimize entropy production. Good for the institutions perhaps, but not necessarily for the system as a whole since they may then become vulnerable to obsolescence and atrophy.

The problem arises as an inevitable consequence of codification itself. Knowledge that has been codified, as we have already seen, is knowledge that can be stored – on stone tablets, on microfiche, on paper, on computer tape, etc. It loses the transience of knowledge stored in the neural cells of a living brain. Its durability can be impressive: the Hammurabi code has been preserved for nearly 6,000 years since it was first set out on stone tablets in the Mesopotamian basin. In one sense, we are not about to forget the Hammurabi code; it forms part of our archaeological heritage. But in another sense, that is effectively all that the code has become for us today: archaeology. It has little to offer by way of practical guidance to twentieth-century man; as knowledge it is obsolete.

As well as being stockable, codified and abstract knowledge can travel faster and further than the uncodified sort; it can thus diffuse rapidly across space to contemporaries as well as durably over time to descendants. Yet the more it roams the I-space, the further such knowledge moves from a given institutional base that it was feeding and sustaining and into institutional alternatives that over time may come to constitute competing transactional modes. It is the SLC that works this effect: slowly in the lower regions of the I-space (in $\bar{A}\bar{C}$) and quite rapidly in the upper regions (in AC).

Dealing with institutional obsolescence

Obsolescence expresses the impact of unforeseeable future events upon the viability of a given transactional structure. No amount of past investment can protect an institution from obsolescence when changing circumstances bring it about. A saddle might be designed to last a thousand years, yet it could still never compete against the motor car when it arrived on the scene. The onset of institutional obsolescence thus restores a certain viability to competing institutional alternatives as they crystallize out of the operation of the SLC, and this quite independently of whatever accumulated investments might have been channelled into existing institutions to prolong their existence. Codification and abstraction accelerate the process of obsolescence since knowledge having reached AC in the I-space will move faster about the space, cross-pollinating these competing alternatives. The action of the SLC, then, ensures that the forces of renewal in the I-space sooner or later triumph over those of preservation.

Perhaps another way of approaching the trade-off between institutional memory and obsolescence is to look at what happens when one invests in uncodified knowledge. Here the storage of information is a difficult business, for the commodity itself is highly perishable; oral traditions, for example, are notorious for the unreliability of their transmissions.[115] Yet paradoxically their very lack of structure gives them a resilience and a power of adaptation which are often not available in the case of more rigidly codified practices. They survive by a process of incremental and informal adjustment to changing circumstances that is often quite unconscious. Myths, for instance, gain much of their power from their plasticity; they are constantly being modified and reinterpreted to serve the needs of the present. Where myths are transmitted by word of mouth, this plasticity is enhanced.

The recording and storing of codified knowledge, by contrast, creates an institutional commitment, an inertia that is frequently highly resistant to change; not only are the chances of obsolescence increased by the rigidity of knowledge-preserving structures themselves, but its consequences are made more damaging by the social legitimacy that the very existence of such structures may bestow upon past practices.

Codification, however, is only one of the variables that affects the obsolescence of the knowledge base. Its degree of abstraction is another. The more concrete the circumstances that have been codified into a given rule, the greater the tensions that arise when circumstances change but the rule remains in force. Conversely, the more general and abstract the scope of the rule, the easier it will be to adapt or interpret it to suit new circumstances.

Recall from Chapter 3 that abstract knowledge gains in utility in proportion to the number of concrete instances in which it finds application. This would seem to suggest that the further up the U-space towards A we locate the knowledge base, the larger the region in the space that obsolescence has to capture before such knowledge effectively atrophies.

In sum, we might say that institutional obsolescence can be fought in two ways. The first is by keeping institutionalized transactions sufficiently vague and uncodified that they can be adapted unconsciously to new circumstances as they arise. The second is by codifying their governing principles at a sufficient level of generality and abstraction that broad classes of present and future contingencies might still be accommodated without undue strain.

These two ways of combating institutional obsolescence work within different time-frames and are often complementary. While both involve codification as a critical transactional variable, the first is primarily interested in preserving the social integrity of a transaction in the diffusion process – a problem for the C-space – whereas the second is mostly concerned with the epistemological robustness of a transaction's information base and hence with its degree of generality. It therefore looks to the E-space.

Style versus governance

The C- and the E-spaces are two of the three planes – the third being the U-space – that make up the I-space, the conceptual tool through which we apprehend the data field. The C-space orients us towards the communicative aspects of a transaction, the way that actors hoard or share information with each other. How these choose to respond to the constraints and opportunities in which their information environment places them, how far they avail themselves of the institutional structures at hand, tells us something of their *transactional style*.

In transacting with each other, actors pursue their own interests, albeit constrained by their adopted principles. Loosely speaking, we might think of principles as expressive of a broader, more universalistic class of interests – what Rousseau called the *volonté générale* to distinguish it from the more particularistic and atomized *volonté de tous*.[116] Principles and interests can be ranked along ĀA in the E-space according to the degree of generality and abstraction they can demonstrate. It is reasonable to assume that the more general or universalistic a given principle or interest proves to be, the larger the transactional population whose interests it can claim to serve. The E-space therefore helps us to focus on the nature and extent of the interests served by a particular transaction and on the effectiveness of a given set of institutional arrangements for protecting and promoting these[117] – in short, to concentrate on its *governance*.

These two aspects of a transaction, its style and its governance, are intimately intertwined and for this reason have not always been adequately distinguished from each other. We therefore discuss governance in the next section.

5.9: GOVERNANCE

The scope of a transaction

The distinction we are making between the style and governance of a transaction is potentially, as we shall presently see, an important one and it has been overlooked by the existing literature on transaction costs.[118] Governance – the process of identifying and reconciling the different interests to be served through a given transaction – is one of the two variables that affect the *scope* of a transaction, the other being the range and diversity of activities that it can accommodate. We can effectively describe transactional scope by means of a diagram (Figure 5.4) in which the number of different interests to be served by a given governance structure are positioned on a vertical axis and the range of activities that can serve such interests are positioned on the horizontal axis. This allows us to distinguish between governance structures that are focused on a narrow range of activities but that serve a broad range of potential interests (for example, social security agencies), and those that display the opposite characteristics, namely, of serving a narrow range of interests but of doing so through a wide range of different activities (for example, a closely held conglomerate firm).

The range of interests to be served and the range of activities that serve

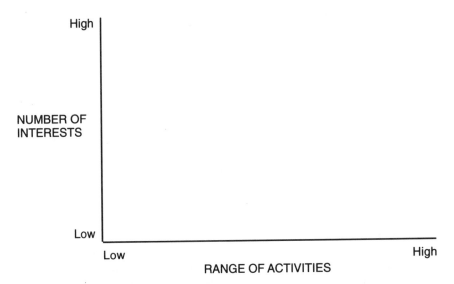

Figure 5.4 Transactional scope

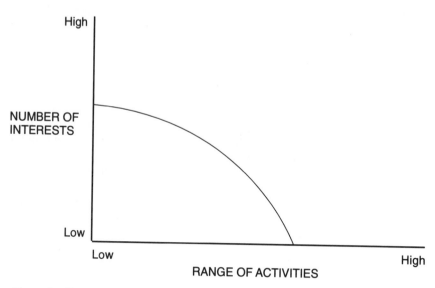

Figure 5.5 The transaction possibility frontier

these can reciprocally determine each other. One could, for instance, start with a given activity and ask whose interests might be served by pursuing it, or, reversing the sequence, one could start with a specific set of interests and ask what types of activity best serve these. Either way we end up transacting at a specific location in the two-dimensional space just described; whether in fact a transaction can feasibly be accommodated by a particular governance structure at that location will be given by its *transaction possibility frontier* (Figure 5.5), the boundary within which a transaction can be coordinated from inside the structure at an acceptable cost, and beyond which some other form of governance will be needed. In many regions of the space, the frontier is a blur rather than a line, a situation that gives rise to border disputes between competing forms of governance.

An increase in transactional capacity brought about either by an organization's growth or an increase in its resource base has the effect of pushing its transaction possibility frontier outward and away from the origin, and of increasing the volume of transactions that can be internalized by its chosen governance structure, whatever that might be.

Transactional *style* then describes how that capacity is utilized: is a given transaction, for example, most effectively handled by completely decentralizing it – as in a market – or should some impersonal form of hierarchical control be maintained – i.e., as in a bureaucracy? Should highly personalized methods of coordination be sought – in which case we approximate fiefs or clans – or is the information involved sufficiently codified or diffused not to require these?

Three points should be made about this way of approaching the issue. Firstly, transaction costs associated with the *process* of governance itself – the identification and reconciliation of divergent interests or levels of interest – are to be distinguished from those associated with the *technical coordination* of a diverse range of activities. In much of the transaction cost and agency literature, the interests to be served by a governance structure tend to be taken as given rather than as problematic, with 'higher' level corporate interests then appearing as somehow more legitimate than lower level ones. In most instances discussed it turns out to be the agent, not the principal, who is considered a source of potential problems and therefore has to be monitored and controlled. Where he acts on interests that diverge from those of boss, his behaviour gets labelled 'opportunistic', and the governance challenge naturally becomes one of keeping his opportunism in check. The interests of the firm then reduce to those of the principal. These, in effect, become the 'higher' purposes that the governance structure is designed to protect.[119] By taking interests as given and unitary – i.e., as well-codified profit maximization rather than as more fuzzy and diffuse social responsibility – it becomes possible to de-politicize transactions and concentrate instead on their efficiency characteristics.[120]

Secondly, a decision to internalize a transaction, to bring it within the transaction possibility frontier of a given governance structure, is partly a response to governance constraints – the activity so internalized must demonstrably serve a defined set of interests – but it is in no way reducible to a choice of transactional style – that is, to a choice between markets, bureaucracies, fiefs, and clans, since these are equally available *outside* the chosen governance structure. The implicit association of internal transactions with bureaucracies and of external ones with markets is a dangerous simplification first performed by Coase (1937) and subsequently kept alive by Williamson himself.[121]

To illustrate: in a command economy, the only legitimate type of external transaction available to the typical state-owned firm is a bureaucratic one, not a market one. In a market economy, by contrast, many large firms choose to conduct even intra-firm transactions – the allocation of capital between competing divisions, buying and selling between divisions, the allocation of employees to jobs, etc. – through largely self-regulating internal markets.

Thirdly, reconciling diverging interests on the one hand and integrating and coordinating the diverse activities required to serve them on the other, and all within a single transactional structure, both call for abstraction but of different kinds. The first type of abstraction acts on the motivational structure of transactional actors, aligning their preferences and values with each other by means of a unifying *vision*;[122] the second acts on their disposition to achieve mutual coordination through the creation of a coherent *strategy*. Vision and strategy can either reinforce each other or they can work against each other. Effective governance partitions the I-space

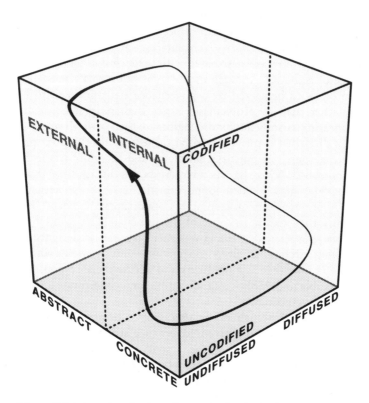

Figure 5.6 Internal and external organization in the I-space

along the abstraction dimension into internal transacting populations, those that can be reached and made to share a unifying vision, and external populations that cannot. The larger and more diverse the internal transacting population, the more abstract the vision must be. External transacting populations are then parametrized and pushed further out along the abstraction dimension. Strategy then effectively drives the SLC of the newly created internal population – whether it be a firm or another type of organization – through a judicious mix of transactional styles some of which will connect it at various points along the abstraction dimension to external populations. Figure 5.6 indicates how our transactional categories, activated by the SLC, give rise both to elements of internal organization and to external transactional structures.

An example

A concrete example will help to illustrate the difference between governance and style.

The local branch of a large international firm is located at some distance out of town. Until recently, its employees were obliged to come into the city at lunchtime for lack of adequate catering facilities provided at the workplace, a procedure that was both costly and time consuming and a source of grumbling and dissatisfaction throughout the local organization.

The firm, mindful of its image and the need to retain staff, then decided to establish a canteen on the premises in order to resolve the issue. As a purely financial proposition, a catering facility was of dubious attraction given that it would probably only serve one meal at midday, and this only to a limited number of people. The question for the firm's management was whether to have the organization itself provide the catering service in-house or to have an outside firm bid for the catering contract. That management was prepared to address the issue at all implied that it was willing to extend the firm's transactional scope, if only by accommodating an expanded set of interests: those of employees. But how far should such scope be extended?

Were the firm to opt for the second course and go for external contracting, the situation would be fairly straightforward and would leave its organizational structure unaffected. Part of the firm's own premises might be let to the successful bidder on an arm's-length basis and employees would be charged a market price for their meals that reflected the convenience to them of not having to travel into town. On the other hand, opting for the first course by providing an in-house catering facility, whether on a purely commercial or a partly subsidized basis, would amount to a further extension of the firm's transactional scope, an internalization of activities that it was not originally designed to undertake, but which, through its effects on staff morale, might have a beneficial long-term impact on its strategy.

The extension of scope brought about by the first option, however, occurs along both the activity axis of Figure 5.4 and its governance axis. We can approach the governance issue by asking whose interests are being served by the provision of a canteen on the premises. The short answer seems to be 'the employees'. Obviously they stand to benefit most directly from such an arrangement since they are spared the time, cost, and effort of going into town for their midday meal. But do not the firm's shareholders and its other stakeholders also benefit? Fewer lunchtime delays might occur, staff morale might improve, and, by allowing employees more flexibility in their choice of mealtime, overall productivity might go up, and with it, the firm's profits.

To the extent that the interests of employees have to be accommodated by the firm if it is not to be penalized, it is led to extend the range of interests to which it is willing to respond as well as the range of activities through which it does so. Employees, in effect, become acknowledged as *stakeholders* with a legitimate impact on governance. Indeed, if they ever became the most powerful stakeholder in the organization so that all other interests were subordinated to their own, then the organization would become indistinguishable from the Yugoslav labour-managed firm.[123]

Now assuming that the firm accepts to extend its activities in this way – and by implication the range of interests that it serves – it then has to decide how the canteen will be managed. And if, as is sometimes the case with large international firms, this one tends to be ponderous and bureaucratic, it may feel that its current way of managing things will have to be modified in the case of the canteen if it is ever to become financially viable. Perhaps it will have to decentralize day-to-day control over catering decisions – purchasing, the choice of menu, etc. – to an extent that would be quite unacceptable in other parts of its organization. Alternatively, it may feel that if this new undertaking is to have the required impact on staff morale, employees should be actively involved in its management through a committee structure and regular consultations. Hard upon the heels of a decision concerning its transactional scope, then – should this kind of organization be getting into the catering business at all, whether directly or through subcontracting? – the firm confronts a choice of transactional style.

Governance, strategy, and style

Questions of scope tend to be dealt with at that level in an organization responsible for governance – the board of directors in an enterprise, the council of bishops, the cabinet, etc. The key issues to be decided at this level are what range of interests should legitimately be served by the transactional structure – the problem of governance – and what range of activities best serve these – the choice of an appropriate strategy. Governance and strategy choices are strongly interlinked: changes in the one are likely to entail changes in the other with the causal lines of influence moving in both directions. Problems of transactional style, on the other hand, are usually left to executive discretion: change the people in charge of implementing a chosen strategy and they will often wish to modify the style in which the relevant transactions are conducted in a direction that they personally feel more comfortable with.

Governance and strategy on the one hand, and style on the other, allow a transacting group to forge its own identity over time. Strategy, to be effective, must navigate between the constraints set by governance considerations on the *legitimacy* of organized action, and those set by the transactional styles available on the *capacity* for such action. In short, interests must be reconciled using the resources available. Where governance has a broad focus, and must accommodate a wide variety of diverse or divergent interests, it will seek to work to a set of abstract values and universal principles that all transacting parties can subscribe to.[124] Since these can never be fully realized in practice, the organization's perceived effectiveness – up to a point at least – will be linked more to the integrity of its chosen procedures than to any specific outcomes. Where, on the other hand, governance has a narrow focus and only one or a few interests to serve, it will be oriented to concrete goals, to specific outcomes, and to efficiency considerations. Abstract values and principles might then appear to take a back seat and a more pragmatic cost–benefit approach will predominate.

The problem of organizational growth

Economic organizations work to a narrower governance focus than, say, political or religious organizations. Paradoxically, however, as they grow, they often come to exceed the transactional capacity of those styles associated with a narrow focus, such as fiefs and clans. They then seek out transactional styles – bureaucracies and markets – that promise greater efficiency, but in doing so are inevitably led to broaden the range of stakeholder interests to which they must respond. Not all these stakeholders, however, are internal to the organization when it is narrowly construed as a firm, in spite of the influence they are able to exert on its transactional structure.

The character of economic organizations can thus be transformed and at the same time subtly undermined by a quest for transactional efficiencies, which, by provoking a change in transactional style, increase capacity by imperceptibly bringing about a shift from narrow to broad governance. The consequence of the shift is either a politicization of the governance structure which becomes an arena for bargaining between an expanded set of competing interests, or an increasing emphasis on process rather than performance – the plague of many a state bureaucracy.[125]

Only rarely can firms escape this dilemma as they grow. If they do so it is because they have been able to infuse into their situation a coherent and energizing vision behind which ostensibly competing interests can align themselves with no loss of transactional efficiency. Such a strategic vision helps to articulate the interests to be served by a given transactional structure in a non-conflictual way, to specify the range of activities through which they will be served, and to identify the transactional styles most appropriate for pursuing such activities. Whether we choose to label it a founding myth, a tradition, a utopia, or whatever, a well-crafted vision exerts a strong influence on the evolution of a culture whether at the level of a small group, an organization, or a nation-state. It becomes a solvent that keeps the process congruent with the requirements of effective performance.

Culture itself, the pattern created by institutionalized transactions as they evolve in the I-space, is the subject of the next chapter.

5.10: CONCLUSION

Recapitulation

The contribution of this chapter to the book's general theme will now be briefly summarized. Information moves through the SLC largely in anticipation of or in giving effect to social exchanges. Movement in the data field has a cost that is best contained by creating structures for the accommodation of recurrent exchanges where efficiency matters. Social exchanges constrained by efficiency considerations we call transactions, and the general purpose structures that they inhabit we call institutions. Organizations are concrete embodiments of institutional arrangements adapted to particular cases.[126]

To be viable as transactional structures, institutions must adequately reflect the information environment in which the exchanges they claim to govern might take place. This chapter has identified four ideal–typical transactional structures amenable to institutionalization. Each is listed and briefly described in Table 5.1.

The action of the SLC is continuously redistributing information in the I-space and hence affecting the viability of each of these structures. The assignment of transactions will therefore shift between them partly as a passive response to the influence of the SLC itself and partly in more active attempts to forestall the erosive action of the cycle through investments in institutionalization.

The SLC, by continuously modifying their information environment, acts directly on transactional options in the I-space. It also acts on them indirectly by extending or contracting the range of interests along the abstraction dimension that a given transactional structure can coherently serve. The issue of governance, therefore, is to be distinguished from that of transactional choice although the two remain intimately related through the action of the SLC.

Governance issues effectively partition the I-space along the abstraction dimension into a transacting population that subscribes to a given set of objectives and others that do not. Governance in a sense motivates the creation of organization. Organization, in turn, operates through interlinked transactional structures, reconfiguring them as circumstances in the data field dictate. For this reason, the decision to internalize a transaction – i.e., to bring it within a given framework of governance – is not reducible to a choice of transaction structure as such.

Limitations of institutional economics

Differences between the transaction cost and the neoclassical approach to economizing are by now well documented[127] and will not be dealt with further here. Of more importance to our discussion perhaps is that the differences between the approach to transactions outlined in this chapter and that adopted by the new institutional economists such as Oliver Williamson are numerous and potentially significant. We shall deal with three.

Firstly, although the New Institutional Economics acknowledges the important role played by information in the choice of transactional arrangements, by focusing primarily on the information asymmetries that might exist between parties – i.e., on the diffusion characteristics of a transaction – rather than on the degree of codification or abstraction of relevant transactional data, it has been led to concentrate its attention on effects rather than on causes. Codification and abstraction are, of course, referred to, but in essentially atheoretical terms. They are dealt with under the general categories of 'uncertainty' and 'atmosphere'; beyond occasional references to the tacit nature of certain kinds of knowledge, an appreciation of their crucial link to communicability and hence to the social possibilities of information sharing remains generally undeveloped.

The consequence of this neglect is that transactional choices have been framed purely in terms of their centralization characteristics, at first by concentrating on the end points of a centralization–decentralization continuum – i.e., on hierarchies and markets – and then later on intermediate forms.[128] Much transactional richness related to codification or abstraction phenomena escapes such a formulation so that even when an intermediate transactional form is introduced – Ouchi talks of clans, Butler of federations – it is perceived to be little more than an infill between markets and hierarchies.[129] The whole exercise thus remains strictly one-dimensional. Only information diffusion is brought into play.

Secondly, the markets and hierarchies paradigm implies, but does not develop, a dynamic theory of information flows. Expressions such as 'information impacting', 'opportunism', and 'strategic behaviour' are highly suggestive and, in my view, somewhat Schumpeterian in flavour. But they are pressed into the service of an essentially static theory of transactional assignment. A mechanistic rather than an evolutionary perspective still informs too much of the analysis.[130] The SLC shows that creative destruction is at work in the I-space, and applies no less to transactional structures than to other economic goods. Information flows activate new structures and cause older ones to atrophy. Some institutional investment helps to reinforce existing structures and to slow the process down, some merely helps to accelerate it. In this view, markets attain moments of stability – i.e., equilibrium – but in historical time: not only is the attainment of equilibrium path dependent so that the specific trajectory of the SLC as it approaches the market region of the I-space matters, but transactional activity, even once it has reached the market region and *pace* equilibrium theorists, has no built-in tendency to remain there. The learning that occurs in markets is as likely to move it away from equilibrium as towards it in a 'logic of collective action' that was first described by Michels and then by Olson.[131]

Finally, in the absence of a conceptual scheme that could factor out governance issues from transactional ones, the new institutional economists have tended to conflate the two: hierarchies are treated as a matter of course as internal to firms, and markets as institutions that are external to firms. Hybrid forms, to be sure, exist between these polar alternatives, and in such cases one talks of bilateral governance.[132]

None of this is wrong as such, but it paints an incomplete picture: *all* transactional forms may exist inside or outside particular governance structures such as firms and in each case they are amenable to varying degrees of institutionalization. Governance objectives may be served by either internal or external transactions, and any particular mix or transaction style will reflect, on the one hand, efficiency considerations and the availability of internal and external structures, and on the other, the distribution of power among stakeholders within the governance framework. The simple dichotomy created by the markets and hierarchies paradigm between internal and external transactions may turn out in fact to have but a limited institutional application; namely, to the joint-stock firm. Indeed, the boundary that separates the inside from the outside of such an organization already presupposes a highly codified transactional environment. Inject a measure of fuzziness and ambiguity into that environment, however, and the boundary may well dissolve or appear as nothing more than a gradient.[133] We discuss this further in the context of the case presented in Chapter 7.

Institutional economics: the way forward

In spite of such limitations, the New Institutional Economics research programme, given its willingness to acknowledge the central role played by information in the economic process, constitutes a marked advance over what is on offer from the neoclassical orthodoxy. There, information retains the status of the luminiferous ether of classical physics before Einstein: a ubiquitous medium that admitted of a mechanical account of action at a distance and kept the world conveniently Newtonian.

Institutional economics, however, needs a more explicit and dynamic theory of information flows if it is to make more than a dent in the neoclassical defences. Having established that there exist credible institutional alternatives to markets, it needs to show how information production and exchange underpins them all, shaping their internal evolution as well as how they collaborate and compete. In effect, what is needed is a theory of social learning that extends beyond the individual or the organization[134] to encompass more complex institutional settings. Such a theory, I believe, is foreshadowed in Douglass North's historical studies of institutions. It now needs further development.

The SLC takes a step in the direction of such a theory, one that encompasses neoclassical forms of learning – moves towards equilibrium – as a special case. The kind of learning promoted by the SLC we might call *meta-learning*;[135] it is quite at odds with the Pavlovian kind of learning associated with efficient markets. This, to be sure, occurs, but it gradually gives way to experience-based reflection (absorption and impacting) and to an accumulation of insights (scanning) that move well-positioned individuals away from a mindless equilibrium passively endured and towards new opportunities opened up by creative data processing strategies.

Only in one phase of the SLC – the diffusion phase – can information gradually come to acquire the characteristics required by efficient markets, and that phase is temporary. Elsewhere, understanding the exchange process requires an appreciation of the specific circumstances under which information is structured (codified and abstracted from data) and shared (diffused) among social agents. A structural approach to the information problem leads us to the kind of institutional analysis presented in this chapter. It is distinguishable from a structuralist approach by its contingent and constructivist operation.[136] A process approach, by contrast, would lead us to a cultural analysis; culture, under most definitions, having something to do with the *way* that experience is structured and shared within and between groups. Structure and process are not exclusive perspectives. We turn to process next.

Chapter 6

Culture as economizing

ABSTRACT

Various students of culture take the structuring and sharing of information as central to their definition of culture. Structuring involves codification and abstraction and sharing involves diffusion. It follows from such definitions that a political economy of information implies a theory of culture and that cultural processes can be viewed as attempts at economizing on social information processing.

The SLC integrates a number of anthropological perspectives on culture – i.e., materialism, idealism, structuralism, culturalism, etc. – which, when analysed statically, have appeared to be in opposition to one another.

In the I-space, we distinguish between centripetal and centrifugal cultures. The first confine their transactions to a narrower region of the I-space than the second. With cultural evolution cultures tend to become more centrifugal and complex. Cultural convergence, the idea that cultures increasingly come to resemble each other over time, is easier to operationalize with centripetal than with centrifugal cultures. However, it contradicts the premises of cultural evolution.

The effectiveness of a given set of institutions as information economizing devices also depends on the level of cultural evolution. Institutions require structures for their governance and these trace out boundaries that separate in-groups from out-groups, thus creating distinctive cultures. If institutions define the means through which social attempts at information economizing will be effected, governance structures specify the ends to which such economizing will be applied.

The quest for information economies is one of the key drivers of cultural evolution. If we represent a culture in the I-space as a given configuration of institutions, then it becomes apparent that inter-institutional links, no less than intra-institutional ones, will be subject to attempts at economizing. In other words, a culture as a whole can be taken as an expression of economizing activity, a point that calls into question the almost exclusive focus of conventional economics on market institutions alone.

6.1: INTRODUCTION

Definitional issues

Culture has always been something of a portmanteau term on which scholars from diverse disciplines could each hang up their own preferred meaning. The use of the term by organization theorists such as Deal and Kennedy, Schein, or Hofstede, for example, when discussing corporate values and practices, differs substantially from that by cultural anthropologists like, say, Malinowski, Kroeber, Sahlins, Harris, Douglas, or Hall.[1] To devise a working definition of culture that will satisfy specialist and non-specialist alike is probably an impossible task and it will not be attempted here. What will be is the use of the cultural concept as an integrating device for pulling together the different strands of thought we have been developing.

The term 'culture' first made its appearance in our discussion in Chapter 3 when we described the C-space, a creation that brought together the codification and diffusion dimensions of the I-space. There, we justified our use of the term – at least provisionally – by observing that culture has something to do with the way that information is structured and shared within and across definable populations. Codification could thus be made to serve as a proxy measure for structuring, and diffusion could do duty for sharing. The focus in Chapter 3 was on communication processes and for the limited purposes of that discussion our working definition of culture was adequate.

The progress of our discussion since then, however, calls for a more extended treatment of the concept. As we learnt in Chapter 2, for example (that is to say, even before our discussion got under way), the structuring of information involves abstraction as well as codification so that the phenom-enon of abstraction should also figure in any detailed discussion of culture. It is implicit in the work of Durkheim and Mauss and it underlies Talcot Parsons's distinction between particularistic (concrete) and universalistic (abstract) cultures.[2] In our own day, Habermas's discussion of systems and life-worlds draws heavily upon the difference between abstract and concrete forms of thought.[3]

Another consideration that must also now be taken on board is that culture evolves over time. How effectively might such evolution be account-ed for by our dynamic analysis of information flows in Chapter 4? Is the behaviour of the SLC at least consistent with what has been written concerning cultural evolution?

Finally, in the preceding chapter we concluded that any discussion of institutions is of a piece with a broader cultural discourse. What is the nature of the link, then, between institutional structures and cultural processes? What are the influences that the one might exert upon the other?

Linking culture and political economy

If we can address these issues satisfactorily, in effect we shall be able to build a bridge between a political economy of information, such as we have sketched out in the preceding chapters, and the culture concept. Indeed, I believe that we can go further, since in the final analysis, as I shall argue, the one reduces to the other. The implications of such an exercise are far reaching: for in such a case cultures taken at whatever level, no less than the individual agent, the organization, or the institution, become an expression of attempts at economizing. How convincingly does current economic theory account for such a possibility?

In this chapter, the theorizing that has been poured so far into this book reaches its high-water mark. On occasions we shall be using economic terms drawn from the institutional economics literature to talk not about economics but about culture. Some readers may choose to interpret the terms of a discourse as little more than a linguistic convenience – after all, many different disciplines survive some degree of overlap in the vocabularies they each employ; for others, however, it may presage what Kuhn labelled a 'Gestalt switch',[4] a sudden and unanticipated rearrangement of existing and common elements that provokes a change in the pattern that is perceived.

6.2: APPROACHES TO CULTURE

Some definitions

Any term which lacks a single and well-tested theoretical foundation lends itself to sweeping and often quite unwarranted interpretations that have the effect of pulling it hither and thither as different users compete to appropriate it for their own purposes. Such has been the case with the term 'culture'. An early view of culture, for example, as the psychic unity of mankind, was advanced by Tylor;[5] it is suggestive but far too vague to be of much use since by such a definition culture becomes simultaneously everything and nothing. At best Tylor is pointing to the mental experiences people hold in common. But then Jung's theory of the collective unconscious also becomes a theory of culture as well as being a psychological theory, unless further qualifications are added.[6]

In spite of adumbrations of a general theory of culture in the works of Boas, Sapir, Benedict, Linton, Bateson, Kluckhohn, and White,[7] progress towards greater precision and clarity has not been easy. Its inherent vagueness and elusiveness have helped the term to slip its anthropological moorings and to drift towards the shores of organizational theory and of the popular management literature.[8] This has been of more help in spreading a general awareness of the importance of cultural phenomena than in promoting any real understanding of them.

Anthropologists themselves still tend to oscillate between two different approaches to the phenomenon of culture. The first, originally associated with the name of Radcliffe-Brown,[9] takes culture to be an expression of social structure and function with kinship patterns and their associated network of social relations becoming both the means and the object of cultural transmission: structure transmits culture and culture, in turn, transmits structure.

The second approach views culture as a patterned cognitive order that has evolved historically; a set of norms and roles – cognitive variables – that proscribe or regulate behaviour. The pattern view of culture is associated with the name of Kroeber.[10] After reviewing several hundred definitions of culture, Kroeber and Kluckhohn were able to distil from them a single essential feature. Culture is pattern transmitted by symbols – a product of action which conditions further action.[11]

The gap that separates the structural–functional and the cognitive approaches to culture does not appear to be unbridgeable. The theory of social structure, for example, stresses the part played by implicit or explicit roles in the standardization of behaviour and thought. In so doing, it builds its analysis on two intangibles very close to the pattern theorist's heart: social values and the psychological interests of the individual. In a sense, therefore, a social structure theory of culture rests upon a pattern theory that it has internalized. The two theories turn out to offer complementary perspectives rather than competing ones. Group structure has a cognitive basis and there is every reason to believe that cognition in turn is shaped at least in part by social structural and functional considerations. As Kelly has put it, 'People belong to the same cultural group not only because they behave alike, nor because they expect the same things of others, but especially because they construe their experience in the same way.'[12] To secure this common sharing of experience, a group must establish articulated mechanisms for the selection, structuring, and transmission of valued meanings; in a word, *culture-specific institutions* that contribute to the creation of a stable and meaningful order for group members.

Reconciling structural–functional and cognitive theories of culture in this way leads to a perception of cultural processes as the structuring and sharing of information within a given group through ordered social relationships. The transactional strategies through which such information exchange is conducted either express or are constrained by a normative order, and when transactions are recurrent, they gradually build up patterned institutional arrangements designed to preserve and reinforce such a normative order, or, more rarely, to adapt it to changing circumstances.[13]

Information structuring, information sharing: can any reader fail to spot the parallels between these two cultural variables and those of codification, abstraction, and diffusion that we have been using as building blocks for a political economy of information? The major difference, of course, between the existing discourse on culture and our own is that although the former has identified these two variables as fit and proper candidates for a theory of culture, it has not as yet effectively articulated such a theory. The I-space claims to do just that. It articulates an explicit set of relationships between the variables that can simultaneously accommodate a static–institutional perspective with its focus on structure as well as a dynamic–evolutionary one focusing on process.

That pre-literate and literate cultures tend to operate at different levels of codification and abstraction is by now a commonplace in the anthropological literature; that this difference has some effect on the scope for social exchange and its institutionalization has also been duly noted.[14] Yet these observations were never resolved into an explicit theoretical relationship that subjected information sharing behaviour by actors in different social settings to the specific cognitive and communicative resources available to them.

Claude Lévi-Strauss was one of the first to subordinate the social to the cognitive[15] and to acknowledge that even within a single culture, the symbolic could vary in its capacity to structure the social order. The relationship that might obtain between a set of symbols and various elements of the social structure was neither determinate nor one to one. The same symbols and structural elements might show up in different cultures but the way that the first was mapped onto the second might vary considerably from one to the other.

In his discussion of symbolic production Lévi-Strauss did not evoke codification as a variable; the possibility that a single culture could operate at different points on a codification scale was therefore left unexplored.[16] So, in consequence, was the contingent nature of symbolic production itself. Few anthropologists, in fact, have taken symbolizing activity, as we have done, explicitly to vary in its degree of codification and abstraction. For Sapir, to cite one example, one level of symbolic production, language, was the main constituent of culture: 'it is obvious that language has the power to analyse experience into theoretically dissociable elements and to create that world of the potential integrating with the actual which enables human beings to transcend the immediately given in their individual experiences and to join in a larger common understanding ... This common understanding constitutes culture.'[17] The primacy accorded to language by Sapir at the cultural level finds an echo in the work of Jacques Lacan operating at the level of individual psychological processes.[18] Language, however, as our discussion of the E-space made clear, occupies a fairly narrow bandwidth on the codification scale and does not offer the only, or often even the most, appropriate path towards a 'larger common understanding'.

Hall's approach

Edward Hall, perhaps more than other cultural anthropologists, has explored the cognitive potential of the codification scale, but without attempting to link his findings in any systematic way to information sharing behaviour.[19] As we have already seen, the distinction he draws between high context and low context cultures corresponds to two different points on our codification and abstraction dimensions, respectively located in $\bar{A}\bar{C}$ and in AC; the distinction lends itself to theoretical developments that go well beyond what Hall actually attempts.

High context – i.e., concrete, uncodified – actions, Hall sees as rooted in the past, slow to change and highly stable.[20] Another way of saying this is that uncodified transactions lack the definition or structure that facilitate abstraction and hence rapid symbolic manipulation and transformation. High context thought partly owes its durability to the fact that it is non-propositional and hence non-refutable. Yet it also lacks the information storage mechanisms available to more codified forms of exchange; any stability it enjoys is in effect dynamic in nature. As we saw in the preceding chapter, it is precisely because it *can* change, often in ways invisible to the transacting parties themselves, that it remains mostly stable, imperceptibly adapting itself to new situations as circumstances require.

In high context cultures, people avoid verbalizing what they can take for granted, and typically this covers a large part of their daily interactions. Recall that systematic preference for the implicit communication style associated with high context has been interpreted by Bernstein, working in a British context, as a class phenomenon. The 'restricted codes' used by a working-class community for its discourse place beyond its reach the broader, more abstract patterns of interaction that a middle-class community drawing on an 'elaborated code' can enter into.[21] By making his coding behaviour a class phenomenon, Bernstein implicitly explains it as a differential access to educational opportunities within a culture: one uses implicit codes because one has no easy access to explicit ones. Culture, then, becomes class culture; not so much a psychic unity as envisaged by Tylor as a psychic differentiation based on institutional discrimination. Hall, by contrast, treats coding less as a restriction externally imposed on the individual – although it must be such to some extent – than as a free if unconscious collective choice with broad societal consequences for institutional practices and cultural patterns:

> High context cultures make a greater distinction between insiders and outsiders than low context cultures do. People raised in high context systems expect more of others than do participants in low context systems. When talking about something that they have on their mind, a high context individual will expect his interlocutor to know what is bothering him, so that he doesn't have to be specific. The result is that he will talk around and around the point, in effect putting all the pieces in place except the crucial one. Placing it properly – this keystone – is the role of his interlocutor. To do this for him is an insult and a violation of his individuality.[22]

Japanese society offers an interesting example of a high context culture.[23] The nation as a whole displays a marked preference for the use of restricted

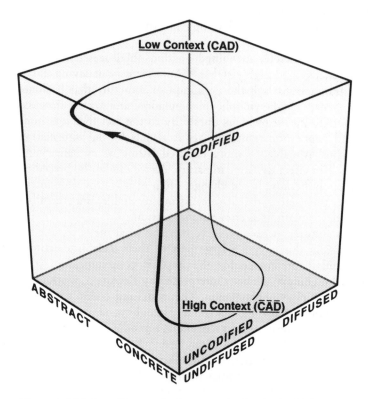

Figure 6.1 High and low context communication in the SLC

codes. Yet differences in coding practice among socio-economic groups can hardly be said to form the basis of any class divisions in Japan: survey after survey reveals that some 90 per cent of Japanese perceive themselves to belong to the middle class.[24] If they have access to elaborated codes, they still prefer to use restricted ones. Japan's experience of restricted codes suggests that, interesting as it is, Bernstein's thesis may not travel easily beyond British shores.

According to Hall, high context in contrast to low context communication is 'economical, fast, efficient and satisfying'.[25] He also notes that it requires a great deal of prior transactional investment since it takes time to build up a shared context and understanding between communicating parties. Yet whether this in fact makes high context communication any more burdensome than low context communication is not clear. After all, do not *all* forms of communication require such prior investment? Is not the key difference between codified and uncodified transactions that in the latter, effectiveness requires a mastery of context whereas in the former it requires a mastery of codes? These two ways of investing, of course, yield quite different benefits.

Investing in context, for example, facilitates smooth intra-group processes; investing in codes, on the other hand, promotes effective inter-group exchanges. The trade-off can be thought of as one between depth and range of exchange. Just as an implicit, high context transactional style would prevent relevant messages from reaching the more extensive populations of out-groups, so a persistent use of the more impersonal style of low context transactions would gradually erode the intimate solidarity of an in-group.[26]

The point is illustrated in Figure 6.1. Here the SLC provides us with guidance as to what our coding strategy should be. High context communication is located, as one might expect, in the region of the I-space labelled $\bar{C}\bar{A}\bar{D}$; low context communication is in CAD. In a low context mode, we see that not only is discourse likely to be more codified, it is also likely to draw on more abstract categories. Our earlier discussion of governance, moreover, leads us to expect that the range of interests served by low context discourse are likely to be articulated in less particularistic ways than in the high context case where intra-group values and common interests show greater overlap and can be implicitly taken for granted.

Needless to say, there are numerous instances in day-to-day transactions when the principle of least effort will keep knowledge implicit and uncodified. As Hall himself observes, the map of one's home town is held in one's head rather than carried about in one's pocket.[27] It does not depict every street and those that it does are stored in fragments. These are then gradually pieced together through successive encounters with particular places, buildings, landmarks, and so on. The resulting mental map is a personal aid built up over long stretches of time through continuous personal involvement. Yet outside a familiar territory it has little to offer. In a new and unexplored environment an external prop – a chart, a written guide, or a scaled map – becomes essential.

An inarticulate, common-sense world, locked up in one's head, forms part of a person's cultural unconscious and is often treated by its possessor as if it were innate rather than contingent, a kind of 'everybody knows ...' knowledge that is rarely challenged in his daily commerce with things and people. For this reason, irrational or untenable notions, implicitly held in common within a culture, often come to acquire an aura of normality, not to say inevitability. Unrefuted because they are not sufficiently explicit to be tested, they came to form a constituent part of a group's cognitive repertoire, its life-world. They remain dormant and usually undisturbed, immersed in the cultural unconscious and gently coasting along until they hit something that brings them to awareness and forces their explicitation. The something may be nothing other than the physical world itself which, like a reef, pierces through the fragile hull that protects the life-world and keeps it afloat.[28] But it may also be another hull, freighted with the competing assumptions held by an out-group or another culture. The collision between two fully laden hulls we call a culture clash.

Internalization

Hall's discussion of high and low context extends to issues of internalization.[29] He notes that social controls, for example, are internalized by the individual in some cultures, expressing themselves through the workings of his own conscience, whereas in others, such controls remain external to the individual, being explicitly embodied in general rules and regulations that are applied to him from outside and then socially enforced.

Our discussion of governance in the preceding chapter associated internalization with a cluster of interests and values that are specifically served by a governance structure operating within a definable boundary. Internalizing, in effect, means bringing transactions inside the boundary the better to serve the interests and values behind them through unified governance. Externalizing, of course, may still serve the same interests and values where internal transaction costs are too high. The governance structure around which the boundary is drawn is defined by the specific purpose that it serves and by the population submitting to it. Such a population is made up of individual data processors: these can range from the amoebas to individual human beings, and from a small group right up to the nation-state and beyond. The larger and more diverse the population subjected to a particular governance structure, the more abstract the articulation of interests and values that it serves must become if it is to achieve any cohesiveness.

Generalizing somewhat, we might say that wherever some degree of organization is required for the cultural pursuit of either common or compatible interests and values, the problem of governance is posed and with it that of control. The concept of internalization then posits a transactional discontinuity along the $\bar{A}A$ axis of Figure 6.1 which defines what constitutes an inside and an outside with respect to the interests and values served at a given level of abstraction.

Hall does not exploit the theoretical opportunities opened up by his discourse. He does not forge any theoretical links between his discussion of high and low context on the one hand and his discussion of internalization on the other. He narrowly confines his attention to two points on our codification scale, one in $\bar{C}$, the other in C. The power of the codification variable, working in harness with abstraction and diffusion, to inform a cultural analysis of institutions and governance structures through the action of the SLC thus remains unutilized.

Mary Douglas

In the field of cultural anthropology, Mary Douglas has perhaps come closest to establishing an articulate relationship between a cognitive and a social order.[30] By integrating cultural classification systems and power relationships, her 'grid and group' analysis echoes in a striking way the transactional categories that we have identified in the I-space.[31] Grid and group, however, as analytical categories, are not free of ambiguity; their empirical coverage is fairly loose. The result is a weak institutional typology from which no strong conclusions can follow. Moreover, as we have already seen, Douglas cannot tell us anything about how a social system might evolve over time within the grid and group framework. Her typology is essentially a static one. Our own framework, being essentially a spatiotemporal theory of data processing and exchange, covers much the same ground as Douglas's, but by drawing upon a more abstract and rigorously derived set of information and communication concepts, it goes further and is able to put forward a refutable set of propositions concerning cultural and institutional evolution. The associations offered by grid and group between belief systems and different forms of social organization remain weak and largely unexplained in the absence of an explicit theory of data processing and communicative behaviour; the explanatory vacuum has been filled by Douglas with stylizations which are interesting but of limited application.

A culturalist perspective is not the only one from which an integration of the cognitive and social order can be undertaken. An early, if ambitious, attempt was made by the French structuralist school.[32]

The structuralist perspective

For structuralists, codification turns out to differ in one important respect from what has been advanced in Chapter 2. There, we argued that codification and abstraction are the activities of an individual mind guided by both social *and* idiosyncratic circumstances. Much collective cognitive structuring takes place along $\bar{D}D$ and reflects a common physiological species-specific heritage: certain things we know in common about the world; we do so because at a primitive level we are led to structure it through the same perceptual apparatus. We probably all experience gravity and breathing in similar ways, and up to a point we can refer to them in a manner that is universally intelligible.

Yet where exactly is that point? Can it be really said that a !Kung tribesman and a Chicago physiologist *interpret* their respective experiences of gravity and breathing so similarly that they will subsequently be led to use the same coding strategies in articulating them? Beyond the most primitive level of experience, are they not in fact talking of different things so that mutual understanding will require that the coding strategies respectively used be shared?

Our position is that it is the *communicative* properties of codes that lead to their being shared, and the extent to which such sharing is possible then defines a variety of transactional arrangement as described in the previous chapter. The structuralist, by contrast, places the largest part of the burden for the social sharing of experience on the common structuring rather than on the communicative properties of codes. All codification and abstraction then becomes collective codification and abstraction and analysis reduces to finding those binary oppositions – between life and death, culture and nature, etc. – which remain invariant across cultures and across different forms of social organization. Idiosyncratic circumstances still have a role to play, but not in guiding the acts of codification and abstraction themselves; they only help to translate commonly held codes into a diversity of specific social customs and forms of organization.[33]

The structuralist sees the same binary oppositions appearing and reappearing in all epochs and in all cultures;[34] they may then attach themselves to different symbols, yet where these are iconic – i.e., images – they are often drawn from the same repertoire of forms. This almost platonic quest for universal unchanging codes has had a considerable influence on the development of linguistics where, through the work firstly of Saussure and his followers and then later of Noam Chomsky, the idea of a transformational grammar giving us access to the universally shared deep structures of the mind has gained many adherents.[35] The main discernible difference between the deep structures posited by structural linguistics and Jung's archetypes of the collective unconscious is that the latter, being images, appear to operate as organizing Gestalten at a lower level of codification and abstraction than the former and hence allow much greater scope for further idiosyncratic articulation by the individual – personal construing as Kelly would put it.[36] Thus if transformational grammars offer a reverse path from the concrete verbal productions of a linguistic group to the universal deep structures of the mind, so Jungian psychology works back from the idiosyncratic utterances of the individual to the underlying archetypes.

From our theoretical perspective, structuralism appears to hypothesize the existence of collective abstract codifications in region CAD of Figure 6.1 that are rooted in physiology rather than in the operation of the SLC. At best, their trajectory in the I-space originates in the region of the concrete and proceeds towards the abstract – i.e., moving from $\bar{A}$ to A – but in D, that is, collectively within the target population as a whole (Figure 6.2). Diffusion, or information sharing, enters the picture not as anything that could affect the trajectory of codification and abstraction activities themselves, but as a triggering device that sets in motion cognitive processes which are at some deep level already wired in.

To be sure, the structuralist hypothesis illustrated in Figure 6.2 is not in any way excluded from consideration by our theory of information flows, and the argument that codification and abstraction are to some extent constrained by physiology is one that we have ourselves put forward in Chapter 2. Yet this only places the hypothesis within the realm of possibility. It does not make it probable nor even plausible. If he/she is to improve the hypothesis's prospects, the structuralist must meet two challenges. Firstly, he/she must be willing to put forward more testable propositions than has

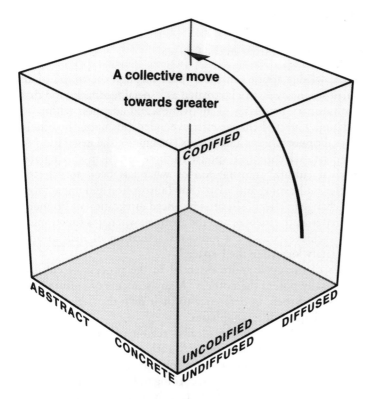

Figure 6.2 Structuralism in the SLC

been done thus far concerning whatever link he/she discerns between universal codes and the specific social practices and structures within which they are embedded – many of Claude Lévi-Strauss's structuralist inter-pretations remain, to say the least, fanciful, their much-vaunted inner coherence or logic notwithstanding. Secondly, the structuralist must provide a convincing account of the relationship that obtains between the *evolution* of codes and that of social structure. How do mental structures maintain their mapping onto social practices as these change and gain in complexity? Does the link get broken? Does it become contingent? Structuralism for the time being remains too static and deterministic adequately to deal with cultural evolution and the workings of the SLC.

6.3: CULTURE AND THE SOCIAL LEARNING CYCLE

Locating different views of culture in the I-space

Recall that new knowledge appears in the I-space through the action of an SLC. For our purposes the cycle can be treated as a social feedback loop that facilitates the evolutionary processes of innovation and adaption within an interacting population. Cultural change effectively depends upon the timely detection of external opportunities and threats (scanning), the generation of variety and appropriate selection in response to these (problem-solving and abstraction), efficient cultural transmission of what has been so selected (diffusion), and relevant learning and adaptation (absorption and impacting). Adaptive cultural change in effect calls for a balanced integration of Popper's three worlds, the material, the mental, and the abstract; when it is functioning smoothly an SLC achieves this by a judicious activation of institutional structures appropriately located in the I-space.[37]

Are some phases of the cycle more essential to the process of cultural change, or more causally potent than others? Many students of culture have argued that this is so but then, in deference to their own theoretical biases, they each go on to pick quite different phases.

Located in what we might call the idealist region of the I-space, for example – i.e., in A – we encounter cultural anthropologists like Goodenough, for whom all culture is cognitive and conceptual, and more 'real' as a private than as a public phenomenon.[38] According to Goodenough, culture consists of the concepts and models that individuals use to organize and interpret their everyday experience. Pattern theorists such as Kroeber, in so far as they might be inclined to accept this anthropological variant of methodological individualism, would then be required to subordinate the emergence of social organization in D to the personal symbolizing activities of individuals in Ḋ. Anthropologists following Durkheim or Sumner, on the other hand, would convert personal concepts and models into by-products of social organization and the interests of society.[39] In the latter case institutions exert an autonomous causal influence that runs from Popper's World 3 towards Worlds 2 and 1, and from D towards Ḋ.

Marx in *The German Ideology* is ensconced in C̄ĀD̄. He sees social organization as 'evolving out of the life processes of definite individuals',[40] a move in which World 1 exerts a powerful causal influence on Worlds 2 and 3 and in which any reciprocal influence is either weak or non-existent. World 3 for Marx is in fact 'superstructure', resting upon the material foundations provided by World 1, but itself exerting little causal influence upon it. It follows that a complete SLC as we have described it has no basis in reality; the 'reifications' that we create for ourselves in World 3 exercise a largely illusory influence on the other two worlds. This, in a nutshell, is the materialist argument. We shall now explore it further in order to bring into sharper focus the way that we interpret the operation of culture in the I-space.

The materialist perspective

Neither structuralists, idealists, nor pattern theorists occupy as restrictive a position in the I-space as do materialists, Marxist or otherwise. Structuralists occupy the region around CAD and are therefore concerned with abstract universal codes. In explaining how these came into being the structuralist may invoke universal social (Durkheim) or biological (Lévi-Strauss) factors. Idealists will occupy locations in CA but they will spread themselves out along the D̄D dimension according to how individualistic they are in their orientation. Pattern theorists, by contrast, do not locate themselves *a priori* in any particular part of the I-space since the personal symbolizing activity of individuals could originate in either local or non-local phenomena, have either concrete or abstract causes, and operate at different levels of codification.

Not so materialists. They are called upon to perform two distinct but related forms of reduction. Firstly they must reduce the abstract to the concrete – in the anthropological case, the symbolic to the biological. By itself this might not appear to distinguish them much from structuralists who argue that universal codes have a biological basis; that is, that at some level we are all 'wired up' in the same way. Yet to structuralists this is no reduction, for they inject pre-extant universal structures into a physical substratum so as to organize the latter, so to speak, from above. They are not required to take such universal structures as epiphenomenal to the functioning of the physical processes in which these happen to be embedded.

Materialists, by contrast, have to take what is concrete and spatiotemporally local as their point of departure, which, in addition to reducing the symbolic to the biological – a move from C to C̄ – also tends to particularize it, 'definite individuals in concrete circumstances' as Marx would put it. This particularization constitutes the second type of reduction. As a consequence, materialists refuse any concessions at all to culture as a potentially autonomous level of analysis. Culture is to be thought of as a set of practical, instrumental responses to concrete biological necessities and functional interests unmediated by symbolic interpretation.[41] Culture in the hands of the materialist becomes ephiphenomenal, no longer able to account for the social dynamic itself; at best it constitutes an environment within which immediate biological purpose unfolds. In sum, in addition to reducing the symbolic to the physical, the cultural materialist reduces the general to the particular – or to a collection of particulars since like the idealist, the materialist can choose a number of positions along D̄D.

The materialist position rests upon two supporting premises. On the one hand, materialists hold that only the immediately given is *real* and can exert any sort of influence on the organism. As one moves out of the here and now, one escapes into abstract constructions that are but distorted reflections of local circumstances, the mainspring of social action. The independent reality that Pythagoras attributed to abstract numbers or that Plato imputed to the Phileban solids, for example, has no place in a materialist's concrete universe.

The second supporting premise relates to *interests*. If the abstract realm is the locus of cultural mystification clad in religious or ideological garb, then it is the material interests of those who have a stake in the prevailing social order – or, to be more specific, in the ways that scarce resources are socially distributed to specific individuals or groups – that provide the distorting reflections just mentioned as well as the motive force to deflect the focus of any cultural discourse away from concrete particulars in Ā and towards abstract principles in A. Marvin Harris, tearing down the thin symbolic veil that conceals this operation from us, claims that:

> The demystification of world religion begins with this simple fact: Confucianism, Taoism, Buddhism, Hinduism, Christianity and Islam prospered because the ruling elites who invented or co-opted them, benefited materially from them. By spiritualizing the plight of the poor, these world religions unburdened the ruling class of the obligation of providing material remedies for poverty. By proclaiming the sacredness of human life and the virtue of compassion towards the humble and the weak, they lowered the cost of internal law and order.[42]

For Harris, the end point of this cynical exercise in economizing on social transaction costs is state formation, the abstract and codified institutional expression of particular interests.

> Once the state becomes a functional reality, its components resonate within a single gigantic amplifier. The more powerful the ruling class, the more it can intensify production, increase population, wage war, expand territory, mystify peasants and increase its power still further. All neighbouring chiefdoms must either rapidly pass the threshold of state formation, or succumb to the triumphant armies of the new social Leviathan.[43]

As material conditions vary, so naturally enough will the forms of social organization to which they give rise. In comparing hunter-gatherer societies, for example, with 'big-man' redistributive systems, Harris notes that in the first case egalitarianism is rooted in the openness of resources, the simplicity of the tools of production, the lack of non-transportable property and the mobile structure of the band. In hunter-gatherer societies, Harris continues,

> Friction can easily be resolved by the movement of the aggrieved parties to new camp sites or those of their relatives. Since there are no standing crops, permanent houses, or heavy equipment, the question of who gets

up and moves away and who stays is of little significance. Hence extremes of subordination and superordination are unknown.[44]

Big-manship, by contrast, is a political-economic instrument for the intensification of production.

> Village-level big men play a central role in cultural materialist theories concerning the origins of advanced forms of inequality. These big men act as the 'nodes' of three important institutional complexes: they intensify production; they carry out redistribution of the resultant temporary harvest surplus and trade goods; and they use their prestige and material wealth to organize trading expeditions and military engagements ... The expansion of the managerial aspects of these functions rapidly leads to permanent and severe forms of hierarchy which eventually culminates in there being differential access to strategic resources; this in turn lays the basis for the emergence of class and the state.[45]

Harris versus Douglas

Mary Douglas, who could not be accused of being soft on materialism, has none the less also argued that infrastructural conditions can have an important impact on the way that people construct their world:

> It makes a great deal of difference to the quality of social life if people are sharing resources which seem to be expanding, dwindling or static ... If the Nuer believe themselves to be husbanding a static livestock population, and the Dinka an expanding one, this would be another explanation for why the latter take social control more lightly. Economic expansion and restriction turn out to be much more significant variables affecting cosmology than absolute population density as such.[46]

The examples cited by Douglas, however, differ from those given by Harris in two important respects. Firstly, what constitutes reality is not immediately given by the concrete situation of social actors but is symbolically mediated. Beliefs, symbolically articulated hypotheses, come into play as a mediating variable and in a 'tolerant' environment, non-viable beliefs will not necessarily become the target of immediate adverse selection. Belief may be subject to nothing more demanding than Simon's law of 'satisficing' which, in the typical case, allows them to subsist even if they are no more than minimally rather than optimally adapted to a given situation.[47] Thus not only are phenomena such as economic expansion or contraction known only symbolically rather than directly, but furthermore they retain a tentative hypothetical character and may not be subjected to particularly rigorous testing.

The second difference between the examples given by Harris and Douglas has to be inferred from the first and concerns the functioning of interests. If material conditions act directly and unforgivingly on belief systems then by implication so do material interests; in the I-space they both originate in Ā even if they subsequently give rise to symbolizing in A. The direction of causation is well established. If on the other hand their effect on belief systems is symbolically mediated then one can allow for interests to reflect cognitive as well as material constraints and thus to originate at different points along ĀA in the I-space. They may come to shape the physical basis of perceptions in Ā but if they happen to originate, say, at a point close to A then the movement turns out to run in the opposite direction to that hypothesized by the materialist; namely, from A towards Ā. The argument is not so much that interests do not shape symbolizing activity – we leave this issue open – but that such interests may enjoy a measure of autonomy of their own at different levels of abstraction and are not of necessity held in thrall to local material conditions.

The materialist thesis would convince more if it claimed less. That material circumstances often have a way of imposing themselves few would deny. But only in subsistence economies – from which cultural materialists seem to draw much of their evidence – do they have any real scope to impose themselves restrictively on social cognition. And even here, the sheer diversity of belief systems encountered in broadly similar material environments hardly argues for fettered cognition.

There is a mechanistic flavour to the materialist argument that deprives our cognitive aparatus of any freedom of manoeuvre – freedom, for instance, to *interpret* our situation and our problems, freedom to devise *alternative* ways of addressing them. Yet the 'system of needs' according to Sahlins 'must always be relative, not accountable as such, by physical necessity, hence symbolic by definition'.[48] Kelly's construct theory echoes this argument when it asserts that 'it is in the similarity of the construction of events that we find the basis for similar action by different actors and not in the identity of the events themselves'.[49] Information structuring and sharing thus acquire a logic and an autonomy of their own which, whilst interacting with the material base and often subject to its lawlike dictates – we all without exception experience the laws of gravity and the need for oxygen – are not yet enslaved by it.

Culture, then, is not superstructure as the materialist would have us believe. If it were, the I-space as a whole would indeed become epiphenomenal. World 1 would hold sway over World 2 and World 3 to such an extent that the path of the SLC would be as predictable as that of De la Mettrie's *Homme Machine* set in a Laplacean universe.[50] Given a detailed enough knowledge of initial physical and social conditions its trajectory in the I-space would reduce to a simple matter of computation – doubtless tedious ones. In a purely physical process, culture, as an autonomous level of explanation, has no useful role to play: where action can only occur mechanically and not informationally (see Chapter 1), culture becomes superfluous.

The autonomy of the cultural object

Culture only becomes meaningful as a level of analysis once it is accepted that symbolizing activity, whether abstract or concrete, always originates in World 2, the world of the mind.[51] It may then externalize its products by embedding them in artefacts or in the social structure, but the mind and not merely the physical brain remains the locus of what we have termed codification and abstraction,[52] a structuring process in which the constitutive elements and relations of the cognitive object are identified and elaborated (see Chapter 2). Through the operation of the SLC the cognitive object so structured acquires a life and a mobility of its own that unshackle it from the spatiotemporal limitations imposed by individual and local circumstances, and allow it to participate in a wider community of social transactions to whose repertoire it contributes. In doing so, it moves out of the two-dimensional E-space and into the three-dimensional I-space to become a cultural as well as a cognitive product. The C-space and the U-space are thereby also activated, the first establishing the social possibilities for information sharing and the second the interplay of social interests and values that might motivate such sharing. Interests and values, then, make their appearance in the I-space but as symbolically mediated variables that can take on a range of values along the $\bar{A}A$ scale and not just as a parameter confined to $\bar{A}$.[53] The cultural object, in consequence, is not burdened by its past or by its physical origins as the materialist would have us believe, but is free to combine with other cultural objects to form systems that have a logic of their own and whose evolution in the I-space can be explained largely in cultural terms rather than in the purely physical ones of biology or of a behaviourist psychology. To quote Leslie White:

> Culture is a class of things and events dependent upon symbolizing ... Culture determines itself ... a process *sui generis* ... Environments merely permit or prohibit the existence of certain elements or features of a culture; they do not determine them.[54]

Yet in freeing man from the bondage of his material circumstances, does culture not then proceed to ensnare him in a web of symbols no less constraining? Should we not agree with Leslie White when he goes on to say that 'although physically and biologically a thermodynamic system, man is, and remains, a puppet of his culture'.[55] In sum, if material conditions and the physical needs – i.e., interests – they impose upon us do not have the power to coerce us to the extent that materialists believe, does it necessarily follow that the symbol systems through which, as men, we make good our escape emancipate us to the extent that we imagine?

Culture in the hands of a Kroeber or a Lévi-Strauss may have acquired some autonomous explanatory power but it remains in effect no less deterministic for that. Indeed, developmental psychologists like Bruner[56] would have it invading our very perceptual apparatus, thus completely reversing the causal relationship posited by materialists to exist between ideas and physical processes. To quote Hall once more:

> Culture has always dictated where to draw the line separating one thing from another. These lines are arbitrary, but once learned and internalized, they are treated as real.[57]

This is hardly the kind of thinking that allows individual cognition an unfettered right to roam through the I-space.

The challenge of endogenous cultural change

The culturalist account of human behaviour and custom is not new; it has as respectable an ancestry as the materialist account in anthropology. As far back as 1889, for example, Frans Boas was interpreting the cultural phenomenon as the imposition of conventional meanings on the flux of experience that determined our very perception of the external world.[58] And the privileged vehicle for achieving this moulding of thinking and perception was to be language, given to the individual from outside. Not much emancipation here.

It would appear, then, that if man can escape becoming a prisoner of his material circumstances he may yet be trapped and coerced by the way he is made to construe these. To be sure, within certain ecological limits beyond which, in Popper's phrase, 'reality kicks back', he might retain some relative freedom of construal that is likely to vary from culture to culture. But once he has committed himself to a particular interpretation of his experience, whether freely or under social constraint, a certain cognitive inertia sets in that further curtails his freedom to change his mind and to explore alternative formulations.

The problem is that neither materialist nor idealist theories of culture, where these are strongly deterministic, allow much scope for endogenous cultural change in social systems. Change is taken as originating outside the system; either it brings about alterations to a culture's material conditions which then mechanically work their way through to the shared perceptions and cognitions whereby such conditions are apprehended – the materialist approach to cultural change – or external change first affects construal before filtering through to social practice – the idealist position.

Yet it would be misleading to brand all theories of culture as deterministic. Even Harris, for example, speaking for the materialists, does not exclude non-deterministic lines of influence running from World 3 to World 2 to World 1. He just does not think that they are of much importance in the general order of things. At best they amount to a form of cultural drift in which unintended and unrecorded changes seep through the pores of the cultural reproduction apparatus, gradually bringing about a differentiation in the cultural practices of initially homogeneous groups.

Douglas, defending an idealist position, also sees man as essentially free in his choice of interpretative schemes. And once the mechanistic restrictions of strong determinism have been lifted and reciprocal influences are allowed between Worlds 1, 2 and 3 – say along the lines described in our discussion of the E-space in Chapter 2, and further developed in our presentation of the SLC in Chapter 4 – then possibilities exist within a social system for *endogenous* cultural change that go well beyond what might be expected when either Popper's World 1 or his World 3 is taken to be causally dominant – allegedly the only interesting cases of change available under strong determinism.

Strong versus weak realism

The system's capacity for cultural change is now further enhanced if we trade in a *strong realist* position, the belief that our knowledge of the world is absolute – whether it is immediately given by our senses as the materialists would have it, or mediated by *a priori* abstract categories as claimed by idealists – for what we might call a weak realist position. Weak realism, like strong realism, takes the world as real rather than as a pure fabrication of our symbolizing minds, but differs from the latter in arguing that our knowledge of it retains an irreducibly provisional character.

Popper, one of the main proponents of weak realism, holds that although we can never attain absolute truths, we can approach them by generating bold hypotheses that survive as knowledge through a continuous process of testing, corroboration, and adjustment, in which false knowledge gradually gets weeded out.[59] Popper believes that the inductive inference that acts as a bridge between a multiplicity of concrete particulars and abstract generalizations has no epistemological validity as such – as Hume realized two centuries ago, it simply cannot yield fully reliable knowledge. A hypothesis, no matter how well corroborated by rigorous testing, is always open to subsequent falsification and for that reason has to remain provisional – we might, borrowing from Simon, talk of 'epistemological satisficing' to describe the conditional acceptance of a hypothesis that is deemed 'good enough' in the light of current evidence. In this way the door is left open for alternative constructions, and these, under certain circumstances, can become harbingers of change.

From a weak realist perspective, therefore, a cultural repertoire of symbols can never be fully closed or self-contained but must remain open to two radically different types of transformations:

1   Those that occur initially in the E-space alone and through which new symbols or symbol systems emerge as provisional knowledge through a process of hypothesis generation and testing. They were described in

Chapter 2. While these are confined to an isolated E-space, however, they remain uncommunicated and hence the property of individual minds. Until the diffusion dimension has been activated, they have no cultural implications beyond those that hold for individual behaviour. In an isolated E-space, hypothesis generation and testing is either an asocial or a private affair. Change, to be sure, occurs, but it does not propagate.

2   Those which operate through the U- and C-spaces as well as the E-space and thus activate the I-space as a whole. Here any new symbols or symbol systems forged in the first type of transformation now encounter a culture's existing repertoire embedded in social and institutional practice: they survive the encounter either by getting assimilated in established structures without disturbing them, by dislodging members of the repertoire that are vulnerable to challenge, or by finding unoccupied niches in which they can thrive. In other words, hypothesis testing and corroboration now become a social as well as an epistemological process.

Weak realism subjects new cultural knowledge to the rigours of selection throughout the SLC. Where it survives it spreads into new environments in which it tries to occupy protected niches; from these it might then seek out new populations in the I-space. The diffusion of new knowledge can then be thought of as a competitive process in which cultures vie with each other for dominance.[60] In this struggle, material conditions now appear as ecological limits beyond which selection becomes particularly ferocious. Sahlins has associated these limits with the physical environment itself. It imposes its constraints on symbolizing activities, yet leaves each of them free to develop their own internal logic in the I-space in competition with other logics.[61]

Does such competition between cultural logics have a metalogic of its own? In other words, does cultural evolution have a discernible direction to it irrespective of which particular cultural logic achieves dominance at a given moment? To this question we turn next.

6.4: CULTURAL CONVERGENCE: A REINTERPRETATION

Biological versus cultural evolution

Culture has at times been described as the pursuit of evolution by non-biological means. Biological evolution is a slow business. The pace at which it proceeds depends upon random mutations in the genome surviving the many and varied ordeals inflicted upon them by an indifferent environment. Intergenerational learning at the genetic level – otherwise known as Lamarckian inheritance – is not possible since none of the experience acquired by one generation can be biologically transmitted to the next. Only information contained in the germ cells is transmitted and such information is not modified by ontogenetic learning. Biological evolution thus proceeds firstly through an apparently random generation of genetic variety by means of mutations, and secondly through the survival of those genetic variants best adapted to the specific environments in which they find themselves.[62] Over short time-frames the resulting changes are scarcely perceptible: biologically speaking, for instance, man is not much different today from what he was 100,000 years ago. Whatever differences we see between men, such as racial features when they are taken collectively, or eye colour if taken individually, are those which have been 'tolerated' by the widely different environments that make up the human habitat.[63]

Twentieth-century man, however, differs from prehistoric man in virtually every respect other than biology. Why? Because modern man, unlike other animal species, has succeeded in insulating himself from the immediate selective pressures of his environment to an extent that was unimaginable even 200 years ago. The best measure of this insulation from selection is the change in an individual's life expectancy at birth. Two centuries ago life expectancy in Western Europe was about 30 years of age and someone who survived his fifth birthday could expect to live up to the age of 45–50. Today, life expectancy at birth is over 70 in most European countries, and in a country like France it has reached 77 years of age.[64] In the space of two centuries life expectancy in Western Europe has more than doubled.[65]

Recent improvements in life expectancy owe virtually everything to cultural evolution and almost nothing to biological evolution. Unlike the latter, cultural evolution turns out to be Lamarckian; that is to say, the learning accumulated by one generation is at least in part available to its successor. Recall that culture is a process of structuring and sharing information within a given population. When that population extends itself over time across generations, transmitted information nourishes a social memory in which experiences with survival value are preserved by one generation and act to mitigate the selective actions of the environment for its descendants. Once information with survival value is preserved outside the genome – in cultural artefacts, customs, institutions, etc. – cultural evolution can begin to act on the organism's environment as well as on the organism itself. The effect is cumulative; outside the genome evolution can act at a much faster rate. It is not so much that the organism has improved its biological fitness to survive in a given environment – although better health care and nourishment certainly improve such fitness – but rather that culture, mediated by technology and social practice, now interposes itself between the organism and the environment in such a way as to reduce the stringency of the selection process. Culture, if you will, in the shape of cities, social security offices, and frozen foods, acts as a protective belt against the buffetings of a raw and unforgiving nature. And the more effective the belt, the greater the variety of cultural practices that will be tolerated rather than weeded out by the selection process.

Given that culture is a socially inherited response to a specific range of environmental conditions, one could reasonably expect cultural practices to reflect that range. Polynesian culture, for example, differs from Eskimo culture in ways that can be readily explained by differences in climate, in the availability of natural resources, in population density, and so on. A materialist, citing the above example, would be quick to argue that differences in physical circumstances must be taken as a direct cause of variations in cultural practice; similar circumstances call forth similar practices. A culturalist would reply that in each case environmental influences, although doubtlessly present, remain quite indirect since what the materialist calls physical circumstances have to be symbolically construed and interpreted by those who experience them before they are capable of eliciting any response. Cultural variety may therefore still be present even when physical causes are held constant. The coupling between a culture and its physical setting, then, must be considered for most purposes a loose one.

Yet what grounds do we have for believing that cultural variety can be maintained over time? Marx and Marxists, for example, have taken physical circumstances themselves, no matter how varied these may be at the outset, as subject to a gradual process of homogenization. It is the spread of the very technologies that decouple social organizations from the local constraints imposed by natural settings that account for this. To take a specific example, in hot climates peasants are accustomed to taking a three- or four-hour break in the middle of the day in order to avoid having to toil in the fields in the intense heat. In pre-industrial societies where the majority of people still work in agriculture, therefore, long midday breaks may constitute valid work norms for the culture as a whole. With industrialization, however, not only do fewer people work in the fields but for modernizing sectors of the economy, readily available air conditioning technology makes a three- or four-hour break in the middle of the day as irrelevant as it is dysfunctional.[66] Over time, therefore, the working day is likely to become altered in a direction that reflects the options opened up by mechanical ventilation technology.

Do cultures converge?

The rapid spread of industrialization and of modern technology leads to a generalization of the conclusion to be drawn from the above example: people located in what were originally very diverse cultures find themselves, by degrees, confronting increasingly similar physical circumstances. A materialist, committed to the view that similarities in physical circumstances lead to similarities in ways of thinking, will deny that such circumstances might be construed differently due to individual variations in personality and cognition. The only genuine source of cultural variety must be sought in changes in material conditions. Today cultural variety is being eroded by the very ability of modern technology to interpose an artificial environment between a given social group and its immediate habitat; and this is particularly so where that technology is subject to rapid diffusion processes.

The belief that industrialization eliminates cultural variety over time is labelled the *convergence hypothesis*. A given cultural order – usually the most technologically or materially advanced – is perceived to be the end state which all other cultures consciously or unconsciously aspire – or are driven – to reach. It is then taken as a model. Within the model culture itself, earlier stages may then come to be seen as an inevitable preparation for later stages, so that social evolution acquires a strongly teleological flavour. The convergence hypothesis in effect globalizes what Butterfield called the 'Whig interpretation of history'.[67]

Marx's belief in the inevitability of a universal communist order reached through determinate historical stages might be considered a political variant of the convergence hypothesis. And both Tönnies's and Durkheim's views of the modernization process, each in its own way, are predicated upon convergence. The first explored the gradual depersonalization of social life that occurs when societies move from a *Gemeinschaft* to *Gesellschaft* order, from community to organization.[68] The second stressed the increasing rationalization of society that follows the division of labour as the mechanical solidarity of the primary group comes to be replaced by the organic solidarity of the secondary group.[69]

Some versions of the convergence hypothesis emphasize the rationality-inducing properties of modern industrial technologies and their associated technostructures – i.e., the people and organizations required to run them.[70] The technical performance requirements of a modern petrochemical plant, for example, impose a formidable discipline on the way that the relevant physical processes are conceived and on how one can organize people to handle them. Other versions of convergence prefer to stress the economic factors that fertilize the growth of universal rationality, Rostow's theory of economic take-off and catch-up being a case in point.[71]

Can theories of cultural convergence be depicted in the I-space? In spite of their number and variety, most of them exhibit two common traits.

The first is that they all involve a shift away from institutional arrangements that thrive on predominantly concrete and uncodified forms of thought (i.e., fiefs and clans), and a move towards structures – bureaucracies or markets – that draw upon more abstract and codified ways of thinking. We can represent this shift most succinctly as a move in the I-space as in Figure 6.3.

The second is that most of them require the SLC, taken here as a generator of social innovation and change, either to come to a halt in an identifiable region of the I-space or, at least, to confine its cyclical activities primarily to that region.

Thus, for example, following different paths, both Marx and Durkheim

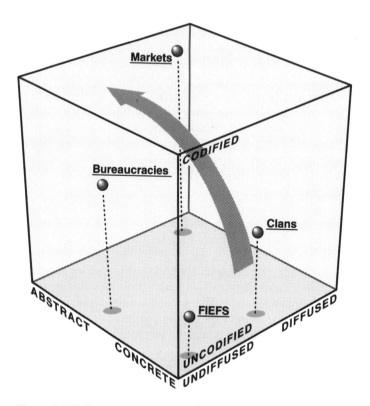

Figure 6.3 Cultural convergence in the I-space

alight on a bureaucratic cultural order as that on which all social evolution ultimately converges, the first having started from a feudal order in the fief region and the second from a state of mechanical solidarity in the clan quadrant.[72] And given their monopolistic and hierarchical organization, Galbraith's large technostructures are also assignable to the bureaucratic region of the I-space.

Others such as Rostow, by contrast, see a market order as the point of arrival of convergent evolution. By combining the decentralizing power of modern communications with the rationalizing force of modern technology, they effectively transform market processes into the solvent of a single global economic order. For some members of this group such as the marketing specialist Theodore Levitt, it is global consumers who have today become the agents of convergence.[73] He points to the popularity of Kentucky Fried Chicken in Kuala Lumpur and Tokyo as well as to the spread of sushi bars in New York as evidence for the globalization of consumer markets.

Although not specifically framed to explain it, the convergence hypothesis has become topical in recent years on account of the Japanese phenomenon.

Many are led to ask whether Japan's impressive economic performance over the last century is an expression of convergent evolution, a process of catching up which is bound to come to a halt as the country achieves parity with earlier industrializers, or is it rather attributable to some unique set of cultural traits, which, being beyond the reach of imitation by outsiders, in fact challenge the whole concept of convergence?

The analysis presented in Chapters 2 and 3 lends a certain plausibility to a hypothesis that has all cultures sooner or later converging on a market order. If we can agree that all cultural processes are ultimately about the structuring and sharing of information within and between groups, then it would seem reasonable to assume that in so far as modernization promotes a greater codification and abstraction of social exchange, it has also to come to terms institutionally with the forces of information diffusion that are thereby set in motion. New codes thus get shared and collectively absorbed to an extent that transcends cultural boundaries (see Figure 6.4).

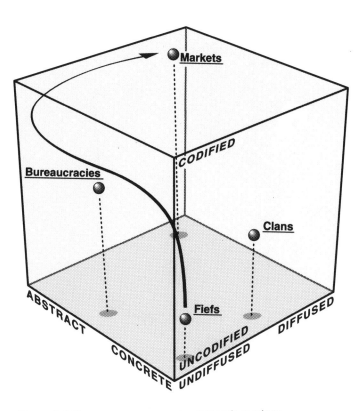

Figure 6.4 Convergence as a move towards markets

The need for divergence

Converging cultures, however, pay a price for pursuing an increasingly common path in their respective evolution, for with the resulting loss of cultural variety comes a diminution in their collective capacities to innovate and evolve. Recall that variety originates in those components of the SLC that are missing from Figure 6.4 – namely, absorption, impacting, and scanning, the latter being a move in the I-space which generates uniqueness on the left and for that reason must be regarded as a major source of individuation and differentiation for individuals, for products, and, of course, for cultures. A plausible model of cultural *evolution*, then, would require the restoration of the SLC's missing components and with them a degree of movement in the I-space that is quite incompatible with convergence as we have just described it; namely, convergence to a specific point or region of the I-space.

Allowing the SLC to operate its Buddhist cycle of birth, death, and rebirth, however, presents its own difficulties. Are we going to argue, for example, that in advanced industrialized societies market culture is shortly due to be

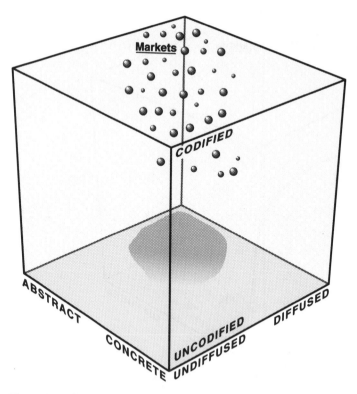

Figure 6.5a Culture as transactional scatter: the US

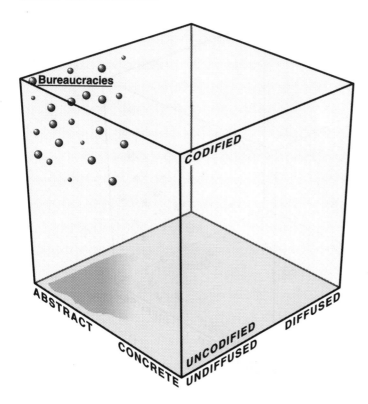

Figure 6.5b Culture as transactional scatter: France

replaced by a clan culture and thence by some kind of refeudalization of society as the SLC moves into the fief region? Are we further going to assert that at some indefinite time in the future we shall re-enter a bureaucratic phase? It all sounds absurdly mechanical and implausible. We shall clearly need to draw more subtle inferences than these from the operations of the SLC if we are going to make any progress.

For a start, we need to realize that a culture is never a unitary object with a single specific location in the I-space, but rather a scatter of points representing either individual transactions or clusters of transactions that are channelled, where these are available, through the appropriate institutional structures. As we saw in the previous chapter, these compete and collaborate from different locations in the I-space. The pattern created by the scatter and the configuration of activated institutions will give a cultural order its particular 'signature' and an identifiable centre of gravity in the I-space without in any way allowing the first to be reduced to the second; scatter and centre of gravity each remain distinctive attributes of a culture. Simplifying somewhat, we might say that if the second allows us to locate a culture's core

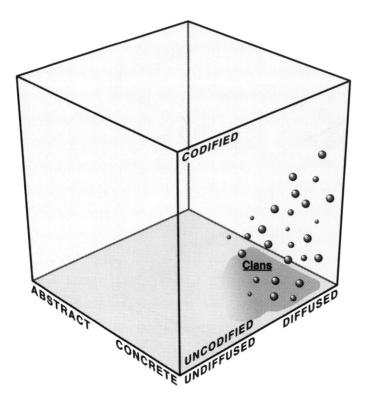

Figure 6.5c Culture as transactional scatter: Great Britain

values in the I-space, the first measures the cultural tolerance that has developed around these core values.

To illustrate such an interpretation of culture in the I-space, four distinctive scatter patterns and centres of gravity are schematically shown in Figures 6.5(a) to (d), one each for the US, France, Britain, and China. If we now take the case of the US, for example, it can be seen that whilst the cultural centre of gravity is firmly located in the market region of the I-space, many of the country's institutions might be assignable elsewhere: the Federal Reserve system is a bureaucracy; Congress operates more like a clan; many unions remain fiefdoms; and so on. In the case of Britain, by contrast, although market institutions are clearly present as in the case of the US, the country's cultural centre of gravity is arguably much closer to the clan region, the experience of Thatcherism notwithstanding. Many institutional practices – Parliament, the lack of a written constitution, the 'establishment' and the London club – proclaim a greater commitment to shared perceptions and values among small groups. France, with its strong *dirigiste* and state traditions, is more plausibly a bureaucratic culture than either the US or

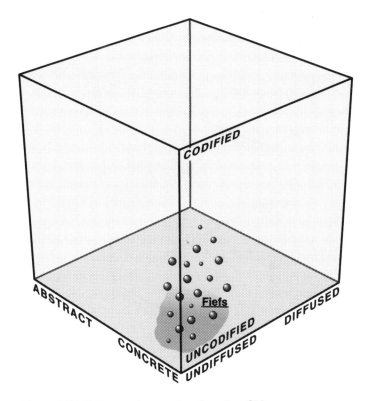

Figure 6.5d Culture as transactional scatter: China

Britain, but again, one which is not without a goodly stock of institutions located in clans and markets.[74]

Centripetal and centrifugal cultures

Locating a culture in the I-space solely through its centre of gravity tells us certain things about it but usually not enough. If we are to avoid the false economies of stereotyping we also need to know something about how widely scattered in the space its institutions turn out to be relative to its centre of gravity. This will then allow us to distinguish between *centripetal* cultures, those whose institutions are closely bunched together in the I-space, and *centrifugal* cultures, those whose institutions are widely dispersed. The two types of culture are illustrated in Figures 6.6(a) and (b). It turns out that in a totally centripetal culture, scatter ceases to matter and the centre of gravity in the I-space carries all the information we need. Conversely, in a totally centrifugal culture with little or no discernible centre of gravity it is the pattern of scatter and not the centre of gravity that holds the relevant information.

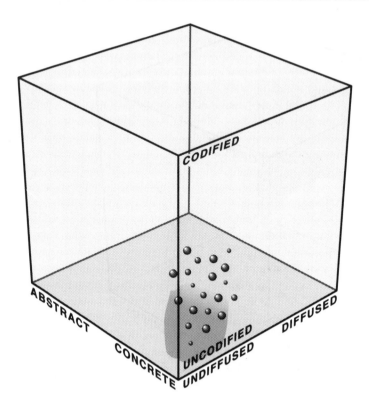

Figure 6.6a A centripetal culture in the I-space

How do we account for this difference between centripetal and centrifugal cultures? One explanation might concern the available technologies. If the appropriate communication infrastructure is not available to handle highly codified forms of exchange at a distance, for example, people will be confined for the most part to face-to-face communications in the lower regions of the I-space. Under such circumstances, they may find it less profitable to invest in the acquisition of abstract codes since being limited to highly localized transactions they may have scant opportunities to use them. Communication constraints of this kind still confine many undeveloped societies to fief or clan forms of organization and promote associated cultural values. Seen thus, centrifugalism expresses an extension of transactional possibilities opened up by technological evolution and modernization. The move from *Gemeinschaft* to *Gesellschaft* records simultaneously an increase in the degree of scatter of transactional points in the I-space – a reflection of the enhanced exchange possibilities – as well as a shift further up the space of the culture's centre of gravity. It is probably fair to say that the upward shift in the centre of gravity has

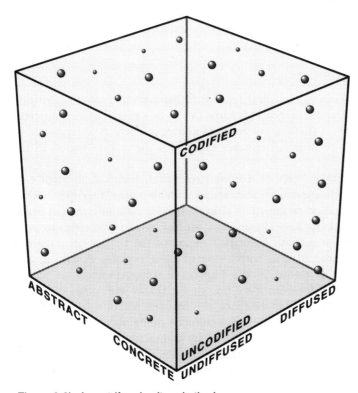

Figure 6.6b A centrifugal culture in the I-space

attracted more attention from students of culture than the increase in transactional scatter.

A second possible explanation is that the degree of transactional and institutional scatter in the I-space is to some extent the expression of deliberate cultural choices – more likely in the case of centripetal than centrifugal cultures. Technologies and institutions that might have extended transactional possibilities are discarded for ethical or practical reasons. Centripetalism then expresses a cultural or an ideological bias whereby transactions that might have been accommodated in quite different regions of the I-space are deliberately channelled – sometimes quite coercively – through a particular location.[75]

The idea is to turn culture into a unitary object in the I-space rather than a scatter of points. Marxism-Leninism, for example, could be thought of as an ideology designed to promote a centripetal cultural order in the bureaucratic region of the space. In the next chapter, we consider in more detail how the attempt worked out in the case of China and what problems it poses for post-communist societies. So-called market cultures, for their part, can be no less centripetal when in turn they seek indiscriminately to convert unadapted forms of social and economic exchange into market transactions.[76]

Reinterpreting convergence

Armed with the centripetal/centrifugal distinction, we are now in a position to rethink cultural convergence. It turns out to be open to quite a different interpretation from the one put forward above, one which today seems to have as its task to bring all cultures tidily into the market region of the I-space.

The modernization theories that we have so far discussed all involve an increase in codification and abstraction, which taken together with a centripetal orientation terminate in either a bureaucratic or a market order. For this to occur, as we have already seen, the SLC would have either to come to a halt in the bureaucratic or market region of the I-space or to operate within a very confined area within one of these regions. A culture as a patterned scatter of points in the I-space, however, presents us with a particular difficulty, for even if we find that it shares with other cultures a common centre of gravity in the space, this by itself will now be insufficient to establish their similarity. After all, a culture's *configuration* in the I-space, the unique institutional pattern created by transactional scatter, may well turn out to be what gives it its particular character. And, as we have already seen, the greater the degree of transactional scatter – i.e., the more centrifugal the culture – the greater is likely to be the part played by its configuration rather than its centre of gravity in accounting for its character. Convergence between centrifugal cultures must then be argued either on the ground that centripetal forces are at work that militate against or override the transactional choices opened up by modern technology – and such forces have to be ideologically motivated – or on the assumption that such cultures are effectively moving towards identical configurations in the I-space. But note that convergence between cultures is now required to bring about a *coincidence of patterns* rather than merely one of locations in the I-space, and this is not only a much less likely outcome, given the intrinsic complexity of cultural configurations, but also a much more difficult one to explain convincingly.

Convergence as cultural pattern-matching shares with convergence as-coinciding-locations an additional difficulty: neither account can cope with a continuously operating SLC. The assumption must therefore be that when convergence has been achieved, the cycle is tamed; it is either brought to a halt or rendered incapable of generating divergence between cultures once more. In neither case, then, are the absorption, impacting, and scanning components of the cycle – the sources of random destabilizing movement in the I-space; the source of singular insight and innovation – allowed to act as a stimulus to cultural differentiation. Recall however that the SLC, an aggregate of many smaller cycles, can adopt any number of configurations in the I-space, each of them moving knowledge clockwise. It can therefore act upon each scatter point in a cultural scatter individually, imposing upon it a trajectory uniquely determined by the particular set of barriers and forces that it confronts on its own. For this reason not only is a centrifugal culture's configuration at time t_1 unlikely to be exactly the same as what it was at time t_0, but it is also impossible to predict from the latter; the degrees of freedom involved are just too great.[77]

But if convergence as now described is so difficult to achieve or to stabilize once achieved, is there any sense in which it can still be said that cultures converge as they modernize? The passage from a centripetal to a centrifugal cultural order, we believe, holds the key to effective modernization. It amounts to a profound social and institutional transformation that cultures certainly experience in common as they evolve. Yet it is one that *increases* variety rather than reducing it, accelerating cultural evolution and the pace of the SLCs that bring it about. Whatever identity might then be achieved between two centrifugal patterns coinciding in the I-space remains nothing more than a coincidence. In this perspective, modernizing cultures, if they converge at all, do so less in pursuit of some homogeneous institutional order yearned for by centripetalists, than in a common quest for ways of dealing with variety and change.

Centripetalism seeks out harmony and balance in preference to complexity and change. In its search for a total and stable cultural order, it is as likely to draw inspiration from equilibrium models of market processes as from hierarchical models of administrative procedures. Such models admit of change, of course, but of the local and incremental kind, of the kind that operates within a given institutional framework rather than across competing frameworks. When they are called upon to handle the totality of a culture's transactions, as is the case when they are applied centripetally, these models may then come under considerable strain. For they are not designed to handle evolutionary change, the sort that is disequilibrating, paradigmatic, and which, if it is to succeed, as Schumpeter well understood, must destroy in order to create.

Managing the SLC

If cultural evolution, as we are arguing, turns out to be centrifugal in the I-space, using technology to link up ever larger and more diverse populations in an ever-increasing diversity of transactional arrangements, then cultural values must coexist in a pluralistic fashion and become equally subject to selection. They must consequently be made to compete and collaborate with each other. In doing so they will activate the SLC, which, operating as a gigantic feedback loop – in actual fact as a countless multitude of such loops

– is continuously generating, testing, and distributing new knowledge in response to problems perceived.

Managing its SLCs then becomes a culture's most challenging task. Push transactional competition between different regions of the I-space too far[78] and the social fabric tears apart under the strain of centrifugal forces that cannot be institutionally channelled or constrained. On the other hand, too good a fit between diverse transactional systems rekindles the forces of centripetalism and impairs a culture's capacity to adapt to change and evolve. To borrow a term from modern mathematics, a centripetal cultural order is a strong attractor in the I-space, imposing a single type of governance, a limited set of interests and values to be served, and strong restrictions on the institutional means for serving them. A centrifugal cultural order, by contrast, tolerates the coexistence of multiple levels of governance serving a diversity of interests that range from those of the individual right through to those of the nation-state and above. Correlatively it actively promotes a multiplicity of institutional arrangements for the servicing of such interests.

Centrifugalism at some level has to take it on faith that order emerges out of chaos and for that reason it accepts the presence of turbulence, variety, and change in the I-space as indispensable elements of any worthwhile learning process.

6.5: CULTURE AS INSTITUTIONAL PATTERN

Technology and institutionalization

Culture is the institutionalized application of intelligence to socially driven thermodynamic processes, an attempt to minimize the production of entropy within a given social order. In Chapter 5 we interpreted institutionalization as a device that imparts a measure of stability and economic viability to broad classes of transactions in the I-space.[79] Institutions act as 'attractors' for uncommitted transactions, competing or collaborating in the data field to capture them. It would be reasonable to suppose, therefore, that institutions are not merely a reflection of where transactional activity happens to be found in the I-space and so in some sense passive vessels for their containment. They must also be considered causal agents of social evolution in their own right, actively playing their part in giving a culture its centripetal or centrifugal orientation.

There has been a tendency by certain observers to link cultural evolution to that of institutions and to find in the extensive diffusion of complex and modern institutional structures across cultural boundaries *prima facie* evidence for the convergence hypothesis. Since, however, in the preceding section we advanced an alternative formulation of the convergence hypothesis, one based on the identity of transactional configurations in the I-space rather than on that of transactional location, we need to examine with care the possible contribution made by institutionalization, if any, to the process of convergence as we now conceive it.

A pertinent question that might be asked, for instance, is whether institutions as social technologies are capable of rapid and effective diffusion by imitation.[80] And if institutions themselves wax or wane through the effects of the SLC as was suggested in Chapter 5, what, if anything, then gives to a cultural configuration of institutions its stability? A tenable theory of convergence requires satisfactory replies to both these questions.

The issues raised can be subtle. Consider by way of illustration the one concerning social technologies. It is not always easy to distinguish between physical and social technologies. It is tempting to associate the first with hardware – things that you can drop on your foot – and the second with software and organization. Yet it is equally possible to adopt a different approach and to define a technology as being social to the extent that it facilitates or impedes certain patterns of social exchange by specifying viable procedures for the structuring and sharing of information. Thus, under such a definition a telephone would be no less of a social technology than a joint-stock company but a refrigerator would not; or again, a local area network (LAN) would qualify whereas a particle accelerator would fail to.

Obviously as we ourselves have been using the terms, social and physical technologies are not mutually exclusive. In pre-industrial subsistence economies, for example, transactional objectives are modest and the social technology available to facilitate exchange is unsophisticated. In such circumstances we would expect the physical and technical constraints on population density and distribution to predominate and to severely limit the scope for social interaction beyond small primary groups. Opportunities for systematic codification, abstraction, and diffusion will consequently be few and far between so that not only may a patriarchal household structure make fief transactions the dominant form of social exchange, but for want of competing alternatives it may turn them into an institutional paradigm for the social system as a whole. Where this happens a leader becomes a father not only to his progenies but to all his followers; he can exact from them the unconditional obedience that fathers in patriarchal families expect from their children.[81] Should some degree of physical mobility now be available to followers, however, it will have the effect of tempering demands for unconditional submission. They might, after all, be able to walk out: a clan form of organization, reflecting a greater decentralization of power, may then replace the fief. Yet in both cases the essentially centripetal nature of the culture will keep reasserting itself: the more codified and abstract social technologies that would allow a greater degree of transactional scatter and choice in the I-space simply remain unavailable.

In more complex, differentiated societies, with larger, simultaneously more geographically concentrated *and* dispersed populations, transactional objectives become more varied and a number of institutional paradigms that could serve them may then coexist, sometimes competitively, to offer a measure of choice. Patriarchal forms of personalized control will gradually come to lose their perceived efficacy and individuals may then be led to associate in various ways to secure their needs. The social stability that went with a single unchanging transactional order will now be eroded by an awareness of the contingent nature of things and perhaps by a growing conviction that they could sometimes be better. In Europe in the late Middle Ages, the hold of the manorial economy as a transactional paradigm located in the fief region of the I-space was gradually weakened by the combined effects of a revival of commerce, improvements in long-distance communications, the growth of cities, and the centralization of administrative power in the royal bureaucracy. Each of these changes entailed an evolution in social technologies. The fief as a transactional form did not, of course, immediately disappear; but it now had to coexist with other equally viable and competing transactional structures such as the medieval guild (a clan) and the royal treasury (a bureaucracy).[82]

Institutional competition or collaboration

With the onset of institutional pluralism, transactional assignments over time come to lose their givenness; undermined by subtle shifts in interpersonal perceptions and understandings, by power plays, and by the actions of the SLC itself they acquire a contingent character. Centrifugal forces then distribute transactions over ever-wider regions of the I-space, at first tentatively if not covertly, but as time passes with genuine prospects of stability and hence of institutionalization appearing on the horizon. New cultural patterns slowly crystallize, fed by a growing volume of transactions whose own viability is now enhanced by the prospect of imminent institutionalization. Emerging patterns express all at once the physical or material circumstances in which social exchange occurs, the sunk-cost constraints imposed by prior transactional investments, the exchange potential opened up by current rates of transactional investment, and the constructive and destructive role of the SLC.

The strength of any given cultural pattern – that is, its distinctiveness in the I-space – owes something to the coherence with which the values and beliefs that give it its social legitimacy come together. Yet these do not float in free space; they remain tethered to the existing institutional structures that are distributed in the I-space, and through them they form relationships between themselves that, as we have seen, are either collaborative or competitive. These structures effectively provide the channels through which the SLC runs its course, activating large tracts of the I-space in the case of centrifugal cultures, and only small pockets of it in the case of centripetal ones.

But what is meant exactly by collaborative or competitive relationships between existing institutional structures? And must the valency of the linkages that characterize two otherwise identical cultural patterns also be similar to satisfy the requirements of convergence? One example of a collaborative linkage between different regions of the I-space would be the one that exists between, say, market institutions and the regulatory agencies devised to ensure their efficient functioning. Here, an investment in the market region of the space is actually enhanced by a complementary investment in bureaucracy. To illustrate: few American industries feel as encumbered by regulatory agencies as its banking industry.[83] In addition to three federal regulators – the Federal Reserve System, created by Congress in 1913, the Office of the Comptroller of the Currency, established in 1863 to help finance the American Civil War, and the Federal Deposit Insurance Corporation, set up under Roosevelt's 1933 Banking Act – there is a regulator of the country's credit unions, as well as the Federal Home Loan Bank System. At the state level regulators are met also – fifty of them in all – responsible for charting banks and other depositary institutions. Banks may compete with each other in various financial markets, but they do so within a framework of rules set by bureaucratic state agencies. Why? – because the conditions that produce efficient markets (freedom of entry and exit, numerous players, abundant flows of market information, etc.) do not arise spontaneously and, once created, have to be painstakingly maintained. Recall that under the action of the SLC, markets will sooner or later give way to clans[84] which in the particular example of the banking industry would translate into an oligopolistic market structure: a few powerful players informally managing to replace a competitive relationship with one that is partly collaborative. The promotion of efficient markets – efficient at least in the neoclassical sense – thus entails some minimum investment in bureaucracy and a measure of hierarchical coordination, no matter how irksome these might be to individual players.

A second example of collaborative linkage between institutions located in different regions of the I-space is provided by the frequent need to secure a degree of charismatic leadership for clan organizations characterized by instability; this involves a simultaneous investment in fiefs and clans. In the early Middle Ages in Europe, for instance, the medieval monarch was considered a *primus inter pares*, and continually vying with powerful princes and barons for political ascendancy. The feudal order was decentralized and unstable. Over time in France and in Britain the King's Peace gradually replaced manorial jurisdiction and the grounds of the monarch's legitimacy shifted from election or conquest to investiture by the Church. He became endowed with quasi-divine powers,[85] which in England, since the time of Henry VIII, were themselves somewhat reined in by the concept of the 'King-in-Parliament', an institution that restitutes some power to the clan region at the expense of the fief. Collaboration then gives way to competition between institutions, albeit now of a more controlled and synergistic kind.

Not all institutional linkages in the I-space, however, are so conveniently synergistic. Some are antagonistic and actually hinder transactional efficiency. Nepotism in an administration, for instance, is a survival of the personalized network of loyalty and obligations characteristic of the fief region but operating within the impersonal rational–legal structure required of a bureaucracy. Recall that the increase in codification entailed by a move up the I-space from fiefs towards bureaucracies may still preserve in people's minds, whether in the form of their unconscious habits or in the values that they hold implicitly, an uncodified collective memory of earlier transactional forms. The Tudor revolution in government in sixteenth-century England originated in large part in the separation it achieved – first initiated by Cardinal Wolsey and taken further by Thomas Cromwell – between the monarch's *personal* sphere of influence and that which he exercised as constitutional head of state. Competence and professionalism rather than blind personal loyalty or connections became the criteria to reckon with in staffing the growing state bureaucracy. Nepotism and professionalism gradually came to be perceived as incompatible approaches to the problem of state administration. One or the other had to be chosen. Nepotism, of course, was not done away with overnight – indeed it took another three centuries to fully professionalize the British Civil Service – but its influence was severely curtailed.[86]

A second instance of antagonistic linkages has already been mentioned: that which obtains when the clan-like behaviour of an industrial cartel, based upon an invisible network of interpersonal commitments between a small number of players, robs a market of its allocative efficiency – in what Adam Smith used to refer to as a conspiracy against the public.

Cultural logic and cultural order

A cultural pattern in the I-space becomes internally consistent and stable when its constituent institutional linkages and related transactional investments are mutually reinforcing and any antagonistic linkages that might emerge are suppressed. Drawing on the connectionist perspective developed in Chapter 2 with its emphasis on excitatory and inhibitory linkages in neural activation patterns, one might even in such a case speak of a *cultural logic* in which different parts of the transactional structure are either jointly activated or mutually exclusive. Where such a logic consistently favours the activation of a particular pattern, whether centripetal or centrifugal, one might then speak of a *cultural order*. The pattern thus favoured may act as an attractor for a particular region of the I-space. For example, a capitalist order is generally thought of as a cultural pattern of transactions that is centrifugally spread out throughout the I-space but whose overall logic is designed to protect and enhance the transactional viability of the market region; a feudal order generates a cultural logic that aims to achieve the same for the fief region, and so on.

A cultural logic may survive the generative or destructive effects of the SLC by shifting to new institutions as they emerge in the I-space, selecting these on the basis of their pattern-preserving properties. It may thus exhibit what Ross Ashby calls *ultra-stability*.[87]

A cultural order is perhaps what we as individuals most readily take for granted in our daily behaviour. It remains, for the most part, an implicit structure that has been internalized and unconsciously guides our approach to transactions and governance. Sahlins's comment on market transactions is apposite:

> Market decisions leave the impression that production is merely the precipitate of an enlightened rationality. The structure of the economy appears as the objectivised consequence of practical behaviour, rather than a social organization of things, by the institutional means of the market, but according to a cultural design of persons and goods.[88]

A cultural logic, providing it encounters no competing alternative that might threaten its ascendancy, makes a cultural order appear inevitable; it becomes part of an individual's life-world. Unless it is challenged and thus brought to awareness, a cultural order forms a large part of what Hall has termed the 'cultural unconscious':

> The cultural unconscious, those out-of-awareness cultural systems that have yet to be made explicit, probably outnumber the explicit systems by a factor of one thousand or more – such systems have various features or dimensions which are governed by the order, selection and congruence rules ...
>
> Significant portions of extension systems still function out of awareness ... and therefore fall within the scope of out-of-awareness culture ... Culture is therefore very closely related, if not synonymous with what has been defined as 'mind'.[89]

If we follow this line of reasoning, then it appears that a cultural order, to function smoothly, requires that individuals internalize and develop diverse transactional capacities in different regions of the I-space in order to activate the particular cultural logic associated with that order. In doing this they need to be guided by a value system that can accommodate itself to expected outcomes – broad and diverse in the case of a centrifugal culture, much less so in the case of a centripetal one – and that will mobilize them to take corrective action when outcomes get out of line with expectations. When this happens, we can say that the cultural order has become *meaningful* for transacting individuals. To quote Sahlins once more: 'Meaning is the specific property of the anthropological object. Cultures are meaningful orders of persons and things.'[90]

Adaptation and the cultural order

To be meaningful, however, does not necessarily mean to be adequate. A cultural order may have deep significance for its members and yet, when considered objectively, still reflect a poor degree of adaptation between their respective Worlds 1, 2, and 3. A lack of adaptation need not imply any *subjectively* experienced conflict between Popper's three worlds as construed by an individual, although obviously it does not exclude it. To understand this we must link adaptation to a culture's evolutionary possibilities.

We shall say that a cultural order lacks adaptation if the way that Worlds 1, 2, and 3 are integrated together by its members lowers the culture's survival prospects below what they would otherwise be. To illustrate: it frequently happens that the collective W2s and the W3s constructed within a given culture do not allow an effective exploitation of the development possibilities offered by W1. Many sub-Saharan African countries, for example, sit on abundant natural resources – more than sufficient to meet their present or future economic needs – yet these remain undeveloped. Why? Because particularistic values and tribal forms of organization hinder adaptive moves through the SLC towards the creation of institutions requiring greater codification and abstraction, institutions located in W3 that could respond adaptively to threats and opportunities residing in W1.[91] Other cultures – Japan, Singapore, Hong Kong – with virtually no material resources of their own have achieved levels of social and economic developments which are the envy of the Third World largely because their collective W2s and W3s allowed them to favourably reconceptualize their W1 situation. They could thus achieve through trade and the maintenance of a strongly external orientation the development of a domestic resource base that would be quite inconceivable under more traditional formulations.[92]

By giving an epistemological interpretation to the phenomenon of cultural adaptation we are able to link it to the evolutionary properties of the SLC. Recall from Chapter 4 that the SLC describes a form of social learning in which new knowledge enters a social system – in this case a culture – in response to felt problems. New knowledge is structured, tested, abstracted, diffused, absorbed, and impacted through the operation of a gigantic feedback loop whose particular configuration in the I-space is shaped by the distribution of institutions that accelerate or block the relevant knowledge flows.

Cultural adaptation can then be given two distinct and complementary meanings. Under the first, knowledge that survives the action of the SLC should enhance a social system's cultural survival prospects. False knowledge should be gradually selected out of the system and valid knowledge retained. Under the second, the specific distribution of institutions in the I-space that give effect to a given cultural logic and hence to a particular configuration of the SLC, within certain bounds should also enhance the system's survival prospects. How these bounds might be set, however, needs a word of explanation.

Metabolizing cultural knowledge: the problem of complexity

The distinction that we drew in the preceding section between centripetal and centrifugal cultures translates in practice into one between small and large SLCs. A small SLC, clearly, occupies a small region of the I-space and a large SLC a large region; yet what this specifically means for social practice will depend on what particular region of the space is activated. We know from our earlier discussions that in a centripetal culture, social institutions operate within a narrow compass of transactional styles and values. Centripetal cultures perform best when confronted with limited and specialized tasks – such is the case with the army, the Church, or, in pre-industrial societies, fishing or hunting communities[93] – in an environment whose boundaries they either enact or control.[94] They can then keep the world at bay and with it any threatening changes or competing transactional alternatives. This will obviously be easier in those regions of the space where information flows are not hard to manage. There is more scope, for example, for achieving centripetalism in $\bar{C}$ than in C, and, one might suspect, in $\bar{A}$ than in A, although under the right circumstances it might also be achieved elsewhere.[95]

Centrifugal cultures by contrast are open to the world, to its complexity, and, by implication, to change. They are pluralistic. If centripetal cultures minimize their need for adaptation by choosing an ecological niche, by specializing, and by keeping the complexities of the world at bay by boundary maintenance strategies, centrifugal cultures adapt by scanning, by codifying and by abstracting – in evolutionary parlance, by generating variety, by selection, and by generalization. Centripetal cultures aim to minimize the amount of variety generated and to hold on to what exists already in preference to what is possible: they are intrinsically conservative. Centrifugal cultures, by contrast, maximize the generation of variety and are more strongly oriented towards what is possible than towards what already exists. The former place the accent on remembering; the latter are happy to allow forgetting. The one faces the past; the other the future.

Selective remembering and forgetting express the cultural metabolism by means of which information is processed. In the light of our discussion could it be said that centripetal cultures, with the emphasis they place on conservation, metabolize information more slowly than centrifugal ones?

Cultures, like individuals, have to be able to forget in order to learn so that forgetting must be considered an essential component of any credible adaptation process. In Chapter 3, for example, we referred to the neurologist Luria, who, in *The Mind of a Mnemonist*, vividly described the individual who remembers everything and who is, in effect, incapable of forgetting anything. Such a person is in deep trouble in trying to come to terms with the complexities of the world for he cannot shed data. It accumulates and remains in storage, ready to intervene as noise in any future information processing activity, cluttering up all efforts at selection – codification, abstraction – which impart a measure of order to experience.[96]

High context cultures, being less naturally oriented towards codification and abstraction, may be particularly prone to such data overload. Because they lack articulated cognitive strategies for processing large volumes of data, however, it tends to leak out from the system in a random fashion; the oral traditions described in Chapter 3, for instance, indicate how data losses are incurred across generations by faulty transmission. High context cultures for this reason become protective and ritualistic with respect to their data with the result that everything is preserved whatever its actual or potential relevance. Such indiscriminate efforts at remembering inevitably slow down the data metabolism of a culture.

The centripetal tendencies of high context cultures may therefore have several causes. One has already been identified in the shape of a culture's spatiotemporal characteristics and the communicative constraints these place upon it. Here, we are advancing a second: a high context culture, permanently threatened with data overload owing to its inability to metabolize it fast enough, may seek to keep novel data at bay through boundary maintenance strategies that keep the SLC small and manageable.[97] It will then limit or devalue any new data that its members are exposed to, particularly where such data cannot be handled within the existing transactional infrastructure.

So long as boundaries are maintained, the viability of centripetal cultures, whether high or low context, will depend primarily on how well they have adapted to their chosen ecological niche – i.e., on how well their Worlds 2 and 3 exploit their different World 1 possibilities. Yet once the boundaries are breached, for whatever reason, centrifugal forces are set in motion which gradually rob Worlds 2 and 3 of their facticity. These are now required to accommodate several possible life-worlds some of which will come to acquire the character of competing hypotheses, alternative ways of constructing the cultural order.

More often than not the forces of centrifugalism will triumph over those of centripetalism. One example of how these forces confront each other was given by Daniel Lerner in his classic *The Passing of Traditional Society* where he recounts the cultural transformation of a Turkish village trapped in the orbit of a new and fast growing modern metropolis, in this case the city of Ankara.[98] Yet the triumph of centrifugalism is by no means a foregone conclusion. Where a cultural order is particularly well adapted to its ecological niche it may survive the onslaught of competing cultural hypotheses. Consider once more the case of military culture. Society as a whole may evolve towards greater liberalism and a plurality of social values, beliefs, institutions, etc.; yet given the stringency and the dangerous nature of the task that a modern army may be called upon to perform – and often at very short notice, as the rapid mobilization of half a million US troops in the Persian Gulf in the autumn of 1990 amply demonstrated – military culture is required to remain steadfastly formal and hierarchical, and hence centripetal, in its transactional style if it is to retain its effectiveness. An army, to be sure, will have its fiefdoms and its clans. It may even operate through markets on the fringes of the organization. Its institutional core, however, rests upon a single, unchanging set of values: rule-based hierarchical authority and unconditional obedience.

Military culture is a specialized niche culture with boundary maintenance problems of its own – like the Catholic Church it is constantly required to reassess how much of the external world to admit within the boundary. But wherever it enjoys a high degree of perceived social legitimacy, it can more than hold its own as an institution within a wider centrifugal cultural order.

Maintaining cultural identity

If centripetal and centrifugal cultures metabolize transactional data in different ways – the former aiming at its retention and the latter at its elimination – does this affect the way that they each use data to forge their respective identities?

It is probably easier to understand a centripetal culture's approach to identity than a centrifugal one's. Something achieves identity when it can be contextualized (that is, placed in a stable network of elements and relations); it then acquires location and duration. When individuals or groups struggle to maintain their identity they do so either by retaining an attachment to certain spatial locations in their environment such as a region or a city, or by retaining in memory certain events that are meaningful to them – i.e., by commemorating them. Both methods store data in ways that confirm them in who they are.

A centripetal culture's approach to the problem of identity given its conservative bias is more likely to place the accent on custom and tradition than a centrifugal one's. Tradition, for example, is important to the preservation of military values as well as of religious ones. It is particularly important to the identity of high context cultures. For this reason perhaps, an anthropologist like Boas tended to focus almost exclusively on tradition – the *Völkergedanken* – as the privileged vehicle for the cultural transmission and preservation of cultural identity.[99] But what of centrifugal cultures? If these adapt by forgetting as much as by remembering, are they helped or hindered in the maintenance of identity by the deliberate shedding of data? And, if helped, where does this leave tradition?

It is worth reminding ourselves that in centrifugal cultures, forgetting is not necessarily a random process but a selective and evolutionary one in which new and better-adapted knowledge replaces older and less-adapted knowledge through the action of the SLC. New knowledge establishes its viability by handling everything that was handled by old knowledge *and more*. It gets retained, in short, when it has demonstrated greater explanatory powers than old knowledge, either by dealing more penetratingly with those specific phenomena addressed by the old knowledge or by convincingly increasing the range of phenomena that can be handled within the framework of a single explanatory scheme.[100]

Another way of saying the same thing is that new knowledge achieves greater generality or *abstraction* than old knowledge. This implies that centrifugal cultures, by degrees, tend to shift their centres of gravity away from Ā and towards A, thus providing us with the vital clue we are after:

> *centrifugal cultures shed data and achieve their forgetting by moving towards a more abstract cultural order as they spread out in the I-space, an order from which they increasingly derive their identity.*

The concrete spatiotemporal events that are the source of their tradition are in effect constantly being reinterpreted in ways that increase their generality and move them away from Ā. They achieve ultra-stability by operating an abstract cultural logic only loosely coupled to the contingencies of concrete events.

Abstraction and centrifugalism

It is their growing powers of abstraction that give centrifugal cultures their strength, that extend their reach to ever-larger transactional populations and that thereby make them a constant threat to centripetal cultures, particularly where these are high context and hence close to Ā.

But low context centripetal cultures close to A are equally vulnerable. What kind of cultures might these be? Those described by Durkheim as being characterized by organic solidarity in fact come close to fitting the bill. Durkheim associated organic solidarity with the division of labour and a centrifugal abstract order, yet this order becomes frozen in Durkheim's thinking by its links with the sacred. It lacks that provisional quality that would keep it open to revision.[101] Organic solidarity can therefore just as easily lead to a centripetal bureaucratic order as to a centrifugal one; witness Marxist-Leninist bureaucracies naively trying to channel every conceivable type of transaction through their ill-adapted administrative apparatus – and all in the name of an abstract utopia quite disconnected from the real world.[102]

Centrifugal cultures, as they reach out ever further towards A, are led to reconceptualize the distinction they previously drew between in-groups and out-groups in both a more abstract and a more fluid way; and as transactional populations increase in size, they are then called upon to reconcile the diverging interests within and between such groups. Their approach to the problem of governance, therefore, will also differ from that adopted by centripetal cultures. To this topic we turn in the next section.

6.6: THE PROBLEM OF GOVERNANCE IN CULTURAL PERSPECTIVE

Transacting with strangers

Almost by definition, an out-group is made up of people who may be known to in-group members but who enjoy more limited rights to consideration than the in-group and much less right to any in-group loyalty. They may share certain values and attitudes in common with in-group members but the initial presumption must be against it. In the typical case the out-group member is a stranger and the stranger as a transactional actor will tend to be depersonalized. What is known about him/her is what is known of people in general, and this does not always inspire confidence. An in-group's own pride and self-esteem frequently rest on a mildly deprecating stereotyping of outsiders. The stranger will therefore not be trusted as readily as in-group members and for this reason uncodified transactions between in- and out-groups will prove to be problematic, sometimes requiring from each of them a large prior investment; where such transactions are non-recurrent, they will only occasionally be justified by the prospective returns they offer. Given the difficulties of uncodified exchange with out-groups it seems plausible to assume that any transactions that involve them will tend to gravitate towards the upper regions of the I-space where they can be made explicit and can form the object of a written agreement.

The assumption receives some support from the fact that it has recently been made in reverse by the New Institutional Economics to explain the existence of firms. Where transactions are so vague that contracts cannot be written or monitored using codified means they are internalized by organizations and subsequently subjected to less explicit form of governance. For this to happen, of course, some prior investment in organizational capacity – i.e., in uncodified face-to-face exchanges within collaborative networks – allowing such transactions to be handled non-contractually must already have taken place.[103] The new theory of the firm then argues that firms can be described as a nexus of less codifiable internalized transactions.[104]

Devising suitable governance arrangements for transacting with strangers greatly extends the population that one can interact with so that a move towards C as we saw in Chapter 3 entails simultaneously a move towards D. But we know from Chapter 2 and from our discussion of governance in Chapter 5 that it is also a move towards A, a move which in low context, centrifugal cultures can be readily accommodated, but which in high context, centripetal cultures may well be perceived as threatening.

The collective self

In a sociological tradition that goes back to Durkheim, cultural evolution has been depicted as a move from Ā to A, from concrete, particularistic values and exchange relationships to abstract, universalistic ones. In their day Karl Marx, Max Weber, Karl Polanyi and, more recently, Fernand Braudel have each commented on the power of impersonal market relationships to dissolve closely knit and particularistic feudal structures. Marx's distinction between the forces and relations of production and the lags that could occur between them represents an attempt to furnish a material basis for such cultural and institutional evolution in the I-space.[105] Drawing on the physics of his day Marx perceived the driving force behind social evolutionary processes to be matter and energy, i.e., labour powers and material well-being, spatiotemporally located in Ā. For this reason, therefore, governance arrangements could never really serve anything other than concrete and specific interests. Moves towards A were for Marx escapes into superstructure, abstract reifications designed to mask the material self-seeking nature of social action. Yet the self that was doing the seeking was a collective self; concrete interests were not individual interests but those of a given *class*, so that with Marx we are always operating in D rather than in Ḋ in the I-space. The creative tensions that might occur between collective and individual thought and which trigger the scanning phase of the SLC are either without social consequences, or signify nothing more than a competition between different types of collective representation within an individual mind.

Durkheim, like Marx, allowed little scope for individual cognitive autonomy. Collective consciousness invades the individual from outside through a socialization process that provides him with the building blocks with which he will construct his life-world.[106] His personal identity, in effect, becomes a mirror image of the collective identity of the groups to which he belongs.[107]

> The collective consciousness is the highest form of the psychic life since it is the consciousness of the consciousness. Being placed outside of and above individual and local contingencies, it sees things only in their permanent and essential aspects which it crystallizes into communicable ideas ... it alone can furnish the mind with the moulds which are applicable to the totality of things and which make it possible to think of them.[108]

The individual's thoughts and experiences are thus channelled into a set of concepts and categories that match those of the surrounding social order, into a stable apodictic mental universe that he subsequently inhabits with little possibility of escape.

Such, at least, is the case in societies regulated by what Durkheim calls mechanical solidarity, pre-industrial societies in which the homogeneity of mental categories has not yet been disturbed by the division and specialization of roles or the depersonalization and abstraction of relationships that is entailed by an extension of the transactional population. Organic solidarity poses a different set of problems. For where exactly, we could ask, might the 'collective' of collective consciousness originate in an industrial society characterized by a division of labour, multiple affiliations, and increasingly impersonal relationships? Is it in the family? In the street corner gang? At school? Should we then view an urban subculture, for instance, as a partitioning off of a single pre-extant collective mind or as an autonomous locus of collective consciousness in its own right? And would any mental discontinuities between such a subculture and the wider society in which it is embedded begin to break the givenness of the latter's own collective cognitive structures?

Givenness, after all, whether cognitive or otherwise, suggests a lack of options, boundaries so tightly drawn around existing categories that little or no exploration outside them is deemed possible. If such boundaries are determined by a group's material conditions, as Marx believed, then only a change in its material circumstances can effectively redraw them. Their quality of givenness, however, will not necessarily be threatened by the change. Nor will it disappear in Durkheim's depiction of social evolution as a move from mechanical to organic solidarity. Evolving categories, to be sure, become more abstract, more codified – they are characterized by Habermas as a 'linguistification of the sacred'[109] – and for that reason can expand the size of the population for which they have validity. Durkheim, however, in contrast to Marx, roots that validity in religious truths rather than in material conditions, truths that condition an individual's life-world – and by implication the collective consciousness. Dealing with values rather than interests, religious truths are not open to question or to revision. Where they fracture, therefore, they disintegrate, not to be replaced by new and better truths but by a state of *anomie* or normlessness.

The provisional character of collective representation

An alternative approach to the construction of social categories is given by Popper in *The Open Society and its Enemies*. Social categories are free conceptualizations that originate in individual rather than collective thought but that gradually gain currency through a mixture of testing, negotiation, and adjustment.[110] They may in this way become more abstract even while retaining a provisional quality. In an open society social adherence to them will for that reason also be more tentative so that drawing clear boundaries which give a single unambiguous contour to collective consciousness is in practice probably not possible. Too many competing or overlapping formulations stand in the way.

If we follow Popper, then, the distinction we have drawn between transactions internal to a group and those which link it to particular out-groups must also appear provisional, although perhaps more so in a centrifugal than in a centripetal culture. In the latter case, as we have already indicated, the boundary that fences off internal from external transactions is designed to act as a screen protecting an in-group from any information and communication overload which might overwhelm its capacity to categorize or to organize. The in-group in effect erects a filter between itself and the outside world that will influence what its members will attend to and what they will ignore, achieving a selectiveness which economizes on transactions while establishing a distinct cultural identity for the group.

Yet maintaining transactional barriers against penetration from outsiders will not always be sufficient to secure the survival of a centripetal culture. On occasion it will also be threatened by centrifugal forces operating from within its boundaries, forces which act to reassign various institutional elements of the culture to different regions of the I-space.

Centrifugal pressures are sometimes the result of a rapid increase in the number of group members and their subsequent differentiation from each other. Beyond a certain group size, the transactional economies available to the in-group from a specific institutional arrangement begin to erode and lead to the formation of subgroups with possibly divergent interests and governance requirements, and thus to new in-group–out-group relationships. Transactional and information processing styles must then adjust to a more complex governance process so that any change in the size of the cultural unit is likely to provoke movements along all three dimensions of the I-space. More abstract governance structures, for example, may have to be devised further along A in order to regulate inter-group relations on the basis of commonly held general interests, while the more specific concrete interests of newly created subgroups may require forms of governance closer to $\bar{A}$.[111] How far control of transactions is then decentralized – i.e., diffused along $\bar{D}D$ – within any one of the governance frameworks created will then be a function of the transaction costs imposed by the information environment – i.e., a function of codification and abstraction – as well as of the distribution of power among group members.

An example: the growth of the firm

We can illustrate with an example of organizational growth the transformation of a centripetal into a centrifugal culture that follows an increase in the size of the transactional population. Many high technology firms founded by tough, single-minded entrepreneurs have an internal culture that could be characterized as fief-like. The charismatic and personal power of a founder or a founding team pervades the firm in its early years while it is still small and trying to get itself established. Employee loyalty to the founders is intense and the feeling that people have of participating in a technological crusade against formidable odds can sometimes elicit extraordinary levels of effort and performance. Commitments are intensely personal and are constantly being reaffirmed in the daily face-to-face encounters made possible in a small organization.

With the growth of the firm, however, and a subsequent increase in the number of its employees, the founder's charismatic power now has to be channelled down through the organization through ever-longer lines of communication. One day he/she will start meeting people who claim to be working for him/her but that he/she has never seen before. Their commitment to the founder's success may no longer be so easily sustainable on the basis of personal loyalty or enthusiasm alone. The founder may then begin to install organizational control systems which can maintain the required level of employee effort when he/she is attending to other things. And since the founder cannot actually be everywhere at once, he/she is led, by degrees, to fall back on a panoply of impersonal administrative routines that can handle the complexities of organizational growth.

Suddenly a bureaucratic transactional style is vying with a fief one as the firm shifts from being a purely centripetal culture in fiefs – 'this is the way we do things around here'[112] – to being more of a centrifugal one, with some transactions originating at the top of the organization continuing to be located in fiefs and others – perhaps the majority – now being assigned to bureaucracies.

With continued growth of the firm, further structural differentiation will eventually take place. A functional organizational structure, for example, the most direct expression of the bureaucratic style, might give way to a multidivisional one in which autonomous divisions compete for investments by the strategic centre of the organization,[113] much as would independent firms in an external capital market. In this phase a market culture begins to make its appearance in certain parts of the firm, and what used to be decried as bureaucratic in-fighting for resources is suddenly transformed into a regulated and legitimate competitive process.

One point should be noted concerning the example just presented. The firm as it grows does not necessarily dispense with fief transactions as it adopts bureaucratic ones, or with the latter as it then proceeds to grow an internal market culture. If it did then it would in effect remain centripetal even as it grew and shifted its cultural centre of gravity in the I-space. In a centrifugal culture a diversity of transactional styles are allowed to coexist in different parts of the firm and at different levels within it. The problem of governance, as we saw in Chapter 5, does not necessarily reduce to choosing exclusively between the different transactional styles being activated; it is rather one of how to make them all work together.

Recall from Chapter 5 that organizations grow by internalizing transactions. In the transaction cost literature this amounts to saying that they are brought under a unified and hierarchical structure of governance. Our own analysis casts doubts on this way of thinking about governance. A governance *process* is needed to bring multiple and divergent stakeholder interests into mutual alignment and thus to give purpose and coherence to organized action. Where these interests express themselves through a diversity of transactional styles – the case of a centrifugal culture – they may in fact be beyond the reach of single unified governance structure. Even within the firm an accommodation often has to be sought between particularistic and universalistic interests so that it may be more realistic to depict the governance process as a bringing into play and a balancing out of several governance structures, each of which may be expressing interests at a different level of generality and abstraction. In short, we are hypothesizing that achieving unity of governance through a single structure rather than through process – we might say, through uniformly applied formal rules rather than through shared vision – will be productive of a centripetal culture; a centrifugal culture, to be effective, may require multiple and overlapping governance structures *even within a single firm*.

The abstraction of inter-group transactions

Returning to our discussion of centripetalism, we conclude that unless a culture is operating in a relatively static environment, unchallenged by internal or external developments, we shall see the boundary between internal and external transactions continuously shifting and being redrawn, a diversity of styles being activated, and by implication, with them, fairly transient and elusive articulations of the collective consciousness. Only where there is little physical, occupational, or social mobility, and individuals remain disposed to go on defining themselves by means of unchanging social categories, is the Durkheimian view of collective consciousness, whether it be concrete or abstract in character, likely to retain any force. Moreover, where multiple levels of governance are tolerated along $\bar{A}A$ – as we have just seen, a more likely possibility in centrifugal than in centripetal cultures (see Figure 6.6b) – collective consciousness, even if comparatively stable to start with, comes to acquire an irreducibly contingent character destructive of such stability.

It was argued in the previous chapter that inter-group transactions might require more abstract or universalistic governance structures than intra-group transactions. By implication, then, external transactions will always tend to present a more abstract character than internal ones. Such a conclusion has some interesting consequences, for if external transactions trigger a move towards A in the I-space and away from $\bar{A}$, then the action of the SLC will also push such transactions towards C and away from $\bar{C}$. The idea, in effect, generalizes Bernstein's sociolinguistic hypothesis concerning the use of restricted codes with in-groups and elaborated codes with out-groups.[114] But considered from an evolutionary perspective in fact it goes much further, for it entails the less obvious proposition that *it is the interaction with out-groups that motivates the creation of codified abstract knowledge; transacting with in-groups tends to keep knowledge concrete and uncodified.*

Let us develop this line of thinking further. We start with the uncontroversial proposition that the members of any in-group taken at random will always be vastly outnumbered by the members of all the out-groups that it can relate to and through which it can gain its specific identity. The idea is made all the more plausible if we are prepared to treat an in-group's remote ancestors and descendants as members of its out-group population on the grounds that the process of inter-personal face-to-face communication by means of which an in-group achieves its cohesiveness is effectively unavailable to them.

Now the essential point is this: transactional knowledge that has to be tested with culturally uncommitted out-groups, by dint of this fact alone, enjoys a more extensive and rigorous corroboration than that which can be confined to in-group transactions. When such knowledge survives its tests, it achieves a greater level of generality: being tested in a plurality of different groups it will also be tested in a diversity of settings which taken together transcend the limitations imposed by any one group's idiosyncratic circumstances. What can then be most plausibly retained as epistemologically valid is what can be abstracted from large numbers of external transactions. In addition to being more abstract, such knowledge will also be more codified: lower levels of trust between in-group and out-group, as well as the difficulties of personalizing transactional relationships, will require a greater degree of explicitness in the exchange process.

The codification, diffusion, and abstraction of exchange relationships mutually reinforce one another. If external transactions are indeed more codified than internal ones, their constitutive knowledge will diffuse more rapidly beyond the in-group and to the transactional population as a whole; it will therefore not only be tested at the in-group's interface with its immediate transactional partners but in a plurality of out-groups simultaneously, many of which will be located well beyond this interface. The process of corroborating transactional knowledge and of enhancing its generality is thus further facilitated by codification and the more extensive diffusion that it helps to bring about.

A second consideration, this time of a more behavioural kind, also contributes to making out-group transactions more abstract than in-group ones. Impersonal transactions with out-groups evoke a more deliberative and critical attitude than the more informal but also more affect-laden and committing transactions conducted within an in-group. Thus whereas a somewhat dubious and cost-ineffective in-group transaction might well be 'reprieved' out of a sense of social solidarity, questionable out-group transactions will usually be allowed to 'die' if they fail to meet the joint expectations of the transacting parties. Not only, by dint of the variety of settings, then, are the knowledge and assumptions of transacting parties more rigorously tested in out-group than in in-group transactions, but test failures when they occur are more ruthlessly weeded out by the parties. If objective knowledge is the product of inter-subjective processes, as argued by Popper,[115] then one has to cross more difficult terrain to reach inter-subjective consensus with an out-group than one does with an in-group; the transactional knowledge that accumulates through out-group exchanges is less prone to the distortions of social bonding and groupthink.[116]

While increased levels of interaction between a given in-group and a plurality of out-groups move transactionally relevant knowledge towards greater codification, abstraction, and diffusion in the I-space, at the same time they also test the implicit premises on which much other related in-group knowledge rests. The test can sometimes be painful and can go as far as to threaten the in-group's very stability or identity in cases where it fractures the life-world of its members. A centripetal culture, where it has the power to do so, may then respond to such pain or the threat of it by firstly drawing ever tighter boundaries around itself and then by reducing the density of threatening exchanges with out-groups. It may even beat a retreat from A back towards Ā once more, towards its founding myths and sacred places. A centrifugal culture, by contrast, is more likely to respond to the pain adaptively, with readjustments to its life-world and its founding premises, shedding some old knowledge in order to accommodate the new; some ability to relativize its situation will allow it to maintain its progression towards A in spite of such adjustments. A centrifugal culture, according to this line of argument, has a greater capacity to learn from its mistakes than a centripetal one.

An example: the case of Japan

Japan provides us with an interesting illustration of the difficulties that confront a culture having to balance out in a cognitively coherent fashion the conflicting claims of in-groups and out-groups. Centrifugal cultural forces have been at work in Japanese society since the Meiji restoration – some, indeed, would argue since well before[117] – and they have endowed the country with the full panoply of institutions required of a modern industrialized nation. Yet, arguably, many of these institutions do not really function according to the logic of a centrifugal cultural order: their assignment in the I-space would display less scatter than it would in the case of western institutions operating at a similar level of development. They must contend with a strongly inward-looking cultural bias that solves the problems of the in-group at the expense of out-group interests. This particularistic orientation of Japanese culture is especially visible when interested out-groups are non-Japanese. The country's pattern of behaviour in international trade disputes is one illustration of this cultural bias; its frequent tiffs with the United States – the ultimate centrifugal culture – provoked by the latter's perception of Japan as a free rider in matters of defence and foreign policy, is another.[118]

In the international arena Japan is far from being the only country to put special interests before general principles and obligations. France, for example, through a skilful exploitation of the EC's Common Agricultural Policy, has successfully managed to protect its farmers at the expense of other, sometimes more deserving, claimants and often in violation of its own espoused free trade principles. Yet in a country like France, whatever the merits of the case might be, at least the claims of out-groups are acknowledged and possibly even *understood*. In Japan those claims – especially when they come from abroad – are met with incomprehension. Typically, the Japanese response is that Japan's culture is opaque and hard for foreigners to understand – a polite way of saying that barriers to entry into the in-group are higher than they are elsewhere, and that on the other side of these barriers the in-group may be doing quite nicely, a state of affairs quite in line with the natural order of things.

Foreign observers of Japan, however, rarely comment on the barriers to *exit* from the in-group: corporate employment practices, language, the very modest amount of international experience of most Japanese managers, etc. Until very recently, Japan's links with the outside world have been conducted primarily through trade rather than through direct foreign investment. This has served to limit the country's exposure to out-group interaction and hence to blunt its sensitivity and responsiveness to out-group expectations. It thus has few ways of adequately conceptualizing them.

One implication of our analysis – for which Japan stands as a counter example – is that where transactions with out-groups are sufficiently dense, abstract knowledge is more likely to be internalized from outside as a given than generated from within the in-group itself. In such cases the cohesiveness of the group's collective consciousness may weaken. It will not happen without tensions or conflicts, since alternative ways of construing an externally given abstract order may still compete for the allegiance of in-group members. Cleavages in the collective consciousness will then reflect the choices made by various subgroups within the in-group, not only redrawing once more the boundary between in- and out-groups, but also mapping out a possible trajectory for an emerging centrifugal order.

Harmony versus conflict in the cultural order

Marvin Harris has criticized Anglo-Saxon structural-functionalism for failing to acknowledge the fragmented and conflict-laden nature of the collective mind. In Parsons's work for example, according to Harris, the idealist bias is evident in the requirement that a *shared* cognitive orientation and a *shared* articulated set of goals be functional prerequisites for survival when in fact all around us we see complex societies riven by bitter class, ethnic, and regional conflict.[119]

In a centrifugal order, of course, shared cognitive orientations and objectives at one level of cultural aggregation might perfectly well coexist with conflict at another. To require harmony of the whole is in effect to advocate a centripetal cultural order. For social harmony turns out to be a core value of centripetalism, whether it be conceived of as the outcome of perfectly competitive market processes – i.e., the invisible hand – or of an all-seeing and coordinating hierarchical authority. Such 'harmony' does not process conflict so much as repress it or ignore it; efficient markets are then justified on the grounds of Pareto optimality, hierarchical coordination on the grounds of impartiality, and so on.

Underlying the harmony model of social process in a centripetal culture is a quest for equilibrium, for a stable, unchanging social order that eliminates painful and divisive uncertainties. Centrifugal cultures, by contrast, aim to exploit conflict and uncertainty constructively, making use of them as drivers of adaptive change. For conflict to play a constructive role in social evolution it has to be contained within certain bounds but not eliminated. The governance challenge then becomes to devise structures that can operate flexibly within those bounds.

Harris, like other Marxists, seeks a centripetal order, a harmonious end state to the process of human development in which class conflict will have been eliminated by the destruction of one class by another. Classes in Marxist theory are not taken as temporary groupings in the I-space but as durably real W3 entities with built-in and irreconcilable class interests. These have the effect of converting the class struggle into a zero-sum game with historically determined winners and losers. Marxist historicism, the ineluctable laws through which capitalism replaces feudalism and communism replaces capitalism, is in fact profoundly anti-evolutionary since not only does the whole process of the class struggle unwind as predictably as a watch-spring, effectively closing off the future as a horizon of open possibilities, but, having unwound, it then comes to rest in a static state of social harmony and remains in that state thereafter. History in fact comes to an end.[120]

Constructing a flexible identity

If we can feel free to redraw the boundary separating in-groups from out-groups in response to developments that take place in the I-space, why cannot Harris? The reason is that our evolutionary perspective gives us a freedom of manoeuvre that is not available to him. Recall that for Harris collective consciousness and group identity derive directly from the group's material situation and its concrete physical needs, whereas for us they vary with the way in which a group chooses to construe its situation. Internalizing new abstract categories may either enhance or undermine a group's power of construal, but whatever conflicts result therefrom are rooted in cognitive processes that are always subject to revision and usually only loosely connected to the group's material base. It is precisely through such a constant reconceptualizing and redrawing of our categorial boundaries that our individual and collective identities are forged; we are thus able to escape both a parochial materialism that would confine our 'interests' to whatever fills our bellies, as well as a utopian idealism in thrall to cognitive categories of its own creation.

Not everyone successfully escapes: cognitively speaking, many are destined to remain stuck in their village while others roam through interplanetary space. But let us not pretend that what separates the elders of an Anatolian hamlet from an international team of business executives running the global operations of a large aerospace firm can be accounted for solely or even mainly by objective differences in their material interests. For the key to what distinguishes the two groups lies in the way they each construe things: the first group has internalized a narrow set of concrete categories that define most of the world outside the village as an out-group, whereas the second has internalized an abstract world view that greatly expands the range and variety of groups with which it has the option of interacting.

The crucial point is this: identity owes as much to the range of groups one *could* belong to as to those one *does* belong to.[121] Identity, like information, is thus also a function of the power to *select* and, like information, can be more or less abstract, codified, or shared – i.e., diffused – according to the number of possible states that are available to the individual to choose from. In an abstract universe, individuals have the option of construing themselves more broadly than they can when they believe themselves to be strictly confined to a unique spatiotemporal location and a specific set of concrete circumstances. How well they are able to exercise that option depends on their ability to bring the universal abstract categories they have mastered to bear on their concrete circumstances in order to integrate them together, a move from A towards Ā in the I-space.

Much Jungian psychology is concerned with this integrative capacity of the individual and with its consequences for the development of his/her personality.[122] Where the ability to use abstractions in this integrative fashion fails, the individual is left with a number of concrete, unintegrated identities, fragments of multiple and sometimes colliding selves.[123] The truly practical person, therefore, is not the materialist ridiculed by Sahlins and extolled by Harris; it is someone equally at home with abstract and with concrete categories and capable of applying abstract theories, sometimes imported in from remote mental locations, to immediate and pressing issues. The sociologist Kurt Lewin once quipped that 'there is nothing so practical as a good theory'. There is also nothing so theory-laden as good practice.

The language of participants versus the language of observers

To summarize. Out-groups are a codified abstraction that provoke a transactional discontinuity along the $\bar{A}A$ dimension of the I-space. On one side of the discontinuity we have the concrete, personalized, implicit categories used for transactions within the in-group; on the other side the abstract, impersonal, explicit transactional categories that the in-group uses with the out-group.

Have we not, in effect, already encountered this in-group/out-group distinction in Chapter 3 in our discussion of emic and etic codes?

In anthropology the emic codes studied have been those of selected in-groups (participants), and the etic codes used in such studies those of one particular out-group (observers). By chance the out-groups in question have often mostly consisted of anthropologists seeking to test out ready-made abstract categories derived from their discipline, whereas the in-groups selected have turned out to be Kalahari bushmen or other suitably pre-industrial people working to a quite different agenda.

Now the behaviour of bushmen can be something of a puzzle to the untutored eye; their rain dances and burial rites do not readily make sense to the outsider. How, then, should the diligent field anthropologist go about making sense of what she sees? Those who support the emic approach claim that understanding the bushmen means getting onto their wavelength and, as far as possible, getting to see the world as they do – preferably by becoming a bushman oneself. Only by doing this, by putting onself, so to speak, in the bushman's shoes – a figure of speech if ever there was one – can rain dances and burial rites *really* make sense to an outsider. But this means abandoning any detached and objective etic categories that one brings to the task as an observer and trading them in for the participant's own emic categories. Understanding bushmen then ceases to be the outcome of an application of *a priori* abstract categories to a given segment of reality which they can successfully process, and becomes rather the fruit of what those writing in the tradition of interpretative sociology refer to as *Verstehen*, an implicit and intuitive grasp of meaning that is achieved following the absorption and impacting (the *ar, i* phase of the SLC) of emic categories used by participants.[124]

Those who opt for an etic approach see in such a strategy a total relativism and a renunciation of scientific procedure. The language of participants, to be sure, can be observed – albeit only etically – but cannot in itself yield any genuine and objective understanding of the bushman's situation. An emic interpretation will tell us something of how a participant *construes* his situation, but only objectively determined circumstances can convincingly explain his actual behaviour. His own construal has little or no explanatory power of itself. In short, if we ask a Kalahari bushman to tell us what he is doing, he will tell us what he *thinks* he is doing. But this for an etic observer may be far removed from what he is *really* doing.

Harris, discussing Mary Douglas's analysis of ancient Israelite purification rites, succinctly states the case for an etic approach:

> It is true that the pig had an anomalous etic status for the ancient Israelites (as well as for many other ancient and modern peoples of the near and Middle East), but the source of this anomalous status is not the binary code of an archaic mental calculus; rather it is the practical and mundane cost/benefit of raising pigs under marginal or inappropriate infrastructural conditions.[125]

Harris, however, fails to see that defining 'infrastructural conditions' will in fact involve him in importing his own abstract categories into the analysis and that these are not objectively given but possibly as tentative in their own way as the 'archaic mental calculus' that he deprecatingly refers to. What will be accepted by Harris's professional colleagues as constituting 'infrastructure' may well depend upon which branch of anthropology they have been trained in (will economic anthropologists, for instance, frame their definitional requirements in the same way as, say, cultural anthropologists or physical anthropologists?), on the stringency of the tests this branch requires in establishing abstract categories of infrastructure, on its particular research traditions, and so on. Thus the language of observers, although possibly better corroborated and of greater generality than that of participants – at least in those cases where it forms part of an established scientific tradition – may not turn out to be of an inherently different nature. It will simply have progressed further towards A along the ĀA dimension. Harris of course hotly contests this:

> Idealist strategies claim that 'all knowledge is ultimately emic'. To deny the validity of etic description is in effect to deny the possibility of a social science capable of explaining sociocultural similarities or differences. To urge that the etics of scientific observers is merely one among an infinity of other emics, is to urge the surrender of our intellects to the supreme mystification of total relativism.[126]

If we understand Harris correctly, then, there are those who 'think' they know – the participants – and those who *really* know – the observers. The difference between the two groups is that the latter have access to 'objective' data on, say, infrastructural conditions and other features of the participants' *real* situation whereas the latter do not. And what, we might ask, are the etic categories that Harris is trying to shield from 'supreme mystification'? His answer is revealing:

> Only by recognizing the difference between emic and etic definitions of such concepts as exploitation and surplus can a demystified substantivist strategy avoid the sterile relativism of the Boasian program.[127]

The integration of emic and etic discourse

The danger that emic description poses for Harris is that if it is accepted as valid description then, as he puts it himself, 'All the basic assertions of Marxism about the nature of objective historical processes are thereby rendered null and void.'[128]

The weakness in Harris's position stems from his failure to recognize that what is provisional is not necessarily relative in the sense that anything goes. Paul Feyerabend has made the slogan 'anything goes' into the rallying cry of epistemological anarchists,[129] and Feyerabend himself, to be consistent, could not reasonably grant any less a scientific status to the Kalahari bushmen's own musings than he would to Harris's. All genuine knowledge is sourced locally and validated locally; universally valid knowledge moving frictionlessly across cultural boundaries is an illusion held in place by social acts of cognitive coercion – the scientific community itself, according to Feyerabend, being today one of the main agents through which such coercion is exercised.

The relativist asks us to believe that *all* movements in the E-space towards greater codification and abstraction are socially determined and at root nothing more than an expression of power processes, institutionalized or otherwise, at work in a social system; all logic is therefore a social logic and all corroboration of new knowledge is a socially derived validation process. In other words, all epistemologically significant movement along $\bar{A}A$ in the I-space is dictated by what takes place in the D region where knowledge is collectively held. Individual movement along $\bar{A}A$ in $\bar{D}$ is certainly possible but remains quite without consequence for the creation of new knowledge unless it is first filtered through diffusion barriers set up between $\bar{D}$ and D and operated by powerful groups, themselves located in D. Cognitively speaking, then, the individual proposes but it is society rather than nature that effectively disposes and thus conditions the way in which he/she will activate his/her individual E-space. Epistemological anarchists deplore such cognitive coercion and advocate free movement in the E-space, unhindered by social constraints – hence their cry 'anything goes'. *Plus royaliste que le roi*, they want to push relativism to its limits in order to release individuals from the cognitive bonds that tether them to society and block their creativity.

Realists like Popper and Lakatos, whilst recognizing the role played by social forces in accelerating or slowing down movement in the E-space, argue that in the long run it will always be nature and not society that disposes. As Popper puts it, sooner or later 'reality kicks back' if it is allowed to.[130] The move towards abstraction retains an irreducibly provisional quality while at the same time slowly gaining in objectivity; it thus avoids both the evolutionary blind alley of a relativist position which denies the possibility of epistemological progress and the dogmatism of the Marxists with their privileged access to the essence of things.

Better-corroborated provisional etic knowledge thus becomes unambiguously preferable to poorly tested emic knowledge. Yet since we have placed both of these on a single continuum going from Ā to A and allowed some two-way movement along it, does any insuperable barrier prevent us from shifting between both types of knowledge if we so wish to providing that we satisfy the epistemological conditions of validity for movement in the E-space? After all, it may only be in the highly local and uncomplicated world of Kalahari bushmen that the need to abstract may be only weakly felt and that there might be little to motivate any movement from Ā to A. In most other societies, what is sought is an epistemologically valid integration of emic and etic discourses rather than a domination of one by the other.

The emphasis on epistemological validity is crucial. If Harris chooses to 'see' exploitation every time he 'observes' a blue-collar worker, he is entitled to do so – in some cases, we might do so too – but he should not anoint his insight with a scientific status unless it meets certain minimum conditions of intersubjective testability, problems of social validation notwithstanding. Failing this, quite in contradiction with Harris's own thesis, his 'observation' amounts to the ultimate appropriation of the etic by the emic. We can share his concern that it should not happen.

The economics of discoursing

If, as we are arguing, there is no unbridgeable epistemological divide between emic and etic discourse, or, in Bernstein's terminology, between restricted and elaborated codes, then any choice one is called to make between them boils down to what one is trying to achieve in the I-space and at what cost. Mastering codes that move one from Ā to A sacrifices richness for structure. If it concurrently involves a move from C̄ to C it may increase the out-group population that one can communicate with – assuming that it possesses the relevant codes. But if implicit in-group codes are also lost in the process of shedding data and moving up the I-space towards C then one may no longer be able to communicate effectively with a given in-group. Of course communicative capacity can always be maintained in different regions of the E-space, but only through increased investments. These will not always be forthcoming.

The coding choices made, therefore, ultimately turn out to be economic ones, having to do with the allocation of scarce cognitive and communicative resources to alternative transactional possibilities. Governance and institutional structures in the I-space offer anchoring points with respect to which efforts at economizing might be undertaken. Economizing behaviour in the I-space in fact produces all the features that in other circumstances we would associate with industry structure, such as barriers to entry, economies of scale, market concentration, etc. These certainly constrain but do not determine the range of cultural activities that are possible, activities whose horizons are constantly being reconfigured and extended by the action of the SLC.

The approach that we have adopted relativizes the concept of in-group and out-group so that what passes for an internal transaction at one moment could well be reclassified as an external one the next. It does not follow that the distinction between the two types of group has no validity. Discontinuities in information flows certainly affect the ways that existing transactional and governance structures get reinforced or eroded; but these in any case must be understood as not much more than islands of temporary stability set in what is essentially a dynamic process with the SLC continually overlaying existing structures with new ones and then eroding or dislodging the old ones. The almost caste-like distinction that has been drawn between emic and etic categories can only really convince within the framework of a static epistemology. When information flows in the I-space reach a certain velocity they rob the distinction of much of its epistemological force. Etic discourse may, as we have argued above, be better corroborated than emic discourse – and this is why we would not wish to deny the value of etic discourse – but there is something more than faintly patronizing in the view that some kind of epistemological 'power of the keys' has been given to those who happen to hold the etic view. One of Popper's contributions has been to show that there is no reason to treat emic categories as any less scientific than etic ones. They may be less extensively corroborated than the latter but provided they can eventually be made to meet the epistemological requirements of refutability – and debate continues to rage over what these might be – they are just as capable of approaching the truth.

Recapitulation

To conclude. The production and exchange of information is a cultural activity that is subject to economizing. If governance structures define both the populations and the *ends* towards which efforts at economizing will be applied, institutions define some of the *means* through which such efforts will be effected. The U-space allows us to relate the degree of abstraction of governance objectives – i.e., their generality – to the size of the population whose interests they serve. It can be inferred that the larger the population to be served by a given type of governance arrangement, the more abstract must the articulation of its interests become if these are to command wide allegiance. The population whose behaviour might be regulated by a given governance structure, however, need not always be the one whose interests or values are effectively served by it. Nor need a given set of interests necessarily be associated with a single level of governance along ĀA; multiple, overlapping governance structures that integrate a diversity of individual and group interests are also possible – and in many cases desirable too. We associate these with centrifugal cultural forms.

From our discussion the nature of cultural centripetalism now becomes easier to grasp. It expresses a certain exclusiveness with respect to interests, values, and population served. Centripetalism will feel more comfortable if it operates at but one level of abstraction – which can vary – and it will therefore tend to opt for a single point on the ĀA scale of Figure 6.6a. By implication it will also seek to work through a single type of governance structure. It is centripetalism's narrow governance focus – motivated by ideology when located in A and by self-interests when located in Ā – that explains its preference for a single institutional form through which to pursue its objectives over those alternatives available singly or in combination in the I-space. Centripetalism possibly survives more easily in Ā than in A since in that location, being less universalistic and claiming less generality, it is also less refutable. It remains, however, no less vulnerable in the long run to the erosive action of the SLC than the more centrifugal forms of governance that it shuns.

6.7: CONCLUSION

Culture as an economic activity

In this chapter we have extended the theoretical analysis presented in the first five chapters to cultural processes. The quest for a political economy of information has in effect led us to a theory of culture in which economizing in the production and exchange of information holds a central place. Economizing in time, in space, and in energy, to be sure, also have their place in any theory of culture, but analysed independently of information economies they lead us up the blind alley of materialism. Returning for a moment to our modified production function of Chapter 1 (see Figure 1.8) we might say that if orthodox economics focuses its attention on the horizontal axis at the expense of the vertical one – concentrating on physical resources and neglecting informational ones – materialism tries to do away with the vertical axis altogether as an element of analysis.

Information economizing is taken here to be a dynamic concept driven by the SLC; only when it pauses in the appropriate regions of the I-space – i.e., markets or bureaucracies – does it allow for maximization of the neoclassical or the bureaucratic kind. The quest for information economies is one of the key drivers of cultural evolution: the generation (hypothesis formulation) and selection (hypothesis testing) of socially useful variety and its diffusion and absorption within a population.

One popular theory of cultural evolution, the convergence hypothesis, we found not to stimulate evolution at all but rather its opposite. Expressed as a centripetal coming to a point in the I-space, cultural convergence effectively brings the SLC to a halt, and with it any possibility of evolutionary change. Were cultural evolution to be conceived of as a matching of centrifugal patterns in the I-space, on the other hand, the SLC could still function and evolutionary change would still occur. Yet, as we have seen, the probability of any two such patterns actually matching becomes vanishingly small as societies gain in complexity and differentiation.

The SLC is the solvent of centrifugal evolutionary forces; its reach is being extended ever further by modern communication technology to new populations.[131] In the process existing transactional structures get eroded and new exchange possibilities are opened up.

But whose interests should be served by these new possibilities? Or put another way, how do we identify the social groupings on whose behalf economizing might be sought? This, of course, is the problem of governance, and in a centrifugal culture it is complicated by the fact that multiple interests operating at different levels of abstraction and population aggregation compete and collaborate. If one level of governance strongly predominates – whether it achieves its dominance through competition or collaboration – the result is likely to be a centripetal cultural order, universalistic if it is located at the abstract end of the ĀA dimension, particularistic if located at the concrete end. If, on the other hand, different levels of governance simultaneously exert pressure as they well might in a centrifugal culture, then social disintegration threatens if transactional resources turn out to be insufficient to meet all their claims. Individual and social identity then get fractured and the culture may retreat into centripetalism to nurse them. If the SLC is effectively to run its course through the I-space irrigating it with new knowledge, a balance must somehow be struck between competing levels of governance which either fosters collaboration or allows for some measure of coexistence between them, not necessarily peaceful, but not unnecessarily destructive either.

The implications for economic analysis

At this point we must ask the question that we have so far asked at the end of every chapter except the introductory one: what implications, if any, do the contents of this chapter hold for the way we think about economic processes? Our reply will be quite general.

The New Institutional Economics conceives of institutions as devices for economizing on transaction costs. Although the transaction cost literature has tended to focus almost exclusively on economic institutions such as firms and markets, a sufficiently broad conception of transactions would in principle allow any social institution such as the family or the Church to be accommodated within an economizing framework.[132]

But could *relations* between institutions variously located in the I-space be so accommodated? It seems possible. Williamson himself, for example, introduces the concept of bilateral governance to deal with cases such as joint ventures in which independent governance structures collaborate in pursuit of shared objectives.[133] In the particular case discussed by Williamson, the structures in question – i.e., firms – would most likely be located in close proximity in the I-space for they are essentially institutions of the same kind. Yet this is hardly a prerequisite for all kinds of inter-institutional collaboration. Do we not, for example, see institutionalized collaboration between Parliament (clans) and the Crown in British political life (fiefs)? Or informal collaboration between families (say, clans) and schools (bureaucracies) over the education of children? Is a concern for economizing on the exchange processes any less present in such arrangements than it is in commercial life?

A network of institutions, each subject to the economizing imperative – both internally and in its external relations – in fact provides the basis for the broader competitive or collaborative cultural configurations that extend themselves in the I-space. If institutions, therefore, are crystallizations of the social need to economize on exchange, then so must culture be now taken as an *institutional pattern* in the I-space.

To make culture as a whole the subject of economic analysis, however, moves us somewhat beyond the position of the New Institutional Economics. Culture, of course, cannot be reduced to a particular level of governance such as the nation-state, or to any specific set of institutions designed for, say, the conduct of macroeconomic policy such as a central bank, a ministry of finance, and a state statistical office. It is at work both inside and outside such entities. Culture as we have described it in this chapter is both more diffuse and at the same time more complex than what is internal to any given social grouping; it is characterized by patterns of institutions and transactions that are shaped by the action of SLCs as they navigate through different levels of governance.

By subjecting this shifting kaleidoscopic entity to the economizing imperative, we effectively reverse the traditional relationship between economics and anthropology. The latter discipline has speciated and built a whole subdiscipline on the argument that economic exchange has a cultural dimension to it which makes it the proper focus for an economic anthropology. Such an argument, however, leaves the focus of economic analysis itself essentially untouched. Market exchange still remains at the core of the economist's and now the economic anthropologist's concern. Anthropological insights into the varied circumstances in which market exchange occurs may undoubtedly deepen our understanding of the process and even help to draw disciplinary boundaries around it – doubtless to the satisfaction of economists, who, like other professionals, are territorial creatures. But they do little to extend the scope of economics itself.

Yet if, as we have argued in this book, economizing is a constituent attribute of *all* forms of social exchange then the almost exclusive preoccupation of orthodox economists with markets, whether on account of their analytical tractability or simply of the discipline's initial focus, has to be misplaced. The New Institutional Economics has cogently argued this point;

here we merely take the line of thinking that it has initiated to its logical conclusion: cultural processes as a whole are a fit subject for economic analysis.

Culture, we are arguing, is nothing other than a set of organizational and institutional arrangements created for the social production and exchange of useful information. By means of the I-space we have presented a dynamic theory of information production and exchange processes ordered along the three critical dimensions of abstraction, codification, and diffusion. Does not our proposed extension of economic thinking to the cultural domain place the analysis of information processes at the top of the economic agenda? And does it not call for a much deeper understanding of the information phenomenon in its physical and social manifestations than economists reared in the neoclassical tradition have been willing to countenance?

Towards a new economic paradigm

The prevailing economic paradigm has in effect fathered two quite distinct economic orders, not one as is commonly supposed by critics of the neoclassical orthodoxy. The first is based on markets: the free enterprise economy; the second on hierarchy: the command economy. In spite of important differences between them, they share as siblings certain characteristics, two of which are worth emphasizing.

The first is that each in its own way takes information production and exchange as a given: information is well codified and readily available where it should be: in the heads of all economic agents in the case of the market economy; in the head of a single central coordinator in the case of the command economy. Recent theorizing has allowed for search costs and for temporary informatiom asymmetries in the economic system, but these do not destabilize the paradigmatic assumptions of long-run equilibrium and allocative efficiency.[134]

The second characteristic shared by the two economic orders is their centripetalism. Transactional arrangements in the I-space which are essentially contingent on a particular trajectory of the SLC – i.e., path dependent – and on the information environment activated by that trajectory are taken by each to be normative and universal in scope thus fostering ideologies such as Marxism-Leninism in support of hierarchy, and 'Reaganomics' or 'Thatcherism' in support of markets.

A more penetrating examination of the information phenomenon, of the contingent nature of transactions that feed upon it, and of the evolutionary properties of the knowledge it gives rise to would yield a much more centrifugal concept of the economic order, indeed one now coextensive with a culture taken as a totality. In effect, it would lead to what we might call a Braudelian approach to the analysis of the economic process, one that admits of richness, variety, and complexity. Braudel, surveying the development of capitalism through the lens of the economic historian, explicitly resisted the temptation of reducing it to a market order.[135] Capitalism, in the pages of his three-volume work on the subject, is nothing less than the operation of the SLC in human affairs, countless information flows set in motion by developments in technology, social organization, geographical discovery, competitive struggles, and the myriad opportunities they open up and foreclose for individuals or groups. For the French historian, capitalism, far from being equatable with the centripetalism of a neoclassical market order, was *par excellence* the highest expression of a centrifugal order. Braudel supported his thesis with detailed and painstaking historical research. We arrive at a similar conclusion to his by way of theoretical analysis.

The real contest, from the perspective we have adapted, is not between the ideology of markets and that of hierarchies as alternative ordering principles for economic action but between a centripetal and a centrifugal cultural – and hence economic – order. And since, according to our analysis, only the first can properly be called ideological, this contest cannot be framed as one between competing ideologies. Rather it has to be seen as one between an ideological and an evolutionary order. It effectively reaffirms the distinction that Popper has already made between a closed and an open society,[136] but it does so this time on information grounds.

In a centrifugal 'capitalist' economic order there is room for clans and fiefs as well as for markets and hierarchies. Each institutional form will have its own way of economizing and of being efficient, and each will establish an appropriate level of governance as a function of the size of the population whose interests are being served. The very multiplicity of governance levels in a centrifugal system, however, renders the economic concept of efficiency problematic when dealing with the system as a whole since efficiency can only ever be properly gauged when effort is directed towards a unitary set of objectives. As Schumpeter well understood, an evolutionary economic process may display effective economizing behaviour at the global level without necessarily yielding efficiencies of an engineering kind.[137] Centripetal ideologies located in the upper regions of the I-space find it hard to live without unambiguous efficiency measures; yet if the wrong ones are constructed the economic system as a whole becomes distorted and stunted. In the next chapter we examine this issue in more detail through a case study which allows us to illustrate how the conceptual scheme that we have developed in this book finds application in the real world.

Chapter 7

Case study – socialist transformations

ABSTRACT

The I-space has potential as an analytical tool for the diagnosis of social and political change. Its use can be illustrated by comparing the modernization process in China, Japan, and Central and Eastern Europe.

The Confucian tradition has tended to give particular prominence to the exercise of personal power. The shift in China to a Marxist-Leninist order did not fundamentally alter this tendency. Mao Zedong, in his day, behaved as imperiously as his Qing predecessors. The economic reforms currently under way have their origins in attempts to curb Mao's personal power after the disasters of the Great Leap Forward in the late 1950s. China, however, still lacks the cultural disposition to create an impersonal institutional order, whether of the market or the bureaucratic kind. For this reason the country continues to operate primarily out of the lower regions of the I-space.

Japan is also culturally more comfortable in the lower regions of the I-space, albeit in clans rather than, like China, in fiefs. Japan, however, operates its institutions more centrifugally than China does. As was suggested in the preceding chapter, a centrifugal cultural order facilitates the process of modernization. At the level of the individual enterprise, it facilitates organizational learning.

When the countries of Eastern and Central Europe fell to communism after the Second World War, they were already located much further up the I-space than were either China or Japan or, indeed, the USSR. The development challenge that they currently face, therefore, is not to move up the space but to move horizontally towards markets from a well-codified bureaucratic order. The danger they run in doing so, is that in their concern to achieve a market order they make it centripetal and hence block the action of the SLC. A well-functioning SLC would bring them down the I-space once more into the clan region. Here they would encounter a decentralizing China that is experimenting with a new economic order that we may label *Network Capitalism*. In that country, a centripetal cultural order centred on fiefs is giving way to a more centrifugal cultural order centred on clans. The lesson that its modernizing experience holds for Eastern and Central Europe is that markets are but a brief moment in a broader, more centrifugal capitalist process. They should not, therefore, be approached centripetally.

7.1: INTRODUCTION

Two years that changed the world

The two-year interval between the summers of 1989 and 1991 was a memorable one for the communist movement. On the night of 4 June 1989, the Chinese leadership responded to demands for less corruption within party ranks and for more democracy by massacring protesting students in and around Tiananmen Square. Estimates of casualties range from the high hundreds to the low thousands. Several thousand more were then arrested. Executions followed.

Two months later the massive outflow of young people from East Germany voting with their feet led to the collapse of the Berlin Wall and with it to the general collapse of the forty-year-old Soviet hegemony over Eastern Europe.

In August 1991, with Mikhail Gorbachev away from Moscow on vacation, a group of party conservatives attempted to get hold of the Soviet state apparatus. The coup failed and the Soviet political system then came apart at the seams.

Few people at the beginning of 1989 could have predicted such outcomes. China, following the pragmatic economic policies that its octogenarian leader Deng Xiaoping initiated in 1978, appeared all set to continue liberalizing in the wake of rapid growth and to become another 'Asian miracle'. Economic liberalization has indeed been maintained; political liberalization, however, remains in the deep freeze. In Eastern Europe and in the Former Soviet Union (FSU), political liberalization has been patchy and has rekindled nationalist and ethnic animosities which had lain dormant under Soviet rule and the pressures of east–west confrontation. Economic liberalization, on the other hand, has been more visible at the grass roots than in the upper reaches of the economic structure itself, with small traders occupying the interstices of a decaying economic structure.

Various interpretations of the events in Tiananmen Square have been put forward, many of them bearing more than a passing resemblance to the 'Oriental despotism' hypothesis advanced in the 1950s by Karl Wittfogel and foreshadowed by Marx and later by Lenin.[1] Max himself first formulated his views of Asiatic society with regard to India. He argued that an unqualified despotism first appeared in completely Oriental societies based on an agrarian order with large state-operated works of water control and a system of dispersed village communities interlocked with an agro-hydraulic economy. Applied to contemporary China, the Oriental despotism hypothesis held that a long tradition of absolutist rule based on the state's responsibility for the creation and maintenance of a large-scale physical and economic infrastructure made it impossible for the Chinese leaders to accept that economic and political decentralization might be related. Deng's commitment to economic reform had been misunderstood in a liberal west that took such a relationship for granted: it did not imply any correlative commitment to political evolution. Ironically, Marx would have been able to anticipate Deng's response and its passive acceptance by the Chinese population, for in his opinion Oriental despotism smothered all 'historical energy' and the willingness to engage in meaningful political struggle.[2]

The collapse of Honecker's regime in the former East Germany is easier to grasp in retrospect if one takes into account the state of the FSU at the time. By 1989, the cost of maintaining its East European empire had become prohibitive given the country's own secular economic decay. The Soviet rate of growth had been in decline for nearly two decades according to official figures, and according to CIA estimates had actually turned negative. Given internal turmoil in its own republics and the rising political and economic costs of armed intervention in Warsaw Pact countries – i.e., increased needs for social and political control and renewed confrontation with the west – the Soviet Union could no longer afford to protect unpopular regimes in its client states. Marxism-Leninism, it was argued, was an ideology that had been imposed on Eastern Europe from outside and was quite alien in spirit to the region's earlier political traditions – not all of which, it should be said, pointed in the direction of political or economic liberalism. When the external force that kept it in place weakened, those traditions reasserted themselves – sometimes with a destabilizing vengeance.

The sudden collapse of the Marxist-Leninist order in the FSU has not yet found an explanation that commands wide consensus. Thus although occasional reference will be made in this chapter to developments in the FSU and some policy issues discussed with reference to them, they will not be analysed in any detail. Our discussion of western communism will focus primarily on Central and Eastern Europe.

Towards a cultural interpretation

Many of the explanations put forward for what has happened in China and Eastern Europe have a strong culturalist flavour. China's social and political traditions do not lend themselves to modern-style democratization – something, it is held, that also holds for the Arab world as well as for most other Asian countries – whereas those in Eastern Europe do, albeit perhaps to a lesser extent than in the older democracies of Western Europe and North America. Yet whether culture can really be the argument-stopper that it is sometimes called upon to play must be open to doubt. The fact that a culture can evolve and transform itself – witness the cultural metamorphosis that has occurred over the past fifteen years in the Iberian Peninsula – is a source of difficulty for the culturalist hypothesis: either things change because the culture itself has changed or things do not change because the culture is not yet ready for it. Culture is made to explain everything and consequently explains nothing.

Might the I-space allow us to go beyond such tautologies in our use of culture as an explanatory variable? This chapter aims to show that it can. Indeed, our purpose is more ambitious than that. It is to show that as an analytical tool, the I-space can be used to derive policy prescriptions which, strange as they might appear from more conventional perspectives, are in fact based on sound reasoning.

And a new policy orientation is urgently required: both for post-communist regimes and for reform-minded communist regimes such as those of China and Vietnam that seek to mitigate the more negative effects of a pure command economy whilst holding on to some of its main features. In both kinds of regime, the state-owned enterprise sector is currently in intensive care – kept alive by a drip feed of state subsidies that weakens the economy as a whole – and the fast burgeoning private sector has become a breeding ground for corruption and sharp practices by well-positioned bureaucrats who are turning many ordinary people against the market as a potential solution to their problems. In this chapter we use the I-space to challenge the prevailing policy assumption that for such regimes the road to economic reform is one that leads from a bureaucratic order to a market one. We shall show that while markets are indeed an essential part of any realistic policy put forward, they remain but a part and then perhaps not even the most important one.

Our strategy consists in briefly comparing the modernization of China and Japan in the I-space and applying our findings to an analysis of the challenges currently facing Eastern Europe and the FSU. Both China and Japan encountered a highly confident and expansive west in the nineteenth century and each responded to the experience with attempts at modernizing their institutions – with very different results.[3] Yet although, of the two, only China plausibly conforms to Wittfogel's thesis of Oriental despotism, both form part of the same 'culture area' with a Confucian and Buddhist inheritance acting as a important solvent of social and political practice.

The material presented in this section is based largely on my own work with Chinese industrial enterprises over a five-year period from 1984 to 1988 inclusive, as well as on that of my colleague John Child. We both, in succession, ran the China–EC Management Programme (which has now become the China–Europe International Business School) located in Beijing. The programme was initially under the wing of the State Economic Commission and then later under the Commission for the Reform of the Economic Structure. From this vantage point we both enjoyed a degree of access to Chinese state-owned enterprises which, from a data collection point of view, must be rated as unique.[4]

Since we are covering much material in little space, what is on offer here is clearly little more than illustrative of the I-space's potential as an explanatory framework. An individual *theory* is judged to be useful if it changes the way we think about things, about other theories or facts; is judged to be valid if it offers testable predictions and then survives their testing without being fatally damaged in the process. A theoretical *framework* such as the I-space, by contrast, has a broader vocation. It is judged to be useful if it is a source of fruitful theories, and it is judged to be valid if it is a source of valid theories. Only a few theories are put forward in what follows and these are not tested. We believe them to be testable, however, but until they have been subjected to more systematic scrutiny than is possible here, the case for them must rest on their coherence and plausibility rather than on their empirical corroboration.

Whether the I-space, beyond being a source of new theories, has any paradigmatic value as a way of organizing these theories into a meaningful master pattern is a matter taken up in the concluding chapter of the book.

7.2: CHINA'S MODERNIZATION

The historical setting

For two hundred years, China has experienced some difficulty locating itself in a world which it could not dominate. The Macartney embassy of 1793 to Beijing well illustrated the confident self-sufficiency of an empire closeted up in a world of its own in decline. Lord George Macartney was bringing with him gifts from George III, together with requests for trade and representation. In an edict addressed to the British monarch, which has become a classic of its kind, the Chinese emperor, Ch'ien-Lung, then in the fifty-seventh year of his reign, gently put the barbarian king in his place:

> The Celestial Court has pacified and possessed the territory within the four seas. Its sole aim is to do its utmost to achieve good government and to manage political affairs, attaching no value to strange jewels and precious objects. The various articles presented by you, O King, this time are accepted ... in consideration of the offerings having come a long distance with sincere good wishes. As a matter of fact, the virtue and prestige of the Celestial Dynasty having spread far and wide, the kings of the myriad nation come by land and sea with all sorts of precious things. Consequently there is nothing we lack ... We have never set much store on strange ingenious objects, nor do we need any more of your country's manufactures.[5]

Until the opium wars of the middle of the nineteenth century, the Chinese claims to moral and cultural superiority had gone largely unchallenged by an expansive west. Early attempts by Jesuit missionaries such as Matteo Ricci and Michele Ruggieri to use the prestige of western science as an aid to the digestion of a Christian religious message met a fierce resistance from the literati. The more discerning among them, such as Fang Yi Zhi (1611–1671), were able to tease out whatever was of scientific value in the Jesuits' offering and to reject the rest. Fang himself judged westerners to be skilled at enquiring and probing, but quite incapable of grasping the basic mysteries of the universe.[6]

In the eighteenth century, the secular qualities of Confucianism held great appeal for the French *philosophes* who were by conviction readily disposed to admire a country in which a stable and secure social order had been achieved unbolstered by religion. Perhaps the Chinese had good reason, then, to feel pleased with themselves. The available evidence indicates that by European standards, China's people were well-off. The per capita income levels computed for China at the end of the eighteenth century by Paul Bairoch and quoted by Braudel[7] give a figure of 228 US dollars (measured in 1960 dollars). This compares favourably with a European per capita income of 213 dollars at the same period. The Confucian stress on rationality subsequently found a ready echo in the strivings of the Enlightenment, and, later, the Chinese imperial system of examinations used for recruitment into the Mandarinate served as an inspiration for some of Napoleonic France's educational reforms.

China's system of government has been described by Max Weber as patrimonial. Imperial authority was charismatic, and officialdom, the pillar of public order and the state, was held to partake of that charisma.[8] A Confucian ideology thus placed the emphasis on the exercise of personal power operating through a single continuous hierarchy descending from the emperor at the top and reaching down into the smallest and remotest village of the empire.

Only it did not really reach. The old Chinese saying that 'Heaven is high and the Emperor is far' effectively summed up how the local peasants and merchants tended to view imperial edicts and decrees emanating from the Dragon Throne. What kept China together was a cellular social structure – a vast tissue of comparatively isolated and self-contained villages or groups of villages – embedded in a cohesive common culture, rather than an efficient rational–legal bureaucratic administration coordinating different elements of the body politic from afar. Had the country enjoyed a more developed and differentiated social and political structure, it must be doubted whether the ruling elite, whose preoccupations were primarily aesthetic and who were not permitted, as Balazs has nicely put it, to 'impoverish their personalities in specialization',[9] could have held the country together. Levenson, discussing the amateur ideal in Ming and early Qing society, suggests that Chinese officials were amateurs in office: 'They were trained academically, but not directly for specific tasks to be undertaken; whatever the case among aides in official yamens, mere hirelings without the proper Confucianist claim to leadership, the higher-degree-holding members of the bureaucracy – the ruling class par excellence – were not identified with expertise. The prestige of office depended on that fact.'[10]

Two features of the system effectively conspired to keep China's social structure cellular: firstly, a lack of any transport infrastructure of the type that might facilitate extensive horizontal communications and commercial exchanges among citizens beyond their immediate locality; secondly, a low rate of literacy. The written language was the only effective tool of communication that could span myriad local dialects and it was hard to master – even the ideograms inscribed on Shang dynasty oracle bones (1400–1050 BC) exceed 2,500 in number. A tiny group of literati at the top of the administrative pyramid could thus exercise, through their virtual monopoly on written means of communication, a modest degree of control over a large number of self-sufficient cells that usually found it easier to comply, even if perfunctorily, than to achieve the degree of horizontal coordination among themselves required to mobilize any resistance.[11]

Moreover, since the countries on China's borders generally posed few threats, there was little of the external pressure that had been experienced by nascent European states to strengthen the system as a whole by dissolving the cellular structure and to replace it with something more solid.[12]

Learning from the west?

China's encounter with an expanding west challenged the country's comfortable self-sufficiency. Confining British traders to the city of Canton (today Guangzhou) at the mouth of the Pearl river in order that they could be watched suggested that outside Peking the imperial writ did not run very far. China's coastal regions had always been more open to foreign cultures and influences than its interior provinces – a disposition viewed as treasonable by the more conservative elements in the imperial bureaucracy – and it was in these regions that Europe's maritime powers, Portugal, Spain, Holland, and Britain, first made their presence felt, at a comfortable distance from the country's centre of power. China's inability to respond either forcefully or coherently to the growing foreign presence in its territories was symptomatic of a dynasty in decline. The opium wars of 1839–42 and 1856–60 had shown that Confucian moral suasion would neither awe nor deter foreign intruders and that it was no substitute for effective military power, and, by implication, for the type of strong state that could develop and project it. The Taiping rebellion, for example, was one reflection of the west's disruptive influence: it was a peasant rebellion against the Manchu, the Mandarin, and the foreigner. The rebellion began in 1850 in the hills of Kwangsi near Canton and spread throughout central China. It was not suppressed until 1864 – and not without foreign assistance in the shape of a joint Anglo-French expeditionary force.[13]

Following China's repeated humiliation at the hands of European powers in the nineteenth century, the development challenge, as many Chinese would-be reformers then perceived it at the beginning of the twentieth century, was to learn from foreigners the secret of building a strong state whilst remaining untainted by their morals or their philosophy. The belief that the two could be kept separate had given rise to the slogan 'Chinese learning for the essential principles, Western learning for practical applications',[14] and to the growth of the self-strengthening movement at the end of the nineteenth century.

The passing of the old order brought about by Sun Yat-sen's Republican Revolution of 1911 did not lead to the abandoning of personal ways of exercising power. The rational–legal institutions that could have helped to 'routinize' the charisma of the emperor and subsequently given legitimacy to the new order were simply not available. The struggle to fill the power vacuum that was created by the demise of the Qing dynasty first took the form of warlordism in the 1920s and of a civil war in the 1930s fought between communists led by Mao Zedong on the one hand and nationalists led by Chiang Kai-shek on the other, a civil war which, barring an interlude in which the warring parties joined forces to fight the Japanese, did not come to a halt until the communist takeover of 1949.

The communist regime aimed to make a clean sweep of the past and to give China a new identity. Marxism-Leninism might be a foreign borrowing, but, now augmented and indigenized as Mao Zedong thought, it would take China beyond merely playing 'catch-up' with the west; through a powerful new philosophy it would also restore China's historical claim to moral superiority.[15] Paradoxically, however, Marxism-Leninism could never have succeeded in China had it not in many respects been convergent with the Confucianism that it replaced. The year 1949 may have ushered in a revolution from below in sociological terms,[16] but the discernible philosophical continuities between the new ideology and the one that it replaced – both share a dogmatic assurance that they possess the blueprint for a politically and socially just society based on the benevolent leadership of a centralized state[17] – arguably made the subsequent social and cultural transformation of the country evolutionary rather than revolutionary. As a senior party cadre once quipped to a western reporter, 'Confucius preached loyalty to the emperor. We can interpret this as loyalty to the state and to the Communist Party.'[18]

It was the personalized, charismatic, and hierarchical style of leadership that he successfully adopted, following the Long March of 1934–5 and the setting up of his base in Yanan (Shaanxi Province) in late 1936, which secured for Mao Zedong his power base within the Communist Party – a stylistic continuity with the imperial past that Mao's close collaborators would subsequently find themselves anxious to counter.[19] An opportunity presented itself with the excesses of the Great Leap Forward of 1958–9 when Mao's romantic enthusiasm and his somewhat capricious will-to-power were tragically shown to be no substitute for the kind of careful rational planning that Marxism-Leninism appeared to require if it was to fulfil its promise.

Stalin's forced industrialization of the USSR in the 1930s, inspiring as it was bound to be for prospective 'late developers',[20] was an easy policy to misunderstand and a hard one to follow. Sloppily implemented by China's illiterate peasants with little more than a few mindless slogans acting as their guide, Mao's hopelessly utopian vision resulted in the world's greatest famine ever. Millions died of starvation – Riskin's estimates range from 15 to 30 million[21] – and although in a discussion with Lord Montgomery, Mao was later to attribute the failure of the Great Leap Forward to 'inexperience, waste, and bad organization at the lower echelons' of the Communist Party,[22] as Marshal Peng Teh-hui (the defence minister) commented, 'In the view of some comrades, putting politics in command was a substitute for everything ... But putting politics in command is no substitute for economic principles, much less for concrete economic measures'.[23] The manifest failure of Mao's policies in the early 1960s allowed the party to initiate moves that aimed to limit his personal power. Many of China's current policies have their roots in the actions initiated by the country's leading pragmatists during the early 1960s to limit the damage created by the Great Leap. The much-vaunted Four Modernizations, for example, officially proclaimed to be the centrepiece of Chinese policy in early 1978, originated in Zhou Enlai's Report on the Work of the Government, made to the Third National People's Congress (NPC) in December 1964, in which he asserted that the Communist Party must 'strive to build China into a powerful socialist state with a modern agriculture, modern industry, modern national defence, and modern science and technology'.[24]

The power of charisma

In practice, it proved to be no easier to routinize Mao's charisma after the failure of the Great Leap Forward than it had been to routinize the emperor's after the advent of the Republic in 1911. For all the efforts of those who directed it, the Marxist-Leninist bureaucratic structure that had been created in the 1950s and closely modelled on the Soviet one remained stubbornly patrimonial; it lacked the essential attributes of economic rationality and legality that impart stability and legitimacy to impersonal administrative rule. It offered a natural arena for factionalism and opportunistic behaviour, and for the emergence of what Gouldner, in another context, has labelled a 'mock bureaucracy'.[25] Largely for this reason, Mao, sensing that his position was under threat, was able to counter the attempt to replace personal by bureaucratic rule by drawing on the full power of his charisma. It found its most destructive expression in the Great Proletarian Cultural Revolution that he launched in 1966.

The events of this period are well documented and need not be repeated here. Suffice it to say that the Cultural Revolution, conceived of by Mao as a cataclysmic episode that would reach into the 'very souls' of the Chinese population,[26] soon spun out of control with warring factions of Red Guards fighting each other in Mao's name.[27] What became virtually an undeclared civil war was only brought to a halt when the army was called in during the autumn of 1967 to restore order and allow the economy to function. The 'turmoil' was officially presented by Mao's successors as having gone on until Mao's death in 1976, so that the pursuit of the Four Modernizations, which was then resumed, could then be presented by the new leadership as the continuation of a policy that had been interrupted, rather than as the challenge to the Maoist inheritance that in fact it amounted to. Mao himself was then charitably depicted as a well-intentioned old man who in his dotage had fallen under the evil influence of his younger wife, Jiang Qing, and the Gang of Four.

Mao's personal rule had been the cause of untold suffering in China: economic during the Great Leap Forward; economic, social, and moral during the Cultural Revolution. The post-Mao leadership was now determined to play down the role of ideology, which had isolated China from the outside world no less than it had been at the time of the 1793 Macartney mission, and to pursue more pragmatic policies. More than anything else, it was determined to do away once and for all with the caprice of personal rule, and to work within a stable framework of laws and institutions. Reform was to be the order of the day, pragmatic reform shielded from ideological attacks by Mao's own dictum that 'practice was the sole criterion of truth' and his exhortation to 'seek truth from facts'.

Policy reorientations

Although never explicitly presented as such to foreigners, the economic reforms initiated by the Third Plenum of the Eleventh Central Committee of the Chinese Communist Party in December 1979 were at least philosophically inspired by the Hungarian reforms of 1968 – the New Economic Mechanism (NEM) – where they were not closely modelled on them. These in turn drew much of their own legitimacy from Lenin's New Economic Policy (NEP) of 1921–8.[28] Two years after the October Revolution of 1917 in Russia, and following the ravages of 'war communism' (1918–20), it had become obvious to all but the most doctrinaire Marxists that a command economy would need some form of accommodation with market processes if it was to function at all, at least in the early phases of its construction. Marx himself had left the door open for this eventuality by concentrating much of his wrath on monopoly capitalism rather than on 'petty commodity traders'.[29] However, Lenin, in the somewhat coy phrase of Su Xing, the deputy editor of the People's Liberation Army's newspaper *Red Flag*, 'was the first in the annals of Marxist political economy to confirm the existence of commodities and currency in a socialist society'.[30] Ideology therefore appeared to pose no insuperable obstacles to the presence of markets in a communist state providing that they occupied a clearly subordinate role and posed no institutional threat to what was still intended to be predominantly a hierarchically organized bureaucratic order. They were viewed as little more than a lubricant, a stimulus to greater efficiency. Chen Yun, party elder and conservative, had clearly stipulated that central planning should predominate, with market forces as a 'useful supplement, not harmful on the whole'.[31] In post-Mao China, then, party loyalists would be reassured by the official slogan that 'the market regulates prices and the state regulates the market'.

The party was to remain very much in charge. In fact the market, as understood in the west, was not much in evidence in the first raft of economic reforms undertaken in China, those that were initiated in agriculture in Sichuan Province in 1978. They were experimental and limited in scope. Farms were to be de-collectivized and allowed to produce for the market as well as for the state. Once production for state quotas had been completed, peasant families – now once more the basic production unit – were free to produce what they liked and sell it on rural markets at higher prices. The response to these modest measures was a considerable increase in agricultural production and a rapid growth in rural incomes. The experiment was then extended to the rest of the country so that by the end of 1983 it had become nationwide.

It is important to note the very local character of these early reforms. The markets created by the reforms were rural ones – of the type that predominated during the Qing dynasty – and the extra food produced was mostly for local consumption. The Maoist quest for local self-sufficiency had effectively maintained the cellular structure inherited from the country's imperial past and blocked the interregional integration of markets. Market integration was in any case never going to be easy in a country where as late as 1985 36 per cent of villages had no passable road for vehicles and where on average there was only one truck for every 3,375 farmers.[32] Contrary to the popular western vision of China as a single vast market of over a billion people, therefore, it would be probably fairer to describe it as a million markets of a thousand people each.

The mechanics of economic reform

As the agricultural reforms gathered pace, Chinese policy-makers turned their attention to industry. Revitalizing state-owned enterprises (SOEs) was the most urgent requirement if the goal of quadrupling 1980 gross industrial and agricultural output value by the year 2000, as put forward at the 12th National Congress of the Chinese Communist Party in 1982, was to be met.[33] Collective and family businesses might be left to their own devices but 85 per cent of urban workers were employed by SOEs, and in this sector from 1957 to 1977 the value added per unit of capital had dropped by 40 per cent.[34] But such revitalization was going to be a far more delicate matter, politically speaking, since unlike agricultural reform, industrial reform, to be effective, would require administrative decentralization. This was carried out as a two-step process, the first one consisting of a delegation of administrative authority over enterprises to provincial and city level administrations, the second one consisting of a decentralization of economic powers to enterprise managers.[35]

As early as 1979 over one hundred state-owned enterprises in Sichuan Province had been granted some discretion by central government over their production and marketing activities. They had also been allowed some retention of profits and depreciation funds, both of which they had hitherto handed over to the state as legitimate owner of the business. By the end of 1980 most provinces were running experiments in enterprise management covering some 6,600 SOEs. By the end of 1982 a contract responsibility system similar to the one that had been introduced in agriculture in 1980 was being tried out in an attempt to clarify the rights and duties of industrial firms.[36]

The first of the two steps towards administrative decentralization, namely the transfer of responsibility for the management of all but the largest state-owned enterprises from the central government in Beijing to provincial governments and to city governments, was not free of ambiguities and potential contradictions. Along with the transfer of responsibilities, and in compensation for it, went access to a significant part of the revenues generated by these enterprises. Yet state ownership was state ownership whether the property rights it bestowed were exercised at the centre or at the periphery of the system. No ideological principle, therefore, appeared to be at issue in these measures at the time when they were enacted.

Administrative delegation in China was in fact a periodic response to an age-old dilemma: centralize and see the economy stagnate under the bureaucracy's dead hand; decentralize and face chaos as the particularistic forces of local interests overwhelm the bureaucratic machine's ability to control them. The dilemma was symptomatic of the country's lack of an administrative infrastructure through which the centre could extend its writ, a situation which plagued the communist regime no less than the imperial dynasties and the republic that had preceded it. Local interpretation and implementation of ambiguously worded instructions or regulations emanating from a distant centre varied widely and effectively blocked the administrative integration and coordination that we have come to associate with the modern nation-state. Ironically, then, to a greater extent even than in the FSU, Marxist-Leninist practice as interpreted and applied in China bred economic irrationality and incoherence throughout industry. Far from speeding up the modernization of state structures, however, it only served to perpetrate the rule of a patrimonial bureaucracy and an imperial system of governance quite at odds with the country's actual development needs.

Administrative delegation within the state apparatus, as we have just seen, was not the only reform measure envisaged. In October 1984, a key policy document was issued by the Party Central Committee entitled 'China's Economic Structure Reform',[37] increasing enterprise autonomy in certain areas beyond what had been initiated in 1979, and permitting certain prices to float. In February 1985, SOEs were granted the discretion to plan their own technological developments, and in September 1985, large and medium-sized SOEs were given the freedom to pursue their own marketing policies. That year also saw the generalization of a fiscal reform that had been introduced experimentally in 1983 and in which profit remittances to the state were replaced by a 55 per cent tax on profits.

These measures had the effect of moving the centre of gravity of the reform process from the countryside into the cities, the heartland of the bureaucracy's power base and, by implication, of any resistance that the changes might provoke.

As with the agricultural reforms, the decentralization of decision-making power to industrial enterprises and to those who managed them turned out to be extremely modest by western standards. Under the old, centralized system, an enterprise manager had no discretion whatsoever over what went on in his firm. He was in effect little more than a technician required to implement a meticulously detailed set of instructions emanating from an industrial bureau supervising his sector and concerning every conceivable aspect of his business. There were national bureaux, provincial bureaux, and city level bureaux whose job it was to integrate numerous requirements coming from different parts of the state bureaucracy – the State Planning Commission, the State Economic Commission, the Sectoral Ministries, the Territorial Authorities, etc. – and pass them on to the various enterprises under their care in the form of a coherent set of instructions. The Chinese Communist Party, whose own organization shadowed the state structure at every level both inside and outside the enterprise, was there to see that these instructions were carried out in line with government policy. Yet since many of these instructions were actually in conflict with one another or turned out to be unfeasible – as, for example, when a provincial or city administration arbitrarily imposed on firms in its charge production quotas that were additional to those established by the State Planning Commission – managers could rarely be held responsible for failing to implement them; they often experienced little trouble therefore in renegotiating them to suit their firm's actual capacities or – more plausibly – their own personal inclinations. The systematic renegotiation and erosion of plan targets by enterprise managers is a pervasive feature of all communist economies; it has been baptized the 'soft budget constraint' by the Hungarian economist Janos Kornai;[38] it is nothing more than a reflection of the deeply rooted irrationalities that plague all attempts at central planning.

With the enterprise reforms, all this was now set to change. In future, managers would have greater discretion to make decisions on matters such as product mix and prices but would henceforth be held directly responsible for their firm's profits and losses.

Before this could happen, of course, the term profit itself had to be rendered operationally meaningful. Since, until 1984, all profits made by a state-owned firm were handed over to the state[39] and all losses incurred by the enterprise were made good by state subsidies, remitted profits could hardly serve as an incentive to effort and efficiency. Managerial and worker motivation was now to be fostered by allowing firms to hold on to their profits and to remit to the state what was called an income tax – in western parlance a corporate tax. As we saw earlier, this was fixed at 55 per cent of pre-tax profits. Post-tax enterprise profits were then to be allocated in roughly equal parts to three funds, one from which worker bonuses could be paid, one for employee welfare expenditures – medical facilities, housing, schools, etc. – and one for investment in new technology and equipment.

But how convincingly could profit be used as a yardstick for measuring performance? After all, profit in a market system has another function than simply rewarding effort: that of acting as a signal for the efficient allocation of scarce resources. It can only act in this way in conjunction with a price system which makes a credible distinction between the revenue generated by a sale and the costs effectively incurred in securing the sale. Properly measured and generalized, profit then becomes a faithful reflection of the forces at play in the economic system as a while. A resource allocation process triggered by differences in profitability between alternative possibilities will be less wasteful of a society's resources than one which is insensitive to such differences. It is said to exhibit a greater degree of economic rationality. Prices, in the People's Republic of China (PRC) as in other centrally planned economies, were so far from being able to contribute coherently to the resource allocation process that a significant number of SOEs had become 'value subtractors'; i.e., the value of their inputs, when measured at world prices, exceeded the value of their outputs using the same measures.

Prices, however, whatever the ambitions of Chinese reformers, were still considered politically too 'hot' to touch. Any attempt to correct decades of accumulated distortions, it was argued, would lead to social unrest and threaten the stability of the regime. Prices therefore were to be reformed at a later date. Yet since it was clear that in the meantime, given the new freedoms granted to enterprise managers, some firms would be making – and holding on to – windfall profits and others would be incurring unsustainable losses purely on account of irrationalities in the price system, an 'adjustment tax' would be set for each firm by its supervising bureau to ensure that profitability would be equalized across all the firms in its care so that none would either benefit or suffer too much.[40] The level of the adjustment tax was set by negotiations between an individual firm and its supervising bureau. The tax was considered necessary since worker bonuses inside each firm were tied to its reported profits and workers might find it hard to believe, given the prevailing pricing practices, that the firm's profitability or lack of it was in any way a reflection of their own performance. If the reforms were to work, they had to be perceived as fair by those called upon to implement them.

The preferred instrument for bringing about decentralization to enterprises was the contract, a Chinese variant on western Management by Objectives (MBO) techniques often pretty far removed from the voluntary arm's-length process that industrial societies commonly associate with contracting. Until the 6th National People's Congress of May 1984, SOEs were controlled through a 'Director Responsibility System Under the Leadership of the Party'. At Deng Xiaoping's suggestion the congress replaced this mechanism with a 'Director Responsibility System'. It was followed in 1986 and 1987 by the introduction of a bewildering array of responsibility systems, the most common of which was the 'Contract Management Responsibility System' in which enterprise targets were set four years in advance to coincide with the last four years of the 7th Five-Year Plan (1987–90).[41] All these responsibility systems shared a common feature: they shifted the risk for performance on to the contractor and rewarded or penalized him/her accordingly. In each case a contract would be drawn up between an enterprise manager and the bureau responsible for its supervision. The contract would specify production targets of certain goods and services that the firm was expected to meet in order to fulfil the state plan in its sector. The state would set the price at which these had to be made available to the state distribution system and would also specify product and technical changes to be carried out by the firm in its next planning period. Once its plan targets had been met the firm was free to produce for the market. For this part of its production, however, the firm had to secure its own inputs as best it could outside the plan – for its planned output it was guaranteed supplies by the state – and to find its own distribution outlets.

Delegation versus decentralization

The above discussion offers but a small sample of what has been an extensive and complex process. Many important features of the reforms not relevant to the next section's discussion – such as the opening up of the country to foreign trade (the Open Door Policy) and the creation of Special Economic Zones (SEZs) – have been omitted. Since the reforms are an ongoing process no judgement on their future prospects can be final. Something, however, can be said about the pattern that was beginning to emerge in the state-owned sector by the end of the 1980s, a pattern that endures in the 1990s.

To grasp the pattern, a conceptual distinction must be drawn between delegation and decentralization. In casual discourse the two terms are rarely distinguished; yet this must be done if the challenge of industrial reform in China is to be fully grasped.

In a regime of delegation an agency relationship is established in which an agent is granted some discretion concerning the means he will use to serve the interests of a principal. The principal articulates his interests as a set of goals that the agent is required to pursue. The relationship established between principal and agent is a hierarchical one, expressed within organizations through an employment contract and between organizations through long-term contracts or other institutional means. A hierarchical relationship facilitates the monitoring of the agent by the principal and monitoring is necessary to forestall the opportunistic behaviour by the agent – i.e., the substituting of the agent's own goals for those of the principal.

In a regime of decentralization, by contrast, the agent is free to pursue his own goals since some degree of goal congruence is assumed to exist between principal and agent.[42] Thus the latter, in pursuing his own interests, also serves those of his principal. Monitoring may still be necessary to ensure that goal congruence actually obtains but this will be a much lighter business than with delegation. The relationship may have to be regulated but not necessarily by hierarchical means. This is the 'invisible hand' argument for a decentralized market order. Thus in principle, although it pushes decisions towards the base of a decision pyramid, delegation retains a strong element of hierarchical coordination whereas decentralization moves the system further towards horizontal self-regulation. The first requires a certain minimum volume of vertical information flows so that the top of the pyramid can monitor the base; the second, a larger volume of horizontal information flows to allow for a mutual adjustment of the different elements at the base of the pyramid.

The territorial delegation of power to provinces and cities attempted by the Chinese leadership at the beginning of the 1980s to revitalize the economy very quickly ran up against the fact that the Chinese state lacked the communication and information mechanisms that would allow it to control the delegation process effectively. Administrative regulations emanating from the centre were more often than not contradictory or ambiguous in their phrasing, just as they had been in earlier times. And local interpretation of central government instructions, in the absence of a physical presence representing the centre, could always be moulded to fit in undisruptively with local interests. Furthermore, the information relayed back to the centre and on which much of its own policy formulation depended was in turn either ambiguous or distorted. The centre had therefore to be physically present locally to some degree if the system was to function at all – hence the endless 'inspection tours' by central government organs having to rely on their own eyes and ears to sense what was really going on down at the base.[43]

In part, the need for personalized forms of control resides in Chinese culture itself: a deeply rooted preference for an implicit communication style in which much is left unsaid puts a premium on face-to-face relationships where a tone of voice, a gesture, and the context itself become important aids to the proper interpretation of a message.[44] Furthermore, the near total absence of a viable legal system in China creates a powerful incentive to avoid destructive conflict through such interpersonal forms of accommodation.[45] Until 1979, the country did not even have a published criminal code[46] and as late as 1985, according to the Minister of Justice, it had less than 10,000 lawyers.[47] For this reason civil disputes are dealt with mostly through mediation. Of the 68,000 civil disputes that passed through the Shanghai Jurisdiction Bureau in 1985, for example, 66,000 were handled through mediation and the rest through the courts. At the time, the city boasted 40,000 mediators; most were retired workers or teachers who worked unpaid. They were, of course, also untrained.

Yet the need for corrective personalized interaction must also be attributed in good measure to the intrinsic irrationality in a Marxist-Leninist order of the messages emanating from the centre. The all-seeing bureaucrat coordinating things from the centre according to a rational plan turned out in the PRC – as indeed in other centrally planned economies – to be neither all-seeing nor able to coordinate much of anything.

To illustrate: the socialist system of accounting, introduced in the mid-1950s, was designed to serve the needs of the state as it had done in ancient times – in the Qing dynasty, accountants were government officials responsible to the emperor. In practice, as an aid to the structuring and interpretation of financial data, it is much closer to a book-keeping than to an accounting system, and as a book-keeping system it offers three variants that a firm can choose from: debit–credit (the western system); receiving–paying (the traditional Chinese system); plus–minus (a hybrid).[48] The ability of such an accounting system to deliver a 'true and fair view' of an organization's financial position is, to say the least, pretty weak, and any supervising agency that placed undue reliance on a firm's financial reporting system for the purpose of coordination and control would drown in a sea of fragmentary and contradictory data that it could neither master nor understand. What sense, for example, could it make of the fact that for each of six years running, the Beijing No. 2 Automobile Manufacturing Plant had remitted profits to the state that were twice the book value of its fixed assets?[49] If markets were 'blind' – the conservative planner Chen Yun's oft repeated criticism of the market order – then, it would appear, so were the state officials sitting atop an unreconstructed patrimonial bureaucracy.

As a consequence of this absence of effective administrative control mechanisms, what had been originally intended to be a limited delegation of power in which the interests of the centre would continue to be served by provincial and city governments quickly transformed itself into a *de facto* decentralization in which the latter felt free to pursue their own local interests beyond the reach of central controls. Recently developed SOEs thus became a valuable resource for local authorities, a resource that could be squeezed for financial contribution towards, say, projects that had been locally approved but denied central government funding. The available evidence indicates that such 'squeezing' increased significantly in the aftermath of the 1984–6 enterprise reforms.[50]

A second problem that plagued attempts at economic decentralization was that local interests remained steadfastly local. Decentralization in a properly functioning market system quickly leads to coordination based upon a rapid horizontal flow of information between economic agents. The spatial extent of the market is in effect established by the number of agents that can be reached in a timely fashion by such information. Absent the horizontal flow of information, and the self-regulating quality of market processes disappears. Information under the new economic regime in the PRC, however, was no more inclined to flow horizontally between territorial units such as cities or provinces than it had been to flow vertically between such units and the centre. An age-old concern with self-sufficiency and local autonomy – which Mao himself had done much to reinforce – tended to block such flows. The traditional cellular structure of Chinese society was reasserting itself through the reforms. In the language of the I-space: not markets, not hierarchies, but clans and fiefs.

The local quest for autonomy manifested itself in several ways. One was a revival of local protectionism that blocked the flow of imports and exports across provincial boundaries. In 1985, for example, the Shanghai city authorities issued an edict forbidding the export of beer to other provinces by local breweries; it also pressured local retailers against selling beer not produced locally. And in 1988, to take another example, Hunan Province set up its own customs patrols along its provincial boundaries to stop its peasants from selling their pigs in neighbouring Guangdong Province at the higher prices available there.

Another area in which local autonomy found expression was in the reduction of tax remittances to the central government: from over 70 per cent in the early 1980s to just over 25 per cent in 1989.[51] China's central government has today a smaller share of total tax revenues than any country in the world – even in a country as decentralized as the United States, the federal share of tax revenues is 60 per cent. In effect, the Chinese government practises 'tax farming', as did the Qing dynasty before it,[52] using provincial and city administrations to collect predetermined amounts of revenues whose levels are set largely independently of taxable capacity, given the central administration's inability to assess this. Local authorities, better informed of local taxable capacity, are then free to collect and retain revenues well in excess of the central government's targets. The government's loss of fiscal control to provincial authorities was also being matched by its loss of monetary control. Under central planning, the creation of credit had been securely tied to the plan and control of the money supply was located in the Ministry of Finance. With the reduction in the scope of central planning, firms were increasingly required to secure the financial resources they needed through local borrowing. Provincial and city branches of the People's Bank of China and other state banks were far more responsive to the pressures that could be put on them by local authorities than by Beijing, pressures that would lead to lending to non-viable enterprises with little prospect of repayment. Thus the creation of credit passed increasingly under local control and in many respects quite explicitly: one could, for example, read in the *China Daily* that appeared on 4 April 1985 that 'Hebei Province is taking drastic measures to soak up an excess currency supply after pumping too much money into circulation last year.'[53]

The 'drastic measures' undertaken by provincial governments were not always economically sophisticated. Shandong Province, for example, in a bid to soak up an excess 1.5 billion yuan in circulation at the beginning of 1985, 'ordered retailing departments at all levels to boost clothing production and sales, to put more pork and eggs on the market, to develop food processing industry, and to push the sale of jewelry'.[54]

The refeudalization of state-owned enterprises

To summarize, the most telling way in which newly acquired local autonomy worked against the market-oriented thrust of the reforms as a whole resided in the control that the latter gave to local authorities over the firms and other state organizations in their care. Indeed, with devolution such firms became 'their' property, to be exploited by them for local purposes as they saw fit. As Bai Jimian, secretary of the Shaanxi Provincial Party Committee, put it in a letter to the *People's Daily* in 1986, 'Some leaders regard the departments or units entrusted to them by the Party as independent kingdoms ... and have turned the relationship between the leader and the led into one of feudal personal attachment.'[55] The centre had in effect granted local authorities industrial fiefs, and in circumstances that often promoted a kind of industrial feudalism: firms seeking protection from competition – i.e., from better-quality products imported from outside the locality, from the workings of the new bankruptcy law, etc. – would informally pledge loyalty and obedience to their local supervising bureau and do its bidding, often well beyond the provisions of any 'contract' that their managers might have signed. The price of such protection could be high. A 1986 survey by inspectors from the State Council in Shaanxi and Sichuan Provinces discovered that more than ninety different kinds of 'forced contributions' had been levied on state-run or collective enterprises, robbing them of 5 per cent to 15 per cent of their annual income. Contributions fell into three categories: the funding of urban construction projects by local governments, donations to various 'foundations' set up by local organizations, and extortions for personal favours by local agencies with regulatory power over firms. The vulnerability of collective and township enterprises to this kind of behaviour was even greater than that of SOEs for, unlike the latter, they could not recover their losses through subsidies from the state. The same survey, for example, reported that 137 collective enterprises in Sichuan Province were forced to contribute 49 per cent of their total profits to various local agencies.[56]

The potential for bureaucratic interference by external agencies in enterprise management in the PRC is hard for a westerner to imagine. If anything, the enterprise reforms have increased this potential. Prior to the reforms, the industrial bureau supervising a firm provided it with 'one umbrella' that could shelter it from 'many gods'. Following the reforms, looser relations with the bureau removed the umbrella, thus allowing the 'many gods' direct access to the firm.[57] In many cases it became little more than a lemon to be squeezed for resources, and the more profitable it was the more intensive became the squeeze. Local administrative bodies known as the 'mothers-in-law' (MILs) would swoop down upon a hapless firm for 'inspections', charging a fee here, imposing a fine there, or, in the absence of any more profitable opportunities, requesting a banquet for its officials.[58] Often these MILs would insist on maintaining an office and staff permanently on a firm's premises with costs and salaries being charged to the enterprise. One firm of 3,000 people that I visited in the summer of 1987 had to 'accommodate' twenty-two different MILs in this fashion![59]

The refeudalization of the Chinese enterprise was by no means a uniform phenomenon. The more capitalistic provinces such as Guangdong and Fujian gave their firms considerably greater margin for manoeuvre than, say, the northern or western Chinese provinces. Yet, generally speaking, the intended decentralization of power to enterprise managers from the centre was more often than not converted into a much more limited delegation of power from the local authority that now owned it.[60] The separation of the firm from its supervising bureaucracy did not take place – the organizational tissue was continuous across the state–firm interface. Even if both parties wanted it, a separation would be extremely painful. The mutual interdependencies were too great. If the firm sought the protection of the local authorities against the waywardness of the economic environment, the latter in turn depended on SOEs for the performance of many municipal functions. SOEs, for example, were responsible for the provision of 75 per cent of all houses and flats built between 1982 and 1987.[61] Most were also required to provide their workers and dependants with medical services, schooling, transport, and recreational facilities. Given such independence, therefore, the enterprise manager found himself, no less than before, renegotiating targets set and quotas allocated by his organizational superiors. The skilled negotiator in this system was the one who had built up a network of personal relationships (*guanxi*) among the power brokers outside and immediately above the firm. To be a skilled manager without being at the same time a skilled negotiator did not get one very far in Deng's China, enterprise reforms notwithstanding.

The internal management of state-owned enterprises

The internal management of state-owned enterprises appeared for the most part to be only slightly affected by the reforms. A study of eleven Beijing-based SOEs indicated that while there had occurred a modest decentralization of authority from state bodies to firms, inside the firm a recentralization had taken place.[62] Agency theory would account for such recentralization in terms of the increasingly uncertain local environment that enterprise managers confronted under the reforms,[63] and a time study of six enterprise directors concluded that whatever centralization existed in their firms, it was of a highly personalized nature.[64] It also appeared that irrationality in the firm's external environment bred irrationality in its internal environment. 'Internal contracting' took place in many enterprises, at the instigation of their supervising bureaux – they themselves responding to central government directives. It was extended to different units within the organization using the same principles as those that obtained between the firm and its supervising bureaucracy. A firm's production workshops, for example, would 'sell' their products to each other at a volume and at a transfer price set by the firm's top management. If one workshop managed to sell its output to other units in the firm at a volume in excess of the targets that had been set it would be allowed to keep the surplus 'profit' this produced, using it for bonus and welfare payments to its members. The trick for senior managers, then, was to establish an internal transfer pricing system that would be fair to all. In practice, this proved to be almost impossible in the absence of a credible market price that could act as a focusing mechanism for intra-organizational negotiations. Some workshops would strike it lucky, even being able to build their own exclusive sports facilities out of the profits made in this way, while others lost out and were penalized. Unsurprisingly, a feeling of unfairness was pervasive in many enterprises that practised internal contracting in this way, and often one of the main concerns of senior enterprise management was to ensure either that everyone got pretty much the same bonus regardless of the workshop he happened to work for, or at least that rewards going to different units did not get too far out of line with each other. Industrial logic hardly got a look in.

One important reason for the lack of coherence of internal management systems, as we have just seen, was that the absence of a rational price system outside the enterprise deprived the latter of any meaningful signals for the calibration of its internal accounting, planning, and control systems. Nobody who had to work within the system could ever afford to place too much faith in the accuracy or relevance of the accounting information produced by the firm. We have already alluded to the fragmentary nature and questionable usefulness of much of this data. But there was another, more sinister, reason for caution: cases were reported in which a firm's accountant was physically assaulted by workers if he probed too carefully the figures given out by a workshop on its output.[65] Such information, therefore, could hardly form a credible basis for evaluating individual or collective performance. Partly as a consequence of this, any evaluation that might be attempted had to be subjective and for the most part arbitrary, thus placing considerable personal power in the hands of those called upon to perform it. Usually, the best way to avoid intractable conflicts with a firm's workforce was to avoid making discriminatory performance evaluations altogether. For want of reliable performance data, then, a deeply entrenched egalitarianism operating at the enterprise level tended to survive all attempts at eradicating it. Indeed, if anything, the available evidence suggests that in certain respects the reforms tended to reinforce it. Although working with a sample of firms that was too small to yield a statistically significant result, Child, in a 1990 replication of a 1985 study, not only saw little or no variation in bonus levels paid out to workers, but also noted a considerable narrowing of differential earnings between enterprise directors and the lowest-paid non-apprentice workers compared to the earlier study.[66]

Outside the state-owned sector

If the economic reforms gave disappointing results within state-owned enterprises, the same cannot be said of collective and township enterprises, and of small private firms. These were smaller than state-owned firms and much less favoured in terms of the technology or the quality of the human resources that they were allocated by the state. For this reason, and because they were much more numerous and spatially scattered, they tended to escape more easily the attention of the supervising bureaucracy. The Shanghai tax authorities, for example, in one of their sweeps on 'registered individual businessmen' – they seized the books of 10,361 of these – established that 86 per cent of them were dodging their taxes.[67]

The absence of material privileges enjoyed by these firms was often more than compensated for by the extra freedom that they enjoyed, a freedom made doubly secure by the fact that the majority operated in rural areas often beyond bureaucratic reach. How else could the Kunshan Television Factory, started by peasants in Jiangsu Province in 1984 with a total investment of 4.5 million yuan, have produced 36 million yuan's worth of black and white television sets and a profit of 3 million yuan by 1986? As *The Economist* pointed out in its 1987 Survey of China's Economy, this made the company nearly twenty times more productive per unit of capital employed than the giant Baoshan steelworks located fifty miles outside Shanghai – and infinitely more profitable, since the latter was making a loss.[68]

In the small enterprise sector in China, a crude but genuine capitalist order has been in the making since the early 1980s, more often than not *in spite of* the reforms rather than because of them. Private and collective firms – the latter in many cases private firms in disguise – began slowly to 'hollow out' the SOEs they had so long been dominated by, some by acting as subcontractors to them, others, particularly in downstream consumer markets, by becoming their direct competitors. The consequent loss of relative economic power by SOEs has been startling: between 1978 and 1991 the SOE sector's contribution as a proportion of total industrial output dropped from 80 per cent to 55 per cent. In the same period, the collective sector's contribution grew from 19.8 per cent to 35 per cent, and that of the individual/private sector grew from 0.2 per cent to 5.1 per cent.

We conclude this section by noting the irony in China's present situation. Enterprise reforms that had been intended to revitalize the state sector had the probable effect of weakening it further by creating a virtually private sector nimble enough to compete with it. China's SOEs, like those of the post-socialist economies of Eastern and Central Europe and the CIS, are finding it very difficult to adapt themselves to a more marketing-oriented environment. Yet in China, the SOE sector, in contrast to the situation, say, in the CIS, may never have been large enough to act as a brake on grass-root reforms once these have taken hold. To illustrate this point, we compare the size distribution of Chinese firms with those of the two most 'liberal' socialist economies of the 1980s (see Table 7.1).

The structures of central planning in China may, as Child has suggested,[69] have been 'sedimented'[70] in the state-owned sector, thus reducing its capacities of adaptation to a market environment. But this merely left the field free for the small, adaptive, rurally based firms to sow the seeds of a new capitalist order. It is because China is a 'late developer',[71] with 75 per cent of its population still living in rural areas, that it has been able to dismantle the apparatus of central planning that continues to hinder the growth of such an order in other socialist countries.

Table 7.1 Comparative size distribution of Chinese firms

Size of firm by no. of employees	Size distribution (%)		
	China (1982)	Yugoslavia (1981)	Hungary (1981)
5–33	59.2	6.6	2.2
34–75	19.5	15.8	4.8
76–189	12.2	32.1	18.7
190–243	8.5	12.0	65.1
+243	0.6	33.5	9.2

7.3: INTERPRETATION

The role of bureaucracy in the modernization process

How might the I-space help us to make sense of China's various attempts at modernization and in particular the one it initiated in 1978 and continues today? Can it add anything to what we already know?

In addressing this issue we shall start from a simple but plausible premise: particularistic cultural values and an underdeveloped communication infrastructure locate all pre-modern societies in the lower region of the I-space, where fief and clan forms of organization predominate. Modernization might then plausibly be interpreted as a gradual progression up the space, towards a greater degree of codification and abstraction of social and economic exchange and a more explicit articulation of social structure. Durkheim registers the move through the progressive division of labour, Tönnies in terms of the depersonalization of social relationships, and Weber through the growth of rational–legal forms of administration and economic activity.[72]

It is worth noting in passing that Marx's oft-quoted description of capitalist development is shown in the I-space to be incomplete in one important respect. His 'stages' model of development has a feudal order giving way to a market order in various European countries at some point between the late fifteenth century and the end of the eighteenth century.[73] Yet a market society itself could only properly be built on the back of a strong bureaucratic and mercantile state which itself emerged in Europe as a distinct stage during a phase of absolutism. The evolution of market society then followed the progressive decentralization of economic power from the absolutist state to a new group of actors, a rising bourgeoisie that operated within a framework of laws and institutions still codified and controlled by the state. In Europe, in other words, the move was initially from a feudal economic order with power concentrated in fiefs – the governance of small numbers in the I-space – to one in which the crown gradually gained the ascendancy, consolidating its dominion over much larger populations, both by its monopoly of the means of coercion – i.e., a standing army that had to be paid for and equipped – and by the creation of a rational–legal administration that could finance such means as well as complement them in the projection of royal power. As J.F. Bosher put it, the new bureaucracies that emerged in Europe during the seventeenth and eighteenth centuries became 'the ultimate administrative weapon' whereby nation-states were forged.[74] This evolving absolute state was located in the region of the I-space labelled bureaucracy.[75] It was only as the self-regulating power of markets became better understood and hence itself amenable to some form of indirect state supervision that an absolute, or sometimes less-than-absolute, monarch was willing to trade in his tight direct control of domestic economic activity and foreign trade in return for a more arm's-length and looser relationship

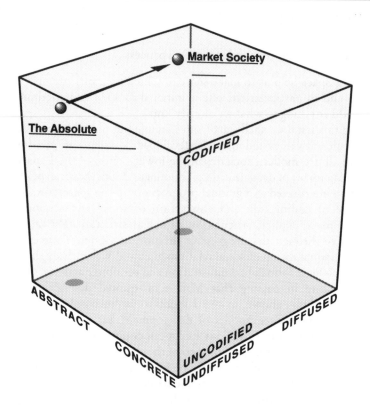

Figure 7.1 From the absolute state to market society

with a larger set of economic agents – a move to the right in the I-space (Figure 7.1).[76] Holland was the first European nation to take this path, followed by Britain and then France.

The communist revolutions in Russia and China occurred in pre-modern societies, something that puzzled doctrinaire Marxists who had expected them to take place in developed capitalist nations[77] – Marx had after all depicted communism as a stage beyond capitalism towards which all market societies were being propelled by ineluctable historical laws. Yet our use of the I-space should spare us any sense of surprise at what actually happened: a Marxist-Leninist order is but one possible institutional outcome of an attempt to move out from fiefs and into bureaucracies; if Europe's earlier industrial experience is any guide, it corresponded to the absolutist phase of a modernization process, one in which codified, abstract, and hierarchical forms of control predominate. Markets, if anything, would *follow* this phase, rather than precede it. They would do so fitfully and messily in most cases, thus marking the transition from a centripetal to a centrifugal order. In sum, Marx believed that he had identified the organizing and ideological principles of a post-industrial society. Transformed by Lenin into a programme, however, it became a blueprint to be followed by pre-modern ones.[78]

The challenge of moving up the I-space

Our earlier discussion of the social learning cycle in Chapter 4 emphasized the conflict-laden nature of moves up the I-space. The acts of codification and abstraction force explicit choices between alternatives which subsequently often erode the discretionary power of those making decisions. Max Weber describes the outcome as a routinization of charisma in which power that resides in persons is by degrees partly transferred to impersonal institutions and to roles.[79] A second source of conflict associated with a move up the I-space results from increasing pressures to decentralize – a natural consequence of forces set in motion by the inherent diffusibility of codified and abstract data. When codified decisions, and the abstract knowledge on which they are based, become visible to all and amenable to analysis, and hence to challenge or questioning, the very ubiquity of data used erodes the bureaucratic monopoly on decision-making.

Although only careful research could settle the points, one could possibly argue that the FSU was more beset by the second kind of conflict – arising from pressures to decentralize – than the first, whereas in the case of China, although pressures to decentralize have been ever present, the conflicts associated with the processes of codification and abstraction themselves have predominated.[80] We shall briefly discuss the case of the FSU in section 7.6. Here we explore further China's attempts to move up the I-space. They have for the most part been frustrated.

At first sight it may seem strange to suggest that China has experienced any problem at all in moving up the I-space towards a bureaucratic order. Had not the country's celestial bureaucracy, after all, been a source of inspiration for the *philosophes* of the Enlightenment and most notably for Voltaire? Had not the Chinese mandarinate provided a model of secular administration for Europe's emerging nation-states?[81]

It is not always easy to peer through the cultural veil and see what is really going on in a society radically different from one's own. The wrong signals get picked up and amplified. They are then interpreted through the use of inappropriate models. The 'etic' language used by outside observers can also sometimes leave participants in a culture perplexed and unable to provide corrective insights. China has a long history of being misunderstood by the west – and vice versa. So it was that the Chinese administrative model so admired two hundred or so years ago was characterized by two distinctive features which, had they been properly understood at the time, might have somewhat tempered European enthusiasm for them:

1   It subjected a simple and cellular agrarian society to an imperial form of governance that had quite different aims from those of the nation-state. Simplifying somewhat and drawing on Kant's Categorical Imperative we might say that one of the distinguishing features of the nation-state is that it is required to treat its members partly as ends – at least in theory – whereas an empire treats them as means. When applied to the Chinese case, the function of the central administration in this second scheme was to secure just enough social and economic stability to collect the rice tax, the principal source of imperial revenue – a policy that Heckscher labels *provisioning* to distinguish it from more mercantilist alternatives.[82] In effect, a tiny mandarinate in Beijing sat atop a vast mound of peasants from which they were quite detached and which they controlled indirectly through a small class of lower gentry, themselves domesticated by their own aspiration to upward mobility. The absence in imperial China – in contrast to Japan – of any thriving and independent merchant class made a move up into the state bureaucracy the only viable career option for young talent.[83]

2   Moves up the codification scale through imperial edicts and regulations were based on ritualistic rather than on rational–legal principles. A formalism uninformed by the power of abstraction thus governed official transactions. Patrimonialism kept the Chinese bureaucracy particularistic; impersonal rules, expressing a belief in a universalistic abstract order, found little application in a system based upon personal power games. Any institutional development that might take place further up the I-space remained precarious and subject to frequent lapses back down the I-space. The reliance on personal power and inter-personal accommodation characteristic of fiefs would always be pre-ferred. The effective administrative reach of Qing bureaucracy (particularly late Qing), appearances to the contrary notwithstanding, was extremely limited.[84]

The most notable and systematic attempts made by China in our own century to move up the I-space towards a more codified and abstract form of governance occurred after 1949, following the communists' arrival in power and the creation of the People's Republic. Marxist-Leninist doctrine offered a comforting explanation for China's failure to modernize where Japan had succeeded – the continued depredations of the western imperialist powers from the opium wars onwards inflicted on a country weakened by a moribund political system[85] – as well as a programme to address the issues – the creation of a Soviet-inspired command economy based on a rational allocation and equitable distribution of resources performed by an omnis-cient bureaucracy.[86] This bureaucracy, however, was beholden to a charis-matic leader, Mao Zedong, who was not slow to realize that whatever institutionalization of the country's political and administrative life might be required for the effective exercise of central bureaucratic control could only act as a constraint on his personal ideological vision and on the personal power he was depending on to implement it – a constraint consciously sought by his collaborators after the fiasco of the Great Leap Forward and the several million deaths by starvation that accompanied it. His charisma was under threat. The move up the I-space from fiefs to bureaucracies implied by such institutionalization, whatever its ideological colours, can only be successfully achieved at the expense of personal power since it is rule-governed. It was labelled by Max Weber 'the routinization of charisma'.[87]

The cultural revolution

Mao's response, as is well known, was to resist the move, and, proclaiming that the revolution was being sapped from within, to go over the heads of his bureaucratizing rivals and draw on his massive popular support by launching the Great Proletarian Cultural Revolution of 1966.[88] He used the media to extend the reach of his individual power in the fief region to the Chinese population as a whole and thereby attempted to establish a form of direct personal rule which, if successful, would largely dispense with the amplifying powers of impersonal and codified bureaucratic controls that appeared to threaten his personal freedom of manoeuvre further up the I-space.[89] In Fairbank's words, 'Mao was able to do this because of the imperial prerogatives that he had accumulated as the charismatic and sacrosanct great leader, above the law and unbound by precedent or custom. This in turn was possible because he presided over a regime based on his personality and ideology, not on law.'[90]

Charismatic leadership, however, can often only retain the loyalty of its followers by cleaving to a strategy of vagueness and ambiguity. To remain effective it must appear oracular and avoid at all costs even a slight codification of its pronouncements lest in pleasing some it offends others. Yet, at a time when social tensions and divisions in China were running high, Mao's studied equivocations became a source of violent and destructive conflict, not least between his followers themselves, each group interpreting his Delphic pronouncements to suit its own interests.

Mao's bold attempt to extend through mass mobilization the reach of personal governance typical of fiefs towards the right in the I-space, towards ever-larger populations of would-be followers, rapidly led him into the clan region of the space. It proved to be disastrous. Clans gain much of their cohesiveness first by carefully distinguishing an 'in-group' from other 'out-groups' on the basis of some shared belief or value, and second by resolving problems arising within the former by a process of mutual adjustment which is often carried out at the expense of the latter. In China, things quickly got out of control as radical and conservative factions of Red Guards, each professing its allegiance to Mao, clashed in different parts of the country.[91]

The ideological and social tensions that prevailed at the time then quickly transformed the clan region into a terrain for a Hobbesian 'war of all against all'. Within two years of launching the Cultural Revolution, Mao, confronting what was a virtual civil war, was led to disband the Red Guards and send them down to the countryside for 're-education'. He had discovered the limits to his personal power.[92]

Once more up the I-space

The economic reforms set in motion two years after Mao's death in 1976 constituted another major attempt by the Chinese leadership to help the country escape from the fief region and to move up the I-space. China's continued backwardness, now made painfully visible to all by an 'open door' policy which gradually brought the country back into the real world following ten years of self-imposed isolation, was attributed by many in the Chinese leadership to a vestigial feudalism that promoted arbitrary and personal rule and blocked the emergence of modern institutions. Unlike earlier moves up the I-space, however, which sought to establish a centripetal bureaucratic order based on Marxist-Leninist ideology, this one aimed at some measure of decentralization that would bring the country somewhere between the market region and the bureaucratic region of the I-space – that is, further to the right along the diffusion dimension. Marxism-Leninism, it was explained, was to remain firmly in the saddle, but for pragmatic reasons market processes were to be given a freer rein.

Beyond the reach of the central bureaucracy, or for that matter of conservative provincial ones, markets of a kind therefore took hold – in the countryside, in small collective enterprises, in rural townships, and in some of the more liberal provinces of the south such as Guangdong or Fujian. In those organizations subject to closer administrative control, however, such as state-owned enterprises, the economic irrationalities of Marxism-Leninism were either maintained intact or carried over in some suitably disguised form into the new order. The result, as always, was interpersonal accommodation, a resort to the use of personal power rather than impersonal rule, either to solve pressing problems that the system could not address or to respond to emerging opportunities. It was accompanied this time by a spectacular growth in corruption as opportunities for the practice of arbitrage between the planning and the embryonic market system proliferated. The attractive power of a centripetal culture in fiefs was once more reasserting itself in those sectors of the economy in greatest need of modernization and of a rational–legal order, those that remained most directly under the sway of an unreconstructed patrimonial bureaucracy.

The Iron Law of Fiefs

To conclude this section, we note that whereas the institutions located in markets become progressively clan-like if the market learning available to economic agents is idiosyncratic in nature and impacted – Roberto Michels termed this 'The Iron Law of Oligarchy' (it becomes 'oligopoly' when applied to economic rather than political processes)[93] – those located in bureaucracies collapse into fiefs where the codified information they draw upon cannot be processed with enough economic or administrative rationality to stabilize transactions and institutionally embed them in the upper regions of the I-space. We may call this 'The Iron Law of Fiefs'.[94] It is illustrated in Figure 7.2.

An important difference to note between these two 'laws' is that whereas the first actually follows the SLC around the I-space and may merely reflect the inevitable impacting of a learning-by-doing process as subgroups – i.e., nascent clans – within a market acquire idiosyncratic uncodified knowledge through absorption, the second represents a regression with respect to the

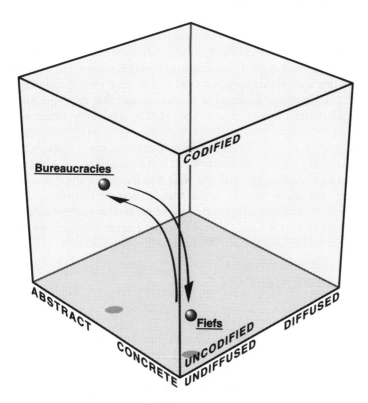

Figure 7.2 The Iron Law of Fiefs

SLC and thus effectively acts as a block to learning. The iron laws of oligarchies and fiefs, although both involving moves down the I-space towards personalized forms of exchange, in effect represent quite different responses to the challenge of social evolution.

Our analysis is not without its little ironies. Was it not, after all, the main appeal of Marx's 'stages' model, for those endorsing its claim to be a scientific expression of historical laws – its historicism – that by putting their faith in a Marxist-Leninist programme which would usher in the final stages of human development, i.e., communism, they were placing themselves on the side of progress? Just as capitalism had provided an escape from the shackles of feudalism, so communism would lead the world beyond the dehumanizing exploitations of capitalism.[95]

The I-space, however, as used here, indicates firstly that there is nothing necessarily progressive about historical stages, conceived as a sequence of centripetal cultural traits, since an SLC, even as it moves forward, can bring us down the space once more towards earlier institutional forms that a stages model had sought to discard; secondly, and perhaps more importantly, it also suggests that the adoption of a Marxist-Leninist order is the best way to throw whatever progress such stages might have to offer into reverse. Under such an order, the SLC is, in effect, run backward. For want of economic rationality, communism leads right back into feudalism wherever the culture in which it is being applied is itself well disposed towards transacting in fiefs. Today in China this hypothesis applies in full to the state-owned industrial sector and with diminishing force to a private sector that now operates towards the right in the I-space, beyond the reach of a feudally structured hierarchy.

The dualistic nature of the Chinese economic reforms itself violates the provisions of the stages model and stands in need of an explanation. After all, Japan at the time of its encounter with the west was also as a culture heavily invested in fiefs and many would argue that in certain respects it has remained so. Yet it has become a paradigm case of successful modernization. How did it manage to escape China's fate? Can the I-space offer a plausible account of the Japanese phenomenon? We turn to this question next.

7.4: JAPAN'S MODERNIZATION

Comparisons with China

There is one striking parallel between China's encounter with a confident and expansionary Europe and Japan's with a confident and expansionary America: in both cases the country was already under some degree of internal stress. The Qing dynasty in China had entered into the declining phase of what Chinese historians call the country's 'dynastic cycle'.[96] Given the pressures of population growth and the increasingly frequent peasant revolts

– the government had barely managed to put down the great White Lotus Rebellion after almost ten years of fighting – 'The surprising fact', Perkins remarked, 'is that China held together at all.'[97] In Japan, by the time that the US Commodore Perry's Black Ships appeared in Edo Sound in 1853 to challenge the country's 250-year-old seclusion policy, the Tokugawa *Bakufu*, the Shogun's military government, wracked by social dislocations and fiscal crises, was in a state of secular decay. Its internal problems were further compounded by the invidious comparisons that could now be drawn between on the one hand the technological and military potential that the west was displaying in the country's main harbour, and on the other what could be mustered by the Shogunate after two and a half centuries of isolation punctuated only by tiny doses of 'Dutch Learning' centred on the annual visit of a Dutch merchantman to the island of Deshima in the middle of Nagasaki harbour.[98] As happened in Qing China, then, the intrusion of foreigners hastened the Tokugawa regime's destruction.[99]

From there on, in any comparison between the two countries, it is the differences that predominate. Not only was Japanese feudalism more decentralized than the Chinese variety but the country's commercial and financial centres, Edo (now Tokyo) and Osaka, were far more developed and sophisticated than their equivalent in China.[100] By 1853, Japan was already in an advanced state of transition from an agrarian to a mercantile economy and even manufacturing was well advanced in certain sectors.[101]

Moreover, for historical reasons, Japanese culture appeared more willing and capable of absorbing western industrial practice than China's was. Although in both cases there was a concern not to be overwhelmed and contaminated by foreign practice – the Japanese expression *Wakon Yosei*, translated as 'Western Technology but Japanese Spirit', replaced *Wakon Kansai* ('Japanese Spirit, Chinese Technique'), an expression that had done duty several centuries earlier when the country had taken China as its model[102] – in China the modernizers were a tiny, almost invisible minority within an entrenched and very conservative ruling elite, whereas in Japan, after the collapse of the *Bakufu* and the restoration of the Meiji emperor in 1868, the elite as a whole became committed to a process of rapid modernization.[103] It would achieve it, in the words of the new government's Charter Oath of 1868, by 'seeking knowledge throughout the world'.[104]

Thus where in China even demonstrably useful western technologies such as railways and steam navigation elicited fierce resistance from a proud class of literati, ignorant of the outside world and indifferent to it, in Japan, a dispossessed samurai-turned-entrepreneur class was even willing to borrow foreign institutions – military, educational, political, etc. – if these could be made to contribute to a strengthening of the country and secure for it a greater measure of security and autonomy in the future. The pursuit of *Fukoku Kyohei* – 'Rich country, strong army' – required a wholehearted acceptance of western models;[105] therefore the 'Japanese spirit', whatever else it might be, was a phenomenon highly accommodating of foreign influence.

The result was that in Japan 'learning from the west' became a collective enterprise initiated at the top of the system and pursued systematically and with gusto. In China, by contrast, it represented episodic and isolated initiatives by individuals and small groups carried out in the teeth of resistance from the top, as well as from the mandarinate as a whole which often viewed foreign borrowings as close to treason.

In China, therefore, systematic state-sponsored modernization had to await the arrival of a communist regime following a revolution from below. In Japan, a revolution from above allowed it to get under way eighty years earlier, soon after the Meiji restoration.[106]

The western development model most prominently on offer to China at the time its revolution was incubating in the 1920s and 1930s was Marxism-Leninism, an ideology applied with apparently promising results first by Lenin and then by Stalin in a young and optimistic USSR. Japan, by contrast, in its quest for useful ideas and models from the west, encountered the Victorian economic liberalism of the 1870s; in Japanese hands it then got alloyed with a strong mercantile orientation that placed national above individual interests. Meiji entrepreneurs such as Eiichi Shibusawa, for example, have been labelled 'community centred';[107] largely guided by his conviction that his country needed fertilizer, Shibusawa risked a fortune to start a fertilizer company in a way that was far from being economically rational. Shibusawa advocated the ideals of *bushido* (the way of the warrior) in business: public service, loyalty, magnanimity, courage, and honesty were to characterize the modern businessman.[108] Japan's orientation towards the market did not therefore imply a passive acceptance of a market order and of the nightwatchman state of classical liberal theory. There are few modern industries in Japan today that do not owe their existence to government initiative. Indeed, the powerful role accorded to the state in Japan's modernization has led some western observers in the 1970s to characterize Japan as a 'developmental state',[109] one which is 'purpose-governed' (*telocratic*) rather than 'rule-governed' (*nomocratic*).[110] The challenge, as the country's leaders interpreted it, was to secure an honourable place in the pecking order of nations. The challenge was largely viewed in military terms for the first forty-five years of the twentieth century, and in economic terms thereafter, when the trick became to find ways of harnessing the dynamizing energy of market forces in a controlled manner to the creation of a strong state. China, as it turns out, is thus not the only Asian society that has striven to subordinate markets to hierarchies.

Not all the western institutions through which Japan has sought to implement its developmental goals have been freely borrowed. Some – independent trade unions, antitrust legislation, etc. – were imposed on the country by the Supreme Commander for the Allied Powers (SCAP), during the seven-year American occupation at the end of the Pacific war. Yet just as a Confucian cultural order remained clearly discernible through the Marxist-Leninist trappings acquired by the People's Republic of China, so it was manifest in post-war Japan in the ways that the institutions of liberalism were effectively operated.[111]

Here we run into a difficulty. For the same Confucianism which has been invoked by Chinese reformers to explain the country's backwardness and its slowness to modernize is also cited as an energizing factor in accounts of the Japanese and other East Asian miracles. In a Chinese value survey carried out in twenty-two countries, for example, Hofstede and Bond[112] showed that Asian countries are pretty selective in their pursuit of Confucian values. Some are oriented towards the future, and towards perseverance and thrift; others towards the present and the past. Only the former are associated with economic growth; Bond and Hofstede label the culture of the former 'Confucian dynamism'.[113] They do not exactly call the culture of the latter 'Confucian torpor' but their article does indicate that as a *causa causans*, Confucianism, not unlike Christianity in the hands of Max Weber,[114] can be pretty fissiparous. Clearly, if culture can be made to explain so much, then in effect it may end up explaining very little.[115]

The Japanese enterprise system

Nowhere is the dilemma posed by the culturalist approach more apparent than in western interpretations of the remarkable post-war performance of large Japanese enterprises. To grasp the issue we need to briefly recapitulate some of the main and well-known features of the Japanese enterprise system.

As most students of the Japanese enterprise system are at pains to point out, far from being a modern expression of some deeply rooted cultural tradition, many features of the system are in fact a post-war creation. Some of them were built on the willingness of an eager learner to take seriously the pronouncements of senior US executives and academics such as Deming and Juran concerning American organizational practices – more seriously, indeed, than most American managers were willing to take them.[116] To be sure, traditional values played an important part when it came to adapting foreign practice or pronouncements to Japanese circumstance, but at the turn of the century, for example, these values were hardly indicative of what was to follow. Lockwood, discussing the protection of labour in Japan at the time, points out that:

> By 1890 Japan had begun to repeat the ugly if now familiar history of the Industrial Revolution in the West. There was no regulation of hours or wages, or of child labour. There were no labour standards of any sort, except for general laws relating to property and contracts. Factory operatives commonly worked eleven to fourteen hours, day or night, and of course at a pittance. These were mostly girls, aged fourteen to twenty,

hired from the countryside by practices which bordered often on seduction. Typically they were lodged in factory dormitories on a three year contract. As many as 50% are said to have deserted within six months. Labour efficiency was correspondingly low. The old system of financial paternalism carried over into modern industry, with its reciprocal obligations of protection and subordination. But it soon lost most of its kindliness and humanity in the cold calculations of industrial capitalism.[117]

As late as the 1920s, the Japanese firm was a locus of confrontations and conflicts, largely the product of tensions created by the country's accelerated process of modernization. Progress in labour legislation in Japan owed much to external influence and criticism, and in particular to the International Labour Organisation formed in 1919. Although Japan joined the organization at the outset – in fact, it established the first permanent delegation – Japan insisted that Japanese industry required special latitude in labour matters.[118]

It will be clear from the foregoing that the Japanese enterprise system is the outcome of a complex interplay of cultural, institutional, and situational factors which admits of no simple interpretation.

In the west, the prevailing conception of a firm derives from the joint-stock company – had the partnership structure retained its dominance, the organizational history of the twentieth century might have been very different. The joint-stock company requires that we draw the organizational boundary fairly tightly around its employees and that we place the resulting whole at the service of shareholder interests.[119] This may not be the most useful way to conceptualize the Japanese firm. It might best be viewed as a set of concentric circles that express varying degrees of reciprocal commitment between stakeholders located at various distances from an organizational core – a nexus of obligations only some of which can be considered contractual.[120] The differences between the western and the Japanese concept of the firm are schematized in Figure 7.3.[121]

In the central circle of the Japanese enterprise system are to be found the firm's managers and permanent employees. Here reciprocal commitment is at its most durable and intense. In the outer circle are to be found the least-committed stakeholders, members of the general public, etc.[122] In the middle circle are located close customers, suppliers, temporary workers, bankers, and, if the firm is a member of a *Kereitsu* or enterprise grouping, other firms in the *Kereitsu*.

Such a concentric arrangement is somewhat reminiscent of the distinction drawn by the first Tokugawa government between Tokugawa's Ieyasu's trusted vassals, the *Fudai Daimyos*, and the *Tozama* or Outside Lords.[123] It also brings out another feature of the Japanese firm that is strongly expressive of a national trait: its particularism. Organizational outcomes are skewed to

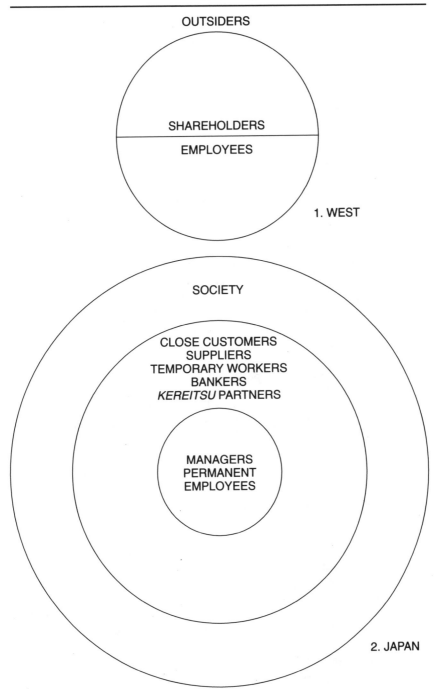

Figure 7.3 Western (above) versus Japanese (below) concepts of the firm

benefit groups that one is committed to – often at the expense of a more general interest or principle – and the extent of that commitment is a function of which circle among the concentric three a given group occupies. The universalism implicit in the Christian parable of the good Samaritan has no application in this scheme. A stranger can never be a neighbour and must not be allowed to occupy any of the circles.[124]

Such exclusiveness raises the question of how an individual gets to penetrate any of these charmed circles. If Japanese organizational practices are any guide, the answer is by a process of socialization, with those located in the inner circle being the target of the most important and durable efforts of socialization. In the case of employees this is made possible by the recruitment and employment practices of the large Japanese firm, which, as is well known, firstly recruits people of particular age and education to fill general vacancies rather than specified jobs; secondly makes lifetime employment an ideal to be striven for; and finally gives age and length of service priority consideration as promotion criteria.[125] As Dore and other observers of Japanese organizations remind us, such practices have only ever covered the permanent employees of the larger enterprises and thus extend at most to a third of the country's labour force; nevertheless their influence has been pervasive throughout the economy in the post-war years,[126] both as a source of norms for others to adopt and as a set of privileges to be competed for.

One effect of Japanese employment practices has been to replace the workings of the labour market in the inner circle by a process somewhat like the quasi-voluntary submission to authority practised in the late Roman Empire and early Middle Ages and known as a 'commendation':[127] the firm extends its protection to core employees in return for their loyalty and compliance. The same deal is on offer in the middle circle but at a much lower level of commitment. Here we find temporary employees who might one day become permanent employees but who for now have to absorb fluctuations in employment levels, effectively acting as a buffer that protects the inner core of workers and allows the firm to make good to them its promise of job security.

The same goes for subcontractors. Some protection from the vagaries of competitive market contracting is traded for loyalty and dedication by the subcontracting firm. Japanese firms operate with far fewer subcontractors than their American counterparts, even though subcontracting accounts for a much greater percentage of value added. Relationships with subcontractors are of the non-market kind. Indeed, 'relational contracting'[128] has been put forward by Dore as a viable alternative to both vertical integration and market contracting.[129] Price, then, plays a minor – although not negligible – role in such relationships since what counts above all is attitude and commitment.

Reciprocal commitment in the inner circle has to be built up on the basis of trust and a mutual alignment of values, something which takes time and effort. Why is trust needed? Because both sides are investing in what Williamson calls a *transaction-specific investment*; that is, one which cannot be transferred at low cost to parties external to the transaction and the benefits of which can only be realized to the extent that the relationship between the buyer and the seller is maintained.[130] A new employee, for example, knows that his loyalty to the firm will only be repaid in the later stages of his career. In the early years, in accordance with the principle of *nenko joretsu* (promotion according to seniority), he will progress at the same rate as his colleagues (she, however, will not!) whatever his individual talent and skills, and only as he reaches early middle age will his responsibilities and rewards begin to reflect his earlier performance. In this way, destructive inter-group competition is avoided.[131]

Likewise, if the firm knows that it will be committing itself to a new entrant over the length of his career, then it will have to be particularly attentive to its recruitment processes. Mistakes could be very costly. For this reason, the first two or three years of employment after leaving school or university remain somewhat provisional for both sides.[132] A fair amount of job hopping might take place at that time as both firm and recruit seek a better 'fit' – a job mobility survey carried out by Robert Cole from 1970 to 1971 in Yokohama indicated that inter-firm job changes were at their highest in the 16–25 age groups and fell off rapidly thereafter.[133] After a short while, then, new employees are expected to settle down and make a commitment. Beyond a certain point, job moves are perceived as symptomatic of a questionable capacity for loyalty and thus carry penalties such as lower status and salary in the recruiting firm.

In spite of this early but limited job mobility, firms take enormous pains in their recruiting procedures to ensure that candidates will fit in with their company's culture. School teachers and university professors are often put on retainers by firms to put forward promising candidates. The latters' family backgrounds will each be carefully investigated for possible signs of problems or delinquency – a task often entrusted to an agency which specializes in such matters and which makes discreet enquiries of teachers, professors, and possibly neighbours[134] – and if one of these is accepted into the company, he will be subjected to a rigorous training programme lasting anything from six weeks to three months, the central theme of which will concern *seichin*, or spirit, often involving Zen meditation, group living, and 25-mile endurance walks.[135] He will also be given what western recruits entering a firm at the same level would consider pretty menial jobs before being assigned a more responsible post.

Why are recruits willing to put up with such arduous initiation rites? A western firm that tried to submit school-leavers or graduates that it wished to recruit to such a demanding regime on the basis of 'jam tomorrow' would quickly find them being lured away by competitors offering a more attractive package. There are in fact signs that this is beginning to happen in Japan and that in response larger firms are gradually moving towards a system of pay that gives as much weight to merit as to seniority. This is partly as a result of demographic pressures, and partly because of the growing number of western firms setting up and entering the labour market with a different kind of offering.

Yet by and large, in the larger enterprises – those which drive the system – alternative employment opportunities with equivalent career prospects are simply not on offer. Firm A will not be much interested in recruiting someone socialized to firm B's way of doing things. Such employment is considered disruptive rather than enriching. Diversity of experience and exposure is not much prized when it has taken place outside the firm, and general academic qualifications are not rated as anything more than an index of raw potential – useful in assessing school-leavers or graduates fresh from university but useless as an indicator of potential value to the firm of a 30-year-old manager or professional with six or seven years' employment behind him.

Mastering the culture of an organization's inner circle is considered to be the business of a lifetime and is viewed as one of the key determinants of an employee's career prospects. It follows that the longer a person stays with the firm, the greater his experience of the firm and its ways of doing things and hence the greater his value to the firm. Such hefty transaction-specific investments by employees in their organization impose, as we have already seen, their own economic logic: that returns on such investments are measured in terms of payment and progression within the firm according to seniority. An individual's commitment to life-long firm-specific learning would weaken considerably if individual performance was the dominant consideration in deciding on pay and promotion. For this reason, employees are rewarded more for their inputs than for their outputs – at least in the early years when people are required to invest in firm-specific learning up-front. Equally important, it is also a logic that tends to view employee performance more as a group or an organizational phenomenon than as an individual one. In contrast to the individualist perspective that shapes western employment practices, a Confucian one sees man as socially determined.[136]

Cultural consequences of the Japanese enterprise system

What are the organizational consequences of structuring the employment relation in this way? They are numerous and we shall limit our discussion to three of them.

The first is that it fosters a personalized hierarchical dependency. Since an employee finds it unprofitable to look outward to a labour market for his salvation, he looks upward to his superiors. The latter's attitude towards his subordinates is supposed to be informed by a Confucian benevolence institutionalized in the *Oyabun–Kobun* (parent–child, boss–follower) relationship in which senior managers within a firm act as lifetime mentors to newly entering employees.[137] Such paternalism is scorned in the west but welcomed in Japan. It offers some measure of protection to vulnerable employees; it also has its rewards for senior managers since it allows them to build up a loyal following within the firm.[138] Unsurprisingly it also contributes to the intense factionalism to be found in the upper reaches of Japanese enterprises.[139]

Feelings of dependency are fostered in many different ways in the large Japanese firm and exploit a personality orientation that some see as having its origins in domestic child-rearing practices.[140] These breed 'other-directedness' rather than 'inner-directedness' and actively discourage the quest for individual autonomy and responsibility that is a hallmark of the western Judeo-Christian tradition.[141]

Over time, the Japanese firm becomes something of a total institution for its employees, providing holidays for the family, schooling for the children, and a number of welfare services that in Europe or the US would be considered the responsibility of the political community.[142] In this way are the invisible webs that tie an individual to his workplace spun. Few alternative options exist to pull him away from his organizational attachments once these are formed. Often, only a feeling of mutual trust between employer and employee prevents those links from being experienced as coercive by the latter. For little by way of countervailing power is available to him – witness Kamata's powerful indictment of the quasi-military lifestyle that a firm like Toyota imposes on a worker.[143] The union that he belongs to is an enterprise union whose senior ranks are frequently as dependent as he is on the firm for their own future career prospects; as Cole points out, it is difficult under such circumstances for the union to represent effectively the interests of its members as distinct from the interests of the company.[144] A worker's leisure hours are also often appropriated by the firm. A wife views her husband's early return from work – or from group drinking with colleagues – with alarm since it signals that all is not well between her husband and colleagues at the workplace. His organizational identity in effect becomes a hegemon that inhabits the very core of his soul to the exclusion of all other contenders.

The second consequence is that a heavy firm-specific investment in the mastery of organizational culture by employees creates a high trust culture with a much lighter need for formal control systems than in, say, the more pluralistic American firm which employees of much more varied backgrounds move into and out of, and in which high trust is consequently much harder to establish. Kagono and his co-workers, for example, in a comparative study of Japanese and US organizational characteristics, found Japanese firms to be more centralized but less formal and rule bound,[145] and Kono has noted that whereas a fair amount of formal planning takes place in Japanese firms, formal implementation mechanisms are lacking.[146] To be sure, formal control systems are not in short supply in the Japanese firm, but they tend to be more at the service of the individual worker himself than of his supervisor. In their comparative study of ITT under Harold Geneen and Matsushita, Pascale and Athos argue that the difference between the two firms with respect to management control processes was that whereas in the American firm there was nowhere to hide – i.e., whatever a manager did would be made visible by Geneen's unforgiving reporting structure – in the Japanese firm there was nothing to hide.[147]

Kono, in a study of the strategy and structure of large Japanese firms, has observed that there is much less of a concern with organizational structure as such in Japanese firms than in western ones and that fewer of them have divisionalized their operations. Japanese management thus appears to be more concerned with process than with structure.[148] Control is exercised implicitly through carefully planned socialization processes rather than through an undue reliance on formal reporting relationships. For this reason the type of contractual orientation incarnated in written job descriptions hardly exists in the Japanese firm. Task definition and execution are the responsibility of the group or the section (*Kacho*), not of the individual – i.e., managers were trusted and were not pried upon. The concept of the specialized professional role is comparatively undeveloped in the Japanese enterprise and only finds an echo in the market for lower-level technical skills. Dore, for example, in his 1969 study of Hitachi and English Electric (now GEC), pointed out that in the British firm a skilled engineer tended to think of himself primarily as, say, an electrician who happened to be working for English Electric, whereas in the Japanese firm he thought of himself as a Hitachi man who happened to have the skills of an electrician.[149]

Unsurprisingly, in a downturn, the Japanese firm found it much easier to reassign its workforce new jobs even if these were sometimes quite unrelated to their existing technical skills than did the English firm, which even in good times found itself plagued by job demarcation disputes between competing trades. The lower degree of job formalization in Hitachi gave the firm considerable flexibility in the deployment of its workforce both at the level of the individual job and at that of the organizational task. Such flexibility allowed the Japanese firm to meet its commitment to lifetime employment.

The third consequence of Japanese employment practices is that they breed a particularistic ethic in the workforce that is placed unconditionally at the service of the firm's future growth and prosperity rather than a universalistic ethic that might at times set abstract individual principles in opposition to those of an employer. The Japanese firm takes great pains to present itself to its employees and outsiders as being at the service of society, but in fact it derives no universal rules or principles from such an orientation. A cynic might interpret it as an attempt to legitimate enterprise profits by fostering a belief that what is good for Toshiba or Canon is good for Japan. The underlying motive remains at root utilitarian rather than moral.

Such particularism can be a source of blind and indiscriminate loyalty by employees, sometimes leading them to break the law in the service of their firm – e.g., as when two Hitachi employees were caught trying to steal proprietary technology from IBM in the mid-1980s and when employees of a Toshiba subsidiary were discovered to be selling militarily sensitive precision grinding technology to the Soviet Union in defiance of COCOM regulations.[150] It is no accident that one of the most popular plays with Japanese audiences remains the historical *Tale of the Forty-Seven Ronin*, a story of leaderless Samurai who out of loyalty to their lord (*giri*) sacrificed their reputations, their fathers, their wives, their sisters, their righteousness, and finally their lives, dying by their own hands.[151]

Particularism shows up again in inter-firm relationships[152] and, if a firm is prominent enough, in its dealings with certain government agencies such as the Ministry of International Trade and Industry (MITI). If a market order expresses a belief in universalistic values, in the impartial application of competition-promoting rules, and in the impersonal selection of winners and losers by the market process itself, an industrial policy, by contrast, serves particularistic values and expresses a concern with specific outcomes skewed towards identified beneficiaries or classes of beneficiaries. It is part of MITI's creed that the two orientations are not fundamentally incompatible, as is assumed in western thinking, but are in fact both phases of a single evolutionary process. The infant industry argument, for example, has been invoked by ministry men to justify lavishing particularistic care on their chosen firms until they are strong enough to fend for themselves in international competitive markets – and win of course.[153]

MITI's behaviour towards firms and industries only provides one illustration of the selective intimacy that suffuses government–enterprise relationships in Japan. Others could be cited. If in the US, for example, an enduring liberal belief in the 'minimal state'[154] conspires to keep firms and governments at arm's length from each other, in Japan much more conspires to bring them closer together. And few things do so more than the practice of *Amakudari* – literally, 'descending from heaven' – through which senior civil servants, on taking early retirement, find a pleasant and prestigious post already prepared for them in one of their 'client' firms. It has been jestfully suggested that given the greater affluence found in business than in the bureaucracy and the declining prestige of the bureaucracy in Japan – greatly accelerated by recent scandals – bureaucrats who move into business should be referred to as *amaagari*, that is, 'ascending to heaven'.[155] Government and enterprises – particularly large ones – are thus not wholly distinct and separable structures but effectively form part of a single hierarchical continuum, albeit one that is more loosely coupled than popular western perceptions of Japan Inc. would have us believe.

Summary

Our overview of the main features of the Japanese enterprise system and its development has been cursory and hardly does justice to its complexity and sophistication. We have barely touched on the broader institutional environment within which the system is set. As always, the temptation is to expand a chapter into a book. The features that we have highlighted, nevertheless, should allow us some comparison with those of the Chinese state-owned enterprises that we discussed in sections 7.3 and 7.4. We turn to this next.

7.5: INTERPRETATION

Chinese state-owned firms and Japanese firms compared

A frequent complaint that is heard in China from the western joint venture partners of Chinese state-owned enterprises is that the latter's workers are employed for life, promoted strictly on the basis of seniority, and rewarded more for adopting a 'correct' political attitude than for their performance. Moreover, these partners will go on to observe, since the firm's assets are owned by the state, no one seems to be overly concerned with enterprise profitability.

These are not the only characteristic features that Chinese and Japanese firms turn out to have in common: in a more general way both appear to practise a form of corporate socialism rooted in the Confucian belief that the individual is essentially a product of his social situation and that if the enterprise can provide him with a secure and stable community as a reference group, his values and his performance will be enhanced. Such meliorism is by no means unique to Confucian culture. In Great Britain, for example, as early as 1800, Robert Owen had bought the great mills at New Lanark where he proceeded to put into practice his creed that 'men's character is made for them and not by them'. By 'character', Owen did not mean the individual disposition of each person, but the make-up of moral and social ideas that might be infused into a community by education and environment. Owenite socialism was to become an important influence on the British working-class movement[156] as well as on the paternalistic employment practices of firms like Cadbury Brothers Ltd, Rowntree, and Lever Brothers.[157]

The paradox is that many of the organizational practices that have been invoked as an explanation for the poor economic performance of Chinese firms also seem to turn up – albeit in less ideological garb – as critical success factors in accounts of the competitive performance of the Japanese enterprise. We must therefore either acknowledge a contradiction or recognize that our interpretation of the facts is incomplete.[158]

In addressing this issue a good point of departure might be to ask how Japanese and Chinese firms compare in the I-space. From our description in the previous section it could plausibly be argued that like the Chinese firm, the Japanese firm is heavily invested in the lower regions of the I-space where inter-personal relations remain implicit, much exchange uncodified, and where trust and shared values loom large in any explanation of employee behaviour.

Arguably there are also differences between Chinese and Japanese firms: a greater willingness to seek consensus and to invest in it in the case of the Japanese firm, coupled with a stronger disposition to share knowledge with colleagues, probably locates it closer to the clan region of the I-space than the Chinese firm. In the latter, opportunistic behaviour at all organizational levels – an attempt by individuals or groups to move to the left in the space and exploit the fief region for their own purposes – is more evident.[159] The Japanese firm takes great pains to forestall opportunistic behaviour by its employees. Opportunism, if anything, characterizes the behaviour of the firm itself in relation to its competitors – at which point it is relabelled 'strategic behaviour' since the competitive advantage it secures for the enterprise is thereby deemed legitimate.[160]

A more important difference perhaps is that the cultural and institutional investments of the Japanese firm, in marked contrast to those of the Chinese firm, do not coop it up in the lower regions of the I-space. No 'Iron Law of Fiefs' is at work, sapping its economic rationality.[161] By adopting western accounting and planning and control systems, and by setting them in a market context which could give an intelligible meaning to cost and price signals, the Japanese firm has successfully managed to codify many of its organizational practices and thus spread itself further up the I-space than the Chinese firm.

In sum, while it continues to maintain a transactional bias in favour of clans – as we have already seen, it applies formal control systems with a much lighter touch than western firms[162] – the Japanese firm, together with the country that provides it with its primary institutional environment, has effectively acquired a centrifugal culture.

Different challenges, different responses: the influence of history

What evidence would we cite to support our claim that Japan has spread itself out in the I-space? Simply this: the country today displays a much greater capacity for economic rationality, learning, and adaptation than China has until recently. Institutional and economic practices borrowed from the west from the 1870s onward were capable of being stabilized further up the I-space because they did not suffer from the debilitating particularisms and irrationalities of the Marxist-Leninist creed. In China the particularisms latent in its borrowed ideology further compounded those already manifest in the national culture itself. In Japan, on the other hand, the universalistic orientation of the liberal economic ideology it imported – not all of its institutional borrowings had the stamp of liberalism – effectively worked *against* the country's cultural disposition to particularism. Both markets and rational–legal bureaucracies are the institutional embodiment of universalistic values; they can only be made to operate effectively if particularistic practices are in good part forsaken.

Like other modernizing cultures, China, no less than Japan, also struggled to understand and then to absorb universalistic values. Why then did Japan succeed where China failed?

One important reason, if we leave the country's 250-year seclusion to one side, is that Japan has historically been much more open to external forces and influences than China ever was. From the beginning of the Chou dynasty (1028 BC) China was a powerful state surrounded by tributary statelets from which it felt that it had little to learn. According to the dogma of the Chinese religion of Heaven, all the countries of the world were subject to the Chinese emperor, the Son of Heaven. There could be no such thing as other independent states.[163] To the Chinese mind, therefore, it was inconceivable that beyond its geographical horizon there might exist civilizations to rival its own, civilizations that operate on different principles and from which China might benefit. As Needham put it, when discussing China's twenty centuries of contact with the west prior to the European scientific revolution,

> Contacts there were, interchanges of ideas and techniques certainly occurred, but never in such profusion as to affect the characteristic style of China's civilization and hence her science. In the light of this, it is no exaggeration, then, to speak of the 'isolation' of China, or, alternatively, of the rest of the world from her; culturally that was something very real.[164]

A second possible reason might be added to the first. The pressure to develop or adopt technologies which might embody abstract universal principles was largely absent in China until the middle of the nineteenth century. According to Elvin, China by 1300 had developed selected technologies to a point where industrialization comparable to Europe's eighteenth-century Industrial Revolution was possible. It never happened. As late as 1793, the emperor's apparent disdain for the gifts brought to him by the Macartney mission was intended to indicate that in a country where muscle power was plentiful and virtually free, technology and the rationality that it imposes on its users was little prized and indeed considered by many – not, it should be noted, the emperor himself – to be little more than a source of baubles and playthings for the imperial court. The social and political pressures that in Europe had led to the scientific revolution, the precursor of the Industrial Revolution, were absent.[165] In contrast to the emergent nation-states of Europe, in China the state viewed itself primarily as a collector rather than a creator of wealth – did not the rice tax institutionally express a physiocratic belief that the country's main source of wealth resided in the land rather than in useful knowledge and artefacts? The belief was not entirely unfounded. China's intensive agriculture could keep many more people alive than European agriculture. The result was an over-supply of human labour which made the use of machines uneconomical. Thus, in contrast to Europe, technology had little scope for developing to a level which would justify mass production; to be sure, the earliest machines were somewhat quicker and more efficient than human labour, but they required too much investment to be competitive.[166] The result was that scarcely any of the technical knowledge and skills accumulating at the imperial court found its way into general commercial applications. Little of it was codified for general use, and for that reason, little diffused.

Japan, by contrast, was poor in natural resources, and prior to its civil wars in the sixteenth century had sat for several centuries at the feet of its cultural mentor, China. From the Middle Kingdom it had absorbed Buddhism and Confucianism, many of its technologies, its written characters, and much of its art. In all cases it had adapted its cultural imports to suit local conditions, often – as it was later to do with the west – improving upon them as it went along.[167]

Japanese culture has always perceived itself as vulnerable and fragile and for that reason appears to be blessed with a built-in disposition to learn from others and to do so creatively. It imitates, to be sure, but it imitates innovatively rather than slavishly, always carefully evaluating what it sees, and then subsequently improving on its chosen model with some discernment.[168] Japan's cultural capacity to absorb foreign technology and ideas at the time of the Meiji restoration, in spite of 250 years of isolation, was greater than China's. The expression *Wakon Yosei* ('Western Technology but Japanese Spirit') produced far fewer obstacles to genuine learning than *t'i yung*, the Chinese equivalent.[169] China had more to unlearn. It still does.

Western economic rationality, then, first entered Japan through some of the foreign ideas that the latter systematically borrowed. Since 1862 the Shogunate itself, despite its reputation for conservatism, had been sending students abroad, bringing foreign technologies into Japan, employing foreign language and science teachers, and generally encouraging 'western learning' (*yogaku*). And in the Meiji era that followed, the policy was continued; it was summed up in the new emperor's Charter Oath of 1868 in the prescription that 'knowledge was to be sought throughout the world'. As Passin notes, the mood was strongly utilitarian, westernizing and individualistic.[170] As the country's modernization progressed, however, economic rationality also further imposed itself through the need to export and to compete abroad in order to pay for the inputs essential to the modernization process. The country's almost total lack of domestic sources of the raw materials required for a modern economy – petroleum, iron ore, coal, and non-ferrous ores – placed it at a disadvantage which could only be overcome with special effort, providing a unifying challenge to all Japanese.[171]

Viewed as a move from *Gemeinschaft* to *Gesellschaft*, Japan's move up the I-space has followed a similar trajectory to that taken by the European countries between the sixteenth and the nineteenth centuries; many would argue that it did not move as far up the space towards an impersonal order as western countries did, yet the orientation and pace of its progression were similar. By contrast, in this century the two communist giants, the Soviet Union and China, started out along the same path but were then stalled for ideological reasons.

Like other successful modernizers, Japan first built up a strong state bureaucracy under a mercantilist banner and is only now slowly beginning to decentralize – we defer to the end of the chapter our discussion of whether this is leading the country towards a genuine market order.[172] Before the war its investment in the structures of a strong state found expression in military adventurism; in the post-war period the belief in a strong state survived, entrenched in a mercantilist creed which today remains a source of discord with countries that have moved the institutional centre of gravity of their economic system further to the right in the I-space and are therefore more deeply imbued with market values than Japan today appears to be. Culturally speaking, the Japanese institutional order remains heavily invested in clans and, to a lesser extent, in bureaucracies.

For all that, the country shows all the signs of having escaped the centripetal forces that continue to plague China – less so in south China, where a capitalist if not a market order has begun to take root, than in other parts of the country – and of having become a centrifugal culture. In spite of important cultural differences that remain latent beneath the surface, in terms of its level of development, at least, we have little difficulty in thinking of Japan as a 'westernized' country.

The hypothesis being advanced here is that a centrifugal institutional order is an essential feature of a successfully completed process of modernization. Centrifugal cultures enjoy a greater capacity to learn than centripetal ones since they have institutional structures distributed throughout the I-space to facilitate the processing and transmission of information. Their SLCs are consequently broader and less subject to blockages. Yet, however centrifugal it becomes, a culture's centre of gravity in the I-space will continue to influence the way that it operates its learning cycle and hence its configuration in the space.

To illustrate the point consider the difference between Japan, whose cultural centre of gravity, as we have just argued, remains located in clans, and the United States, whose cultural centre of gravity is located in markets. Both today might be considered centrifugal cultures, but they will remain so only in so far as they successfully manage to counterbalance the attractive forces of clans and markets respectively. These forces act with increasing intensity on the SLC as it approaches the relevant region and with decreasing intensity as it moves away from it (see Figure 7.4). Thus, for example, the American

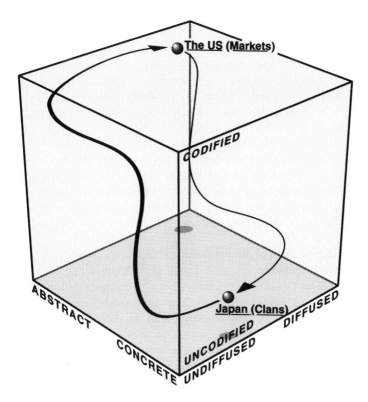

The US (Markets)

CODIFIED

ABSTRACT

Japan (Clans)

DIFFUSED

CONCRETE   UNCODIFIED   UNDIFFUSED

Figure 7.4 America and Japan in the SLC

cultural bias towards markets works in favour of the codification, abstraction, and diffusion of information, as exemplified in the practices of what Williamson calls the economic institutions of capitalism – the Securities and Exchange Commission, the Antitrust Division of the United States Department of Justice, the United States Federal Trade Commission, etc. By contrast, the Japanese cultural bias towards clans encourages the rapid absorption of readily available codified information and its subsequent impacting in a more implicit form within restricted groups whose property it then becomes. Japanese trading companies, the *sogo shoschas*, to cite but one example, are institutionally organized for the systematic collection and analysis of global market and technological data on a scale unimaginable in western firms, as are government bodies such as Jetro and MITI.[173]

Were the US bias in favour of markets or the Japanese bias in favour of clans to turn centripetal – that is, to convert a cultural preference for given transactional style into a basis for excluding competing institutional alternatives – then the SLC, whose scope is set by the diversity of transactional forms available to it in the I-space, would either shrink or come to a halt.

The Japanese firm as a learning organization

Returning now to our earlier comparison between Chinese state-owned enterprises and Japanese firms, we are now in a better position to understand what distinguishes them from each other. Whereas both operate on the basis of a particularistic socialist or neo-Confucian ethic in the lower region of the I-space, the Japanese firm, embedded in what is becoming an increasingly centrifugal culture, has stabilized a number of organizational practices further up the codification scale and, in contrast to the Chinese state-owned firm, has thus become something of a *learning organization*, responding in a rational fashion to abstract and codified as well as to concrete and uncodified signals emanating from its internal and external environments.[174] The Chinese state-owned enterprise, on the other hand, for want of economic rationality, of a viable abstract and codified transactional order, remains stuck in fiefs.

The growing centrifugalism of Japanese culture does not alter the fact that its core values remain anchored in clans. Today Japan's prevailing cultural orientation must rate as a major contributor to the country's conflict with cultures whose own core values locate them in the market region of the I-space. The enduring particularism of clans, with its partitioning of the world into in-groups and out-groups, makes it impossible to give any impartial consideration to the claims of the outsider, no matter how legitimate, over those of the insider: no appeal to universal values can be entertained. In the words of one of the critics of Japan's clannishness, 'The Japanese system and what is left of the international free trade system are incompatible because the latter requires adherence to rules that the administrators cannot afford to accept without undoing their complex network of informal relations, known as *jinmyaku*. Deals can be made within the system, but the introduction of rules that applied to everyone would weaken and eventually destroy it.'[175]

The result is a gradual polarization of in-group–out-group relations – with Japan supplying the in-groups and its trading partners the out-groups – as well as ever-increasing friction and mutual incomprehension. Those who believe in cultural convergence see the problem as a passing phenomenon that will disappear as Japan progresses centripetally in the I-space towards a full-fledged market order. Those who see in centrifugalism an alternative to convergence as an explanation of cultural evolution, one in which a culture's centre of gravity does not inevitably become displaced as it spreads itself out in the I-space, are not so sure.

We now briefly examine what lessons our comparative analysis of China's and Japan's modernization holds for the post-communist economies of Eastern Europe and by implication for the fledgling Commonwealth of Independent States (CIS). Although the following section will be less descriptive and more impressionistic than those that preceded it – we are, after all, trying to capture a target that has been moving ever faster since 1989 – the I-space will once again serve as our guide.

7.6 POST-COMMUNISM IN EASTERN EUROPE

Introduction

The collapse of the Soviet Empire in Eastern Europe was swift, massive, and unexpected. It had been apparent for some time that the command economies in Europe were in decline relative to their free market competitors and that they were failing to satisfy the aspirations they had fostered, but when the end came it did so with such speed that it took pretty much all western observers by surprise. Three and a half years on, the dust thrown up by the institutional collapse of communism has not yet settled. The contours of the new order that is being erected on the rubble of the old one are barely discernible. There are blueprints, of course, but they may be a poor guide to what is actually happening on the building site. Furthermore, there are many blueprints and even more architects, each trying to get his project approved and implemented. There is this time no master planner, however, no omniscient coordinator to pull it all together. After all, is planning not what the ex-command economies have been trying to escape from?

Such a turbulent state of affairs counsels caution to those who would attempt to describe and interpret it. The fuzziness and unreliability of the data available do not allow anything more than a very sketchy outline of some key issues at this stage and a very tentative hypothesis to explain them. The views expressed, however, although of necessity only provisional given the paucity of reliable data that can be marshalled in their support, will be forcibly presented. They are the fruit of an interaction between an evolving theoretical perspective and personal field experiences that resonate together and that amplify what would otherwise be weakly held convictions. Whether these would enjoy a high degree of empirical corroboration is an issue that could only be settled by systematic and detailed field research. Whether such field research is itself a justifiable enterprise is a matter for the reader to judge.

The road to 1989

That a totally centripetal Marxist-Leninist order, located in bureaucracies in the I-space, may be impossible to achieve in practice had already begun to impress itself upon Lenin within two years of the October revolution of 1917, during the period of 'War Communism' (1918–20) when the need for planning was repeatedly proclaimed but no national plan could actually be drawn up.[176] By 1921 he was paying a belated tribute to the power of markets with the introduction of his New Economic Policy (NEP). Markets would be allowed to function widely, but only as a temporary expedient during a phase of transition from a capitalist to a communist system. The application of the market mechanism was thus presented as a short-term concession, justified by the primitive socio-economic conditions prevailing in Russia at the time. In an underdeveloped country dominated by peasant agriculture and 'petty commodity production', a longer transition period between capitalism and socialism would be required.[177] The social democratic wing of Marxism, however, began to view markets less as a temporary device and more as an essential adjunct to the planned economy.[178]

The NEP period was brought to an end with the introduction of the first five-year plan (1928–32) and the forced collectivization of agriculture. A command economy was installed and justified as corresponding to the next stage on the road to communism, the socialist stage. It was Stalin who created, maintained, and disseminated the new model of socialism. In this model, state ownership of the means of production replaces private owner-ship and the whole national economy is administered as if it were one giant firm – in effect implementing the Marxist vision of 'one nation – one factory'.[179] In fact, in contrast to the vaunted economic equivalence claimed for the allocative mechanisms of socialist and market exchange by Oskar Lange and Abba Lerner,[180] state planning as implemented by Stalin aimed at abolishing economic exchange altogether. Stalin took it for granted, as he indicated in his book *Economic Problems of Socialism in the USSR* (1952), that under full communism, financial relations between state enterprises would be abolished and replaced by direct exchange of products; that is to say, without the intermediation of money.[181]

Yet Marxism-Leninism, the intellectual elixir which would allow advanced capitalist countries – and most notably Germany – to progress and move beyond the last level of 'antagonistic' historical stages and to enter into their communist inheritance,[182] had effectively been administered to a pre-modern economy which on some estimates had no more than 0.5 per cent of its labour force employed in manufacturing at the time of the October revolution.[183] At the turn of the century, Russian industrial workers had been a branch of the peasantry rather than a distinct social group, and as such had engaged in non-agrarian pursuits known as *promysly*. Seventy per cent of workers classified as industrial in Russia held jobs in industrial enterprises located in rural areas.[184]

When after the Second World War the countries of Eastern Europe fell to communism, it could reasonably be assumed that since some of them, pre-war, had already reached an advanced stage of industrialization – at least in comparison with Russia in 1917 – they would become a natural socialist showcase for workers being exploited in the capitalist west. As it turned out, however, the communist collapse of 1989 was most complete in those countries – East Germany, Czechoslovakia, Poland, Hungary – which before the war had been the most advanced. Elsewhere – Bulgaria, Romania,

Yugoslavia and, more recently, in the former republics of the Soviet Union – the communists retained enough power and influence to slow things down. It seemed, then, if anything, as if there was an inverse relationship between a society's level of development and its propensity to communism.

The painful business of shifting paradigms

The revolutions of 1989 in Eastern Europe accelerated the search for an accommodation with markets in the Soviet Union itself. This search had already been initiated in April 1985 at the Plenary Meeting of the CPSU Central Committee with the introduction of *perestroika* or restructuring.[185] A sudden acceleration in the country's secular economic decline – Abel Aganbegyan, economic adviser to Mikhail Gorbachev, estimated that the Soviet Union had been a no-growth economy since the early 1970s[186] – exacerbated by mounting ethnic unrest and secessionist tendencies in many of the republics, had put economic reform at the top of the political agenda. But economic reform, for those reared on the orthodoxies of Soviet ideology – and that included Mikhail Gorbachev himself – could only mean some new variant on the NEP in which markets would be introduced as a complement to, rather than as a replacement of, what already existed, as a way of injecting a new vigour and efficiency into the ailing planned economy. Markets would then act as a support to central planning and help to make it more efficient: in contrast to the way things function in a liberal economy they would thus remain at the service of a bureaucratic order rather than the other way round. Centripetal cultures fight for their corners, and the Soviet Union did so, right up to the last moment, until its final demise in August 1991.

In post-communist Eastern Europe, on the other hand, the presumption was now in favour of a western model and that was taken to mean a market order *tout court*. The problem was how to get there. Few people in the region under the age of seventy had anything more than folk memories of what markets actually involve in terms of personal risk and effort, and for the person in the street the word typically conjured up nothing more intellectually challenging by way of an image than a cornucopia of consumer goods – everyday items that had been unavailable for the better part of forty-five years and which for that reason populated his/her every fantasy. For those with some understanding of the problem, however, the existing economic terrain hardly promised a smooth ride to markets. It was littered with the toxic debris of forty-five years of central planning: an antiquated physical infrastructure, overmanned state-owned enterprises producing goods that nobody wanted at unrealistic prices, and most importantly perhaps, an enterprise culture that fostered caution and a quest for personal security instead of innovation and risk-taking.[187]

The replacement of the Ostmark by the Deutschmark in the ex-GDR in 1990 at a parity of one to one powerfully illustrated the difficulties that lay ahead for would-be reformers. Overnight, consumer demand for East German goods collapsed as West German goods became freely available. Overnight, the putative market value of many East German firms manufacturing such goods was virtually driven to zero.

The reformer's answer to this precarious state of affairs in different Eastern European countries was to try to move towards a market economy through a four-part programme of market transformation:

1   By establishing or maintaining price stability through tight monetary and fiscal policies.
2   By creating a set of market-clearing relative prices through the ending of price controls, the elimination of subsidies, and the opening of the economy to international trade.
3   By ending the restrictions on private economic activity and introducing new commercial and tax laws.
4   By disciplining state enterprises.

In practice, the latter measure would prove to be the hardest. SOEs had to be subjected to the discipline of the market: by allowing private firms and importers to compete; by eliminating subsidies, cheap credits, and tax concessions; by ending borrowing on the basis of central bank guarantees; by antitrust policies to break up the industrial giants; and by forcing loss-makers to close.[188] Most countries tackled the issue of state enterprises by drawing up a massive programme of privatization: state-owned enterprises were to be forced to sink or swim in competitive markets by a shift into private ownership. Several reasons motivated this decision. Firstly, the need to bring down state budget deficits in order to attract foreign funds meant that subsidies to unprofitable state-owned enterprises would have to be brought speedily to an end. Of course this immediately raised the issue of how to establish *which* firms were unprofitable in the absence of reliable price signals. The difficulty of establishing the profitability of a state-owned firm, however, merely strengthened the case for rapid mass privatization since all measures of profit in the absence of a genuine market test were now suspect and it was almost impossible to gauge the true opportunity cost to the economy of keeping a firm going. By quickly pushing these firms into the market, a genuine market test would bootstrap itself into being.

Secondly, to continue to prop up such firms would merely help to shield inefficient monopolies from the winds of competition, prevent new and more dynamic firms from entering the market, and thus postpone the advent of a market order.

Thirdly, these firms were increasingly perceived to have become convenient refuges for many of the old *nomenklatura*, the party faithful of the *ancien régime*, and hence – as has turned out to be the case in Yeltsin's Russia – potential bastions of resistance to the reform process as a whole. In many Eastern European countries, the communist old boy network remains strong, obstructing reform by design or by incompetence; the popular pressures of rising expectations required that the firms be either privatized or dismantled as quickly as possible lest the reforms lose their momentum and whatever popular support they enjoy.

Although the details vary, the reform policies devised by different East European countries have been broadly similar. Poland has travelled fastest and furthest down this road and has endured the most pain in doing so. At the time of writing, the consensus among observers is that the country may be turning a corner. More than 60 per cent of its labour force is now employed in the private sector – up from 45 per cent in 1990 – and the private sector now produces about 45 per cent of GDP. By government figures, the number of registered private companies is more than 200,000 and some estimates of the number of unincorporated businesses reach 1.5 million.[189] The case of the ex-GDR has to be treated separately since it has benefited from massive financial support from the ex-West Germany – paradoxically, this has been a source of some massive additional problems since it has reduced the willingness of workers and managers alike to endure the pain necessary to economic restructuring. The Treuhandanstalt, for example, the government agency charged with privatizing the east's old state-owned enterprises, has spared many non-viable firms the fate of liquidation, keeping them alive at a huge cost to the German public purse.[190]

Can you teach an old dog new tricks? The problem of state-owned enterprises

The main inspiration behind the East European reforms has been Anglo-Saxon market philosophy in its neoclassical form. The cold war has only one victor, the United States, and its triumph has been made all the more visible by the superior performance of its military technology in the 1990–1 Gulf War as compared with that of the Soviet Union's. What could be more natural, then, for those seeking a new model and a new ideology to guide them through what promises to be a dangerous and turbulent period, than to embrace the beliefs of those who can deliver such a performance? Accordingly we find Harvard University's Jeffrey Sachs firmly in the saddle as the leading western adviser to the economic reformers of Eastern Europe; Vaclav Klaus, former Czechoslovakia's finance minister, was Chicago trained; and the World Bank and IMF, both champions of a liberal market order, have been achieving visibility almost everywhere in the region.

Three years into the reforms, however, faith in markets is better justified by a stroll through the maze of street traders peddling their wares in the centre of Warsaw or Prague than by any visit to a state-owned firm. The standard of living in Eastern Europe as a whole has dropped, unemployment has risen, and social and ethnic tensions have increased as people seek out scapegoats for their plight. As yet, with the possible exception of Poland –

and here the signals are still mixed – there is only a glimmer of light at the reform end of tunnel.

During this period it has also become increasingly apparent that once the smaller SOEs in commerce and services have been disposed of, few, if any, of the larger state-owned firms that remain are likely to be viable on their own in a market economy. Some will be lucky and find foreign joint venture partners – indeed many already have – but the majority will either have to close down or continue to survive on state subsidies. In the planned economy, most were in reality little more than branch plants, extensions of the sectorial ministries to which they ultimately reported. Even in the ex-GDR, where they were grouped into large *Kombinate* – which in turn served as industrial models for Romania and post-1968 Czechoslovakia – the locus of decision-making power was in the Unions of State Enterprises (Vereinigung Volkseigener Betrieber),[191] the bureaucratic body to which the *Kombinate* reported, rather than in the latter themselves. Most of the activities that in the west we consider to be the job of a firm's top management – formulating strategies, giving direction to the firm's innovative activities, developing investment policies, etc. – were thus located outside the enterprise and in various parts of its supervising bureaucracy. As a consequence, given a firm's lack of scope and autonomy and its strong vertical dependencies, there was little internal *managerial* coordination of its production activities with external conditions; furthermore, given the fragmented and cloistered nature of the bureaucracies located above it and on which the firm depended, often there was no effective coordination of those strategic activities essential to its survival either. The positive and negative results of the system were neatly summed by Granick in a four-country comparison of state-owned enterprises:

Positive results
1 A high degree of concentration of enterprise effort on those aspects of performance which were accorded greater priority by the central managers of the industrial system.
2 Probably a high degree of intensity of work effort by managerial personnel in the enterprises, at least so long as the degree of *plan ambition* (degree of difficulty of achieving the targets for the key success indicators) did not grossly exceed an optimum level.

Negative results
1 A high degree of suboptimization by enterprise managers, who concentrated entirely on achieving *specific indicators* of performance which were quantified in their annual plans, at the expense of neglecting aspects of performance which were non-quantified, were primarily of longer run significance, or which had their main effects upon other enterprises.
2 A low level of contribution by enterprise managers to the quality of central planning; enterprise managers were given strong incentives to

manipulate the information they provide so as to minimize the degree to which their enterprise plan targets would be raised in future years.[192]

For state-owned enterprises to be viable in a market economy they need firstly to master for themselves the skills of strategic management and then to exercise them within a framework of corporate governance adapted to their new circumstances. The lucky ones, those that have found foreign joint venture partners to teach them these skills, will probably survive, albeit virtually under foreign ownership. Most, however, will not be so lucky and without outside help they will not be able to change. The rigid internal structures they inherit from their socialist past militate against it, and their much shrunken resource base is at present too slender to absorb the costs involved. Most important of all, perhaps, is the fact that their corporate culture, the intangible vessel in which past beliefs and practices have been 'sedimented',[193] is likely to fiercely resist the profound changes in attitudes and values required to bring about a successful organizational renewal. And current indicators are that enterprise managers are more likely to offer such resistance than their workers.[194]

A theoretical perspective

Privatization is currently taken to be one of the key policy instruments of a successful transformation of decrepit planned economies into market economies in Eastern Europe. Only by restoring enterprises to private ownership, it is argued, can a competitive climate be created and managers be given an incentive to perform. State ownership, in the event, turned out to be no ownership at all since firms as such could not be bankrupted and the state therefore was never compelled to bear the risk of residual ownership. In the absence of credible price signals, moreover, a firm's economic health could not be assessed and this further deprived the state of any legitimate grounds for closing down a non-performing firm. Its only option was to endlessly pump subsidies into loss-making firms on the ground that external economies and benefits probably compensated for internal diseconomies. It turned out that only the state itself as residual risk bearer could eventually be bankrupted and of course this is precisely what was beginning to happen. The basic premise that underpins the move to privatization is that since in a market a firm has to sink or swim unbuoyed by state subsidies, firms would learn to swim since now their very survival was at stake.

In a sense what we have here is essentially a neoclassical economist's view of the firm: a frictionless point on a production function adapting instantly to unambiguous and freely available market signals. It is a strictly behaviourist perspective which has the market ringing bells – i.e., emitting price stimuli – and the firm salivating in response. The function of the market, then, is to act as a source of stimuli, bearers of information on external realities, to which firms are expected to instantly adapt. Note that from this perspective the firm is not required to spend time *interpreting* the stimuli: to the neoclassical economist, the firm, as a dot on a production function, is conditioned to respond mechanically to external forces without taking the processing of data as in any way problematic. If data processing does occur, it is black box and yields outputs consistent with perfect foresight and rationality. The timely and intelligent response by firms to market signals then leads to market equilibrium and socially efficient outcomes. Where a firm is wanting in timeliness or intelligence, it ceases to be. We shall label this neoclassical approach to market learning, *N-learning*.[195]

A more Darwinian view of the firm, not necessarily incompatible with the neoclassical one, comes out of organizational theory. Known as the population ecology model,[196] it takes firms to be information processors whose ability to learn is restricted by bounded rationality. They can indeed adapt to market signals but only within a certain range, bracketed by internal data processing capacities as well as by the structural inertia of previously processed data (i.e., past experience). Markets then become an evolutionary selection mechanism that eliminates firms that fail to adapt – often the older ones, already set in their ways, or the weaker elements among the younger ones – and redistributes resources to firms, the more adaptable or the younger ones, that can cope with the necessary learning. Organizational evolution and change can therefore be thought of as the joint product of birth and death processes among firms and of internal transformation within existing firms. In contrast with the neoclassical perspective, then, the population ecology one does leave room for creative adaptation, for learning of the far from equilibrium kind, and for novelty. For birth and death processes are a function of how tolerant the environment turns out to be of less-than-optimal adaptation. Some socio-economic environments are more 'forgiving' of given behaviour patterns than others, and some allow time for exploration and mistakes, as well as for average performance. In such cases, the way that a firm processes and interprets environmental stimuli begins to matter. Only in totally unforgiving environments, where no 'slack' is available for learning and adaptation, does the population ecology approach reduce to the neoclassical one.

A gloomy hypothesis

An organizational ecology perspective on the economic transformations taking place in Eastern Europe would lead to the following provocative thought: newly created markets in the region are emitting signals that call for responses which, although well within the adaptive range of many newly created small firms, effectively extend beyond the typical state-owned firm's capacities for organizational adaptation. Partly shaped by policy-makers of the neoclassical persuasion, such markets have become unforgiving for such firms. They thus risk becoming the killing fields for most state-owned enterprises, and privatization will be the path that leads them there.

It may be that this is too gloomy a view of how markets are being made to function in Eastern Europe since we ourselves in the west do not use markets quite so unforgivingly as selection devices. Yet it is not market *practices* but market *ideology* that is making the running in Eastern Europe at present. Policy prescriptions are in the hands of economists, lawyers, and accountants, many of whom treat markets no less centripetally than Marxist-Leninists in their time treated bureaucracy, and some of whom passionately believe in N-learning as the most effective strategy for promoting socially optimal outcomes. In the next section we draw on our earlier discussion of China and Japan and on the I-space itself to try to better understand the nature of the options currently facing Eastern Europe and the CIS.

7.7: EASTERN EUROPE: AN INTERPRETATION

China and Eastern Europe compared

In section 7.3 we briefly outlined 'The Iron Law of Fiefs': bureaucratic failure channels transactions down into the fief region whenever rationality – a capacity to abstract from and to adequately codify recurring regularities in social and economic exchange – is insufficiently present to stabilize the institutionalization of exchanges in the region of the I-space labelled 'bureaucracies'. Another way of phrasing this would be to say that in situations where these two transactional forms compete with each other, the centripetal pull of fiefs sometimes proves to be stronger than the centripetal pull of bureaucracies. In a centrifugal cultural order, these transactional forms in fact collaborate rather than compete; they effectively counter-balance each other so that neither comes to dominate the cultural order at the expense of the other.

Does the Iron Law of Fiefs help to explain the problems encountered in dealing with the reform of state-owned enterprises in Eastern Europe as we have hypothesized that it does in China? There is plenty of evidence that inter-personal accommodation and the exercise of personal power still predominate within state-owned enterprises trying to cope with the irrationalities of the central planning mechanism[197] and the managerial mentalities that it generated, and that 'soft budget constraints' and 'investment hunger' continue to exert their influence in Eastern Europe as in China.[198] Moreover, the numerous personal fiefdoms that were lodged inside the state bureaucracy[199] appear to have survived the upheavals of the past three years in Eastern Europe as well as in the newly independent republics of the CIS.

Yet in contrast to China, which was an agrarian economy still operating under a quasi-feudal regime when the communists came to power in 1949, most Eastern European countries by the beginning of the Second World War had developed rational–legal institutions further up the I-space, and some, notably the GDR and Czechoslovakia before the war, had ranked among the most developed of capitalist economies, enjoying the advantages of both a modern infrastructure and an educated and skilled labour force. The Iron Law of Fiefs, therefore, if it was anywhere at work following the post-war communist takeover of Eastern Europe, in some countries at least – more in Czechoslovakia than in Hungary, and more in Hungary than in Bulgaria – would be operating against the transactional inertia of prior institutional and cultural investments established further up the I-space, an inertia that would counterbalance the centripetal pull of fiefs and thus would salvage a much larger chunk of an earlier rational–legal order in the upper regions of the I-space. How this order had in practice distributed transactions between bureaucracies and markets, that is to say, how far socio-economic institutions had been decentralized, largely depended on a particular country's liberal inheritance.

At first sight, then, Eastern Europe's more advanced state of industrialization gave its institutional reform problems a very different stamp from those of China's. Whatever ideology, if any, it draws on for its inspiration, the main challenge facing the PRC is still not fundamentally different from that facing any other modernizing country: it is to blend *Gemeinschaft* and *Gesellschaft*[200] cultural orders, to build up at least a few stable rational–legal institutions, and to add to the prevailing stock of particularistic values a number of more universalistic ones – in short, to first spread some of its institutional investments further up the I-space and *then* to let the codification–diffusion law take its course and gradually bring about the decentralization necessary to the creation of a modern economy. China's historical tragedy has been that with little understanding of western ways, it borrowed a development model which, for want of the necessary economic rationality, would constantly move it in the opposite direction, dragging it down the I-space and breeding a particularism that was guaranteed to bring it back – culturally, if not economically – to its point of departure. Its salvation since 1978 has been that the bureaucratic reach of fief forms of governance being limited, large chunks of economic activity in the rural areas and in the townships have successfully escaped the scrutiny of both central and local government. Given that the 'private' sector – i.e., collective, township, and family businesses – enjoys several times the rate of growth prevailing in the state sector and that the latter continues to stagnate, an ever-larger proportion of agricultural and industrial output now emerges from informal, self-regulating activities that are slowly crystallizing into a network of small local markets. The lack of any legal framework or physical infrastructure that could shift goods and information in large volumes on a national scale, however, continues to undermine attempts at market integration and keeps such markets as exist operating much lower down the I-space than do their western equivalents. Economic exchange in China, therefore, even in the private sector, remains far more local, personalized, and uncodified than it would if efficient market institutions and infrastructure were available.

Eastern Europe, on the other hand, heir to an important stock of pre-war institutional investments further up the I-space that pre-dates the advent of Marxism-Leninism, has been better able to counter its re-feudalizing tendencies – better, indeed, than many of the new republics of the CIS which, in their socio-economic and cultural characteristics, are more similar to China than they are to Eastern Europe. The challenge the region faces, therefore, is not so much moving *up* the I-space – in spite of the fact that in some measure the Iron Law of Fiefs remains at work in the region – as moving horizontally further to the right in it and towards markets.

The need for a Schumpeterian approach

But, as a policy description, is this so very new? From what has been said so far there seems at first sight to be little to distinguish what the I-space prescribes for Eastern Europe and what is already being advocated by western policy-advisers crowding the finance and economics ministries of the different countries in the region. For our framework to demonstrate its value are we not entitled to expect that it will take us further? What can it add to current offerings?

Recall from the previous section that the current policies being advocated for Eastern Europe have a strong centripetal flavour. The idea is to move the region's new cultural order into the market region, and, through the development of institutions designed to promote market efficiencies of the neoclassical kind – a securities and exchange commission, a bankruptcy law, antitrust instruments – to keep it there. We have labelled this process N-learning and have hypothesized that few state-owned firms, if any, will survive the ordeal without massive infusions of aid either from the state or from foreign investors. Even then a large number of survivors are likely to remain in intensive care for a long time to come – a 1992 OECD study measures the recovery period in decades rather than in years,[201] consuming scarce organizational resources that could be better employed elsewhere. What Eastern Europe needs, however, is not expensive terminal care in neoclassical market equilibrium for geriatric enterprises that cannot hope to make it, but an invigorating dose of Schumpeterian 'creative-destruction'. Whether we are then led to place the accent on the word 'creative' or on the word 'destruction' will depend on the economic system's capacity to *learn* and *adapt*. To distinguish it from N-learning, we have labelled such a capacity *S-learning*, in honour of Schumpeter, and we interpret it as the ability *to operationalize the SLC as a whole*. It is a capacity for S-learning that urgently has to be built up in Eastern Europe if economic renewal is to occur. The prescriptions of S-learning are quite different from those of

N-learning: as in the latter case, they involve a move towards markets; but they then move the reform process beyond markets and towards new institutional investments in the lower regions of the I-space. In this respect they help to distinguish the policy perspective presented here from others currently on offer.

S-learning is expressive of a capitalist process and can only effectively operate in a centrifugal culture. It therefore needs institutional structures located throughout the I-space if it is to fully activate an SLC and with it the six components of an effective innovation and renewal process (see Chapter 4).

The capitalist processes activated by S-learning can have different centres of gravity in the I-space. We might, for instance, associate market capitalism – the kind that operates in efficient equity and bond markets – more readily with the market region of the I-space than we would industrial or managerial capitalism with its scale economies and its large administrative hierarchies. This might be more closely associated with bureaucracies in the I-space and with transactions internal to firms.

Both forms of capitalism just cited would be assignable in the upper reaches of the I-space and many would argue that these are the only kinds of capitalism on offer. Should we accept such an argument, we would then be left with a dilemma.

The PRC has achieved a 12 per cent GNP growth rate in 1992 and a recent recalculation of the country's economic ranking by the IMF and the World Bank – one based on purchasing power parities (PPP) rather than GNP – has transformed it into the world's third largest economy.[202] Now, as we have argued above, China's growth has been fuelled by institutional and cultural processes located much further down the I-space than has been the case with western countries when they industrialized. We are thus invited to account for this growth either by arguing that it is not capitalist in nature or by identifying brands of capitalism whose centres of gravity can be located lower down the I-space. Under the first option we are led to acknowledge the existence of economic mechanisms that are superior to capitalism in generating growth, but since they are manifestly not Marxist-Leninist we have no idea what they might be. Under the second we are led to seek out those features of a centrifugal culture that, while located in the lower part of the I-space, none the less contribute to a capitalist process.

Entrepreneurial and network capitalism: the re-personalization of exchange

What would be the characteristic features of capitalistic processes lower down the I-space?

The first is that they would be a small firm phenomenon, driven by family businesses and township or collective enterprises, and linked through a dense network of subcontracting arrangements.

The second would make them non-contractual in orientation. Exchange relationships would be collaborative rather than competitive and based on broader notions of reciprocity and mutual obligation than are commonly found in market contracting.

The third is that in contrast to capitalistic processes operating further up the I-space, these would operate as far as possible beyond the reach of state bureaucracies. The law and state regulations would be perceived as a hindrance rather than a help and this would limit the scope of transactions that could be undertaken. Thus capitalist processes further down the I-space seek a low profile and for this reason economic growth remains external to the firm; it is achieved by new players entering the market rather than through the organizational growth of existing players.

The fourth and final feature that we might associate with such capitalistic processes is that they would be better equipped to handle uncodifiable uncertainty than codifiable risk. In this sense they exhibit entrepreneurial qualities that are absent further up the I-space. In the lower region of the I-space, uncertainty is *absorbed* through the gradual build-up of trust relationships rather than *reduced* through the writing of contracts. This requires some sharing of values and beliefs by transacting parties and implies a considerable up-front investment in face-to-face relationships.

Within firms, the transactional style associated with this type of capitalism is that of fiefs; working relationships are based on personal loyalty and commitment. Between firms, the transactional style is that of clans: a mutual adjustment of players to each other based on negotiations and a shared orientation. In their more codified and less personalized form these two transactional styles give rise to bureaucracies and markets, or, in our new terms, to managerial and market capitalism. In the lower regions of the I-space, however, they produce, respectively, *entrepreneurial capitalism* to regulate intra-firm relationships, and *network capitalism* to regulate inter-firm relationships.

If we leave to one side those transactional forms which in this discussion we have associated with internal organization, that is to say managerial and entrepreneurial capitalism, we are left with markets and network capitalism as distinctive ways of ordering a firm's external economic relationships. Armed with these two institutional orders, we are now in a position to expand the 'Iron Law of Fiefs' hypothesis outlined in section 7.3.

Recall that Chinese state-owned firms were dragged back into the fief region as a result of their being unable to move up the I-space towards a stable bureaucratic order. Recall further that small entrepreneurial family businesses, township firms, and collective enterprises moved towards the right in the lower region of the I-space; from the clan region they could then establish exchange relationships with each other beyond the reach of the bureaucratic gaze.

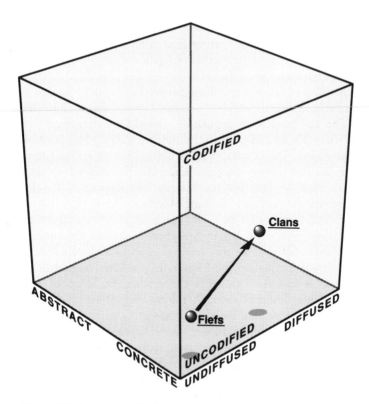

Figure 7.5 Network capitalism

What we see in China's small firm sector is the natural complement to the Iron Law of Fiefs. Being unable for infrastructural, institutional, and cultural reasons to move up the I-space, these small firms are building a capitalist order that operates at a lower level of codification than the western market variant (see Figure 7.5). Redding has labelled this variant on capitalism *Chinese Capitalism*,[203] because he sees it at work among the overseas Chinese of South-East Asia. We shall use the term *Network Capitalism* to mark the fact that it is a generic phenomenon, as much at work in the family workshops of the 'Third Italy', the relational contracting of the Japanese firm,[204] or the 'old boy' networks of the City of London.

A question that might be asked is whether network capitalism represents a way station along a new trajectory towards market capitalism – i.e., convergence by another route – or a stable institutional order in its own right. Our discussion of convergence in Chapter 6 led us to reject the centripetal view of cultural development implicit in a 'stages' approach. And as we suggested above, a centrifugal cultural order is quite consistent with a transactional bias towards one particular region of the I-space. One could

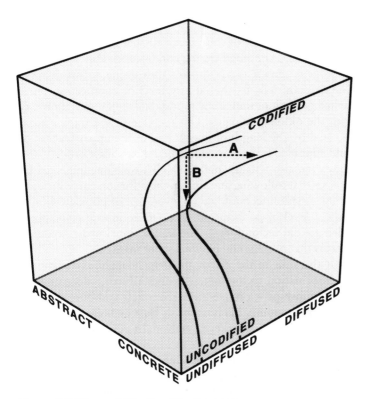

Figure 7.6 IT as a shift in the diffusion curve

then imagine a selective move up the space of certain institutional practices which leaves intact the transactional centre of gravity of the whole.

Another crucial variable cautions us against viewing network capitalism too hastily as a 'pre-modern' variant of market capitalism and due to disappear when the latter takes root: technology. The large-scale transactional infrastructures that populate the upper regions of the I-space are in large part the product of communications technologies that were created in the second half of the nineteenth century: the railways and the telegraph. Chandler had described in detail how large managerial hierarchies emerged to take advantage of the extended possibilities for coordination offered by these new technologies.[205] To be cost-effective, however, the uses of these technologies required a high degree of codification in exchange and a consequent depersonalization of relationships. Only in this way could transacting in large numbers – a precondition for mass production – be secured.

The new information technologies, by massively increasing the volume of data that can be processed and transmitted per unit of time, effectively reduce the pressure to codify. Where the fax replaces the telex and the video-conference replaces the telephone, we shall see a *repersonalization* of exchange relationships which then operate much further down the I-space. The impact of information technology on the codification, abstraction, and diffusion of knowledge is shown as a rightward shift in the diffusion curve of Figure 7.6. The diagram tells us that at any level of codification more people can be reached per unit of time using modern information technology than could be with the old technologies. This increase in the transactional population is indicated by the length of line A, and in the upper reaches of the I-space it would appear to favour an extension of the market order.

The diagram, however, also tells us something else, this time indicated by line B. This line tells us that following any shift in the diffusion curve brought about by modern information technologies, a given size of population may be reached at a lower level of codification – i.e., using more personalized means – than under the old technologies. The transactional order favoured by this second effect is that of clans and networks, not markets.

We conclude that the shift in the diffusion curve brought about by the spread of modern information technologies favours a further decentralization of economic relationships – a move away from fiefs and bureaucracies – but that such decentralization is likely to be at least as favourable to the spread of network capitalism as to market capitalism. In a centrifugal cultural order, of course, these institutional forms are as likely to be complementary to each other as they are to be competitive. Only if they get imbued with ideology are they likely to become antagonistic to each other.

What implications can we draw from the above discussion with reference to Eastern Europe? We have argued that SOEs in Eastern and Central Europe are less subject to the Iron Law of Fiefs than are Chinese SOEs. They are therefore more stably located in bureaucracies. The main challenge of the reforms, therefore, has been framed in terms of shifting these firms to the right in the I-space towards the market region. Yet an overpreoccupation with the problems of SOEs and with the need to usher in market capitalism has led policy-makers to neglect the possibilities of network capitalism and the small firms that make it possible. As in China, it is network capitalism rather than market capitalism that is taking root in the debris of the planned economy in post-socialist societies. An ideological commitment to market capitalism takes network capitalism to be a transient phenomenon, incapable of delivering the rates of growth required to pull Central and Eastern Europe out of its communist past, and due to melt away as soon as the institutions necessary to the proper functioning of market capitalism have been put in place in the upper part of the I-space. Nevertheless, the successes of network capitalism in those cultures where it has been allowed to flourish should alert us to the fallacy that we commit when we reduce as multifaceted a phenomenon as capitalism to a market order.

7.8: CONCLUSION

Linking a theoretical framework to the real world

Unlike a specific theory, a general conceptual framework cannot be directly tested empirically; it follows that it cannot be directly refuted empirically either.[206] The I-space is just such a framework. Its inaccessibility to direct testing, however, does not completely disconnect it from the real world for it can still be a source of theories and hypotheses that are themselves amenable to empirical tests. Where these are not forthcoming then the framework remains stuck in a metaphysical limbo which is quite incapable of acting on the world as we know it.

A framework's value can be gauged by the number and quality of testable theories that it can spawn which subsequently become well corroborated. Since generating such theories is a vast enterprise in itself, the best we could hope for in this chapter was to explore one small area of application and to show what kind of theorizing is possible. To then go on to test whatever theories come out of the exercise would take us well beyond the purpose of this book, which is to present the framework and to provide a modest illustration of its potential fruitfulness.

I have chosen as an illustrative theme the collapse of communism both because it is highly topical and hence can demonstrate the utility of a good explanatory framework but also because it is an arena in which a good number of explanatory theories still compete for allegiance. Since these are numerous and varied, I will not enumerate them but will single out those that might help to throw our own contribution into relief.

The modernization process in the I-space

The backcloth to our discussion is the process of social and economic modernization taken as a progressive complexification of the social order and the integration of ever-larger populations into viable political governance structures. The sheer pressure of numbers involved in more extensive forms of social and economic exchange have traditionally called for higher degrees of codification of transactions with a collateral differentiation of roles, a progressive division of labour, and a gradual depersonalization of social relationships that extend beyond the primary group. Social theorists have variously labelled the resulting transformation a move from mechanical to organic solidarity,[207] from *Gemeinschaft* to *Gesellschaft*,[208] or a move towards the 'cash nexus'.[209] For us these transformations, however defined and however performed, all involve some degree of movement up the I-space towards greater codification. Others, prominent among them Talcot Parsons, have also stressed the parallel shift that occurs from particularistic to universalistic values – what we would describe in the space as a move towards an abstract order and away from the concrete immediacy of the here and now.[210]

We recall from our discussion of the SLC in Chapter 4 that a move towards a codified abstract order sets in motion forces for the diffusion of information within a target population that either has to be allowed for or has to be actively countered. If allowed for, we sooner or later obtain a liberal order with the bulk of social decision-making decentralized to markets – both political (i.e., the competition being for votes) and economic. If countered, we require that the agencies of centralization effectively control the diffusion of information and channel it towards designated and privileged recipients. At the societal level such agencies might well be the state itself and its institutions.

Theories of modernization, explicitly or otherwise, are usually agreed that social evolution requires a move towards greater codification and abstraction in the I-space. Where they differ is on how far this necessarily entails a decentralization of power based on the inherent diffusibility of codified and abstract information. And the reason for their differences is not hard to see: codification and abstraction appear at first sight to be merely the cognitive expression of individual thought processes whereas the diffusion of knowledge invokes the concept of power relations in social exchange. Where cognition is treated independently of social power, then the cognitive trajectory expressing social evolution towards greater codification and abstraction, as indicated in the E-space, might appear to be determined by cognitive considerations alone and merely to reflect how far given individuals or groups have progressed in their thinking. Such is, for example, the position adopted by 'internal' histories of science which explain advances in a particular field almost exclusively in terms of the internal logic of the scientific problems it addresses, leaving out of consideration the influence on that logic of wider social forces.[211]

As soon as the diffusion dimension is brought into play, however, it becomes apparent that what can be thought and what can be communicated are in fact heavily intertwined. And since what can be communicated is never independent of the distribution of power in a social system, it becomes plausible to argue that decisions taken on how far to control the availability of transactional knowledge within a population must inevitably affect the way that codification and abstraction themselves are performed and in what area of political endeavour cognitive investments will be sanctioned. Political and economic control of the diffusion of knowledge, then, by shaping the cognitive and communicative strategies of individual agents, affects the social system's ability to evolve epistemologically. Whether such evolution is also progressive remains a controversial question that we must leave to one side.

Caution is needed here. By equating the exercise of power with the ability to control the diffusion of transactional knowledge we appear to be transforming centripetalism into a phenomenon that can only occur on the left of the I-space. It may well be that in practice a centripetal cultural order is easier to maintain in fiefs or bureaucracies where power is concentrated; but certain societies, notably the US, take information sharing seriously enough to institutionalize it and thus to make sure that it takes place. The Freedom of Information Act or the legal restrictions placed on insider trading, to take two examples, together with the institutionalized emphasis on openness and transparency in political and economic transactions, all point to a centripetal bias towards markets, which, although not strong – the US, along with other western industrialized countries, remains a centrifugal culture – has an effect on the way that an SLC will operate at the national level.

Centripetal versus centrifugal approaches to modernization

Could the seventy-year-long ideological tug of war between a hierarchical and a market order account for the centripetal quality of the policies, both political and economic, that had been designed to bring either of them about? Is a belief in an omniscient socialist state in effect any more absurd than a belief in an omniscient free market?

The basic difference between a theory of modernization derived from the operation of the SLC in the I-space and those derived from an ideological belief in either markets or hierarchies is that the latter tend to promote a centripetal model of institutional development and the former a centrifugal one. The difference is consequential. Centripetalism of whatever kind is inevitably led to describe complex social transformations as the linear progression of a point in the I-space, which, when pausing for a few centuries to take a breather, produces 'stages' of development: i.e., feudalism, absolutism, capitalism, if one is a liberal; slavery, feudalism, capitalism, socialism, if one is a Marxist. European history certainly lends itself to such a schematization, which is probably why a Eurocentric world view might occasionally be tempted to crystallize these stages into historical or development laws.[212] The mechanistic flavour of this intellectual operation is well brought out by some remarks made by Immanuel Wallerstein who, explaining how he came to formulate his Euro-conditioned thesis of a 'Modern World System', claimed that he had been inspired by the analogy with astronomy, 'which purports to explain the laws governing the universe, although (as far as we know) only one universe has ever existed'. Wallerstein then continued:

> What do astronomers do? As I understand it, the logic of their argument involves two separate operations. They use the laws derived from the study of smaller physical entities, the laws of physics, and argue that (with perhaps certain specified exceptions) these laws hold by analogy for the system as a whole. Second, they argue a posteriori. If the whole system is

to have a given state at time y, it most probably had a certain state at time x.[213]

What starts out, then, as a descriptive convenience, in some hands becomes transformed by degrees into an imperative prescription based on a conviction that ineluctable historical processes can be nudged along a little by fostering only the growth of those institutions in the I-space consistent with the location of the next stage scheduled to make its appearance. Centripetalism distrusts any institutional investments carried out outside that location. It treats them as potential competitors that have lost out – or are about to lose out – to historical forces, and at best views them as vestiges to be tolerated rather than actively built up. Marx might credit capitalism with sweeping away the cobwebs of feudalism across the globe, but he could afford to be generous: he believed that socialism was about to visit the same fate upon capitalism and that he himself was on the side of history.[214]

From an I-space perspective a centripetal cultural order fails to promote the institutional diversity that facilitates social learning and adaptation. China's centripetal move into a Marxist-Leninist bureaucratic order after 1949 is instructive in this respect. By simultaneously trying to do away with the feudal vestiges of the 'old China' while espousing the economic irrationalities of the planned economy, it found itself falling between two stools, being neither able to construct and stabilize a set of rational–legal institutions in the codified region of the I-space, nor able legitimately to return to established traditions located in the fief region. It was only when Deng Xiaoping blessed the pursuit of 'socialism with Chinese characteristics' in 1978, thereby endorsing the use of a greater measure of economic rationality in the conduct of the country's affairs, that a more centrifugal accommodation between the upper and lower regions of the I-space became possible, this time driven by pragmatism rather than ideology. The outcome was a gradual decentralization towards clans.

To turn what is possible into a reality, however, remains arduous. The enduring particularism of Chinese culture continues to undermine the growth of institutions based on universalistic values: an independent judiciary and the impersonal rule of law, a central bank that is not at the beck and call of the ministry of finance or the party, a press that promotes the free flow of information and ideas, etc., still have to make their appearance in the PRC.

Yet arguably, Japan could also still be characterized as a particularistic culture. Many observers would claim that such particularism is at the root of its continued inability or reluctance to contribute to the construction of a universalistic international economic order. Van Wolferen, for example, notes in Japan 'the near absence of any idea that there can be truths, rules, principles, or morals that always apply, no matter what the circumstances'.[215] Particularism, however, has not prevented the country from building up a viable set of institutions in the upper reaches of the I-space. In spite of the continued pull of fiefs and clans, Japan has undoubtedly become more *centrifugal*, and possibly more so than a number of western countries that may have overinvested in bureaucracies and markets and that have consequently seen their capacities for S-learning subsequently eroded. Their own institutionalized centripetalism may thus be creating a distorting lens through which they look at Japan. They keep looking out for a market culture similar to their own and for that reason fail to detect the emergence of a learning culture, centred on clans and increasingly aligned with the possibilities of network capitalism.

Conclusion: the lesson from China for Eastern Europe?

The hypothesis that emerges from our discussion in this chapter is that in China a centripetal cultural order is slowly giving way to a centrifugal one, and that this evolution is accompanied by a decentralization of economic power, a shift in the I-space from fiefs to clans. The Tiananmen Square episode and its aftermath has confronted the Chinese leadership with a choice not dissimilar to that faced by other modernizing economies in Asia: either a coercive return to a centripetal variant of Marxism-Leninism, or a looser arrangement in which some economic decentralization is offered in return for continued political control by the centre. Economic pragmatism has in effect become the order of the day: as we have seen, the decentralization of institutional development is occurring at a lower level of codification perhaps than was experienced in western countries, but it appears to remain centrifugal enough to promote something like S-learning.

The hypothesis, reformulated as a move by China towards network capitalism, helps to explain why in spite of the continuing presence of large, mostly stagnant state-owned firms centripetally assigned to bureaucracies – but in effect, as we have seen, operating in fiefs – and in spite of the chaos and corruption that continue to sap the Chinese leadership's Confucian quest for harmony, the country continues to turn in one of the fastest rates of economic growth in the world.

What lessons, then, if any, does China's modernization experience hold for Eastern Europe as it struggles free of the centripetal shackles of Marxism-Leninism? Simply this: avoid trading-in one set of shackles for another: those of a centripetal market order. The I-space takes the emergence of centrifugal cultures, whatever the transactional bias that they might display, as the distinguishing mark of modernity; in such cultures, to be sure, markets play an essential role but by no means an exclusive one. Centrifugalism promotes S-learning; by locating institutions throughout the I-space it stimulates the flow of new knowledge throughout a culture. S-learning is creative destruction; it is therefore both a pain and a joy, continuously dislodging parts of what has gone before and replacing them with something new. S-learning, as a capitalistic process, goes on throughout the I-space, in fiefs no less than in markets. An N-learning approach to modernization and development, one that would paint us into the north-east corner of the I-space in a quixotic search for a total market order, would breed only alienation, as Marx himself well understood, a state from which all possibilities for S-learning – and hence for capitalism itself – have been squeezed out. Death, by any other name.

Chapter 8
Conclusion

ABSTRACT

Economic growth and development today is limited less by the availability of physical resources than by environmental constraints on their utilization. Increasingly, it is the output rather than the input side of the physical transformation process that is causing concern. Putting the lid on economic growth, however, would create intense conflicts between societies at different levels of development. Yet this need only be so if we continue to think of our planetary resource endowments in purely physical terms.

In Chapter 1 we saw that under certain circumstances information resources can effectively be substituted for physical ones but that whatever substitution occurs is the fruit of a *learning* process. Orthodox economics cannot convincingly handle such learning since it takes the information environment of economic agents as being exogenously given. It is, of course, this givenness that allows market institutions to be cast in such a favourable light.

Our analysis does not call into question the utility of market institutions. Problems only appear when these are handled centripetally and set in competition with alternative institutional arrangements. The information perspective that we have adopted in this book points to a need to broaden the economic agenda to accommodate non-market institutional forms as complements rather than alternatives to markets.

The new technologies introduced by the information revolution point in the same direction. They are increasing our cognitive capacity to process and transmit data and thus effectively reducing the pressure on us to economize on data processing resources. As a consequence it is becoming ever more feasible to transact efficiently from positions lower down the I-space where relations can once more be personalized. In effect, in pursuit of such personalized transactions, western firms are building up the processes of network capitalism *inside* their organizations.

Our theorizing in this book has been applied at the level of individual human agents and of groupings of such individuals. We hypothesize that it also applies at the level of processes – physical, biological, and psychological – that go to make up such individuals. If so, then the I-space becomes a tool for exploring the way that nature as a whole economizes on information processing.

8.1: THE LIMITS TO NEOCLASSICAL GROWTH

The edition of *The Economist* that spanned the two weeks from 21 December 1991 to 3 January 1992 – a bridge between two fateful years in Europe's post-war history – commented that environmentalists

> are suspicious of economic growth, because they think it will use up too much of the world's natural resources. This is turning many of them against free trade, because free trade means more growth. They are appalled by the thought that the world's population will double in the coming century, because that will eat up resources even faster. The physical earth is becoming more important to them than the people who live on it.[1]

Citing the collapse of communism in Eastern Europe and the Soviet Union, the leader went on to assert, however, that 'there is now no alternative to the free market as the way to organize economic life'. Another article in the same edition helped to clarify for the attentive reader specifically how free markets 'organize economic life', claiming that 'Neoclassical economics is now international orthodoxy'.[2]

The fixity of physical resources, however, has always sat uncomfortably with the horizontal supply curves required by competitive markets. These promise a level of abundance that the earth is in no position to deliver. Orthodox economists, of course, are in no way discomfited since they can always retreat behind the usual 'as if' assumptions: in competitive markets economic agents will behave *as if* supplies were infinitely elastic. Environmentalists, however, could then reply with some justification that since the supply of physical resources is manifestly not elastic to the extent required by efficient markets, economic agents are behaving *as if* they were being irrational. Economic rationality, they will argue, at least that of the neoclassical variety, may not offer the surest path to ecological salvation.

The argument in favour of limiting our consumption of natural resources has been around since the time of Malthus.

In the past two decades it has undergone a subtle shift. In 1971, a study carried out by Donella and Denis Meadows for the Club of Rome[3] forecast a gradual exhaustion of certain key resources on which successful industrial-ization was thought to depend. The limits to economic growth, the authors hypothesized, were set by the finite availability of specific resources. The case was well presented and well received by the general public; its point for some, however, was somewhat blunted by the realization that technological change could always replace physical inputs as they increased in scarcity by more abundant ones. After all possibilities for technical substitution have run their course, the world may indeed one day run out of resources; but not in our lifetime; not even in our children's.

Nevertheless, in the late 1980s new constraints on humanity's rate of economic growth and development appeared, this time not linked to the *availability* of physical resources but to their *transformation* into consumable goods and services. Greenhouse gases, which threaten to significantly raise the surface temperatures of our planet, and the depletion of the life-protecting ozone layer in the upper atmosphere by the over-production of CFCs are both the by-products of excessive and ecologically destabilizing output levels rather than of any growing scarcity of inputs. According to the new arguments, then, even if physical resources were as abundant as horizontal supply curves pretend that they are, and whether on account of technological substitution or not, we would still face limits to economic growth based on the fact that their unrestricted conversion into outputs has been poisoning our planet for some time and is continuing to do so at an increasing pace. Environmental Malthusianism is thus even more restrictive than the earlier version: the limits to growth are not set by supply constraints so much as by the irreducible waste generated by these supplies; it is not so much a question of what the earth can provide but of what it can absorb.

Putting a lid on growth or indeed reversing it – as some environmentalists advocate – would have a devastating effect on global social and economic development. At a stroke it would convert the economic process into a vast zero-sum game both within and between different societies. Suddenly we would all find ourselves fighting for a share of a fixed or a shrinking pie, and although demographic growth every year would continue to push up the number of claimants – some demographers forecast a doubling of the world population between 1990 and the year 2020 – the size of the pie, if it is fixed by the new ecological imperative, could no longer be increased without making it inedible for all.

The deep irony is that at the very moment that, with the demise of Marxism, many thought that distributional issues could finally be taken off the economic agenda, they are once more being thrust under our nose. Socialism had made the equitable distribution of wealth primarily an ethical issue; the environmental revolution appears set to convert it increasingly into a practical matter of survival if a Hobbesian 'war of all against all' is not to tear the planet apart. Unsurprisingly, many people remain reluctant to abandon the positive-sum game perspective fostered by neoclassical and Keynesian models of economic growth.

The basic message of this book is that over the long term they may not have to. It is only our obsessive preoccupation with *physical* resources that makes future economic growth appear zero-sum, and neither a neoclassical, nor a Keynesian, nor indeed a Marxist approach to the problem offers any useful change of perspective.

Yet go back for a moment to the production function of Figure 1.8. It describes the basic premise around which the concepts presented in this book have been built. What does it tell us? Simply this: that in producing a given level of output, any constraints on the consumption of physical inputs can

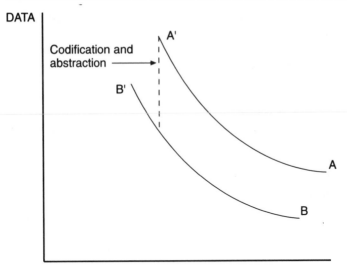

Figure 8.1 The information production function

be circumvented by an increased consumption of data inputs and that any restrictions imposed on the use of the latter by the limitations of our data processing apparatus – i.e., bounded rationality, etc. – can in turn be overcome through codification and abstraction by converting data into information (see Figure 8.1). The limitations on global output imposed upon us by emerging ecological constraints on physical processes – associated with greenhouse gases, pollution, the depletion of the ozone layer, etc. – are certainly not imaginary; they have to be taken seriously. But they are far from constituting the absolute limitations on growth that a conventional economic perspective makes them out to be. They can be circumvented by our proven ability to make novel and effective use of data and information; that is to say, by our ability to *learn*.

Figure 8.1 shows the required learning to be of two kinds: (1) *Experiential learning* described by a gradual substitution of data for physical resources; this is the kind of integrative and incremental learning described by learning or experience curves in manufacturing and it moves one up the curve AA′ towards the left. (2) *Conceptual learning* in which information is extracted from data in a discontinuous fashion – a downward movement in the diagram from A′ to B′. The first kind of learning economizes on physical resources through a gradual process of data substitution; the second economizes on the data itself. Combined, they lead us towards the origin in the diagram and thus over time towards an ever-smaller consumption of physical and data inputs for a given level of output.

I believe that Figure 8.1 provides the foundations for a new way of thinking about the role of knowledge in economic processes, one whose constituent elements are described in Chapters 2 to 6 of this book. Let us briefly recapitulate what these are.

8.2: RECAPITULATION

In conformity with the Principle of Least Action, physical systems act to preserve themselves and survive over time, i.e., to fight the forces of entropy that threaten their integrity. Data processing systems – cells, individual human beings, social systems – can effectively reduce their rate of entropy production by minimizing the consumption of physical resources such as space, time, or energy that they require for a given level of activity.[4] As we have seen, they do this firstly by increasing their level of data processing activity – i.e., by moving up the transformation curve AA′ of Figure 8.1 and replacing physical inputs by data inputs in their productive activities – and secondly, within the data processing operations themselves, by reducing the volume of data to be handled. Through acts of codification and of abstraction, data processing systems metabolize the data they encounter into information and knowledge, thus keeping themselves decongested and open to the absorption of new experiences. Their metabolism functions all the better where the data inputs are themselves already low in entropy. Properly deployed, codification and abstraction give a data processing system access to low entropy sources; that is, those with a greater initial capacity to do work.[5] Such systems are not omnivorous, however, since their ability to process particular kinds of data is partly dictated by the physical substrate of their cognitive apparatus – frogs, for example, do not see the same world as we do,[6] and our own has been greatly expanded by the technological amplification of our five senses – and partly conditioned by prior data processing experiences held in memory.

The E-space, presented and discussed in Chapter 2, takes codification and abstraction as two distinct yet interrelated ways of economizing on cognitive effort. Codification economizes on the quantity of data required to form categories; abstraction economizes on the number of categories required to apprehend phenomena. The first gives form to the particular case and the second, by giving generality to a particular form, extends its applicability to new cases. These will now be apprehended by the cognitive apparatus from the outset as more 'organized' phenomena and hence as low entropy inputs. The mix of cognitive economies achieved through codification and abstraction by the individual data processor over time, as well as their extent, expresses this learning style.

The codification and abstraction of experience, by converting it into a low entropy input, i.e., knowledge, makes it simultaneously more accessible and useful to others as well as inherently more diffusible. Other things being equal, knowledge that has achieved a highly codified and abstract state will diffuse through a population of data processors faster than knowledge that remains immersed in the data that gave rise to it. The U- and C-spaces of Chapter 3 show why: not only does codified and abstract knowledge enjoy a greater degree of utility, but it is easier to transmit down a communication channel at speed without information losses.

The U- and C-spaces also show, however, that other things are in fact rarely equal and that in addition to the cognitive bias of senders that may place them in a part of the E-space from which effective communication becomes problematic, receivers may either lack the necessary prior investments in codes and concepts required to understand a message, or lack the values that may attune them to the potential relevance of a message – in short, the right orientation is wanting.

Social information processing, therefore, far from being able to assume a frictionless and instantaneous 'Newtonian' flow of well-codified abstract data in the information plenum as required by the prevailing economic orthodoxy, is in fact characterized by numerous blockages that express what are often irreducible differences in cognition and values between individuals and groups.

In Chapter 4 we brought individual (E-space) and social information processing (U- and C-spaces) together to create a three-dimensional I-space through which to apprehend the spatiotemporal distribution and flow of data in the data field. By doing this it becomes possible to examine the creation of new knowledge as an emergent property of the field itself. Whether it was generated through an import of fresh external data into the field from outside or through a reconfiguration of data already in the field, it was hypothesized that radically new knowledge would generally flow clockwise in the I-space through a social learning cycle (SLC) made up of six components: scanning, problem-solving, abstraction, diffusion, absorption and impacting. The cycle might be described as an attractor that could be either shaped or dissolved by the pattern of institutional structures that channel the flow of data of the I-space. It has points both of minimum entropy at which new knowledge structures are most articulated and coherent, and of maximum entropy at which such structures are absorbed and digested by a population of data processors, getting dissolved in the process.

The SLC is a creative destroyer: in order to accommodate new knowledge that is epistemologically incompatible or incommensurate with what is currently on offer, it often dislodges existing cognitive investments distributed throughout the I-space, eroding or weakening the institutional structures that house them as it does so.

The institutional structures through which social information processing takes place were presented and discussed in Chapter 5. They are themselves partly products and partly causes of the data field. Although in practice many institutional possibilities and combinations of possibilities are discernible we distinguished four 'ideal types':[7] markets, bureaucracies, clans, and fiefs.

Markets and bureaucracies deal with well-codified and abstract data, differing only with respect to its diffusion – markets favour information sharing, bureaucracies not – whereas fiefs and clans work with uncodified and concrete, contextual data, with fiefs exhibiting a centralizing bias that is much weaker in clans.

All social systems of any size will require a mix of these institutional types. The values and beliefs that reside in a system, however, when combined with the distribution of power within it, will give prominence to certain institutional forms over others and confer on the SLC that activates the system a distinctive signature. In Chapter 5 we also took social interests as important determinants of institutional choice. Effective governance requires a good fit between the generality of social interests pursued – i.e., their degree of abstraction – and the location in the I-space of the institutional structures selected to serve them.

It might be said that the more abstract and universal the interests to be served by a given set of institutions, the larger the population of data processors that can potentially be brought under a unified system of governance, always providing that the institutions so activated have actually been located in the I-space and integrated with each other in a way that favours unified governance. Where this is not the case, the SLC can become blocked or stunted and certain groups will evolve outside the governance structure and in opposition to it.

In Chapter 6, the structuring and sharing of information were taken to be the defining characteristics of a cultural process. Codification, abstraction, and diffusion underlie the production and exchange of information, so that a political economy of information and a theory of culture become in effect indistinguishable from each other.

Cultural systems act centripetally or centrifugally in the data field – i.e., their constituent institutions compete or collaborate from different locations in the I-space with varying degrees of strength. A culturally inspired configuration of institutions provides data processors with situated responses as well as itself making a contribution to the interplay of forces and flows in the data field. Yet, by making the ubiquity of well-codified abstract information a prerequisite for efficient economic transactions, neoclassical economics either confines the economic problems of society exclusively to the market region of the I-space, thus relegating the study of other regions to sociologists or anthropologists, or, if it does explore other regions, it is mainly with a view to finding ways of shifting any plausibly economic transactions that inhabit them into the market region. The efficiency available in bureaucracies, fiefs, or clans is then defined as suboptimal or second best with respect to economic outcomes available in markets, outcomes that, as we have seen, implicitly depend on the nature of the information environment that regulates transactions. How the definition of economic efficiency itself might vary with changes in the information environment is not addressed. Thus whereas a theory of culture makes economic explanation contingent on the information environment, orthodox economic theory, by parametrizing the information environment at the outset, effectively converts theory of culture into an alternative to economic explanation.

Parametrizing transactionally relevant information in this way has been one of the main reasons that the neoclassical orthodoxy has been unable to cope with economic and institutional change.[8]

8.3: N- AND S-LEARNING

What consequences flow from the occultation of information by orthodox economics? Firstly, by taking the information environment as exogenously given, it takes market exchange by assumption as being the only transactionally efficient institutional order on offer. Other forms of exchange might still have to be tolerated but only in the absence of a viable market option. If, it is argued, the economic problem of society is taken to be the allocation of scarce resources[9] then let us not add to society's problems by turning information, the vital lubricant of the allocation process, into a resource that is itself subject to scarcities. Dealing with physical scarcities is challenge enough as it is.

Unsurprisingly, given the nature of the basic assumptions, efficient markets usually turn out to be the most desirable of locations in the I-space. And since casual empiricism indicates that industrialized countries have more of them than do pre-industrial ones – i.e., stock exchanges, commodity exchanges, bond markets, etc. – it seems reasonable to assume that efficient markets are what development effectively requires. Taken as it stands, the belief that in many countries adding efficient markets to the panoply of existing institutions is uncontroversial and unlikely to do much harm. If intelligently followed it is even likely to do some good. It is when the plea for efficient markets goes centripetal, when markets are viewed as adequate *alternatives* to most if not all existing institutions, that the problems start. All non-market solutions become instances of 'market failure', a situation to be tolerated rather than sought. Williamson's quip that 'in the beginning there were markets'[10] says it all.

The belief that development, whether short term or long term, is about ever more codification, abstraction, and diffusion of information – i.e., a conscious attempt to move away from the origin in the I-space – is what I have labelled in Chapter 7 the N-learning hypothesis. It finds its way into theories of short-term economic behaviour such as the rational expectation hypothesis[11] or the more evolutionary stage-models of economic growth, whether these move us towards a bureaucratic order but no further (as with Marx's or Durkheim's) or beyond it towards a market one (as with, say, Rostow).[12] In the first case we move towards greater codification and abstraction but not necessarily towards greater diffusion. In the second we progress along all three dimensions of the I-space, thus completing half an SLC. In the latter case, the emerging market order becomes a focus for teleonomic explanations of development processes[13] and implicitly underpins all beliefs in the convergence hypothesis.

N-learning was contrasted in Chapter 7 with S-learning where development, instead of constituting an adaptive response to the irresistible pull of centripetal forces emanating from the market region of the I-space – a transactional black hole that vacuum cleans the I-space of all other forms of exchange – expresses a steady densification of transactions and transactional structures throughout the I-space. Development in an S-learning regime thus becomes a product of centrifugalism and of the SLCs that make it possible. It requires a continuing evolution and renewal of most existing structures rather than their elimination.

N-learning and the economic orthodoxy to which it gave rise have proved to be a powerful paradigm and one that even in the face of a riding tide of criticism has proved hard to dislodge.[14] Its detractors account for its continued incumbency by the lack of a convincing alternative that might compete with it; after all, they argue, it takes a theory to beat a theory.[15] Like a Ptolemaic model barnacled with epicycles, therefore, it will continue to serve until something better comes along.

The absence of a competing theory, however, is not the whole story. The neoclassical model's staying power is in no small part due to the fact that it effectively remains a convincing description of efficient market processes. The dissatisfaction it gives rise to is not due to its failure to adequately account for market behaviour: it is traceable to the implicit assumption that in accounting for market behaviour it has put forward a satisfactory explanation of the economic problem of society. Non-market forms of exchange are then either treated as 'second best' solutions – the 'market failure' approach – or they become the sociologist's or the anthropologist's problem, not the economist's.

It is only if the economic agenda can be broadened to accommodate transactional orders other than markets – i.e., fiefs, clans, bureaucracies – as economically worthy in their own right that the explanatory scope of the neoclassical model will be judged insufficient. Not wrong; just insufficient.

A start has been made in the direction of agenda broadening by the new institutional economics, and the award of the Nobel Memorial Prize for Economics in 1991 to Ronald Coase, one of the founders of the new field, is a pointer of things to come. Yet there is still a long way to go. Institutional economics posits internal organization as an alternative to markets for the governance of economic transactions but does so largely within a neoclassical equilibrium framework. Furthermore, it rests its case on the scarcity of information, not on its form. It is a theory of information asymmetry – and hence of diffusion – which frequently alludes to the problems of codification and abstraction but does not articulate them theoretically. For this reason, when Ouchi talks of clans, for example, he places this transactional form along a one-dimensional continuum that has markets at one end and hierarchies at the other. In effect, Williamson and Ouchi[16] each invoke the diffusion dimension of the I-space in their analysis, but the diffusion dimension alone. It offers them a theory of information exchange which they are unable to relate to a theory of information production. The transactional contingencies that we have described in this book and which give rise to different institutional orders can only be fully apprehended if they rest on an integrated and articulate theory of information production and exchange. We have traced the contours of what such a theory might look like in these pages but much work remains to be done to give it formal coherence.

If and when a new theory emerges, N-learning will not thereby have been confuted; neoclassical economics will continue to offer us the most convincing account we have to date of market-driven behaviour. But it will have to be incorporated into a broader explanation of economic processes, one that is free to roam throughout the I-space, unbeholden to the market region. To the extent that theories with greater explanatory power are to be preferred to those with less, one that convincingly endogenizes information and at the same time extends the reach of economic theorizing to forms of exchange that had been left out of account by the neoclassical orthodoxy inevitably threatens the incumbency of the latter.

So what might the I-space explain that the neoclassical model does not? Obviously any answer given here has a highly provisional character since refutable hypotheses have yet to be derived from the framework and tested. But we can at least try to motivate the enterprise.

In three areas, the I-space promises a richer and more realistic account of economic exchange than neoclassical models:

1   By converting the data of economic transactions into variables operating along the dimensions of codification, abstraction, and diffusion, the I-space endogenizes information in a way that restores a certain realism to the behaviour of the economic agent. He/she is still an economizer but now aims to save on data processing as well as on physical effort since he/she is constrained to do so both by personal bounded rationality and by limits on the computability of the problems encountered.[17] This much, of course, was already known. What the I-space highlights is how far the agent's strategies for economizing on data processing reflect the contingencies of his/her information environment and the institutional arrangements available.

2   The convenient equating of transactions external to organizations such as firms with market governance and transactions internal to them with hierarchical or bureaucratic governance disappears in the I-space. The challenge of effective governance is to define and serve the interests of a

given transactional population and to align its members behind a particular interpretation of such interests. Yet these interests can in theory be served by *any* of the transactional forms identified in the I-space, whether singly or in combination. Just as there is competition and collaboration between different institutional forms in the I-space, so there is between different levels of governance, each being a function of the generality of the interests to be served and the size of the population that can be aligned behind it.[18] The complexities of economic agency cannot be wished away through the reductionist strategy of first converting a diversity of transactional populations into a unitary economic actor – i.e., the firm or the individual – and then deciding that the actor's data processing is strictly 'black box' and ceases to be the economist's problem where it departs from assumptions of perfect rationality.[19]

3   By taking the level of governance – i.e., the generality of the interests defined and the size of the transactional population whose interests are to be served – as a variable rather than as an institutional given we effectively activate a competition between the particularistic and universalistic values that serve a given set of interests as well as between institutional configurations that might express such values. Many models of development assume that in such a contest universalistic values will come to predominate because procedural rationality has the edge over substantive rationality in complex situations.[20] Japan's own experience of modernization challenges this view, as does the particularistic brand of network capitalism emerging in China and discussed in the previous chapter. Universalistic values, to be sure, have emerged in both countries. But do they predominate?[21]

It is the flow of data along the three dimensions of the I-space which, by activating the SLC and promoting S-learning, makes it difficult to durably associate a particular level of governance with a particular institution or set of institutions. S-learning is creative destruction at work. It is the essence of capitalism as described by Schumpeter and as understood by Marx. The neoclassical orthodoxy by equating capitalism with markets, a single staging post along the SLC, ignores its evolutionary character. Dynamic competition brings about irreversible transformations which are not captured by equilibrium models.[22] Indeed, Fernand Braudel, studying capitalism from a historical perspective, presents it as the *antithesis* of efficient markets. His whole thesis is that capitalism cannot be reduced to a market order *tout court*, that it is an ancient, multifaceted phenomenon that effectively coexisted with various modes of production, sometimes working in harmony with them and at others not.[23] Pelikan describes capitalism as a *class* of regimes taking a regime as a set of institutional constraints on the decision-making of agents.[24] Braudel cites the case of Imperial China to show that the existence of markets may be a necessary but hardly a sufficient condition for the emergence of capitalism – a thesis that the current Chinese leadership would doubtless warmly applaud. Markets in China have always been strictly local and small scale; above them the state has kept a close watch. Capitalism, the ability of individuals to exploit new knowledge in ways that transcend the limitations of space and time, never had much chance. If it has a chance today, it will be building, as we saw in Chapter 7, on markets that continue to approximate local networks, albeit now augmented by the possibilities of information technology, rather than on markets of the neoclassical variety. Such network capitalism is centred on the clan region of the I-space.

Economic evolution, like other forms, is driven by the generation of novelty and variety and then by selection from it. Economic models that focus centripetally on one transactional form to the exclusion of others – bureaucracies in the case of mercantilism and Marxism-Leninism, markets in the neoclassical case – perform a premature selection on a necessary institutional variety that is never given the opportunity to emerge. Our case study of the preceding chapter indicated that premature selection may have important practical consequences. The single-minded pursuit of a neoclassical market order in Eastern Europe and the ex-Soviet Union, for example, by stifling the institutional variety necessary for S-learning to take root, may turn out to inhibit rather than to stimulate capitalist processes. And paradoxically, reforming China, if it succeeds in effectively accommodating embryonic markets in a culture that still remains strongly invested in clans and fiefs, may get closer to successfully operating an SLC than post-communist Europe. The Marxist-Leninist proclamations of the ageing Chinese leadership notwithstanding, China will harbour the institutional variety necessary for genuine capitalist evolution. At the time of writing, neither China nor Vietnam are making explicit institutional choices. But by allowing a variety of new and old institutional forms to coexist – albeit in a muddled sort of way – they are also allowing selection mechanisms to work their magic over a wider set of options than a more centripetal approach would allow. In Vietnam, a totally moribund state-owned sector is being allowed to wither away as market processes are taking root. In China, state-owned firms are for the most part in intensive care and many are gradually hollowing themselves out deliberately by contracting out an increasing proportion of their activities to collective or private firms. Markets in the latter case are not being rammed down the throats of state-owned firms through a mechanical process of privatization; they are coming in, so to speak, by invitation. And nowhere faster than in the southern provinces of Guangdong and Fujian, today almost beyond the reach of a conservative central bureaucracy. The visit of Deng Xiaoping to these provinces in January 1992, and in particular to the quasi-capitalistic enclave of Shenzhen bordering Hong Kong, was a nice way of letting it be known that some ideological neglect can be benign.[25]

8.4: A THEORY FOR THE AGE OF INFORMATION

Beyond opening up new theoretical perspectives on certain established economic problems, the I-space also throws light on one of the most important phenomena of our time, one that has as yet received no satisfactory treatment by the neoclassical orthodoxy: the information revolution.

At first sight the claim is hardly surprising since the I-space purports to be a framework for describing the production and exchange of information. If it cannot handle the information revolution, it might be asked, what can it handle? What might surprise, however, given some of the basic characteristics of this revolution, is the type of prediction derivable from the framework. Let us examine one or two of these by way of illustration.

Two simple features underpin what Carlota Perez has labelled the new 'techno-economic paradigm':[26]

1   A massive increase in the volume of data that can be *processed* by technological means per unit of time.
2   A massive increase in the volume of data that can be *transmitted* by technological means per unit of time.

The physical evidence for the information revolution can be seen everywhere: from the ubiquitous PCs that populate the desks of every office to the myriad electronic games on sale for six-year-olds and older in western department stores.

How do we register the effects of the information revolution in the I-space? *By a shift of the codification–abstraction–diffusion curve towards the right in the space.* In the language of economists we can think of this shift as an extension of a given population's transaction possibility frontier. It has two consequences, shown in Figure 8.2.

The first is that for a given level of codification and abstraction a larger diffusion population can be reached in a given unit of time. This is shown as line A in the figure. The consequence of this interpretation is that fewer relays are necessary in the data transmission process to eliminate noise and ambiguity from the system but that those that remain need to share a common set of codes and abstract concepts to be effective.

The second consequence derives from the fact that increases in data processing and transmission capacities reduce cognitive pressures to economize. With no extra effort the production and exchange of information between agents can thus occur at a lower level of codification and abstraction than hitherto: videoconferencing replaces the written report and the hand-scribbled fax the laconic telex. The new computing and communication technologies are avid consumers of data and they can digest great quantities of it in an unrefined form.[27] Thus for a specified diffusion population with

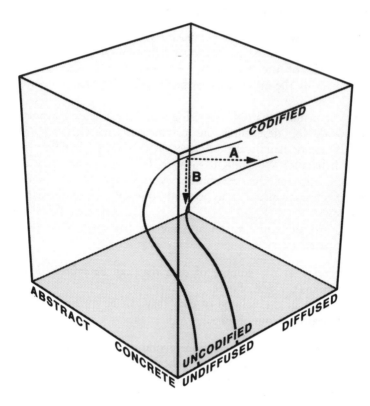

Figure 8.2 Shifting the codification–abstraction–diffusion curve to the right in the I-space

a given degree of spatial scattering, communication will be increasingly repersonalized. Many of the qualities of face-to-face exchange that had been lost through codification and abstraction will now be restored independently of spatial distance. The idea is depicted by line B in the figure. It has in fact already been given a name: high tech – high touch.[28]

In economic organizations both consequences come together: fewer communication relays means fewer people between the top and the base to receive, interpret, reformulate, and retransmit messages – i.e., fewer middle managers and much flatter yet reachable hierarchies; but it also means a greater capacity at the base to absorb and master at an implicit level the abstract codes used at the top and hence a much better educated labour force.[29] Simplifying somewhat, we might say that if the organizational revolution which brought forth deep managerial hierarchies in the first seventy years of the twentieth century aimed at de-skilling the workforce through a systematic codification of organizational practice and a depersonalization of organizational relationships, a full exploitation of the information revolution will require a re-skilling of the workforce in order to manage deep SLCs through S-learning strategies.

The cultural implications of this transformation are only just now coming to be understood. It was the advent of the railways and the telegraph that created the conditions for the development of large managerial hierarchies.[30] These two communication technologies facilitated moves up the codification scale and instituted bureaucratic and market transactions on a scale that had been hitherto unimaginable. The large-scale organization that emerged from this process generated its own distinctive technological trajectory since certain types of production required capital and managerial inputs that were quite beyond the reach of the small or even medium-sized firm.

The PC, the fax, and the videorecorder, by contrast, are technologies which, on account of their data processing and transmission capacities, favour moves back down the codification scale and towards more concrete forms of exchange – into the region of the I-space where fief and clan transactions predominate. The production systems that they are associated with – flexible manufacturing, CIM, etc. – are correspondingly less concerned with standardization (codification and abstraction) and mass production (diffusion) and more concerned with flexibility and small-scale production.

Firms which today find themselves overinvested in the more codified regions of the I-space are paying a price. Neither bureaucracies nor markets can deal comfortably with discontinuous change. They reduce rather than absorb uncertainty by trying to bracket it and convert it into calculable, i.e., codifiable, risk. Clans and fiefs on the other hand, operating lower down the I-space, confront uncertainty on its own terms, absorbing it through social relationships that promote trust and commitment rather than a narrow adherence to rules.

Correcting for this overinvestment does not require organizations to jettison the gains they have secured for themselves over the past hundred years or so in the upper region of the I-space. It calls on them rather to expand their overall transactional capacities through the internal development of what we have called a centrifugal culture, one in which personal and impersonal forms of exchange can mutually invigorate each other. Many large firms in quest of entrepreneurial renewal in the lower part of the I-space are today exploring clan and fief forms of organizational practice through networking and 'intrapreneurial' practices.[31] They are in effect building network capitalism from the inside and, in contrast to the Chinese case, they are approaching it from the market rather than from the clan region.

Our earlier discussion of convergence cautions against viewing network capitalism as an 'attractor', a stable institutional order towards which both industrialized western firms and Chinese family firms will be propelled by the imperatives of information technology. As we saw in the previous chapter, it is at best one transactional option among others in modern capitalism's ever-evolving institutional repertoire.

8.5: EXTENSIONS

One final thought before bringing this concluding chapter to a close.

The basic proposition that has guided the theory outlined in this book is that nature economizes and that if we, as data processing animals, are found to economize it is because we are part of nature.[32] In spite of parallels that might be drawn, therefore, between our own attempts at theorizing and, say, Giddens's theory of structuration or Habermas's theory of communicative action,[33] the I-space aims to capture territory that extends beyond the social. It would be reasonable, therefore, to probe its claim to generality by asking to what extent it has application to data processing phenomena beyond the human sphere. Does the SLC, for example, have its counterpart in either biological or purely physical processes? Do the transactional structures of markets, bureaucracies, clans, and fiefs appear in some guise or other outside human society?

To answer such questions satisfactorily would require much research and probably several other books. We can, however, map out some future avenues of enquiry by setting down markers.

A point to note is that we have been at pains to use the term 'data processing *agents*'. Although the term can apply to individual human beings, in economics it also applies to firms and in some theories of international relations it is made to apply to nation-states.[34] The assumption of methodological individualism in economics, however, is that these uses of the term are but a linguistic convenience since the situated individual remains 'where the action is'. Methodological individualism denies the explanatory power of social facts: institutions and all forms of organization above the level of the individual emerge as an unintended consequence of human action.[35] It also denies, by a timely invocation of the rationality assumption, the relevance of forms of biological and physical organization below the level of the individual. The rationality invoked does not have to be of the synoptic kind required by the neoclassical approach – this amounts to denial of historicity and of the unique and irreversible role of individual acts. Yet even Hayek's more situated rationality ignores the stochastic effects of infra-human processes on human action.[36]

A second restriction placed on the use of the term 'data processing agent' in economics complements the first and originates in the discipline's perception of itself as a social science. Unlike the natural sciences, which deal with the objective interaction of inert matter and energy, the social sciences deal with meaning and interpretation. One cannot infer where an individual is heading for simply by looking back at where he has come from and extrapolating forward as in a mechanical explanation: one has to interpret his *intentions*. The constant temptation for neoclassical economics to forget the problem of meaning in its pursuit of a Newton-inspired market equilibrium has made it a target of criticism both from within the discipline and from outside it.

Economic agents are 'intentional systems'[37] capable of representing the world to themselves with varying degrees of adequacy. Since the thinking subject can be de-coupled from the immediacy of his environment, his thinking has the possibility of becoming more self-contained; he consequently acquires a measure of autonomy with respect to his environment.[38] Yet the thinking subject not only represents the *actual* world to himself, but also, through his imagination, *possible* worlds. Their elicitation, however, may owe more to the eruption of internally driven mental or biological processes than to any externally imposed situational rationality.[39] Human creativity, for example, may thus originate in singularities which are rooted in the physical rather than the social and which for that reason escape the restrictions of methodological individualism.

If we are to use the I-space outside the human sphere, we may be required to dissolve the boundary that separates the physical from the social. At a methodological level, neoclassical economics did so a century ago in order to allow some of the models and metaphors of the natural sciences to encroach upon the realm of the social sciences. We might wish to go further, but in doing so we must realize that this may allow meaning, hitherto a distinctive – indeed a defining – characteristic of the human realm, to slip its social mooring and wander about through the physical world. Thus not only would physical and biological processes shape the evolution of meaning, but the latter would also be able to act upon the former.

Let us be cautious here. It is easy to fall prey to notions of cosmic consciousness which would impart to our evolutionary production function an unsustainable and quite unnecessary teleological quality. Meaning as used here is nothing other than the restoration of context to data processing, the application of sensitivity to a total situation. In biological processes, for example, sensitivity to context gives rise to the idea that environmental pressures compel selection and that the search processes are directed, or *orthogenetic*.[40]

In Chapter 1 we argued that much of modern molecular biology is built upon the concept of data processing and that so is a good part of modern physics.[41] But are biological and physical data processors capable of producing and absorbing *meanings* as well as data? The question is a controversial one since it seems to impute a capacity for intelligence to non-human agents, an idea that today creates fewer problems in biology than it does in physics where it remains associated with the animism of a Whitehead or a Waddington. Recall from Chapter 3 that data was considered meaningful if it brought about changes in a data processing agent's overall disposition to respond; that is to say, to durable changes in its internal states. In this sense even machines might be considered primitive manufacturers and consumers of meaning in so far as they exhibit a capacity to *learn*. If we choose to deny this approach to meaning then we are making it almost by definition a property of consciousness and of consciousness alone.

The ability of inanimate data processors to cope with context has become a complex and controversial issue within the artificial intelligence community.[42] Without getting involved – the end of a long book hardly seems the place to do so – we leave the reader with the thought that if nature acts informationally as well as energetically, the point of departure that we gave ourselves in Chapter 1,[43] then might it not be our incurable anthropocentrism that makes us persist in believing that we are the sole and privileged recipients of whatever meaning naturally available information imparts? Yet if data processors other than man are to be found in nature, and if these are indeed discovered to be producers and exchangers of meaning as well as of raw data, then we hypothesize that the theoretical perspectives offered by the I-space, and, albeit suitably modified, by the structures and processes that it activates, will apply. The codification, abstraction, and diffusion of data will thus turn out to be fundamental expressions of the way that nature, as well as man within it, chooses to economize.

Notes

INTRODUCTION

1 This is a case of what Samuel Bowles and Herbert Gintis have labelled *contested exchange* in their *Schooling in Capitalist America*, New York: Basic Books, 1976. An exchange is contested when the good exchanged possesses an attribute that is valuable to the buyer, costly to provide, and is at the same time difficult to measure or otherwise not subject to determinate contractual specification. Contested exchange markets do not generally clear in competitive equilibrium.

2 The term 'black box' can be viewed here as a euphemism for a pig in a poke.

3 A. Giddens, *The Constitution of Society: Outline of the Theory of Structuration*, Cambridge: Polity Press, 1984.

1 ORIENTING THOUGHTS ON INFORMATION

1 C. Freeman and C. Perez, 'Structural Crises of Adjustment: Business Cycles and Investment Behaviour', in G. Dosi *et al.* (eds) *Technical Change and Economic Theory*, London: Pinter Publishers, 1988.

2 Ibid., pp. 47–48.

3 F. Kodama, 'Technology Fusion and the New R and D', *Harvard Business Review*, July–August 1992, pp. 70–78.

4 L. Walras, *Elements of Pure Economics: or the Theory of Social Wealth*, Philadelphia: Orion Editions, 1984, p. 65 (author's italics).

5 K. Arrow, 'Information and Economic Behaviour'. Lecture presented to the Federation of Swedish Industries, Stockholm, 1973. Reprinted in *The Economics of Information: Collected Papers of Kenneth J. Arrow*, Cambridge, Mass.: The Belknap Press of Harvard University Press, 1984, pp. 136–152. See also G. Akerlof, 'The Market for "Lemons": Qualitative Uncertainty and the Market Mechanism', *Quarterly Journal of Economics* 84, 1970, pp. 488–500.

6 R. Coase, 'The Problem of Social Cost', *Journal of Law and Economics*, 3(1), October 1960, pp. 1–44.

7 Efficiency here is taken in the economist's sense of Pareto efficiency defined as that allocation of resources that no individual agent has any economic interest in improving upon.

8 J. Farrell, 'Information and the Coase Theorem', *Economic Perspectives*, I(2), Fall 1987, pp. 113–129. See also W. Samuelson, 'Comments on the Coase Theorem', in Alvin Roth (ed.) *Game Theoretic Models of Bargaining*, New York: Cambridge University Press, 1985, pp. 321–340.

9 K. Arrow, 'Economic Welfare and the Allocation of Resources for Invention', in

The Rate and Direction of Inventive Activity, Princeton, New Jersey: Princeton University Press, 1962, pp. 609–625.

10 Hayek (1945) stressed the informational role of prices in coordinating the activities of dispersed economic agents. F. Hayek, 'The Use of Knowledge in Society', *American Economic Review*, September 1945, pp. 519–530.

11 S. Grossman and J. Stiglitz, 'On the Impossibility of Informationally Efficient Markets', *American Economic Review*, 70(3), June 1980, pp. 393–408.

12 J. Stiglitz, 'Information and Economic Analysis: A Perspective', *The Economic Journal*, 1983, p. 22.

13 Ibid.

14 J. Marschak, 'Remarks on the Economics of Information', in *Contributions to Scientific Research in Management*, Los Angeles: Western Data Processing Center, University of California, 1959, pp. 79–98; G. Stigler, 'The Economics of Information', *Journal of Political Economy*, 69, 1961, pp. 213–225; A. Alchian, 'Information Costs, Pricing, and Resource Unemployment', *Western Economic Journal*, 7, 1969, pp. 109–128; R. Radner, 'The Evaluation of Information in Organizations', in J. Neyman (ed.) *Proceedings of the Fourth Berkeley Symposium on Mathematical Statistics and Probabilities*, Vol. I, Berkeley and Los Angeles: University of California Press, 1961; J. Hirschleifer, 'The Private and Social Value of Information and the Reward to Inventive Activity', *American Economic Review*, 61, 1971, pp. 547–561; M. Rothschild, 'Models of Market Organization with Imperfect Information: A Survey', *Journal of Political Economy*, 81, 1973, pp. 1283–1308; A. Spence, *Market Signalling*, Cambridge, Mass.: Harvard University Press, 1973; K. Arrow, *Essays in the Theory of Risk Bearing*, Chicago: Markham, and Amsterdam: North-Holland, 1971; K. Arrow, *The Limits of Organization*, New York: Norton, 1974.

15 P. Duhem, *La Théorie Physique: Son Objet, sa Structure*, Paris: Rivière et Cie, 1914 (translated 1953 by Philip Weiner as *The Aim and Structure of Physical Theory*, Princeton, N.J.: Princeton University Press. Reprinted (1962) New York: Atheneum). See also I. Lakatos, *Philosophical Papers: Vol. 1, The Methodology of Scientific Research Programmes; Vol. 2, Mathematics, Science and Epistemology*, Cambridge: Cambridge University Press, 1978.

16 K. Popper, *The Logic of Scientific Discovery*, London: Hutchinson, 1959.

17 T. Kuhn, *The Structure of Scientific Revolutions*, Chicago: The University of Chicago Press, 1962.

18 Kuhn refers to this use of the term paradigm as a 'disciplinary matrix'. See T. Kuhn, 'Second Thoughts on Paradigms', in F. Suppe (ed.) *The Structure of Scientific Theories*, Urbana: The University of Illinois Press, 1974, pp. 459–482.

19 Stiglitz, 'Information and Economic Analysis', p. 26.

20 The vulnerability of the competitive paradigm is today increasingly acknowledged. Rutherford (1984) holds that the 'problem facing economists amounts to nothing short of explaining the state of knowledge or expectations' (p. 377), and Loasby has commented that 'it is now becoming widely recognized that many of the central unresolved problems in economics turn on questions of knowledge' (Loasby 1986, p. 41). See M. Rutherford, 'Rational Expectations and Keynesian Uncertainty: A Critique', *Journal of Post Keynesian Economics*, 6(13), Spring 1984, pp. 377–387; B. Loasby, 'Organization, Competition, and the Growth of Knowledge', in R. Langlois (ed.) *Economics as a Process: Essays in the New Institutional Economics*, Cambridge: Cambridge University Press, 1986. Both are quoted in T. Lawson, 'The Relative Nature of Knowledge and Economic Analysis', *The Economic Journal*, 97, December 1987, pp. 951–970.

21 Schumpeter, for example, praised Walras's work on the grounds that its

mathematical rigour approximated that found in physics. See J. Schumpeter, *History of Economic Analysis*, London: Allen and Unwin, 1954.

22 See A. Pais, *'Subtle is the Lord . . .': The Science and the Life of Albert Einstein*, Oxford: Oxford University Press, 1982; *Inward Bound: Of Matter and Forces in the Physical World*, Oxford: Oxford University Press, 1986.

23 P. Mirowski, *More Heat than Light: Economics as Social Physics, Physics as Nature's Economics*, Cambridge: Cambridge University Press, 1989, p. 3.

24 Ibid., p. 35. See also P. Harman, *Energy, Force and Matter*, Cambridge: Cambridge University Press, 1982, p. 158.

25 Mirowski *op. cit.*, p. 66; D.W. Theobald, *The Concept of Energy*, London: Spon, 1966, p. 98; N. Nersessian, *Faraday to Einstein*, Dordrecht: Martinus Nijhoff, 1984.

26 P.M. Allen and J.H. McGlade, 'Evolutionary Drive: The Effect of Microscopic Diversity, Error Making and Noise', *Foundations of Physics*, 17(7), July 1987.

27 I. Prigogine, *From Being to Becoming: Time and Complexity in the Physical Sciences*, New York: W.H. Freeman and Co., 1980.

28 W.S. Jevons, *Principles of Economics*, London: Macmillan, 1905, p. 50. Quoted in Mirowski *op. cit.*, p. 219.

29 Walras refers to such feedback as a 'tâtonnement'; see Walras, *op. cit.*

30 Allen and McGlade, *op. cit.*

31 H.B. Acton, 'Comte' in J.O. Urmson and J. Rée (eds) *The Concise Encyclopedia of Western Philosophy and Philosophers*, London: Unwin Hyman, 1989, p. 63.

32 Ibid.

33 D. Dennett, *Brainstorms: Philosophical Essays on Mind and Psychology*, Sussex: Harvester Press, 1981.

34 Arrow, *The Limits of Organization*.

35 This burden has recently been reimposed on economic man to become a source of bounded rationality. See H.A. Simon, *Administrative Behaviour: A Study of Decision-Making Processes in Administrative Organization*, New York: The Free Press, 1957.

36 The generalization of institutional choices beyond the market option in circumstances when information deficiences rob it of its optimal properties goes by the name of 'mechanism design'. See R.B. Meyerson, 'Mechanism Design', in J. Eatwell *et al.* (eds) *Allocation, Information, and Markets*, The New Palgrave, London: Macmillan, 1989, pp. 191–206.

37 Hayek, 'The Use of Knowledge'.

38 Arrow, 'Information and Economic Behaviour'; Akerlof *op. cit.*

39 See for example the discussion of 'sunspot' equilibria by Cass and Shell (1983). D. Cass and K. Shell, 'Do Sunspots Matter?', *Journal of Political Economy*, 91, pp. 193–227.

40 For discussions on the cognitive limitations see J. March and H.A. Simon, *Organizations*, New York: John Wiley and Sons, 1958; D. Kahneman, P. Slovic and A. Tversky, *Judgment under Uncertainty: Heuristics and Biases*, Cambridge: Cambridge University Press, 1982; R. Hogarth and M.W. Reder (eds) *Rational Choice: The Contrast between Economics and Psychology*, Chicago: The University of Chicago Press, 1987.

41 R. Coase, 'The Nature of the Firm', *Economica*, N.S. 4, 1937, pp. 386–405. O.E. Williamson, *Markets and Hierarchies: Analysis and Antitrust Implications*, New York: The Free Press, 1975.

42 R.K. Merton, *Social Theory and Social Structure*, New York: The Free Press, 1957.

43 See P.M. Allen, 'Evolution: Why the Whole is Greater than the Sum of the Parts',

Unpublished manuscript, International Ecotechnology Research Centre, Cranfield Institute of Technology (undated); and I. Prigogine and I. Strengers, *Order out of Chaos: Man's New Dialogue with Nature*, Toronto: Bantam Books, 1984.

44 Mathematical Chaos is not the first challenger of such theories: the quantum theory confronted them in the 1920s and 1930s.

45 Ian Percival, 'The Order in Chaos', *New Scientist*, 8 July 1989.

46 Allen and McGlade *op. cit.*

47 P.M. Allen, 'Towards a New Science of Complex Systems', in *The Science and Praxis of Complexity*, Tokyo: United Nations University Press, 1985.

48 Evolutionary models have recently made their appearance in economics. Their orientation is quite different, however, from the one adapted here. See for example D. Hamilton, *Evolutionary Economics: A Study of Change in Economic Thought*, New Brunswick: Transaction Publishers, 1991; R. Nelson and S.G. Winter, *An Evolutionary Theory of Economic Change*, Cambridge, Mass.: The Belknap Press of Harvard University Press, 1982; J. Foster, *Evolutionary Macroeconomics*, London: Allen and Unwin, 1987.

49 J. Davidse, 'Characteristics of Growth and Limitations in Electronics', *Technological Forecasting and Social Change*, 24, 1983, pp. 125–135.

50 R.M. Solow, 'Growth Theory and After', *American Economic Review*, 78(3), June 1988.

51 Business people, however, have not been slow to grasp that information rather than matter is becoming the focus of exchange rather than a support for it. For under 5 US dollars, Fuji offers consumers a roll of 35mm ASA 400 film housed inside a top quality *disposable* camera. Millions of these have been sold in Japan and they are now entering the US market. Or again, Kimberley-Clark spent 10 million US dollars out of a 35 million US dollar launch-marketing budget for a new disposable nappy on locating three-quarters of the year's 3.5 million new American mothers, then directly mailing each of them. The firm reckons that its new database is more valuable than the raw materials that go into its nappies. Examples like these have become commonplace.

52 Arrow, 'Information and Economic Behaviour'.

53 The role of services in world trade may already be under-represented. Many services flow across borders in the form of intra-firm trade. Only some of these service flows give rise to direct payments, thus making their way into the statistical records.

54 The survival of Marxism-Leninism in China is no longer taken as an expression of popular support for the ideology. Its protagonists are concerned with personal survival rather than welfare maximization. For an interpretation of the failure of the Chinese reforms relevant to the issue under discussion, see M. Boisot and J. Child, 'The Iron Law of Fiefs: Bureaucratic Failure and the Problem of Governance in the Chinese Economic Reforms', *Administrative Science Quarterly*, December 1988, as well as Chapter 7 of this book.

55 Marx was a classical economist who was overtaken by the marginalist revolution.

56 The terms 'knowledge', 'information', and 'data', however, tend to be used interchangeably in much economic analysis. Is there for example any operational difference between perfect information, perfect knowledge, and perfect foresight? Between data processing and information processing? The issue comes to a head when one is asked to specify what exactly passes between two individuals in the act of communication. Is it knowledge? Information? Or data? Failure to clarify the terms used sometimes leads to some pretty loose thinking, as for example with Fritz Machlup who, in his *Production and Distribution of*

Knowledge in the USA, not only conflates knowledge and information but also, directly as a consequence of this, production and distribution as well. Thus on page 7 he informs the reader that 'producing knowledge will mean, in this book, not only discovering, inventing, designing, and planning, but also disseminating and communicating'. See F. Machlup, *The Production and Distribution of Knowledge in the USA*, Princeton, New Jersey: Princeton University Press, 1972.

57 K.R. Popper, *Realism and the Aim of Science*, London: Hutchinson, 1983.

58 See Arrow, *The Limits of Organization*, p. 30.

59 The debate that opposes realists, constructivists, and empiricists concerns the adequacy of the link between external data and a knowing subject. Does the link, for example, provide us with objective knowledge *of* an external world and, if not, on what basis do we assume that latter's existence? Our own analysis, as will become apparent in the latter chapters, aligns with the realists, albeit in a qualified way. For a fuller discussion of these issues see K.R. Popper, *Objective Knowledge: An Evolutionary Approach*, Oxford: The Clarendon Press, 1972; R. Boyd, 'On the Current Status of Scientific Realism', *Erkenntnis*, 19, 1983, pp. 45–90, reprinted in R. Boyd *et al.* (eds) *The Philosophy of Science*, Cambridge, Mass.: MIT Press, 1991.

60 It should be stressed that a data processing entity need be neither conscious nor even biological. See D. Brooks and E. Wiley, *Evolution as Entropy: Towards a Unified Theory of Biology*, Chicago: The University of Chicago Press, 1986.

61 Physicists believe that at energies much higher than that of plasma, particles cease to be distinct and hence do not yield data. Only in the primordial Big Bang would have such energies existed. A few billion-billionths of a second after the Big Bang the universe would have expanded and cooled enough for particles – and with them the forces that bind them to each other – to crystallize out. See J.D. Barrow, *The World within the World*, Oxford: Oxford University Press, 1990; D. Layzer, *Cosmogenesis: The Growth of Order in the Universe*, Oxford: Oxford University Press, 1990.

62 The Anthropic Principle is one attempt to build bridges between the natural and the social sciences. It states that the laws that regulate physical processes must be of such a nature as to make possible our own existence as observers. See J.D. Barrow and F.J. Tipler, *The Cosmic Anthropic Principle*, Oxford: Oxford University Press, 1986.

63 D. Brooks and E. Wiley, *op. cit.*, p. 106.

64 B.O. Küppers, *Information and the Origin of Life*, Cambridge, Mass.: The MIT Press, 1990; E. Morin, *La Méthode: Vol. 1, La Nature de la Nature*, Paris: Seuil, 1977.

65 Brooks and Wiley *op. cit.*, p. 89. See also I. Prigogine, G. Nicolis and A. Babbyantz, 'Thermodynamics of Evolution', *Physics Today*, 25(11), 1972, pp. 23–28, 25(12), pp. 38–44.

66 Jon Elster, *Leibnitz et la Formation de l'Esprit Capitaliste*, Paris: Aubier, 1975.

67 *Actien* in archaic Dutch (translated as 'action' in French and English) was a product of mass, velocity, and time. But it also connoted the shares of the newly chartered joint-stock trading companies. Action was thus conceived of as having abstract value. For a discussion of this point, see Mirowski *op. cit.*, p. 120.

68 Barrow *op. cit.*, pp. 80–81.

69 Barrow and Tipler *op. cit.*, p. 149.

70 I.B. Cohen, *The Conservation of Energy and the Principle of Least Action*, New York: Arno, 1981.

71 Mirowski *op. cit.*, p. 80.

72 '[I]f one drops the idea that learning and doing are separate activities then the distinction between moving along and shifting production functions loses its force'. See R. Nelson, 'Production Sets, Technological Knowledge, and R and D: Fragile and Overworked Constructs for Analysis of Productivity Growth?', *American Economic Association*, 70(2), May 1980, pp. 62–71.

73 The correlation between choice of factors and historical period is not a rigorous one. Although he was writing in the twentieth century, the arguments of Joseph Schumpeter's production function were also land and labour.

74 A. Maddison, in his book *Phases of Capitalist Development* (New York: Oxford University Press, 1982), has noted the comparatively unimportant role of investment prior to, say, 1826, compared with the astonishing correlation between investment and productivity growth in industrialized countries since then.

75 Mirowski *op. cit.*

76 H. Chenery, 'Process and Production Functions from Engineering Data', in W. Leontief (ed.) *Studies in the Structure of the American Economy*, New York: Oxford University Press, 1976, pp. 229, 301, 317. Quoted in Mirowski *op. cit.*, pp. 331–332.

77 Daniel Bell, 'Models and Reality in Economic Discourse', in D. Bell and I. Kristol (eds) *The Crisis in Economic Theory*, New York: Basic Books, 1981; Daniel Bell, 'Thinking Ahead', *Harvard Business Review*, May–June 1979.

78 Institutional associations can acquire ideological colouring: witness the controversy sparked off by Robert Solow's aggregate production function in which it was suggested that profits on 'capital' represent the return to a factor of production as imputed by the market. See R. Solow, 'Growth Theory and After'.

79 That is to say, acts with direction rather than purpose. The distinction between teleological and teleonomic action is discussed in J. Monod, *Le Hasard et la Nécessité: Essai sur la Philosophie Naturelle de la Biologie Moderne*, Paris: Seuil, 1970.

80 For a somewhat novel interpretation of how such learning evolves and is maintained see R. Sheldrake, *A New Science of Life: The Hypothesis of Formative Causation*, London: Paladin, 1983.

81 R. Van Wyk, 'Technological Change. A Macroperspective', *Technological Forecasting and Social Change*, 15, pp. 281–296, 1979.

82 H.R. Maturana and F.J. Varela, *Autopoiesis and Cognition: The Realization of the Living*, Boston: D. Reidel, 1980.

83 Brooks and Wiley *op. cit.*, p. 77.

84 The complexity perspective is over a century old in biology. See for example L. Dollo, 'Les Lois de l'Evolution', *Bull. Belge. Géol.*, 7, 1893, pp. 164–167; R.A. Fisher, *The Genetical Theory of Natural Selection*, Oxford: The Clarendon Press, 1930; H.F. Blum, *Time's Arrow and Evolution*, 3rd edn, Princeton: Princeton University Press, 1968; J. Maynard-Smith, 'The Structure of Neo-Darwinism', in C.H. Waddington (ed.) *Towards a Theoretical Biology*, Vol. 2, pp. 82–89, Chicago: Aldine Publishing Co., 1970; B. Rensch, *Biophilosophy*, New York: Columbia University Press, 1971; R. Gruner, 'On Evolution and its Relation to Natural Selection', *Dialogue*, 16, 1977, pp. 708–714.

85 Brooks and Wiley *op. cit.*, p. 36.

86 S.N. Salthe, *Evolving Hierarchical Systems: Their Structure and Representation*, New York: Columbia University Press, 1985.

87 N. Eldredge, *Unfinished Synthesis: Biological Hierarchies and Modern Evolutionary Thought*, New York: Oxford University Press, 1985.

88 Brooks and Wiley *op. cit.*, pp. 89, 356.
89 Ibid., p. 29.
90 G. Nicolis and I. Prigogine, *Exploring Complexity: An Introduction*, New York: W.H. Freeman and Co., 1989, p. 14.
91 Ibid., p. 8.
92 Since it incorporates the universe as a whole, this must be the ultimate aggregate production function.
93 The concept of codification is developed in Chapter 3.
94 Brooks and Wiley *op. cit.*, p. 32.
95 Brooks and Wiley are at pains to point out that in contrast to prevailing views that consider evolution to be a *negentropic* phenomenon, they take evolution to be an entropic process, but one in which realized variation lags behind the maximum entropy allowed by an expanding phase space. It is the lag that gives rise to organization in spite of the fact that realized variation and the entropy maximum are both increasing. See Brooks and Wiley *op. cit.*, p. 38. For a discussion of evolution as negentropy see E. Schrödinger, *What is Life?*, Cambridge: Cambridge University Press, 1967.
96 The discovery, for example, that certain materials can act as superconductors at temperatures well above the boiling point of nitrogen (–196°C) might be a good instance of such a shift. It offers potentially large savings in energy but remains a laboratory curiosity until it is better understood. The seeking of understanding, however, immediately moves us away from horizontal movements in the space and back on to the saw-toothed curve of Figure 1.7.
97 Spatial economics continues to be the poor relation within the discipline. It will stay so as long as the neoclassical approach treats firms as points on a production function in a world of zero transport costs.
98 Mirowski *op. cit.*
99 P. Hawken, *The Next Economy*, New York: Holt, Rinehart and Winston, 1983, p. 11.
100 J. Heskett, *Managing in the Service Economy*, Cambridge, Mass.: Harvard Business School Press, 1986, p. 160.
101 George Gilder, *The Quantum Revolution in Economics and Technology*, New York: Simon and Schuster, 1989.
102 The focus is reflected in conventional accounting systems which, for example, continue to take direct labour as their point of reference. This, however, along with the material transformation it effects, accounts for an ever-decreasing proportion of a firm's costs. See J. Wheatley, 'How Costs Lead Firms Astray', *Management Today*, June 1980; and H.T. Johnson and R. Kaplan, *Relevance Lost: The Rise and Fall of Management Accounting*, Cambridge, Mass.: Harvard Business School Press, 1987.
103 J.B. Quinn, *Intelligent Enterprise: A New Paradigm for a New Era*, New York: The Free Press, 1992.
104 See C. Perez, 'Microelectronics, Long Waves, and World Structural Change: New Perspectives for Developing Countries', *World Development*, 13(3), 1985, pp. 441–463. We find in this argument echoes of Marx's well-known distinction between the forces of production and the relations of production. For him, too, crisis and conflict resulted from any mismatch between them. K. Marx, *Capital: A Critique of Political Economy*, Vol. 1, London: Lawrence and Wishart, 1972.
105 Marc Blaug, *Economic Theory in Retrospect*, Cambridge: Cambridge University Press, 1978, pp. 24–29.
106 K. Marx, *Capital*, Vol. 1.
107 H.A. Simon, 'The Logic of Heuristic Decision Making', in N. Rescher (ed.) *The Logic of Decision and Action*, Pittsburgh: University of Pittsburgh Press, 1967,

pp. 1–20; reprinted in H.A. Simon, *Models of Discovery*, Dordrecht, Holland: D. Reidel Publishing Co., 1977.

108 E. Morin, *Le Paradigme Perdu: La Nature Humaine*, Paris: Editions du Seuil, 1973.

109 The Principle of Least Action as we have seen can be made to serve either orientation depending on the temporal horizon chosen.

110 D. North, *Structure and Change in Economic History*, New York: W.W. Norton & Co., 1981.

111 V. Gordon Childe, *Man Makes Himself*, London: L.A. Watts, 1951.

112 M. Jacob, *The Cultural Meaning of the Scientific Revolution*, New York: Alfred Knopf, 1988.

113 We are using the term in the sense intended by Von Mises. See L. Von Mises, *Socialism: An Economic and Sociological Analysis*, Indianapolis: Liberty Classics, 1981, p. 22.

114 In a sense we are extending the so-called Anthropic Principle in a new direction. The Principle states that any plausible explanation of the universe must be capable of accommodating us as observers. Our production function further argues that it must also be capable of accommodating us as economizers. In this way economic man finds his place *in* nature rather than outside it as in the neoclassical model. See Barrow and Tipler *op. cit.*

2 THE STRUCTURING OF INFORMATION

1 G.M. Edelman, *Neural Darwinism: The Theory of Neuronal Group Selection*, Oxford: Oxford University Press, 1987, p. 14.

2 P.S. Churchland, *Neurophilosophy: Towards a Unified Science of the Mind/Brain*, Cambridge, Mass.: The MIT Press, 1989.

3 Ibid., p. 1.

4 See R. Dawkins and J. Krebs, 'Animal Signals: Information or Manipulation?', in J.R. Krebs and N.B. Davies (eds) *Behavioural Ecology: An Evolutionary Approach*, Oxford: Basil Blackwell, 1978; R. Llinás, '"Mindness" as a Functional State of the Brain', in C. Blakemore and S. Greenfield (eds) *Mind Matter*, Oxford: Basil Blackwell.

5 Churchland *op. cit.*, p. 77.

6 See respectively: R.C. Shank, 'The Role of Memory in Language Processing', in C.N. Cofer (ed.) *The Structure of Human Memory*, San Francisco: Freeman, 1976, pp. 162–189; M. Minsky, 'A Framework for Representing Knowledge', in P.H. Winston (ed.) *The Psychology of Computer Vision*, New York: McGraw-Hill, 1975, pp. 211–277; D.A. Norman and D.G. Bobrow, 'On the Role of Active Memory Processes in Perception and Cognition', in C.N. Cofer (ed.) *The Structure of Human Memory*, San Francisco: Freeman, 1976, pp. 114–132; see also D.E. Rumelhart, 'Notes on a Schema for Stories', in D.G. Bobrow and A. Collins (eds) *Representations and Understanding*, New York: Academic Press, 1975, pp. 211–236.

7 J.A. Feldman and D.H. Ballard, 'Connectionist Models and their Properties', *Cognitive Science*, 6, 1982, pp. 205–254.

8 J.H. Jackson, 'On Localization', in *Selected Writings*, Vol. 2, New York: Basic Books (original work published in 1869); A.R. Luria, *Higher Cortical Functions in Man*, New York: Basic Books, 1966. Other contributors to the PDP perspective were D.O. Hebb, *The Organization of Behaviour*, New York: Wiley, 1949; K.S. Lashley, 'In Search of the Engram', in *Society of Experimental Biology*

Symposium No. 4: Psychological Mechanisms in Animal Behaviour, London: Cambridge University Press, 1950, pp. 478–505; F. Rosenblatt, *Principles of Neurodynamics*, New York: Spartan, 1962; and O.G. Selfridge, 'Pattern Recognition in Modern Computers', *Proceedings of the Western Joint Computer Conference*, 1955.

9 See T.J. Sejnowski, 'Open Questions about Computation in Cerebral Cortex', in J.L. McClelland and D.E. Rumelhart, *Parallel Distributed Processing: Explorations in the Microstructure of Cognition*, Vol. 2, Cambridge, Mass.: The MIT Press, 1988, pp. 372–389.

10 R.L. Gregory, *Mind in Science: A History of Explanations in Psychology and Physics*, Middlesex, England: Penguin Books, 1981.

11 Aaoki and Siekevitz liken the developing brain to a highway system which evolves with repeated use. Roads that are less travelled will eventually be abandoned and those that are used most will be broadened and strengthened. Also new roads will be built where they are needed. See C. Aaoki and P. Siekevitz, 'Plasticity in Brain Development', *Scientific American*, 259(6), December 1988, pp. 34–42.

12 Physicists misleadingly use the communication metaphor when they talk of 'messenger particles'.

13 H. Nyquist, 'Certain Factors Affecting Telegraph Speed', *Bell System Technical Journal*, April 1924, p. 324; R.V.L. Hartley, 'Transmission of Information', *Bell System Technical Journal*, July 1928, p. 535; C.E. Shannon, 'The Mathematical Theory of Communication', *Bell System Technical Journal*, July and October, 1948.

14 Churchland *op. cit.*, p. 396.

15 D.A. Norman, 'Reflections on Cognition and Parallel Distributed Processing', in McClelland and Rumelhart *op. cit.*, Vol. 2, pp. 531–546, p. 534.

16 Edelman *op. cit.*, p. 38.

17 T.H. Bullock, 'Signals and Neural Coding', in *The Neurosciences: A Study Program*, New York: Rockefeller University Press, 1967, pp. 347–352.

18 See, for instance, G.U. Underwood, *Strategies for Information Processing*, London: Academic Press, 1978; J.R. Anderson, *Cognitive Skills and their Acquisition*, Hillsdale, New Jersey: Lawrence Erlbaum Associates, 1981; D.A. Norman, 'Twelve Issues for Cognitive Science', in D.A. Norman (ed.) *Perspectives on Cognitive Science*, Hillsdale, New Jersey: Lawrence Erlbaum Associates, 1981, pp. 265–295.

19 Edelman *op. cit.*, p. 38.

20 Z. Pylyshyn, *Computation and Cognition*, Cambridge, Mass.: The MIT Press, 1984.

21 Feldman and Ballard *op. cit.*, p. 208.

22 For the development of the theory see G.M. Edelman, 'Group Selection and Phasic Reentrant Signalling: A Theory of Higher Brain Functions', in G.M. Edelman and V.B. Mountcastle, *The Mindful Brain: Cortical Organization and the Group-Selective Theory of Higher Brain Functions*, Cambridge, Mass.: The MIT Press, 1978, pp. 51–100; G.M. Edelman, 'Group Selection as the Basis for Higher Brain Function', in F.O. Schmitt *et al.*, *Organization of the Cerebral Cortex*, Cambridge, Mass.: The MIT Press, 1981, pp. 535–563; G.M. Edelman and G.M. Reeke, 'Selective Networks Capable of Representative Transformations, Limited Generalizations, and Associative Memory', *Proc. Natl. Acad. Sci. U.S.A.*, 79, 1982, pp. 2091–2095; G.M. Edelman and L.H. Finkel, 'Neuronal Group Selection in the Cerebral Cortex', in G.M Edelman *et al.*, *Dynamic Aspects of Neocortical Function*, New York: Wiley, 1984, pp. 653–695.

23 Edelman, *Neural Darwinism*, p. 43.

24 Churchland *op. cit.*, p. 35.

25 Yet even this approach needs cautious interpretation. As Churchland has warned, 'Models of learning and memory that invest all the processing complexity in *connections*, and next to none in the neuron itself, may well find that the model must postulate many more units than the nervous system has.' Ibid., p. 36.

26 J.L. McClelland, D.E. Rumelhart and G.E. Hinton, 'The Appeal of Parallel Distributed Processing', in J.L. McClelland and D. Rumelhart, *Parallel Distributed Processing: Explorations in the Microstructure of Cognition*, Vol. 1, Cambridge, Mass.: MIT Press, 1986, p. 31.

27 Some of these rules go back to the work of D.O. Hebb, *The Organization of Behaviour*, New York: Wiley, 1949.

28 J.L. McClelland and D.E. Rumelhart, 'An Interactive Activation Model of Context Effects in Letter Perception: Part 1. An Account of Basic Findings', *Psychological Review*, 88, 1981, pp. 375–407; D.E. Rumelhart and J.L. McClelland, 'An Interactive Activation Model of Context Effects in Letter Perception: Part 2. The Contextual Enhancement Effect and Some Tests and Extensions of the Model', *Psychological Review*, 89, 1982, pp. 60–94.

29 Churchland *op. cit.*, p. 72.

30 Edelman, *Neural Darwinism*, p. 6.

31 D.E. Rumelhart and J.L. McClelland, 'PDP Models and General Issues in Cognitive Science', in J.L. McClelland and D. Rumelhart, *Parallel Distributed Processing*, Vol. 1, p. 135.

32 Churchland *op. cit.*, p. 464.

33 T.J. Sejnowski, in J.L. McClelland and D.E. Rumelhart, *Parallel Distributed Processing*, Vol. 2, p. 380.

34 J.J. Hopfield, 'Neurons with Graded Response have Collective Computational Properties like those of Two-state Neurons', *Proceedings of the National Academy of Sciences, U.S.A.*, 81, 1984, pp. 3088–3092; G.E. Hinton and T.J. Sejnowski, 'Learning and Relearning in Boltzmann Machines', in J.L. McClelland and D.E. Rumelhart, *Parallel Distributed Processing*, Vol. 1; P. Smolensky, 'Information Processing in Dynamical Systems: Foundations of Harmony Theory', in J.L. McClelland and D.E. Rumelhart, *Parallel Distributed Processing*, Vol. 1. See also the parallel drawn between cooperative search and thermodynamics by S. Kirkpatrick, C.D. Gelatt and M.P. Vecchi, 'Optimization by Simulated Annealing', *Science*, 220, 1983, pp. 671–680.

35 C.E. Shannon, 'The Mathematical Theory of Communication'. Edelman *op. cit.*

36 Tensor network theory has become a useful mathematical tool for carrying out such operations. See W.H. Pitts and W.S. McCulloch, 'How We Know Universals: The Perception of Auditory and Visual Form', *Bulletin of Mathematical Biophysics*, 9, 1947, pp. 127–147, for an early application of the idea that representations are vectors in coordinate space and that computations are vector to vector transformations. The vector matrix approach was also used by Rosenblatt in 1962: F. Rosenblatt, *Principles of Neurodynamics*, New York: Spartan Books, 1962. For more recent work see T. Kohonen *et al.*, 'A Principle of Neural Associative Memory', *Neuroscience*, 2, 1977, pp. 1065–1076; J.A. Anderson and M.C. Moser, 'Categorization and Selective Neurons', in G.E. Hinton and J.A. Anderson (eds) *Parallel Models of Associative Memory*, Hillsdale, New Jersey: Lawrence Erlbaum Associates, 1981, pp. 213–236; D.H. Ballard, 'Cortical Connections and Parallel Processing: Structure and Function', *Behavioural and Brain Sciences*, 9(1), 1986; A. Pellionisz and R. Llinás, 'Tensor

Network Theory of the Metaorganization of Functional Geometrics in the Central Nervous System', *Neuroscience*, 16, 1985, pp. 245–273.

37 W. Weaver, 'Recent Contributions to the Mathematical Theory of Communications', in C.E. Shannon and W. Weaver, *The Mathematical Theory of Communication*, Urbana: The University of Illinois Press, 1949, p. 9.

38 Shannon and Weaver *op. cit.*.

39 Symbols in the sense used here imply conventions regulating their use and how they combine. To that extent to select the repertoire of symbols from which messages will be formulated is to precode the message.

40 This is known as the ergodic hypothesis.

41 For a discussion of entropy, see Chapter 1.

42 See A. Newall and H.A. Simon, *Human Problem Solving*, Englewood Cliffs, New Jersey: Prentice-Hall, 1972, p. 792. Newall and Simon discuss 'chunking' as a problem-solving strategy. We shall see in Chapter 4 that problem-solving and coding are equivalent.

43 Conan Doyle's fiction is perhaps the most harmless of the examples that come to mind. History furnishes ready examples of dramatic information failures – failures to detect crucial signals that were judged to be banal and inconsequential at the time. Thus much of the data that prefigured a Japanese attack on Pearl Harbor in 1941 was already in the hands of US intelligence when the Japanese struck, and knowledge that the Soviet Union had installed medium-range missiles on the island of Cuba was in the possession of the US intelligence network two months before the crisis blew up in October 1961. In both cases, the data was disregarded. In our own day a similar failure to interpret the relevant signals as informative explains the belated response of the western powers to the military threat posed by Iraq. See G.T. Allison, *The Essence of Decision: Explaining the Cuban Missile Crisis*, Boston: Little, Brown, 1971; R. Wohlstetter, *Pearl Harbor: Warning and Decision*, Stanford: Stanford University Press, 1962.

44 Bayesians assume that this *a priori* statistical disposition gradually improves the message's goodness of fit with the statistical structures of the real world through a process of learning by experience. See C. Howson and P. Urbach, *Scientific Reasoning: A Bayesian Approach*, La Salle, Illinois: Open Court, 1989.

45 In *Neural Darwinism* Edelman distinguishes between a *primary* repertoire, acquired in the course of ontogenetic development, and a *secondary* repertoire that reflects the idiosyncratic build-up of experience.

46 J.S. Bruner, 'On Perceptual Readiness', *Psychological Review*, 64, 1957, pp. 123–152.

47 G.A. Miller, 'The Magical Number Seven, Plus or Minus Two: Some Limits on our Capacity for Processing Information', *Psychological Review*, 63(2), March 1956, pp. 81–96.

48 E. Hicks, 'On the Rate of Gain of Information', *Quarterly Journal of Experimental Psychology*, 4, 1952, pp. 11–26.

49 D.E. Rumelhart *et al.*, 'Schemata and Sequential Thought Processes in PDP Models', in J.L. McClelland and D.E. Rumelhart, *Parallel Distributed Processing: Explorations in the Microstructure of Cognition*, Vol. 2, Cambridge, Mass.: The MIT Press, 1988, pp. 7–57.

50 Edelman, *Neural Darwinism*, p. 3.

51 See J.S. Bruner, J.J. Goodnow and G.A. Austin, *A Study of Thinking*, New York: John Wiley, 1956; A. Moles, *Information Theory and Esthetic Perception*, Urbana: University of Illinois Press, 1968, p. 57.

52 A western alphabet consumes fewer bits of information than do, say, Chinese characters. This is why the latter are harder to computerize; word processors are

still rare in Japan on account of the problems posed by *Kanji*, the several thousand characters of Chinese origin that are the backbone of written Japanese.

53 Moles *op. cit.*

54 Ibid., p. 126.

55 We shall not concern ourselves with the issue of whether one way or level of knowing has some epistemological primacy over others – i.e., the thesis of *reductionism*.

56 J.R. Searle, 'Minds and Brains without Programmes', in C. Blakemore and S. Greenfield (eds) *Mindwaves*, Oxford: Basil Blackwell, 1987.

57 Ibid., p. 19.

58 Moles's discussion of aesthetics, Ch. 7, *op. cit.*

59 A similar measure is used in computer science to measure programming effort. The relationship between a computer program's running time and the size of its input is called the *time complexity* of a program. But here it is inputs over time rather than outputs over time that are used as measures. For a discussion see R. Penrose, *The Emperor's New Mind: Concerning Computers, Minds, and the Laws of Physics*, London: Vintage, 1989; and B.O. Küppers, *Information and the Origin of Life*, Cambridge, Mass.: The MIT Press, 1990.

60 The creation of new knowledge is the subject of Chapter 4.

61 Penrose, *op. cit.*, p. 143.

62 E. Rosch and B. Lloyd, *Cognition and Categorization*, Hillsdale, New Jersey: Lawrence Erlbaum Associates, 1978.

63 Edelman, *Neural Darwinism*, p. 244.

64 See our discussion at the end of the previous section.

65 Gregory *op. cit.*, p. 273.

66 Also the amount of information needed to *change* an existing category will be much greater than the amount of information needed to create it in the first place – a further contribution to cognitive conservatism. For a decision theoretic treatment of this issue see Volkema, 'Problem Formulation in Planning and Design', *Management Science*, 29(6), June 1983, pp. 639–652.

67 G.E. Hinton *et al.*, 'Distributed Representations', in J.L. McClelland and D.E. Rumelhart, *Parallel Distributed Processing*, Vol. 1, pp. 77–109.

68 A.M. Uttley, 'Conditional Processing in a Nervous System', in *Mechanization of Thought Processes*, London, 1959.

69 Howson and Urbach *op. cit.*

70 Edelman, *Neural Darwinism*, p. 32.

71 Churchland *op. cit.*, p. 256.

72 Minsky *op. cit.*

73 Edelman, *Neural Darwinism*, p. 245. Crick has also argued that the 'feature detectors' that form the basis of perception are likely to be inborn but they become tuned up by experience, especially during certain critical periods of development. See Crick, in J.L. McClelland and D.E. Rumelhart, *Parallel Distributed Processing*, Vol. 2, p. 369.

74 Those who, in the tradition of Locke, Berkeley, and Hume, argue that all knowledge of matters of fact, as distinct from that of purely logical relations between concepts, is based on experience.

75 N.R. Hanson, *Patterns of Discovery*, Cambridge: Cambridge University Press, 1965.

76 Technology may well begin to replace the senses in the classification of phenomena that are well within their reach, but require specialized training. Objective computerized tests, for example, are challenging the delicate and subjective art of judging wines by mouth. Developed by the Dutch Food

Analysis Institute in Zeist, for example, the new tests employ chemical detection to identify wines by area and by variety. See *The Economist*, 15 March 1986, 'By Computer'. Likewise the 'nose' whose special talent in the perfume industry is to memorize some 4,000 basic smells, both natural and chemically produced, is also under threat from progress in artificial intelligence. *The Economist*, 29 June 1985, 'Why French Noses are Best'.

77 C.S. Pierce argued that when a scientist seeks to explain a phenomenon, there are in fact an indefinite number of hypotheses to be tried. He does not, however, canvas the whole range but restricts himself to a few plausible ones. Pierce believed that he was guided by a 'tropism for truth'. For a discussion of this issue see Churchland *op. cit.*, p. 250.

78 Bruner *et al. op. cit.*, p. 145.

79 Smolensky *op. cit.*, p. 257.

80 Edelman, *Neural Darwinism*, p. 25.

81 Hinton *et al. op. cit.*, p. 78.

82 Ibid., p. 107.

83 D.E. Rumelhart and J.D. McClelland, 'PDP Models', p. 131; see also D.R. Hofstadter, *Gödel, Escher, Bach: An Eternal Golden Braid*, New York: Basic Books, 1979.

84 Abstraction, as an economizing activity, does not necessarily aim at optimal solutions since their attainment would itself often require an uneconomic amount of data processing – that is, processing data running well beyond what is contained in perceived recurrent regularities alone. Heiner illustrates the point with the algorithm used for Rubik's Cube. The algorithm is acknowledged to be less efficient than an optimal solution. But, then, how does one choose the optimum from 43 trillion theoretical possibilities? See R.A. Heiner, 'The Origin of Predictable Behaviour', *American Economic Review*, 73(4), 1983, pp. 560–574.

85 C. Morris, *Signification and Significance*, Cambridge, Mass.: The MIT Press, 1964; C.S. Pierce, 'Questions Concerning Certain Faculties Claimed for Man', *Journal of Speculative Philosophy*, Vol. 2, 1868, pp. 103–114; U. Eco, *A Theory of Semiotics*, Bloomington: Indiana University Press, 1979.

86 This definition comes from R. Harrod, *Money*, London: Macmillan, 1969.

87 Logics do not *have* to be thought of as dealing with well-coded phenomena, whether concrete or abstract. The 'fuzzy' logic of Lofti Zadeh, for example, makes its assignments according to a 'yes', 'no', or 'maybe' principle, leaving a rough edge around the phenomena it structures.

88 For an empirically derived typology of cognitive styles very aligned with what we are discussing here, but inspired by Jung's psychological types, see I. Briggs Myers, 'Introduction to Type: A Description of the Theory and Application of the Myers–Briggs Type Indicator', Palo Alto: Consulting Psychologists Press, 1987; see also C.G. Jung, *Collected Works: Vol. 6, Psychological Types*, Princeton, New Jersey: Princeton University Press, 1971.

89 M. Polanyi, *Personal Knowledge: Towards a Post-Critical Philosophy*, London: Routledge and Kegan Paul, 1958.

90 Munro points out that as representations of the world become more symbolic, stimuli become more discreet. He quotes Shepard and Podgorny (1975) 'Whereas we can continuously shift a colour (for example blue) in brightness, hue, and saturation until it becomes as similar as we wish it to any other colour (for example green), we cannot continuously deform a word "blue" to another word "green" without passing through intermediate configurations that are not colours at all' (pp. 189–190): P.W. Munro, 'State Dependent Factors Influencing

Neural Plasticity: A Partial Account of the Critical Period', in J.L. McClelland and D.E. Rumelhart, *Parallel Distributed Processing*, Vol. 2, pp. 471–502; R.N. Shepard and P. Podgorny, 'Cognitive Processes that Resemble Perceptual Processes', in W.K. Estes (ed.) *Handbook of Learning and Cognitive Processes*, Hillsdale, New Jersey: Lawrence Erlbaum Associates, 1975, pp. 189–237.

91 Polanyi *op. cit.*

92 Thus Heisenberg, reminiscing on developments in the quantum theory in the period 1926–1927, observed that 'we couldn't doubt that [quantum mechanics] was the correct scheme but even then we didn't know how to talk about it ... [these discussions left us in] a state of almost complete despair', in O. Gingerich (ed.) *The Nature of Scientific Discovery: A Symposium Commemorating the 500th Anniversary of the Birth of Nicolaus Copernicus*, Washington: Smithsonian Institution Press, 1975, pp. 556–573. Quoted by A.I. Miller, *Imagery in Scientific Thought: Creating 20th Century Physics*, Cambridge, Mass.: The MIT Press, 1987, p. 150.

93 One classic formulation of how this reciprocal influence is socially mediated goes by the name of the Sapir–Whorf hypothesis. See E. Sapir, *Culture, Language, and Personality*, Berkeley: University of California Press, 1957; and B.L. Whorf, *Language, Thought, and Reality*, New York: Wiley, 1956.

94 J.H. Flavell, *The Developmental Psychology of Jean Piaget*, Princeton, New Jersey: D. Van Nostrand Co., 1963.

95 J.S. Bruner, *Beyond the Information Given: Studies in the Psychology of Knowing*, London: George Allen and Unwin, 1974.

96 J.S. Bruner, 'The Growth of Representational Processes in Childhood', paper presented at the 18th International Congress of Psychology, Moscow, 1966; reprinted in J.S. Bruner, *Beyond the Information Given*, pp. 313–324.

97 Polanyi *op. cit.*, p. 98.

98 Miller has adopted this approach in his study of scientific creativity – see A.I. Miller *op. cit.*

99 S. Zuboff, *In the Age of the Smart Machine: The Future of Work and Power*, Oxford: Heinemann, 1988.

100 Bruner, *Beyond the Information Given*; Gregory *op. cit.*

101 P. Langley *et al.*, *Scientific Discovery: Computational Explorations of the Creative Process*, Cambridge, Mass.: The MIT Press, 1987. It should be emphasized once more, however, that both forms of innovation ultimately have the effect of saving on data processing. Concepts consume data no less than percepts.

102 D.E. Rumelhart *et al.*, 'A General Framework for Parallel Distributed Processing', in J.L. McClelland and D.E. Rumelhart, *Parallel Distributed Processing*, Vol. 1, p. 57.

103 Quoted in Gregory *op. cit.*, p. 519.

104 F.C. Bartlett, *Remembering*, Cambridge: Cambridge University Press, 1932.

105 K.R. Popper, *The Logic of Scientific Discovery*, London: Hutchinson, 1959.

106 Bruner, *Beyond the Information Given*, p. 233.

107 J. Ziman, *Public Knowledge: The Social Dimension of Science*, Cambridge: Cambridge University Press, 1968.

108 This derivation may be quite indirect – see Popper, *The Logic*.

109 The notion that perceptual objects are concrete objects while conceptual objects are abstract ones goes back to Frege. See G. Frege, *The Foundations of Arithmetic*, transl. J.L. Austin, Oxford: Blackwell, 1953 (originally published 1884).

110 Churchland *op. cit.*, p. 268. See also P.K. Feyerabend, 'How to be a Good

Empiricist: A Plea for Tolerance in Matters Epistemological', in *Philosophy of Science, The Delaware Seminar*, Vol. 2, B. Baumrin (ed.), pp. 3–39, New York, 1963; and M. Hesse, 'Is there an Independent Observation Language?', in *The Nature and Function of Scientific Theories*, R. Colodny (ed.), Pittsburgh: University of Pittsburgh Press, 1970, pp. 36–77.

111 Hanson *op. cit.*

112 Bruner, *Beyond the Information Given*, pp. 234–235.

113 Edelman, *Neural Darwinism*, p. 247. See also R.J. Herrnstein, 'Stimuli and the Texture of Experience', *Neurosci. Biobehav. Rev.*, 6, 1982, pp. 105–117; R.J. Herrnstein, 'Riddles of Natural Categorization', *Philosophical Transactions of the Royal Society London (Biology)*, 308, 1985, pp. 129–144; R.J. Herrnstein *et al.*, 'Natural Concepts in Pigeons', *Journal of Experimental Psychology and Animal Behavioural Processes*, 2, 1976, pp. 285–301; J. Cerella, 'Visual Classes and Natural Categories in the Pigeon', *Journal of Experimental Psychology and Human Perception*, 5, 1979, pp. 68–77.

114 K.R. Popper, *Objective Knowledge: An Evolutionary Approach*, Oxford: The Clarendon Press, 1972; K.R. Popper and J.C. Eccles, *The Self and its Brain: An Argument for Interactionism*, London: Routledge and Kegan Paul, 1977; P. Munz, *Our Knowledge of the Growth of Knowledge: Popper or Wittgenstein?*, London: Routledge and Kegan Paul, 1985.

115 See R. Boyd *et al.*, *The Philosophy of Science*, Cambridge, Mass.: MIT Press, 1991.

116 We only retain in memory a tiny fraction of the data that we process. There is now good psychological evidence for the existence of short-term memory stores with retention times of the order of a second at most. Simon and Newall *op. cit.*, p. 798.

117 Douglas and Isherwood present consumer goods as a communication system that renders 'visible and stable the different categories of culture' enabling its members to 'make and maintain social relationships'. See M. Douglas and B. Isherwood, *The World of Goods: Towards an Anthropology of Consumption*, Middlesex: Penguin Books, 1978, pp. 59–60; J. Baudrillard, *Le Système des Objets*, Paris: Gallimard, 1968.

118 H.A. Simon, 'A Behavioural Model of Rational Choice', in H.A. Simon (ed.) *Models of Man*, New York: Wiley, 1957.

119 A.R. Luria, *The Mind of a Mnemonist*, London: Jonathan Cape, 1969.

120 K.R. Popper, *Realism and the Aim of Science*, London: Hutchinson, 1983.

121 And even here opinions are divided. See for example I. Lakatos, *Philosophical Papers: Vol. 1, The Methodology of Scientific Research Programmes*, Cambridge: Cambridge University Press, 1978; P. Feyerabend, 'Against Method', in *Minnesota Studies for the Philosophy of Science*, 4, Minnesota: University of Minnesota Press, 1970. The so-called Quine–Duhem thesis suggests that only clusters of theories can ever be tested. Quine argued that any hypothesis can in principle be protected by making suitable and sometimes large-scale adjustments in the background theoretical network. W.V.O. Quine, *Word and Object*, Cambridge, Mass.: The MIT Press, 1960.

122 Popper's doctrine of falsifiability, in which competitors seek to refute newly discovered knowledge, loses much of its force when applied to technology: an individual or a firm that can bring about a technical effect that others *cannot* repeat secures wealth rather than opprobrium. Popper, *The Logic*, 1959.

123 R. Boyd and P.J. Richerson, *Culture and the Evolutionary Process*, Chicago: The University of Chicago Press, 1985, pp. 82, 172.

124 Churchland *op. cit.*, p. 368.

125 D. Kolb, *The Learning Style Inventory: Technical Manual*, Boston, Mass.: McBer and Co., 1976.

126 D.M. Wolfe and D.A. Kolb, 'Career Development, Personal Growth, and Experiential Learning', in D.A. Kolb, I.M. Rubin and J.M. McIntyre (eds) *Organizational Psychology: A Book of Readings*, Englewood Cliffs, New Jersey: Prentice-Hall, 1979, pp. 535–563.

127 J.S. Bruner, *The Process of Education*, Cambridge, Mass.: Harvard University Press, 1960; J.S. Bruner, *On Knowing: Essays for the Left Hand*, New York: Atheneum, 1966; O.J. Harvey, D. Hunt and H. Schroeder, *Conceptual Systems and Personality Organization*, New York: John Wiley and Sons, 1961.

128 J. Singer, 'The Importance of Day Dreaming', *Psychology Today*, 1(II), 1968, pp. 18–26; J. Kagan *et al.*, 'Information Processing in the Child: Significance of Analytic and Reflective Attitudes', *Psychological Monographs*, 78(1), 1964; J. Kagan and N. Kogan, 'Individual Variations in Cognitive Processes', *Carmichael's Manual of Child Psychology* (3rd edition), Vol. 1, P.H. Mussen (ed.), New York: John Wiley and Sons, 1970.

129 Kolb *op. cit.*, p. 541.

130 Langley *et al.*, p. 37.

131 Ziman *op. cit.*

132 E. Durkheim, 'The Dualism of Human Nature and its Social Condition', in K. Wolff (ed.) *Emile Durkheim*, Columbus: Ohio State University Press, 1960 [1914], pp. 325–4?

133 Volkema *op. cit.*

134 R.W. Clarke, *Einstein: The Life and Times*, London: Hodder and Stoughton, 1973. Clarke attributes the expression to Banesh Hoffman who worked with Einstein.

135 T. Kuhn, *The Structure of Scientific Revolutions*, Chicago: The University of Chicago Press, 1962.

136 In trying to clarify Kuhn's sometimes confused use of the term 'paradigm', Masterman finds three distinct levels at which the word can be used. The broadest is the 'metaphysical' in which a paradigm refers to an unquestioned presupposition. More restrictive is Kuhn's 'disciplinary matrix', the shared commitments of a disciplinary community including its symbolic generalizations, beliefs, values, etc. These correspond to Masterman's own sociological paradigms. Finally there is the 'exemplar' or what Masterman calls an 'artifact' or a 'construct paradigm' referring to the concrete accomplishment of a scientific community. The first level comes close to what Holton describes as 'themata', durable heuristics originating within an individual and refractory to puzzle-solving activity. M. Masterman, 'The Nature of a Paradigm', in I. Lakatos and A. Musgrave (eds) *Criticism and the Growth of Knowledge*, Cambridge: Cambridge University Press, 1970, pp. 59–90; G. Holton, *Thematic Origins of Scientific Thought: Kepler to Einstein*, Cambridge, Mass.: Harvard University Press, 1973; D.L. Eckberg and L. Hill Jr, 'The Paradigm Concept and Sociology: A Critical Review', *American Sociological Review*, 44, December 1979, pp. 925–937.

137 Polanyi *op. cit.*, p. 81.

138 S. Freud, *Introductory Lectures on Psychoanalysis*, Middlesex: Penguin Books 1973.

139 Jung *op. cit.*

140 G.A. Kelly, *A Theory of Personality: The Psychology of Personal Constructs*, New York: W.W. Norton and Co., 1963.

141 D. Bannister and F. Fransella, *Inquiring Man*, Middlesex: Penguin Books, 1966, p. 31. Although Bruner has charged construct theory with being too mentalistic,

it constitutes one of the few attempts to develop a unitary view of man.

142 Kelly *op. cit.*

143 These are adapted from Bruner's determinants of the strength of a perceptual hypothesis. See J.S Bruner, 'Personality Dynamics and the Process of Perceiving', in R.R. Blake and G.V. Ramsey, *Perception – An Approach to Personality*, New York: Ronald Press, 1951.

144 Popperian corroboration of the narrowly epistemological kind, resting upon data and categories uncontaminated by social processes, is clearly not the only ground we have for entertaining a perceptual hypothesis or adopting a construct. Our social situation, or our openness to the influence of a peer group or an authority figure, will also play a part. One might even go further and argue as Lakatos and, more forcefully, Feyerabend have done that what constitutes corroboration is itself in part socially determined. See Lakatos *op. cit.*; Feyerabend *op. cit.*; see also M. Hollis and S. Lukes, *Rationality and Relativism*, Oxford: Basil Blackwell, 1982.

145 I. Hacking, 'Experimentation and Scientific Realism', *Philosophical Topics*, 13, 1982, pp. 71–87.

146 How far this is so depends on the particular case and also on the cognitive style of the theorist. Einstein, for example, was more inclined to give superordinate constructs free play in his thinking than was, say, Rutherford. See Pais *op. cit.*

147 J. Piaget, *Plays, Dreams, and Imitations in Childhood*, New York: W.W. Norton and Company, 1962.

148 P. Berger and T. Luckmann, *The Social Construction of Reality: A Treatise in the Sociology of Knowledge*, Middlesex: Penguin Books, 1966. See also A. Schutz, *The Phenomenology of the Social World*, London: Heinemann, 1972.

149 This, of course, is precisely the line adopted by those who view innovations as the ineluctable product of social forces and the *zeitgeist*.

150 Personality factors as we have already seen will also dictate our preference for concrete or abstract constructs. See K. Goldstein, *The Organism*, New York: American Book Co., 1939.

151 Bannister and Fransella *op. cit.*

152 See our earlier discussion in section 2.2.

153 Evolutionary progress also requires that this variety be kept within limits, otherwise chaos rather than evolution will be the result. The establishment of technical and scientific standards in a field of knowledge may reduce variety but still facilitate progress. Pre-revolutionary France, for example, prior to the introduction of the metre as the country's standard unit of length, boasted about 700 different measures often varying from town to town. The metre, conceived as 'a means of spreading Enlightenment and Fraternity among all people', had to be perfect, universal, and permanent. Hence the decision that it should be a fraction of the Meridian – in effect the ten-millionth part of the distance from the pole to the equator. The urge to variety, however, was not quickly dispelled by such universalism and the metre took about ten years to get itself established as a standard.

154 For a discussion of this point see K.R. Popper, *The Open Society and its Enemies: Vol. 1, Plato; Vol. 2, Hegel and Marx*, London: Routledge and Kegan Paul, 1945; see also Munz, *op. cit.*

155 L. Walras, *Elements of Pure Economics: or the Theory of Social Wealth*, Philadelphia: Orion Editions, 1984.

156 For a discussion see J.W. Dean, 'The Dissolution of the Keynesian Consensus', in D. Bell and I. Kristol, *The Crisis in Economic Theory*, New York: Basic Books, 1981, pp. 19–34.

157 F. Hayek, 'The Use of Knowledge in Society', *American Economic Review*, September 1945, pp. 519–530.

158 A. Postlewaite, 'Asymmetric Information', in J. Eatwell, M. Milgate and P. Newman (eds) *Allocation, Information, and Markets*, The New Palgrave, London: Macmillan, 1987, pp. 35–38.

159 Simon, 'A Behavioural Model'.

160 A good introduction to this flourishing area of economics is given by T. Eggertsson in *Economic Behaviour and Institutions*, Cambridge: Cambridge University Press, 1990.

161 Heiner has pointed out that 'Greater uncertainty will cause rule governed behaviour to exhibit increasingly predictable regularities so that uncertainty becomes the basic source of predictable behaviour.' He goes on to suggest that existing economic models work on the opposite assumption by implicitly upgrading the competence of agents to handle the data processing complexity associated with the presence of uncertainty. They are then made to pursue quite implausible optimization strategies that in effect place all the data available to them in their respective E-space at the service of a single possible outcome. Simon views such strategies as expressive of *substantive rationality* and contrasts them with those, more oriented towards the systematic application of rules, that express *procedural rationality*. The first kind of rationality inhabits the south-west region of the E-space, the second kind the north-east region. See R.A. Heiner, 'The Origin of Predictable Behaviour', *American Economic Review*, 73(4), 1983, pp. 560–574; and H.A. Simon, 'Rationality in Psychology and Economics', in R.M. Hogarth and M.W. Reder, *Rational Choice: The Contrast between Economics and Psychology*, Chicago: The University of Chicago Press, 1986, pp. 25–40.

162 D.K.H. Begg, *The Rational Expectations Revolution in Macroeconomics: Theories and Evidence*, Oxford: Philip Allan, 1982. Rational expectations is a theory of macroeconomic learning that holds firstly that people use *all* the data available to them in shaping their expectations about the future course of economic variables and not just past data on prices – in our parlance, they draw such data from all parts of the E-space. It then goes on to argue that in their use of data, people tend to learn from past mistakes so that a progressively better fit is achieved between expectations and actual outcomes brought about by the manipulation of policy variables. The rational expectations hypothesis rests on the assumption that government cannot hoard data or its coding strategies for any length of time. Sooner or later, people catch on and adjust their behaviour accordingly. The type of learning implied is one that moves individuals towards ever-better hypotheses concerning the behaviour of a few well-coded and abstract variables such as inflation or price movements; and, of course, in moving individuals in this way, such learning also moves markets towards equilibrium.

The theory of rational expectations has empirical content. It has found support in the behaviour of financial markets and those of certain commodities. Yet the fact that corroboration for the theory is drawn from such a circumscribed area of economic activity, and one that is institutionally located so close in the E-space to the north-east corner where efficient markets reside, robs the theory of much explanatory scope and raises many questions concerning the way it develops its core assumptions.

163 In the 1930s, the early institutionalists such as John Commons had sought to replace economics as an abstract theory with something more concrete that took into account the existence of institutions and other features of the social structure that were lost to view in the neoclassical perspective. The economic agenda of the

early institutionalists would have shifted the discipline in the E-space from the north-east to the north-west corner where data, although more concrete, remains highly coded. The new institutionalists such as Oliver Williamson, by contrast, aim to broaden the economic agenda by adding to what has already been achieved under the neoclassical paradigm, models of economic behaviour that occupy regions of the E-space less demanding of economic man's powers of coding and abstracting.

With its emphasis on transaction costs – broadly reducible in the view of most of its advocates to information costs – institutional economics holds an implicit view of information processes that come closest to those that have been made explicit in this chapter and that will be further developed in the rest of the book. Institutional economics shares our concern to make economic man a more red-blooded creature, to get him out of his solitary confinement in the north-east corner of the E-space and allow him to wander. The underlying aim of the new institutional economics is to develop a body of economic theorizing that can cope with a more complex and hopefully more interesting economic agent. Our own concern in this book is less explicitly economic: it is to develop further our understanding of how information is processed and shared by such an agent and simply to indicate the possible implications his/her behaviour might have for economic theorizing. See J.R. Commons, *Institutional Economics*, Madison: University of Wisconsin Press, 1934; O.E. Williamson, *Markets and Hierarchies: Analysis and Antitrust Implications*, New York: The Free Press, 1975.

164 For a discussion of Methodological Individualism, see M. Blaug, *The Methodology of Economics: or How Economists Explain*, Cambridge: Cambridge University Press, 1992, pp. 206–219.

3 THE SHARING OF INFORMATION

1 cf. Chapter 1.

2 Institutionalization is further investigated in Chapter 5.

3 M. Polayni, *Personal Knowledge: Towards a Post Critical Philosophy*, London: Routledge and Kegan Paul, 1958.

4 U. Eco, *Opera Aperta*, Milan: Bompiani, 1962.

5 L. Wittgenstein, *Tractatus Logico-Philosophicus*, London: Routledge and Kegan Paul, 1961.

6 This was acknowledged by the later Wittgenstein. See *Philosophical Investigations*, Oxford: Basil Blackwell, 1968.

7 D.R. Brooks and E.O. Wiley, *Evolution as Entropy: Towards a Unified Theory of Biology*, Chicago: The University of Chicago Press, 1986. For an alternative view of entropy in the communication process see C.E. Shannon and W. Weaver, *The Mathematical Theory of Communication*, Urbana: The University of Illinois Press, 1949.

8 J.S. Bruner, 'On Perceptual Readiness', *Psychological Review*, 64, 1957, pp. 123–152.

9 M. Harris, *Cultural Materialism: The Struggle for a Science of Culture*, New York: Vintage Books, 1979.

10 Ibid.

11 The Correspondence Theory of Truth received its modern formulation in the work of Alfred Tarski. See A. Tarski, 'Der Wahrheitsbegriff in den formalisierten Sprachen', *Studia Philosophica I*, 1935, pp. 261–405; see also a discussion of Tarski in R. Boyd, 'Confirmation, Semantics, and the Interpretation of

Scientific Theories', in R. Boyd, P. Gasper and S.D. Trout (eds) *The Philosophy of Science*, Cambridge, Mass.: The MIT Press, 1992, pp. 3–35.

12 See D.C. Dennett, 'Intentional Systems', *Journal of Philosophy*, LXVIII(4), 1971, pp. 87–106.

13 M. Argyle, *Social Interaction*, Atherton: Methuen, 1969, p. 437; see also D. Bannister and F. Fransella, *Inquiring Man*, Middlesex: Penguin Books, 1966, p. 126.

14 Harris *op. cit.*

15 K. Marx, *Economic and Philosophical Manuscripts of 1844*, London: Lawrence and Wishart, 1970.

16 W. Abernathy and J.M. Utterback, 'Patterns of Industrial Innovations', in M.L. Tushman and W.L. Moore (eds) *Readings in the Management of Innovation*, Boston: Pitman, 1982, pp. 97–108.

17 C. Freeman and C. Perez, 'Structural Crises of Adjustment: Business Cycles and Investment Behaviour', in G. Dosi *et al.* (eds) *Technical Change and Economic Theory*, London: Pinter Publishers, 1988, pp. 38–66.

18 A striking example of the difference in diffusibility between coded and uncoded design traditions is offered by the evolution of the Gothic style between the twelfth and fifteenth centuries. Although the basic coded elements of the style – the flying buttress, the ribbed vault, the pointed arch – diffused to Britain, Italy, Germany from the Ile de France where they originated, much of the spirit and ideas which had inspired the development of early French Gothic stayed behind or were misunderstood. Anyone who doubts this should compare the cathedral of Amiens, where the style received its classic formulation, with those at Salisbury, Orvieto or even Cologne. Building upon the coded elements of style received from France, each country exploited its 'misunderstanding' creatively and went on to develop a design tradition of its own. See N. Pevsner, *The Englishness of English Art*, Middlesex: Penguin Books; R. Wittkower, *Allegory and the Migration of Symbols*, Boulder, Colorado: Westview Press, 1977.

19 Shannon and Weaver *op. cit.*

20 J. Vansina, *Oral Tradition: A Study in Historical Methodology*, Middlesex: Penguin Books, 1965; see also J. Goody, *The Interface between the Written and the Oral*, Cambridge: Cambridge University Press, 1987.

21 See Chapter 2.

22 Shannon and Weaver *op. cit.*

23 Ibid.

24 A. Moles, *Information Theory and Esthetic Perception*, Urbana: University of Illinois Press, 1968.

25 Ibid.

26 Ibid., p. 130.

27 The mechanics through which these two steps are carried out in a research setting are described in detail in K.D. Knorr-Cetina, *The Manufacture of Knowledge: An Essay on the Constructivist and Contextual Nature of Science*, Oxford: Pergamon Press, 1981. For an example of how this two-step process might work in reverse, see E. Katz and P.F. Lazarsfeld, *Personal Influence*, Glencoe, Illinois: The Free Press, 1955.

28 The sociology of knowledge, translating the term *Wissenssoziologie* first coined by Max Scheler in Germany in the 1920s, broadly aims to deal with everything that passes for knowledge in human thought but from a sociological perspective, one that is concerned with the way that subjective meanings become externalized into objective and hence shared facticities. In short, the sociology of knowledge looks at communication constraints and at the effects these exert on the creation

and sharing of knowledge and on the different ways of knowing that result. See M. Scheler, *Schriften zur Soziologie und Weltanschauunglehre*, Vols 1–3, Leipzig, 1923 and 1924; K. Manheim, *Ideology and Utopia*, Routledge and Kegan Paul, 1960.

29 D. MacKay, *Information, Mechanism and Meaning*, Cambridge, Mass.: The MIT Press, 1969, p. 24.

30 Note the parallel between Mackay's definition of meaning and Popper's dispositional view of knowledge. See K.R. Popper, *Realism and the Aim of Science*, London: Hutchinson, 1983, p. xxxv.

31 The life-world is defined by Alfred Schutz as the 'unexamined ground of the Natural World View'. See A. Schutz and T. Luckmann, *The Structure of the Life-World*, London: Heinemann, 1974, p. 3.

32 M. Sahlins, *Culture and Practical Reason*, Chicago: The University of Chicago Press, 1976, p. 102.

33 F. Braudel, *Civilisation Matérielle, Economie et Capitalisme, XVe–XVIIIe Siècle: Tome 1, Les Structures du Quotidien*, Paris: Armand Colin, 1979, p. 352.

34 E.M. Rogers and F.F. Shoemaker, *Communication in Innovation: A Cross Cultural Approach*, New York: The Free Press, 1971.

35 G. Tarde, *Les Lois de l'Imitation*, Paris: Collection Ressources, 1979.

36 A number of contemporary authors such as René Thom have extended the role they would give to imitation as a unifying mechanism beyond human society to nature as a whole. See R. Thom, *Stabilité Structurelle et Morphogenèse: Essai d'une Théorie Générale des Modèles*, Paris: Intereditions, 1977.

37 In putting forward this view, Tarde foreshadowed much contemporary thinking on the growth and development of scientific thought. See for example S. Toulmin, *Human Understanding*, Oxford: Clarendon Press, 1972; D. Campbell, 'Evolutionary Epistemology', in P.A. Schlipp (ed.) *The Philosophy of Karl Popper*, La Salle, Illinois: Open Court Publishing, 1974.

38 A.P. Usher, 'Technical Change and Capital Formulation', in *Capital Formation and Economic Growth*, National Bureau of Economic Research, 1955, pp. 523–550. Tarde made the same point. See G. Tarde *op. cit.*, p. ix.

39 J.A. Schumpeter, *The Theory of Economic Development*, London: Oxford University Press, 1961 [1934].

40 The Japanese seemed to have mastered this 'strategy of the Tortoise' rather sooner than their western competitors. Japan's innovation policies are discussed in R.E. Caves and M. Uekusa, *Industrial Organization in Japan*, Washington, DC: The Brookings Institution, 1976.

41 See for an example drawn from science the description of Henri Poincaré by the psychologist E. Toulouse and discussed by Miller. E. Toulouse, *Henri Poincaré*, Paris: Flammarion, 1910; A. Miller, *Imagery in Scientific Thought: Creating 20th Century Physics*, Cambridge, Mass.: The MIT Press, 1987; see also G. Holton, *The Scientific Imagination: Case Studies*, Cambridge: Cambridge University Press, 1978. For an example of unconscious invention in the field of mathematics see S.A. Papert, 'The Mathematical Unconscious', in J. Wechsler (ed.) *On Aesthetics in Science*, Cambridge, Mass.: The MIT Press, 1978.

42 Alexander Fleming's work on lysozyme, for example, was not thought to justify his election to the Royal Society. It paved the way, however, for the chance observation that was to lead to the discovery of penicillin. Fleming's biographer, Macfarlane, described the sequence of events that led to the discovery as having an 'almost unbelievable improbability' (p. 247). Yet as Fleming himself later commented, 'I was just playing.' See F. Bustina, *Diez Años de Amistad con Sir Alexander Fleming*, Madrid: Editorial M.A.S. 1961, p. 56; and G. Macfarlane,

Alexander Fleming: The Man and the Myth, Oxford: Oxford University Press, 1984.

43 E. Durkheim and M. Mauss, *Primitive Classification*, London: Cohen and West, 1963 [1903].

44 T. Shibutani, 'Reference Groups as Perspectives', *American Journal of Sociology*, 60, 1955, pp. 562–570.

45 For illustrations of this kind of behaviour see I.L. Janis, *Groupthink: Psychological Studies of Policy Decisions and Fiascos*, Boston: Houghton Mifflin Co., 1982. For a cultural treatment of the same phenomenon see M. Douglas, *Natural Symbols: Explorations in Cosmology*, Middlesex: Penguin Books, 1973.

46 This point was forcefully made by Jules Henry in *Culture against Man*, Middlesex: Penguin Books, 1972.

47 H. Scarbrough and J.M. Corbett, *Technology and Organization: Power, Meaning and Design*, London: Routledge, 1992.

48 cf. Chapter 2.

49 P. Berger and T. Luckmann, *The Social Construction of Reality: A Treatise in the Sociology of Knowledge*, Middlesex: Penguin Books, 1966.

50 F. Hayek, 'The Use of Knowledge in Society', *American Economic Review*, September 1945, pp. 519–530. For a more anthropological discussion of the same phenomena see C. Geertz, *Local Knowledge: Further Essays in Interpretative Sociology*, New York: Basic Books, 1983.

51 Schutz and Luckmann *op. cit.*, p. 68.

52 Shannon and Weaver *op. cit.*

53 F. Tönnies, *Community and Association*, London: Routledge and Kegan Paul, 1955; E. Durkheim, *The Division of Labour in Society*, New York: The Free Press, 1933.

54 J.S. Bruner, *Beyond the Information Given: Studies in the Psychology of Knowing*, London: George Allen and Unwin, 1974; J.H. Flavell, *The Developmental Psychology of Jean Piaget*, Princeton, New Jersey: Van Nostrand and Co., 1963.

55 To say that abstract categories of culture bound his knowledge does not imply that they determine it. As Geertz has observed, 'Nothing has done more, I think, to discredit cultural analysis than the construction of impeccable depictions of formal order in whose actual existence nobody can quite believe'; G. Geertz, *The Interpretation of Cultures: Selected Essays*, New York: Basic Books, 1973, p. 18.

56 Polanyi *op. cit.*, p. 53.

57 Scheler *op. cit.*

58 Tarde *op. cit.*

59 Bruner, *Beyond the Information Given*, p. 439.

60 E. Leach, *Culture and Communication: The Logic by Which Symbols are Connected*, Cambridge: Cambridge University Press, 1976.

61 Vansina *op. cit.*, p. 102.

62 Harris *op. cit.*, p. 340.

63 George Orwell, *1984*, Middlesex: Penguin Books.

64 Scarbrough and Corbett *op. cit.* See also M. Foucault, *Histoire de la Folie à l'Age Classique*, Paris: Editions Gallimard, 1972.

65 Among non-Marxists, an efficiency view of the control of information flows is put forward by institutional economists such as Oliver Williamson and organization theorists such as Simon and March, whereas a more libertarian view – associated with Friedrich Hayek – is that no attempt at the control of information flows can ever be complete; thus neither straight coercion nor

Machiavellian manipulation can be effective communication strategies over the long run. Without taking sides in this debate, one might simply note that in those social systems that are continually innovating and creating new knowledge – that is, performing acts of codification at different points along the scale – information flows are set in motion that sooner or later overwhelm any filtering mechanisms designed to contain them. Individual acts of codification, however, constrained in the data they can draw upon as well as by their position along the diffusion scale, can never be the free expression of untrammelled thought. Even when it is at its most creative, the human mind roams across cognitive territory the topography of which is largely shaped by others. Only if the available freedom of manoeuvre is used wisely, and in ways that acknowledge the nature of the terrain, will cognitive exploration prove fruitful. See O.E. Williamson, *The Economic Institutions of Capitalism: Firms, Markets, Relational Contracting*, New York: The Free Press, 1985; J. March and H.A. Simon, *Organizations*, New York: John Wiley and Sons, 1958; F.A. Hayek, *The Counter-Revolution in Science: Studies on the Abuse of Reason*, Indianapolis: The Liberty Press, 1979.

66 Marx *op. cit.*

67 See A. Shaikh, 'Abstract and Concrete Labour', in J. Eatwell, M. Milgate and P. Newman (eds) *Marxian Economics*, The New Palgrave, London: Macmillan, 1990; G. de Vivo, 'Labour Power', in J. Eatwell, M. Milgate and P. Newman, *op. cit.*

68 Berger and Luckmann *op. cit.*, p. 66.

69 The distinction between universalistic and particularistic orientations was developed by Parsons. See T. Parsons, *The Social System*, London: Routledge and Kegan Paul, 1951.

70 P. Bridgeman, *The Logic of Modern Physics*, London: Macmillan, 1927.

71 It will be noted that we are placing the dependent variable along the horizontal axis in violation of mathematical conventions. This reflects a clash between two logics: the first, mathematical, explicitly requires the dependent variable along the vertical axis; the second is implicit and it expects communication processes to be represented as a horizontal phenomenon. My own experience of working with these concepts is that people find them more accessible if the second logic, the implicit one, is allowed to predominate. I shall therefore continue to use it here and throughout the book.

72 Hayek, 'The Use of Knowledge'.

73 C. Castañeda, *A Separate Reality*, New York: Simon and Schuster, 1971. Bourdieu labels such prestige 'Symbolic Capital'. See P. Bourdieu, *Esquisse d'une Théorie de la Pratique, Précédé de Trois Études d'Ethnologie Kabyle*, Geneva: Librairie Droz, 1972.

74 B. Bernstein, *Class, Codes, and Control: Vol. 1, Theoretical Studies towards a Sociology of Language*, London: Routledge and Kegan Paul, 1971.

75 L. Walras, *Elements of Pure Economics: or the Theory of Social Wealth*, Philadelphia: Orion Editions, 1984 [1926].

76 Vansina *op. cit.*

77 One revealing indicator of the preference for local news in industrial societies is the absence of a wholly national newspaper in the US.

78 Bourdieu refers to this kind of local knowledge as *habitus*. See Bourdieu *op. cit.*, Ch. 2.

79 Polanyi *op. cit.*

80 Tarde *op. cit.*

81 We are not claiming that the abstraction has to be *derived* from the statistical

base; only supported by it. We thus avoid getting involved in 'Hume's Problem' as Popper refers to it.

82 R. Gregory, *Mind in Science: A History of Explanations in Psychology and Physics*, Middlesex: Penguin Books, 1981, pp. 146–148.

83 K.R. Popper, *The Logic of Scientific Discovery*, London: Hutchinson, 1959.

84 Schutz and Luckmann *op. cit.*, pp. 23–25.

85 This is the position of P. Feyerabend in *Against Method: Outline of an Anarchistic Theory of Knowledge*, London: Verso, 1975. For a somewhat less polemical presentation of the case for relativism, see B. Barnes and D. Bloor, 'Relativism, Rationalism and the Sociology of Knowledge', in M. Hollis and S. Lukes (eds) *Rationality and Relativism*, Oxford: Basil Blackwell, 1982.

86 E. Husserl, *Ideas: General Introduction to Pure Phenomenology*, London: Collier–Macmillan, 1962.

87 See the discussion in D. Martindale, *The Nature and Types of Sociological Theories*, London: Routledge and Kegan Paul, 1967.

88 E. Hall, *Beyond Culture*, New York: Doubleday, 1976.

89 Bernstein *op. cit.*

90 Polanyi *op. cit.*, p. 378. The external observer of purely physical phenomena has also been having a hard time at the quantum scale.

91 An example of how this 'common firmament' comes under strain when traditions diverge is given by David Hull's description of the clash between Darwinists and Cladists. See D. Hull, *Science as a Process: An Evolutionary Account of the Social and Conceptual Development of Science*, Chicago: The University of Chicago Press, 1988; the issue is also discussed by Knorr-Cetina *op. cit.*

92 Foucault *op. cit.*

93 P. Munz, *Our Knowledge of the Growth of Knowledge: Popper or Wittgenstein?*, London: Routledge and Kegan Paul, 1985, p. 160.

94 This multiple overlay of alternative codifications has its counterpart in the natural sciences. Take, for example, Hugh Everett III's 'Many-Worlds Interpretation' of quantum mechanics. See H. Everett III, '"Relative State" Formulation of Quantum Mechanics', in *Review of Modern Physics*, 29(3), July 1957, pp. 454–462.

95 Tarde *op. cit.*, p. 31.

96 G.A. Kelly, *A Theory of Personality: The Psychology of Personal Constructs*, New York: W.W. Norton and Co., 1963, p. 95.

97 The technical problem of information sharing is addressed in section 3.11.

98 In the words of Paul Feyerabend, 'anything goes'.

99 Popper, *Realism*.

100 K.R. Popper, *The Open Society and its Enemies: Vol. 1, Plato; Vol. 2, Hegel and Marx*, London: Routledge and Kegan Paul, 1945.

101 Tarde, *op. cit.*, p. 95. As Tarde then goes on to point out, to innovate one must be able to some extent to escape society. As he puts it, one must become '*suprasocial*' (p. 95).

102 Competitive coding is also hypothesized to operate at the neurological level. See D.E. Rumelhart and D. Zipser, 'Feature Discovery by Competitive Learning', in D.E. Rumelhart and J.L. McClelland (eds) *Parallel Distributed Processing: Explorations in the Microstructure of Cognition*, Cambridge, Mass.: The MIT Press, 1986, pp. 151–193.

103 Workable rather than optimal solutions are what followers are seeking since at the leading edge of technical research optimality remains a concept of dubious practical application. See H.A. Simon, *The New Science of Management Decision*, New York: Harper and Row, 1960.

104 On the Copernican revolution, see E.J. Dijksterhuis, *The Mechanization of the World Picture: Pythagoras to Newton*, Princeton, New Jersey: Princeton University Press, 1986; T.S. Kuhn, *The Copernican Revolution: Planetary Astronomy in the Development of Western Thought*, Cambridge, Mass.: Harvard University Press, 1957. On the decline of creation doctrines and the rise of Darwinism, see M.B. Foster, 'The Christian Doctrine of Creation and the Rise of Modern Natural Science', *Mind*, 43, 1934, pp. 446–468; E. Mayr, *The Growth of Biological Thought: Diversity, Evolution, and Inheritance*, Cambridge, Mass.: The Belknap Press of Harvard University Press, 1982.

105 Weber takes the capacity to generate an extraordinary discourse as the decisive characteristic of charisma. See Max Weber, *Economy and Society*, G. Roth and C. Wittich (eds), Berkeley: University of California Press, 1978.

106 As Whitehead put it, 'The greatest invention of the nineteenth century was the invention of the method of invention.' A.N. Whitehead, *Science in the Modern World*, Lowell Lectures, 1925, New York: Mentor Books, 1948.

107 Schumpeter *op. cit.*

108 Usher *op. cit.*

109 Since the end of the Second World War, for example, the Japanese have learnt to adapt creatively the advanced technologies they imported from the west and, indeed, in many ways to improve upon them. Only an obsessive concern with neat categorizations that kept invention and imitation well apart as conceptual schemes blinded western companies – greatly to their cost – to the incremental creative powers of Japanese firms. Since these were not original inventors, it was blithely assumed, they could only be cheap imitators incapable of catching up. See C. Johnson, *MITI and the Japanese Miracle: The Growth of Industrial Policy, 1925–1975*, Stanford, California: Stanford University Press, 1982; B.R. Martin and J. Irvine, *Research Foresight: Priority Setting in Science*, London: Pinter Publishers, 1989.

110 Katz and Lazarsfeld, for example, in an important study on consumer behaviour, showed that in many product markets the diffusion of an innovation is a two-step process involving an initial communication through the media to established opinion leaders in a community, and then, subsequent to their own adoption of a new product or service, its gradual spread through face-to-face discussions and imitation to the rest of the community. Opinion leaders were always the first to hear about and adopt a new trend. They were generally in touch and known by the others to be 'in the know'. Whether it was for an item of information or judgements on a new product or a passing fashion, members of the community depended upon these opinion leaders for guidance. Katz and Lazarsfeld *op. cit.*

111 A. de Tocqueville, *De la Démocratie en Amérique*, Paris: Gallimard, 1986.

112 See L. Dumont, *Homo Hierarchicus: Le Système des Castes et ses Implications*, Paris: Gallimard, 1966.

113 An example of the latter is furnished by Copernicus's reputed reluctance to publish his heliocentric theory. Koestler put this down to fear of ridicule as much as to concern with the reaction of the Church. See A. Koestler, *The Sleepwalkers: A History of Man's Changing Vision of the Universe*, Middlesex: Penguin Books, 1959, p. 204.

114 Bourdieu *op. cit.*

115 Galileo's forced recantation of the new cosmology in the face of Church opposition serves to remind us that our own culture was not always as receptive to the diffusion of new ideas as we like to believe.

116 G. Duby, *Guerriers et Paysans: VIIe–XIIe Siècle: Premier Essor de l'Economie*

Européenne, Paris: Gallimard, 1973.
117 Tarde *op. cit.*
118 Berger and Luckmann *op. cit.*, p. 104.
119 Tarde describes it as 'Une grammaire, un code, une constitution implicite ou écrite, une industrie regnante, une poétique souveraine, un catechisme: tout cela, qui est le fond *catégorique* des sociétés, est l'oeuvre lente et graduelle de la *dialectique* sociale.' Tarde *op. cit.*, p. 182.
120 Labour, sexuality, and territoriality, by virtue of their pervasiveness, are the natural foci of such efforts at institution building.
121 For an application of the transaction cost perspective to institutions see D. North, *Institution, Institutional Change and Economic Performance*, Cambridge: Cambridge University Press, 1990.
122 Parsons *op. cit.*
123 Where this personal utility can accommodate a social welfare function we move towards universalism. It need not therefore be assumed that personal utility inevitably translates into self-seeking or strategic behaviour. For a discussion of how self- and group-interests come together in the utility function of an individual, see H. Margolis, *Selfishness, Altruism and Rationality: A Theory of Social Choice*, Chicago: The University of Chicago Press, 1982.
124 Berger and Luckmann *op. cit.*, p. 121.
125 Bourdieu *op. cit.*
126 Hence the fate that befalls ideologies such as Marxism-Leninism that fail to achieve the status of a non-testable religion. Jam next week has always been a much safer thing to promise than jam tomorrow when jam today is unavailable.
127 Archaeology provides us with numerous examples of artefacts that have been manufactured with identical technologies and diffused throughout a culture area, but which still exhibit basic aesthetic differences and divergent cultural sensibilities. As Tarde clearly saw, total imitation is an unattainable ideal.
128 O.E. Williamson, 'Hierarchical Control and Optimum Firm Size', *Journal of Political Economy*, 75, April 1967, pp. 123–138.
129 Brooks and Wiley *op. cit.*
130 Vansina *op. cit.*, p. 37.
131 The move from informal to formal organization as a firm grows in western industrial societies has similarities to the move to a written tradition in oral cultures. See Goody *op. cit.*
132 Vansina *op. cit.*, p. 33.
133 Ibid., p. 28.
134 Ibid., p. 69.
135 For a treatment of property rights relevant to this perspective, see T. Eggertsson, *Economic Behaviour and Institutions*, Cambridge, Cambridge University Press, 1990.
136 Vansina *op. cit.*, p. 33.
137 Ibid., p. 36.
138 The function of branding, of course, is to restore the primacy of message provenance over both message consistency and a too discriminating use of the personal utility function.
139 Tarde *op. cit.*
140 E. Durkheim, *Le Suicide*, Paris: Presses Universitaires de France, 1930, p. 281.
141 Piaget takes the terms 'assimilation' and 'accommodation' as the twin poles of any biological or social learning process. See J. Piaget, *Biologie et Connaissance: Essai sur les Relations entre les Régulations Organiques et les Processus Cognitifs*, Paris: Gallimard, 1967.

142 For an illustration of this process in the context of Turkey's modernization, see D. Lerner, *The Passing of Traditional Society*, Glencoe, Illinois: The Free Press, 1958.

143 E. Durkheim, *The Division of Labour in Society*, New York: The Free Press, 1964 [1983]. This is what Durkheim terms *mechanical solidarity*.

144 Berger and Luckmann *op. cit.*, p. 106.

145 The term is Giddens's. See A. Giddens, *The Constitutions of Society: Outline of the Theory of Structuration*, Cambridge: The Polity Press, 1984.

146 Shannon and Weaver *op. cit.*

147 See Hägerstrand for a discussion of the spatial constraints on communications. T. Hägerstrand, *Innovation as a Spacial Process*, Chicago: The University of Chicago Press, 1976.

148 For an explanation of why diffusion is placed on the horizontal axis, see note 71 above.

149 J. Ziman, *Public Knowledge: The Social Dimension of Science*, Cambridge: Cambridge University Press, 1968.

150 Our view of common sense differs from Einstein's who defined it as that stock of prejudices acquired before the age of eighteen. Prejudices are in fact acquired over a lifetime. It also ignores the distinction drawn by Giddens between Common Sense and Mutual Knowledge. See Giddens *op. cit.*

151 Thus the grounds for choosing among different types of common sense are not fundamentally different from those which help us select from among competing scientific theories: how much of the world do they each explain?

152 cf. Chapter 2.

153 Polanyi *op. cit.*, p. 300.

154 Schutz and Luckmann *op. cit.*, p. 270.

155 Many examples can be drawn from the history of science: Bruno, Copernicus, Galileo, etc.

156 We are using here the definition of value proposed by Walras. See Walras *op. cit.*, pp. 66–67.

157 The orientation towards proprietary knowledge of a scientific nature differs from that adopted towards technology. With appropriability secured, the latter will be traded for money whereas the former will be traded for esteem and recognition – this might of course be cashed in for money at a later date. For a discussion of science as exchange, see W. Hagstrom, *The Scientific Community*, New York: Basic Books, 1965. For an alternative conception of how appropriability functions in science, see Knorr-Cetina *op. cit.*

158 Matching the distribution of knowledge *within* a group is not the same as matching it *between* groups. We address this issue in Chapters 5 and 6.

159 The free lunch approach to communications is precisely what distinguishes the neoclassical economist from the neo-Austrian.

160 Moles *op. cit.*, p. 78.

161 Ibid., p. 84.

162 See Chapter 2.

163 Polanyi *op. cit.*, p. 86. Giddens argues that much of it does not have to be articulated to be transmissible. It simply cannot itself be talked about. See Giddens *op. cit.*

164 How far new telecommunication technologies will be able to substitute for face-to-face exchanges with no impoverishment in the quality of the exchange is a subject of much debate.

165 See Hall *op. cit.*

166 Giddens *op. cit.*, p. 4.

167 Pierrre Cardin *haute couture* dresses, for example, were soon joined by Pierre Cardin ready to wear for women, ready to wear for men, accessories, and new household furniture and decorative items. Can we soon expect to see Pierre Cardin kitchenware, household utensils, street furniture – and ready mixed concrete?
168 In this game corporate advertising might be considered a halfway house.
169 See R.K. Merton, 'Priorities in Scientific Discovery', *American Sociological Review*, 22(6), December 1957, pp. 635–659; J.R. Ravetz, *Scientific Knowledge and its Social Problems*, Middlesex: Penguin Books, 1973.
170 Since writing this statement, I have grown less confident of its force. Is it sustainable in a regime of HDTV and virtual reality? I will only retract, however, when I can fully experience a sky diving holiday without leaving the comforts of my living room.
171 Zuboff's researches, however, do not suggest that a reduced need for codification readily translates into a reduced need for abstraction. S. Zuboff, *In the Age of the Smart Machine: The Future of Work and Power*, Oxford: Heinemann, 1988.
172 Bernstein *op. cit.*
173 Bernstein's use of the term 'restricted code' has been criticized by Labov even in cases as non-specialized as those of street-corner gangs. See W. Labov, 'The Logic of Nonstandard English', *Georgetown Monographs on Language and Linguistics*, 22, 1969, pp. 1–22, 26–31.
174 Our use of the term 'field' is closer to the geographer's than to that of the data processing specialist; in particular the geographer's concept of the Mean Information Field coming out of the work of Hägerstrand seems well aligned with our own use of the term. See T. Hägerstrand, 'Aspects of the Spatial Structure of Social Communication and the Diffusion of Information', Papers of the Regional Science Association, 1966, pp. 27–42; R. Abler, J. Adams and P. Gould, *Spatial Organization: The Geographer's View of the World*, Englewood Cliffs, New Jersey: Prentice-Hall, 1971.
175 For a discussion of the latter relationship see P. Mirowski, *More Heat than Light: Economics as Social Physics, Physics as Nature's Economics*, Cambridge: Cambridge University Press, 1989.
176 A. Sandmo, 'Public Goods', in J. Eatwell, M. Milgate and P. Newman (eds) *Allocation, Information and Markets*, The New Palgrave, London: Macmillan, 1989, pp. 254–266.
177 M. Blaug, *Economic Theory in Retrospect*, Cambridge: Cambridge University Press, 1978.
178 K. Marx, *Capital: A Critique of Political Economy*, Vol. 1, Part 3, London: Lawrence and Wishart, 1970.
179 Marx was an early adherent to Darwin's theory of Natural Selection. His admiration for Darwin gave rise to the myth that he wrote to him asking permission to dedicate *Das Kapital* to him. The myth has since been debunked. See R. Colp, 'The Myth of the Marx–Darwin Letter', *History of Political Economy*, 14, 1982, pp. 461–482.
180 Hayek, 'The Use of Knowledge'.
181 A good overview of the issues is given in J. Eatwell, M. Milgate and P. Newman (eds) *Allocation, Information and Markets*.
182 R. Nelson and S. Winter, *An Evolutionary Theory of Economic Change*, Cambridge, Mass.: The Belknap Press of Harvard University Press, 1982; J. Foster, *Evolutionary Macroeconomics*, London: Allen and Unwin, 1987.
183 A. Alchian and H. Demsetz, 'Production, Information Costs, and Economic Organization', *American Economic Review*, 62, 1972, pp. 777–795; D. North *op. cit.*

184 Hayek, 'The Use of Knowledge'.
185 This point is implicit in the work of Von Foerster, Atlan, Nicolis, Prigogine, and Morin. See H. Von Foerster, 'On self organizing systems and their environments', in Yovitz and Cameron (eds) *Self Organizing Systems*, London: Pergamon Press, 1960, pp. 31–50; H. Atlan, *Entre le Cristal et la Fumée: Essai sur l'Organisation du Vivant*, Paris: Seuil, 1979; G. Nicolis and I. Prigogine, *Exploring Complexity: An Introduction*, New York: W.H. Freeman and Co., 1989; E. Morin, *La Méthode: La Nature de la Nature*, Paris: Seuil, 1977.
186 See Chapter 1. Systems which conserve their energy are known in physics as Hamiltonian systems.

4 DYNAMIC BEHAVIOUR: THE SOCIAL LEARNING CYCLE

1 R. Sheldrake, *The Presence of the Past*, London: Fontana, 1988. According to Sheldrake, 'Morphic fields, like the known fields of physics, are non material regions of influence extending in space and continuing in time. They are localized in and around the systems they organize.' Somewhat recalling Aristotelian essentialism, Sheldrake argues that each kind of natural system has its own kind of field. Thus there is an insulin field, a beech field, a swallow field, and so on (pp. xxii–xxiii).
2 P. Duhem, *La Théorie Physique: Son Objet, sa Structure*, Paris: Marcel Rivière et Cie, 1914.
3 One variant of essentialism is due to Plato who held that there are really existing abstract entities or forms, of which physical objects are but imperfect copies.
4 Lacan, to take an example from a different field, has been accused of giving too much primacy to the verbal in his approach to psychoanalysis. See J. Lacan, *Ecrits*, Paris: Seuil, Vol. 1 1966, Vol. 2 1971.
5 For some this move is a *sine qua non* of the scientific enterprise. The façade of the Social Science Research Building at the University of Chicago bears Lord Kelvin's famous dictum 'If you cannot measure, your knowledge is meagre and unsatisfactory'. Referred to in T.S. Kuhn, 'The Function of Measurement in Modern Physical Science', *Isis*, 52, 1961, pp. 161–193.
6 M. Polanyi, *Personal Knowledge: Towards a Post-Critical Philosophy*, London: Routledge and Kegan Paul, 1958, p. 195.
7 The personality factors that shape the personal element were discussed in Chapter 2. For a telling example see Fleck's 1935 monograph on the discovery of the link between the Wassermann reaction and syphilis. L. Fleck, *Genesis and Development of a Scientific Fact*, Chicago: The University of Chicago Press, 1979 [1935]. Fleck's work in many ways anticipates that of Kuhn's on paradigms. See T.S. Kuhn, *The Structure of Scientific Revolutions*, Chicago: The University of Chicago Press, 1962.
8 Kuhn, *The Structure*.
9 Ibid.
10 The theory of cognitive dissonance argues that where the conflict is indeed intra-personal, our cognitive apparatus works to minimize the distance between A and not-A. See L. Festinger, *A Theory of Cognitive Dissonance*, Palo Alto, California: Stanford University Press, 1957.
11 How hard it is to acknowledge A when one is theologically committed to not-A! It was only in 1992 that the Church finally brought itself to admit that it had been mistaken in its treatment of Galileo. See also J. Gernet, *Chine et Christianisme: Action et Réaction*, Paris: Gallimard, 1982.

12 The convergence of mechanical and electronic technologies in mecatronics and more recently in nano-technologies could yet make a nonsense of this remark.

13 G. Révész, *Thinking and Speaking*, Amsterdam, 1954, p. 3.

14 E. Sapir, 'Conceptual Categories in Primitive Languages', *Science*, 74, 1931, p. 578.

15 cf. Chapter 2.

16 The formula is $\Delta R = -K \log_2 n$. See A. Moles, *Information Theory and Esthetic Perception*, Urbana: University of Illinois Press, 1968, p. 154.

17 J.S. Bruner, J.J. Goodnow and G.A. Austin, *A Study of Thinking*, New York: John Wiley and Sons, 1956.

18 See A. Pais, *'Subtle is the Lord...': The Science and the Life of Albert Einstein*, Oxford: Oxford University Press, 1982. For an original interpretation of the crisis provoked by the quantum theory, see D. Bohm, *Wholeness and the Implicate Order*, London: Routledge, 1980.

19 'Following Alfred Landé, I propose to say that something exists, or is real, if and only if it can be kicked and can in principle kick back; to put it a little more generally, I propose to say that something exists, or is real, if and only if it can *interact* with members of World 1, with hard physical bodies', K.R. Popper, *The Open Universe: An Argument for Indeterminism*, London: Hutchinson, 1982, p. 116.

20 The term is borrowed and adapted from Williamson for whom impacting 'exists in circumstances in which one of the parties to an exchange is much better informed than is the other regarding underlying conditions germane to the trade, and the second party cannot achieve information parity except at great cost – because he cannot rely on the first party to disclose the information in a truly candid manner', O.E. Williamson, *Markets and Hierarchies: Analysis and Antitrust Implications*, New York: The Free Press, 1975, p. 14. Clearly our own use of the term is more neutral than Williamson's. It decouples the problem of disclosing knowledge which is deeply embedded from the ethical disposition of the knower.

21 cf. Chapter 2.

22 The structural conflict that opposes nominalists and realists has taken many forms and goes back to scholastic philosophy. Abelard attempted to reconcile realist and nominalist positions in his *Sic et Non* but, despite his immense influence, he met with little success. See E. Gilson, *La Philosophie du Moyen Age: Tome 1, Des Origines Patristiques à la Fin du XIIème Siècle*, Paris: Payot, 1944.

23 cf. Chapter 2. A.I. Miller, *Imagery in Scientific Thought: Creating 20th Century Physics*, Cambridge, Mass.: The MIT Press, 1987; P. Langley, H. Simon, G. Bradshaw and J. Zytkow, *Scientific Discovery: Computational Explorations of the Creative Process*, Cambridge, Mass.: The MIT Press, 1987; G. Holton, *Thematic Origins of Scientific Thought: Kepler to Einstein*, Cambridge, Mass.: Harvard University Press, 1973.

24 G. Holton, *The Advancement of Science and its Burdens: The Jefferson Lectures and Other Essays*, Cambridge: Cambridge University Press, 1986.

25 Ibid.

26 Langley *et al., op. cit.*

27 Bohm *op. cit.* See also his *Causality and Chance in Modern Physics*, London: Routledge and Kegan Paul, 1984.

28 Duhem *op. cit.*

29 See R. Wohlstetter, *Pearl Harbor: Warning and Decision*, Stanford, California: Stanford University Press, 1962; G.T. Allison, *The Essence of Decision: Explaining the Cuban Missile Crisis*, Boston: Little, Brown, 1971.

30 Tragically for the US, that is; Britain regarded America's entry into the war as a deliverance.

31 Physical space is implicitly present only along the diffusion dimension.

32 L. Walras, *Elements of Pure Economics: or the Theory of Social Wealth*, Philadelphia: Orion Editions 1984 [1926], p. 65.

33 J.S. Bruner, 'On Perceptual Readiness', *Psychological Review*, 64, 1957, pp. 123–152.

34 Ibid.

35 See M. Scheler, *Die Wissenformen und die Gesellschaft*, Leipzig: Der Neue Geist, 1926, pp. 56ff.

36 W. James, *Principles of Psychology*, Vol. II, New York: Henry, 1890, p. 289.

37 Bruner *op. cit.*

38 J.S. Bruner and J.L. Postman, 'On the Perception of Incongruity: A Paradigm', *Journal of Personality*, No. 18, September 1949.

39 Kuhn, *The Structure*.

40 See, for example, I. Lakatos and A. Musgrave (eds) *Criticism and the Growth of Knowledge*, Cambridge: Cambridge University Press, 1970; I.B. Cohen discusses the problematic nature of the term 'revolution', noting that 'the notion that a revolution in astronomy attended the publication of Copernicus's *De Revolutionibus* in 1543 was a fanciful invention of eighteenth century historians of astronomy; it was popularized to such an extent that the Copernican revolution became the paradigmatic revolution in science'. Yet as Cohen points out, 'critical examination of the evidence by historians has shown that the revolution was not at all Copernican, but was at best Galilean and Keplerian'. I.B. Cohen, *Revolution of Science*, Cambridge, Mass.: The Belknap Press of Harvard University Press, 1985, p. x.

41 Cf. Chapter 1.

42 J. Schmookler, 'Economic Sources of Inventive Activity', *Journal of Economic History*, March 1962, pp. 1–20.

43 For an illustration of how such networks operate, see H.M. Collins, 'Tacit Knowledge and Scientific Networks', in B. Barnes and D. Edge (eds) *Science in Context: Readings in the Sociology of Science*, Milton Keynes: The Open University Press, 1982.

44 I. Prigogine, *From Being to Becoming: Time and Complexity in the Physical Sciences*, New York: W.H. Freeman and Co., 1980.

45 Polanyi *op. cit.*, p. 301.

46 G. Macfarlane, *Alexander Fleming: The Man and the Myth*, Oxford: Oxford University Press, 1985. Pasteur's discovery of asymmetric fermentation offers another example; see R. Dubos, *Pasteur and Modern Science*, New York: Doubleday, 1960. For a lighthearted discussion of the role of prior preparedness in scientific discovery, see R.S. Root-Bernstein, *Discovering: Inventing and Solving Problems at the Frontiers of Scientific Knowledge*, Cambridge: Mass.: Harvard University Press, 1989.

47 This cognitive conservatism does not necessarily brand them as 'puzzle-solvers'. New paradigms can just as easily emerge from the idiosyncratic nature of perception as from an innate disposition to try something new. See T.S. Kuhn, *The Copernican Revolution: Planetary Astronomy in the Development of Western Thought*, Cambridge, Mass.: Harvard University Press, 1957, and A. Koestler, *The Sleepwalkers: A History of Man's Changing Vision of the Universe*, Middlesex: Penguin Books, 1959.

48 J. Piaget, *Biologie et Connaissance: Essai sur les Relations entre les Régulations Organiques et les Processus Cognitifs*, Paris: Gallimard, 1967.

49 C.E. Shannon and W. Weaver, *The Mathematical Theory of Communication*, Urbana: The University of Illinois Press, 1949.

50 H.A. Simon, 'Scientific Discovery and the Psychology of Problem Solving', in R. Colodny (ed.) *Mind and Cosmos*, Pittsburgh: University of Pittsburgh Press, 1966, pp. 22–40.

51 L. Laudan, *Progress and its Problems: Towards a Theory of Scientific Growth*, Berkeley: University of California Press, 1977.

52 Langley *et al.*, *op. cit.*

53 Ibid.

54 Collins *op. cit.* For a discussion of internal versus external accounts of science see I. Lakatos, 'History of Science and its Rational Reconstructions', in R.C. Buck and R.S. Cohen (eds) P.S.A. *Boston Studies in the Philosophy of Science*, 8, 1970, pp. 91–135, Dordrecht: Reidel. For a critique of the internal view, albeit an implicit one, see R.K. Merton, 'Insiders and Outsiders: A Chapter in the Sociology of Knowledge', *American Journal of Sociology*, 77, July 1972, pp. 9–47.

55 Turing labelled such non-computability the 'halting problem'. See A. Turing, 'On Computable Numbers with an Application to the Entscheidungsproblem', in *Proceedings of the London Mathematical Society* (Ser. 2), 42, pp. 230–265; a correction, 43, 1937, pp. 544–546. See also G.J. Chaitin, 'Information-Theoretic Computational Complexity', *IEEE Transactions, Information Theory* 20(10), 1974.

56 Langley *et al.*, *op. cit.*

57 H.A. Simon, 'Does Scientific Discovery have a Logic?', *Philosophy of Science*, 40, 1973, pp. 471–480.

58 J.S. Bruner, *On Knowing: Essays for the Left Hand*, New York: Atheneum, 1965.

59 Or for that matter any other epistemic community that makes use of them.

60 Where choice is predicated upon incommensurate alternatives, the act of choosing may result in a serious loss of information.

61 Thus, for example, whereas Copernican astronomy displaced Ptolemaic astronomy, the theory of relativity merely subsumed Newtonian mechanics as a special case.

62 Object constancy is discussed in E. Hilgard, R.C. Atkinson and R.L. Atkinson, *Introduction to Psychology*, New York: Harcourt Brace Jovanovich, 1971.

63 Duhem *op. cit.*; W.V.O. Quine, *Word and Object*, Cambridge, Mass.: The MIT Press, 1960.

64 I. Lakatos, 'Falsification and the Methodology of Scientific Research Programmes', in Lakatos and Musgrave *op. cit.*, pp. 91–196.

65 The consistency requirement is much less rigorous outside the field of science. In the realm of art, for example, its violation may even be experienced as an enrichment.

66 That is, it falls on the wrong side of Popper's demarcation criterion separating science from pseudo-science. K.R. Popper, *The Logic of Scientific Discovery*, London: Hutchinson, 1959.

67 See section 4.10.

68 This is why so often in science, the initial reception given to a new theory depends on its 'elegance' or aesthetic appeal. 'Aesthetic sensibility plays the part of the delicate sieve', according to Poincaré, and Heisenberg, paraphrasing Niels Bohr, equated the language of poetry and physics: 'when it comes to atoms, language can be used only as in poetry. The poet is not nearly so concerned with describing facts as with creating images and establishing mental connections ...

Quantum theory ... provides us with a striking illustration of the fact that we can fully understand a connection though we can only speak of it in images and parables ...' H. Poincaré, *Science and Method*, New York: Dover, n.d. [1908]; W. Heisenberg, *Physics and Beyond*, New York: Harper and Row, 1971, p. 210. Both quotes in J. Wechler, *On Aesthetics in Science*, Cambridge, Mass.: The MIT Press, 1981, pp. 1, 4.

69 P.K. Feyerabend, *Against Method: Outline of an Anarchistic Theory of Knowledge*, London: Verso, 1975.

70 'Share of mind' is a corporate strategy concept.

71 Weber's 'formal' rationality corresponds in many respects with Simon's procedural rationality. Yet paradoxically, whereas Weber associates formal rationality with economic calculation, Simon links the latter to substantive rationality. Space does not allow us to elucidate the way that these two authors use their terms. Our own use of them will be apparent. See M. Weber, *Economy and Society*, Berkeley: University of California Press, 1968, p. 85; H.A. Simon, 'Rationality in Psychology and Economics', in R.M. Hogarth and M.W. Reder (eds) *Rational Choice: The Contrast between Psychology and Economics*, Chicago: The University of Chicago Press, 1986, pp. 25–40.

72 K.R. Popper, *Realism and the Aim of Science*, London: Hutchinson, 1983; I. Lakatos, *Philosophical Papers: Vol. 1, The Methodology of Scientific Research Programmes*, Cambridge: Cambridge University Press, 1978.

73 K.R. Popper, *Realism*.

74 See, for example, E.M. Rogers and F.F. Shoemaker, *Communication of Innovation: A Cross Cultural Approach*, New York: The Free Press, 1971.

75 Kuhn, *The Structure*; Pais *op. cit.*

76 Holton, *Thematic Origins*.

77 A challenge that behaviourists such as J.B. Watson and B.F. Skinner regarded as hopeless. What goes on in C̄ should be treated as a black box: see J.B. Watson, *Behaviourism*, London: K. Paul, 1928; B.F. Skinner, *Science and Human Behaviour*, New York: Macmillan, 1953.

78 Duhem *op. cit.*

79 Bloor takes such embedding as a justification for materialism. His materialism, however, differs substantially from Marvin Harris's. See D. Bloor, *Knowledge and Social Imagery*, Chicago: The University of Chicago Press, 1976.

80 Williamson *op. cit.*

81 F.A. Hayek, 'The Use of Knowledge in Society', *American Economic Review*, September 1945, pp. 519–530.

82 We shall avoid the dualist controversy in which the issue is one of deciding whether W2 is reducible to W1.

83 This point is emphasized by Mowery and Rosenberg when they stress the contribution made by basic research know-how to the process of technology assimilation. See D.C. Mowery and N. Rosenberg, *Technology and the Pursuit of Economic Growth*, Cambridge: Cambridge University Press, 1989.

84 For a general discussion of the issue of consciousness in intelligent machines see the collection of essays edited by J. Haugeland in *Mind Design: Philosophy, Psychology, Artificial Intelligence*, Cambridge, Mass.: The MIT Press, 1982.

85 R. Gregory, *Mind in Science: A History of Explanations in Psychology and Physics*, Middlesex: Penguin Books, 1981, p. 299.

86 Ibid., p. 317.

87 Economists likewise distinguish between 'embodied' and 'disembodied' technical change, the latter diffusing best practice more rapidly than the former. See R.M. Solow, 'Investment and Technical Progress', in K. Arrow, S. Karbin and P.

Suppes (eds) *Mathematical Methods in the Social Sciences*, Stanford, California: Stanford University Press, 1960. As can be seen in the next paragraph we have another use for the term 'disembodied'.

88 In the case of the individual the population of data processing agents becomes neuronal cells. As we argue in the conclusion there is no reason in principle why the I-space and the SLC should not apply to biological entities at the molecular level. All that is required is that they be data processors. See J.M. Von Neumann, *The Theory of Self-Reproducing Automata*, Urbana: The University of Illinois Press, 1966.

89 cf. Chapter 2.

90 Popper, *The Logic*.

91 Lakatos, *Philosophical Papers*, Vol. 1. Popper later did admit it. 'We can falsify only *systems of theories* and ... any attribution of falsity to any particular statement within such a system is always highly uncertain' (p. 187), in *Realism*.

92 Feyerabend *op. cit.*, and T.S. Kuhn, *The Essential Tension: Selected Studies in Scientific Tradition and Change*, Chicago: The University of Chicago Press, 1977.

93 See K. Thomas, *Religion and the Decline of Magic*, Middlesex: Penguin Books, 1971.

94 Bloor *op. cit.*

95 Einstein's 'apartness' has been discussed by Pais *op. cit.*

96 Polanyi *op. cit.*

97 R. Smullyan, *Forever Undecided: A Puzzle Guide to Gödel*, Oxford: Oxford University Press, 1987.

98 Much has been made of this point in the study of madness and mental institutions. See M. Foucault, *Histoire de la Folie à l'Age Classique*, Paris: Gallimard, 1972; E. Goffman, *Asylums: Essays on the Social Situation of Mental Patients and Other Inmates*, Middlesex: Penguin Books, 1968.

99 Popper, *The Open Universe*.

100 C. Howson and P. Urbach, *Scientific Reasoning: The Bayesian Approach*, La Salle, Illinois: Open Court, 1989.

101 F.A. Yates, *Giordano Bruno and the Hermetic Tradition*, London: Routledge and Kegan Paul, 1964.

102 Shannon's level C. See Shannon and Weaver *op. cit.*

103 Festinger *op. cit.*

104 Rogers and Shoemaker *op. cit.*

105 Until recently technological knowledge tended to get hoarded and scientific knowledge to get diffused. Of late the dividing line between the two has become increasingly blurred. See, for example, N. Rosenberg, 'Science and Technology in the Twentieth Century', in G. Dosi, R. Gianetti and P.A. Toninelli, *Technology and Enterprise in a Historical Perspective*, Oxford: The Clarendon Press, 1992, pp. 63–96.

106 J.M. Keynes, *The General Theory of Employment, Interest and Money*, London: Macmillan, 1936.

107 See I. Kirzner, *Perception, Opportunity and Profit*, Chicago: The University of Chicago Press, 1979; and I. Kirzner, 'Uncertainty, Discovery and Human Action', in I. Kirzner (ed.) *Method, Process and Austrian Economics: Essays in Honour of Ludwig von Mises*, Lexington, Mass.: D.C. Heath, 1982.

5 INSTITUTIONS

1 O.E. Williamson, *Markets and Hierarchies: Analysis and Antitrust Implications*, New York: The Free Press, 1975.

2 For some of the cognitive processes involved see P. Johnson-Laird, *Mental Models: Towards a Cognitive Science of Language, Inference, and Consciousness*, Cambridge: Cambridge University Press, 1983.

3 Williamson *op. cit.*; R. Coase, 'The Nature of the Firm', *Economica*, 4, 1937, pp. 386–405; J.R. Commons, *Institutional Economics*, Madison: University of Wisconsin Press, 1934.

4 W. Ouchi, *Theory Z: How American Business Can Meet the Japanese Challenge*, Reading, Mass.: Addison-Wesley Publishing Co., 1981.

5 M. Douglas, *How Institutions Think*, London: Routledge and Kegan Paul, 1987.

6 Without going so far as to use the term 'subordination', George Duby illustrates the argument from design in his study *Les Trois Ordres ou l'Imaginaire du Féodalisme*, Paris: Gallimard, 1978.

7 Williamson *op. cit.*; W. Ouchi, 'Markets, Bureaucracies and Clans', *Administrative Science Quarterly*, 25(1), March 1980, pp. 129–141.

8 This was *the* economic problem as framed by Hayek. See F.A. Hayek, 'The Use of Knowledge in Society', *American Economic Review*, 35, 1945, pp. 519–530.

9 L. Walras, *Elements of Pure Economics: or the Theory of Social Wealth*, Philadelphia, Orion Editions, 1984 [1926].

10 This is the problem of adverse selection first signalled by Akerlof and later generalized by Wilson. See G. Akerlof, 'The Market for "Lemons"', *Quarterly Journal of Economics*, 84(3), August 1970, pp. 488–500; C. Wilson, 'The Nature of Equilibrium in Markets with Adverse Selection', *Bell Journal of Economics*, II, Spring 1980, pp. 108–130.

11 See Braudel's discussion of European fairs. F. Braudel, *Civilisation Matérielle, Economie et Capitalisme XVe–XVIIIe Siècle: Tome 2, Les Jeux de l'Echange*, Paris: Armand Colin, 1979, pp. 63–75; for a more general discussion of the role of markets in ancient times, see K. Polanyi, C.M. Arensberg and H.W. Pearson (eds) *Trade and Market in the Early Empires: Economies in History and Theory*, Chicago: Gateway Edition, 1957.

12 Perhaps one should add 'sooner or later'. One should also add that much of the focus of rational expectation theorists has been on the behaviour of government as a privileged possessor of information. This in no way weakens the point that we are making. See T.J. Sargent, *Rational Expectations and Inflation*, New York: Harper and Row, 1986.

13 Hayek, *op. cit.*

14 In a real estate slump, for example, asking prices can be a quite misleading indicator of market prices. We are back in a *souk*, but one which sells higher value items. Efficiency-eroding transaction costs are correspondingly higher.

15 Contrast with adaptive expectations where the focus is on past prices.

16 W. Ross Ashby, *An Introduction to Cybernetics*, London: Methuen, 1956.

17 Market equilibria built upon faulty assumptions are known as *sunspot equilibria*.

18 See R.E. Lucas and T.J. Sargent (eds) *Rational Expectations and Econometric Practice*, Minneapolis: University of Minnesota Press, 1980. As Sheffrin puts it, 'Expectations are rational if, given the economic model, they will produce actual values of variables that will, on average, equal the expectations. Expectations will diverge from actual values only because of some unpredictable uncertainty in the system. If there were no unpredictable uncertainty, expectations of variables

would coincide with the actual values – there would be *perfect foresight*. The rational expectations hypothesis differs from perfect foresight because it allows for uncertainty in economic systems.' S.M. Sheffrin, *Rational Expectations*, Cambridge: Cambridge University Press, 1983.

19 Williamson *op. cit.*

20 It is worth noting that in non-market societies, insider trading is viewed with much more indulgence than in market societies. Compare Wall Street's reaction to Ivan Boeski with Hong Kong's to Ronald Li. For the argument that Hong Kong is less of a market society than commonly supposed, see Chapter 7.

21 Paul Henri Dietrich, Baron d'Holbach, *Système de la Nature*, Paris, 1770.

22 A. Smith, *An Inquiry into the Nature and Causes of the Wealth of Nations*, London, 1776.

23 Nor did he argue that individual interests are invariably selfish. See A. Smith, *The Theory of Moral Sentiments*, London, 1759. For a recent reformulation of this view see H. Margolis, *Selfishness, Altruism, and Rationality: A Theory of Social Choice*, Chicago: The University of Chicago Press, 1982.

24 Contrast this approach to social rationality with J.J. Rousseau's, where the *volonté de tous* could never produce a coherent *volonté générale*. To secure socially optimal outcomes, therefore, the state had to be introduced as a social arbitrator, as a custodian of a *volonté générale* constantly under threat from the *volonté de tous*. Markets could not be expected to do the job. Rousseau, *Du Contrat Social*, Paris: Garnier-Flammarion, 1966.

25 For a critique of what market values can produce in terms of social suffering, see K. Polanyi, *The Great Transformation: The Political and Economic Origins of our Time*, Boston: Beacon Press, 1944. Margolis has recently hypothesized that individual and group interests coexist in the individual's utility function in ways that are consistent with neoclassical outcomes. See Margolis *op. cit.*

26 An early exponent of such an ideology was Herbert Spencer who has been labelled a social Darwinist before Darwin. See his *The Man versus the State*, Middlesex: Penguin Books, 1969 [1884].

27 See the discussion in R. Firth (ed.) *Themes in Economic Anthropology*, London: Tavistock Publications, 1970.

28 The equilibrium view is visible in the work of sociologists like Talcot Parsons. For a critique see A. Gouldner, *The Coming Crisis of Western Sociology*, London: Heinemann, 1970.

29 Williamson *op. cit.*, p. 20.

30 See Chapter 3.

31 G.G. Hamilton (1984) distinguishes between the ascriptive way that the term 'role' is used in patrimonial bureaucracies such as the Imperial Chinese one, and its achievement orientation in rational–legal bureaucracies of the Weberian kind. See G.G. Hamilton, 'Patriarchalism in Imperial China and Western Europe: A Revision of Weber's Sociology of Domination', *Theory and Society* 13, 1984, pp. 393–425.

32 See Chapter 7.

33 Rousseau *op. cit.*

34 M. Weber, *The Theory of Social and Economic Organization*, New York: The Free Press, 1964.

35 For a description of how such an administrator would proceed, see E. Barone, 'The Ministry of Production in the Collectivist State', in F.A. Hayek (ed.) *Collectivist Economic Planning*, London: Routledge and Kegan Paul, 1935, pp. 247–290. Originally published in Italian in *Il Giornale degli Economisti*, 1908.

36 See K. Arrow, *Social Choice and Individual Values*, New Haven, Connecticut: Yale University Press, 1963.

37 See J.A. Jackson (ed.) *Professions and Professionalization*, Cambridge: Cambridge University Press, 1970.

38 Clan and bureaucratic professional transactions often work in tandem in organizations such as hospitals or schools. Since they both occupy a similar position on the diffusion scale it would appear that one of the defining characteristics of professionalism is information asymmetry – see A.M. Carr-Saunders and P.A. Wilson, *The Professions*, London: Frank Cass and Co., 1964.

39 The term has become strongly associated with the strategy work of Michael E. Porter. See his *Competitive Advantage: Creating and Sustaining Superior Performance*, New York: The Free Press, 1985.

40 J.A. Schumpeter, *The Theory of Economic Development: An Inquiry into Profits, Capital, Credit, Interest and the Business Cycle*, London: Oxford University Press, 1961 [1934].

41 One is reminded of Sir John Hick's dictum that the returns to monopoly are 'a quiet life'.

42 G. Clark, 'The Social Foundations of States', in F.L. Carsten (ed.) *The New Cambridge Modern History: Vol. V, The Ascendancy of France, 1648–1688*, Cambridge: Cambridge University Press, 1961.

43 In those parts of the former Soviet Union where local access to education was limited, authoritarian government persists – witness the Central Asian republics.

44 As M. Warner points out, with 1.5 per cent of the population undergoing higher education, China trails other Third World countries in its educational investments. See M. Warner, 'China's Managerial Training Revolution', in M. Warner (ed.) *Management Reforms in China*, London: Pinter Publishers, 1987, pp. 73–85.

45 Williamson *op. cit.*

46 R. Michels, *Political Parties*, New York: Dover 1959.

47 M. Olson, *The Logic of Collective Action: Public Goods and the Theory of Groups*, Cambridge: Mass.: Harvard University Press, 1971. For the policy implications of Olson's thesis see M. Olson, *The Rise and Decline of Nations: Economic Growth, Stagflation, and Social Rigidities*, New Haven, Connecticut: Yale University Press, 1982.

48 R. Axelrod, *The Evolution of Cooperation*, New York: Basic Books, 1984.

49 A.D. Chandler, *The Visible Hand: The Managerial Revolution in American Business*, Cambridge, Mass.: The Belknap Press at Harvard University Press, 1977.

50 Williamson *op. cit.*

51 Ouchi, 'Markets, Bureaucracies, and Clans'.

52 R.J. Butler, 'Control through Markets, Hierarchies, and Communes: A Transactional Approach to Organizational Analaysis', in A. Francis, J. Turk and P. Willman (eds) *Power, Efficiency and Institutions: A Critical Appraisal of the 'Markets and Hierarchies Paradigm'*, London: Heinemann, 1983, pp. 137–158.

53 G.B. Richardson, 'The Organization of Industry', *The Economic Journal*, LXXXII (Supplement), 1972, pp. 882–896.

54 E. Hall, *Beyond Culture*, New York: Doubleday, 1976.

55 The difference between risk and uncertainty was articulated by Frank Knight. The first is measurable and hence insurable, the second is not. See F. Knight, *Risk, Uncertainty, and Profit*, New York: Houghton Mifflin Co., 1921.

56 Contrast in this respect the kind of discernment required of clan transactions with those imputed to markets by rational expectation theory.

57 T.J. Johnson, *Professions and Power*, London: Macmillan, 1972.
58 Thus clan tranactions require a greater degree of involvement than, say, *network* transactions, the latter standing halfway between clans and markets. For a sociological description of networks, see B. Marin and R. Mayntz (eds) *Policy Networks: Empirical Evidence and Theoretical Considerations*, Frankfurt am Main: Campus Verlag, 1991.
59 See, for example, J.G. Riley, 'Competition with Hidden Knowledge', *Journal of Political Economy*, 93, October 1985, pp. 958–976.
60 Chandler *op. cit.*
61 For an application of game theory to industrial organization, see J. Tirole, *The Theory of Industrial Organization*, Cambridge, Mass.: The MIT Press, 1988.
62 Although he only uses the word 'guild' three times in the entire book, Henri Pirenne's *Medieval Cities* remains one of the best short introductions to the culture of these organizational forms. See H. Pirenne, *Medieval Cities: Their Origin and the Revival of Trade*, Princeton, New Jersey: Princeton University Press, 1925.
63 The crisis in the US health service provides one example of this new perspective.
64 In biology, species represent the lowest level of genuine discontinuity above the level of the individual. Taxonomists assemble species into genera and higher taxa. See E. Mayr, Chapter 6 in *The Growth of Biological Thought: Diversity, Evolution, and Inheritance*, Cambridge, Mass.: The Belknap Press of Harvard University Press, 1982.
65 C.G. Jung, *The Archetypes of the Collective Unconscious. Collected Works*, Princeton, New Jersey: Princeton University Press, 1954.
66 Hayek *op. cit.*
67 M. Sherif, 'Superordinate Goals in the Reduction of Intergroup Conflict', *American Journal of Sociology* 63, 1958, pp. 349–358.
68 How such a team might function is well described in T. Kidder, *The Soul of a New Machine*, New York: Avon Books, 1981; for a more sobering view see J. Goodefield, *An Imagined World: A Study of Scientific Discovery*, London: Hutchinson, 1981.
69 M. Douglas, *Natural Symbols: Explorations in Cosmology*, Middlesex: Penguin Books, 1973; Chapter 2, this volume.
70 B. Bernstein, 'Social Class and Psycho-therapy', *British Journal of Sociology*, 15, 1964, pp. 54–64.
71 M. Weber, *Economy and Society: An Outline of Interpretative Sociology*, Berkeley: University of California Press, 1978.
72 See M. Bloch, *La Société Féodale*, Paris: Albin Michel, 1939.
73 Ibid.
74 M.M. Postan, *The Medieval Economy and Society*, Middlesex: Penguin Books, 1975.
75 Pirenne *op. cit.*
76 M. Granet, *La Féodalité Chinoise*, Oslo: Institut pour l'Etude Comparative des Civilisations, 1952.
77 K. Marx, *Economic and Philosophical Manuscripts of 1844*, London: Lawrence and Wishart, 1970.
78 G.B. Sansom, *Japan: A Short Cultural History*, London: Barrie and Jenkins, 1946.
79 Until 1825 and the coronation of Charles X, French kings were deemed to possess miraculous healing powers activated by a laying of hands. See M. Bloch, *Les Rois Thaumaturges*, Paris: Gallimard, 1983 [1921].
80 Polanyi *op. cit.*

81 The New Testament suggests that even twelve is one too many!

82 M. Weber, *On Charisma and Institution Building*, Chicago: The University of Chicago Press, 1968.

83 Ibid.

84 Bloch, *La Société Féodale*. See also G. Duby, *Guerriers et Paysans: VIIe–XIIe Siècle, Premier Essor de l'Economie Européenne*, Paris: Gallimard, 1973.

85 These may be either concrete, as in myth, or abstract: see M. Eliade, *Images et Symboles: Essai sur le Symbolisme Magico-religieux*, Paris: Gallimard, 1952.

86 This is not to say that they were not also terrified of him. See I. Deutcher, *Stalin: A Political Biography*, Middlesex: Penguin Books, 1966.

87 The blood line, however, remains a fragile transmission belt in the case of religious charisma: Khomeini the son, for example, does not appear to command the same devoted following in Iran as Khomeini the father.

88 Weber, *Economy and Society*.

89 Douglass North has explored this hypothesis empirically in a historical context. See D. North, *Structure and Change in Economic History*, New York: W.W. Norton and Co., 1981.

90 M. Boisot, *Information and Organization: The Manager as Anthropologist*, London: HarperCollins, 1994.

91 The shift to open systems architecture in the computer industry offers many interesting parallels to the example under discussion here.

92 Douglas, *Natural Symbols*.

93 B. Bernstein, *Class, Codes and Control. Vol. 1: Theoretical Studies towards a Sociology of Language*, London: Routledge and Kegan Paul, 1971.

94 Hall *op. cit.*

95 Douglas, *Natural Symbols*, p. 80.

96 As Langley and his co-workers point out, of course, both data- and theory-driven theories are partial theories. See P. Langley, H.A. Simon, G.L. Bradshaw and J.M. Zytkow, *Scientific Discovery: Computational Explorations of the Creative Process*, Cambridge, Mass.: The MIT Press, 1987, p. 24.

97 R.K. Merton, *Social Theory and Social Structure*, Glencoe, Illinois: The Free Press, 1957.

98 John Commons took the transaction to be the basic unit of microeconomic analysis, an approach which deflected subsequent analysis away from transactional patterns – J.R. Commons *op. cit.*

99 D. North, *Institutions, Institutional Change and Economic Performance*, Cambridge: Cambridge University Press, 1990.

100 Ibid.

101 Polanyi *op. cit.*, p. 224.

102 A. Giddens, *The Constitution of Society: Outline of the Theory of Structuration*, Cambridge: Polity Press, 1984, p. 375.

103 North, *Institutions*.

104 See C. Macpherson, *The Political Theory of Possessive Individualism: Hobbes to Locke*, Oxford: Oxford University Press, 1962.

105 A. Schutz and T. Luckmann, *The Structures of the Life-World*, London: Heinemann, 1974.

106 R.L. Gregory, *Mind in Science: A History of Explanations in Psychology and Physics*, Middlesex: Penguin Books, 1981, p. 311.

107 This was the point made by Coase in 1937 with respect to the choice between firms and markets. See R. Coase *op. cit.*

108 J.A. Schumpeter, *Capitalism, Socialism, and Democracy*, New York: Harper and Row, 1942.

109 To our knowledge ethical costs have not been taken on board by the transaction cost literature.

110 North, *Institutions*.

111 H.A. Simon, *Models of Bounded Rationality*, 2 vols. Cambridge, Mass.: The MIT Press, 1982.

112 To argue that knowledge has a physical substratum is not to argue for a *reduction* of knowledge to physical processes.

113 See, for example, I.M. Kirzner, *Perception, Opportunity, and Profit: Studies in the Theory of Entrepreneurship*, Chicago: The University of Chicago Press, 1979.

114 Michels *op. cit.*

115 See Chapter 3, and J. Vansina, *Oral Tradition: A Study in Historical Methodology*, Middlesex: Penguin Books, 1965.

116 Rousseau *op. cit.*

117 See M. Boisot, 'Markets and Hierarchies in Cultural Perspective', *Organization Studies*, Spring 1986.

118 See, for example, L. Putterman (ed.) *The Economic Nature of the Firm: A Reader*, Cambridge: Cambridge University Press, 1986; T. Eggertsson, *Economic Behaviour and Institutions*, Cambridge: Cambridge University Press, 1990.

119 Such a view is implicit in Williamson's treatment of the subject. See Williamson *op. cit.*

120 See A. Francis, 'Markets and Hierarchies: Efficiency or Domination?', in Francis *et al.*, *op. cit.*, pp. 105–116.

121 Coase *op. cit.*; Williamson *op. cit.* and *The Economic Institutions of Capitalism: Firms, Markets, Relational Contracting*, New York: The Free Press, 1985.

122 Under the assumption of methodological individualism a corporate vision would either not be necessary or would emerge naturally from the interaction of the employees themselves. Yet such a vision can plausibly be taken as an emergent property of the organization's own processes. See H. Mintzberg, 'Crafting Strategy', *Harvard Business Review*, July–August, 1987; G. Hamel and C.K. Prahalad, 'Strategic Intent', *Harvard Business Review*, May–June, 1989.

123 J. Vanek, *The Economics of Worker's Management: A Yugoslav Case Study*, London: Allen and Unwin, 1972. What distinguishes the Japanese from the Yugoslav firm is that in the former, stakeholder power is located in the managerial group, not in the labour force as a whole. See T. Hanami, *Labour Relations in Japan Today*, Tokyo: Kodansha International, 1981.

124 Habermas argues that while interests can vary according to situations, values are stable across situations. He criticizes utilitarians for reducing the latter to the former. Yet values, in their comparative stability, may simply reflect the law of large numbers: the lowest common denominator of what does not vary. See Habermas, *The Theory of Communicative Action*, Vol. 1, Cambridge: Polity Press, 1984, p. 172.

125 We have here another variant of the distinction made by Simon between substantive and procedural rationality. See H.A. Simon, 'Rationality in Psychology and Economics', in R.M. Hogarth and M.W. Reder (eds) *Rational Choice: The Contrast between Economics and Psychology*, Chicago: The University of Chicago Press, 1986, pp. 25–40.

126 North, *Institutions*.

127 Eggertsson *op. cit.*

128 O.E Williamson, *The Economic Institutions*.

129 Ouchi, 'Markets, Bureaucracies, and Clans'; Butler *op. cit.*

130 This is not the case in the institutional approach adopted by Douglass North. And what Williamson terms the 'Fundamental Transformation', the conversion

of a large-numbers bidding situation into one of bilateral supply, exhibits a strong path dependency. See Williamson, *The Economic Institutions*, p. 61.

131 Michels *op. cit.*; Olson, *The Logic*.

132 Williamson, *The Economic Institutions*.

133 Much of the current management literature alludes to the increasing fuzziness of the organizational boundary. Both people and productive factors are able to position themselves on different orbits with respect to the firm's organizational core. For a discussion of these points see Charles Handy, *The Age of Unreason*, London: Business Books, 1989; J.B. Quinn, *Intelligent Enterprise: A Knowledge and Service Based Paradigm for Industry*, New York: The Free Press, 1992.

134 Such learning is foreshadowed in the kind of inter-firm collaboration taking place in the so-called 'Third Italy'. See M. Best, *The New Competition: Institutions of Industrial Restructuring*, Cambridge: The Polity Press, 1990; M. Piore and C. Sabel, *The Second Industrial Divide*, New York: Basic Books, 1984.

135 We might think of meta-learning as the institutional equivalent of what Argyris and Schön refer to as 'Double Loop Learning' and Bateson termed 'Deutero-learning'. See C. Argyris and D. Schön, *Organizational Learning: A Theory of Action Perspective*, Reading, Mass.: Addison-Wesley, 1978; Gregory Bateson, *Steps towards an Ecology of Mind: Collected Essays in Anthropology, Psychiatry, Evolution and Epistemology*, St Albans, Herts: Paladin, 1972.

136 Giddens *op. cit.*

6 CULTURE AS ECONOMIZING

1 T. Deal and A. Kennedy, *Corporate Cultures: The Rites and Rituals of Corporate Life*, Middlesex: Penguin Books, 1982; G. Hofstede, *Culture's Consequences: International Differences in Work-Related Values*, Beverly Hills: Sage Publications, 1980; B. Malinowski, *A Scientific Theory of Culture and Other Essays*, New York: Oxford University Press, 1961; A.L. Kroeber, *Anthropology*, New York: Harcourt, Brace, 1948; M. Sahlins, *Culture and Practical Reason*, Chicago: University of Chicago Press, 1976; M. Harris, *Cultural Materialism: The Struggle for a Science of Culture*, New York: Vintage Books, 1980; M. Douglas, *Purity and Danger*, London: Routledge and Kegan Paul, 1966; E. Hall, *Beyond Culture*, New York: Doubleday, 1976; C. Geertz, *The Interpretation of Cultures*, New York: Basic Books, 1973; E. Schein, *Organizational Culture and Leadership*, San Francisco: Jossey-Bass, 1992.

2 E. Durkheim and M. Mauss, *Primitive Classification*, London: Cohen and West, 1963 [1903]; T. Parsons, *The Social System*, London: Routledge and Kegan Paul, 1951.

3 J. Habermas, *The Theory of Communicative Action*, 2 vols, Cambridge: Polity Press, 1981, 1987.

4 T. Kuhn, *The Structure of Scientific Revolutions*, Chicago: University of Chicago Press, 1962.

5 E.B. Tylor, *Primitive Culture: Researches into the Development of Mythology, Philosophy, Religion, Language, Art and Custom*, London: J. Murray, 1971.

6 There is of course no reason why Jung's theory should not be a theory of culture.

7 F. Boas, *The Mind of Primitive Man*, New York: The Free Press, 1938 [1911]; D. Manddlebaum (ed.) *Selected Writings of Edward Sapir*, Berkeley and Los

Angeles, 1949; R. Benedict, *Patterns of Culture*, London: Routledge and Kegan Paul, 1935; R. Linton, *The Study of Man*, New York: Appleton Century, 1936; G. Bateson, *Naven: A Survey of the Problems Suggested by a Composite Picture of the Culture of a New Guinea Tribe Drawn from Three Points of View*, Cambridge: Cambridge University Press, 1936; C. Kluckhohn, *Culture and Behaviour*, New York, 1962; L. White, *The Science of Culture*, New York: Farrar, Straus, 1949.

8 Deal and Kennedy *op. cit.* For a practical example, see P.R. Harris and R.T. Moran, *Managing Cultural Differences*, Houston: Gulf Publishing Co., 1979.

9 A.R. Radcliffe-Brown, *Structure and Function in Primitive Society*, London: Cohen and West, 1952.

10 Kroeber *op. cit.*

11 As the two authors put it, culture is 'patterns explicit and implicit, of and for behaviour acquired and transmitted by symbols, constituting the distinctive achievement of human groups, including their embodiments in artefacts; the essential core of culture consists of traditional (i.e., historically derived and selected) ideas and especially their attached values; culture systems may, on the one hand, be considered a product of action, on the other as conditioning elements for further action'; A. Kroeber and C. Kluckhohn, *Culture: A Critical Review of Concepts and Definitions*, Papers of the Peabody Museum of American Archaeology and Ethnology, Vol. 47, Cambridge, Mass.: Harvard University Press, 1952, p. 181.

12 G.A. Kelly, *A Theory of Personality: The Psychology of Personal Constructs*, New York: W.W. Norton and Co., 1963, p. 94.

13 The 'more rarely' needs stressing. As Gouldner has written: 'Parsons' conception of men as "eager tools" willingly pursuing whatever goals have been "internalized" in them, largely derives from the stress he places upon "socialization" as a value imprinting mechanism; his stress upon socialization implicitly defines men as value-*transmitting* and value-*receiving* rather than as value-*creating* creatures. Here, then, the very agency that is the source of men's humanness, socialization, is also the agency that eternally makes man a tool to pursue the ends of others; man is thus alienated in the very process of becoming human'. A.W. Gouldner, *The Coming Crisis of Western Sociology*, London: Heinemann, 1970, p. 192.

14 See, for example, J. Goody, *The Logic of Writing and the Organization of Society*, Cambridge: Cambridge University Press, 1986.

15 C. Lévi-Strauss, *La Pensée Sauvage*, Paris: Plon, 1962; C. Lévi-Strauss, *Les Structures Elémentaires de la Parenté*, Paris: Plon, 1949.

16 Lévi-Strauss, *Les Structures.*

17 E. Sapir, 'Language', *Encyclopaedia of the Social Sciences*, 9(33), pp. 155–169, quoted in Sahlins *op. cit.*, p. 22.

18 J. Lacan, *Ecrits*, Vol. 1, Paris: Seuil, 1966.

19 Hall *op. cit.*

20 Ibid., p. 93.

21 B. Bernstein, *Class, Codes, and Control: Vol. 1, Theoretical Studies towards a Sociology of Language*, London: Routledge and Kegan Paul, 1971.

22 Hall *op. cit.*, p. 113.

23 See, for example, C. Nakane, *Japanese Society*, Middlesex: Penguin Books, 1973; T.S. Lebra, *Japanese Patterns of Behaviour*, Honolulu: The University Press of Hawaii, 1976; C. Moore (ed.) *The Japanese Mind: Essentials of Japanese Philosophy and Culture*, Tokyo: Charles E. Tuttle Co., 1967.

24 See, for example, E. Vogel, *Japan as No. 1: Lessons for America*, Tokyo: Charles

E. Tuttle Co., 1979, p. 120.

25 Hall *op. cit.*, p. 101.
26 Durkheim's distinction between organic and mechanical solidarity is of the same nature – see E. Durkheim, *The Division of Labour in Society*, New York: The Free Press, 1964 [1893].
27 Hall *op. cit.*
28 K.R. Popper, *Realism and the Aim of Science*, London: Hutchinson, 1983.
29 Hall *op. cit.*, p. 27.
30 Mary Douglas, *Natural Symbols: Explorations in Cosmology*, Middlesex: Penguin Books, 1978.
31 In critical sociology, Habermas's Theory of Communicative Action also comes close. See Habermas *op. cit.*
32 J. Piaget, *Structuralism*, Routledge and Kegan Paul, 1971.
33 Harris *op. cit.*, pp. 167–168.
34 Ibid.
35 F. de Saussure, *Cours de Linguistique Générale*, Paris: Payot, 1972 [1915]; N. Chomsky, *Aspects of the Theory of Syntax*, Cambridge, Mass.: The MIT Press, 1965.
36 C.G. Jung, *The Archetypes of the Collective Unconscious. Collected Works*, Princeton, New Jersey: Princeton University Press, 1954.
37 See Chapter 5.
38 W. Goodenough, *Description and Comparison in Cultural Anthropology*, Chicago: Aldine Publishing Co., 1970.
39 E. Durkheim, *The Division of Labour in Society*, New York: The Free Press, 1983 [1933]; W.C. Sumner, *Folkways*, Boston, 1906.
40 K. Marx and F. Engels, *The German Ideology*, London: Lawrence and Wishart, 1965, pp. 36–37.
41 Sahlins *op. cit.*, p. 73.
42 Harris *op. cit.*, p. 110.
43 Ibid., p. 102.
44 Ibid., p. 81.
45 Ibid., p. 92.
46 Douglas, *Natural Symbols*, p. 131.
47 H.A. Simon, *Reason in Human Affairs*, Oxford: Basil Blackwell, 1983.
48 Sahlins *op. cit.*, p. 150.
49 Kelly *op. cit.*
50 J.O. De la Mettrie, *L'Homme Machine*, Princeton, 1960 [1748].
51 M.A. Boden, *Artificial Intelligence and Natural Man*, London: The MIT Press, 1987, p. 444.
52 Hall suggests that mind and culture are virtually synonymous terms. See Hall *op. cit.*
53 Recall from Chapter 5 that it is only when a transactional population is dichotomized into an internal and an external group that some interests and values get parametrized – those of the external group.
54 White *op. cit.*
55 Ibid.
56 J.S. Bruner, *Beyond the Information Given*, London: George Allen and Unwin, 1974, p. xx.
57 Hall *op. cit.*, p. 230.
58 Sahlins *op. cit.*, p. 670.
59 Popper *op. cit.*
60 Richard Dawkins labels the units of cultural inheritance – those which struggle

to survive across generations – 'memes'. They are hypothesized to be analogous to the particulate gene and in a similar way to be naturally selected by virtue of their 'phenotypic' potential for survival and replication. See R. Dawkins, *The Extended Phenotype: The Gene as the Unit of Selection*, Oxford: Oxford University Press, 1982, p. 290; see also R. Boyd and P.J. Richerson, *Culture and the Evolutionary Process*, Chicago: The University of Chicago Press, 1985.

61 Sahlins *op. cit.*

62 Exactly how random genetic mutations are in reality remains a matter of debate among biologists – see R. Dawkins, *The Blind Watchmaker*, Middlesex: Penguin Books, 1986.

63 See T. Dobzhansky, *Mankind Evolving: The Evolution of the Human Species*, New Haven, Connecticut: Yale University Press, 1962.

64 *The World Bank Atlas*, The World Bank, Washington, DC, 1988.

65 These figures are computed from those given by P. Laslett, *The World We have Lost*, London: Methuen and Co., 1971, p. 97; see also C.M. Cipolla, *The Economic History of World Population*, Middlesex: Penguin Books, 1965.

66 I have seen this happen in both China and Spain.

67 H. Butterfield, *The Whig Interpretation of History*, Middlesex: Penguin, 1931; Talcot Parsons could never quite free himself from the belief that the US provided the cultural model which all other cultures should seek to emulate.

68 E. Tönnies, *Community and Association*, London: Routledge and Kegan Paul, 1955.

69 Durkheim *op. cit.*

70 That is, Galbraith's. See J.K. Galbraith, *The New Industrial State*, London: Hamish Hamilton, 1967.

71 W.W. Rostow, *The Stages of Economic Growth: A Non-communist Manifesto*, Cambridge: Cambridge University Press, 1960.

72 K. Marx, *Capital*, London: Lawrence and Wishart, 1970; Durkheim *op. cit.*

73 T. Levitt, 'The Globalization of Markets', *Harvard Business Review*, May–June 1983.

74 The recent scandals at Lloyd's suggest that such a 'high trust' environment may not survive the advent of a competitive international market for services.

75 For an example of how the Lyon textile industry was frog-marched by the state into becoming a bureaucratic culture when it had been a clan one, see M. Piore and C. Sabel, *The Second Industrial Divide*, New York: Basic Books, 1984.

76 Such was the case, for example, with Thatcherism in its unadulterated form.

77 This is not to say that local predictions are not possible. It is the culture's total configuration in the I-space that is beyond the reach of prediction.

78 Transactional competition should not be confused with market competition.

79 D. North, *Institutions, Institutional Change and Economic Performance*, Cambridge: Cambridge University Press, 1990. As North puts it, institutions lower transaction costs.

80 Organization theorists have labelled this process 'Institutional Isomorphism'. B. DiMaggio and W.W. Powell, 'The Iron Cage Revisited: Institutional Isomorphism and Collective Rationality in Organizational Fields', *American Sociological Review*, 82, 1983, pp. 147–160.

81 Unsurprisingly, it is in those remoter parts of China least touched by the modernization of communications that feudal forms of exploitation remain at their most intense.

82 See, for example, G. Elton's discussion of the separation of crown finances from those of the royal household. G. Elton, *Reform and Reformation: England 1509–1558*, London: Edward Arnold, 1977.

83 *The Economist*, 25 August 1990, p. 65.
84 See Chapter 5.
85 M. Bloch, *Les Rois Thaumaturges*, Paris: Gallimard, 1983 [1921].
86 Elton *op. cit.*
87 W. Ross Ashby, *An Introduction to Cybernetics*, London: Methuen, 1956.
88 Sahlins *op. cit.*, p. 166.
89 Hall *op. cit.*, p. 166.
90 Sahlins *op. cit.*, p. x.
91 Residing in W1 but not necessarily originating there: the European Community's Common Agricultural Policies, for example, a W3 phenomenon, are known to have a debilitating effect on African farming practices.
92 I am aware of course that the environmental problems that plague industrialized societies do not exactly suggest a harmonious alignment between our own W1, W2, W3s.
93 Durkheim labels the organizational form required to pursue simple homogeneous tasks in pre-industrial societies, 'mechanical solidarity'.
94 K. Weick, *The Social Psychology of Organizing*, Reading, Mass.: Addison-Wesley, 1979.
95 This will hopefully be developed further in a future volume.
96 A.R. Luria, *The Mind of a Mnemonist*, London: Jonathan Cape, 1969.
97 Note that a 'small and manageable' SLC in clans has quite different characteristics from those it would have in fiefs, markets, or bureaucracies.
98 D. Lerner, *The Passing of Traditional Society*, New York: The Free Press, 1958.
99 Sahlins *op. cit.*, p. 69.
100 K.R. Popper, *The Logic of Scientific Discovery*, London: Hutchinson, 1959.
101 Durkheim *op. cit.*
102 Ibid.; see also Habermas's discussion of Durkheim, Mead, and Spencer in Habermas *op. cit.*
103 O.E. Williamson, *The Economic Institutions of Capitalism: Firms, Markets, Relational Contracting*, New York: The Free Press, 1985.
104 S. Cheung, 'The Contractual Nature of the Firm', *Journal of Law and Economics*, 3(1), 1983, pp. 1–21.
105 K. Marx, *A Contribution to the Critique of Political Economy*, London: Kegan Paul, 1904. See the author's preface.
106 Habermas takes collective consciousness and life-world to be almost interchangeable terms. Habermas *op. cit.*, Vol. 2.
107 Mead shared Durkheim's view of the relationship between personal and collective identity – see G.H. Mead *op. cit.*, p. 200; see also Habermas *op. cit.*, p. 58.
108 E. Durkheim, *The Elementary Forms of the Religious Life*, London: Allen and Unwin, 1915, p. 444; quoted in Harris *op. cit.*, p. 167.
109 Habermas *op. cit.*, Vol. 2.
110 K.R. Popper, *The Open Society and its Enemies: Vol. 1, Plato; Vol. 2, Hegel and Marx*, London: Routledge and Kegan Paul, 1945.
111 A Marxist would argue that such general interests are but concrete interests in disguise. Subscribing to them creates 'false consciousness'.
112 Deal and Kennedy *op. cit.*
113 A.D. Chandler, *Strategy and Structure: Chapters in the History of the American Industrial Enterprise*, Cambridge, Mass.: The MIT Press, 1962.
114 Habermas makes essentially the same point using the concepts of *social* integration (restricted codes) and *systematic* integration (elaborated codes). Habermas *op. cit.*, Vol. 2, p. 163.

115 K.R. Popper, *Objective Knowledge: An Evolutionary Approach*, Oxford: The Clarendon Press, 1972.

116 P. Munz, *Our Knowledge of the Growth of Knowledge: Popper or Wittgenstein?*, London: Routledge and Kegan Paul, 1985; I.L. Janis, *Groupthink: Psychological Studies of Policy Decisions and Fiascos*, Boston: Houghton Mifflin Co., 1982.

117 See, for example, R. Bendix, 'Preconditions of Development: A Comparison of Japan and Germany', in R. Dore (ed.) *Aspects of Social Change in Modern Japan*, Princeton, New Jersey: Princeton University Press, 1967. Bendix does not impute any liberal orientation to the country; he does, however, stress the country's openness to change. See also R. Bendix, 'A Case Study in Cultural and Educational Mobility: Japan and the Protestant Ethic', in N.J. Smelser and S.M. Lipset (eds) *Social Structure and Mobility in Economic Development*, Chicago: Aldine Publishing Co., 1966.

118 K. Van Wolferen, *The Enigma of Japanese Power: People and Politics in a Stateless Nation*, London: Macmillan, 1989.

119 Harris *op. cit.*. See also Gouldner's criticism of Parsons, in Gouldner *op. cit.*

120 That it should do so is surprising given Marx's early admiration for Darwin.

121 Mead refers to the set of such groups as the 'generalized other'. Mead *op. cit.*, pp. 152–163.

122 C.G. Jung, *The Integration of the Personality*, London: Routledge and Kegan Paul, 1940.

123 The implication of these multiple identities for our concepts of rationality are explored by Jon Elster and others in J. Elster (ed.) *The Multiple Self: Studies in Rationality and Social Change*, Cambridge: Cambridge University Press, 1985; see also R. Ornstein, *Multimind: A New Way of Looking at Human Behaviour*, London: Macmillan, 1986.

124 It is close to what Jung means by *empathy*. See C.G. Jung, *Collected Works: Vol. 6, Psychological Types*, Princeton, New Jersey: Princeton University Press, 1971. Discussed in M. Jacoby, *Individuation and Narcissism: The Psychology of Self in Jung and Kohut*, London: Routledge, 1985; see also the discussion in Habermas *op. cit.*, Vol. 1, p. 107.

125 Harris *op. cit.*, p. 192.

126 Ibid., p. 45.

127 Ibid., p. 238.

128 Ibid., p. 236.

129 P.K. Feyerabend, *Against Method: Outline of an Anarchistic Theory of Knowledge*, London: Verso, 1975.

130 Lakatos is more cautious than Popper in his assessment of how ferociously reality kicks back. His 'research programmes' act as convoys that can protect many a weak theory from the isolated raider. I. Lakatos, *Philosophical Papers: Vol. 1, The Methodology of Scientific Research Programmes*, Cambridge: Cambridge University Press, 1978.

131 For some of the social and organizational problems this poses, see J. Child and R. Loveridge, *Information Technology in European Services: Towards a Microelectronic Future*, Oxford: Basil Blackwell, 1990.

132 For one example, see Becker. Although not quite a transaction cost economist he is close to their thinking. G. Becker, *A Treatise on the Family*, Cambridge, Mass.: Harvard University Press, 1981.

133 Williamson *op. cit.*

134 See for example A. Alchian and H. Demsetz, 'Production, Information Costs, and Economic Organization', *American Economic Review*, 62, 1972, pp. 777–795. The authors do not take the firm to be an instance of market failure attributable to

information asymmetries. Rather they see the firm as an alternative market in which information asymmetries are gradually whittled down.

135 F. Braudel, *Civilisation Matérielle, Economie et Capitalisme, XVe–XVIIIe Siècle*, Vol. 1, Paris: Armand Colin, 1979, pp. 8–9.

136 Popper, *The Open Society*.

137 J.A. Schumpeter, *Business Cycles: A Theoretical, Historical, and Statistical Analysis of the Capitalist Process* (abridged), New York: McGraw-Hill, 1964 [1939].

7 CASE STUDY – SOCIALIST TRANSFORMATIONS

1 K.A. Wittfogel, *Oriental Despotism: A Comparative Study of Total Power*, New York: Vintage Books, 1981 [1951].

2 Ibid., p. xxiii.

3 Frances V. Moulder, *Japan, China and the Modern World Economy: Towards a Reinterpretation of East Asian Development ca. 1600 to 1918*, Cambridge: Cambridge University Press, 1977.

4 For details of the enterprise reforms see M. Boisot and J. Child, 'The Iron Law of Fiefs: Bureaucratic Failure and the Problem of Governance in the Chinese Economic Reforms', *Administrative Science Quarterly*, 33, December 1988, pp. 507–527.

5 Ssu-yū Teng and John K. Fairbanks (eds) *China's Response to the West: A Documentary Survey, 1839–1923*, Cambridge, Mass.: Harvard University Press, 1979, p. 19.

6 J. Gernet, *Chine et Christianisme: Action et Réaction*, Paris: Gallimard, 1982, p. 83; see also W.J. Peterson, 'Fang I-Chih's Western Learning', in W.T. de Bary (ed.) *The Unfolding of Neo-Confucianism*, New York: Columbia University Press, 1975, pp. 398–399.

7 F. Braudel, *Civilisation Matérielle, Economie et Capitalisme, XVe–XVIIIe Siècle; Tome III, Le Temps du Monde*, Paris: Armand Colin, 1979: pp. 460–461.

8 M. Weber, *The Religion of China: Confucianism and Taoism*, New York: The Free Press, 1951, p. 32.

9 E. Balazs, *La Bureaucratie Céleste: Recherches sur l'Economie et la Société de la Chine Traditionelle*, Paris: Gallimard, 1968; J.R. Levenson, 'The Amateur Ideal in Ming and Early Ch'ing Society: Evidence from Painting', in J.K. Fairbank (ed.) *Chinese Thought and Institutions*, Chicago: The University of Chicago Press, 1957, p. 321.

10 Levenson *op. cit.*

11 Balazs *op. cit.*

12 W. Eberhard, *A History of China*, London: Routledge and Kegan Paul, 1950.

13 I.C.Y. Hsu, *The Rise of Modern China*, Hong Kong: Oxford University Press, 1982.

14 Cited in J. Fairbank, E.O. Reischauer and A.M. Craig, *East Asia: The Modern Transformation*, Boston, 1965, p. 177.

15 Hence Mao's boast that he would overtake Britain within ten years.

16 For an elucidation of the term 'revolution from below', see B. Moore Jr, *Social Origins of Dictatorship and Democracy: Lord and Peasant in the Making of the Modern World*, Middlesex: Penguin Books, 1966.

17 D. Howard Smith, *Confucius and Confucianism*, London: Paladin, 1974; J. Levenson, *Confucianism and its Modern Fate: A Trilogy*, Berkeley: University of California Press, 1958.

18 'China's Leaders Recognize Merits of Confucianism', *Asia Wall Street Journal*, 18 January 1984.
19 S. Karnow, *Mao and China: Inside China's Cultural Revolution*, Middlesex: Penguin Books, 1972; E. Snow, *Red Star over China*, Middlesex: Penguin Books, 1978.
20 The concept of the 'late developer' is proposed by Dore to explain Japan's modernization. See R. Dore, *British Factory – Japanese Factory: The Origins of National Diversity in Industrial Relations*, Berkeley: University of California Press, 1973.
21 C. Riskin, *China's Political Economy*, Oxford: Oxford University Press, 1987.
22 Karnow *op. cit.*, p. 110.
23 Ibid.
24 D. Barnett, *China's Economy in Global Perspective*, Washington, DC: The Brookings Institution, 1981, p. 13.
25 A. Gouldner, *Patterns of Industrial Bureaucracy*, Glencoe, Illinois: The Free Press, 1954.
26 *People's Daily* (Beijing), 21 May 1967.
27 H.Y. Lee, *The Politics of the Cultural Revolution: A Case Study*, Berkeley: University of California Press, 1978.
28 E.H. Carr, *The Bolshevik Revolution: 1917–1923*, Middlesex: Penguin Books, 1966.
29 K. Marx, *Capital*, London: Lawrence and Wishart, 1970.
30 Su Xing, 'Understanding China's Socialist System', *Beijing Review*, No. 47, 19 November 1984.
31 *The Economist*, 26 July 1986.
32 'Roads Could Pave Way to Strong Rural Economy', *China Daily*, 15 April 1985.
33 'Major Events of the Past Decade', *Beijing Review*, 24 November 1986.
34 'China at Thirty Five', *Behind the Headlines*, P. Evans and David Zweig.
35 Ibid.
36 J. Child, *Managing in China during the Age of Reform*, Cambridge: Cambridge University Press, 1994, Ch. 2, p. 11.
37 Ibid., Ch. 2, p. 13 – Communist Party of China 1984.
38 J. Kornai, *Growth, Shortage and Efficiency: A Macrodynamic Model of the Socialist Economy*, Oxford: Basil Blackwell, 1982, p. 27. I had occasion to see the soft budget constraint in action when doing research on state-owned firms in China. In one firm the planned target was renegotiated downwards just enough to show the higher authorities the profit level above which bonuses could legally be paid to the workforce. In this case the supervising bureau played the role of a gamekeeper turned poacher.
39 In exercising its ownership rights, the state was in fact requiring a dividend payout in excess of 100 per cent since firms were also made to hand over depreciation payments and therefore could only replace worn-out physical assets at the state's pleasure.
40 W.A. Byrd, 'Contractual Responsibility Systems in Chinese State Owned Industry: A Preliminary Assessment', in N. Campbell (ed.) *Advances in Chinese Industrial Studies*, Greenwich, Connecticut: JAI Press, 1991, pp. 7–36; see also G. Tidrick and C. Chen (eds) *China's Industrial Reforms*, Oxford: Oxford University Press, 1987.
41 Child *op. cit.*, Ch. 2, p. 13; Byrd *op. cit.*, p. 13.
42 Note that a *congruence* of goals does not amount to an *identity* of goals. In the latter case there would be no motive for market exchange. See also J.E. Stiglitz, 'Principle and Agent', in J. Eatwell, M. Milgate and P. Newman (eds) *Allocation*,

Information, and Markets, The New Palgrave, London: Macmillan, 1989, pp. 241–253.

43 Inspection tours did not come into being with the reforms in the PRC. They are an inheritance of the 1950s.

44 'Family Network', *China Daily*, 27 September 1986.

45 'Corruption Foul and Fair', *The Economist*, 21 December 1985.

46 'By Law or by Cadres?' *The Economist*, 21 December 1985.

47 'State Trains Paralegals to Assist Business', *China Daily*, 16 March 1985.

48 Lu Zu-Wen, 'The Evolution of China's Accounting System Paves the Way for Opening to the Outside World', Mimeo, University of International Business Economics, Beijing, 1985.

49 *China Daily*, 8 March 1986.

50 Child *op. cit.*, Ch. 4, p. 16; *Beijing Review* 1989, in Child *op. cit.*.

51 'Survey of China's Economy', *The Economist*, 1 August 1987.

52 S. Mann, *Local Merchants and the Chinese Bureaucracy, 1750–1950*, Stanford, California: Stanford University Press, 1987, p. 4.

53 'Hebei Vows to Soak up Excess in Money Supply', *China Daily*, 4 April 1985.

54 'Excess Money Strategy – Sell More', *China Daily*, 23 April 1985.

55 *People's Daily*, 18 April 1986.

56 'Too Many Hands in Factory Pockets', *China Daily*, 11 September 1986.

57 Child *op. cit.*, Ch. 4, p. 17.

58 A banquet in China is a copious meal of between eight and eighteen dishes to be shared between eight and eighteen people.

59 For a more detailed description of the managerial problems of Chinese state-owned enterprises see M. Boisot and G.L. Xing, 'The Nature of Managerial Work in the Chinese Enterprise Reforms: A Study of Six Directors', *Organization Studies*, 13(2), Spring 1992, pp. 161–184.

60 See J. Child and Y. Lu, 'Industrial Decision Making under China's Reforms 1985–1988', *Organization Studies*, 11, 1990, pp. 321–351.

61 'Survey of China's Economy', *The Economist*, 1 August 1987.

62 Child and Lu *op. cit.*; see also J. Child and Y. Lu, 'Institutional Constraints on Economic Reform: The Case of Investment Decisions in China', Research Paper in Management Studies, University of Cambridge, August 1992.

63 K.M. Eisenheart, 'Agency Theory: An Assessment and Review', *Academy of Management Review*, 14, 1989, pp. 57–74.

64 Boisot and Xing *op. cit.*

65 I myself saw workshop control documents in which planned and actual figures reported for a variety of components were identical to four decimal places. A zero variance seemed to be the rule rather than the exception.

66 J. Child, 'The Structure of Earnings in Chinese Enterprises and Some Correlates of their Variation', in J. Child and M. Lockett (eds) *Reform Policies and the Chinese Enterprise*, Advances in Chinese Industrial Studies, Vol. 1(A), Greenwich, Connecticut: JAI Press, 1990; see also Walder, who holds that egalitarianism has been the prime motive behind an indiscriminate distribution of bonus payments to workers with little regard to their performance. A.G. Walder, 'Wage Reform and the Web of Factory Interests', *The China Quarterly*, No. 109, 1987, pp. 22–41.

67 'So Taxing', *The Economist*, 8 April 1989.

68 *The Economist*, 'Survey of China's Economy, 1 August 1987.

69 Child, *Managing in China*, Ch. 1, p. 14.

70 S.R. Clegg and D. Dunkerley, *Organization, Class, and Control*, London: Routledge, 1980.

71 Dore op. cit.
72 E. Durkheim, *The Division of Labour in Society*, New York: The Free Press, 1983 [1933]; F. Tönnies, *Community and Association*, London: Routledge and Kegan Paul, 1955 [1887]; M. Weber, *Economy and Society*, Berkeley: University of California Press, 1978.
73 Marx op. cit.
74 J. Bosher, *French Finances, 1770–1795: From Business to Bureaucracy*, Cambridge: Cambridge University Press, 1970.
75 The move from feudalism to absolutism can be best depicted in the I-space by extending the population located along the diffusion dimension. A fief exercises its dominion over a relatively small number of people. Modern methods of accounting and administration allowed one particular fief, that of the monarch, to extend its reach to a much larger group, which then became the nation-state. See N. Elias, *The Civilizing Process: Vol. 2, State Formation and Civilization*, Oxford: Basil Blackwell, 1939. For an application of this line of thinking to the English case, see G.R. Elton, *Reform and Reformation: England 1509–1558*, London: Edward Arnold, 1977.
76 For a general treatment of this issue see D.C. Coleman, 'Economic Problems and Policies', in F.L. Carsten (ed.) *The New Cambridge Modern History: Vol. V, The Ascendancy of France*, Cambridge: Cambridge University Press, 1961; S. Skalweit, 'Political Thought' in the same volume; P. Anderson, *Passages from Antiquity to Feudalism*, London: Verso, 1974.
77 Carr op. cit.
78 V.I. Lenin, *What is to be Done? Burning Questions of our Movement*, Beijing: Foreign Language Press, 1975.
79 M. Weber, *On Charisma and Institution Building*, Chicago: The University of Chicago Press, 1968.
80 This would explain why in the USSR pressures for reform have more of a political thrust than in China, where a more economic orientation predominates. The clamour for democracy that was heard in Tiananmen Square found little echo among the population at large and could therefore be silenced with impunity.
81 Balasz op. cit.
82 A. Heckscher, *Mercantilism*, 2 vols, London: Macmillan, 1955 [1935].
83 Balasz op. cit.; Mann op. cit. See also Túng-Tsu Ch'ü, 'Chinese Class Structure and its Ideology', in J.K. Fairbank (ed.) *Chinese Thought and Institutions*, Chicago: The University of Chicago Press, 1957.
84 According to Susan Mann, merchants became key members of what Max Weber termed the informal 'liturgical' structures of local governance. Members of the Qing dynasty's local elite, somewhat like the citizens of ancient Athens, were called upon to perform important public services at their own expense on behalf of the state. This was a direct response to the limits of bureaucratic control, and in particular to the high administrative costs of bureaucratic tax collection. See Mann op. cit., pp. 13–15.
85 V.I. Lenin, *Imperialism, the Highest Stage of Capitalism: A Popular Outline*, Beijing: Foreign Language Press, 1975.
86 Lenin, *What is to be Done?*
87 M. Weber, *On Charisma*.
88 Lee, op. cit.; J.K. Fairbank, *The Great Chinese Revolution: 1800–1895*, London: Pan Books, 1987.
89 There is evidence that large tracts of the rural areas, where the media were absent, escaped Mao's spell; F. Butterfield, *China: Alive in the Bitter Sea*, London: Hodder and Stoughton, 1982.

90 Fairbank *op. cit.*, p. 337.
91 Lee *op. cit.*
92 Fairbank *op. cit.*
93 R. Michels, *Political Parties*, New York: Dover Publications, 1959; M. Olson, *The Logic of Collective Action: Public Goods and the Theory of Groups*, Cambridge, Mass.: Harvard University Press, 1971.
94 Boisot and Child *op. cit.*
95 K.R. Popper, *The Open Society and its Enemies*, 2 vols, London: Routledge and Kegan Paul, 1945.
96 See, for example, Yü-chüan Wang, 'The Rise of the Land Tax and the Fall of Dynasties in Chinese History', in J.R. Levenson (ed.) *Modern China: An Interpretative Anthology*, New York: Macmillan, 1971, pp. 130–154.
97 D.H. Perkins, *Agricultural Development in China: 1368–1968*, Chicago: The Aldine Press, 1969.
98 G. Sansom, *A History of Japan: 1615–1867*, Tokyo: Charles E. Tuttle Co., 1963.
99 G. Allen and A. Donnithorne, 'The Modernization of the Economy', in *Western Enterprise in Far East Economic Development: China and Japan*, London: Allen and Unwin, 1954.
100 W.W. Lockwood, *The Economic Development of Japan: Growth and Structural Change*, Princeton, New Jersey: Princeton University Press, 1968; G.B. Sansom, *Japan: A Short Cultural History*, London: Barrie and Jenkins, 1946.
101 G. Allen and A. Donnithorne *op. cit.*
102 E. Wilkinson, *Misunderstanding: Europe vs. Japan*, Tokyo: Chuokoron-sha, 1981, pp. 112–113.
103 J. Hirshmeyer and T. Yui, *The Development of Japanese Business: 1600–1980*, London: Allen and Unwin, 1981.
104 R. Dore, 'Japan as a Model of Economic Development', in *Modern Japanese Society.*
105 Allen and Donnithorne *op. cit.*
106 Moore *op. cit.*
107 Dore, 'Japan as a Model of Economic Development'. The quote is from G. Ranis.
108 J. Hirshmeyer, 'The Japanese Spirit of Enterprise (1867–1970)', Seminar in Smaller Industries Development, Nagoya International Training Centre, Japan International Cooperation Agency, 15 May 1978.
109 C. Johnson, *MITI and the Japanese Miracle: The Growth of Industrial Policy, 1925–1975*, Stanford, California: Stanford University Press, 1982.
110 These two terms were coined by G.A. Kelly, 'Who Needs a Theory of Citizenship?', *Daedalus*, Fall 1979, p. 25.
111 R. Dore, *Taking Japan Seriously: A Confucian Perspective on Leading Economic Issues*, London: Athlone Press, 1987.
112 G. Hofstede and M.H. Bond, 'Confucius and Economic Growth: New Trends in Culture's Consequences', *Organizational Dynamics*, 16(4), 1988, pp. 4–21.
113 Ibid.
114 M. Weber, *The Protestant Ethics and the Spirit of Capitalism*, London: Unwin University Books, 1930 [1904–5].
115 For a fuller treatment of Hofstede's approach, see *Culture's Consequences: International Differences in Work-Related Values*, Beverly Hills, California: Sage Publications, 1980.
116 See, for example, E. Vogel, *Japan as No. 1: Lessons for America*, Tokyo: Charles E. Tuttle Co., 1979.
117 Lockwood *op. cit.*

118 Ibid., p. 558.
119 R. Tricker, *Corporate Governance*, Aldershot: Gower, 1984.
120 S. Cheung, 'The Contractual Nature of the Firm', *Journal of Law and Economics*, 3(1), April 1983, pp. 1–21.
121 The concentric rings are a corporate adaptation of a model of inter-personal relationships in Japan put forward by C. Nakane, *Japanese Society*, Middlesex: Penguin Books, 1973, pp. 5–14.
122 These are considered stakeholders in so far as they are customers. Of course some customers will be more committed than others.
123 Sansom, *A History of Japan*.
124 For a discussion of particularism and universalism, see T. Parsons, *The Social System*, London: Routledge and Kegan Paul, 1951, pp. 61–63.
125 R. Clarke, *The Japanese Company*, New Haven: Yale University Press, 1979.
126 Dore, *British Factory*. There is currently a debate on the future of this system.
127 M.M. Postan, *The Medieval Economy and Society*, Middlesex: Penguin Books, 1975.
128 V.P. Goldberg, 'Rational Exchange: Economics and Complex Contracts', *American Behavioural Scientist*, 23(3), January–February 1980, pp. 337–352.
129 R. Dore, *Flexible Rigidities: Industrial Policy and Structural Adjustment in the Japanese Economy 1970–80*, London: The Athlone Press, 1988, p. 77.
130 O.E. Williamson, *The Economic Institutions of Capitalism*, New York: The Free Press, 1985, p. 62.
131 Hirshmeyer *op. cit.*
132 H. Passin, *Society and Education in Japan*, Tokyo: Kodansha International, 1965.
133 Robert E. Cole, *Work Mobility and Participation: A Comparative Study of American and Japanese Industry*, Berkeley: University of California Press, 1979, p. 69.
134 Dore, *British Factory*.
135 F.L.K. Hsu, *Iemoto: The Heart of Japan*, Cambridge, Mass.: John Wiley and Sons, 1975.
136 L. Pye, *Asian Power and Politics: The Cultural Dimension of Authority*, Cambridge; Mass.: The Belknap Press of Harvard University Press, 1985.
137 Clarke *op. cit.*
138 This relationship is similar in certain respects to the *Sempai–Kohai* (senior–junior) relationship; see T. Rohlen, *For Harmony and Strength*, Berkeley: University of California Press, 1974.
139 Nakane *op. cit.*
140 For a penetrating discussion of such practices, see T. Doi, *The Anatomy of Dependence*, Tokyo: Kodansha International, 1977; see also W. Caudill and H. Weinstein, 'Maternal Care and Infant Behaviour in Japan and America', *Psychiatry*, 32, 1969, pp. 12–43.
141 D. Riesman, *The Lonely Crowd: A Study of the Changing American Character*, New Haven, Connecticut: Yale University Press, 1961.
142 Dore, *British Factory*.
143 S. Kamata, *Japan in the Passing Lane*, New York: Pantheon Books, 1982.
144 R.E. Cole, *Japanese Blue Collar: The Changing Tradition*, Berkeley: University of California Press, 1971.
145 T. Kagono *et al.*, *Nihon Kigyo no Senryaku to Soshiki* (Strategy and Structure of Japanese Business), Tokyo: Organization Science, Summer 1981.
146 T. Kono, *Strategy and Structure of Japanese Enterprises*, London: Macmillan, 1984.

147 R.T. Pascale and A. Athos, *The Art of Japanese Management: Applications for American Executives*, New York: Warner Books, 1981.

148 Kono *op. cit.*

149 Dore, *British Factory.*

150 COCOM (Coordinating Committee) is the international organization that supervises certain types of western trade with communist countries.

151 R. Benedict, *The Chrysanthemum and the Sword*, London: Routledge and Kegan Paul, 1967.

152 R. Caves and M. Uekusa, *Industrial Organization in Japan*, Washington, DC, The Brookings Institution, 1976.

153 Johnson *op. cit.*; see also D.I. Okimoto, *Between MITI and the Market: Japanese Industrial Policy for High Technology*, Stanford, California: Stanford University Press, 1989.

154 R. Nozick, *Anarchy, State and Utopia*, Oxford: Basil Blackwell, 1974.

155 G.L. Curtis, 'Big Business and Political Influence', in E.F. Vogel (ed.) *Modern Japanese Organization and Decision-Making*, Tokyo: Charles E. Tuttle Co., 1979.

156 G.D.H. Cole and Raymond Postgate, *The Common People: 1746–1946*, London: Methuen, 1949.

157 A. Chandler, *Scale and Scope: The Dynamics of Industrial Capitalism*, Cambridge, Mass.: Harvard University Press, 1990.

158 This is not the first time that we confront the paradox. J. Abbeglen, in *The Japanese Factory*, Glencoe, Illinois: The Free Press, 1958, also cited this feature to explain the *lower* productivity of Japanese enterprises as compared with US ones. See R.M. Marsh and H. Manari, *Modernization and the Japanese Factory*, Princeton, New Jersey: Princeton University Press, 1976.

159 Boisot and Xing *op. cit.*

160 Strategic behaviour is discussed in O.E. Williamson *op. cit.* The term also bears some relation to the concept of 'strategic intent' as developed by C.K. Prahalad and G. Hamel. See G. Hamel and C.K. Prahalad, 'Strategic Intent', *Harvard Business Review*, May–June 1989.

161 Boisot and Child *op. cit.*

162 Pascale and Athos *op. cit.*; Kono *op. cit.*

163 Eberhard *op. cit.*

164 C. Ronan, *The Shorter Science and Civilization in China: An Abridgement by Colin Ronan of Joseph Needham's Original Text*, Cambridge: Cambridge University Press, 1978, p. 59.

165 Ibid.; M. Elvin, *The Pattern of the Chinese Past*, Stanford: Stanford University Press, 1974.

166 Eberhard *op. cit.*, pp. 245–246.

167 This is perhaps most evident in its architecture. See R.T. Paine and A. Soper, *The Art and Architecture of Japan*, Middlesex: Penguin Books, 1955.

168 See M. Peck, 'Technology', in H. Patrick and H. Rosovsky (eds) *Asia's New Giant: How the Japanese Economy Works*, Washington, DC: The Brookings Institution, 1976, pp. 582–583.

169 I.C.Y. Hsu, *The Rise of Modern China*, Hong Kong: Oxford University Press, 1982, p. 360.

170 Passin *op. cit.*, pp. 67–68.

171 L.B. Krauss and S. Sekiguchi, 'Japan and the World Economy', in Patrick and Rosovsky *op. cit.*, pp. 383–458.

172 That this is no deterministic development path is evidenced by the fact that the United States followed quite a different trajectory.

173 For a description of the *Sogo Shoscha*, see A.K. Young, *The Sogo Shoscha: Japan's Multinational Trading Companies*, Tokyo: Charles E. Tuttle Co., 1979.

174 R. Garratt, *The Learning Organization*, London: Fontana, 1987; P.M. Senge, *The Fifth Discipline: The Art and Practice of the Learning Organization*, London: Century Business, 1990.

175 K. Van Wolferen, *The Enigma of Japanese Power: People and Politics in a Stateless Nation*, London: Macmillan, 1989, p. 431.

176 T. Kowalik, 'Central Planning', in J. Eatwell, M. Milgate and P. Newman (eds) *Problems of the Planned Economy*, London: Macmillan, 1990.

177 W. Brus, 'Market Socialism', in Eatwell, Milgate and Newman *op. cit.*, pp. 164–177; see also Communist International, *Programme of the Communist International*, London: Communist International, 1929.

178 K. Kautsky, *Die proletarische Revolution und ihr Programm*, Stuttgart: I.H.W. Dieta Nachfolger, 1922.

179 M. Ellman, 'Josif Vissarionovich Stalin', in Eatwell, Milgate and Newman *op. cit.*, p. 251.

180 O. Lange and F.M. Taylor (eds) *On the Economic Theory of Socialism*, Minneapolis: University of Minnesota Press, 1938; A.P. Lerner, 'A Note on Socialist Economics', *Review of Economic Studies*, 4, 1936, pp. 72–76.

181 Ellman *op. cit.*, p. 251.

182 E. Gellner, 'Economic Interpretation of History', in J. Eatwell, M. Milgate and P. Newman (eds) *Marxian Economics*, The New Palgrave, London: Macmillan, 1990, pp. 148–158.

183 Carr *op. cit.*

184 R. Pipes, *The Russian Revolution: 1899–1919*, London: Fontana, 1992 – see footnote 26, p. 107.

185 A. Aganbegyan, 'Perestroika', in Eatwell, Milgate and Newman, *Problems*, pp. 1–12.

186 *The Economist*, 'Survey of the Soviet Economy', 9 April 1988.

187 J. Child and L. Markoczy, 'Host Country Managerial Behaviour and Learning in Chinese and Hungarian Joint Ventures', *Journal of Management Studies*, 30, 1993.

188 'Eastern Europe's Economies', *The Economist*, 13 January 1990.

189 *The Economist*, 4 April 1992, 'Pioneers of Capitalism', p. 73; also 'Coming Along More Nicely', 9 January 1993, p. 38.

190 *The Economist*, 'The Visible Treuhand', 21 March 1992.

191 B. Csikás-Nagy, *Revue de l'Est*, III(I), 1972, p. 25, in D. Granick, *Enterprise Guidance in Eastern Europe: A Comparison of Four Socialist Economies*, Princeton, New Jersey: Princeton University Press, 1975, p. 140; Granick himself somewhat questions this interpretation.

192 Granick *op. cit.*, p. 476.

193 Clegg and Dunkerley *op. cit.*

194 See Y. Aharoni and L. Lachman, 'Can the Collective Manager's Mind be Nationalized?', *Organization Studies*, 3(1), 1982, pp. 33–46.

195 M. Boisot, 'Schumpeterian Learning versus Neoclassical Learning: Development Options for Post-Communist Societies', in S. Birley and I.C. MacMillan (eds) *International Perspectives on Entrepreneurship Research*, Amsterdam: North-Holland, 1992, pp. 6–31.

196 M. Hannan and J. Freeman, *Organizational Ecology*, Cambridge, Mass.: Harvard University Press, 1989.

197 A. Kozminski, 'Framework for Comparative Studies of Management in Post-Socialist Economies', *Studies in Comparative Communism*, 4, 1991, pp. 413–424;

J. Winiecki, 'Obstacles to Economic Reform of Socialism: A Property-Rights Approach', *The Annals of the AAPSS*, 507, 1990, pp. 65–71.

198   Albeit with important difference. See D. Granick, 'The Industrial Environment in China and the CMEA Countries', in Tidrick and Chen *op. cit.*, pp. 103–131.

199   T. Laky, 'Enterprises in a Bargaining Position', *Acta Oeconomica*, 3–4, 1979, pp. 227–246; T. Laky, 'Realities and Potentialities of the Autonomous Sector', in B. Dallago, G. Ajani and B. Grancelli (eds) *Privatization and Entrepreneurship in Post Socialist Countries*, London: Macmillan, 1992.

200   Tönnies *op. cit.*

201   *The Economist*, 'Crossing the East–West Chasm', 16 May 1992.

202   See *The Economist*. *The Economist*'s own calculations make China the world's second largest economy.

203   G. Redding, *The Spirit of Chinese Capitalism*, Berlin: Walter de Gruyter, 1990.

204   Dore, *Flexible Rigidities*.

205   A.D. Chandler, *The Visible Hand: The Managerial Revolution in American Business*, Cambridge, Mass.: The Belknap Press of Harvard University Press, 1977.

206   A consequence of the Duhem–Quine thesis. For a discussion see Chapter 2.

207   Durkheim *op. cit.*

208   Tönnies *op. cit.*

209   Marx *op. cit.*

210   Parsons *op. cit.*

211   See I. Lakatos, 'History of Science and its Rational Reconstructions', in R.C. Buck and R.S. Cohen (eds) P.S.A. *Boston Studies in the Philosophy of Science*, 8, Dordrecht: Reidel, 1971, pp. 91–135. The case for a more 'external' approach to science is illustrated by a case study in B. Wynne, 'Physics and Psychics: Science, Symbolic Action and Social Control in Late Victorian England', in B. Barnes and S. Shapin (eds) *Natural Order: Historical Studies of Scientific Culture*, Beverly Hills: Sage Publications, 1979, pp. 167–186.

212   Of course the problem starts when one moves outside Europe. Marx never entirely succeeded in fitting an 'Asiatic Mode of Production' into his stages. See R. Jessop, 'Mode of Production', in Eatwell, Milgate and Newman, *Marxian Economics*, pp. 289–296.

213   I. Wallerstein, *The Modern World System: Capitalist Agriculture and the Origins of the European World Economy in the Sixteenth Century*, New York: Academic Press, 1974, p. 7.

214   K. Marx and Friedrich Engels, *Selected Works*, Vol. 2, Moscow: Foreign Language Publishing House, 1962.

215   Van Wolferen *op. cit.*, p. 9.

8 CONCLUSION

1   'The Hole He Left Behind', *The Economist*, 21 December 1991–3 January 1992.

2   'Universities Compared: Cambridge Versus Cambridge', *The Economist*, 21 December 1991–3 January 1992, p. 43.

3   D.H. Meadows, D. Meadows, J. Randers and W.W. Behrens III, *The Limits to Growth: A Report on the Club of Rome's Project on the Predicament of Mankind*, London: Earth Island, 1972.

4   Varela calls these *autopoeitic systems*. See F.J. Varela, *Principles of Biological Autonomy*, New York: North-Holland, 1980.

5   R. Penrose, *The Emperor's New Mind: Concerning Computers, Minds, and the*

Law of Physics, London: Vintage, 1989, p. 412.

6 J.Y. Lettvin, H.R. Maturana, W.S. McCulloch and W.H. Pitts, 'What the Frog's Eye Tells the Frog's Brain', *Proceedings of the IRE*, 47(11), November 1959, pp. 1940–1959.

7 M. Weber, *The Theory of Social and Economic Organization*, New York: The Free Press, 1964.

8 See J. Elster, *Explaining Technical Change: Studies in Rationality and Social Change*, Cambridge: Cambridge University Press, 1983.

9 L. Robbins, *An Essay on the Nature and Significance of Economic Science*, London: Macmillan, 1935.

10 O.E. Williamson, *Markets and Hierarchies: Analysis and Antitrust Implications*, New York: The Free Press, 1975, p. 20.

11 D.K. Begg, *The Rational Expectations Revolution in Macroeconomics: Theories and Evidence*, Oxford: Philip Allan, 1982.

12 W.W. Rostow, *The Stages of Economic Growth: A Non-Communist Manifesto*, Cambridge: Cambridge University Press, 1960. See also J. Johanson and L.G. Mattson, 'Interorganizational Relations in Industrial Systems: A Network Approach Compared with the Transaction Cost Approach', in G. Thompson, J. Frances, R. Levacic and J. Mitchell (eds) *Markets, Hierarchies, and Networks: The Coordination of Social Life*, London: Sage Publications, 1991.

13 In contrast to teleology, teleonomy is oriented but not goal-directed. See J. Monod, *Le Hasard et la Nécessité: Essai sur la Philosophie Naturelle de la Biologie Moderne*, Paris: Seuil, 1970. For a specific application of the concept of teleonomy see M. Koppel and H. Atlan, 'Les Gènes: Programme ou Données? Le Rôle de la Signification dans les Mesures de la Complexité', in F.F. Soulié (ed.) *Les Théories de la Complexité: Autour de l'Oeuvre d'Henri Atlan*, Paris: Seuil, 1991, pp. 188–204.

14 In spite of his arguments in favour of S-learning, the later Schumpeter believed that the SLC would eventually come to a halt in the bureaucratic region of the I-space and that the state would then take over. See J.A. Schumpeter, *Capitalism, Socialism, and Democracy*, New York: Harper and Row, 1942.

15 The quip is Herbert Simon's.

16 Williamson, *op. cit.*; see also W. Ouchi, 'Markets, Bureaucracies, and Clans', *Administrative Science Quarterly*, 25(1), 1980, pp. 129–141.

17 H.A. Simon, *Reason in Human Affairs*, Oxford: Basil Blackwell, 1983.

18 W. Streek and P. Schmitter, 'Community, Market, State – and Associations? The Prospective Contribution of Interest Governance to Social Order', in G. Thompson, J. Frances, R. Levacic and J. Mitchell (eds) *Markets, Hierarchies and Networks: The Coordination of Social Life*, London: Sage Publications, 1991.

19 M. Lippi, 'On the Dynamics of Aggregate Macroequations: From Simple Microbehaviour to Complex Macrorelationships', in G. Dosi *et al.* (eds) *Technical Change and Economic Theory*, London: Pinter Publishers, 1988, p. 171.

20 The theoretical grounds for this view can be found in R.A. Heiner, 'The Origin of Predictable Behaviour', *American Economic Review*, 73(4), 1983, pp. 560–574.

21 Another example drawn from my own experience in China will illustrate the point even more forcefully.

   In 1987 I found myself in the small steel town of Baotu in Inner Mongolia giving a seminar to a local engineering firm. My Chinese hosts had arranged for a Sunday visit to a Lama temple located three hours' drive north of Baotu in the hills. We travelled in a military jeep. Since Inner Mongolia is one of the poorest regions in China with little infrastructure, for most of the journey there was no road at all to drive on and we had to use a dried-up river bed as a track. The temple was located at the top of a winding valley and was flanked by a small hamlet of fairly run-down brick houses. Its remarkable architecture apart, two things immediately struck me on arrival at our destination. The first was that most of the village houses were sprouting television aerials. The second is that nearly all the village youths were wearing jeans.

I was reminded of Daniel Lerner's book *The Passing of Traditional Society* which I had read some years earlier in which he described the modernization of village life in a small hamlet just outside Ankara, a modernization brought about largely by modern roads, a bus service, and the transistor radio. But that was Turkey and this was rural China. Beijing was at least fifteen hours away by a combination of car and train. The absence of any physical transport infrastructure, however, had not prevented the influences of the outside world – and since the 'Open Door' policy, a world bigger than China – from penetrating the remotest village hamlet.

Contrast this experience with that of a colleague of mine exploring the Xinghai plateau in the late 1970s; that is, *before* the PRC had inaugurated its 'Open Door' policy. He had been allowed into the province because he was accompanied by his Chinese-born wife who was trying to trace some of her more distant relatives. On arrival in one village, the elders approached the couple and after a few polite exchanges came out straight with what had been preoccupying them: some young kids calling themselves 'revolutionary guards' had shown up in a few of the neighbouring hamlets some time back, talking a lot about a character called Mao. Could the foreign guests please give the elders more information on this person since they knew nothing about him?

22 That is to say, they are path dependent.
23 'Pour cette zone qui n'est pas la vraie économie du marché, mais si souvent sa franche contradiction, il me fallait un mot particulier. Et celui qui se présentait irrésistiblement, c'était bien celui de capitalisme'. F. Braudel, *Civilisation Matérielle, Economie et Capitalisme, XVe–XVIIIe Siècle: Tome 2, Les Jeux de l'Echange*, Paris: Armand Colin, 1979, p. 9.
24 P. Pelikan, 'Can the Innovation System of Capitalism be Outperformed?', in G. Dosi *et al.* (eds) *Technical Change and Economic Theory*, London: Pinter Publishers, 1988, pp. 370–398. See also L. Huwicz, 'Centralization and Decentralization in Economic Processes', in A. Eckstein (ed.) *Comparison of Economic Systems*, Berkeley: University of California Press, 1971.
25 During his visit, Deng predicted that Guangdong Province, with a population of 70 million, would become Asia's fifth 'dragon'. *Financial Times*, 15 March 1992; Alexander Nicoll, 'Deng Xiaoping: Tiny Dynamo at the Heart of the Party'.
26 C. Perez, 'Microelectronics, Long Waves, and World Structural Change', *World Development*, 13(3), 1985, pp. 441–463.
27 See S. Macdonald, 'Information Networks and the Exchange of Information', in C. Antonelli (ed.) *The Economics of Information Networks*, Amsterdam: North-Holland, 1992.
28 J. Naisbitt, *Megatrends: Ten New Directions Transforming our Lives*, New York: Warner Books, 1982, pp. 30–31.
29 S. Zuboff, *In the Age of the Smart Machine: The Future of Work and Power*, Oxford: Heinemann, 1988.
30 A.D. Chandler, *The Visible Hand: The Managerial Revolution in American Business*, Cambridge, Mass.: The Belknap Press of Harvard University Press, 1977.

31 G. Pinchot III, *Intrapreneuring*, New York: Harper and Row, 1985.

32 E. Morin, *Le Paradigme Perdu: La Nature Humaine*, Paris: Editions du Seuil, 1973.

33 Giddens's theory of structuration holds that social relations are structured across time and space in virtue of a duality of structure taken as both the medium and the outcome of the conduct it recursively organizes. Giddens identifies three types of structure: (1) structures of signification, (2) structures of domination, and (3) structures of legitimation. These might be taken to occur respectively along the three dimensions of codification, diffusion, and abstraction. See A. Giddens, *The Constitution of Society: Outline of the Theory of Structuration*, Cambridge: Polity Press, 1984. Habermas distinguishes between *system* and *life-world*, the former being more codified and abstract than the latter; see J. Habermas, *The Theory of Communicative Action*, 2 vols, Cambridge: Polity Press, 1984, 1987.

34 For an interesting approach to treating the state in this way, see E.A. Nordlinger, *On the Autonomy of the Democratic State*, Cambridge, Mass.: Harvard University Press, 1981.

35 Carl Menger outlined the principles of methodological individualism in 1883. He labelled them 'the composite method'. C. Menger, *Problems of Economics and Sociology*, Urbana: The University of Illinois Press, 1963 [1885].

36 Akerlof and Yellen (1985), for example, show that individual behaviours which are only marginally non-maximizing can induce a significant effect on macro-economic outcomes. G.A. Akerlof and J.L. Yellen, 'A Near-Rational Model of the Business Cycle', *Quarterly Journal of Economics*, 100, 1985, pp. 803–838; see also G. Silverberg, 'Modelling Economic Dynamics and Technical Change: Mathematical Approaches to Self-Organization and Evolution', in G. Dosi *et al.* (eds) *Technical Change and Economic Theory*, London: Pinter Publishers, 1988, p. 532.

37 D. Dennett, 'Intentional Systems', *Journal of Philosophy*, LXVIII(4), 1971, pp. 87–106.

38 See B. Shannon, 'Réflexion sur la Complexité de la Cognition Humaine', in F.F. Soulié (ed.) *Les Théories de la Complexité: Autour de l'Oeuvre d'Henri Atlan*, Paris: Seuil, p. 308.

39 This is the radical subjectivist position that Littlechild contrasts with that of the neoclassical and the Austrian school. See S. Littlechild, 'Three Types of Market Processes', in R.N. Langlois (ed.) *Economics as a Process: Essays in the New Institutional Economics*, Cambridge: Cambridge University Press, 1986; see also G.L.S. Shackle, *Imagination and the Nature of Choice*, Edinburgh: Edinburgh University Press, 1979; L. Lachmann, *Capital, Expectations, and the Market Process*, Kansas City: Sheed, Andrews and McMeel, 1977.

40 Silverberg, in Dosi *op. cit.*, p. 539; see also A.J. Lotka, *Elements of Mathematical Biology*, New York: Dover, 1956.

41 Penrose *op. cit.*; B.O. Küppers, *Information and the Origin of Life*, Cambridge, Mass.: The MIT Press, 1990; see also R. Thom, *Esquisse d'une Semiophysique Physique Aristotélienne et Théorie de Catastrophes*, Paris: Intereditions, 1988.

42 For a general introduction to some of the issues, see M.A. Boden, *Artificial Intelligence and Natural Man*, London: The MIT Press, 1987, especially part 5.

43 A perspective obviously shared by physicists such as Brillouin when they claim that information controls and organizes energy flows, and by Boltzmann himself who had the ambition to become the Darwin of the evolution of matter. See L. Brillouin, *La Science et la Théorie de l'Information*, Paris: Masson, 1959; L. Boltzmann, *Populäre Schriften*, Leipzig, 1905.

Bibliography

Aaoki, C. and P. Siekevitz, 'Plasticity in Brain Development', *Scientific American*, 259(6), December 1988

Abbeglen, J., *The Japanese Factory*, Glencoe, Illinois: The Free Press, 1958

Abernathy, W. and J.M. Utterback, 'Patterns of Industrial Innovations', in M.L. Tushman and W.L. Moore (eds) *Readings in the Management of Innovation*, Boston: Pitman, 1982, pp. 97–108

Abler, R., J. Adams and P. Gould, *Spatial Organization: The Geographer's View of the World*, Englewood Cliffs, New Jersey: Prentice-Hall, 1971

Acton, H.B., 'Comte', in J.O. Urmson and J. Rée (eds) *The Concise Encyclopedia of Western Philosophy and Philosophers*, London: Unwin Hyman, 1989, p. 63

Adams, W. and J.W. Brock, 'Integrated Monopoly and Market Power: System Selling, Compatibility Standards, and Market Control', *Quarterly Review of Economics and Business*, 22(4), pp. 29–49, 1982

Aganbegyan, A., 'Perestroika', in J. Eatwell, M. Milgate and P. Newman (eds) *Problems of the Planned Economy*, London: Macmillan, 1990, pp. 1–12

Aharani, Y. and L. Lachman, 'Can the Collective Manager's Mind be Nationalized?' *Organization Studies*, 3(1), 1982, pp. 33–46.

Akerlof, G., 'The Market for "Lemons"; Qualitative Uncertainty and the Market Mechanism', *Quarterly Journal of Economics*, 84(3), 1970, pp. 488–500

Akerlof, G.A. and J.L. Yellen, 'A Near-Rational Model of the Business Cycle', *Quarterly Journal of Economics*, 100, 1985, pp. 803–838

Alchian, A., 'Information Costs, Pricing, and Resource Unemployment', *Western Economic Journal*, 7, 1969, pp. 109–128

Alchian, A. and H. Demsetz, 'Production, Information Costs, and Economic Organization', *American Economic Review*, 62, 1972, pp. 777–795

Allen, G. and A. Donnithorne, 'The Modernization of the Economy', in *Western Enterprise in Far East Economic Development: China and Japan*, London: Allen and Unwin, 1954

Allen, P.M., 'Towards a New Science of Complex Systems', in *The Science and Praxis of Complexity*, Tokyo: United Nations University Press, 1985

Allen, P.M. 'Evolution: Why the Whole is Greater than the Sum of the Parts', Unpublished manuscript, International Ecotechnology Research Centre, Cranfield Institute of Technology (undated)

Allen, P.M. and J.H. McGlade, 'Evolutionary Drive: The Effect of Microscopic Diversity, Error Making and Noise', *Foundations of Physics*, 17(7), July 1987

Allison, G.T., *The Essence of Decision: Explaining the Cuban Missile Crisis*, Boston: Little, Brown, 1971

Anderson, J.A. and M.C. Moser, 'Categorization and Selective Neurons', in G.E.

Hinton and J.A. Anderson (eds) *Parallel Models of Associative Memory*, Hillsdale, New Jersey: Lawrence Erlbaum Associates, 1981, pp. 213–236

Anderson, J.R., *Cognitive Skills and their Acquisition*, Hillsdale, New Jersey: Lawrence Erlbaum Associates, 1981

Anderson, P., *Passages from Antiquity to Feudalism*, London: Verso, 1974

Argyle, M., *Social Interaction*, Atherton: Methuen, 1969

Argyris, C. and D. Schön, *Organizational Learning: A Theory of Action Perspective*, Reading, Mass.: Addison-Wesley, 1978

Arrow, K., 'The Economic Implications of Learning by Doing', *Review of Economic Studies*, 29, 1962, pp. 155–173

Arrow, K., 'Economic Welfare and the Allocation of Resources for Invention', in *The Rate and Direction of Inventive Activity*, Princeton, New Jersey: Princeton University Press, 1962, pp. 609–625

Arrow, K., *Social Choice and Individual Values*, New Haven, Connecticut: Yale University Press, 1963

Arrow, K., *Essays in the Theory of Risk Bearing*, Chicago: Markham, and Amsterdam: North-Holland, 1971

Arrow, K., *The Limits of Organization*, New York: Norton, 1974

Arrow, K., 'Information and Economic Behaviour', *The Economics of Information: Collected Papers of Kenneth J. Arrow*, Cambridge, Mass.: The Belknap Press of Harvard University Press, 1984, pp. 136–152

Atlan, H., *Entre le Cristal et la Fumée: Essai sur l'Organisation du Vivant*, Paris: Seuil, 1979

Axelrod, R., *The Evolution of Cooperation*, New York: Basic Books, 1984

Balazs, E., *La Bureaucratie Céleste: Recherches sur l'Economie et la Société de la Chine Traditionelle*, Paris: Gallimard, 1968

Ballard, D.H., 'Cortical Connections and Parallel Processing: Structure and Function', *Behavioural and Brain Sciences*, 9(1), 1986

Bannister, D. and F. Fransella, *Inquiring Man*, Middlesex: Penguin Books, 1966

Barnes, B. and D. Bloor, 'Relativism, Rationalism and the Sociology of Knowledge', in M. Hollis and S. Lukes (eds) *Rationality and Relativism*, Oxford: Basil Blackwell, 1982

Barnett, D., *China's Economy in Global Perspective*, Washington, DC: The Brookings Institution, 1981

Barone, E., 'Ministry of Production in the Collectivist State', in F.A. Hayek (ed.) *Collectivist Economic Planning*, London: George Routledge and Sons, 1935

Barrow, J.D., *The World within the World*, Oxford: Oxford University Press, 1990

Barrow, J.D. and F.J. Tipler, *The Cosmic Anthropic Principle*, Oxford: Oxford University Press, 1986

Bartlett, F.C., *Remembering*, Cambridge: Cambridge University Press, 1932

Bateson, G., *Naven: A Survey of the Problems Suggested by a Composite Picture of the Culture of a New Guinea Tribe Drawn from Three Points of View*, Cambridge: Cambridge University Press, 1936

Bateson, G., *Steps towards an Ecology of Mind: Collected Essays in Anthropology, Psychiatry, Evolution and Epistemology*, St Albans, Herts: Paladin, 1972

Baudrillard, J., *Le Système des Objets*, Paris: Gallimard, 1968

Becker, G., *A Treatise on the Family*, Cambridge, Mass.: Harvard University Press, 1981

Begg, D.K.H., *The Rational Expectations Revolution in Macroeconomics: Theories and Evidence*, Oxford: Philip Allan, 1982

Bell, D., 'Thinking Ahead', *Harvard Business Review*, May–June 1979

Bell, D., 'Models and Reality in Economic Discourse', in D. Bell and I. Kristol (eds) *The Crisis in Economic Theory*, New York: Basic Books, 1981

Bendix, R., 'A Case Study in Cultural and Educational Mobility: Japan and the Protestant Ethic', in N.J. Smelser and S.M. Lipset (eds) *Social Structure and Mobility in Economic Development*, Chicago: Aldine Publishing Co., 1966

Bendix, R., 'Preconditions of Development: A Comparison of Japan and Germany', in R. Dore (ed.) *Aspects of Social Change in Modern Japan*, Princeton, New Jersey: Princeton University Press, 1967

Benedict, R., *Patterns of Culture*, London: Routledge and Kegan Paul, 1935

Benedict, R., *The Chrysanthemum and the Sword*, London: Routledge and Kegan Paul, 1967

Berger, P. and T. Luckmann, *The Social Construction of Reality: A Treatise in the Sociology of Knowledge*, Middlesex: Penguin Books, 1966

Bernstein, B., 'Social Class and Psycho-therapy', *British Journal of Sociology*, 15, 1964, pp. 54–64

Bernstein, B., *Class, Codes, and Control: Vol. 1, Theoretical Studies towards a Sociology of Language*, London: Routledge and Kegan Paul, 1971

Best, M., *The New Competition: Institutions of Industrial Restructuring*, Cambridge: The Polity Press, 1990

Bhide, A., 'Vinod Khosla and Sun Microsystems A, B, and C', Harvard Business School Cases 9–390–049/050/051

Bijker, W.E., 'The Social Construction of Bakelite: Towards a Theory of Invention', in W.E. Bijker, T.P. Hughes and T. Pinch (eds) *The Social Construction of Technological Systems: New Directions in the Sociology and History of Technology*, Cambridge, Mass.: The MIT Press, 1993

Blaug, M., *Economic Theory in Retrospect*, Cambridge: Cambridge University Press, 1978

Blaug, M., *The Methodology of Economics: or How Economists Explain*, Cambridge: Cambridge University Press, 1992

Bloch, M., *La Société Féodale*, Paris: Albin Michel, 1939

Bloch, M., *Les Rois Thaumaturges*, Paris: Gallimard, 1983 [1921]

Bloor, D., *Knowledge and Social Imagery*, Chicago: The University of Chicago Press, 1976

Blum, H.F., *Time's Arrow and Evolution*, 3rd edn, Princeton: Princeton University Press, 1968

Boas, F., *The Mind of Primitive Man*, New York: The Free Press, 1939 [1911]

Boden, M.A., *Artificial Intelligence and Natural Man*, London: The MIT Press, 1987

Bohm, D., *Wholeness and the Implicate Order*, London: Routledge and Kegan Paul, 1980

Bohm, D., *Causality and Chance in Modern Physics*, London: Routledge and Kegan Paul, 1984

Boisot, M., 'Markets and Hierarchies in Cultural Perspective', *Organization Studies*, Spring 1986

Boisot, M., 'Industrial Feudalism and Enterprise Reform – Could the Chinese Use Some More Bureaucracy?', in M. Warner (ed.) *Management Reforms in China*, London: Pinter Publishers, 1987

Boisot, M., 'The Long March towards Bureaucratic Rationality', in D. Goodman and G. Segal (eds) *China at Forty: Mid-Life Crisis?*, Oxford: The Clarendon Press, 1989

Boisot, M., 'Schumpeterian Learning versus Neoclassical Learning: Development Options for Post-Communist Societies', in S. Birley and I.C. MacMillan (eds) *International Perspectives on Entrepreneurship Research*, Amsterdam: North-Holland, 1992

Boisot, M., *Information and Organization: The Manager as Anthropologist*, London: HarperCollins, 1994

Boisot, M. and J. Child, 'The Iron Law of Fiefs: Bureaucratic Failure and the Problem of Governance in the Chinese Economic Reforms', *Administrative Science Quarterly*, 33, December 1988, pp. 507–527

Boisot, M. and J. Child, 'Network Capitalism: The Strength of Weak Markets', Paper presented at the Cambridge Conference on China, March 1994

Boisot, M. and G. Xing, 'The Nature of Managerial Work in the Chinese Enterprise Reforms: A Study of Six Directors', *Organization Studies*, 13(2), Spring 1992, pp. 161–184

Boltzmann, L., *Populäre Schriften*, Leipzig, 1905

Bosher, J., *French Finances, 1770–1795: From Business to Bureaucracy*, Cambridge: Cambridge University Press, 1970

Bourdieu, P., *Esquisse d'une Théorie de la Pratique, Précédé de Trois Etudes d'Ethnologie Kabyle*, Geneva: Librairie Droz, 1972

Bowles, S. and H. Gintis, *Schooling in Capitalist America*, New York: Basic Books, 1976

Boyd, R., 'On the Current Status of Scientific Realism', *Erkenntnis*, 19, 1983, pp. 45–90. Reprinted in R. Boyd *et al.* (eds) *The Philosophy of Science*, Cambridge, Mass.: MIT Press, 1991

Boyd, R., 'Confirmation, Semantics, and the Interpretation of Scientific Theories', in R. Boyd *et al.* (eds) *The Philosophy of Science*, Cambridge, Mass.: The MIT Press, 1992, pp. 3–35

Boyd, R. and P.J. Richerson, *Culture and the Evolutionary Process*, Chicago: The University of Chicago Press, 1985

Boyd, R., P. Gasper and S.D. Trout (eds) *The Philosophy of Science*, Cambridge, Mass.: MIT Press, 1991

Braudel, F., *Civilisation Matérielle, Economie et Capitalisme, XVe–XVIIIe Siècle*, 3 vols, Paris: Armand Colin, 1979

Bridgeman, P., *The Logic of Modern Physics*, London: Macmillan, 1927

Briggs Myers, Isabel, 'Introduction to Type: A Description of the Theory and Application of the Myers–Briggs Type Indicator', Palo Alto: Consulting Psychologists Press, 1987

Brillouin, L., *La Science et la Théorie de l'Information*, Paris: Masson, 1959

Brooks, D.R. and E.O. Wiley, *Evolution as Entropy: Towards a Unified Theory of Biology*, Chicago: The University of Chicago Press, 1986

Bruner, J.S., 'Personality Dynamics and the Process of Perceiving', in R.R. Blake and G.V. Ramsey, *Perception – An Approach to Personality*, New York: Ronald Press Co., 1951

Bruner, J.S., 'On Perceptual Readiness', *Psychological Review*, 64, 1957, pp. 123–152

Bruner, J.S., *The Process of Education*, Cambridge, Mass.: Harvard University Press, 1960

Bruner, J.S., *On Knowing: Essays for the Left Hand*, New York: Atheneum, 1965

Bruner, J.S., 'The Growth of Representational Processes in Childhood', Paper presented at the 18th International Congress of Psychology, Moscow, 1966; reprinted in J.S. Bruner, *Beyond the Information Given*, pp. 313–324

Bruner, J.S., *Beyond the Information Given: Studies in the Psychology of Knowing*, London: George Allen and Unwin, 1974

Bruner, J.S. and J.L. Postman, 'On the Perception of Incongruity: A Paradigm', *Journal of Personality*, No. 18, September 1949

Bruner, J.S., J.J. Goodnow and G.A. Austin, *A Study of Thinking*, New York: Wiley, 1956

Brus, W., 'Market Socialism', in J. Eatwell, M. Milgate and P. Newman (eds) *Problems of the Planned Economy*, London: Macmillan, 1990, pp. 164–177

Bullock, T.H., 'Signals and Neural Coding', in *The Neurosciences: A Study Program*, New York: Rockefeller University Press, 1967, pp. 347–352

Burnham, J., *The Managerial Revolution*, Bloomington: Indiana University Press, 1960

Bustina, F., *Diez Años de Amistad con Sir Alexander Fleming*, Madrid: Editorial M.A.S., 1961

Butler, R.J., 'Control through Markets, Hierarchies, and Communes: A Transactional Approach to Organizational Analysis', in A. Francis, J. Turk and P. Willman (eds) *Power, Efficiency and Institutions: A Critical Appraisal of the 'Markets and Hierarchies Paradigm'*, London: Heinemann, 1983, pp. 137–158

Butterfield, F., *China: Alive in the Bitter Sea*, London: Hodder and Stoughton, 1982

Butterfield, H., *The Whig Interpretation of History*, Middlesex: Penguin, 1931

Byrd, W.A., 'Contractual Responsibility Systems in Chinese State Owned Industry: A Preliminary Assessment', in N. Campbell (ed.) *Advances in Chinese Industrial Studies*, Greenwich, Connecticut: JAI Press Inc., 1991, pp. 7–36

Campbell, D., 'Evolutionary Epistemology', in P.A. Schlipp (ed.) *The Philosophy of Karl Popper*, La Salle, Illinois: Open Court Publishing, 1974

Carr, E.H., *The Bolshevik Revolution: 1917–1923*, Middlesex: Penguin Books, 1966

Carr-Saunders, A.M. and P.A. Wilson, *The Professions*, London: Frank Cass and Co., 1964

Cass, D. and K. Shell, 'Do Sunspots Matter?', *Journal of Political Economy*, 91, 1983, pp. 193–227

Castañeda, C., *A Separate Reality*, New York: Simon and Schuster, 1971

Caudill, W. and H. Weinstein, 'Maternal Care and Infant Behaviour in Japan and America', *Psychiatry*, 32, 1969, pp. 12–43

Caves, R.E. and M. Uekusa, *Industrial Organization in Japan*, Washington, DC: The Brookings Institution, 1976

Cerella, J., 'Visual Classes and Natural Categories in the Pigeon', *Journal of Experimental Psychology and Human Perception*, 5, 1979, pp. 68–77

Chaitin, G.J., 'Information-Theoretic Computational Complexity', *IEEE Transactions, Information Theory*, 20(10), 1974

Chandler, A.D., *Strategy and Structure: Chapters in the History of the American Industrial Enterprise*, Cambridge, Mass.: The MIT Press, 1962

Chandler, A.D., *The Visible Hand: The Managerial Revolution in American Business*, Cambridge, Mass.: The Belknap Press of Harvard University Press, 1977

Chandler, A.D., *Scale and Scope: The Dynamics of Industrial Capitalism*, Cambridge, Mass.: Harvard University Press, 1990

Chenery, H., 'Process and Production Functions from Engineering Data', in W. Leontief (ed.) *Studies in the Structure of the American Economy*, New York: Oxford University Press, 1953, pp. 229, 301, 317

Cheung, S., 'The Contractual Nature of the Firm', *Journal of Law and Economics*, 3(1), April 1983, pp. 1–21

Child, J., 'The Structure of Earnings in Chinese Enterprises and Some Correlates of their Variation', in J. Child and M. Lockett (eds) *Reform Policies and the Chinese Enterprise*, Advances in Chinese Industrial Studies, Vol. 1(A), Greenwich, Connecticut: JAI Press, 1990

Child, J., *Managing in China during the Age of Reform*, Cambridge: Cambridge University Press, 1994

Child, J. and R. Loveridge, *Information Technology in European Services: Towards a Microelectronic Future*, Oxford: Basil Blackwell, 1990

Child, J. and Y. Lu, 'Industrial Decision Making under China's Reforms 1985–1988', *Organization Studies*, 11, 1990, pp. 321–351

Child, J. and Y. Lu, 'Institutional Constraints on Economic Reform: The Case of Investment Decisions in China', Research Paper in Management Studies, University of Cambridge, August 1992

Child, J. and L. Markoczy, 'Host Country Managerial Behaviour and Learning in Chinese and Hungarian Joint Ventures', *Journal of Management Studies*, 30, 1993

Childe, V.G., *Man Makes Himself*, London: L.A. Watts, 1951

Chomsky, N., *Aspects of the Theory of Syntax*, Cambridge, Mass.: The MIT Press, 1965

Churchland, P.S., *Neurophilosophy: Towards a Unified Science of the Mind/Brain*, Cambridge, Mass.: The MIT Press, 1989

Cipolla, C.M., *The Economic History of World Population*, Middlesex: Penguin Books, 1965

Clark, G., 'The Social Foundations of States', in F.L. Carsten (ed.) *The New Cambridge Modern History: Vol. V, The Ascendancy of France, 1648–1688*, Cambridge: Cambridge University Press, 1961

Clarke, R., *The Japanese Company*, New Haven: Yale University Press, 1979

Clarke, R.W., *Einstein: The Life and Times*, London: Hodder and Stoughton, 1973

Clegg, S.R. and D. Dunkerley, *Organization, Class, and Control*, London: Routledge and Kegan Paul, 1980

Coase, R., 'The Nature of the Firm', *Economica*, NS, 4, 1937, pp. 386–405

Coase, R., 'The Problem of Social Cost', *Journal of Law and Economics*, 3(1), October 1960, pp. 1–44

Cohen, I.B., *The Conservation of Energy and the Principle of Least Action*, New York: Arno, 1981

Cohen, I.B., *Revolution of Science*, Cambridge, Mass.: The Belknap Press of Harvard University Press, 1985

Cole, G.D.H. and R. Postgate, *The Common People: 1746–1946*, London: Methuen, 1949

Cole, R.E., *Japanese Blue Collar: The Changing Tradition*, Berkeley: University of California Press, 1971

Cole, R.E., *Work Mobility and Participation: A Comparative Study of American and Japanese Industry*, Berkeley: University of California Press, 1979

Coleman, D.C., 'Economic Problems and Policies', in F.L. Carsten (ed.) *The New Cambridge Modern History: Vol. V, The Ascendancy of France*, Cambridge: Cambridge University Press, 1961

Collins, H.M., 'Tacit Knowledge and Scientific Networks', in B. Barnes and D. Edge (eds) *Science in Context: Readings in the Sociology of Science*, Milton Keynes: The Open University Press, 1982

Colp, R., 'The Myth of the Marx–Darwin Letter', *History of Political Economy*, 14, 1982, pp. 461–482

Commons, J.R., *Institutional Economics*, Madison: University of Wisconsin Press, 1934

Csikás-Nagy, B., *Revue de l'Est*, III(I), 1972, p. 25, in D. Granick, *Enterprise Guidance in Eastern Europe: A Comparison of Four Socialist Economies*, Princeton, New Jersey: Princeton University Press, 1975, p. 140

Curtis, G.L., 'Big Business and Political Influence', in E.F. Vogel (ed.) *Modern Japanese Organization and Decision-Making*, Tokyo: Charles E. Tuttle Co., 1979

David, P., 'Some New Standards for the Economics of Standardization in the Information Age', in P. Dasgupta and P. Stoneman (eds) *Economic Policy and Technological Performance*, Cambridge: Cambridge University Press, 1987

Davidse, J., 'Characteristics of Growth and Limitations in Electronics', *Technological Forecasting and Social Change*, 24, 1983, pp. 125–153

Dawkins, R., *The Extended Phenotype: The Gene as the Unit of Selection*, Oxford: Oxford University Press, 1982

Dawkins, R., *The Blind Watchmaker*, Middlesex: Penguin Books, 1986

Dawkins, R. and J. Krebs, 'Animal Signals: Information or Manipulation?', in J.R. Krebs and N.B. Davies (eds) *Behavioural Ecology: An Evolutionary Approach*, Oxford: Basil Blackwell, 1978

De la Mettrie, J.O., *L'Homme Machine*, Princeton, 1960 [1748]

de Saussure, F., *Cours de Linguistique Générale*, Paris: Payot, 1972 [1915]

de Tocqueville, A., *De la Democratie en Amérique*, Paris: Gallimard, 1986

de Vivo, G., 'Labour Power', in J. Eatwell *et al.* (eds) *Marxian Economics*, The New Palgrave, London: Macmillan, 1990

Deal, T. and A. Kennedy, *Corporate Cultures: The Rites and Rituals of Corporate Life*, Middlesex: Penguin Books, 1982

Dean, J.W., 'The Dissolution of the Keynesian Consensus', in D. Bell and I. Kristol, *The Crisis in Economic Theory*, New York: Basic Books, 1981, pp. 19–34

Dennett, D.C., 'Intentional Systems', *Journal of Philosophy*, LXVIII(4), 1971, pp. 87–106

Dennett, D., *Brainstorms: Philosophical Essays on Mind and Psychology*, Sussex: Harvester Press, 1981

Deutscher, I., *Stalin: A Political Biography*, Middlesex: Penguin Books, 1966

d'Holbach, Baron (Paul Henri Dietrich), *Système de la Nature*, Paris, 1770

Dijksterhuis, E.J., *The Mechanization of the World Picture: Pythagoras to Newton*, Princeton, New Jersey: Princeton University Press, 1986

DiMaggio, B. and W.W. Powell, 'The Iron Cage Revisited: Institutional Isomorphism and Collective Rationality in Organizational Fields', *American Sociological Review*, 82, 1983, pp. 147–160

Dobzhansky, T., *Mankind Evolving: The Evolution of the Human Species*, New Haven, Connecticut: Yale University Press, 1962

Doi, T., *The Anatomy of Dependence*, Tokyo: Kodansha International, 1977

Dollo, L., 'Les Lois de l'Evolution', *Bull. Belge. Géol.*, 7, 1893, pp. 164–167

Dore, R., *British Factory – Japanese Factory: The Origins of National Diversity in Industrial Relations*, Berkeley: University of California Press, 1973

Dore, R., *Flexible Rigidities: Industrial Policy and Structural Adjustment in the Japanese Economy 1970–80*, London: The Athlone Press, 1988

Dore, R., *Taking Japan Seriously: A Confucian Perspective on Leading Economic Issues*, London: Athlone Press, 1987

Dosi, G. and L. Orsenigo, 'Coordination and Transformation: An Overview of Structures, Behaviours and Change in Evolutionary Environments', in G. Dosi *et al.* (eds) *Technical Change and Economic Theory*, London: Pinter Publishers, 1988

Douglas, M., *Purity and Danger*, London: Routledge and Kegan Paul, 1966

Douglas, M., *Natural Symbols: Explorations in Cosmology*, Middlesex: Penguin Books, 1973

Douglas, M., *How Institutions Think*, London: Routledge and Kegan Paul, 1987   ·

Douglas, M. and B. Isherwood, *The World of Goods: Towards an Anthropology of Consumption*, Middlesex: Penguin Books, 1978

Dubos, R., *Pasteur and Modern Science*, New York: Doubleday, 1960

Duby, G., *Guerriers et Paysans: VIIe–XIIe Siècle: Premier Essor de l'Economie Européenne*, Paris: Gallimard, 1973

Duby, G., *Les Trois Ordres ou l'Imaginaire du Féodalisme*, Paris: Gallimard, 1978

Duhem, P., *La Théorie Physique: Son Objet, sa Structure*, 1914, Paris: Rivière et Cie. (Translated 1953 by Philip Weiner as *The Aim and Structure of Physical Theory*, Princeton, New Jersey: Princeton University Press. Reprinted 1962, New York: Atheneum)

Dumont, L., *Homo Hierarchicus: Le Système des Castes et ses Implications*, Paris: Gallimard, 1966

Durkheim, E., *The Elementary Forms of the Religious Life*, London: Allen and Unwin, 1915

Durkheim, E., *Le Suicide*, Paris: Presses Universitaires de France, 1930

Durkheim, E., *The Division of Labour in Society*, New York: The Free Press, 1933

Durkheim, E., 'The Dualism of Human Nature and its Social Condition', in K. Wolff (ed.) *Emile Durkheim*, Columbus: Ohio State University Press, 1960 [1914], pp. 325–34

Durkheim, E., *The Division of Labour in Society*, New York: The Free Press, 1964 [1893]

Durkheim, E. and M. Mauss, *Primitive Classification*, London: Cohen and West, 1963 [1903]

Eatwell, J., M. Milgate and P. Newman (eds) *Allocation, Information and Markets*, The New Palgrave, London: Macmillan, 1989

Eatwell, J., M. Milgate and P. Newman (eds) *Marxian Economics*, The New Palgrave, London: Macmillan, 1990

Eberhard, W., *A History of China*, Routledge and Kegan Paul, London: 1950

Eckberg, D.L. and L. Hill Jr, 'The Paradigm Concept and Sociology: A Critical Review', *American Sociological Review*, 44, December 1979, pp. 925–937

Eco, U., *Opera Aperta*, Milan: Bompiani, 1962

Eco, U., *A Theory of Semiotics*, Bloomington: Indiana University Press, 1979

Edelman, G.M., 'Group Selection and Phasic Reentrant Signalling: A Theory of Higher Brain Functions', in G.M. Edelman and V.B. Mountcastle, *The Mindful Brain: Cortical Organization and the Group-Selective Theory of Higher Brain Functions*, Cambridge, Mass.: The MIT Press, 1978, pp. 51–100

Edelman, G.M., 'Group Selection as the Basis for Higher Brain Function', in F.O. Schmitt *et al.*, *Organization of the Cerebral Cortex*, Cambridge, Mass.: The MIT Press, 1981, pp. 535–563

Edelman, G.M., *Neural Darwinism: The Theory of Neuronal Group Selection*, Oxford: Oxford University Press, 1987

Edelman, G.M. and L.H. Finkel, 'Neuronal Group Selection in the Cerebral Cortex', in G.M. Edelman *et al.*, *Dynamic Aspects of Neocortical Function*, New York: Wiley, 1984, pp. 653–695

Edelman, G.M. and G.M. Reeke, 'Selective Networks Capable of Representative Transformations, Limited Generalizations, and Associative Memory', *Proc. Natl. Acad. Sci. U.S.A.* 79, 1982, pp. 2091–2095

Eggertsson, T., *Economic Behaviour and Institutions*, Cambridge: Cambridge University Press, 1990

Eisenheart, K.M., 'Agency Theory: An Assessment and Review', *Academy of Management Review*, 14, 1989, pp. 57–74

Eldredge, N., *Unfinished Synthesis: Biological Hierarchies and Modern Evolutionary Thought*, New York: Oxford University Press, 1985

Eliade, M., *Images et Symboles: Essai sur le Symbolisme Magico-religieux*, Paris: Gallimard, 1952

Elias, N., *The Civilizing Process: Vol. 2, State Formation and Civilization*, Oxford: Basil Blackwell, 1939

Ellman, M., 'Josif Vissarionovich Stalin', in J. Eatwell, M. Milgate and P. Newman (eds) *Problems of the Planned Economy*, London: Macmillan, 1990

Elster, J., *Leibnitz et la Formation de l'Esprit Capitaliste*, Paris: Aubier, 1975

Elster, J., *Explaining Technical Change: Studies in Rationality and Social Change*, Cambridge: Cambridge University Press, 1983

Elster, J., *Making Sense of Marx*, Cambridge: Cambridge University Press, 1985

Elster, J. (ed.) *The Multiple Self: Studies in Rationality and Social Change*, Cambridge: Cambridge University Press, 1985

Elton, G.R., *Reform and Reformation: England 1509–1558*, London: Edward Arnold, 1977

Elvin, M., *The Pattern of the Chinese Past*, Stanford: Stanford University Press, 1974

Everett, H. III, '"Relative State" Formulation of Quantum Mechanics', in *Reviews of Modern Physics*, 29(3), July 1957, pp. 454–462

Fairbank, J.K., *The Great Chinese Revolution: 1800–1895*, London: Pan Books, 1987

Fairbank, J.K., E.O. Reischauer and A.M. Craig, *East Asia: The Modern Transformation*, Boston, 1965

Fama, E. and M. Jensen, 'Agency Problems and Residual Claims', *Journal of Law and Economics*, 26, June 1983, pp. 327–349

Farrell, J., 'Information and the Coase Theorem', *Economic Perspectives*, I(2), Fall 1987, pp. 113–129

Feldman, J.A. and D.H. Ballard, 'Connectionist Models and their Properties', *Cognitive Science* 6, 1982, pp. 205–254

Festinger, L., *A Theory of Cognitive Dissonance*, Palo Alto, California: Stanford University Press, 1957

Feyerabend, P.K., 'How to be a Good Empiricist: A Plea for Tolerance in Matters Epistemological', in *Philosophy of Science, The Delaware Seminar*, Vol. 2, B. Baumrin (ed.), New York, 1963, pp. 3–39

Feyerabend, P.K., 'Against Method', in *Minnesota Studies for the Philosophy of Science*, 4, Minnesota: University of Minnesota Press, 1970

Feyerabend, P.K. *Against Method: Outline of an Anarchistic Theory of Knowledge*, London: Verso, 1975

Firth, R. (ed.) *Themes in Economic Anthropology*, London: Tavistock Publications, 1970

Fisher, R.A., *The Genetical Theory of Natural Selection*, Oxford: The Clarendon Press, 1930

Flavell, J.H., *The Developmental Psychology of Jean Piaget*, Princeton, New Jersey: D. Van Nostrand Company, 1963

Fleck, L., *Genesis and Development of a Scientific Fact*, Chicago: The University of Chicago Press, 1979 [1935]

Foster, J., *Evolutionary Macroeconomics*, London: Allen and Unwin, 1987

Foster, M.B., 'The Christian Doctrine of Creation and the Rise of Modern Natural Science', *Mind*, 43, 1934, pp. 446–468

Foucault, M., *Histoire de la Folie à l'Age Classique*, Paris: Editions Gallimard, 1972

Francis, A., 'Markets and Hierarchies: Efficiency or Domination?', in Francis, A., J. Turk and P. Willman (eds) *Power, Efficiency and Institutions: A Critical Appraisal of the 'Markets and Hierarchies Paradigm'*, London: Heinemann, 1983, pp. 105–116

Francis, A., J. Turk and P. Willman (eds) *Power, Efficiency and Institutions: A Critical Appraisal of the 'Markets and Hierarchies Paradigm'*, London: Heinemann, 1983

Freeman, C. and C. Perez, 'Structural Crises of Adjustment: Business Cycles and Investment Behaviour', in G. Dosi *et al.* (eds) *Technical Change and Economic Theory*, London: Pinter Publishers, 1988, pp. 38–66

Frege, G., *The Foundations of Arithmetic*, transl. J.L. Austin, Oxford: Basil Blackwell, 1953 [1884]

Freud, S., *Introductory Lectures on Psychoanalysis*, Middlesex: Penguin Books, 1973

Galbraith, J.K., *The New Industrial State*, London: Hamish Hamilton, 1967

Garratt, R., *The Learning Organization*, London: Fontana, 1987

Garud, R. and A. Kumaraswamy, 'Changing Competitive Dynamics in Network Industries: An Exploration of Sun Microsystems' Open Systems Strategy', *Strategic Management Journal*, 14, 1993, pp. 351–369

Gatwell, J., 'Socially Necessary Technique', in J. Eatwell, M. Milgate and P. Newman (eds) *Marxian Economics*, London: Macmillan, 1990

Geertz, C., *The Interpretation of Cultures: Selected Essays*, New York: Basic Books, 1973

Geertz, C., *Local Knowledge: Further Essays in Interpretative Sociology*, New York: Basic Books, 1983

Gellner, E., 'Economic Interpretation of History', in J. Eatwell, M. Milgate and P. Newman (eds) *Marxian Economics*, The New Palgrave, London: Macmillan, 1990, pp. 148–158

Gernet, J., *Chine et Christianisme: Action et Réaction*, Paris: Gallimard 1982

Giddens, A., *The Constitution of Society: Outline of the Theory of Structuration*, Cambridge: The Polity Press, 1984

Gilder, G., *The Quantum Revolution in Economics and Technology*, New York: Simon and Schuster, 1989

Gilson, E., *La Philosophie du Moyen Age: Tome 1, Des Origines Patristiques à la Fin du XIIème Siècle*, Paris: Payot, 1944

Gingerich, O. (ed.) *The Nature of Scientific Discovery: A Symposium Commemorating the 500th Anniversary of the Birth of Nicolaus Copernicus*, Washington, DC: Smithsonian Institution Press, 1975, pp. 556–573

Goffman, E., *Asylums: Essays on the Social Situation of Mental Patients and Other Inmates*, Middlesex: Penguin Books, 1968

Goldberg, V.P., 'Rational Exchange: Economics and Complex Contracts', *American Behavioural Scientist*, 23(3), January–February 1980, pp. 337–352

Goldstein, K., *The Organism*, New York: American Book Co., 1939

Goodefield, J., *An Imagined World: A Study of Scientific Discovery*, London: Hutchinson, 1981

Goodenough, W., *Description and Comparison in Cultural Anthropology*, Chicago: Aldine Publishing Co., 1970

Goody, J., *The Logic of Writing and the Organization of Society*, Cambridge: Cambridge University Press, 1986

Goody, J., *The Interface between the Written and the Oral*, Cambridge: Cambridge University Press, 1987

Gouldner, A., *Patterns of Industrial Bureaucracy*, Glencoe, Illinois: The Free Press, 1954

Gouldner, A., *The Coming Crisis of Western Sociology*, London: Heinemann, 1970

Granet, M., *La Féodalité Chinoise*, Oslo: Institut pour l'Etude Comparative des Civilisations, 1952

Granick, D., *Enterprise Guidance in Eastern Europe: A Comparison of Four Socialist Economies*, Princeton, New Jersey: Princeton University Press, 1975

Gregory, R.L., *Mind in Science: A History of Explanations in Psychology and Physics*, Middlesex: Penguin Books, 1981

Grossman, S. and J. Stiglitz, 'On the Impossibility of Informationally Efficient Markets', *American Economic Review*, 70(3), June 1980, pp. 393–408

Gruner, R., 'On Evolution and its Relation to Natural Selection', *Dialogue*, 16, 1977, pp. 708–714

Habermas, J., *The Theory of Communicative Action*, 2 vols, Cambridge: Polity Press, 1984, 1987

Hacking, I., 'Experimentation and Scientific Realism', *Philosophical Topics*, 13, 1982, pp. 71–87

Hägerstrand, T., 'Aspects of the Spatial Structure of Social Communication and the Diffusion of Information', Papers of the Regional Science Association, 1966, pp. 27–42

Hägerstrand, T., *Innovation as a Spacial Process*, Chicago: The University of Chicago Press, 1976

Hagstrom, W., *The Scientific Community*, New York: Basic Books, 1965

Hall, E., *Beyond Culture*, New York: Doubleday, 1976

Hamel, G. and C.K. Prahalad, 'Strategic Intent', *Harvard Business Review*, May–June 1989

Hamel, G. and C.K. Prahalad, 'Corporate Imagination and Expeditionary Marketing', *Harvard Business Review*, July–August 1991

Hamel, G., Y. Doz and C.K. Prahalad, 'Collaborate with your Competitors – and Win', *Harvard Business Review*, January–February 1989

Hamilton, D., *Evolutionary Economics: A Study of Change in Economic Thought*, New Brunswick: Transaction Publishers, 1991

Hamilton, G.G., 'Patriarchalism in Imperial China and Western Europe: A Revision of Weber's Sociology of Domination', *Theory and Society*, 13, 1984, pp. 393–425

Hanami, T., *Labour Relations in Japan Today*, Tokyo: Kodansha International, 1981

Handy, C., *The Age of Unreason*, London: Business Books, 1989

Hannan, M. and J. Freeman, *Organizational Ecology*, Cambridge, Mass.: Harvard University Press, 1989

Hanson, N.R., *Patterns of Discovery*, Cambridge: Cambridge University Press, 1965

Harman, P., *Energy, Force and Matter*, Cambridge: Cambridge University Press, 1982

Harris, M., *Cultural Materialism: The Struggle for a Science of Culture*, New York: Vintage Books, 1980

Harris, P.R. and R.T. Moran, *Managing Cultural Differences*, Houston: Gulf Publishing Co., 1979

Harrod, R., *Money*, London: Macmillan, 1969

Hartley, R.V.L., 'Transmission of Information', *Bell System Technical Journal*, July 1928, p. 535

Harvey, O.J., D. Hunt and H. Schroeder, *Conceptual Systems and Personality Organization*, New York: Wiley, 1961

Haugeland, J., *Mind Design: Philosophy, Psychology, Artificial Intelligence*, Cambridge, Mass.: The MIT Press, 1982

Hawken, P., *The Next Economy*, New York: Holt, Rinehart and Winston, 1983, p. 11

Hayek, F., 'The Use of Knowledge in Society', *American Economic Review*, 35, September 1945, pp. 519–530

Hayek, F., *Individualism and the Economic Order*, London: Routledge and Kegan Paul, 1949

Hayek, F., *The Counter-Revolution in Science: Studies on the Abuse of Reason*, Indianapolis: The Liberty Press, 1979

Hayek, F. (ed.) *Collectivist Economic Planning*, London: Routledge and Kegan Paul, 1935

Hebb, D.O., *The Organization of Behaviour*, New York: Wiley, 1949

Heckscher, A., *Mercantilism*, 2 vols; London: Macmillan, 1955 [1935]

Hedley, B., 'Strategy and the Business Portfolio', *Long Range Planning* 10(2), 1977

Heiner, R.A., 'The Origin of Predictable Behaviour', *American Economic Review*, 73(4), 1983, pp. 560–574

Heisenberg, W., *Physics and Beyond*, New York: Harper and Row, 1971

Henderson, R.M. and K.B. Cark, 'Architectural Innovation: The Reconfiguring of Existing Product Technologies and the Failure of Established Firms', *Administrative Science Quarterly*, 35, 1990, pp. 9–30.

Henry, Jules, *Culture against Man*, Middlesex: Penguin Books, 1972

Herrnstein, R.J., 'Stimuli and the Texture of Experience', *Neurosci. Biobehav. Rev.*, 6, 1982, pp. 105–117

Herrnstein, R.J., 'Riddles of Natural Categorization', *Philosophical Transactions of the Royal Society London (Biology)*, 308, 1985, pp. 129–144

Herrnstein, R.J. *et al.*, 'Natural Concepts in Pigeons', *Journal of Experimental Psychology and Animal Behavioural Processes*, 2, 1976, pp. 285–301

Heskett, J., *Managing in the Service Economy*, Cambridge, Mass.: Harvard Business School Press, 1986

Hesse, M., 'Is There an Independent Observation Language?', in *The Nature and Function of Scientific Theories*, R. Colodny (ed.), Pittsburgh: University of Pittsburgh Press, 1970, pp. 36–77

Hicks, E., 'On the Rate of Gain of Information', *Quarterly Journal of Experimental Psychology*, 4, 1952, pp. 11–26

Hilgard, E., R.C. Atkinson and R.L. Atkinson, *Introduction to Psychology*, New York: Harcourt Brace Jovanovich, 1971

Hinton, G.E. and T.J. Sejnowski, 'Learning and Relearning in Bolzmann Machines', in J.L. McClelland and D.E. Rumelhart (eds) *Parallel Distributed Processing: Explorations in the Microstructure of Cognition*, Vol. 2, Cambridge, Mass.: MIT Press, 1986

Hinton, G.E. *et al.*, 'Distributed Representations', in D.E. Rumelhart and J.L. McClelland (eds) *Parallel Distributed Processing: Explorations in the Microstructure of Cognition*, Vol. 1, Cambridge, Mass.: MIT Press, 1986

Hirschleifer, J., 'The Private and Social Value of Information and the Reward to Inventive Activity', *American Economic Review*, 61, 1971, pp. 561–547

Hirshmeyer, J., 'The Japanese Spirit of Enterprise (1867–1970)', Seminar in Smaller Industries Development, Nagoya International Training Centre, Japan International Cooperation Agency, 15 May 1978

Hirshmeyer, J. and T. Yui, *The Development of Japanese Business: 1600–1980*, London: Allen and Unwin, 1981

Hofstadter, D.R., *Gödel, Escher, Bach: An Eternal Golden Braid*, New York: Basic Books, 1979

Hofstede, G., *Culture's Consequences: International Differences in Work-Related Values*, Beverly Hills: Sage Publications, 1980

Hofstede, G. and M.H. Bond, 'Confucius and Economic Growth: New Trends in Culture's Consequences', *Organizational Dynamics*, 16(4), 1988, pp. 4–21

Hogarth, R. and M.W. Reder (eds) *Rational Choice: The Contrast between Economics and Psychology*, Chicago: The University of Chicago Press, 1987

Hollis, M. and S. Lukes, *Rationality and Relativism*, Oxford: Basil Blackwell, 1982

Holton, G., *Thematic Origins of Scientific Thought: Kepler to Einstein*, Cambridge, Mass.: Harvard University Press, 1973

Holton, G., *The Scientific Imagination: Case Studies*, Cambridge: Cambridge University Press, 1978

Holton, G., *The Advancement of Science and its Burdens: The Jefferson Lectures and Other Essays*, Cambridge: Cambridge University Press, 1986

Hopfield, J.J., 'Neurons with Graded Response have Collective Computational Properties like Those of Two-state Neurons', *Proceedings of the National Academy of Sciences, U.S.A.*, 81, 1984, pp. 3088–3092

Howard Smith, D., *Confucius and Confucianism*, London: Paladin, 1974

Howson, C. and P. Urbach, *Scientific Reasoning: A Bayesian Approach*, La Salle, Illinois: Open Court, 1989

Hsu, F.L.K., *Iemoto: The Heart of Japan*, Cambridge, Mass.: Wiley, 1975

Hsu, I.C.Y., *The Rise of Modern China*, Hong Kong: Oxford University Press, 1982

Hughes, T.P., 'The Evolution of Large Technological Systems', in W.E. Bijker, T.P. Hughes and T. Pinch (eds) *The Social Construction of Technological Systems*, Cambridge, Mass.: The MIT Press.

Hull, D., *Science as a Process: An Evolutionary Account of the Social and Conceptual Development of Science*, Chicago: The University of Chicago Press, 1988

Husserl, E., *Ideas: General Introduction to Pure Phenomenology*, London: Collier-Macmillan, 1962

Huwicz, L., 'Centralization and Decentralization in Economic Processes', in A. Eckstein (ed.) *Comparison of Economic Systems*, Berkeley: University of California Press, 1971

Irvine, J., *Evaluating Applied Research: Lessons from Japan*, London: Pinter Publishers, 1988

Jackson, J.A. (ed.) *Professions and Professionalization*, Cambridge: Cambridge University Press, 1970

Jackson, J.H., *Clinical and Physiological Researches on the Nervous System*, London: Churchill. Contains a reprinting of 'On the Anatomical and Physiological Localization of Movement in the Brain', first published in *The Lancet*, 1873, i: 84–85.

Jacob, M., *The Cultural Meaning of the Scientific Revolution*, New York: Alfred Knopf, 1988

Jacoby, M., *Individuation and Narcissism: The Psychology of Self in Jung and Kohut*, London: Routledge and Kegan Paul, 1985

James, W., *Principles of Psychology*, Vol. II, New York: Henry, 1890

Janis, I.L., *Groupthink: Psychological Studies of Policy Decisions and Fiascos*, Boston: Houghton Mifflin Co., 1982

Jensen, M. and W. Meckling, 'Theory of the Firm: Managerial Behaviour, Agency Costs, and Capital Structure', *Journal of Financial Economics*, 3(4), October 1976, pp. 305–360

Jessop, R., 'Mode of Production', in J. Eatwell, M. Milgate and P. Newman, *Marxian Economics*, The New Palgrave, London: Macmillan, 1990, pp. 289–296

Jevons, W.S., *Principles of Economics*, London: Macmillan, 1905

Johanson, J. and L.G. Mattson, 'Interorganizational Relations in Industrial Systems: A Network Approach Compared with the Transaction Cost Approach', in G. Thompson, J. Frances, R. Levacic and J. Mitchell (eds) *Markets, Hierarchies, and Networks: The Coordination of Social Life*, London: Sage, 1991, p. 262

Johnson, C., *MITI and the Japanese Miracle: The Growth of Industrial Policy, 1925–1975*, Stanford, California: Stanford University Press, 1982

Johnson, H.T. and R. Kaplan, *Relevance Lost: The Rise and Fall of Management Accounting*, Cambridge, Mass.: Harvard Business School Press, 1987

Johnson, T.J., *Professions and Power*, London: Macmillan, 1972

Johnson-Laird, P., *Mental Models: Towards a Cognitive Science of Language, Inference, and Consciousness*, Cambridge: Cambridge University Press, 1983

Jung, C.G., *The Integration of the Personality*, London: Routledge and Kegan Paul, 1940

Jung, C.G., *The Archetypes of the Collective Unconscious. Collected Works*, Princeton, New Jersey: Princeton University Press, 1954

Jung, C.G., *Collected Works: Vol. 6, Psychological Types*, Princeton, New Jersey: Princeton University Press, 1971

Kagan, J. *et al.*, 'Information Processing in the Child: Significance of Analytic and Reflective Attitudes', *Psychological Monographs*, 78(1), 1964

Kagan, J. and N. Kogan, 'Individual Variations in Cognitive Processes', *Carmichael's Manual of Child Psychology* (3rd edn), Vol. 1, P.H. Mussen (ed.), New York: John Wiley and Sons, 1970

Kagono, T. *et al.*, *Nihon Kigyo no Senryaku to Soshiki* (Strategy and Structure of Japanese Business), Tokyo: Organization Science, Summer 1981

Kahneman, D., P. Slovic and A. Tversky, *Judgment under Uncertainty: Heuristics and Biases*, Cambridge: Cambridge University Press, 1982

Kamata, S., *Japan in the Passing Lane*, New York: Pantheon Books, 1982

Karnow, S., *Mao and China: Inside China's Cultural Revolution*, Middlesex: Penguin Books, 1972

Katz, E. and P.F. Lazarsfeld, *Personal Influence*, Glencoe, Illinois: The Free Press, 1955

Katz, M.L. and C. Shapiro, 'Technology Adoption in the Presence of Network Externalities', *Journal of Political Economy*, 94, 1985, pp. 822–841

Kautsky, K., *Die proletarische Revolution und ihr Programm*, Stuttgart: I.H.W. Dieta Nachfolger, 1922

Kelly, G.A., *A Theory of Personality: The Psychology of Personal Constructs*, New York: W.W. Norton and Co, 1963

Kelly, G.A., 'Who Needs a Theory of Citizenship?', *Daedalus*, Fall 1979, p. 25

Keynes, J.M., *The General Theory of Employment, Interest, and Money*, London: Macmillan, 1936

Kidder, T., *The Soul of a New Machine*, New York: Avon Books, 1981

Kirkpatrick, S., C.D. Gelatt and M.P. Vecchi, 'Optimization by Simulated Annealing', *Science*, 220, 1983, pp. 671–680

Kirzner, I., *Competition and Entrepreneurship*, Chicago: The University of Chicago Press, 1973

Kirzner, I., *Perception, Opportunity, and Profit: Studies in the Theory of Entrepreneurship*, Chicago: The University of Chicago Press, 1979

Kirzner, I., 'Uncertainty, Discovery and Human Action', in I. Kirzner (ed.) *Method, Process and Austrian Economics: Essays in Honour of Ludwig von Mises*, Lexington, Mass.: D.C. Heath, 1982

Kluckhohn, C., *Culture and Behaviour*, New York, 1962

Knight, F., *Risk, Uncertainty, and Profit*, New York: Houghton Mifflin Co., 1921

Knorr-Cetina, K.D., *The Manufacture of Knowledge: An Essay on the Constructivist and Contextual Nature of Science*, Oxford: Pergamon Press, 1981

Kodama, F., 'Technology Fusion and the New R and D', *Harvard Business Review*, July–August 1992, pp. 70–78

Koestler, A., *The Sleepwalkers: A History of Man's Changing Vision of the Universe*, Middlesex: Penguin Books, 1959

Kohonen, T. *et al.*, 'A Principle of Neural Associative Memory', *Neuroscience*, 2, 1977, pp. 1065–1076

Kolb, D., *The Learning Style Inventory: Technical Manual*, Boston, Mass.: McBer and Co., 1976

Kono, T., *Strategy and Structure of Japanese Enterprises*, London: Macmillan, 1984

Koppel, M., and H. Atlan, 'Les Gènes: Programme ou Données? Le Rôle de la Signification dans les Mesures de la Complexité', in F.F. Soulié (ed.) *Les Théories de la Complexité: Autour de l'Oeuvre d'Henri Atlan*, Paris: Seuil, 1991, pp. 188–204

Kornai, J., *Growth, Shortage and Efficiency: A Macrodynamic Model of the Socialist Economy*, Oxford: Basil Blackwell, 1982

Kornai, J., *Vision and Reality, Market and State: New Studies on the Socialist Economy and Society*, Hemel Hempstead: Harvester-Wheatsheaf, 1990

Kowalik, T., 'Central Planning', in J. Eatwell, M. Milgate and P. Newman (eds) *Problems of the Planned Economy*, London: Macmillan, 1990

Kozminski, A., 'Framework for Comparative Studies of Management in Post-Socialist Economies', *Studies in Comparative Communism*, 4, 1991, pp. 413–424

Krauss, L.B. and S. Sekiguchi, 'Japan and the World Economy', in H. Patrick and H. Rosovsky (eds) *Asia's New Giant: How the Japanese Economy Works*, Washington, DC: The Brookings Institution, 1976, pp. 383–458

Kroeber, A.L., *Anthropology*, New York: Harcourt, Brace, 1948

Kroeber, A. and C. Kluckhohn, *Culture: A Critical Review of Concepts and Definitions*, Papers of the Peabody Museum of American Archaeology and Ethnology, Vol. 47, Cambridge, Mass.: Harvard University Press, 1952

Kuhn, T.S., *The Copernican Revolution: Planetary Astronomy in the Development of Western Thought*, Cambridge, Mass.: Harvard University Press, 1957

Kuhn, T.S., 'The Function of Measurement in Modern Physical Science', *Isis*, 52, 1961, pp. 161–193

Kuhn, T.S., *The Structure of Scientific Revolutions*, Chicago: The University of Chicago Press, 1962

Kuhn, T.S., 'Second Thoughts on Paradigms', in F. Suppe (ed.) *The Structure of Scientific Theories*, Urbana: The University of Illinois Press, 1974, pp. 459–482

Kuhn, T.S., *The Essential Tension: Selected Studies in Scientific Tradition and Change*, Chicago: The University of Chicago Press, 1977

Küppers, B.O., *Information and the Origin of Life*; Cambridge, Mass.: The MIT Press, 1990

Labov, W., 'The Logic of Nonstandard English', *Georgetown Monographs on Language and Linguistics*, 22, 1969, pp. 1–22, 26–31

Lacan, J., *Ecrits*, Paris: Seuil (Vol. 1, 1966: Vol. 2, 1971)

Lachmann, L., *Capital, Expectations, and the Market Process*, Kansas City: Sheed, Andrews and McMeel, 1977

Lakatos, I., 'History of Science and its Rational Reconstructions', in R.C. Buck and R.S. Cohen (eds) P.S.A. *Boston Studies in the Philosophy of Science*, 8, Dordrecht: Reidel, 1971, pp. 91–135

Lakatos, I., *Philosophical Papers: Vol. 1, The Methodology of Scientific Research Programmes; Vol. 2, Mathematics, Science and Epistemology*, Cambridge: Cambridge University Press, 1978

Lakatos, I. and A. Musgrave (eds) *Criticism and the Growth of Knowledge*, Cambridge: Cambridge University Press, 1980

Laky, T., 'Enterprises in a Bargaining Position', *Acta Oeconomica*, 3–4, 1979, pp. 227–246

Laky, T., 'Realities and Potentialities of the Autonomous Sector', in B. Dallago, G. Ajani and B. Grancelli (eds) *Privatization and Entrepreneurship in Post Socialist Countries*, London: Macmillan, 1992

Lange, O., 'On the Economic Theory of Socialism', *Review of Economic Studies*, 4 (Pt. I, October 1936, pp. 53–71; Pt. II, February 1937, pp. 123–142)

Lange, O., and F.M. Taylor (eds) *On the Economic Theory of Socialism*, Minneapolis: University of Minnesota Press, 1938

Langley, P., H.A. Simon, G.L. Bradshaw and J.M. Zytkow, *Scientific Discovery:*

Computational Explorations of the Creative Process, Cambridge, Mass.: The MIT Press, 1987

Lashley, K.S., 'In Search of the Engram', in *Society of Experimental Biology Symposium No. 4: Psychological Mechanisms in Animal Behaviour*, London: Cambridge University Press, 1950, pp. 478–505

Laslett, P., *The World We have Lost*, London: Methuen and Co., 1971

Laudan, L., *Progress and its Problems: Towards a Theory of Scientific Growth*, Berkeley: University of California Press, 1977

Lawrence, P. and C. Vlachoutsicos (eds) *Behind the Factory Walls: Decision Making in Soviet and US Enterprises*, Boston, Mass.: Harvard University Press, 1990

Lawson, T., 'The Relative Nature of Knowledge and Economic Analysis', *The Economic Journal*, 97, December 1987, pp. 951–970

Layzer, D., *Cosmogenesis: The Growth of Order in the Universe*, Oxford: Oxford University Press, 1990

Leach, E., *Culture and Communication: The Logic by Which Symbols are Connected*, Cambridge: Cambridge University Press, 1976

Lebra, T.S., *Japanese Patterns of Behaviour*, Honolulu: The University Press of Hawaii, 1976

Lee, H.Y., *The Politics of the Cultural Revolution: A Case Study*, Berkeley: University of California Press, 1978

Lenin, V.I., *What is to be Done? Burning Questions of our Movement*, Beijing: Foreign Language Press, 1975

Lenin, V.I., *Imperialism, the Highest Stage of Capitalism: A Popular Outline*, Beijing: Foreign Language Press, 1975

Lerner, A., 'A Note on Socialist Economies', *Review of Economic Studies*, 4, 1936, pp. 72–76

Lerner, D., *The Passing of Traditional Society*, New York: The Free Press, 1958

Lettvin, J.Y., H.R. Maturana, W.S. McCulloch and W.H. Pitts, 'What the Frog's Eye Tells the Frog's Brain', *Proceedings of the IRE*, 47(11), November 1959, pp. 1940–1959

Levenson, J.R., 'The Amateur Ideal in Ming and Early Ch'ing Society: Evidence from Painting', in J.K. Fairbank (ed.) *Chinese Thought and Institutions*, Chicago: The University of Chicago Press, 1957, p. 321

Levenson, J.R., *Confucianism and its Modern Fate: A Trilogy*, Berkeley: University of California Press, 1958

Lévi-Strauss, C., *Les Structures Elémentaires de la Parenté*, Paris: Plon, 1949

Lévi-Strauss, C., *La Pensée Sauvage*, Paris: Plon, 1962

Levitt, T., 'The Globalization of Markets', *Harvard Business Review*, May–June 1983

Linton, R., *The Study of Man*, New York: Appleton Century, 1936

Lippi, M., 'On the Dynamics of Aggregate Macroequations: From Simple Micro-behaviour to Complex Macrorelationships', in G. Dosi *et al.* (eds) *Technical Change and Economic Theory*, London: Pinter Publishers, 1988, p. 171

Littlechild, S., 'Three Types of Market Processes', in R.N. Langlois (ed.) *Economics as a Process: Essays in the New Institutional Economics*, Cambridge: Cambridge University Press, 1986

Llinás, R., '"Mindness" as a Functional State of the Brain', in C. Blakemore and S. Greenfield (eds) *Mind Matter*, Oxford: Basil Blackwell, 1987

Loasby, B., 'Organization, Competition, and the Growth of Knowledge', in R. Langlois (ed.) *Economics as a Process: Essays in the New Institutional Economics*, Cambridge: Cambridge University Press, 1986

Lockwood, W.W., *The Economic Development of Japan: Growth and Structural*

Change, Princeton, New Jersey: Princeton University Press, 1968

Lotka, A.J., *Elements of Mathematical Biology*, New York: Dover, 1956

Lucas, R.E. and T.J. Sargent (eds) *Rational Expectations and Econometric Practice*, Minneapolis: University of Minnesota Press, 1980

Luria, A.R., *Higher Cortical Functions in Man*, New York: Basic Books, 1966

Luria, A.R., *The Mind of a Mnemonist*, London: Jonathan Cape, 1969

McClelland, J.L., D.E. Rumelhart and G.E Hinton, 'The Appeal of Parallel Distributed Processing', in D.E. Rumelhart and J.L. McClelland (eds) *Parallel Distributed Processing: Explorations in the Microstructure of Cognition*, Vol. 1, Cambridge, Mass.: MIT Press, 1986

McClelland, J.L. and D.E. Rumelhart, 'An Interactive Activation Model of Context Effects in Letter Perceptions: Part 1. An Account of Basic Findings', *Psychological Review*, 88, 1981, pp. 375–407

Macdonald, S., 'Information Networks and the Exchange of Information', in C. Antonelli (ed.) *The Economics of Information Networks*, Amsterdam: North-Holland, 1992

Macfarlane, G., *Alexander Fleming: The Man and the Myth*, Oxford: Oxford University Press, 1984

Machlup, F., *The Production and Distribution of Knowledge in the USA*, Princeton, New Jersey: Princeton University Press, 1972

MacKay, D., *Information, Mechanism and Meaning*, Cambridge, Mass.: The MIT Press, 1969

MacMillan, I., M.L. McCaffery and G.V. Wijk, 'Competitors' Responses to Easily Imitated New Products: Exploring Commercial Banking Product Introductions', *Strategic Management Journal*, 6, 1985, pp. 75–86

Macpherson, C., *The Political Theory of Possessive Individualism: Hobbes to Locke*, Oxford: Oxford University Press, 1962

Maddison, A., *Phases of Capitalist Development*, New York: Oxford University Press, 1982

Malinowski, B., *A Scientific Theory of Culture and Other Essays*, New York: Oxford University Press, 1961

Manddlebaum, D. (ed.) *Selected Writings of Edward Sapir*, Berkeley and Los Angeles, 1949

Manheim, K., *Ideology and Utopia*, London: Routledge and Kegan Paul, 1960

Mann, S., *Local Merchants and the Chinese Bureaucracy, 1750–1950*, Stanford, California: Stanford University Press, 1987

March, J. and H.A. Simon, *Organizations*, New York: John Wiley and Sons, 1958

Margolis, H., *Selfishness, Altruism, and Rationality: A Theory of Social Choice*, Chicago: The University of Chicago Press, 1982

Marin, B. and R. Mayntz (eds) *Policy Networks: Empirical Evidence and Theoretical Considerations*, Frankfurt am Main: Campus Verlag, 1991

Markoczy, L., 'Managerial and Organizational Learning in Hungarian and Western Joint Ventures', Research paper, Judge Institute of Management Studies, University of Cambridge, March 1992

Marris, R., *The Economic Theory of Managerial Capitalism*, Glencoe, Illinois: The Free Press, 1964

Marschak, J., 'Remarks on the Economics of Information', *Contributions to Scientific Research in Management*, Los Angeles: Western Data Processing Center, University of California, 1959, pp. 79–98

Marsh, R.M. and H. Manari, *Modernization and the Japanese Factory*, Princeton, New Jersey: Princeton University Press, 1976

Marshall, A., *Principles of Economics*, London: Macmillan, 1947

Martin, B. and J. Irvine, *Resarch Foresight: Priority Setting in Science*, London: Pinter Publishers, 1989

Martindale, D., *The Nature and Types of Sociological Theories*, London: Routledge and Kegan Paul, 1967

Marx, K., *A Contribution to the Critique of Political Economy*, London: Kegan Paul, 1904

Marx, K., *Economic and Philosophical Manuscripts of 1844*, London: Lawrence and Wishart, 1970

Marx, K., *Capital: A Critique of Political Economy*, London: Lawrence and Wishart, 1972

Marx, K. and F. Engels, *Selected Works*, Vol. 2, Moscow: Foreign Language Publishing House, 1962

Marx, K. and F. Engels, *The German Ideology*, London: Lawrence and Wishart, 1965

Masterman, M., 'The Nature of a Paradigm', in I. Lakatos and A. Musgrave (eds) *Criticism and the Growth of Knowledge*, Cambridge: Cambridge University Press, 1970, pp. 59–90

Maturana, H.R. and F.J. Varela, *Autopoiesis and Cognition: The Realization of the Living*, Boston: D. Reidel, 1980

Maynard-Smith, J., 'The Structure of Neo-Darwinism', in C.H. Waddington (ed.) *Towards a Theoretical Biology* (Vol. 2), Chicago: Aldine Publishing Co., 1970, pp. 82–89

Mayr, E., *The Growth of Biological Thought: Diversity, Evolution, and Inheritance*, Cambridge, Mass.: The Belknap Press of Harvard University Press, 1982

Mead, G.H., *Mind, Self and Society: From the Standpoint of a Social Behaviourist*, Chicago: The University of Chicago Press, 1934

Meadows, D.H., D. Meadows, J. Randers and W.W. Behrens III, *The Limits to Growth: A Report on the Club of Rome's Project on the Predicament of Mankind*, London: Earth Island, 1972

Menger, C., *Problems of Economics and Sociology*, Urbana: The University of Illinois Press, 1963 [1885]

Merton, R.K., *Social Theory and Social Structure*, Glencoe, Illinois: The Free Press, 1957

Merton, R.K., 'Priorities in Scientific Discovery', *American Sociological Review* 22(6), December 1957, pp. 635–659

Merton, R.K., 'Insiders and Outsiders: A Chapter in the Sociology of Knowledge', *American Journal of Sociology*, 77, July 1972, pp. 9–47

Meyerson, R.B., 'Mechanism Design', in J. Eatwell, M. Milgate and P. Newman (eds) *Allocation, Information and Markets*, The New Palgrave, London: Macmillan, 1989, pp. 191–206

Michels, R., *Political Parties*, New York: Dover, 1959

Miller, A.I., *Imagery in Scientific Thought: Creating 20th Century Physics*, Cambridge, Mass.: The MIT Press, 1987

Miller, G.A., 'The Magical Number Seven, Plus or Minus Two: Some Limits on our Capacity for Processing Information', *Psychological Review*, 63(2), March 1956, pp. 81–96

Minsky, M., 'A Framework for Representing Knowledge', in P.H. Winston (ed.) *The Psychology of Computer Vision*, New York: McGraw-Hill, 1975, pp. 211–277

Mintzberg, H., 'Crafting Strategy', *Harvard Business Review*, July–August 1987

Mirowski, P., *More Heat than Light: Economics as Social Physics, Physics as Nature's Economics*, Cambridge: Cambridge University Press, 1989

Moles, A., *Information Theory and Esthetic Perception*, Urbana: University of Illinois Press, 1968

Monod, J., *Le Hasard et la Nécessité: Essai sur la Philosophie Naturelle de la Biologie Moderne*, Paris: Seuil, 1970

Moore, B. Jr, *Social Origins of Dictatorship and Democracy: Lord and Peasant in the Making of the Modern World*, Middlesex: Penguin Books, 1966

Moore, C. (ed.) *The Japanese Mind; Essentials of Japanese Philosophy and Culture*, Tokyo: Charles Tuttle Co., 1967

Morin, E., *Le Paradigme Perdu: La Nature Humaine*, Paris: Editions du Seuil, 1973

Morin, E., *La Méthode: Vol. 1, La Nature de la Nature*, Paris: Seuil, 1977

Morris, C., *Signification and Signifcance*, Cambridge, Mass.: The MIT Press, 1964

Moulder, Frances V., *Japan, China and the Modern World Economy: Towards a Reinterpretation of East Asian Development ca. 1600–1918*, Cambridge: Cambridge University Press, 1977

Mowery, D.C. and N. Rosenberg, *Technology and the Pursuit of Economic Growth*, Cambridge: Cambridge University Press, 1989

Munro, P.W., 'State Dependent Factors Influencing Neural Plasticity: A Partial Account of the Critical Period', in J.L. McClelland and D.E. Rumelhart (eds) *Parallel Distributed Processing: Explorations in the Microstructure of Cognition*, Vol. 1, Cambridge, Mass.: MIT Press, 1986

Munz, P, *Our Knowledge of the Growth of Knowledge: Popper or Wittgenstein?*, London: Routledge and Kegan Paul, 1985

Naisbitt, J., *Megatrends: Ten New Directions Transforming our Lives*, New York: Warner Books, 1982

Nakane, C., *Japanese Society*, Middlesex: Penguin Books, 1973

Nelson, R., 'Production Sets, Technological Knowledge, and R and D: Fragile and Overworked Constructs for Analysis of Productivity Growth?', *American Economic Association*, 70(2), May 1980, pp. 62–71

Nelson, R. and S.G. Winter, *An Evolutionary Theory of Economic Change*, Cambridge, Mass.: The Belknap Press of Harvard University Press, 1982

Nersessian, N., *Faraday to Einstein*, Dordrecht: Martinus Nijhoff, 1984

Newall, A. and H.A. Simon, *Human Problem Solving*, Englewood Cliffs, New Jersey: Prentice-Hall, 1972, p. 792

Nicolis, G. and I. Prigogine, *Exploring Complexity: An Introduction*, New York: W.H. Freeman and Co., 1989

Nolan, P., 'China's Economic Reforms', in J. Eatwell, M. Milgate and and P. Newman (eds) *Problems of the Planned Economy*, London: Macmillan, 1987

Nordlinger, E.A., *On the Autonomy of the Democratic State*, Cambridge, Mass.: Harvard University Press, 1981

Norman, D.A., 'Twelve Issues for Cognitive Science', in D.A. Norman (ed.) *Perspectives on Cognitive Science*, Hillsdale, New Jersey: Lawrence Erlbaum Associates, 1981, pp. 265–295

Norman, D.A., 'Reflections on Cognition and Parallel Distributed Processing', in J.L. McClelland and D.E. Rumelhart, *Parallel Distributed Processing: Explorations in the Microstructure of Cognition*, Vol. 2, Cambridge, Mass.: The MIT Press, 1986, pp. 531–546

Norman, D.A. and D.G. Bobrow, 'On the Role of Active Memory Processes in Perception and Cognition', in C.N. Cofer (ed.) *The Structure of Human Memory*, San Francisco: Freeman, 1976, pp. 114–132

North, D., *Structure and Change in Economic History*, New York: W.W. Norton & Co., 1981

North, D., *Institutions, Institutional Change and Economic Performance*, Cambridge: Cambridge University Press, 1990

Nozick, R., *Anarchy, State and Utopia*, Oxford: Basil Blackwell, 1974

Nyquist, H., 'Certain Factors Affecting Telegraph Speed', *Bell System Technical Journal*, April 1924, p. 324

Okimoto, D.I., *Between MITI and the Market: Japanese Industrial Policy for High Technology*, Stanford, California: Stanford University Press, 1989

Olson, M., *The Logic of Collective Action: Public Goods and the Theory of Groups*, Cambridge, Mass.: Harvard University Press, 1971

Olson, M., *The Rise and Decline of Nations: Economic Growth, Stagflation and Social Rigidities*, New Haven, Connecticut: Yale University Press, 1982

Ornstein, R., *Multimind: A New Way of Looking at Human Behaviour*, London: Macmillan, 1986

Orwell, G., *Nineteen Eighty-Four*, Middlesex: Penguin Books, 1954

Ouchi, W., 'Markets, Bureaucracies and Clans', *Administrative Science Quarterly*, 25(1), March 1980, pp. 129–141

Ouchi, W., *Theory 2: How American Business Can Meet the Japanese Challenge*, Reading, Mass.: Addison-Wesley Publishing Co., 1981

Paine, R.T. and A. Soper, *The Art and Architecture of Japan*, Middlesex: Penguin Books, 1955

Pais, A., *'Subtle is the Lord . . .': The Science and the Life of Albert Einstein*, Oxford: Oxford University Press, 1982

Pais, A., *Inward Bound: Of Matter and Forces in the Physical World*, Oxford: Oxford University Press, 1986

Papert, S.A., 'The Mathematical Unconscious', in J. Wechsler (ed.) *On Aesthetics in Science*, Cambridge, Mass.: The MIT Press, 1978

Parsons, T., *The Social System*, London: Routledge and Kegan Paul, 1951

Pascale, R.T. and A. Athos, *The Art of Japanese Management: Applications for American Executives*, New York: Warner Books, 1981

Passin, H., *Society and Education in Japan*, Tokyo: Kodansha International, 1965

Pavitt, K., 'Some Foundations for a Theory of the Large Innovating Firm', in G. Dosi, R. Giannetti and P.A. Toninelli (eds) *Technology and Enterprise in a Historical Perspective*, Oxford: The Clarendon Press, 1992

Peck, M., 'Technology', in H. Patrick and H. Rosovsky (eds) *Asia's New Giant: How the Japanese Economy Works*, Washington, DC: The Brookings Institution, 1976, pp. 582–583

Pelikan, P., 'Can the Innovation System of Capitalism be Outperformed?', in G. Dosi *et al.* (eds) *Technical Change and Economic Theory*, London: Pinter Publishers, 1988, pp. 370–398

Pellionisz, A. and R. Llinás, 'Tensor Network Theory of the Metaorganization of Functional Geometries in the Central Nervous System', *Neuroscience*, 16, 1985, pp. 245–273

Penrose, E., *The Theory of the Growth of the Firm*, New York: Wiley, 1958

Penrose, R., *The Emperor's New Mind: Concerning Computers, Minds, and the Laws of Physics*, London: Vintage, 1989

Percival, I., 'The Order in Chaos', *New Scientist*, 8 July 1989

Perez, C., 'Microelectronics, Long Waves, and World Structural Change: New Perspectives for Developing Countries', *World Development*, 13(3), pp. 441–463, 1985

Perkins, D.H., *Agricultural Development in China: 1368–1968*, Chicago: The Aldine Press, 1969

Peterson, W.J., 'Fang I-Chih's Western Learning', in W.T. de Bary (ed.) *The Unfolding of Neo-Confucianism*, New York: Columbia University Press, 1975, pp. 398–399

Pevsner, N., *The Englishness of English Art*, Middlesex: Penguin Books, 1956

Pfeffer, J., *The External Control of Organizations: A Resource Dependency View*, New York: Harper and Row, 1978

Piaget, J., *Plays, Dreams, and Imitations in Childhood*, New York: W.W. Norton and Co., 1962

Piaget, J., *Biologie et Connaissance: Essai sur les Relations entre les Régulations Organiques et les Processus Cognitifs*, Paris: Gallimard, 1967

Piaget, J., *Structuralism*, Routledge and Kegan Paul, 1971

Pierce, C.S., 'Questions Concerning Certain Faculties Claimed for Man', *Journal of Speculative Philosophy*, 2, 1868, pp. 103–114

Pinchot, G. III, *Intrapreneuring*, New York: Harper and Row, 1985

Piore, M. and C. Sabel, *The Second Industrial Divide*, New York: Basic Books, 1984

Pipes, R., *The Russian Revolution: 1899–1919*, London: Fontana, 1992

Pirenne, H., *Medieval Cities: Their Origin and the Revival of Trade*, Princeton, New Jersey: Princeton University Press, 1925

Pitts, W.H. and W.S. McCulloch, 'How We Know Universals: The Perception of Auditory and Visual Form', *Bulletin of Mathematical Biophysics*, 9, 1947, pp. 127–147

Poincaré, H., *Science and Method*, New York: Dover, n.d. [1908]

Polanyi, K., *The Great Transformation: The Political and Economic Origins of our Time*, Boston: Beacon Press, 1944

Polanyi, K., C.M. Arensberg and H.W. Pearson (eds) *Trade and Market in the Early Empires: Economies in History and Theory*, Chicago: Gateway Edition, 1957

Polanyi, M., *Personal Knowledge: Towards a Post-Critical Philosophy*, London: Routledge and Kegan Paul, 1958

Popper, K.R., *The Open Society and its Enemies: Vol. 1, Plato; Vol. 2, Hegel and Marx*, London: Routledge and Kegan Paul, 1945

Popper, K.R., *The Logic of Scientific Discovery*, London: Hutchinson, 1959

Popper, K.R., *Objective Knowledge: An Evolutionary Approach*, Oxford: The Clarendon Press, 1972

Popper, K.R., *The Open Universe: An Argument for Indeterminism*, London: Hutchinson, 1982

Popper, K.R., *Realism and the Aim of Science*, London: Hutchinson, 1983

Popper, K.R. and J.C. Eccles, *The Self and its Brain: An Argument for Interactionism*, London: Routledge and Kegan Paul, 1977

Porter, M., *Competitive Advantage: Creating and Sustaining Superior Performance*, New York: The Free Press, 1985

Postan, M.M., *The Medieval Economy and Society*, Middlesex: Penguin Books, 1975

Postlewaite, A., 'Asymmetric Information', in J. Eatwell, M. Milgate and P. Newman (eds) *Allocation, Information, and Markets*, The New Palgrave, London: Macmillan, 1987, pp. 35–38

Prahalad, C.K. and G. Hamel, 'The Core Competence of the Corporation', *Harvard Business Review*, May–June 1990

Prigogine, I., *From Being to Becoming: Time and Complexity in the Physical Sciences*, New York: W.H. Freeman and Co., 1980

Prigogine, I. and I. Stengers, *Order out of Chaos: Man's New Dialogue with Nature*, Toronto: Bantam Books, 1984

Prigogine, I., G. Nicolis and A. Babbyantz, 'Thermodynamics of Evolution', *Physics Today*, 25(11), pp. 23–28, 25(12), pp. 38–44, 1972

Putterman, L. (ed.) *The Economic Nature of the Firm: A Reader*, Cambridge: Cambridge University Press, 1986

Pye, L., *Asian Power and Politics: The Cultural Dimension of Authority*, Cambridge,

Mass.: The Belknap Press of Harvard University Press, 1985

Pylyshyn, Z., *Computation and Cognition*, Cambridge, Mass.: The MIT Press,1984

Quine, W.V.O., *Word and Object*, Cambridge, Mass.: The MIT Press, 1960

Quinn, J.B., *Intelligent Enterprise: A Knowledge and Service Based Paradigm for Industry*, New York: The Free Press, 1992

Radcliffe-Brown, A.R., *Structure and Function in Primitive Society*, London: Cohen and West, 1952

Radner, R., 'The Evaluation of Information in Organizations', in J. Neyman (ed.) *Proceedings of the Fourth Berkeley Symposium on Mathematical Statistics and Probabilities*, Vol. I, Berkeley and Los Angeles: University of California Press, 1961

Ravetz, J.R., *Scientific Knowledge and its Social Problems*, Middlesex: Penguin Books, 1973

Redding, G., *The Spirit of Chinese Capitalism*, Berlin: Walter de Gruyter, 1990

Rensch, B., *Biophilosophy*, New York: Columbia University Press, 1971

Révész, G.,*Thinking and Speaking*, Amsterdam: North-Holland, 1954

Richardson, G.B., 'The Organization of Industry', *The Economic Journal*, LXXXII (Supplement), 1972, pp. 882–896

Riesman, D., *The Lonely Crowd: A Study of the Changing American Character*, New Haven, Connecticut: Yale University Press, 1961

Riley, J.G., 'Competition with Hidden Knowledge', *Journal of Political Economy*, 93, October 1985, pp. 958–976

Riskin, C., *China's Politial Economy*, Oxford: Oxford University Press, 1987

Robbins, L., *An Essay on the Nature and Significance of Economic Science*, London: Macmillan, 1935

Rogers, E.M. and F.F. Shoemaker, *Communication of Innovation: A Cross Cultural Approach*, New York: The Free Press, 1971

Rohlen, T.,*For Harmony and Strength*, Berkeley: University of California Press, 1974

Ronan, C., *The Shorter Science and Civilization in China: An Abridgement by Colin Ronan of Joseph Needham's Original Text*, Cambridge: Cambridge University Press, 1978

Root-Bernstein, R.S., *Discovering: Inventing and Solving Problems at the Frontiers of Scientific Knowledge*, Cambridge, Mass.: Harvard University Press, 1989

Rosch, E. and B. Lloyd, *Cognition and Categorization*, Hillsdale, New Jersey: Lawrence Erlbaum Associates, 1978

Rosenberg, N., 'Science and Technolgoy in the Twentieth Century', in G. Dosi, R. Gianetti and P.A. Toninelli, *Technology and Enterprise in a Historical Perspective*, Oxford: The Clarendon Press, 1992, pp. 63–96

Rosenblatt, F., *Principles of Neurodynamics*, New York: Spartan, 1962

Ross Ashby, W., *An Introduction to Cybernetics*, London: Methuen, 1956

Rostow, W.W., *The Stages of Economic Growth: A Non-Communist Manifesto*, Cambridge: Cambridge University Press, 1960

Rothschild, M., 'Models of Market Organization with Imperfect Information: A Survey', *Journal of Political Economy*, 81, 1973, 1283–1308

Rousseau, J.J., *Du Contrat Social*, Paris: Garnier-Flammarion, 1966

Rumelhart, D.E., 'Notes on a schema for stories', in D.G. Bobrow and A. Collins (eds) *Representations and Understanding*, New York: Academic Press, 1975, pp. 211–236

Rumelhart, D.E. and J.L. McClelland, 'An Interactive Activation Model of Context Effects in Letter Perception: Part 2. The Contextual Enhancement Effect and Some Tests and Extensions of the Model', *Psychological Review*, 89, 1982, pp. 60–94

Rumelhart, D.E. and J.L. McClelland, 'PDP Models and General Issues in Cognitive Science', in D.E. Rumelhart and J.L. McClelland (eds) *Parallel Distributed Processing: Explorations in the Microstructure of Cognition*, Vol. 1, Cambridge, Mass.: The MIT Press, 1986

Rumelhart, D.E. and J.L. McClelland, 'A General Framework for Parallel Distributed Processing', in D.E. Rumelhart and J.L. McClelland (eds) *Parallel Distributed Processing: Explorations in the Microstructure of Cognition*, Vol. 1, Cambridge, Mass.: The MIT Press, 1986

Rumelhart, D.E. and D. Zipser, 'Feature Discovery by Competitive Learning', in D.E. Rumelhart and J.L. McClelland (eds) *Parallel Distributed Processing: Explorations in the Microstructure of Cognition*, Vol. 1, Cambridge, Mass.: The MIT Press, 1986, pp. 151–193

Rumelhart, D.E. *et al.*, 'Schemata and Sequential Thought Processes in PDP Models', in J.L. McClelland and D.E. Rumelhart (eds) *Parallel Distributed Processing: Explorations in the Microstructure of Cognition*, Vol. 2, Cambridge, Mass.: The MIT Press, 1988, pp. 7–57

Rumelt, R., 'Towards a Strategic Theory of a Firm', in R.B. Lamb (ed.) *Competitive Strategic Management*, Englewood Cliffs, New Jersey: Prentice-Hall, 1984

Rutherford, M., 'Rational Expectations and Keynesian Uncertainty: A Critique', *Journal of Post Keynesian Economics*, 6(13), Spring 1984, pp. 377–387

Sahlins, M., *Culture and Practical Reason*, Chicago: The University of Chicago Press, 1976

Salthe, S.N., *Evolving Hierarchical Systems: Their Structure and Representation*, New York: Columbia University Press, 1985

Samuelson, W., 'Comments on the Coase Theorem', in A. Roth (ed.) *Game Theoretic Models of Bargaining*, New York: Cambridge University Press, 1985, pp. 321–340

Sandmo, A., 'Public Goods', in J. Eatwell, M. Milgate and P. Newman (eds), *Allocation, Information and Markets*, The New Palgrave, London: Macmillan, 1989, pp. 254–266

Sansom, G.B., *Japan: A Short Cultural History*, London: Barrie and Jenkins, 1946

Sansom, G.B., *A History of Japan: 1615–1867*, Tokyo: Charles E. Tuttle Co., 1963

Sapir, E., 'Conceptual Categories in Primitive Languages', *Science*, 74, 1931, p. 578

Sapir, E., 'Language', *Encyclopaedia of the Social Sciences*, 9(33), 1933, pp. 155–169

Sapir, E., *Culture, Language, and Personality*, Berkeley: University of California Press, 1957

Sargent, T.J., *Rational Expectations and Inflation*, New York: Harper and Row, 1986

Scarbrough, H. and J.M. Corbett, *Technology and Organization: Power, Meaning and Design*, London: Routledge, 1992

Schein, E., *Organizational Culture and Leadership*, San Francisco: Jossey-Bass, 1992

Scheler, M., *Schriften zur Soziologie und Weltanschauunglehre*, Vols 1–3, Leipzig, 1923 and 1924

Scheler, M., *Die Wissenformen und die Gesellschaft*, Leipzig: Der Neue Geist, 1926

Schmookler, J., 'Economic Sources of Inventive Activity', *Journal of Economic History*, March 1962, pp. 1–20

Schrödinger, E., *What is Life?*, Cambridge University Press, 1967

Schumpeter, J.A., *The Theory of Economic Development: An Inquiry into Profits, Capital, Credit, Interest and the Business Cycle*, London: Oxford University Press, 1961 [1934]

Schumpeter, J.A., *Capitalism, Socialism, and Democracy*, New York: Harper and Row, 1942

Schumpeter, J.A., *History of Economic Analysis*, London: Allen and Unwin, 1954

Schumpeter, J.A., *Business Cycles: A Theoretical, Historical, and Statistical Analysis of the Capitalist Process* (abridged), New York: McGraw-Hill, 1964 [1939]

Schutz, A., *The Phenomenology of the Social World*, London: Heinemann, 1972

Schutz, A. and T. Luckmann, *The Structures of the Life-World*, London: Heinemann, 1974

Searle, J.R., 'Minds and Brains without Programmes', in C. Blakemore and S. Greenfield (eds) *Mindwaves*, Oxford: Basil Blackwell, 1987

Sejnowski, T.J., 'Open Questions about Computation in the Cerebral Cortex', in J.L. McClelland and D.E. Rumelhart (eds) *Parallel Distributed Processing: Explorations in the Microstructure of Cognition*, Vol. 2, Cambridge, Mass.: The MIT Press, 1988, pp. 372–389

Selfridge, O.G., 'Pattern Recognition in Modern Computers', *Proceedings of the Western Joint Computer Conference*, 1955

Senge, P.M., *The Fifth Discipline: The Art and Practice of the Learning Organization*, London: Century Business, 1990

Shackle, G.L.S., *Epistemics and Economies: A Critique of Economic Doctrines*, Cambridge: Cambridge University Press, 1972

Shackle, G.L.S., *Imagination and the Nature of Choice*, Edinburgh: Edinburgh University Press, 1979

Shaikh, A., 'Abstract and Concrete Labour', in J. Eatwell, M. Milgate and P. Newman (eds) *Marxian Economics*, The New Palgrave, London: Macmillan, 1990

Shank, R.C., 'The Role of Memory in Language Processing', in C.N. Cofer (ed.) *The Structure of Human Memory*, San Francisco: Freeman, 1976, pp. 162–189

Shannon, B., 'Réflexion sur la Complexité de la Cognition Humaine', in F.F. Soulié (ed.) *Les Théories de la Complexité: Autour de l'Oeuvre d'Henri Atlan*, Paris: Seuil.

Shannon, C.E., 'The Mathematical Theory of Communication', *Bell System Technical Journal*, July and October 1948.

Shannon, C.E. and W. Weaver, *The Mathematical Theory of Communication*, Urbana: The University of Illinois Press, 1949

Sheffrin, S.M., *Rational Expectations*, Cambridge: Cambridge University Press, 1983

Sheldrake, R., *A New Science of Life: The Hypothesis of Formative Causation*, London: Paladin, 1983

Sheldrake, R., *The Presence of the Past*, London: Fontana, 1988

Shepard, R.N. and P. Podgorny, 'Cognitive Processes that Resemble Perceptual Processes', in W.K. Estes (ed.) *Handbook of Learning and Cognitive Processes*, Hillsdale, New Jersey: Lawrence Erlbaum Associates, 1975, pp. 189–237

Sherif, M., 'Superordinate Goals in the Reduction of Intergroup Conflict', *American Journal of Sociology*, 63, 1958, pp. 349–358

Shibutani, T., 'Reference Groups as Perspectives', *American Journal of Sociology*, 60, 1955, pp. 562–570

Silverberg, G., 'Modelling Economic Dynamics and Technical Change: Mathematical Approaches to Self-Organization and Evolution', in G. Dosi *et al.* (eds) *Technical Change and Economic Theory*, London: Pinter Publishers, 1988, p. 532

Simon, H.A., *Administrative Behaviour: A Study of Decision-Making Processes in Administrative Organization*, New York: The Free Press, 1957

Simon, H.A., 'A Behavioural Model of Rational Choice', in H.A. Simon (ed.) *Models of Man*, New York: Wiley, 1957

Simon, H.A., *The New Science of Management Decision*, New York: Harper and Row, 1960

Simon, H.A., 'Scientific Discovery and the Psychology of Problem Solving', in R. Colodny (ed.) *Mind and Cosmos*, Pittsburgh: University of Pittsburgh Press, 1966, pp. 22–40

Simon, H.A., 'Thinking by Computers', in R. Colodny (ed.) *Mind and Cosmos*, Pittsburgh: University of Pittsburgh Press, 1966

Simon, H.A., 'Does Scientific Discovery have a Logic?', *Philosophy of Science*, 40, 1973, pp. 471–480

Simon, H.A., 'The Logic of Heuristic Decision Making', in N. Rescher (ed.) *The Logic of Decision and Action*, Pittsburgh: University of Pittsburgh Press, 1967, pp. 1–20; reprinted in H.A. Simon, *Models of Discovery*, Dordrecht, Holland: D. Reidel Publishing Co., 1977

Simon, H.A., *Models of Bounded Rationality*, 2 vols, Cambridge, Mass.: The MIT Press, 1982

Simon, H.A., *Reason in Human Affairs*, Oxford: Basil Blackwell, 1983

Simon, H.A., 'Rationality in Psychology and Economics', in R.M. Hogarth and M.W. Reder (eds) *Rational Choice: The Contrast between Economics and Psychology*, Chicago: The University of Chicago Press, 1986, pp. 25–40

Singer, J., 'The Importance of Day Dreaming', *Psychology Today* 1(2), 1968, pp. 18–26

Skalweit, S., 'Political Thought', in F.L. Carsten (ed.) *The New Cambridge Modern History: Vol. V, The Ascendancy of France*, Cambridge: Cambridge University Press, 1961

Skinner, B.F., *Science and Human Behaviour*, New York: Macmillan, 1953

Smith, A., *The Theory of Moral Sentiments*, London: 1759

Smith, A., *An Inquiry into the Nature and Causes of the Wealth of Nations*, London, 1776

Smolensky, P., 'Information Processing in Dynamical Systems: Foundations of Harmony Theory', in D.E. Rumelhart and J.L. McClelland (eds) *Parallel Distributed Processing: Explorations in the Microstructure of Cognition*, Vol. 1, Cambridge, Mass.: The MIT Press, 1986

Smullyan, R., *Forever Undecided: A Puzzle Guide to Gödel*, Oxford: Oxford University Press, 1987

Snow, E., *Red Star over China*, Middlesex: Penguin Books, 1978

Solow, R.M., 'Investment and Technical Progress', in K. Arrow, S. Karbin and P. Suppes (eds) *Mathematical Methods in the Social Sciences*, Stanford, California: Stanford University Press, 1960

Solow, R.M., 'Growth Theory and After', *American Economic Review*, 78(3), June 1988

Spence, A., *Market Signalling*, Cambridge, Mass.: Harvard University Press, 1973

Spencer, H., *The Man versus the State*, Middlesex: Penguin Books, 1969 [1884]

Stigler, G., 'The Economics of Information', *Journal of Political Economy*, 69, 1961, pp. 213–225

Stiglitz, J.E., 'Information and Economic Analysis: A Perspective', *The Economic Journal*, 1983, p. 22

Stiglitz, J.E. 'Principal and Agent', in J. Eatwell, M. Milgate and P. Newman (eds) *Allocation, Information and Markets*, The New Palgrave, London: Macmillan, 1989, pp. 241–253

Streek, W. and P. Schmitter, 'Community, Market, State – and Associations? The Prospective Contribution of Interest Governance to Social Order', in G. Thompson, J. Frances, R. Levacic and J. Mitchell (eds) *Markets, Hierarchies and Networks: The Coordination of Social Life*, London: Sage Publications, 1991

Sumner, W.C., *Folkways*, Boston, 1906

Talmon, J., *The Origins of Totalitarian Democracy: Political Theory and Practice during the French Revolution and Beyond*, Middlesex: Penguin Books, 1952

Tarde, G., *Les Lois de l'Imitation*, Paris: Collection Ressources, 1979

Tarski, A., 'Der Wahrheitsbegriff in den formalisierten Sprachen', *Studia Philosophica I*, 1935, pp. 261–405

Teece, D.J., 'Profiting from Technological Innovation: Implications for Integration, Collaboration, Licensing, and Public Policy', in D.J. Teece (ed.) *The Competitive Challenge: Strategies for Industrial Innovation and Renewal*, Cambridge, Mass.: Ballinger, 1987

Teece, D.J., 'Technological Change and the Nature of the Firm', in G. Dosi *et al.* (eds) *Technical Change and Economic Theory*, London: Pinter Publishers, 1988

Teng, Ssu-yū and John K. Fairbank, (eds), *China's Response to the West: A Documentary Survey, 1839–1923*, Cambridge, Mass.: Harvard University Press, 1979

Theobald, D.W., *The Concept of Energy*, London: Spon, 1966

Thom, R., *Stabilité Structurelle et Morphogenèse: Essai d'une Théorie Générale des Modèles*, Paris: Intereditions, 1977

Thom, R., *Esquisse d'une Semiophysique Physique Aristotélienne et Théorie des Catastrophes*, Paris: Intereditions, 1988

Thomas, K., *Religion and the Decline of Magic*, Middlesex: Penguin Books, 1971

Thompson, G., J. Frances, R. Levacic and J. Mitchell (eds) *Markets, Hierarchies, and Networks: The Coordination of Social Life*, London: Sage Publications, 1991

Tidrick, G. and J. Chen (eds) *China's Industrial Reforms*, Oxford: Oxford University Press, 1987

Tirole, J., *The Theory of Industrial Organization*, Cambridge, Mass.: The MIT Press, 1988

Tönnies, F., *Community and Association*, London: Routledge and Kegan Paul, 1955 [1887]

Toulmin, S., *Human Understanding*, Oxford: The Clarendon Press, 1972

Toulouse, E., *Henri Poincaré*, Paris: Flammarion, 1910

Tricker, R., *Corporate Governance*, Aldershot: Gower, 1984

Túng-Tsu Ch'u, 'Chinese Class Structure and its Ideology', in J.K. Fairbank (ed.) *Chinese Thought and Institutions*, Chicago: The University of Chicago Press, 1957

Turing, A., 'On Computable Numbers with an Application to the Entscheidungs-problem', in *Proceedings of the London Mathematical Society* (Ser. 2), 42, 1937, pp. 230–265; a correction, 43, pp. 544–546

Tushman, M. and L. Rosenkopf, 'Organizational Determinants of Technological Change: Towards a Sociology of Technological Evolution', in B. Staw and L. Cummings (eds) *Research in Organizational Behaviour*, Vol. 14, Greenwich, Connecticut: JAI Press, 1992

Tylor, E.B., *Primitive Culture: Researches into the Development of Mythology, Philosophy, Religion, Language, Art and Custom*, London: J. Murray, 1971

Underwood, G.U., *Strategies for Information Processing*, London: Academic Press, 1978

Usher, A.P., 'Technical Change and Capital Formation', in *Capital Formation and Economic Growth*, National Bureau of Economic Research, 1955, pp. 523–550

Uttley, A.M., 'Conditional Processing in a Nervous System', in *Mechanization of Thought Processes*, London, 1959

Vanek, J., *The Economics of Worker's Management: A Yugoslav Case Study*, London: Allen and Unwin, 1972

Vanek, J., 'The Basic Theory of Financing of Participatory Firms', in J. Vanek (ed.) *Self-Management: Economic Liberation of Man*, Middlesex: Penguin Books, 1975

Vansina, J., *Oral Tradition: A Study in Historical Methodology*, Middlesex: Penguin Books, 1965

Van Wolferen, K., *The Enigma of Japanese Power: People and Politics in a Stateless Nation*, London: Macmillan, 1989

Van Wyk, R., 'Technological Change. A Macroperspective', *Technological Forecasting and Social Change*, 15, 1979, pp. 281–296

Varela, F.J., *Principles of Biological Autonomy*, New York: North-Holland, 1980

Vianello, F., 'Labour Theory of Value', in J. Eatwell, M. Milgate and P. Newman (eds) *Marxian Economics*, London: Macmillan, 1990

Vogel, E., *Japan as No. 1: Lessons for America*, Tokyo: Charles Tuttle Co., 1979

Volkema, C., 'Problem Formulation in Planning and Design', *Management Science*, 29(6), June 1983, pp. 639–652

Von Foerster, H., 'On Self Organizing Systems and their Environments', in Yovitz and Cameron (eds) *Self Organizing Sysems*, London: Pergamon Press, 1960, pp. 31–50

Von Mises, L., *Socialism: An Economic and Sociological Analysis*, Indianapolis: Liberty Classics, 1981

Von Neumann, J.M., *The Theory of Self-Reproducing Automata*, Urbana: The University of Illinois Press, 1966

Walder, A.G., 'Wage Reform and the Web of Factory Interests', *The China Quarterly*, No. 109, 1987, pp. 22–41

Wallerstein, I., *The Modern World System: Capitalist Agriculture and the Origins of the European World Economy in the Sixteenth Century*, New York: Academic Press, 1974

Walras, L., *Elements of Pure Econonics: or the Theory of Social Wealth*, Philadelphia: Orion Editions, 1984 [1926]

Warner, M. (ed.) *Management Reforms in China*, London: Pinter Publishers, 1987

Watson, J.B., *Behaviourism*, London: Kegan Paul, 1928

Weaver, W., 'Recent Contributions to the Mathematical Theory of Communications', in C.E. Shannon and W. Weaver, *The Mathematical Theory of Communication*, Urbana: The University of Illinois Press, 1949, p. 9

Weber, M., *The Protestant Ethics and the Spirit of Capitalism*, London: Unwin University Books, 1930 [1904–5]

Weber, M., *The Religion of China: Confucianism and Taoism*, New York: The Free Press, 1951

Weber, M., *The Theory of Social and Economic Organization*, New York: The Free Press, 1964

Weber, M., *On Charisma and Institution Building*, Chicago: The University of Chicago Press, 1958

Weber, M., *Economy and Society*, G. Roth and C. Wittich (eds), Berkeley: University of California Press, 1968

Wechler, J., *On Aesthetics in Science*, Cambridge, Mass.: The MIT Press, 1981

Weick, K., *The Social Psychology of Organizing*, Reading, Mass.: Addison-Wesley, 1979

Wheatley, J., 'How Costs Lead Firms Astray', *Management Today*, June 1980

White, L., *The Science of Culture*, New York: Farrar, Straus, 1949

Whitehead, A.N., *Science in the Modern World* (Lowell Lectures, 1925), New York: Mentor Books, 1948

Whorf, B.L., *Language, Thought, and Reality*, New York: Wiley, 1956

Wilkinson, E., *Misunderstanding: Europe vs. Japan*, Tokyo: Chuokoron-sha, 1981

Williamson, O.E., 'Hierarchical Control and Optimum Firm Size', *Journal of Political Economy*, 75, April 1967, pp. 123–138

Williamson, O.E., *Markets and Hierarchies: Analysis and Antitrust Implications*, New York: The Free Press, 1975

Williamson, O.E., *The Economic Institutions of Capitalism: Firms, Markets, Rational Contracting*, New York: The Free Press, 1985

Williamson, O.E., 'The Logic of Economic Organization', in O.E. Williamson and S. Winter (eds) *The Nature of the Firm: Origins, Evolution, and Development*, New York: Oxford University Press, 1991

Wilson, C., 'The Nature of Equilibrium in Markets with Adverse Selection', *Bell Journal of Economics*, II, Spring 1980, pp. 108–130

Winiecki, J., 'Obstacles to Economic Reform of Socialism: A Property-Rights Approach', *The Annals of the AAPSS*, 507, 1990, pp. 65–71

Wittfogel, K.A., *Oriental Despotism: A Comparative Study of Total Power*, New York: Vintage Books, 1981 [1951]

Wittgenstein, L., *Tractatus Logico-Philosophicus*, London: Routledge and Kegan Paul, 1961

Wittgenstein, L., *Philosophical Investigations*, Oxford: Basil Blackwell, 1968

Wittkower, R., *Allegory and the Migration of Symbols*, Boulder, Colorado: Westview Press, 1977

Wohlstetter, R., *Pearl Harbor: Warning and Decision*, Stanford, California: Stanford University Press, 1962

Wolfe, D.M. and D.A. Kolb, 'Career Development, Personal Growth, and Experiental Learning', in D.A. Kolb, I.M. Rubin and J.M. McIntyre (eds) *Organizational Psychology: A Book of Reading*, Englewood Cliffs, New Jersey: Prentice-Hall, 1979, pp. 535–563

Wynne, B., 'Physics and Psychics: Science, Symbolic Action and Social Control in Late Victorian England', in B. Barnes and S. Shapin (eds) *Natural Order: Historical Studies of Scientific Culture*, Beverly Hills: Sage Publications, 1979, pp. 167–186

Xing, Su, 'Understanding China's Socialist System', *Beijing Review*, No. 47, 19 November 1984

Yates, F.A., *Giordano Bruno and the Hermetic Tradition*, London: Routledge and Kegan Paul, 1964

Young, A.K., *The Sogo Shoscha: Japan's Multinational Trading Companies*, Tokyo: Charles E. Tuttle Co., 1979

Yü-chüan Wang, 'The Rise of the Land Tax and the Fall of Dynasties in Chinese History', in J.R. Levenson (ed.) *Modern China: An Interpretative Anthology*, New York: Macmillan, 1971, pp. 130–154

Ziman, J., *Public Knowledge: The Social Dimension of Science*, Cambridge: Cambridge University Press, 1968

Zuboff, S., *In the Age of the Smart Machine: The Future of Work and Power*, Oxford: Heinemann, 1988

Zu-Wen, Lu, 'The Evolution of China's Accounting System Paves the Way for Opening to the Outside World', Mimeo, University of International Business Economics, 1985

Index

Abernathy, W. 99
absorption, integrating old and new
    knowledge 207–9, 228, 304;
    restoring richness to experience
    206–7, 291; using new knowledge
    209
abstraction 58–61; alternative to
    shared context 118–20; categorizing
    possible worlds 200–1, 433;
    conceiving and 86, 228; degree of
    57, 304; diffusion of message and
    93; establishes how knowledge can
    be applied 138; facilitated by
    codification 157; fragility of moves
    towards 125–6, 161; function of 57;
    how it differs from codification
    175; intergroup transactions and
    342–4; the power of uncodified
    176–7; as reality versus descriptive
    convenience 175–6; requirements of
    valid 201–2; scale 60; scientific,
    hurdles and 201; versus
    anthropomorphism 177–8
abstraction scale, semiotics and 60
'acceptable to others' 132
'adjustment tax' 371
aesthetic messages 103–4
Aganbegyan, Abel 409
Age of Information, theory for 441–4
Alchian, A. 13
Allen, P.M. 16, 20

America and Japan, in the SLC 405
American Banking industry 329
American Indian reservation, atrophy
    in 141
Anglo-French expeditionary force
    (1864) 364
Ankara 334
anomie 141
Antitrust Division of the United States
    Department of Justice 405
'anything goes' 136
appropriability, codification,
    abstraction and 161; problem of 12
appropriable value, realization of 140,
    157
'appropriate theorizing' 155
'archaic mental calculus' 349
Argyle, M. 97
Aristotle 117, 168
Arrow, K. 12–13, 21
artefacts, information embedded in
    210; knowledge and 99
artificial intelligence 214, 446
Ashby, Ross 240, 331
Athos, A. 398
'atmosphere' 254, 289
atrophy, overwhelming change and
    141
attractor 235, 275, 326, 330, 443
Austrian School 163, 278
authority, of transmitter 114–15

restricted codes 156, 297–8, 342
Ricardo, David 27
Ricci, Matteo 362
'right hands' 250
Riskin, C. 366
Romania 408, 412
Rostow, W.W. 315–16, 436
Rothschild, M. 13
Rousseau, J.J. 88, 280
Rowntree 400
royalty payments, technical licensing and 140
Ruggieri, Michele 362
Rumelhart, D.E. 44, 59
Rwanda *Ubwiiru* 139

Sachs, Jeffrey 411
Sahlins, M. 107, 293, 308, 312, 331, 347
Salthe, S.N. 32
Samuelson, W. 13
Sapir, E. 172, 294
'satisficing' 307, 311
Saussure, F. de 302
scanning 52, 227, 291, 304; blockages to 182–3, 227; difficulty of detecting novelty 192–3; exercise in anticipation 182; idiosyncratic perception and 194; inventiveness versus selectiveness 195; in the I-space 165; meaningful stimuli as violation of expectations 190–1; openness to experience and 58; perceptual recklessness and 191–2; process 114, 116; relaxation strategies and 49; sources of 193–4; stochastic process 194; strategies 143, 173; two-step process 224–5
scarcity, cognitive investment and 157
Schein, E. 293
Scheler, M. 115–16, 191
Schmookler, Jacob 193
Schultz, A. 274
Schumpeter, J.A. 109, 251, 276; creative destruction 325, 417, 439; markets and 289, 357
science, epistemology and 78; history of 171, 177, 192; level of abstraction

in 66, 131; validation procedures in 125, 170, 218
scientific discovery, problem-solving and 196–7
scientific knowledge 122, 170
scientific methodologies, blocking mechanisms and 129
Searle, John 51
Securities and Exchange Commission 405
'sedimented' 380, 413
Sejnowski, T.J. 44
'selected' 109
semantic messages 103–4
semiotics, abstraction scale and 60
semi-tacit domain, mode of knowing 62
Shannon, Claude, communication and 41, 45–6, 51, 203, 246–7; communication system 100–1, 107, 114, 143–4, 196; level A information transmission 142, 184; level B semantic problem 155–6, 161, 179, 184
sharing of codes, between senders and receivers 151
sharing codes, versus sharing context 150–3
Sheldrake, Rupert 167
Shogunate, military government in 389; students sent abroad by 403
Shutz, Alfred 112, 126
'signalling' practices 258
'signature' of cultural order 319
Simon, H.A. 37, 90, 269; law of 'satisficing' 307, 311; scientific creativity 177, 196, 198
Singapore 332
Singer, J. 76
single shot algorithm, information processing strategy 101, 115–16, 129
'slack' 414
SLC 230, 252; America and Japan in 405; battle against entropy 188–9; blocks to movement through 226–9; clockwise flow pattern in